LOO
THE GRIP

A HANDBOOK OF
ALCOHOL INFORMATION

CONTRIBUTORS

Illustrator
Chapter 10. Special Populations. Section on Adolescents
STUART COPANS, M.D.

Dr. Copans, a child psychiatrist, was a lecturer in an alcohol counselor training program, discussing the effects of alcohol abuse on the family—the early signs of what has since become a major professional interest. He has directed a residential adolescent substance abuse program, in a Dartmouth-affiliated teaching hospital, and is currently in private practice and a consultant to schools on issues of adolescents.

JEAN KINNEY, M.S.W.

Jean Kinney, lecturer in community and family medicine at Dartmouth Medical School, was the Associate Director of the Alcohol Counselor Training Program at Dartmouth conducted between 1972 and 1978, the program that was the impetus for this text. Upon the completion of the Alcohol Counselor Training Program, she joined Project Cork, a program established to develop and implement a model curriculum for medical student education. At the completion of Project Cork, the Resource Center that was established joined the Office of Alcohol and Drug Abuse Programs of Vermont Department of Health, and it serves as a resource for substance abuse and health-care professionals statewide and nationally.

Chapter 11. Other Psychiatric Considerations. Section on Co-occurring Psychiatric Illness
FRED C. OSHER, M.D.

Dr. Osher entered the field of psychiatry after serving as the medical director of a detoxification center in Detroit, a setting which sparked his continuing interest in substance abuse issues. He was an early member of the New Hampshire Psychiatric Research Center, which has been a leader in the area of the care of those with psychiatric illness and substance abuse problems. From there he moved to the Substance Abuse and Mental Health Services Administration (SAMHSA), and he has since joined the Institute of Psychiatry and Human Behavior at the University of Maryland in Baltimore, as the director of community psychiatry.

Chapter 2, Alcohol and the Body
Chapter 3, Medical Complications
TREVOR R.P. PRICE, M.D.
Dr. Price is chairman of the Department of Psychiatry, professor and chairman of psychiatry at the Medical College of Pennsylvania, and chair of the council overseeing Project Cork, a program to promote medical education on alcohol and alcoholism. He entered psychiatry after training in internal medicine. His interest in alcohol was sparked during his tenure at Dartmouth Medical School, when he was a member of the faculty for the Alcohol Counselor Training Program.

Chapter 2, Alcohol and the Body. Section on Other Drugs of Abuse
Chapter 3, Medical Complications. Part III. Other Drug Use
Chapter 11, Other Psychiatric Considerations. Section on Psychotropic Medications
DONALD A. WEST, M.D.
Dr. West, associate professor of psychiatry at Dartmouth Medical School, is actively involved in coordinating substance abuse services at the Dartmouth Hitchcock Medical Center and medical director of the short-term psychiatric unit at the Medical Center. He originally came to Dartmouth on a half-year sabbatical from the University of New Mexico, which he spent with the substance abuse treatment team, and the area apparently began to look like home.

By the time a text has reached its Sixth Edition it becomes difficult to sort out and separate the particular contributions of individual people. Those listed above assumed responsibility for revising and updating material for this edition. Much of what remains incorporated here is, however, the product of others who were involved in the counselor training program, who contributed to earlier editions, and whose work remains.

Co-editor, previous editions
GWEN LEATON
Gwen Leaton was involved in the Alcohol Counselor Training Program as a research assistant. Following the completion of the Counselor Training Program, she held positions in several other education and training programs. Gwen was intimately involved in the development of the initial text as well as subsequent revisions. Illness had prevented her participation in this Sixth Edition. Gwen died in early 1999. Through her contributions over the years she continues to be very much present in this edition.

Chapter 10
Adolescents
FREDERICK BURKLE, JR., M.D., M.P.H., FAAP, FACEP

Dr. Burkle, a lecturer to the counselor trainees at Dartmouth Medical School, came to a psychiatry residency program at Dartmouth Medical School after a practice in pediatrics. He long since left chilly New England and is a professor of pediatrics and surgery at the University of Hawaii John A. Burns School of Medicine and professor of public health at the University of Hawaii School of Public Health.

Chapter 10, The Elderly
Chapter 11, Suicide Evaluation and Prevention
RICHARD GOODSTEIN, M.D.

Dr. Goodstein, another member of the training program faculty at Dartmouth, after establishing and directing a Psychiatric Services Crisis Clinic within the Dartmouth Hitchcok Medical Center, moved south. He joined the Carrier Foundation as Vice President of Medical Education, was been on the faculty at the Rutgers Medical School, and is currently senior director of medical partnerships at Merck & Co. in Pennsylvania.

Chapter 10
Adolescents
HUGH MACNAMEE, M.D.

Dr. MacNamee was an associate professor of clinical psychiatry in the Division of Child Psychiatry at Dartmouth until his death in 1984. Much of the material on adolescents incorporated here reflects lectures he gave to the alcohol counselor trainees. His eminently practical stance and uncommon common sense were always much in evidence. Some things really cannot be improved on.

Chapter 5
Sleep Disturbances
PETER HAURI, PH.D.

Dr. Hauri is presently professor of psychology at the Mayo Medical School, administrative director of the Sleep Disorders Center at the Mayo Clinic and a consultant to the Division of Behavioral Medicine in the Department of Psychology and Psychiatry at the Mayo Clinic.

LOOSENING THE GRIP

A HANDBOOK OF ALCOHOL INFORMATION

SIXTH EDITION

Jean Kinney, M.S.W.

Project Cork
Office of Alcohol and Drug Abuse Programs
State of Vermont

Assistant Professor Community and Family Medicine
Dartmouth Medical School

Illustrations by
Stuart Copans, M.D.

Boston   Burr Ridge, IL   Dubuque, IA   Madison, WI   New York   San Francisco
St. Louis   Bangkok   Bogotá   Caracas   Lisbon   London   Madrid   Mexico City
Milan   New Delhi   Seoul   Singapore   Sydney   Taipei   Toronto

McGraw-Hill Higher Education

*A Division of The **McGraw-Hill** Companies*

LOOSENING THE GRIP: A HANDBOOK OF ALCOHOL INFORMATION, SIXTH EDITION

This book is printed on acid-free paper.

1 2 3 4 5 6 7 8 9 0 QPF/QPF 0 9 8 7 6 5 4 3 2 1 0

ISBN 0–07–289106–8

Vice president and editorial director: *Kevin T. Kane*
Publisher: *Edward E. Bartell*
Editorial coordinator: *Kristine K. Fisher*
Senior marketing manager: *Pamela S. Cooper*
Project manager: *Renee C. Russian*
Senior production supervisor: *Sandra Hahn*
Coordinator of freelance design: *Michelle D. Whitaker*
Compositor: *Interactive Composition Corporation*
Typeface: *10/12 Times Roman*
Printer: *Quebecor Book Group/Fairfield, PA*

Freelance cover designer: *Kristyn A. Kalnes*
Cover image: © *Stuart A. Copans, M.D.*

Library of Congress Cataloging-in-Publication Data

Kinney, Jean.
    Loosening the grip : a handbook of alcohol information / Jean
Kinney. — 6th ed.
        p.   cm.
    Includes index.
    ISBN 0–07–289106–8
    1. Alcoholism—United States Handbooks, manuals, etc.
    2. Alcoholism—Treatment—United States Handbooks, manuals, etc.
    I. Title.
    HV5292.K53   2000
    362.292—dc21   99–16744
                                                                   CIP

www.mhhe.com

God of Compassion, if anyone has come to Thine altar troubled in spirit, depressed and apprehensive, expecting to go away as he came, with the same haunting heaviness of heart; if anyone is deeply wounded of soul, hardly daring to hope that anything can afford him the relief he seeks, so surprised by the ill that life can do that he is half afraid to pray; O God, surprise him, we beseech Thee, by the graciousness of Thy help; and enable him to take from thy bounty as ungrudgingly as Thou givest, that he may leave his sorrow and take a song away.

Author Unknown

CONTENTS

PREFACE

Material on alcohol and alcoholism is mushrooming. There are books, articles, scientific reports, pamphlets. On present use, past use, abuse. Around prevention, efforts at early detection, effects on the family, effects on the body. When, where, why . . .

And yet, if you are in the helping business and reasonably bright and conscientious and can find an occasional half hour to read but don't have all day to search library stacks, then it's probably hard for you to lay your hands on the information you need when it would be most helpful.

This handbook is an attempt to partially remedy the situation. It contains what we believe is the basic information an alcohol counselor or other professional confronted with alcohol problems needs to know and would like to have handy. The work here isn't original. It is an effort to synthesize, organize, and sometimes "translate" the information from medicine, psychology, psychiatry, anthropology, sociology, and counseling that applies to alcohol use and alcoholism treatment. This handbook isn't the last word. But we hope it is a starting point.

Preface, Loosening the Grip, First Edition, 1978.

In the period since the publication of the first edition of this handbook, what was then described as rapid growth in the literature has become a veritable deluge. Consequently, the demands upon those in the helping professions are even greater. To be current would entail not only scanning the literature from the disciplines mentioned, but also looking at the many new journals of the alcohol and substance abuse fields.

Since the first edition of *Loosening the Grip* there have been many changes in the alcohol field. Possibly the most notable one is that there is no longer a distinct alcohol field in the way that was true in the 1970s. There is now a field of substance abuse, which represents a merging of the previously separate worlds of alcohol treatment and drug treatment.

CHANGES IN THIS EDITION

The major change in this edition has been the effort to include more information on other drugs. At the same time, the effort has not been to make this a substance abuse text. Alcohol is clearly the point of departure. In our national concern with the problems of "substance use," it must be kept clearly in mind that overwhelmingly the problem, in terms of sheer numbers of people affected, has been, and continues to be, alcohol. While polysubstance use has become the rule, the common denominator is virtually always alcohol. By identifying problems of alcohol use, you'll simultaneously identify those at greatest risk for other drug use. Within the chapter on Special Populations, the groups that are specifically addressed include adolescents, women, and the elderly, and alcohol issues in the workplace are discussed as well. In addition there is a new section devoted to college students. There is also more discussion of the concept of harm reduction and problems attendant to use and abuse.

Since the first edition was published, there have continued to be queries on the title. Yes, there is a story behind it. When Gwen Leaton, my coauthor for the preceeding editions, and I were preparing the original text, an apt title did not leap forth. Somewhere along the line, in casual conversation someone recounted the comment of an alcoholic struggling to get sober. This alcoholic, discussing her drinking in a rather defiant and belligerent fashion said, "If God didn't want me to drink, He'd knock the glass out of my hand!" One of us jokingly commented that we hoped whoever was present had supplied the obviously perfect retort, "He will; all you have to do is loosen your grip." Somehow that metaphor caught the simplicity and the complexity, the ease and the difficulty, the "holding on" and "being held" that are a part of alcohol problems.

An almost mandatory conclusion for book prefaces is an exhaustive listing of "all the persons whose support and assistance . . ." Trusting that families, friends, and professional colleagues know who they are, here there is a slight departure from that tradition. In fact the most significant contributions to this work have been made by individuals whose names and identities, such as the woman in the example just given, are in many instances unknown—substance abuse therapists, those in the 12-step groups, members of the clergy, school counselors, the medical profession—all those who have been responsible for the strides in our collective understanding and clinical practice, all those whose efforts in their professional and private lives make loosening the grip possible.

However, I do need to acknowledge the continuing presence of Gwen Leaton in this work. Gwen was intimately involved in the development of the initial text as well as subsequent revisions. Illness prevented her participation in this revision. Gwen died in early 1999. Through her contributions over the years she continues to be very much present in this work. Having been a two-decades-long collaborative effort, revising the text to eliminate the "we's" was difficult. Those that remain are very appropriate.

Jean Kinney

1

ALCOHOL

Ramses III distributed beer to his subjects and then told them the tingling they felt radiated from him.

ONCE UPON A TIME . . .

Imagine yourself in what is now Clairvoux, high in the Swiss hills. Stone pots dating from the Old Stone Age have been found that once contained a mild beer or wine. The beverage probably was discovered very much like fire—by a combination of nature plus curiosity. If any watery mixture of vegetable sugars or starches, such as berries or barley, is allowed to stand long enough in a warm place, alcohol will make itself.

No one knows what kind of liquor came first—wine, beer, or mead—but by the Neolithic Age it was everywhere. Tales of liquor abound in folklore. One story relates that at the beginning of time the forces of good and evil contested with each other for domination of the earth. Eventually the forces for good won out. But a great many of them had been killed in the process, and wherever they fell, a vine sprouted from the ground. So it seems some felt wine to be a good force. Other myths depict the powers of alcohol as gifts from their gods. Some civilizations worshipped specific gods of wine. The Egyptians' god was Osiris; the Greeks', Dionysius; and the Romans', Bacchus. Wine was used in early rituals as libations (poured out on the ground, altar, etc.). Priests often drank it as part of the rituals. The Bible, too, is full of references to sacrifices including wine.

From ritual uses the drinking of wine spread to convivial uses, and customs developed. Alcohol was a regular part of meals, viewed as a staple in the diet, even before ovens were invented for baking bread. The Assyrians received a daily portion from their masters of a "gallon" of bread and a gallon of fermented brew (probably a barley beer). Bread and wine were offered by the Hebrews on their successful return from battle. In Greece and Rome, wine was essential at every kind of gathering. Alcohol was found to contribute to fun and games at a party, for example, the Roman orgies. Certainly, its safety over water was a factor, but its effects also had something to do with it. It is hard to imagine an orgy where everyone drank water or welcoming a victorious army with lemonade. By the Middle Ages alcohol permeated everything, accompanying birth, marriage, death, the crowning of kings, diplomatic exchanges, treaty signings, and councils. The monasteries became the taverns and inns of the times, and travelers received the benefit of the grape.

The ancients figured that what was good in these instances might be good in others, and alcohol came into use as a medicine. It was an antiseptic and an anesthetic and was used in combinations to form salves and tonics. As a cure it ran the gamut from black jaundice to knee pain and even hiccups. St. Paul advised Timothy, "No longer drink only water, but use a little wine for the sake of your stomach and your frequent ailments." Liquor was a recognized mood changer, nature's tranquilizer. The biblical King Lemuel's mother advises, "Give wine to them that be of heavy hearts." The Bible also refers to wine as stimulating and cheering: "Praise to God, that He hath brought forth fruit out of the earth, and wine that maketh glad the heart of man."

FERMENTATION AND DISCOVERY OF DISTILLATION

Nature alone cannot produce stronger stuff than 14% alcohol. Fermentation is a natural process which occurs when yeasts combine with plants, be it potatoes, fruit, or grains. The sugar in the plants, exposed either to wild yeasts from the air or commercial yeasts, produces an enzyme, which in turn converts sugar into alcohol. Fermentive yeast cannot survive in solutions stronger than 14% alcohol. When that level is reached, the yeast, which is a living thing, ceases to produce and dies.

In the tenth century an Arabian physician, Rhazes, discovered distilled spirits. Actually, he was looking for a way to release "the spirit of the wine," which was welcomed at the time as the "true water of life." European scientists rejoiced in their long-sought "philosopher's stone," or perfect element. A mystique developed, and alcohol was called "the fountain of youth," *eau-de-vie, aqua vitae. Usequebaugh,* from the Gaelic *usige beath,* meaning breath of life, is the source of the word "whiskey." The word "alcohol" itself is derived from the Arabic *al kohl.* It originally referred to a fine powder of antimony used for staining the eyelids and gives rise to speculation on the expression, "Here's mud in your eye!" The word evolved to describe any finely ground substance, then the essence of a thing, and eventually came to mean "finely divided spirit," or the essential spirit of the wine. Nineteenth-century temperance advocates tried to prove that the word "alcohol" is derived from the Arabic *alghul,* meaning ghost or evil spirit.

Distilled liquor wasn't a popular drink until about the sixteenth century. Before that it was used as the basic medicine and cure for all human ailments. Distillation is a simple process that can produce an alcohol content of almost 93% if it is refined enough times. Remember, nature stops at 14%. Start with a fermented brew. When it is boiled, the alcohol separates from the juice or whatever as steam. Alcohol boils at a lower temperature than the other liquid. The escaping steam is caught in a cooling tube and turns into a liquid again, leaving the juice, water, etc. behind. Voila! Stronger stuff—about 50% alcohol.

Proof as a way of measuring the strength of a given liquor came from a practice used by the early American settlers to test their brews. They saturated gunpowder with alcohol and ignited it: too strong, it flared up; too weak, it sputtered. A strong blue flame was considered the sign of proper strength. Almost straight alcohol was diluted with water to gain the desired flame. Half and half was considered 100 proof. Thus 86-proof bourbon is 43% alcohol. Because alcohol dilutes itself with water from

Persia. Malcolm, in his "History of Persia," *relates that wine was discovered in that kingdom in the reign of Janisheed. He attempted to preserve grapes in a large vessel. Fermentation occurred, and the king believed that the juice was poison and labeled it as such. A lady of the palace, wishing to commit suicide, drank from it. She was pleased with the stupor that followed and repeated the experiment until the supply was exhausted. She imparted the secret to the king and a new quantity was made. Hence wine in Persia is called "delightful poison."*
WALTER W. SPOONER
The Cyclopaedia of Temperance and Prohibition, 1891.

Rhazes discovers distilling

the air, 200-proof, or 100%, alcohol is not possible. The U.S. standards for spirits are between 195 and 198 proof.

ALCOHOL USE IN AMERICA

Alcohol came to America with the explorers and colonists. In 1620, the Mayflower landed at Plymouth because, as it says in the ship's log, "We could not now take time for further search or consideration, our victuals having been much spent, especially our bere." The Spanish missionaries brought grapevines, and before the United States was yet a nation, there was wine making in California. The Dutch opened the first distillery on Staten Island in 1640. In the Massachusetts Bay Colony, brewing ranked next in importance after milling and baking. The Puritans did not disdain the use of alcohol as is sometimes supposed. A federal law passed in 1790 gave provisions for each soldier to receive a ration of one-fourth pint of brandy, rum, or whiskey. The colonists imported wine and malt beverages and planted vineyards, but it was Jamaican rum that became the answer to the thirst of the new nation. For its sake, New Englanders became the bankers of the slave trade that supplied the molasses needed to produce rum. Eventually whiskey, the backwoods substitute for rum, superseded rum in popularity. Sour-mash bourbon became the great American drink.

This is a very brief view of alcohol's history. The extent of its uses, the ways in which it has been viewed, and even the amount of writing about it that survives give witness to the value placed on this strange substance. Alcohol has been everywhere, connected to everything that is a part of everyday life. Growing the grapes or grains to produce it is even suspected as the reason for the development of agriculture. Whether making it, using it as a medicine, drinking it, or writing about it, people from early times have devoted much time and energy to alcohol.

WHY BOTHER?

So alcohol happened. Why didn't it go the way of the dinosaurs? Think about the first time you ever tasted alcohol. . . . Some people were exposed early and don't remember the experience of a little sherry in their bottle or rubbed on their gums when they were teething. Some were allowed a taste of Dad's beer or the Christmas Day champagne at a tender age. Some sneaked sips at the first big wedding or party they were around. Some never even saw it until junior or senior high school. Still others were taught from infancy that it was evil and may not have touched it until college or the army took them away from home. And there are some who, for one reason or another, have never touched the stuff. If you are in the majority, however, you probably encountered alcohol in a variation on one of the above themes.

In vino veritas.
PLINY

Maybe you didn't like that first sip of Dad's beer or Aunt Grace's sherry. Rather than admit it, you decided they must know what was good. So you took a sip every time it was offered. *As you're fighting your way to the top, it helps to have a taste of what's up there.*

Perhaps you were around for the preparations for a big party at your house. Ice, soda, and funny-colored stuff in big bottles were lined up with neat things like cherries, oranges, lemons, and sugar. The atmosphere was busy and exciting. When the guests began to arrive, the first thing they got was something from those bottles. Everyone seemed to talk and laugh quite a bit, and after a while no one seemed to see you. Mom left her drink in the kitchen while she served some of those tasty cheese things she let you try earlier. One quick sip. *To keep the party going, keep the best on hand.*

Perhaps people in your home drank on weekends, but not you. Mom and Dad said things like, "When you're of age" or "Wouldn't want to stunt your growth" or "This is a big people's drink." Anyway, you weren't getting any tastes. Somewhere along the school trail, you wound up at a party you had expected to be like all the others you'd been to. Not this time. Someone brought some beer, and everyone else was having some. There might have been a brief flash of guilt when you thought of the folks, but who wants to stick out in a crowd? So you kept up with the gang. Soon you felt as grown-up as you'd ever been. *On your night of nights, add that sophisticated touch.*

Or perhaps your folks never touched the stuff. They were really opposed to alcohol. They gave you lots of reasons: "It's evil," "People who drink get into terrible trouble," "Vile stuff, it just eats you up," or even, "God's against it." Well, you admired your folks, or were scared of them, or you really believed that part about God's stand. Anyway, no one pushed you too much. Then came the army or college. It seemed as though everyone drank something, sometime, somewhere. They weren't dropping dead at the first sip or getting into too much trouble that you could see. Even if there was a little trouble, someone said, "Oh, well, he was just drunk—sowing some wild oats." Lightning didn't strike. You didn't see the devil popping out of glasses. Just the opposite, most of your friends seemed to be having a lot of fun. *When the gang gets together . . . bowling, fishing, sailing, hiking, swimming, everywhere.*

It could be that you grew up with wine being served at meals. At some time you were initiated into the process as a matter of course. You never gave it a second thought. You might have had a religious background that introduced you to wine as a part of your ritual acceptance into adulthood or as a part of your particular church's worship.

With time, age, and social mobility, the reasons for continuing to drink become more complex. It is not unusual to drink a bit more than one can handle at some point. After one experience of being drunk, sick, or hung over, some people decide never to touch the stuff again. For

We take a drink only for the sake of the benediction.
PERETZ

most, however, something they are getting or think they are getting out of alcohol makes them try it again. Despite liquor's real effects on us, most of us search for an experience we have had with it, or want to have with it, or have been led to believe that we can have with its use. *As an essential part of the Good Life, _____ cannot be excelled.*

Theories to explain alcohol use

Those trying to explain drinking behavior have always been more interested in alcoholism than in explaining alcohol use per se. Nonetheless, various theories have been advanced to explain the basic why behind alcohol use. Probably all contain some truth. They are included for historical perspective. They resurface from time to time as "new" ideas and may also be assumed by the uninformed to explain alcoholism.

"It calms me down, helps my nerves. It helps me unwind after a hard day." This explanation can be thought of as the *anxiety thesis*. In part it is derived from Freud's work. Freud had concluded that in times of anxiety and stress, people fall back on things that have worked for them in the past. In theory, the things you will choose to relieve anxiety are those you did when you last felt most secure. That lovely, secure time might last have been at Mom's breast. It has been downhill ever since. In this case, use of the mouth (eating, smoking, drinking) would be chosen to ease stressful situations.

Another version of the anxiety thesis came from Donald Horton's anthropological studies. He observed that alcohol was used by primitive societies either ritually or socially to relieve the anxiety caused by an unstable environment. Drunken acts are acceptable and not punished. The greater the environmental stress, the heavier the drinking. Therefore, in this view, alcohol's anxiety-reducing property is the one universal key to why people drink alcohol. This theory has by and large been rejected as the sole reason for drinking. Indeed, as biological research advances are made and more is learned of the actual effects of the drug alcohol, it can no longer even be said that alcohol reduces anxiety. At best it partially masks anxiety.

Another theory that surfaced was based on the need for a *feeling of power* over oneself or one's environment. Most people don't talk about this, but take a look at the heavy reliance of the liquor industry on he-man models, executive types, and beautiful women surrounded by adoring males. People in ads celebrate winning anything with a drink of some sort.

The *power theory* was explored by researchers in the early 1970s, under the direction of David McClelland. They examined folk tales from both heavy- and light-drinking societies. Their research indicated that there was no greater concern with relief from tension or anxiety in heavy-drinking societies than in those that consumed less. To look at this further they conducted a study with college men over a period of 10 years. Without revealing the reasons for the study, they asked the students to write down their fantasies before, during, and after the consumption of liquor. The stories revealed that the students felt bigger, stronger, more influential, more aggressive, and more capable of great sexual conquest the more they drank. The conclusion was that people drink to experience a feeling of power. This power feeling was seen as having two different patterns, depending on the personality of the drinker. What was called *p-power* is a personal powerfulness, uninhibited and carried out at the expense of others. Social power, or *s-power,* is a more altruistic powerfulness, power to help others. This s-power was found to predominate after two or three drinks; heavier drinking produced a predominance of p-power.

Another theory arose during the late 1960s at the height of the "counterculture" with its wave of drug use, particularly psychedelic drugs. This approach, as discussed by Andrew Weil, claimed that every human being has some need to reach out toward some larger experience. People will try anything that suggests itself as a way to do that, for instance, alcohol, drugs, yoga, or meditation. Some drugs were then commonly said to "blow your mind" or were designated as "mind-expanding drugs." Evidence cited for seeking altered states of consciousness begins with very young children who whirl, or hyperventilate, or attempt in other ways to produce a change in their experience. When they are older, people learn that chemicals can produce different states. In pursuit of these states, alcohol is often used because it is the one intoxicant we make legally available. The "drug scene" was viewed as another answer to the same search. Weil suggested that this search arises from the "innate psychological drive arising out of the neurological structure of the human brain." His conclusion was that we have put the cart before the horse in focusing attention on drugs rather than on the states people seek from them. Thus he suggested that society acknowledge the need itself for an altered state of consciousness and cope with it in a positive rather than a negative way.

Another perspective on factors that may contribute to alcohol use focuses on stresses associated with modern everyday life—be it in the pressures of making it in the corporate world, corporate downsizing, or the changes in family structure. Use of alcohol is seen as one response to stress. Other responses to stress include hypertension, ulcer disease, and migraine headaches. Accordingly, "stress management" became popular as a technique to helping people develop alternative, less destructive means of coping with stress.

Recently a factor that has been considered to shed light on reasons for drinking is the role of expectations, that is, what an individual believes that alcohol will do to or for them. But for the most part, current research is less interested in identifying factors within the individual that motivate alcohol use. Instead, the attention has turned to the social settings in which people find themselves, in order to identify factors associated

If all be true that I do think,
There are five reasons we should drink;
Good wine—a friend—or being dry—
Or lest we should be by and by—
Or any other reason why.

HENRY ALDRICH, Dean of Christ Church, Oxford
Reasons for Drinking, 1689.

with patterns of use. Accordingly, for example, attention is turning to the roles of peers in determining adolescents' decisions to use alcohol, or the influence of parental standards in setting norms for their teenagers' drinking, or the impact of legislative approaches.

In general, the accepted stance now seems to be a "combination of factors" approach. One inescapable fact is that from the very earliest recorded times alcohol has been important to people. Seldon Bacon, former head of the Rutgers School of Alcohol Studies, made a point worth keeping in mind. He called attention to the original needs that alcohol might have served: satisfaction of hunger and thirst, medication or anesthetic, fostering of religious ecstasy. Our modern, complex society has virtually eliminated all these earlier functions. Now all that is left is alcohol the depressant, the mood-altering drug, the possible, or believed, reliever of tension, inhibition, and guilt. Contemporary society has had to create new "needs" that alcohol can meet.

Myths

In thinking about alcohol use, remember that myths are equally important to people. Many think that alcohol makes them warm when they are cold (not so), sexier (in the courting, maybe; in the execution, not so), manlier, womanlier, cured of their ills (not usually), less scared of people (possibly), and better able to function (only if very little is taken). An exercise in asking a lot of people what a drink does for them will expose a heavy reliance on myths for their reasons. Whether factually based or not, myths often influence people's experience of alcohol use, a phenomenon referred to as the "influence of expectancies." Whatever the truth in the mixture of theory and myth, enough people in the United States rely on the use of alcohol to accomplish something for them to support an almost $100,000,000,000 industry.

ALCOHOL PROBLEMS: THE FLY IN THE OINTMENT

Alcohol is many faceted. With its ritual, medicinal, dietary, and pleasurable uses, alcohol can leave in its wake confusion, pain, disorder, and tragedy. The use and abuse of alcohol have gone hand in hand in all cultures. With the notable exceptions of the Muslims and Buddhists, whose religions forbid drinking, temperance and abstinence have been the exception rather than the rule in most of the world.

As sin or moral failing

All excess is ill, but drunkenness is the worst sort.

WILLIAM PENN

Societies have come to grips with alcohol problems in a variety of ways. One of these regards drunkenness as a sin, a moral failing, and the drunk as a moral weakling. The Greek word for drunk, for example, means literally to "misbehave at the wine." An Egyptian writer admonished his drunken friend with the slightly contemptuous "thou art like a little child." Noah, who undoubtedly had reason to seek relief in drunkenness after getting all those creatures safely through the flood, was not looked on kindly by his children as he lay in his drunken stupor. The complaints have continued through time. A Dutch physician of the sixteenth century criticized the heavy use of alcohol in Germany and Flanders by saying "that freelier than is profitable to health, they take it and drink it." Some of the most forceful sanctions have come from the temperance movements. An early temperance leader wrote that "alcohol is preeminently a destroyer in every department of life." As late as 1974, the New Hampshire Christian Civic League devoted an entire issue of its monthly newspaper to a polemic against the idea that alcoholism is a disease. In its view the disease concept gives reprieve to the "odious alcohol sinner."

As a legal issue

Many see the use of liquor as a legislative issue and believe misuse can be solved by laws. Total prohibition is one of the methods used by those who believe that legislation can sober people up. Most legal approaches through history have been piecemeal affairs invoked to deal with specific situations. Excessive drinking was so bad in ancient Greece that "drinking captains" were appointed to supervise drinking. Elaborate rules were devised for drinking at parties. A perennial favorite has been control of supply. In 81 A.D., a Roman emperor ordered the destruction of half the British vineyards.

Bacchus has drowned more men than Neptune.

THOMAS FULLER

   The sin and legal views of drunkenness often go hand in hand. They have as a common denominator the idea that the drunk chooses to be drunk. He is therefore either a sinner or a ne'er-do-well who can be handled by making it illegal to drink. In 1606 intoxication was made a statutory offense in England by an "Act for Repressing the Odious and Loathsome Sin of Drunkenness." In the reign of Charles I, laws were passed to suppress liquor altogether. Settling a new world did not dispense with the problems resulting from alcohol use. The traditional methods of dealing with these problems continued. From the 1600s to the 1800s, attitudes toward alcohol were low-key. Laws were passed in various colonies and states to deal with liquor use, such as an early Connecticut law forbidding drinking for more than half an hour at a time. Another law in Virginia in 1760 prohibited ministers from "drinking to excess and inciting riot." But there were no temperance societies, no large-scale prohibitions, and no religious bodies fighting.

America's response to alcohol problems

Drinking in the colonies was largely a family affair and remained so until the beginning of the nineteenth century. With increasing immigration, industrialization, and greater social freedoms, drinking became less

Give me another whiskey and sasparilla.

Temperate temperance is best.
Intemperate temperance injures the
cause of temperance.

MARK TWAIN

Equal Suffrage. The probable influence
of Women's Suffrage upon the
temperance reform can be no better
indicated than by the following words
of the Brewer's Congress held in
Chicago in 1881:
Resolved, That we oppose always and
everywhere the ballot in the hands of
woman, for woman's vote is the last
hope of the prohibitionists.

WALTER W. SPOONER.
The Cyclopaedia of Temperance and
Prohibition, 1891.

a family affair. Alcohol abuse became more open and more destructive. The opening of the West brought the saloon into prominence. The old, stable social and family patterns began to change. The frontier hero took to gulping his drinks with his foot on the bar rail. Attitudes began to intensify regarding the use of alcohol. These developments hold the key to many modern attitudes toward alcohol, the stigma of alcoholism, and the wet-dry controversy. Differing views of alcohol began to polarize America. The legal and moral approaches reached their apex in the United States with the growth of the temperance movement and the Prohibition amendment in 1919.

Temperance and prohibition   The traditional American temperance movement did not begin as a prohibition movement. The temperance movement coincided with the rise of social consciousness, a belief in the efficacy of law to resolve human problems. It was part and parcel of the humanitarian movement, which included child labor and prison reform, women's rights, abolition, and social welfare and poverty legislation. Originally it condemned only excessive drinking and the drinking of distilled liquor, not all alcoholic beverages nor all drinking. It was believed that the evils connected with the abuse of alcohol could be remedied through proper legislation. The aims of the original temperance movement were largely moral, uplifting, rehabilitative. Passions grow, however, and before long those who had condemned only the excessive use of distilled liquor were condemning all alcohol. Those genial, well-meaning physicians, businessmen, and farmers began to organize their social life around their crusade. Fraternal orders, such as the Independent Order of Good Templars of 1850, grew and proliferated. In a short span of time it had branches all over the United States, with churches, missions, and hospitals—all dedicated to the idea that society's evils were caused by liquor. This particular group influenced the growth of the Women's Christian Temperance Union (WCTU) and the Anti-Saloon League. By 1869 it had become the National Prohibition Party, the spearhead of political action, which advocated complete suppression of liquor by law.

People who had no experience at all with drinking got involved in the crusade. In 1874 Frances Willard founded the WCTU in Cleveland. Women became interested in the movement, which simultaneously advocated social reform, prayer, prevention, education, and legislation in the field of alcohol. Mass meetings were organized to which thousands came. Journals were published; children's programs taught fear and hatred of alcohol; libraries were established. The WCTU was responsible for the first laws requiring alcohol education in the schools, some of which remain on the books. All alcohol use—moderate, light, heavy, excessive—was condemned. All users were one and the same. Bacon, in describing the classic temperance movement, says there was "one word for the action—DRINK. One word for the category of people—DRINKER."

By 1895, many smaller local groups had joined the Anti-Saloon League, which had become the most influential of the temperance groups. It was nonpartisan politically and supported any prohibitionist candidate. It pressured Congress and state legislatures and was backed by church groups in "action against the saloon." Political pressure mounted. The major thrust of all these activities was that the only real problem was alcohol and the only real solution was prohibition.

In 1919, Congress passed the Eighteenth Amendment, making it illegal to manufacture or sell alcoholic beverages. The Volstead Act had 60 provisions to implement Prohibition. The Act was messy and complicated, and no precedent had been set to force the public cooperation required to make it work. Prohibition remained in effect from 1920 to 1933.

Prohibition shaped much of the country's economic, social, and underground life. Its repeal under the Twenty-first Amendment in 1933 did not remedy the situation. While there was a decline in alcoholism under Prohibition, as indicated by a decline in deaths from cirrhosis, it had failed nonetheless. The real problems created by alcohol were obscured or ignored by the false wet-dry controversy. The quarrel raged between the manufacturers, retailers, and consumers on one side and the temperance people, many churches, and women on the other. Those with alcohol problems or dependent on alcohol were ignored in the furor. When Prohibition was repealed the problem of abuse was still there, and those with dependence upon alcohol were still there along with the stigma of alcoholism.

Another approach to alcohol problems is that of the "ostrich." The ostrich stance became popular after the failure of Prohibition and is still not totally out of fashion. Problems arising from conflicting values and beliefs are often handled with euphemisms, humor, ridicule, and delegation of responsibility.

Our inconsistent attitudes toward alcohol are reinforced in subtle ways. For example, consider the hard-drinking movie heroes. There's the guy who drinks and drinks and then calls for more, never gets drunk, out-drinks the bad guys, kills off the rustlers, and gets the girl in the end. Then there's Humphrey Bogart, who is a drunken mess wallowing in the suffering of humanity until the pure and beautiful heroine appears, at which point he washes up, shaves, and gets a new suit, and they live happily ever after.

Drunkenness versus alcoholism

It is important to see that alcohol dependence is not separate from alcohol. Dependence does not spring full-blown from somewhere. It is generally a condition that develops over time. Alcohol is available everywhere. A person really has to make a choice not to drink in our society. In some sets of circumstances one could drink for the better part of a day and never

The front door of the Boston Licensing Board was ripped down by the crush to get beer licenses the day Prohibition ended.

Food without drink is like a wound without a plaster.
BRULL

seem out of place at all. Some brunches have wine punch, Bloody Marys, or café brulêt as their accompaniment. Sherry, beer, or a mixed drink is quite appropriate at lunchtime. Helping a friend with an afternoon painting project or even raking your own lawn is a reasonable time to have a beer. Then, after a long day, comes the pre-dinner cocktail, maybe some wine with the meal. Later, watching a tape with friends, drinks are offered. And surely, some romantic candlelight and a nightcap go hand in hand. For most people this would not be their daily or even weekend fare, but the point is that none of the above would cause most people to raise an eyebrow. The accepted times for drinking can be all the time, anywhere. Given enough of the kind of days we described, the person who chooses to drink may develop problems, because alcohol is a drug and does have effects on the body.

Is alcoholism, which is now termed alcohol dependence, a purely modern phenomenon, a product of our times? There are no references to alcoholics as such in historical writing. The word *alcoholism* was first introduced in 1849. Magnus Huss, a prominent Swedish physician, wrote a book on the physical problems associated with drinking distilled spirits titled *Chronic Alcoholic Illness: A Contribution to the Study of Dyscasias Based on my Personal Experience and the Experience of Others*. (The term *dyscasias* is no longer used. Even then, the meaning of the term was a bit vague, covering a combination of maladies and generally used to describe those thought to have a "poor constitution.") In using the term *alcohol-ism,* Huss was following the common scientific practice of using "ism" as a description of a disease, especially those associated with poisonings. While recognizing the host of medical complications, he thought that the culprit was distilled spirits and not associated with fermented beverages.

While the word alcoholism is a relatively modern one, there are vague references as far back in time as the third century that distinguish between being merely intoxicated and being a drunkard. In a commentary on imperial law, a Roman jurist of that era suggests that inveterate drunkenness be considered a medical matter rather than a legal one. In the thirteenth century James I of Aragon issued an edict providing for hospitalization of conspicuously active drunks. In 1655 a man named Younge, an English journalist, wrote a pamphlet in which he seemed to discern the difference between one who drinks and one who has a chronic condition related to alcohol. He says, "He that will be drawn to drink when he hath neither need of it nor mind to it is a drunkard."

Wine is a bad thing,
It makes you quarrel with your
neighbor.
It makes you shoot at your landlord,
It makes you—miss him.

History of alcohol treatment efforts

The first serious considerations of the problem of inebriety, as it was called, came in the eighteenth and nineteenth centuries. Two famous writings addressed the problem in what seemed to be a new light.

Although their work on the physical aspects of alcohol became fodder for the temperance zealots, both Dr. Benjamin Rush and Dr. Thomas Trotter seriously considered the effects of alcohol in a scientific way. Rush, a signer of the Declaration of Independence and the first Surgeon General, wrote a lengthy treatise with a nearly equally lengthy title, *An Inquiry into the Effects of Ardent Spirits on the Human Body and Mind, with an Account of the Means of Preventing and the Remedies of Curing Them.* Rush's book is a compendium of the attitudes of the time, given weight by scholarly treatment. The more important of the two, and the first scientific formulation of drunkenness on record, is the classic work of Trotter, an Edinburgh physician. In 1804 he wrote *An Essay, Medical, Philosophical, and Chemical, on Drunkenness and Its Effects on the Human Body.* He states: "In the writings of medicine, we find drunkenness only cursorily mentioned among the powers that injure health. The priesthood hath poured forth its anathemas from the pulpit; and the moralist, no less severe, hath declaimed against it as a vice degrading to our nature." He then gets down to the heart of the matter: "In medical language, I consider drunkenness, strictly speaking, to be a disease, produced by a remote cause, and giving birth to actions and movements in the living body that disorder the functions of health." Trotter did not gain many adherents to his position, but small efforts were also being made in the United States at that time and elsewhere.

PORTRAIT OF A MAN WHO SWears He will never HAVe another drink

Around the 1830s, in Massachusetts, Connecticut, and New York, small groups were forming to reform "intemperate persons" by hospitalizing them, instead of sending them to jail or the workhouse. The new groups, started by the medical superintendent of Worcester, Massachusetts, Dr. Samuel Woodward, and a Dr. Eli Todd, did not see inebriates in the same class with criminals, the indigent, or the insane. Between 1841 and 1874, eleven nonprofit hospitals and houses were set up. In 1876 *The Journal of Inebriety* started publication to advance their views and findings. These efforts were taking place against the background of the temperance movement. Consequently, there was tremendous popular opposition from both the church and the legislative chambers. The *Journal* was not prestigious by the standards of the medical journals of that time, and before Prohibition the hospitals were closed and the *Journal* had folded.

Another group also briefly flourished. The Washington Temperance Society began in Chase's Tavern in Baltimore in 1840. Six drinking buddies were the founders, and they each agreed to bring a friend to the next meeting. Within a few months parades and public meetings were being held to spread the message: "Drunkard! Come up here! You can reform. We don't slight the drunkard. We love him!" At the peak of its success in 1844, the membership consisted of 100,000 "reformed common drunkards" and 300,000 "common tipplers." A women's auxiliary group, the Martha Washington Society, was dedicated to feeding and clothing the

Home for the fallen

I'm sorry son, but we can't accept you if you still can walk. Have another bottle or two and come back once you've fallen.

Alcohol is a very necessary article . . . It makes life bearable to millions of people who could not endure their existence if they were quite sober. It enables Parliament to do things at eleven at night that no sane person would do at eleven in the morning.

GEORGE BERNARD SHAW, 1907

poor. Based on the promise of religious salvation, the Washington Temperance Society was organized in much the same way as the ordinary temperance groups, but with one difference. It was founded on the basis of one drunkard helping another, of drunks telling their story in public. The society prospered all over the East Coast as far north as New Hampshire. A hospital, the Home for the Fallen, was established in Boston and still exists under a different name. There are many similarities between the Washington Society and Alcoholics Anonymous (AA): alcoholics helping each other, regular meetings, sharing experiences, fellowship, reliance on a Higher Power, and total abstention from alcohol. The Society was, however, caught up in the frenzies of the total temperance movement, including the controversies, power struggles, religious fights, and competition among the leaders. By 1848, just 8 short years after being founded, it was absorbed into the total prohibition movement. The treatment of the alcoholic became unimportant in the heat of the argument.

Recognition of the alcoholic as a sick person did not reemerge until comparatively recently. The gathering of a group of scientists at Yale University's Laboratory of Applied Psychology (later the Laboratory of Applied Biodynamics) and the Fellowship of Alcoholics Anonymous, both begun in the 1930s, were instrumental in bringing this about. Also in the 1930s a recovering Bostonian, Richard Peabody, first began to apply psychological methods to the treatment of those with alcoholism. He replaced the terms "drunk" and "drunkenness" with the more scientific and less judgmental "alcoholic" and "alcoholism." At Yale, Yandell Henderson, Howard Haggard, Leon Greenberg, and later E. M. Jellinek founded the *Quarterly Journal of Studies on Alcohol* (QJSA)—since 1975 known as the *Journal of Studies on Alcohol.* Unlike the earlier *Journal of Inebriety,* the QJSA had a sound scientific footing and became the mouthpiece for alcohol information. Starting with Haggard's work on alcohol metabolism, these efforts marked the first attempt to put the study of alcohol and alcohol problems in a respectable up-to-date framework. Jellinek's masterwork, *The Disease Concept of Alcoholism,* was a product of the Yale experience. The Yale Center of Alcohol Studies and the Classified Abstract Archive of Alcohol Literature were established. The Yale Plan Clinic was also set up to diagnose and treat alcoholism. The Yale Summer School of Alcohol Studies, now the Rutgers School, educated professionals and lay people from all walks of life. Yale's prestigious influence had far-reaching effects. A volunteer organization, the National Council on Alcoholism (NCA)—now renamed the National Council on Alcohol and Other Drug Dependence (NCADD)— also grew out of the Yale School. It was founded in 1944 to provide public information and education about alcohol, through the joint efforts of Jellinek and Marty Mann, a recovering individual who became the NCA's first president.

On the other side of the coin, Alcoholics Anonymous was having more success in treating alcoholics than was any other group. AA grew, with a current estimated membership of over two million in both America and abroad. Its members became influential in removing the stigma that had so long been an accompaniment of alcoholism. Lawyers, business people, teachers, people from every sector of society began to recover. They could be seen leading useful, normal lives without alcohol. (More will be said in Chapter 9 on the origins and program of AA itself.) The successful recoveries of its members unquestionably influenced the course of later developments.

Public policy and alcohol

Changing perceptions of alcoholism have become the foundation for public policy. Alcoholism is now recognized as a major public health problem. At the center of the federal efforts has been the National Institute of Alcohol Abuse and Alcoholism (NIAAA), established in 1971. The NIAAA at its founding became a major sponsor of research, training, public education, and treatment programs. The legislation creating the NIAAA was a landmark in our societal response to alcoholism. This bill, the Comprehensive Alcohol Abuse and Alcoholism Prevention, Treatment, and Rehabilitation Act of 1970, was sponsored by the late Senator Harold Hughes, himself a recovering person. Beyond establishing the NIAAA, the legislation created what might be called a "bill of rights" for those with alcoholism. It recognized that they suffer from a "disease that requires treatment"; it provided some protections against discrimination in hiring of recovering alcoholics. That protection was further extended through the passage of the American with Disabilities Act of 1990, designed to protect those with handicaps from discrimination.

In a similar vein, the Uniform Alcoholism and Intoxication Treatment Act, passed in 1971 and dealing with the issue of public intoxication, was recommended for enactment by the states. This Act mandated treatment rather than punishment. With it public inebriation was no longer a crime. These legislative acts incorporated the emerging new views of alcoholism and alcohol abuse: it is a problem; it is treatable.

On the heels of this legislation, there was a rapid increase during the 1970s in alcoholism treatment services, both public and private, both residential and outpatient. In addition, each state mandated alcohol (and drug abuse) services that focused on public information and education as well as treatment. Similarly, community mental health centers that received federal support were required to provide alcohol services. Also health insurance coverage began to include rather than exclude alcoholism treatment services for its subscribers.

In the 1990s, concern about rising health-care costs, increases that consistently exceeded the rate of inflation, brought about efforts to limit coverage for many medical services. Alcohol and drug abuse services covered disproportionately felt the ax. Insurance providers were increasingly reluctant to cover residential care. Thus the earlier most common

form of treatment, the "28-day residential program," ceased to be the dominant treatment model. The result has been much more outpatient care and the closing of many inpatient treatment programs because there were an inadequate number of patients to cover operating costs. Many professionals recognize that inpatient care need not be the universal standard. However, it is critically important for some patients.

Alcohol treatment professionals   With the increase in alcohol services, a new professional emerged, the *alcohol counselor.* These professionals formed the backbone of treatment efforts. With the increasing professionalism, the term *counselor* is more commonly being replaced by the term *therapist.* Alcohol counselors' associations were formed in many states. The early distinction of separating alcohol and drug counselors has gone by the boards. In some instances alcohol-drug counselor associations certify alcohol counselors; in others, state licensing boards have been established.

Interest in counselor credentialing began in the mid-1970s. A decade later, physicians in the substance abuse field began to examine the same questions. What qualifications should a physician have to work in the field? Is personal experience, the primary route by which many physicians initially entered, sufficient? The question was answered, just as it had been with alcohol counselors, with a clear No. Thus first steps were taken among physicians to establish a physicians' credentialing process. At this time there are several different physician groups for those professionally involved in the alcohol and drug fields. The largest of these organizations, the American Society on Addiction Medicine (ASAM) has more than 5,000,000 members. In 1986, ASAM began to offer a certification examination for members in the treatment of substance abuse. Other efforts have been launched to create a medical specialty in "addiction medicine," which would be analogous to other medical specialties, such as orthopedics, pediatrics, or family practice, and which would by definition entail a standardized training sequence and a process to award certification. ASAM has been in the forefront of this effort. The creation of a new medical specialty is a long process. It requires the approval and sanction of the Board of Medical Specialties, the national group that oversees the component member boards. Similarly there are credentials for nurses in the substance abuse field. In combination these efforts testify to the concern for creating standards and the recognition of a core knowledge base and associated clinical skills. They represent an effort to bring those medical personnel engaged in the care of alcohol and drug abuse patients fully into the medical mainstream.

Education for all helping professionals on substance abuse has become more common, with a proliferation of workshops, special conferences, courses, and degree programs. Concern about professional education and standards has not been restricted to those whose primary professional involvement is in substance abuse. It has been increasingly recognized that a core knowledge base and associated clinical skills need to be part of any helping professional's training. Thus the federal Alcohol and Drug Institutes and the Center for Substance Abuse Treatment have initiated programs to improve professional education among physicians, nurses, and social workers. These efforts have included designing model curricula, preparing curriculam materials, and working with the associated professional societies to promote the inclusion of education on alcohol and other drugs by these professions.

With the emergence of alcohol-drug treatment as a new health-care service, efforts were initiated to develop standards, not only for treatment personnel, but also for treatment agencies. In 1984, the Joint Committee on the Accreditation of Health Care Organizations first established minimal standards for alcohol rehabilitation programs. Other groups, such as Commission for Accreditation of Rehabilitation Facilities (CARF), have also begun to accredit substance abuse services. These efforts have resulted from, and at the same time contributed to, our society's response to alcohol and other drug use as a major public health problem.

Problems, use, and public policy   The focus on alcoholism during the 1980s broadened to include the larger issues of alcohol problems and alcohol use. Previously, the public's attitude could have been summarized as "the only real alcohol problem is alcoholism and that wouldn't happen to me." Now alcohol problems are not seen as so far removed from the average person. Drunken driving has captured public attention. This alcohol-related problem can potentially touch anyone. The concern about driving while intoxicated seems to have spilled over to intoxication in general. Intoxication has become less acceptable and is as likely to elicit disgust as to be considered funny or amusing. Other alcohol-related issues also have hit the public policy agenda.

An alcoholic is someone you don't like who drinks as much as you do.
DYLAN THOMAS

The lobby for warning labels on alcoholic beverages saw its efforts succeed in 1989. The extent to which these labels have actually had an impact on drinking patterns is unclear, but seemingly modest. However, in 1999 the movement for warning labels took a hit. The Wine Institute, a trade association of California vintners, convinced the Treasury Department's Bureau of Alcohol, Tobacco and Firearms, whose mission is to regulate the marketplace and collect taxes, to allow an "educational label," a 'non-warning' label, for wine. The proposed language is as follows: "The proud people who made this wine encourage you to consult your family doctor about the health effects of wine." (The word "effects" had to be substituted for the originally proposed "benefits.") This initiative was mounted purportedly in response to some research suggesting that consumption of wine in moderate amounts may have protective health benefits, including a reduced risk of heart disease. To take the wine manufacturers at their word, it seemed only "fair" that this information should be publicly available!

Changes in the Dietary Guidelines for Americans, issued periodically by the Departments of Agriculture and Health and Human Services helped open the door for the wine industry's efforts. These guidelines first mentioned alcohol in 1980, cautioning moderate use. The third version, in 1990, added another caveat: that the use of alcohol was not recommended. However in 1996, in light of evidence on potential benefits of moderate use, there was mention made of "a lower risk of heart disease associated with moderate drinking for some individuals," while also noting that "alcoholic beverages have been used to enhance the enjoyment of meals by many societies throughout history." Dietary guidelines aside, this move by the wine industry has not escaped the notice of Congress and public health officials. Efforts are now underway to prevent the introduction of these "educational labels."

Questions are increasingly being raised about alcohol advertising. The advertising budget for 1993 was $775 million dollars, leading to over $90 billion in alcohol sales. The money spent to promote alcohol sales is virtually equal to that spent on advertising for all other beverage advertising combined—from milk, to sodas, to fruit drinks. The suspicion is that advertising does not, contrary to the industry's claims, simply represent companies' efforts to capture a larger share of the existing market by encouraging drinkers to switch brands. Rather it is directed as well to increasing the market size. That means promoting use among those who are nondrinkers or very light drinkers.

Of special concern is the targeting of young people. The use of animated characters is just one case in point. Might the Budweiser frogs be considered an effort to prime the pump for future consumers? Then there is the placement of advertising. Decisions about where to place advertisements are carefully considered by any manufacturer or business. Magazines or television shows can provide very detailed information about their readers or viewers, with a breakdown by age, income, education, geographic region, and ethnicity. This allows advertisers to target very specific populations. It happens that many of the publications selected for alcohol advertising are placed to hit the youth market, including those under 21 years. A substantial proportion of these ads are for liquor. Beyond having these young readers envisioning alcoholic beverages in their futures, one can't imagine that the size of the underage market has totally escaped the beverage industry. Underage drinking represents 10% of all alcohol consumption. Of the estimated total of 36 billion drinks consumed annually in the United States, that means 3.6 billion drinks for those under age 21. That translates into 10 million drinks *daily* by those not legally old enough to consume alcohol.

A related issue is the creation of new beverages that are seen as appealing to younger people. One such example is the wine coolers introduced in the 1980s. More recent arrivals are drinks designed to mimic some old-fashioned nonalcoholic beverages. First introduced in England, they have since crossed the Atlantic. There is Two Dogs Alcoholic Lemonade, Mrs. Pucker's Citrus Brew, Hucker's Alcoholic Cola (with a 15% to 20% alcohol content), or TGIFriday's Lemon Drop Drink with its 40% alcohol content. The newest arrival is "alcopops." These are neon-colored single servings, packaged in test-tube-style plastic vials. Or how about six-packs of "jello-shots"—plastic tumblers of gelatin, fruit flavored and laced with vodka? These have hit the U.S. market and are being stocked on grocery shelves amidst their look-alike traditional nonalcoholic counterparts. Labels typically include cartoon characters or closely resemble the design of many of the old favorites such as Kool Aid.

Beyond targeting the youth market, some companies have developed advertising campaigns directed toward women and minority groups. The content of the ads is another source of concern. Even by advertising standards, many are blatantly sexist, depicting women in a demeaning manner, and promoting the stereotypes of male behavior that contribute to sexual harassment.

Another concern is the alcohol beverage industry's (especially the distillers) sales promotion in developing countries. With a declining domestic market, one way to maintain profits is to increase foreign sales. Along with economic development, many countries have begun to experience a significant increase in alcohol-related problems. Western patterns of alcohol use, now being introduced, are often very different from traditional practices. One question raised by efforts to increase sales in developing countries is an ethical one. Is there any justification for introducing alcohol problems into countries already struggling with the problems of poverty, malnutrition, inadequate health care, high rates of maternal and infant mortality, and illiteracy? There is another even more basic question. This arises in response to breweries now being built in developing countries, usually financed by international groups. Here the concern is not some future rise in alcohol problems. The brewing process itself requires significant amounts of scarce resources—water and grain. Any diversion of water from agricultural use or town/village water supplies, or activities that reduce the amount of grain for food, can have a devastating immediate impact on people's health and well-being.

Health and fitness   Alcohol use in relation to health and fitness has received considerable attention. An ironic twist is the fact that the alcohol manufacturers are spending undisclosed amounts of the almost $1 billion in advertising budgets to sell lower-alcohol-content beverages! Alongside "lite" and near beers and wine coolers, there has been a dramatic growth in sales of sparkling waters and nonalcoholic wines and beers.

Another window on public attitudes is the way in which alcohol use is portrayed in the media, especially television programming. Network film features aired in prime time with alcoholics as major characters are no longer news. Even on the soap operas, while several of the major characters are active alcoholics, there are also some in recovery. Overall, from soaps to cop shows, drinking behavior is portrayed less glamorously, more realistically, and far less frequently than in the past. A major public educational campaign conducted out of the Harvard School of Public Health in collaboration with the media addressed specific alcohol-related themes for attention. For example, the project promoted incorporating the designated driver into prime-time television shows.

Significant changes are underway with respect to the majority view of alcohol's problems and what constitutes appropriate alcohol use. A book published in the mid-1980s, *How to Control Your Social Drinking,* was probably a first. Its introduction noted that it was not intended for alcoholics, for whom controlled drinking is not recommended, but was directed to the social drinker, who, in our drinking society, may find that it is easy to drink more than is intended or healthy. Basically, it offered a compilation of tips for hosts, party-goers, and top-level business executives on techniques to keep consumption down, while discussing the benefits of moderation. Its significance is not that it contained any startling or new information, but simply that it was published and presumably seen as a topic of sufficient general interest to generate book sales.

ALCOHOL COSTS: PAYING THE PIPER

In the United States, statistics on who drinks—what, where, and when—have been kept since 1850. However, comparisons between different historical periods is difficult. One reason is that statistics have only been gathered methodically and impartially since 1950. Another reason is that there have been changes in the way the basic information is organized and reported. A century ago, reports included numbers of "inebriates" or "drunkards." In the 1940s through the 1960s, "alcoholics" were often a designated subgroup. Then came the 1970s and another change. "Heavy drinkers" or "heavy drinkers with a high problem index" began to replace "alcoholics" as a category in reporting statistical information. In 1980 alcohol dependence syndrome emerged as another category. More recently, "binge drinking," meaning five or more drinks per drinking occasion, has become another category used to described drinking patterns. So the task of identifying changes in drinking practices is not an easy one.

Who drinks what, when, and where

Nonetheless, out of the maze of statistics available on how much Americans drink, where they drink it, and with what consequences, some are important to note. It is now estimated that 70% of men and 60% of women are current drinkers, meaning they have used alcohol once in the past year. They comprise about 65% of the adult population. During the 1960s, per capita consumption rose 32%. In the 1970s, despite some ups and downs, consumption basically leveled off, with a peak in consumption in the early 1980s. Since then alcohol consumption has declined. Consumption in 1996 was the lowest since 1964. The decline in total alcohol consumption is almost entirely due to liquor now being less popular. Since 1977 liquor consumption has dropped by 34%. Notably, the decline in liquor sales has not been counterbalanced by a corresponding increase in either wine or beer consumption. The per capita sales of wine and beer have remained fairly steady.

In 1995 the statistically average American consumed the equivalent of 2.17 gallons of pure ethanol, the type of alcohol we find in alcoholic beverages. The statistically average American gets this quota of alcohol through the consumption of 1.7 gallons of liquor, 3.6 gallons of wine, and 25.6 gallons of beer. Because the alcohol content of each varies in terms of absolute alcohol, 30% of the alcohol consumed comes from liquor, 13% from wine, and the remaining 57% from beer.

A word of caution: all of these figures describe the statistically average American. However, it is important to realize that the average American is a statistical myth. The typical American does not in fact drink his or her "statistical quota." First of all, recall that approximately one-third of Americans do not use alcohol at all. The remaining two-thirds show a wide variation in alcohol use. Thus 70% of the drinking population consumes only 20% of all the alcohol. The remaining 30% of the drinkers consume 80% of the alcohol. Most significantly, one-third of that heavy-drinking 30%, or less than 7% of the total population, consumes 50% of all alcohol. Picture what that means. Imagine having 10 beers to serve to a group of 10 people. If you served these to represent the actual consumption pattern described, you'd have the following: Three people would sit empty-handed. Five people would share two beers. That leaves two people to divide up eight beers. Of those two people, one person would take two and the other person would get a whole six-pack!

Drinking patterns

Patterns of alcohol consumption vary according to a number of demographic factors. Among the key factors are the following:

Gender Women are far more likely to be nondrinkers than are men. Those women who do drink consume significantly less than do men who drink. Men are more than four times more likely to be heavier drinkers than women, with 6.5% of men and only 1.4% of women having had 5 or more drinks per occasion at least once in the previous year.

Age Persons over 50 years of age are more likely to be abstainers than those under 50. For both men and women the proportion of heavier drinkers is highest in the 18–29 age group.

A Tale of 10 Beers and 10 People

3 drink none

5 share 2

1 drinks 2

1 drinks 6

Race   Whites have the highest proportion of members who consume alcohol. Only one-third of African-American women and women of Hispanic origin use alcohol. Hispanic men are more than twice as likely as white and African-American males to be involved in heavy drinking, that is, having more than 5 drinks per occasion,

Education   Alcohol use increases for both men and women with higher levels of education. Those with more than 12 years of education are virtually twice as likely to be drinkers as those with less. On the other hand, the reverse is true for the proportion who are involved in heavy drinking occasions. About 6% of those with less than a high school education report heavy drinking, compared to only a third of that—about 2%—of college graduates.

Family income   The proportion of drinkers rises with family income. However, the proportion of heavy drinking episodes is twice as high among those whose household income is below the national median income than for those above this level.

Geographic region   In the South 42% are abstainers, about a third more abstainers than in other regions. The Northeast has the greatest number of drinkers, 80%, and the greatest percentage of weekly drinkers, 38%. For the other areas of the country, weekly drinkers range between 23% and 28%. The Pacific coast states are those with the largest group of heavy drinkers, 5%. If the numbers who abstain are not included in calculating consumption, by those who actually do drink, consumption is highest in the South and lowest in the Northeast.

Marital status   The lowest proportion of drinkers is found among those who are widowed. This is probably related to age, with the widowed being more likely to be older, and thus in the age group with the lowest proportion of drinkers. The proportion of drinkers is essentially the same between those who are married, either separated or divorced, or never married. However, the picture is different when one looks at heavy drinkers. The highest rate of heavy drinking episodes is found among those never married, 8.7%, closely followed by those who are divorced, 7.9%. This is close to four times the rate of heavy drinking found among those who are married or widowed.

Religion   Protestant conservative religious denominations have the lowest percentage of members who drink, 53.6%. The religious groups with the highest proportion of members who use alcohol are Jews, 92%, followed by Catholics, 79%, and liberal Protestant groups, 73%. On the other hand, although Jews have the biggest proportion of drinkers, less than one-tenth of one percent are heavy drinkers. The highest levels of heavy drinking are reported by Catholics and those whose religious affiliation is noted as "other." Both drinking and rates of heavy drinking vary according to the importance placed upon religion. Only half of those who consider religion very important drink, only a third are weekly drinkers, and only 1.5% report occasions of heavy drinking. On the other hand, among those for whom religion is "not at all" or "not really" important, about 53% are weekly drinkers and 9% are heavy drinkers.

How do the changes in drinking patterns in the United States compare to those of other countries? Internationally, alcohol consumption in industrialized countries has generally declined. Of 23 countries, 78% had lower levels of per capita consumption in 1990 than in 1970. Per capita consumption, for example, was virtually halved in Italy, going from 13.7 litres of absolute alcohol in 1970 to 8.7 litres in 1990. Five countries have had an increase in alcohol consumption: Denmark, Finland, Great Britain, Japan, and Luxembourg. Making comparisons to the United States based on per capita consumption is difficult because of the differing percentages of abstainers in various countries. A quarter of men and over a third of women in Ireland are nondrinkers, whereas in Denmark 98% of men and 94% of women drink. So alcohol consumed within a country is spread over very different portions of the population. A far more useful form for reporting such information would be the per capita consumption among the drinking population; alas, no one does this.

The most recent federal estimate is that 7.4% of the total adult population in the United States can be described as either having alcohol abuse or alcohol dependence. Extrapolating from the most recent census figures, we find that 13.8 million persons age 18 and over are "problem drinkers." It is also estimated that 1 out of 5 adolescents 14 to 17 years old has a serious drinking problem, which represents approximately 3 million teenagers. Thus in the United States an estimated 16.8 million people have drinking problems. For every person with an alcohol problem, it is estimated that four family members are directly affected, which means approximately 67.2 million family members are touched by alcohol.

During the 1970s and 1980s, a number of national polls included questions about alcohol problems. During that period an ever-increasing number of those interviewed indicated an alcohol problem in their immediate family. In 1972 less than 1 out of every 10 people (12%) said a member of the immediate family had a problem with alcohol. Six years later, 1 person in 4 (24%) said that an alcohol problem had adversely affected his or her family life. In 1983 that figure rose to 1 out of every 3. Only 1 year later, the figure reported by a Harris poll was that 38% of all households reported being beset by alcohol problems. In 1988, a survey conducted for the NIAAA found that 43% of the population reported having a family member with alcoholism. These changes in large part

Work is the curse of the drinking classes.

OSCAR WILDE, 1946

probably reflect the increased *recognition* by families of alcohol problems in their midst, rather than representing a dramatic rise in the occurrence of these problems.

In terms of which families are affected, those who are separated or divorced are more likely to report a family member with an alcohol problem. Those separated or divorced are three times more likely to report having had an alcoholic spouse. Younger adults are also more likely to report having an alcoholic family member than are older adults. The proportions are 42% for those under age 45 versus 26% of those over age 65. In any of these figures there is not much precision in distinguishing between alcoholics and those who are nonalcoholic but have had alcohol-related problem(s). These nonalcoholic problem drinkers might include the one-time drunken traffic offender who appears in court, or the person who, when drunk for the one and only time in his life, puts his foot through a window and ends up in a hospital emergency room. But the suspicion is that when reporting "troubles" people are not referring to those who miss work after a particularly festive New Year's Eve!

Among those who are alcohol dependent, under 5% are among the homeless, the modern counterpart of what was at one time termed skid row. At least 95% of problem drinkers are employed or zemployable; they are estimated to comprise 10% of the nation's work force. Most of them are living with their families. The vast majority live in respectable neighborhoods and are homemakers, bankers, physicians, sales people, farmers, teachers, computer programmers, and clergy. They try to raise decent children, go to football games, shop for their groceries, go to work, and rake the leaves.

Economic costs versus economic benefits

Although they constitute only a small portion of the drinking population, alcohol abusers and alcoholics combined cost the United States a huge amount of time and money each year. In assessing these costs, government statistics rely heavily on data gathered during the census, conducted every 10 years. The quantity of information generated may take several years to analyze. When dealing with national counts of anything, from population figures, to the numbers of licensed drivers, to the quantity of alcohol sold, the data are almost always an estimate. The figures are derived from the most recent data available or inferred from other numbers. From time to time, the federal government revises the manner in which it may calculate particular figures. Thus changes do not necessarily reflect a decline in alcohol problems and their costs but may instead reflect a different way of gathering the data.

The most recent estimates of the economic costs of alcohol problems are presented in Table 1.1.

TABLE 1.1   SOCIAL COSTS OF ALCOHOL USE, 1995

	Social costs	
	$ (in billions)	%
Reduced productivity in the workplace	78.5	47.3
Reduced productivity in the home	13.4	8.1
Motor vehicle crashes	18.7	11.3
Comorbidities (related illnesses)	14.1	8.5
Unintentional injuries (excluding auto)	11.8	7.1
Crime	11.5	6.9
Fetal alcohol syndrome	5.8	3.5
Treatment for alcoholism	6.4	3.8
Other	5.8	3.5
Total social costs	166.0	100.0

From: NIAAA. *Seventh and Ninth Special Reports to Congress on Alcohol and Health,* *
Rockville MD, 1994 and 1997.

*This chart is organized using the framework from the *Seventh Report,* because the information is organized by categories that made sense to lay people. But the figures are updated with information from the *Ninth Report,* along with the most recent data from a 1998 report by National Institute on Drug Abuse (NIDA) and NIAAA, *Economic Costs of Alcohol and Drug Abuse, 1992.*

The other side of the cost coin is economic revenues. The total tax revenues on alcohol raised by federal and state authorities in 1995 was $17.84 billion. It should be noted that in 1987, federal tax rates on distilled spirits were raised for the first time in 34 years. The tax on liquor was then raised 20%. Nonetheless, alcohol, especially distilled spirits, continues to be a true bargain. Because inflation has outstripped any federal and state tax increases, the real price of distilled spirits has been cut by nearly half. The real costs of beer have dropped 20%, and the cost of wine dropped by almost 25%. Alcoholic beverages have become so inexpensive that their prices are now within the range of many nonalcoholic beverages. While the costs of soda tripled in that period, the costs of alcoholic beverages have not quite doubled, so both are now in the same price range. The net effect of all this is that the typical American can drink more but spend less of the total family income to do it.

How do the social benefits of alcohol use compare to its social costs? Social benefits, in terms of tax revenues, wages, salaries, and income generated directly by the manufacture and sales of alcohol or indirectly via the hospitality industry or philanthropic contributions by the alcohol

beverage industry have not been similarly systematically calculated nor reported on an annual basis. Nor has there been any effort to translate the benefits to individuals from alcohol consumption into dollars.

A rough calculation of the cost-benefits of alcohol can be made by comparing the figures for social costs ($166 billion) and for social benefits, that is, the alcohol-generated tax revenues ($17.85 billion). Thus for every dollar of taxes generated, there is a corresponding cost to society of $9.54. To state the same thing differently, if all of the alcohol sold in the United States in 1995—which was 447,671,720 gallons of ethanol— were treated as if it had all been marketed as gallons of pure alcohol, the social cost would be $370.80 per gallon. The social benefit per gallon under the same reckoning is $39.85. If we were to pretend that all alcohol were sold as fifths of 80-proof liquor, that would represent 5,595,896,500 fifths. The bill to society per fifth would be $29.66 and the benefits in the form of taxes, $3.19 per fifth.

Other attempts have been made to consider the social costs of alcohol use, especially with respect to health-care costs. One study with the provocative title "The taxes of sin: Do smokers and drinkers pay their way?" was concerned with just that question. A variety of costs related to drinking and smoking were examined, for example, things such as the impact of early mortality attributable to smoking and heavy drinking. One result would be that if smokers and drinkers die early, what they have paid into retirement plans or social security in part becomes available to subsidize the benefits of others. The conclusion was that smokers do pay their way. However, those with alcoholism do not. Taxes on alcohol were found to cover about a half of the expenses generated by those who drink heavily.

Personal costs

The personal cost of alcohol problems is tremendous. It is estimated that alcohol-related deaths may run as high as 10% of all deaths annually. The alcoholic's life expectancy is shortened by 15 years. The mortality rate is two and a half times greater than that of nonalcoholics. Those with alcoholism also have a higher rate of violent deaths. Drinking figures prominently into both accidental death and violent death, for alcoholics and nonalcoholics alike. As many as 75% of all unintentional injuries are alcohol-related, including motor fatalities, falls, drownings, fires, and burns.

Motor vehicle fatalities   The number of fatalities involving alcohol has been steadily declining. Between 1985 and 1995, the proportion of all alcohol-related fatalities (either the driver, passenger, or nonoccupant was drinking) fell from 44% to 33.2%. There has also been a sharp decline in the number of fatalities with a drinking driver, going from slightly over 50% in 1986, the highest level, to 39% in 1995. Furthermore, the proportion of young people killed in alcohol-related accidents has dropped even more. In 1979, when such information was first collected, those under 25 accounted for 49% of all alcohol-related fatalities. In 1995, this figure dropped to 32%. Nonetheless, motor vehicle fatalities remain one of the leading causes of death in this age group. Seventy-eight percent of all deaths from accidents in this age group are due to alcohol-related traffic accidents. It has been estimated that per mile driven, the chances for a fatal accident are 8 times greater for an individual with a blood alcohol concentration of 0.10 or higher than for a nondrinking driver. In fatal motor vehicle accidents involving a pedestrian or bicyclist, the odds are greater that it will be they and not the motorist who has been drinking. The severity of injuries and associated length of a hospital stay have also been related to alcohol consumption at levels of 0.10 or above.

Alcohol consumption and the outcome of an accident are related in several other ways. Drinking is likely to decrease the use of protective devices, such as seat belts and, for motorcyclists, safety helmets. For the latter, with intoxicating levels of alcohol, the use of helmets declines by one-third. Also, for those who have been drinking and sustain injuries, emergency medical care may be made more difficult. For accident victims with similar severity of injuries, those who had been drinking had lower blood pressure and lower PCO_2 (the latter is a measure of blood gases and both are indexes for shock). Thus their medical condition was more fragile and likely to lead to problems if resuscitation and/or emergency care were delayed.

Falls Drinking increases the risk of both death and injury from falls. A review of all studies of deaths from falls showed alcohol involved in 15% to 63% of the groups studied. As blood alcohol rises, the greater the risk of falls. Compared to those who have not been drinking, those with a 0.10 blood alcohol content (BAC) have a 3-times greater risk of a fall; with a BAC of 0.16 or above the risk is 60 times higher. Of the injuries commonly associated with falls, fractures of the ribs and vertebrae are 16 times higher for people who are heavy chronic drinkers than for nonproblematic or "social" drinkers. One study following people over a decade found that the likelihood of a fatal fall increased in proportion to the number of drinks an individual had reportedly consumed on a "typical" drinking occasion.

Burns and fire Drinking increases the risk of injury and death by burns and fire. Burns and fires cause about five thousand deaths annually. Half of the people who die in house fires have high BACs. A review of recent studies shows that between 33% and 61% of people who died as a result of burns had been drinking. Approximately one-quarter of burn injuries involved people who were drinking. Alcohol use also appears to have an impact on the outcome of burn injuries. One study found that

THE SCREAMER
...experience the ups and downs of problem drinking.

among burn victims, those with a positive BAC had virtually twice the proportion of fatalities. The likelihood of death increases with higher BACs. In addition, those diagnosed as alcoholic had a 3-times higher rate of mortality and also died with smaller burns. So both alcohol consumption at the time of the fire as well as alcoholism influence survival rates. For home fires involving cigarette smoking, alcohol too is likely to be a factor.

Water mishaps   Drinking is involved in a significant percentage of deaths from drowning. Among boating-related drownings, 45% of the victims had a positive BAC, and 22% were legally intoxicated. Studies have shown that boat operators who are suffering from fatigue due to sun, wind, glare, and wave motion are 10 times as likely to miss course correction signals if they are also legally intoxicated. Boat passengers who have been drinking are at increased risk also. Alcohol also plays a role in diving accidents, many of which result in spinal cord injury and paralysis. Diving injuries that result in spinal cord injury are four times as likely to involve intoxicated divers. Not surprisingly, blood alcohol levels as low as 0.12 impair divers' judgement and at levels of 0.4 impair the ability to perform dives.

Air traffic safety   The impact of alcohol has also been considered with respect to air traffic safety. No accidents have occurred among the major commercial airlines, but alcohol use has been a factor in a small percentage of other aviation accidents. Experimental studies show that alcohol levels as low as 0.025 reduce a pilot's ability to perform essential tasks.

The workplace   Alcohol has been implicated in injuries in the workplace. An Australian study found that among fatal workplace injuries, 65% of those injured had a BAC of 0.05, and another 16% had measurable blood alcohol levels.

Suicide   Alcohol plays a significant role in suicide. Studies indicate that in one-third of suicide attempts, the individual had been drinking. In slightly over one-third of successful suicides the individual had a positive BAC. Drinking is also associated with more lethal means of suicide, particularly the use of firearms. Alcohol is associated more often with impulsive suicides than it is with premeditated suicides.

Violence   Alcohol use is a significant factor in cases of homicide and family violence. It is a much larger factor than is other drug use. In as many as 67% of all homicides either the victim, the assailant, or both had been drinking. Similarly, drinking is often a precipitating factor in child abuse, beatings, and other family violence. It is estimated that alcohol is implicated in two-thirds of cases of family violence. Fifty percent of pa-

If once a man indulges himself in murder, very soon he comes to think little of robbing; and from robbing he comes next to drinking and sabbath-breaking, and from that to incivility and procrastination.

THOMAS DEQUINCEY, 1839

tients treated in emergency rooms as the result of violence-related injuries were drinking within six hours of the incident.

As discussed in the *Ninth Special Report to the U.S. Congress on Alcohol and Health,* there are variations on this theme. The incidence of violence differs with drinking patterns, for example with binge drinkers vs. steady heavy drinkers, and with the acceptance or nonacceptance of violence in families. Similarly, in work on violence and children, what is being discussed as "violence" can encompass or refer to only some of the following: physical abuse, sexual abuse, psychological abuse, neglect, maltreatment, and abandonment.

Crime   Alcohol use is reflected in national crime statistics. Its role in homicide and family violence has been noted. It is a significant factor in assaults in general. For 72% of the perpetrators and 79% of the victims, alcohol was seen as playing a role. Alcohol is involved in both attempted and completed rapes. For 50% of the rapists and for 30% of the victims alcohol was a prominent feature. In cases of robbery, up to 22% of the offenders had been drinking. The current estimate of the total national bill for alcohol-related crimes and misdemeanors is $11.5 billion. The relationship between crime and alcohol use is not wholly clear. For example, are those who have been drinking just more likely to be apprehended? Or, does it reflect patterns of law enforcement?

Health care and alcohol

Alcohol has a significant impact both on health-care delivery and health-care costs. The following list summarizes some significant points:

• Studies have consistently shown that a minimum of 20% of all hospitalized persons have a significant alcohol problem, whatever the presenting problem or admitting diagnosis. That is an absolute minimum. In some institutions, the proportion is apt to be higher. The Veterans Administration estimates that 50% of all VA hospital beds are filled by veterans with alcohol problems.

• In terms of health-care costs, the American Medical Association in 1993 issued a report stating that of the annual $666 billion that Americans spend on health care annually, 1 of every 4 dollars is related to caring for those who are victims of alcohol or other addictions and related problems.

• Some people incur a disproportionate share of health-care costs. One large-scale study of hospital costs found that a small proportion of patients, only 13%, had hospital bills equal to the remaining 87%. The distinguishing characteristic of the high-cost group was not age, sex, economic status, or ethnicity. It was that those people were heavy drinkers and/or heavy smokers. A follow-up study found that high-cost users also had multiple hospitalizations. Patients with a history of alcoholism have significantly more repeated hospitalizations than do those without such a history.

• When health-care costs for untreated alcoholics and their families are compared to those of families without alcohol dependence, the difference is striking. The families with alcohol dependence have 100% greater medical costs. If one looks at the 1-year period prior to treatment for alcoholism, the health-care costs for untreated alcoholism increase to over 300% of those of the general public. Such a pattern of increasing medical care immediately prior to diagnosis is true for many chronic diseases, including diabetes, hypertension, heart disease, and respiratory illnesses.

• It is not only the family unit but also children of those with alcoholism who have higher than anticipated health-care costs. A study conducted by the Children of Alcoholics Foundation found that children of alcoholics had a 25% greater rate of health-care utilization than their peers. Furthermore, if hospitalized, their stay in a hospital was 29% longer; the hospital bill for their care were 36% greater.

• Following alcohol treatment, there is a rapid decline in the total family's health-care costs.

It is unfortunate and ironic that of all these health-care costs, only a small proportion—approximately 13%—represents expenditures for rehabilitation or treatment of the primary alcohol problem. The bulk of the costs are for treatments of alcohol-induced illness and trauma. Equally disturbing is the NIAAA's estimate that approximately 85% of the nation's alcoholics and problem drinkers are not receiving any formal treatment. Even if one were to factor in the members of AA, who enter without involvement in formal treatment (approximately sixty percent of the 2 million members of AA), that only reduces the "untreated" portion by another 5%.

A more recently recognized health-care cost is the expenditures that result from fetal alcohol syndrome (FAS) and fetal alcohol effects (FAE). It was estimated in 1995 that the costs for treatment and the special education, training, and required support services adds over $5 billion to the nation's health-care costs. Furthermore, these infants grow to become children and eventually adults who continue to require care.

If one considers the federal dollars spent on health research, alcohol use is a health concern that has historically gotten short shrift. When compared to other diseases such as heart disease and cancer, the amount of federal research dollars spent on alcohol research is not proportional to the economic costs or to the numbers of those affected. In the early part of the last decade, 15 times more was spent on heart disease research than on alcoholism and alcohol abuse research. And the amount spent on cancer research was 35 times greater, although the associated costs are only three-quarters as great as those associated with alcohol abuse and alcoholism.

One of the big questions is how alcohol and other drug use problems will fare in the rapidly changing U.S. health-care system. Despite

numerous studies that demonstrate that treating alcoholism is cost effective and that any treatment is better than no treatment, alcohol problems along with other drug use often remain the only major disease not routinely covered by health insurance. There is more awareness of the toll that alcohol dependence and alcohol abuse can take in our public and private lives, yet at the same time there remains the bias that such problems are "different" than other medical illnesses. When health-care reform emerged on the national agenda during the first Clinton administration, many national groups submitted position papers to influence how alcohol and other drug problems would be addressed within health-care reform. These statements tried to convey two messages. One was the importance of not having a dual standard of care, one for traditional medical problems and a different one for substance abuse, as if the latter was not a "real" or "legitimate" medical condition. The other point was to emphasize the potential savings that can result if substance abuse is treated, rather than waiting for the emergence of its medical complications. While an overarching national plan was not effected, forces for change were set in motion. Unfortunately, the dual standard of care that was feared has become the norm as managed care has come to dominate the landscape. However, efforts at the state level have begun to turn this around. Some state legislatures have already passed parity bills that require that behavioral health (substance abuse and psychiatric conditions) be covered in a manner equivalent to other medical problems. The degree to which this view prevails will testify to the extent to which we have come to recognize alcohol abuse and other drug problems as health concerns rather than moral issues.

OTHER DRUG USE

We often speak of substance use or abuse as if the particular substance were irrelevant. There are indeed many striking similarities. There are also some major differences between alcohol and other drugs, in terms of patterns of use, attitudes toward use, and how we as a society respond to the associated problems. While drug use and its associated problems should in no way be discounted, the fact remains that alcohol is far and away the "American drug of choice." This is quite evident from the information compiled in Table 1.2, drawn from the most recent National Household Survey. Sometimes this fact gets lost in discussions of "the war on drugs."

Social costs

In 1995 the social costs associated with drug abuse were estimated to be $109 billion. The corresponding figure for alcohol use/abuse is $166 billion. Almost 60% of the costs of drug abuse are attributed to costs within the criminal justice system, as well as costs to others, such as victims of

TABLE 1.2 ALCOHOL AND OTHER DRUG USE, 1996

Type of Drug	Year proceeding survey	
	Millions of People	% of Population*
Alcohol	138.9	64.9
Cigarettes	69.1	32.3
Smokeless tobacco	10.0	4.7
Any illicit drug use	23.2	10.8
Marijuana	18.4	8.6
Cocaine	4.0	1.9
Crack	1.4	0.6
Any psychotherapeutic drugs**	6.7	3.1
Stimulants**	1.9	0.9
Sedatives**	0.7	0.3
Analgesics**	4.5	2.1
Tranquilizers**	2.4	1.1
Inhalants	2.4	1.1
Hallucinogens	3.6	1.7
LSD	2.1	1.0
PCP	0.4	0.2
Heroin	0.5	0.2

From National Institute on Drug Abuse. *The National Household Survey on Drug Abuse: Population Estimates 1996*. Rockville MD: National Institute on Drug Abuse, 1997.
  * Limited to population 14 years and older.
  **Nonmedical use only.

drug-related crime. This is three times the proportion of alcohol-related costs attributed to these items. For drug abuse there are additional costs. In 1993, federal agencies ranging from the Drug Enforcement Administration to the Immigration Service, FBI, Coast Guard, and U.S. Park Service spent $ 3.6 billion on efforts aimed at reducing the supply of drugs.

Crime Within the federal and state prison populations there are striking differences between the relative proportion of crimes attributable to drinking versus drug use. In general alcohol is associated with crimes against people. Compared to other drug use, it is twice as likely to play a role in homicides, 6 times as likely to be implicated in assaults, and 10 times as likely to be a factor in sexual assault. On the other hand, drug use is associated with crimes against property. Other drug use is 8 times more common than alcohol use in robberies, 10 times more common in burglaries, and 10 times more common in larceny/theft, except for auto theft, where the rate is only 2 times as high.

Of the $8.4 billion state and federal correction attributed to alcohol and drug use, 80% of the costs are drug-related. Much of this disparity is because a large portion of drug cases handled by the criminal justice system are simply the result of the drug's illicit status, rather than being associated with other offenses attributable to drug use. Ninety percent of all arrests for marijuana are for simple possession. They are not for dealing, or growing, or crimes committed that are related to marijuana use. In addition, the penalties fall fairly evenly; there is little distinction in sentencing based on the individual's role in the drug trade system. Users and small time dealers have sentences equivalent to those much higher up in the pyramid. And, as one author wryly noted, the people at the bottom have no room to plea bargain or secure lighter sentences if they turn informer. Some of the laws passed that contributed to the rapid rise in the prison population have been the product of emotion and not reason. The most obvious is the distinction that is now made between cocaine as a powder and cocaine in the form of crack. The penalties for use of equivalent amounts are striking. A quantity that as powder would be handled as a misdemeanor in the form of crack leads to a felony charge and a 5-year mandatory prison term.

Drug use patterns

The National Institute on Drug Abuse (NIDA) conducts two regular surveys of substance use, the National Household Survey, that samples the total population, and Monitoring the Future, a survey of high school students and young adults. In general there was an overall decline in illicit substance use during the 1980s. There was overall an almost 50% decline between 1979 and 1992. There was then a brief rise in use, but in 1995 use again began to fall. The other notable trend is that there is a drop in the age of first use over the past decade.

Marijuana   Marijuana is by far the most widely used illicit drug. Nine percent of the total population used marijuana in 1995. However, marijuana use is most common among the young. Eighteen percent of all high school seniors report having used marijuana in 1998. Overall, use declined during the 1980s. Between 1979 and 1985, there was a 33% decline in use among those age 18 to 25, the age group with the highest level of use. However, from 1993 to 1995 there was a sharp up-turn in use. This has since been reversed. Among high school students in 1995 there was a marked decline. For marijuana, as with drugs in general, there has been a trend toward first use at an earlier age.

Marijuana use is more common among men than women, except for those under age 18. With respect to ethnicity, Hispanics have lower levels of use. Among adolescents 12 to 17 years of age, use is significantly higher in metropolitan areas than in nonmetropolitan and rural areas; however, among the 25- to 34-year-old age group there are no such differences, nor are there significant differences between sections of the country. Marijuana, along with tobacco, is sometimes considered a "gateway" drug. Among current marijuana users and those with heaviest use, there is a significantly higher number who report having tried cocaine. With the increasing attention paid to cultivation techniques, marijuana currently often has twice the THC content of the "back yard" varieties of the 1960s. THC, tetrahydrocannabinol, is the psychoactive compound in marijuana.

Cocaine   The use of cocaine peaked in 1985, followed by a marked decline, with the levels of use remaining relatively constant in the 1990s. Cocaine is more common in the young and middle adult age groups, ages 18 to 34, than among younger or older age groups.

Cocaine use, like marijuana, is more common in men, with the exception of those under age 26, where women's use approaches that of men. Racial differences are far less marked for cocaine use, although rates of use are slightly higher for Hispanic males than for other groups. Cocaine use is higher in metropolitan areas, but distinctions based on geography are not dramatic.

The change in the route of administration and the emergence of crack cocaine has been a particular concern. Although any method of cocaine administration is potentially lethal, the dangers increase dramatically with freebasing and smoking rather than snorting (intranasal administration). With freebasing, unlimited quantities can be ingested. While the level of cocaine use has been slowly but continuously declining, paradoxically there has been a marked increase in cocaine-related problems seen in hospitals' emergency rooms. The DAWN (*Drug Abuse Warning Network*) is a federally supported system to track drug-related incidents both in emergency rooms as well as their role in mortality as measured by medical examiners (coroner's) cases. Overall there has been a marked rise in drug-involved cases, with cocaine-related incidents experiencing the most dramatic rise. Between 1975 and 1985, there had been a tenfold increase, from fewer than 1000 incidents per year to approximately 10,000. By the mid-1990s, there was another tenfold increase to over 120,000 emergency room episodes involving cocaine. Thus, the magnitude of problems associated with use grew geometrically, even as actual use declined. While initially attributed to the presence of crack cocaine, the numbers have not gone down as the use of crack cocaine has declined.

Heroin   In the 1980s, heroin use was primarily associated with those referred to as "the dinosaurs," people in their forties and fifties. However, in the past several years, there has been a reemergence of heroin. A new generation of users has emerged, drawn from those in the 13 to 23 year age bracket. This increase in use has been attributed to a lowering of price, to greater purity, to the fact that cocaine street sellers in some areas have begun trafficking in heroin as well, and also to the fact that there is no "generational" memory of heroin use and its problems.

Inhalants   The use of inhalants is a particular cause for concern. This is because use is concentrated among younger adolescents and preadolescents, involves easily available commercial products, and tends to be a group activity. Use can lead to central nervous system damage.

When Jennifer told me she was a heroine addict I thought she was collecting spider-woman comics again.

Nicotine   Since the late 1960s, when 40% of the adult population smoked, there has been a steady decline in nicotine use. Historically men smoked more than women; however, with their higher quitting rates, the gender gap is far less marked. Among younger smokers, there is virtually no gender difference. With respect to racial differences, whites are more likely to smoke than are African Americans or Hispanics. Smoking is also strongly associated with other substance use. Since 1995, there has been a rise in smoking among those ages 18 to 25.

Public perceptions and public polices

Several factors influence the way in which we view and respond to substance use. The single major factor is legal status. Perceptions of a drug's danger are tied more to a drug's legal status than to its pharmacological properties. There are any number of ways in which we see the problems of alcohol use as belonging to a "them" who is different from us. The same thing is true of other drugs, but even more so. Substance use problems are often seen erroneously as existing mostly in urban inner cities, or among minority groups, or within recent immigrant groups. There is a long historical precedent for this.

A drug's illicit status also has a major impact on how federal money is spent. A large proportion of the money spent on the "war on drugs"— and the use of this military metaphor should not be lost—is not for treatment or prevention. It is going to policing efforts, be it the Border Patrol and the Coast Guard, or narcotics divisions in police departments. Similarly, the criminal justice system has seen a dramatic rise in the prison population. As noted, the bulk of this is attributed to drug-related offenses. In part this has been the result of the introduction of mandatory sentences for drug-related offenses. There is concern that members of minority groups are those most likely to find themselves in prison, despite the fact that there are not correspondingly higher rates of use among this population. This raises serious questions about disparities in policing practices and judicial responses that are based on race.

The cloud of illegality plays a role in the perceptions of what constitutes appropriate treatment, such as the use of methadone maintenance in the treatment of heroin addiction, or needle exchange programs as a means of addressing the epidemic of HIV/AIDs, which is tied to the practice of sharing needles. Another topic that is guaranteed to evoke strong responses is discussion of the possible legalization of marijuana use. This is true whether the topic is its prescription for medical use or the suggestion that we decriminalize possession of small amounts for personal use. In the public health field, harm reduction is a very respectable approach. This is predicated on the recognition that while preventing all use may be the long-range goal, in the interim, there are steps that can be taken to reduce the negative consequences associated with use. Designated drivers are a good example of such a response to driving while intoxicated. Harm reduction is seen as problematic when illegal drugs are involved, however. There is the fear among many that this inevitably can be perceived as condoning use. One of the challenges is to create a public health response that can replace fear tactics with facts and that can see people as needing treatment and intervention rather than primarily criminal sanctions. Our criminal justice response must better distinguish between large international cartels engaged in a major economic enterprise and casual users or small-time dealers, many of whom are only trying to support their own habit, in some cases because treatment is not available.

RESOURCES AND FURTHER READING

History and overview

Alcoholics Anonymous: *Alcoholics Anonymous comes of age,* New York: AA World Service, 1957.

Bacon S: The classical temperance movement in the U.S.A. *British Journal of Addiction* 62:5–18, 1967.

Chafetz M: *Liquor, the servant of man.* Boston: Little, Brown & Co, 1965.

DP: The Washingtonians. *AA Grapevine* 27(9):16–22, 1971.

Lender ME, Kamchanappe KR: Temperance tales, antiliquor fiction and American attitudes toward alcoholics in the late 19th and early 20th centuries, *Journal of Studies on Alcohol* 38(7):1347–1370, 1979.

Rorabaugh W: *The alcohol republic: An American tradition,* New York: Oxford University Press, 1979.

Sournia JC: *A history of alcoholism,* Cambridge MA: Basil Blackwell, 1990.

Why people drink

Horton D: Alcohol use in primitive societies. In Pittman DJ, White HR, eds: *Society, culture, and drinking patterns reexamined.* New Brunswick NJ: Rutgers Center of Alcohol Studies, 1991.

MacAndrew C, Edgerton R: *Drunken comportment,* Chicago: Aldine, 1969.

McClelland D, et al: *The drinking man,* New York: The Free Press, 1972.

Weil A: Man's innate need: Getting high. In *Dealing with drug abuse,* Ford Foundation: New York, 1972.

Social costs and social policy

American Medical Association: *Factors contributing to the health care cost problem,* Chicago: AMA, 1993.

Baldwin WA, Rosenfeld BA, Breslow MJ, Buchman TG, Deutschman CS, Moore RD: Substance abuse-related admissions to adult intensive care, *Chest* 103(1):21–25, 1993.

The frequency of intensive care unit (ICU) admissions related to substance abuse was examined. Of 435 ICU admissions, 14% were tobacco related and generated 16% of costs, 9% were alcohol related generating 13% of costs, and 5% were illicit drug related generating 10% of costs. In all, 28% of ICU admissions generating 39% of costs were substance abuse related. Substance abuse-related admissions were significantly longer and more costly than were admissions not related to substance abuse (4.2 days versus 2.8 days; $9,610 vs. $5,890). Frequency of substance abuse-related admission was linked with the patient's insurance status (Medicare, private insurance, uninsured). In the uninsured group, 44% of admissions were substance abuse related (35% to 52%), significantly higher than in the private insurance and Medicare groups, and generating 61% of all ICU costs in the uninsured group. Large fractions of adult ICU admissions and costs are substance abuse related, particularly in uninsured patients (authors' abstract).

Children of Alcoholics Foundation: *Children of alcoholics in the medical system: Hidden problems, hidden costs,* New York: Children of Alcoholics Foundation, 1990.
The Children of Alcoholics Foundation launched the first major study of the effects of parents' alcohol abuse on their youngsters' health-care patterns, utilization rates, and costs of their medical care. The Foundation hypothesized that children from alcoholic families, as compared with other children, would have greater health-care usage, including more frequent admissions to hospitals, longer hospital stays, and higher health-care costs. The study population consisted of dependent children of adults who were in treatment for alcoholism or related disorders between 1984 and 1986 and youngsters from other families. The data was based on claims filed by 1.6 million subscribers under group policies carried by Independence Blue Cross and included analysis by admission rates, length of hospitalizations, and financial costs of inpatient, short procedure unit, and home health care.

Cook PJ, Moore MJ: Violence reduction through restrictions on alcohol availability, *Alcohol Health and Research World* 17(2):151–156, 1993.
Strong associations have been shown between alcohol use and violence and between restrictions on alcohol availability and per capita alcohol consumption. This work reviews studies showing these relationships and explores their effects on rates of violence. Analysis demonstrates that increases in beer excise taxes are associated with reductions in per capita alcohol consumption and decreases in the incidence of violent crime, particularly rape and robbery.

Drucker E: Drug prohibition. *Public Health Report* 114(Jan/Feb):15–29, 1999. (55 refs.)
For the past 25 years, the United States has pursued a drug policy based on prohibition and the vigorous application of criminal sanctions for the use and sale of illicit drugs. The relationship of a prohibition-based drug policy to prevalence patterns and health consequences of drug use has never been fully evaluated. To explore that relationship, the author examines national data on the application of criminal penalties for illegal drugs and associated trends in their patterns of use and adverse health outcomes for the period from 1972 to 1997. Over this 25-year period, the rate at which criminal penalties are imposed for drug offenses has climbed steadily, reaching 1.5 million arrests for drug offenses in 1996, with a tenfold increase in imprisonment for drug charges since 1979.

Today, drug enforcement activities constitute 67% of the $16 billion federal drug budget and more than $20 billion per year in state and local enforcement expenditures, compared with $7.6 billion for treatment, prevention, and research. Despite an overall decline in the prevalence of drug use since 1979, we have seen dramatic increases in drug-related-emergency department visits and drug-related deaths coinciding with this period of increased enforcement. Further, while black, Hispanic, and white Americans use illegal drugs at comparable rates, there are dramatic differences in the application of criminal penalties for drug offenses—African Americans are more than 20 times as likely as whites to be incarcerated for drug offenses, and drug-related emergency department visits, overdose deaths, and new HIV infections related to injecting drugs are many times higher for blacks than for whites. These outcomes may be understood as public health consequences of policies that criminalize and marginalize drug users and increase drug-related risks to life and health.

Greenfield TK, Graves KL, Kaskutas LA: Alcohol warning labels for prevention: National survey findings. *Alcohol Health and Research World* 17(1):67–75, 1993.

After November 1989, federal law required health warning labels on all alcoholic beverage containers sold in the United States. The authors examined the effectiveness of warning labels as a reminder of the hazards of drinking. They found little evidence to indicate changes in behavior attributable to warning labels, except for limiting drinking when about to drive and an increase in conversations about drinking and pregnancy among women of childbearing age.

Gruenewald PJ: Alcohol problems and the control of availability: Theoretical and empirical issues. In Hilton ME, Bloss G, eds: *Economics and the prevention of alcohol-related problems, NIAAA Research Monograph 25*, Rockville MD: National Institute on Alcohol Abuse and Alcoholism, 1993.

This chapter reviews the theoretical and empirical basis of knowledge about alcohol availability and its effects on alcohol consumption and alcohol-related problems. Theoretical approaches considered include those based on: social norms, the distribution of consumption model, consumer demand and the full price of alcoholic beverages, subjective availability, and a theory of routine activities. The empirical literature reviewed includes studies of monopoly versus license systems for the distribution of alcoholic beverages, the geographical density of liquor outlets, hours and days of sale, and laws governing the forms of availability (the principal forms being on-premise and off-premise availability). The author concludes with a discussion of a number of fundamental problems, both theoretical and empirical, to be resolved by future studies of the relationship between alcohol availability and alcohol-related problems.

Hoffmann NG, DeHart SS, Fulkerson JA: Medical care utilization as a function of recovery status, *Journal of Addictive Diseases* 12(1):97–108, 1993.

A sample of 3,572 chemical dependency inpatients aged 25 to 82 years were the subjects of a study to evaluate whether observed reductions in health care costs are associated with successful recovery from alcoholism and other drug dependence, a function of regression to the mean, or ancillary health care during alcoholism/drug abuse treatment. The total number of hospital days were calculated for the year prior to treatment, and one and two years post-treatment. Utilization rates are not significantly different between recovering and relapsed patients prior to treatment; however, the differences between the two groups for the first and second year post-treatment are significant. The recovery patients showed a continued low utilization rate while the relapsed group had considerably higher utilization in both years. Recovery status is an essential factor to consider when determining valid cost-offsets for medical care utilization after alcoholism/drug treatment. (Author abstract.)

Holder HD: Changes in access to and availability of alcohol in the United States: Research and policy implications, *Addiction* 88(Supplement): 67S–74S, 1993.

Recent changes in alcohol availability and access in the United States are reviewed, and the role public policy research played in such changes is discussed. The paper finds that there are two concurrent trends, i.e., increased alcohol availability through changes in wine and spirits structural availability, lower prices and increased outlet densities, and decreased availability and access through higher minimum drinking ages, server intervention and training, server liability, low- and no-alcohol beverages, and warning labels on alcohol containers. This paper discusses these trends and the implications for policy development to which research is an input. (Author abstract.)

Johnston LD; O'Malley PM; Bachman JG: *National Survey Results on Drug Use from the Monitoring the Future Study, 1975–1997. Volume I: Secondary School Students.* Rockville MD: National Institute on Drug Abuse, 1998. (Chapter refs.)

Johnston LD; O'Malley PM; Bachman JG: *National Survey Results on Drug Use from the Monitoring the Future Study, 1975–1997. Volume II: College Students and Young Adults.* Rockville MD: National Institute on Drug Abuse, 1998. (0 refs.)

These volumes report findings from the ongoing research and reporting project entitled Monitoring the Future. Volume I sets forth data on the prevalence and trends in drug use for eighth, tenth, and twelfth grade students. Volume II provides detailed findings for college students and young adult high school graduates 19–32 years old.

Jones NE, Pieper CF, Robertson LS: The effect of legal drinking age on fatal injuries of adolescents and young adults, *American Journal of Public Health* 82(1):112–115, 1992.

This study examined the effect of legal drinking age (LDA) on fatal injuries in persons aged 15 to 24 years in the United States between 1979 and 1984. Effects on pre-LDA teens, adolescents targeted by LDA, initiation at LDA, and post-LDA drinking experience were assessed. A higher LDA was associated with reduced death rates for motor vehicle drivers, pedestrians, unintentional injuries excluding motor vehicle injuries, and suicide. An initiation effect on homicides was identified. Reductions in injury deaths related to drinking experience were not found. In general, a higher LDA reduced deaths among adolescents and young adults for various categories of violent death. (Authors' abstract.)

Manning WG, Keeler EB, Newhouse JP, Sloss EM, Wasserman J: The taxes of sin: Do smokers and drinkers pay their way? *Journal of the American Medical Association* 261(11):1604–1609, 1989.

The authors estimate the lifetime, discounted costs that smokers and drinkers impose on others through collectively financed health insurance, pensions, disability insurance, group life insurance, fires, motor-vehicle accidents, and the criminal justice system. Although nonsmokers subsidize smokers' medical care and group life insurance, smokers subsidize nonsmokers' pensions and nursing home payments. On balance, smokers probably pay their way at the current level of excise taxes on cigarettes; but one may, nonetheless, wish to raise those taxes to reduce the number of adolescent smokers. In contrast, drinkers do not pay their way; current excise taxes on alcohol cover only about half the costs imposed on others. (Authors' abstract.)

National Institute on Alcohol Abuse and Alcoholism: *Ninth Special Report to U.S. Congress on Alcohol and Health,* Washington DC: U.S. Government Printing Office, 1997.

This is the most recent in a series of reports, mandated by the legislation that created the NIAAA, requiring reports to Congress since 1971.

National Institute on Drug Abuse, Office of Applied Studies: *National Household Survey on Drug Abuse: Main Findings 1996.* Rockville MD: Substance Abuse and Mental Health Service Administration, 1996. (0 refs.)

This report represents the main findings from the 1994 National Household Survey on Drug Abuse (NHSDA). It provides data about the prevalence of use of illicit drugs, alcohol, and tobacco for the total population and for four age groups: youth, young adults, middle adults, and older adults. It examines the demographic correlates of the use of illicit drugs, alcohol, and tobacco. The report provides information about frequency and patterns of illicit drug and alcohol use, trends in drug, alcohol, and cigarette use since 1972, problems resulting from use, and perceptions of the risk from using drugs, alcohol, and tobacco. There are 92 tables summarizing the data presented. It is organized into 12 chapters: description of survey; trends from 1979–1996; marijuana; cocaine; inhalants, hallucinogens, and heroin; nonmedical use of prescription drugs; alcohol; cigarettes and smokeless tobacco; problems associated with marijuana, cocaine, and alcohol; drug use patterns; special topics—use by family income, health insurance status, and welfare assistance, prevalence of treatment, use during pregnancy; and mental health problems.

Sinclair JD, Sillanaukee P: The preventive paradox: A critical examination (commentary), *Addiction* 88(5):591–595, 1993.

This commentary reexamines the "prevention paradox" which suggests that even were there an effective "cure" for alcoholism and the numbers of alcoholics in the population greatly diminished, this would have at best a slight impact upon societal costs. In contrast, even a slight decrease in consumption by light and moderate drinkers, inasmuch as they are for more numerous, would prove a much more effective means of reducing total societal costs attributable to alcohol use. The authors point out what they consider to be significant flaws in this perception and reexamine some of the data presented elsewhere in support of their view. (Authors' abstract.)

2

ALCOHOL AND THE BODY

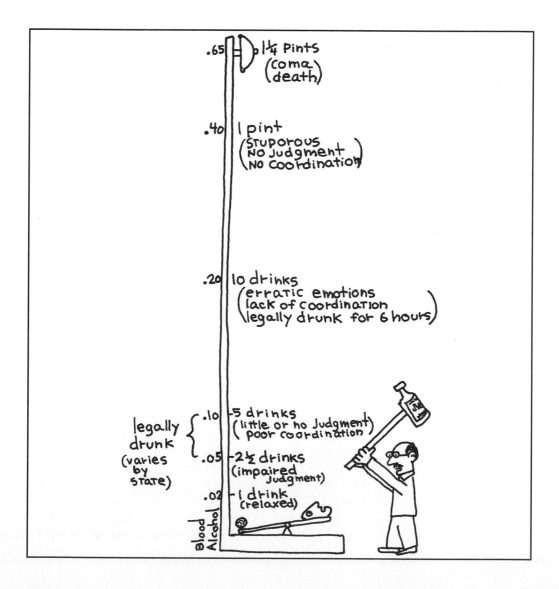

It is now widely recognized that alcohol is more than a beverage. Alcohol is a drug. When ingested, it has specific and predictable physiological effects on the body—any body, every body. Usually attention is paid to the physical impact of chronic use or what happens with excessive use. Often overlooked are the normal, routine effects on anyone who uses alcohol. Let us examine what happens to alcohol in the body—how it is taken up, broken down, and how it thereby alters body functioning.

DIGESTION

The human body is well engineered to take the foods ingested and change them into substances needed to maintain life and provide energy. Despite occasional upsets from too much spice or too much food, this process goes on without a hitch. The first part of this transformation is called digestion. Digestion is like a carpenter who dismantles an old building, salvages the materials, and uses them in new construction. Digestion is the body's way of dismantling food to get raw materials required by the body. Whether alcohol can be called a food was at one time a big point of controversy. Alcohol does have calories. One ounce of pure alcohol contains 210 calories. To translate that into drinks, an ounce of whiskey contains 75 calories and a 12-ounce can of beer contains 150 calories. Alcohol's usefulness as a food is limited, however. Sometimes alcohol is described as providing "empty calories." It does not contain vitamins, minerals, or other essential nutrients. Also, alcohol can interfere with the body's ability to use other sources of energy. As a food, alcohol is unique in that it requires no digestion. Since alcohol is a liquid, no mechanical action by the teeth is required to break it down. No digestive juices need be added to transform it into a form that can be absorbed by the bloodstream and transported to all parts of the body.

ABSORPTION

What happens to alcohol in the body? Surprisingly, absorption of alcohol begins almost immediately with a very small amount taken up into the bloodstream through the tiny blood vessels in the mouth. But the majority goes the route of all food when swallowed—into the stomach. If other food is present in the stomach, the alcohol mixes with it. Here too some alcohol seeps into the bloodstream. Up to 20% can be absorbed directly from the stomach. The remainder passes into the small intestine to be absorbed. The amount of food in the stomach when drinking takes place has important ramifications. Alcohol is an irritant. It increases the flow of hydrochloric acid, a digestive juice secreted by cells of the stomach lining. Anyone who has an ulcer and takes a drink can readily confirm this. This phenomenon explains the feeling of warmth as the drink

	Calories
Beer, 12-oz can	173
Martini, 3 oz, 3:1	145
Olive, 1 large	20
Rum, 1 oz	73
Sherry, sweet, 3 oz	150
Fortified wines	120–160
Scotch, 1 oz	73
Cola, 8 oz	105
Pretzels, 5 small sticks	20

THE JOY OF COOKING

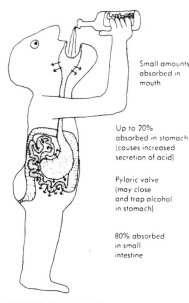

Small amounts absorbed in mouth

Up to 20% absorbed in stomach (causes increased secretion of acid)

Pyloric valve (may close and trap alcohol in stomach)

80% absorbed in small intestine

ABSORPTION OF ALCOHOL

goes down. The presence of food serves to dilute the alcohol and diminish its irritant properties.

The amount of food in the stomach is a big factor in determining the speed with which the alcohol is absorbed by the bloodstream. The rate of absorption is largely responsible for the feeling of intoxication—thus the basis for the advice "Don't drink on an empty stomach." The presence of food slows absorption. How much and how quickly alcohol is absorbed depends both on the total amount of alcohol in the stomach contents and the relative proportion of alcohol to food. The greater the amount of alcohol and the smaller the amount of food in the stomach, the more rapidly the alcohol is absorbed into the bloodstream and the higher the resulting blood alcohol level. A sex-based difference also seems to influence blood alcohol levels. This is related to differing amounts of an enzyme produced by the stomach lining that promotes the breakdown of alcohol (more on this later). Because women have significantly lower levels of this enzyme, more of the alcohol they drink remains available to enter the small intestine and be taken up by the blood. Therefore if women and men consume equivalent amounts of alcohol, women will have a higher blood alcohol concentration.

In addition to the impact of food in the stomach, the rate of absorption varies with the type of beverage. The higher the concentration of alcohol in a beverage (up to 50%, or 100 proof), the more quickly it is absorbed. This partially explains why distilled spirits have more apparent "kick" than wine or beer. In addition, beer contains some food substances that slow absorption. Carbon dioxide, which hastens the passage of alcohol from the stomach, has the effect of increasing the speed of absorption. Champagne, sparkling wines, or drinks mixed with carbonated soda give a sense of "bubbles in the head."

Now, on from the stomach to the pyloric valve. This valve controls the passage of the stomach's contents into the small intestine. It is sensitive to the presence of alcohol. With large concentrations of alcohol, it tends to get "stuck" in the closed position—a condition called pylorospasm. When pylorospasm occurs, the alcohol trapped in the stomach may cause sufficient irritation and distress to induce vomiting. This is what accounts for much of the nausea and vomiting that may accompany too much drinking. A "stuck" pylorus also may serve as a self-protective mechanism. It may prevent the passage into the small intestine of what might otherwise be life-threatening doses of alcohol.

BLOOD ALCOHOL CONCENTRATION (BAC)

In considering the effects of alcohol, several questions come to mind. How much alcohol? And, in how large a person? How fast did the alcohol get there? Is the blood alcohol level rising or declining? Let us consider each of these in turn.

The concentration of alcohol in the blood is the first concern. One tablespoon of sugar mixed in a cup of water yields a much sweeter solution than a tablespoon diluted in a gallon of water. Similarly, a drink with 1 ounce of alcohol will give a higher blood alcohol level in a 100-pound woman than in a 200-pound man. In fact, it will be virtually twice as high. Her body contains less water than his. The second factor is rate of absorption, which depends both on the amount and concentration of alcohol in the stomach and how rapidly it is ingested. So quickly drink a scotch on the rocks on an empty stomach and you will probably be more giddy than if you drink more alcohol more slowly, say in the form of beer after a meal. Even with a given blood alcohol level, there is greater impairment the faster the level has been achieved. Impairment is based on both the amount absorbed and the rate of absorption. Finally, on any drinking occasion, there are different effects for a particular blood alcohol level depending on whether the blood alcohol level is going up or coming down.

Once in the small intestine, the remainder of the alcohol (at least 80%) is very rapidly absorbed into the bloodstream. The bloodstream is the body's transportation system. It delivers nutrients that the cells require for energy and picks up wastes produced by cell metabolism. By this route, too, alcohol is carried to all parts of the body.

Although blood alcohol levels are almost universally used as the measure of alcohol in the body, this does not mean that alcohol merely rides around in the bloodstream until the liver is able to break it down. Alcohol is both highly soluble in water and able to pass rapidly through cell walls. Therefore it is distributed uniformly throughout the water content of all body tissues and cells. For a given blood alcohol level, the alcohol content in the tissues and cells varies in proportion to their amount of water. The alcohol content of liver tissue is 64% of that in the blood; of muscle tissue, 84%; of brain tissue, 75%. It takes very little time for the tissues to absorb the alcohol circulating in the blood. Within 2 minutes brain tissues will accurately reflect the blood alcohol level.

BREAKDOWN AND REMOVAL

The removal of alcohol from the body begins as soon as the alcohol is absorbed by the bloodstream. Small amounts leave unmetabolized through sweat, urine, and breath. The proportion of alcohol in exhaled air has a constant and predictable relationship to the blood alcohol concentration—which is the basis for the use of breathalyzers. These routes, at most, only account for the elimination of 5% of the alcohol consumed. The rest has to be changed chemically and metabolized to be removed from the body.

In 1990, a joint Italian-United States research group, headed by Mario Frezza and Charles Lieber, published new findings on metabolism. These were front page news, particularly because they identified differences between men and women. The breakdown, or metabolism, of alcohol occurs in a multistep process. The first step is its change to acetaldehyde. The enzyme that accomplishes this is called alcohol dehydrogenase, referred to as ADH. Before Frezza and Lieber's work this enzyme was thought to be present and active only in the liver. They, however, identified a gastric form of ADH. The breakdown of alcohol that occurs in the stomach is termed "first-pass metabolism." For nonalcoholic men, the amount of alcohol that can be metabolized by the stomach may be as great as 30% of the alcohol consumed. Nonalcoholic women will metabolize only half that amount in the stomach. Therefore, greater proportions of alcohol enter the bloodstream of women. For both sexes, a history of chronic heavy alcohol use leads to a significant decrease in first-pass metabolism.

The acetaldehyde that is formed is itself acted on in the second step of metabolism, by still another enzyme called aldehyde dehydrogenase. Aldehyde dehydrogenase too is present both in the stomach and liver. Then, very rapidly the acetaldehyde produced is metabolized into acetic acid. This is dispersed throughout the body, where it is broken down in cells and tissues to become carbon dioxide and water. The following diagram illustrates the chain of events:

Alcohol $\rightarrow$ acetaldehyde* $\rightarrow$ acetic acid $\rightarrow$ carbon dioxide and water

Almost any cell or organ can break down the acetic acid that is formed. But only the liver or the stomach can handle the first steps. These first steps depend upon the availability of a substance known as NAD^+, which is essential for the enzyme ADH to act. This substance, or cofactor, is present only in the liver and stomach. The rate of metabolism, that is, how fast metabolism takes place, is determined by the availability of this cofactor. It is not in infinite supply nor immediately present in sufficient quantities to accomplish the metabolism of alcohol in one fell swoop.

As alcohol is oxidized to acetaldehyde, this cofactor NAD^+ is changed; it is converted to NADH. As this occurs, the proportion of NADH to NAD^+ increases. The change in the relative amounts of these two substances has a number of important biochemical ramifications, which are discussed in Chapter 3.

---

* It is at this point that disulfiram (Antabuse®), a drug used in alcoholism treatment, acts. Disulfiram stops the breakdown of acetaldehyde by blocking acetaldehyde dehydrogenase. Thus acetaldehyde starts to accumulate in the system. It is very toxic, and its effects are those associated with an Antabuse reaction. A better term would be acetaldehyde reaction. The toxicity of acetaldehyde usually isn't a problem. It breaks down faster than it is formed. But disulfiram does not allow this to take place so rapidly—thus the nausea, flushing, and heart palpitations. It has been observed that Asians often have such symptoms when drinking. These are probably based on biochemical differences resulting from genetic differences. In effect, some Asians may have a built-in Antabuse-like response.

I'm on an 1800 calorie diet... 10 beers and 25 pretzel sticks.

Generally the rate at which food is metabolized depends on the energy requirements of the body. Experience will confirm this, especially for anyone who has taken a stab at dieting. Chopping wood burns up more calories than watching the VCR. Eat too much food and a storehouse of fat begins to accumulate around the middle. By balancing our caloric intake with exercise, we can avoid accumulating a fat roll. Again, as a food, alcohol is unique. It is metabolized at a constant rate. The presence of large amounts at a particular moment does not prompt the liver to work faster. Despite alcohol's potential as a fine source of calories, increased exercise (and hence raising the body's need for calories) does not increase the speed of metabolism. This is probably not news to anyone who has tried to sober up someone who's drunk. It is simply a matter of time. Exercise may only mean that you have to contend with a wide-awake drunk rather than a sleeping one. He or she is still intoxicated. The rate at which alcohol is metabolized may vary a little between people. It will also increase somewhat after an extended drinking career. Yet the average rate is around 0.5 ounce of pure alcohol per hour—roughly equivalent to one mixed drink of 86-proof whiskey, or a 4-ounce glass of wine, or one 12-ounce can of beer. The unmetabolized alcohol remains circulating in the bloodstream, "waiting in line." The presence of alcohol in the blood, and hence the brain, is responsible for its intoxicating effects.

ALCOHOL'S ACUTE EFFECTS ON THE BODY

What is the immediate effect of alcohol on the various body organs and functions?

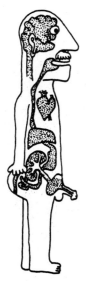

Interferes with brain activity, affecting first judgement, then muscular coordination, then sensory perception

Has few effects on heart or lungs except in high amounts, then may cause death

Interferes with liver's ability to maintain stable blood sugar

Leads to increased production of urine by kidneys

Irritates intestinal system; increases acid secretion by stomach

EEFECTS OF ALCOHOL

Digestive system

As already noted, alcohol is an irritant. This explains the burning sensation as it goes down. Alcohol in the stomach promotes the flow of gastric juices. A glass of wine before dinner may thereby promote digestion by "priming" the stomach for food. But with intoxicating amounts, alcohol impedes or stops digestion.

Circulatory system

In general, acute use of alcohol has relatively minor effects on the circulatory system in healthy individuals. In moderate amounts, alcohol is a vasodilator of the surface blood vessels. The vessels near the skin surface expand, which accounts for the sensation of warmth and flush to the skin that accompanies drinking. Despite the feeling of warmth, body heat is lost. Thus whoever sends out the St. Bernard with a brandy cask to the aid of the snow-stranded traveler is misguided. Despite the illusion of warmth, a good belt of alcohol will likely further cool off the body.

Kidneys

Anyone who has had a couple of drinks may well spend some time traipsing back and forth to the bathroom. The increased urine output is not caused by alcohol's direct action on the kidneys, nor is it due simply to the amount of liquid consumed. This phenomenon is related to the effect of alcohol on the posterior portion of the pituitary gland located at the base of the brain. The pituitary secretes a hormone that regulates the amount of urine produced. When the pituitary is affected by alcohol, its functioning is depressed. Therefore too little of the hormone is released and the kidneys form a larger-than-normal amount of diluted urine. This effect is most pronounced when alcohol is being absorbed and the blood alcohol level is rising.

Liver

The liver is very sensitive to the acute effects of alcohol. (See Chapter 3 for more information about the long-term effects of alcohol on the liver.) It has been demonstrated that for any drinker, not just heavy drinkers, even relatively small amounts of alcohol (1 to 2 ounces) can lead to accumulation of fat in liver cells.

The liver performs an incredible number of different functions—a very important one is its role in maintaining a proper blood sugar level. Sugar (the body's variety, called glucose) is the only source of energy that brain cells can use. Because the brain is the master control center of the body, an inadequate supply of food has far-reaching consequences. When alcohol is present in the system, the liver devotes all of its "attention," so to speak, to metabolizing it. This may well interfere with the normal liver function of maintaining a steady adequate supply of blood sugar. In the liver there is a stored form of glucose (glycogen) that usually is readily available. However, if one has had an inadequate diet, or has not eaten much for a day or two, glycogen may not be present. At such times the liver normally would use a more complicated biochemical process to transform other nutrients such as protein into glucose. This process is called gluconeogenesis. However, in the presence of alcohol this complicated maneuver is blocked. In such cases *hypoglycemia* can result. In a hypoglycemic state there is a below-normal concentration of blood sugar. The brain is deprived of its proper nourishment. Symptoms include hunger, weakness, nervousness, sweating, headache, and tremor. If the level is sufficiently depressed, coma can occur. Hypoglycemia may be more likely to occur and may be more severe in individuals who already have liver damage from chronic alcohol use. But it can occur in otherwise normal people with healthy livers who have been drinking heavily and have not been eating properly for as little as 48 to 72 hours.

In individuals with adequate diets, other metabolic effects of alcohol may cause abnormally high levels of blood glucose. This is called *hyperglycemia,* which is a state similar to that occurring in diabetics.

I have very poor and unhappy brains for drinking: I could well wish courtesy would invent some other custom of entertainment.

OTHELLO (1602–4) ACT 2, SC. 3, 1.

In view of its potentially significant effect on blood sugar levels, the danger posed by alcohol for the diabetic is obvious.

The liver also plays an important role in the metabolism of other drugs. The presence of alcohol can interfere with this role and be responsible for some alcohol-drug interactions. As mentioned before, the liver enzyme ADH is essential to the metabolism of alcohol. Quantitatively, it is the liver's major means of metabolizing alcohol. The liver does have a "backup" system, however. This secondary system is called MEOS (short for microsomal ethanol oxidizing system), and it is located in intracellular structures called microsomes. While termed a backup system for metabolizing alcohol, it is believed that this secondary system only begins to help out significantly in removing alcohol after long-term heavy drinking. It is mentioned here because it is a major system in metabolizing other drugs, including many prescription drugs.

Acutely, the MEOS activity is inhibited dramatically by the presence of alcohol. Therefore other drugs are not broken down at the usual rate. If other drugs in the system have a depressant effect similar to that of alcohol, the central nervous system will be subjected to both simultaneously. However, with some drugs there are additional potential problems. Suppose someone is taking a prescription drug, such as phenytoin (Dilantin) or warfarin sodium (Coumadin), at set intervals and also drinks. The presence of alcohol acutely interferes with the metabolism of the medication; thus when the next scheduled dose is taken, substantial amounts of the earlier dose remain and cumulative toxic effects may occur.*

Central nervous system

The major acute effect of alcohol on the central nervous system (CNS) is that of a depressant. The common misconception that alcohol is a stimulant comes from the fact that its depressant action disinhibits many higher cortical functions. It does this in a somewhat paradoxical fashion. Through the depressant effects of alcohol, parts of the brain are released from their normal inhibitory restraints. Thus behavior that would ordinarily be "censured" can occur. Acute alcohol intoxication, in fact, induces a mild delirium. Thinking becomes fuzzy; and orientation, recent memory, and other higher mental functions are altered. An electroencephalogram (EEG) taken when someone is high would show a diffuse slowing of normal brain waves associated with this mild state of delirium. For the light, occasional drinker these acute effects are, of course, completely reversible. Regular heavy use over time presents a different story.

Precisely how alcohol affects the brain and thereby influences behavior is not fully understood. Research indicates that alcohol exerts a major effect on the physical structure of nerve cell membranes, which in turn

* With chronic long-term alcohol use the activity of the MEOS is speeded up. In this instance the drugs are broken down faster, so higher doses must be administered to achieve a given therapeutic effect. (See Chapter 3 for more about alcohol-drug interactions.)

alters their functioning. These changes may be transient with acute alcohol intake, may persist with chronic use, or may lead to other changes in the structure and function of nerve cells as they compensate and adapt to the continued presence of high levels of alcohol. These effects on nerve cells, directly caused by the presence of alcohol, are presumed to play a major role in causing the behaviors seen with acute intoxication. They are also believed to be the basis for the phenomenon of tolerance and the phenomenon of withdrawal.

Alcohol significantly affects the production and activity of many different neurotransmitters, which are chemical substances in the brain. Neurotransmitters are what allow the cells in the brain to send messages from one cell to another. Thus they are the basis of the brain's communication system. Each cell has a "message sending" end and also a "message receiving" end. Neurotransmitters are what allow messages to cross the spaces between cells, called synapses, and activate the receptors on the "receiving" nerve cell. Several neurotransmitter systems are believed to be particularly important. Alcohol decreases the levels of an inhibitory transmitter, *GABA*, which causes a slowing of the communication across the synapse. Alcohol hastens the breakdown and removal of the neurotransmitter *norepinephrine*. This chemical is known to be involved with activation, stimulation, and the "fight or flight" response to threat. Also alcohol depresses the over-all activity of *serotonin*. Decreased levels of serotonin have been linked through other research to behaviors associated with intoxicated states, depression, anxiety, poor impulse control, aggressiveness, and suicidal behavior. Finally, the presence of alcohol increases the level of endogenous (meaning naturally occurring) opiate-like substances. This in turn leads to increased *dopamine* activity, especially in the part of the brain that is known to be linked to feelings of pleasure and well-being. To further complicate this, alcohol appears to effect the neurotransmitters in some sections of the brain more than those in other sections.

Without question, the CNS, particularly the brain, is the organ system most sensitive to the presence of alcohol. This sensitivity is what being "high," drunk, intoxicated, or impaired is all about. The neurophysiological basis for intoxication is better, but certainly not fully, understood. Without a doubt the intensity of the effect is directly related to the concentration of alcohol in the blood and hence the brain, but even here there are several other influences. The degree of intoxication is also dependent on whether the blood alcohol level is rising, falling, or constant. It is known that the CNS and behavioral effects of a given blood alcohol concentration (BAC) are greater when the blood alcohol level is rising. This is called the *Mellanby effect*. It is as if there were a small "practice effect," or short-term adaptation by the nervous system to alcohol's presence. Thus for a given blood alcohol level, there is more impairment if the blood level is rising than is found with the same BAC when the level of alcohol in the blood is falling.

The drug alcohol is a CNS depressant. It interferes with the activity of various brain centers and neurochemical systems—sometimes with seemingly paradoxical results. A high BAC can suppress CNS function across the board, even to the point of causing respiratory arrest and death. At lower doses it may lead to the activated, giddy, poorly controlled, and disinhibited behaviors that are typical of intoxication. This is not due to stimulation of CNS centers that mediate such behavior. Rather it is attributable to the indirect effect of selective suppression of inhibitory systems that normally keep such behavior in check.

Watch or recall someone becoming intoxicated and see the progression of effects. The following examples refer to the CNS effects in a hypothetical "average" male. Of course the observed effects of differing numbers of drinks over an hour in any given person may vary considerably. However, the type and severity of behavioral effects that do occur are a direct function of the amount of alcohol consumed; they progress in a fairly predictable fashion.

The "drinks" used in the following examples are a little under one-half ounce of pure alcohol, the equivalent of a 12-ounce beer, a 4-ounce glass of wine, or an ounce of 86-proof whiskey. Many generous hosts and hostesses mix drinks with more than 1 ounce of alcohol, even in the context of a quite proper cocktail party. Then there are college fraternity parties. They often ladle out some spiked punch of unknown alcohol content. Or there are the adolescents who, at an impromptu party out in the woods, simply pass the bottle around. So, as you read on, don't shrug off the "ten-drink" section as an impossibility.

One drink   With 1 drink, the drinker will be a bit more relaxed, possibly loosened up a little. Unless he chugged it rapidly, thus getting a rapid rise in blood alcohol, his behavior will be little changed. If he is of average height and weighs 160 pounds, by the end of an hour his blood alcohol level will be 0.02. (The actual measurement is grams %, or grams/100 milliliters. For example, 0.02 g% = 200 mg%.) An hour later all traces of alcohol will be gone.

Two and one-half drinks   With 2½ drinks in an hour's time, your party-goer will have a 0.05 blood alcohol level. He's high. The "newer" parts of the brain, those controlling judgment, have been affected. That our friend has been drinking is apparent. He may be loud, boisterous, making passes. Disinhibited, he is saying and doing things he might usually censor. These are the effects that mistakenly cause people to think of alcohol as a stimulant. The system isn't really hyped up. Rather, the inhibitions have been suspended, due to the depression by alcohol of the parts of the brain that normally give rise to them. At this time our friend is entering the danger zone for driving. With 2½ drinks in an hour, 2.5 hours will be required to completely metabolize the alcohol.

Five drinks   With 5 drinks in an hour, there is no question you have a drunk on your hands, and the law would agree. A blood alcohol level of 0.10 is sufficient to issue a DWI in any state. It is more than enough for states with a lower legal limit for intoxication. By this time the drinker's judgment is nil. ("Off coursh I can drive!") In addition to the parts of the brain controlling judgment, the centers controlling muscle coordination are depressed. There's a stagger to the walk and a slur to the speech. Even though the loss of dexterity and reaction time can be measured, the drinker, now with altered perception and judgment, may claim he has never functioned better. For all traces of alcohol to disappear from the system, 5 hours will be required.

A drunken night makes a cloudy morning.
SIR WILLIAM CORNWALLIS

Ten drinks   This quantity of alcohol in the system yields a blood alcohol content of 0.20. More of the brain than just the judgment, perceptual, and motor centers are affected. Emotions are probably very erratic—rapidly ranging from laughter to tears to rage. Even if your guest could remember he had a coat—which he may not because of memory impairment—he'd never be able to put it on. For all the alcohol to be metabolized, 10 hours will be required. He'll still be legally drunk after 6 hours.

Sixteen drinks—2 six-packs + 4 beers   With this amount of alcohol, the drinker is stuporous. Though not passed out, nothing the senses take in actually registers. Judgment is gone, coordination wiped out, and sensory perception almost nil. With the liver handling roughly 1 ounce of alcohol per hour, it will be 16 hours, well into tomorrow, before all the alcohol is gone.

Twenty drinks—not quite a fifth of whiskey   At this point, the person is in a coma and dangerously close to death. The vital brain centers that send out instructions to the heart and breathing apparatus are partially anesthetized. At a blood alcohol level of 0.40 to 0.50, a person is in a coma; at 0.60 to 0.70, death occurs.

ACUTE OVERDOSE AND TOXICITY

With alcohol as with many other drugs, an acute overdose may be fatal. Usually this occurs when very large doses of alcohol are consumed within a very short period of time. Rapid absorption of the ingested alcohol leads to a rapid and steep rise in BAC. In a relatively brief period, this may lead to loss of consciousness, coma, progressive respiratory depression, and death. Thus a "chug-a-lug" contest can be a fatal game.

In general, the acute lethal dose of alcohol is considered to be from 5 to 8 mg/kg of body weight—the equivalent of about a fifth to a fifth and a half of 86-proof liquor for the typical 155-pound male. Acute doses of

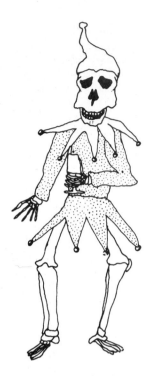

this amount of alcohol can be expected to result in BACs in the range of 0.35 to 0.70. Alcohol overdoses with fatal outcomes are consistently associated with BACs in this range, which is not at all surprising. It is known that a BAC above 0.40 will severely, and all too likely, lethally depress respiratory function.

Of course, the exact lethal dose and BAC in any individual will vary with age, sex, general physical health, and the degree of prior tolerance to alcohol. All things being equal, a very large, healthy, young adult male will tolerate a dose of alcohol that might well be fatal for a small, medically ill, elderly female. This is true, only more so, for the alcohol-dependent person, who has established tolerance, compared with the alcohol-naive novice drinker. Thus the alcoholic person may tolerate an acute dose of alcohol that would kill an otherwise comparable nonalcoholic individual. Although chronic heavy drinking and a high tolerance to alcohol may provide the alcoholic individual with some margin of safety, this protection is finite. Even the most severely dependent person may do himself in by consuming enough alcohol in one drinking bout to raise the BAC to the upper end of the lethal range. Therefore it is probably fair to say that a BAC of 0.70 or higher is certain to be lethal to anyone. The higher the level within the 0.35 to 0.70 range, the greater the risk of death.

Differences in women

Substitute a 120-pound woman in the previous examples, and the weight differential would dramatically speed up the process. A woman and a man who have identical body weights and who both drink the same amounts of alcohol will have different blood alcohol levels. Hers will be higher. Women and men differ in their relative amounts of body fat and water. Women have a higher proportion of fat and correspondingly lower amounts of water. This difference is significant, since alcohol is not very fat-soluble. Her body contains less water than his in which to dilute alcohol, which results in her having a higher concentration of alcohol in her blood.

Simply on that basis, let's contrast a 120-pound woman to our hypothetical 160-pound male drinker. With 1 drink in 1 hour, she would have a BAC of 0.04; 2½ drinks, and her BAC would be up slightly over 0.10. By 5 drinks, she'd have a 0.21 reading. Should she make it through 11 drinks, she'd be in a coma with a blood alcohol level of 0.45.

Beyond body weight and differences in the proportions of fat and water, there are other important differences between men and women with respect to how they handle alcohol. A woman's menstrual cycle significantly influences her rate of absorption and/or metabolism of alcohol. This difference presumably relates to the changing balance of sex hormones and appears to be the result of several interacting factors. During the premenstrual phase of her cycle, a woman absorbs alcohol significantly faster than in other phases of the menstrual cycle. So, pre-menstrually, a woman will get a higher blood alcohol level than she would get from drinking an equivalent amount at other times. In practical terms, a woman may find herself getting high or becoming drunk faster right before her menstrual period. Also, evidence exists that women taking birth control pills absorb alcohol faster and consequently have higher blood alcohol levels.

The differences between men and women in the levels of gastric alcohol dehydrogenase also are significant. Gastric ADH may account for the metabolism of up to 30% of alcohol in males. This means that for men, nearly one-third of the alcohol consumed will be metabolized in the stomach and never pass into the small intestine to be absorbed into the bloodstream. This is not true for women, who have lower levels of gastric ADH. Because of this, significantly less alcohol is metabolized in the stomach and, consequently, more alcohol is available to enter their circulation when the alcohol passes from the stomach to the small intestine. When consuming identical amounts of alcohol, women will have higher blood alcohol concentrations than will men, even if one accounts for differences in their weight and relative proportion of body fat and water.

There are also apparent differences in the metabolism of male and female chronic heavy drinkers. For both men and women with a history of heavy drinking, there is less gastric ADH. Since women have less gastric ADH to start with, and because it declines with heavy alcohol use, there is a veritable absence of gastric ADH among women who drink heavily. Thus for women who have a history of heavy drinking, the amount of alcohol that reaches the bloodstream will be virtually identical to having a dose administered intravenously. The difference in metabolism and the increased demands upon the liver to metabolize alcohol may be one of the mechanisms accounting for women's recognized greater vulnerability to liver disease.

Quite possibly, other important biological differences may exist between men and women in alcohol's effects. Most of the research on the physiological effects of alcohol has been conducted on men, and researchers have assumed their findings to be equally true for women. Though the basic differences between absorption rates of men and women were reported as early as 1932, they were forgotten or ignored until the mid-1970s. The impact of the menstrual cycle was not recognized or reported until 1976! With this failure to examine the effects of the primary and obvious difference between men and women, who knows what more subtle areas have not been considered. Women have been getting short shrift not only in terms of alcohol research. It is equally true in all areas of medical investigation. In light of this the National Institutes of Health is making efforts to promote equal inclusion of women as subjects of biomedical research and in investigations of the clinical trials for new drugs.

Despite biological differences between people, every human body reacts to alcohol in basically the same way. This is true despite the fact that for a given blood alcohol level, a very heavy drinker who has developed tolerance to alcohol may show somewhat less impairment in function than an inexperienced drinker would. This uniform, well-documented response enables the law to set a specific blood alcohol level for defining intoxication. The blood alcohol level can be easily measured by blood samples or a breathalyzer. The breathalyzer is able to measure blood alcohol levels because just as carbon dioxide in the blood diffuses across small capillaries in the lungs to be eliminated as exhaled air, so does alcohol. The amount of carbon dioxide in exhaled air is directly proportionate to that circulating in the bloodstream. The same is true for alcohol. The breathalyzer measures the concentration of alcohol in the exhaled air. From that measurement the exact concentration of alcohol in the blood can be determined.

TOLERANCE

The immediate effects of consumption of the drug alcohol have been described. With continued regular alcohol use over an extended period, changes take place. Tolerance develops, and any drinker, not only the alcohol-dependent individual, can testify to this. The first few times someone tries alcohol, one drink is enough to feel tipsy. With some drinking experience, one drink no longer has that effect. In part this may reflect greater wisdom. The veteran drinker has learned "how to drink" to avoid feeling intoxicated. The experienced drinker has learned to sip, not gulp, a drink and avoids drinking on an empty stomach. The other reason is that with repeated exposures to alcohol, the CNS adapts to its presence. It can tolerate more alcohol and still maintain normal functioning. This is one of the properties that defines alcohol as an addictive drug. Over the long haul the body requires a larger dose to induce the effects previously produced by smaller doses.

Not only does tolerance develop over relatively long spans of time, but there are also rapid adaptive changes in the CNS on each drinking occasion. A drinker is more out of commission when the blood alcohol level is climbing than when it is falling. In a testing situation, if someone is given alcohol to drink and then asked to perform certain tasks, the results are predictable. Impairment is greater on the ascending limb—the rising blood alcohol level, or absorption, phase. As the blood alcohol level drops in the elimination phase, the individual, when similarly tested, will be able to function better with the same blood alcohol content. It is as if one learns to function better with the presence of alcohol after "practice." In fact what probably has happened is that the brain has made some subtle adjustments in the way it functions. Here too there are differences between men and women. Both show greater impairment as

"Medical Declarations" on the alcohol question. The third and final English medical declaration written in 1871. "As it is believed that the inconsiderate prescription of large quantities of alcoholic liquids by medical men for their patients has given rise in many instances to the formation of intemperate habits, the undersigned are of the opinion that no medical practitioner should prescribe it without a sense of grave responsibility. They believe that alcohol, in whatever form, should be prescribed with as much care as any powerful drug. The directions for its use should be so framed as not to be interpreted as a sanction for use to excess, or necessarily for the continuance of its use when the occasion is past."

SPOONER, WALTER W.
The Cyclopaedia of Temperance and Prohibition, 1891.

alcohol levels rise, but there are differences in the kinds of impairment. When intoxicated, women appear to have greater impairment than men for tasks that require motor coordination. Yet, they are superior to men in tasks that require attention. Since driving requires both skills, neither appears the better bet on the highway.

ALCOHOL AS AN ANESTHETIC

Alcohol is an anesthetic, just as depicted in all the old Western movies. But by modern standards, it is not a very good one. The dose of alcohol required to produce anesthesia is very close to the lethal amount. When the vital centers have been depressed enough by alcohol to produce unconsciousness, it only takes a wee bit more to put someone permanently to sleep. Sadly, several times a year almost any newspaper obituary column documents a death from alcohol. Usually the tragedy involves young people chugging a fifth of liquor on a dare or as a prank, or coerced drinking as part of a college fraternity initiation.

OTHER TYPES OF ALCOHOL

In this discussion of alcohol, it is clear that we have been referring to "booze," "suds," "the sauce," "brew," or any of the other colloquial terms for beverage alcohol. To be scientifically accurate, the kind of alcohol discussed is called ethanol, ethyl alcohol, or grain alcohol. Alcohol, if one is precise, is a term used to refer to a family of substances. What all alcohols have in common is a particular grouping of carbon, hydrogen, and oxygen atoms arranged in a similar fashion in the alcohol molecule. They differ only in the number of carbon atoms and associated hydrogen atoms. Each alcohol is named according to the number of carbons it has. Ethanol has two carbon atoms.

The other kinds of alcohol with which everyone is familiar are wood alcohol (methyl alcohol, with one carbon atom), an ingredient of antifreeze, paint thinners, and sterno. The other is rubbing alcohol (isopropyl), comprised of three carbons. This is a common ingredient in perfumes and after-shave, for example. Because of their different chemical makeup, these other alcohols cause big problems if taken into the body. The difficulty lies in differences in rates of metabolism and the kinds of by-products formed. For example, it takes 9 times longer for methanol to be eliminated than it does ethanol. Although methanol itself is not especially toxic, when the liver enzyme ADH acts on it, formaldehyde instead of acetaldehyde is formed. Formaldehyde causes tissue damage, especially to the eyes. The formaldehyde then breaks down into formic acid, which is also not as innocent as the acetic acid produced by ethanol metabolism and can cause severe states of acidosis. Ingestion of methyl

alcohol can lead to blindness and can be fatal; it requires prompt medical attention.

As an interesting aside, the treatment of acute methanol poisoning is one of a handful of situations in clinical medicine where ethanol has a legitimate and important therapeutic role. Administering ethanol to a methanol-poisoned patient slows the rate of methanol metabolism, which results in a reduction of the levels of toxic by-products formed. Why? Because ethanol successfully competes with methanol for the limited amount of liver enzyme ADH required for the metabolism of either variety of alcohol. The rapid administration of ethyl alcohol, while at the same time treating acidosis to correct the body's acid-base imbalance, may ameliorate or entirely eliminate serious complications.

Poisonings from nonbeverage alcohols don't happen only to those alcohol-dependent persons who in desperation will drink anything. Several years ago there was an Italian wine scandal in which table wines were laced with methanol, resulting in more than one hundred deaths. A far more common accident involves the toddler who gets into the medicine cabinet or the teenager or adult who doesn't know that all alcohols are not the same and that some may have dangerous effects.

THE INFLUENCE OF EXPECTATIONS

The focus in this chapter has been on the pharmacological properties of alcohol. The physical changes described, especially alcohol's effects upon the CNS, are directly tied to the amount of alcohol consumed. Pharmacologists refer to this phenomenon as "dose-related" effects. However, our psyche also enters into the equation. Although one's beliefs, wishes, or attitudes cannot negate alcohol's actions, they do have an impact. A person's expectations influence the experience of drinking and how a drinking episode is interpreted. There is increasing literature on this alcohol "expectancy" effect, which examines how beliefs about alcohol's effects influence drinking behavior. Some of these studies involve research situations in which people think they are getting alcohol when, in fact, the drink they consume has none. The explanation for this interaction between pharmacological effects and beliefs is that beliefs are likely to influence what in your surroundings you notice and tune in to while drinking. Thus the person who expects that drinking makes people more aggressive is likely to see others as "asking" for a fight, whereas the person who thinks that drinking enhances sexuality will be attuned to "invitations" for intimacy.

OTHER DRUGS OF ABUSE

The focus has been on alcohol. One might welcome a similar discussion of other drugs of abuse. However, rather than do that, with a consideration of alcohol as a back-drop, let's tease out some of the issues that are important in thinking about any drug of abuse. These include how drugs are taken into the body, how rapidly they are delivered to the brain, how they are metabolized and the kinds of by-products that may be produced in this process, how rapidly they are removed, and the particular neurotransmitters that are affected by their presence. What are the key elements that are significant? The following paragraphs will explore this question.

Route of administration

The term used for how a substance in taken into the body is "route of administration." There are a number of methods, and they apply to all drugs, not just drugs of abuse. For example, prescribed medications may be taken orally. Oftentimes there are further instructions: "Take with eight oz. of water," or "take on an empty stomach," or "take on a full stomach." Sometimes pills have coatings or are gel capsules. These are not simply a drug company's marketing tactic to make them attractive—there is a reason! The particular coating may be selected to assure that the drug passes through the stomach and isn't destroyed by the gastric juices. On the other hand, if the drug is very irritating to the stomach lining, the coating may provide the stomach protection. The route of administration for some medications may be via inhalers, common with asthma or allergy medications. Drugs may be injected. Here, too, there are variations—just under the skin, or into a large muscle, usually the arm or the buttock, or intravenously. Drugs can also be absorbed through the skin, via patches, as in some pain medications or the nicotine patch. A particular route of administration is selected to assure that drugs are delivered efficiently and effectively, so the drug is not removed from the body before it can do its job, and delivered at the proper rate, either as quickly as possible or on a time-released basis.

Apply this efficiency and effectiveness principle to marijuana. When marijuana is smoked in a joint, approximately 30% of the active ingredient that provides the desired effect, THC*, is destroyed by the process of pyrolysis, a chemical change caused by the process of burning. Another 20% to 40% is lost in side stream smoke, the burning that takes place between puffs. You can see that the smoking route of administration does not seem to be very efficient. When smoking a joint, people typically hold their breath. The purpose is to maximize the amount of THC that can enter the bloodstream from the lungs and minimize what is lost in exhaled air. What is taken into the lungs passes into the bloodstream very rapidly. Despite the loss of up to 70% of the psychoactive ingredients, smoking is an effective route to deliver THC in marijuana to the brain. The effects of the drug are felt more immediately than if the

---

* There are 61 different substances found only in marijuana called cannabinoids. There is one, however, that accounts for virtually all of these effects, delta-9-tetrahydrocannabinol. The abbreviation is THC.

marijuana were ingested orally, as happens when it is added to brownies or some other food and has to transverse the digestive system.

The route of administration also has significant import for the kinds of problems that can result from use. With some substance use, dangers that come from how the drug is administered are more significant than the effects of the drug itself. Nicotine is the prime example. Many of the long-term health problems are tied to the *smoking,* not to the nicotine. It is the addictive properties of the nicotine that seduce people into continuing the dangerous practice of smoking. As one physician commented to a smoker, "I really don't object to your drug of choice, but how you deliver it!" Indeed, were all smokers to replace their cigarettes with equivalent daily doses of nicotine delivered via nicotine patches, with the nicotine absorbed through the skin, the rates of respiratory problems, chronic lung disease, bronchitis, emphysema, and lung cancer would decline.

The long-term problems associated with smoking marijuana is not the THC or any of the 60 other cannabinoids. They come from the over 350 other compounds in the smoke, and the "super" exposure to these that is associated with holding the marijuana smoke in the lungs. From the perspective of these smoking effects, one joint is equivalent to far more than one cigarette.

Injection as a route of administration, while among the most efficient, presents significant problems. These come from nonsterile techniques and the accompanying risk of infection. The common practice of sharing needles too is very dangerous. This is, sadly, a very efficient way of transferring blood-borne viruses such as HIV/AIDS and hepatitis B and C.

When drugs are snorted, such as cocaine, the drug is absorbed into the bloodstream from the mucous membranes of the nose. Drugs that are inhaled, or smoked, enter the bloodstream through the lungs. Intravenous administration places the drug directly into the bloodstream. Upon entering the bloodstream the drug is very quickly delivered to the brain.

Site of action

Drugs have different effects on different parts of the brain, including different neurotransmitter systems. The portions of the brain and which systems are affected play a role in producing the effects that are desired and determine the long-term problems, including the level of risk for addiction, as well as the potential for acute problems.

There are problems associated with marijuana use, particularly related to its alterations of perception. While it may contribute to accidents that can cause deaths, there have been no known deaths due to its toxic effects. There is no blood marijuana concentration that is lethal. Essentially, this is because the brain stem, which controls basic body functions such as heart function or respiration, does not contain any of the neurotransmitters that are affected by marijuana.

Solubility in fat and/or water

Drugs differ in whether they are soluble in water and/or fat. Recall how the differences between men and women in their bodies' relative proportion of water and fat influenced their blood alcohol concentrations. All else being equal, with equivalent doses of alcohol, women with proportionately more body fat and less tissue water had higher blood alcohol levels. Whether a drug is fat or water soluble determines how it is distributed in the body and where and how long it is stored. One way in which this is of practical importance is its implications for drug testing. Drugs that are fat soluble leave long-lasting traces in a way that alcohol does not. Thus, detectable amounts of a drug may be present in blood samples due to their slow release from fat stores, long after the last intake of the drug. One can also test hair samples, or fingernails, and identify the presence of a drug through laboratory testing. For alcohol, once the blood alcohol level drops to zero, there is no continuing evidence of recent use as there is with other drugs.

Metabolism

How a drug is metabolized and removed from the body suggests the kinds of problems that may result. As we noted, alcohol is metabolized by enzymes that are produced in the stomach and primarily in the liver, enzymes that are involved in the metabolism of other drugs. Thus if different drugs are present, both requiring the same enzymes, they are in competition, and removal of both is slowed. Another potential problem is the by-products formed during metabolism. Remember the wood alcohol. In some instances there are by-products that are formed by two drugs in combination. Alcohol and cocaine is one example. They form cocaethylene, which is a metabolite that has properties similar to those of cocaine, but in fact may be more toxic to the heart and liver. The formation of this by-product, by acting as a "booster," may make drinking while taking cocaine both more attractive and problem-ridden.

Acute effects of major drug classes

To think of each and every individual drug separately can make absorbing the information overwhelming. Sometimes it seems that daily one hears of a new drug that has hit the street. It is useful to consider different types or classes of drugs that share common features. To know a particular drug's class is to know a considerable amount about how it acts, its effects, the common problems associated with use, especially when combined with how it is taken into the body. All of these factors are important to understanding a drug's effects. The acute effects of the major drug classes are summarized in Table 2.1.

TABLE 2.1   ACUTE EFFECTS OF MAJOR PSYCHOACTIVE DRUG CLASSES

Sedative-Hypnotics

Route of administration:	Usually by mouth; rarely intravenous.
Length of action:	Varies by substance.
Action:	Generally act at receptors of neurons which are linked with or enhance the effects of the GABA (gamma-amino-butyric acid) system. This is the major system that slows neuronal activity. Chloride ion flow into neurons is facilitated either by the GABA system (benzodiazepines) or occurs directly (barbiturates), resulting in sedation.
Desired effects:	Similar to alcohol. Reduction of anxiety; possible elation secondary to decrease in alertness and judgment.
Other acute effects:	Sedation, impaired judgment, impaired operation of vehicles or machinery, respiratory and cardiac depression with overdose (much less likely with benzodiazepines alone).
Interaction with alcohol:	Potentiation of effects, especially respiratory depression. Some degree of cross-tolerance.

Stimulants

Routes of administration:	Cocaine is mostly smoked as "crack."
	Powdered cocaine (cocaine hydrochloride) is snorted intranasally and (rarely) used intravenously or smoked as free base. Amphetamines are taken orally, intravenously, or smoked. Methylphenidate is taken orally.
Length of action:	Cocaine: half-life in plasma approximately one hour. Remains in brain for 2–3 days. Amphetamines: half-life of 6–12 hours. Methylphenidate: half-life about 2 hours.
Action: *Cocaine –*	Affects dopamine, norepinephrine, and serotonin levels. Blocks re-uptake of dopamine, thus prolonging dopamine effects. May enhance dopamine transmission in mid-brain, limbic, and cortical areas of brain. (Cocaine depletes presynaptic dopamine with prolonged use.) Cocaine has toxic effects, particularly on the cardiac, respiratory, and central nervous systems.
Amphetamines and Methylphenidate –	Similar to cocaine. Direct neuron release of dopamine and norepinepherine and blockade of catecholamine re-uptake produce euphoric effects. Various toxic effects on the sympathetic nervous system.
Desired effects:	Increased alertness, feeling of well-being, euphoria, increased energy, reported heightened sexuality.
Other acute effects:	Anxiety, confusion, irritability, potential medical problems (heart, central nervous system, and breathing) with possible death.
Interaction with alcohol:	Alcohol decreases side effects of stimulants (e.g., anxiety) and withdrawal symptoms and is very commonly used with stimulants.

Opioids

Route of administration:	Heroin: Intravenous, snorted, "skin-popped," or smoked. Medications: Taken by mouth, intravenous, or skin patch (fentanyl).
Length of action:	Varies by substance.
Action:	Bind to opiate receptors in specific areas in the central nervous system where they appear to mimic or block normally occurring opiate-like substances.
Desired effects:	The "rush" or "high," a feeling of well-being and intense pleasure, described as "almost orgasmic"; a state of decreased mental and physical awareness and of decreased physical and emotional pain.
Other acute effects:	Sedation, decreased judgment, decreased ability to operate vehicles or machinery, possible respiratory depression if there is an accidental overdose.

TABLE 2.1   (*Continued*)

Interaction with alcohol:	Each potentiates the effects of the other in overdose situations. Possible decreased effect of either when taken by an individual with tolerance to the other (cross-tolerance).

Cannabis

Route of administration:	Smoked, or taken by mouth.
Length of action:	Smoking: 2–4 hours; ingestion: 5–12 hours.
Action:	Usually absorbed through the lungs. Produces effects by binding at receptor sites in the brain that appear to be specific for cannabinoids.
Desired effects:	Sense of relaxation and well-being, euphoria, detachment, modification of level of consciousness, altered perceptions, altered time sense, reported sexual arousal.
Other acute effects:	Slows reaction time and alters perceptions, making it dangerous to operate machinery or drive; panic, anxiety, nausea, dizziness, difficulty in expressing thoughts, paranoid thoughts, depersonalization (a sense of detachment, as if observing oneself).
Interaction with alcohol:	Potentiates depressant effects.

Hallucinogens

Route of administration:	Taken by mouth or smoked.
Length of action:	Varies with the substance: hours to a few days.
Action: *LSD-like drugs –*	(LSD, mescaline, psilocybin, psilocin, and probably DMA, DOT, and DMT)
	Structurally related to serotonin. Probably produces many of its behavioral effects by binding to serotonin receptors.
MDMA-like drugs –	(MDMA, MDA)
	Affects several neurotransmitters, including serotonin but also the adrenergic, cholinergic, and histaminergic sites. Effects seems to be a combination of LSD-like hallucinations and amphetamine-like arousal.
Desired effects:	Increased awareness of sensory input, hallucinations, perceptions of usual environment as novel; altered body image; blurring of boundaries between self and environment; temporary modification of thought processes, claims of special insights, and increased empathy.
Other acute effects: *LSD group –*	Panic attacks. Increased blood pressure, heart palpitations, tremors, nausea, muscle weakness, increased body temperature, ataxia. In some cases accidental death may occur (e.g., believing one can fly and thus jumping).
MDMA group –	Nausea, jaw and teeth clenching, muscle tension, blurred vision, panic attacks, confusion, depression, anxiety, paranoid psychosis, hyperthermia, cardiac arrest.
Interaction with alcohol:	Not well documented.

Phencyclidine (PCP)

Route of administration:	Smoked, taken by mouth, snorted, or injected intravenously.
Length of action:	4–6 hours.
Action:	Behavioral effects believed to be mediated through the N-Methyl-D-Aspartate (ND) excitatory amino acid receptor-channel complex in the brain.
Desired effects:	Visual illusions, hallucinations, and distorted perceptions, feelings of strength, power, and invulnerability, depersonalization, distorted body image.
Other acute effects:	Psychotic reactions; bizarre behavior; outbursts of hostility and violence; feelings of severe anxiety, doom, or impending death; gross incoordination; nystagmus; hypersalivation, vomiting; fever.

(*continued*)

TABLE 2.1   (*Continued*)

Interaction with alcohol:	Not well documented.

Inhalants

Route of administration:	Inhaled.
Length of action:	Varies by substance.
Action:	Poorly understood. Absorbed through lungs. Presumed that inhalants disrupt neural function. Intoxication is similar to the CNS depressants. Nitrites and nitrous oxide cause vasodilatation and increasing cerebral blood flow though remainder of action is unknown.
Desired effects:	
Hydrocarbons –	The "rush," euphoria, behavioral disinhibition, sensation of floating, perceptual disturbances including hallucinations.
Nitrites –	Used to extend or to enhance sexual intercourse, especially in gay, male population; may cause euphoria.
Nitrous oxide –	Euphoria, altered perceptions.
Other acute effects:	
Hydrocarbons –	Cardiac depressants leading to "sudden sniffing death," probably the result of changes in heart rhythms; aspiration; respiratory depression.
Nitrites –	Panic reactions, nausea, dizziness, lowered blood pressure.
Nitrous oxide –	Nausea, vomiting, confusion.
Interaction with alcohol:	Not well researched, but likely to vary with type of substance.

Nicotine

Route of administration:	Smoked, chewed.
Length of action:	Approximately two hours.
Action:	There are specific nicotinic receptors in both the central and peripheral nervous systems. Affects both inhibitory and excitatory elements of a number of neural pathways. May act on some of same pathways as opiates and sedative hypnotics.
Desired effects:	Relaxation, stimulation, social acceptance, image.
Other acute effects:	Dizziness (in the inexperienced), increased heart rate.
Interaction with alcohol:	Negligible.

Anabolic Androgenic Steroids

Route of administration:	Taken by mouth, intramuscular, or patch.
Action:	Bind to hormone-specific receptor complexes in almost every organ system in the body.
Desired effects:	Enhancement of appearance or athletic performance, more self-confidence and self-esteem.
Other acute effects:	Negligible.
Interaction with alcohol:	Not well researched.

Adapted from West D; Kinney J. An overview of substance use and abuse in: *Clinical Manual of Substance Abuse. 2d Edition.* St. Louis, MO: Mosby Yearbook, 1996.

In conclusion

Anything taken into the body has effects. All too often we are discovering these effects to be more harmful than had been previously thought. Chemical additives, fertilizers, pesticides, antibiotics given to livestock destined for the table, and even coloring agents have been questioned. With more information some substances are being recognized as less benign than was supposed. In some instances the federal Food and Drug Administration (FDA) has outlawed or severely restricted use. Let us hope caution with the use of alcohol and other drugs will become as widespread. Many of the acute problems our society encounters with alcohol use in particular may be lessened as uninformed and unconsidered use is replaced by knowledge about the drug we drink.

RESOURCES AND FURTHER READING

Agency for Toxic Substances and Disease Registry: Methanol toxicity, *American Family Physician* 47(1):163–171, 1993.

Methanol is used in a variety of commercial and consumer products. Increased use of methanol as a motor fuel may lead to higher ambient air levels and a greater potential for ingestion from siphoning accidents. Methanol toxicity initially is not characterized by severe toxic manifestations. It represents a classic example of "lethal synthesis," in which toxic metabolites can cause fatality after a characteristic latent period. Methanol is well absorbed following inhalation, ingestion, or cutaneous exposure. It is oxidized in the liver to formaldehyde, then to formic acid, which contributes to the profound metabolic acidosis occurring in acute methanol poisoning. The metabolic products of methanol can produce a syndrome of delayed-onset acidosis, obtundation, visual disturbance, and death. Intravenous sodium bicarbonate therapy should be considered if the patient's blood pH is below 7.2. Treatment is discussed. (Author abstract.)

Alcohol Health and Research World 21(2): (entire issue), 1997.

This thematic issue is devoted to alcohol's effects on the central nervous system. There is a discussion of the neurotransmitters, as well as presentation of the basic mechanisms needed to understand these effects.

Doria JJ: Alcohol metabolism (commentary), *Alcohol Health and Research World* 21(4): 323–323, 1997. (3 refs.)

Gibbons B: Alcohol: The legal drug, *National Geographic* 181(Feb):2–35, 1992.

Directed toward the lay public, this is a very lucid, and authoritative discussion of alcohol, the drug and its effects.

Graham AW, Schultz TK: *Principles of addiction medicine,* 2d edition, Chevy Chase, MD: American Society of Addiction Medicine, 1998.

A comprehensive medical text. Nonmedical personnel will need a "translator."

Kerr JS, Hindmarch I: The effects of alcohol alone or in combination with other drugs on information processing, task performance, and subjective responses (review), *Human Psychopharmacology* 13(1):1–9, 1998. (118 refs.)

This paper reviews the effects of alcohol on human psychomotor performance and cognitive function. It concentrates particularly on effects on reaction time and on skills related to car driving. The effects of alcohol on performance are very variable at low doses (under 1g per kg body weight). The variability is due to the different measures and methods employed by the researchers and to the large interindividual and interoccasional differences in the effects of alcohol. That is, alcohol affects different people in different ways, and it affects the same person differently on separate occasions. Greater performance deficits are observed as the dose increases and as the tasks become more complex. Although results vary, both nicotine and caffeine appear to antagonize the detrimental effects of alcohol on performance. Many other drugs interact with alcohol, the most important of which are sedative agents that can combine synergistically with alcohol to produce profound psychomotor and cognitive impairment. (Author abstract.)

Loke WH: Physiological and psychological effects of alcohol (review), *Psychologia* 35(3):133–146, 1992.

The effects of alcohol on human physiological and psychological processes are reviewed. Among the physiological processes discussed are the effects on the skin, the gastrointestinal tract, and the cardiovascular system. The absorption and distribution pathways of alcohol are also discussed. Psychological effects include vision, muscular coordination, and memory processes. Research indicates that alcohol impairs vision and muscular coordination. It is also noted that no standard system to test the effects of alcohol on reaction time has been developed. (Author abstract.)

Lowinson JH, Ruiz P, Millman RB, Langred JG: *Substance abuse: A comprehensive textbook*, 3d edition, Baltimore MD: Williams and Wilkins, 1997.

A comprehensive medical text. Nonmedical personnel will need a "translator."

Marnell T, ed: *Drug identification bible*, 3d edition, Denver CO: Drug Identification Bible, 1997.

This is a widely used reference volume that endeavors to answer the questions commonly asked by parents, educators, and law enforcement personnel: "What does it look like?" and "What does it do?" It provides information on commonly abused prescription drugs as well as illicit drugs. It addresses the current "drug scene" using color photos, combined with information on street prices, purity, packaging, methods of use, and slang. Two sections are devoted to the identification of tablets and capsules. The section on controlled prescription drugs shows full color/actual size photos of over seven hundred drugs. The section on noncontrolled and over-the-counter preparations lists markings and logo information on approximately nine thousand items. This material is organized for easy reference. The contents are organized as follows: (a) a reprinting of the Controlled Substance Act; (b) prescription drugs:

markings and logos; photos of controlled prescription drugs; use/abuse; (c) illicit drugs—amphetamines, cocaine, designer drugs, heroin, legal highs, LSD, marijuana, PCP, psilocybin mushrooms, Rohypnol—photos, description of use, and slang. The volume concludes with suggested readings, charts of drug detection limits and weight conversion, and an index of drug manufacturers.

Moskowitz H, Burns M: Effects of alcohol on driving performance, *Alcohol Health and Research World* 14(1):12–14, 1990. (24 refs.)

Alcohol impairs driving. That fact, established by epidemiological data together with many controlled studies of alcohol and driving skills, is well known and generally accepted. What is less well understood is that impairment of the most important skills can occur at a very low blood alcohol concentration (BAC). The skills involved in driving a motor vehicle include psychomotor skills, vision, perception, tracking (steering), information processing, and attention. Data from laboratory experiments indicate that all of these functions are impaired by alcohol, although they differ in the extent of their impairment at any given BAC. This article discusses recent research on the effects of alcohol on those brain functions involved in driving a motor vehicle.

Nathan KI, Bresnick WH, Batki SL: Cocaine abuse and dependence: Approaches to management, *CNS Drugs* 10(1):43–59, 1998. (94 refs.)

Cocaine abuse and dependence constitute major health and social problems in the United States and elsewhere. The paper is organized in 6 main sections: (1) overview of cocaine as a drug of abuse, its pharmacologic effects, routes of administration, patterns of use, and clinical symptomatology; (2) epidemiology; (3) medical and psychiatric comorbidity; (4) management, assessment, and treatment; (5) drug therapies, by drug type; and (6) conclusions. (Author abstract.)

3

MEDICAL COMPLICATIONS

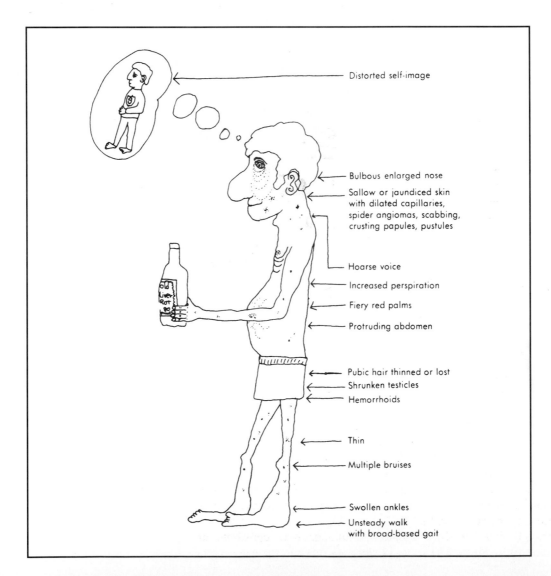

Part I
Advice for the moderate drinker

It probably comes as no great surprise to most people that excessive use of alcohol over a long period can lead to serious problems. What is unfortunately less recognized and appreciated is that, even in moderate amounts, alcohol use can present medical risks. There is no set "dose" of alcohol that reliably can be considered "safe" for people in general or for a single individual throughout his or her life.

Contraindications to moderate use

For some people, in some circumstances, at particular times, what is usually considered moderate alcohol use is too much. The most striking example is the caution against alcohol use during pregnancy. It is becoming more widely appreciated that drinking during pregnancy can cause abnormalities in the infant, a condition called *fetal alcohol syndrome* (FAS), or have some of the associated problems, a condition termed *fetal alcohol effects* (FAE). The woman wishing to conceive should be thoughtful about her drinking. Since many pregnancies are not confirmed until the middle of the first trimester, it is possible that she might ingest harmful levels of alcohol before being aware of her pregnancy. There are other possible adverse consequences of alcohol use during pregnancy. Moderate alcohol use has been linked to an increase in spontaneous abortions. Drinking 1 to 2 drinks per day, for a total of one ounce of alcohol per day, doubles the risk of spontaneous abortions during the second trimester. Nursing mothers, too, are advised to refrain from alcohol use because alcohol can pass through breast milk to the infant. Though maternal alcohol use while nursing does not affect mental development, infants whose mothers consumed one or more drinks per day have been found to have slower rates of motor development.

Even relatively modest alcohol use can create problems for those with cardiac and circulatory problems, e.g., coronary artery disease and/or congestive heart failure, as well as hypertension. High blood pressure in up to 10% of all cases is believed to be the direct result of alcohol use. For those with established hypertension, alcohol use can make management and adequate control of blood pressure more difficult. Moderate drinking also has been found to elevate the level of certain blood fats in individuals with *Type IV hyperlipoproteinemia*.

Others for whom moderate drinking may be unwise may include those with seizure disorders, diabetes mellitus, gout, osteoporosis, and various skin conditions, including psoriasis, as well as those with gastric and duodenal ulcers. The ways in which alcohol may aggravate these conditions are discussed in Part II.

Although none of these medical conditions may constitute an absolute contraindication to using alcohol, all fall into the category of relative contraindications. A glass of wine with meals once or twice a week may present no problem, but several drinks before dinner plus wine with the meal, or an evening on the town, are ill-advised. As a general rule, those being treated for any medical condition ought to inquire about the need to modify temporarily what may be very moderate drinking. In addition to the possibility of alcohol complicating a medical condition, there is the possibility of interactions of alcohol with medications prescribed to treat them.

Alcohol-drug interactions

Wine is at the head of all medicines.
TALMUD: BABABTHRA, 58b

Alcohol-drug interactions may be the area in which the moderate drinker is potentially most vulnerable to problems arising from alcohol use. Alcohol is a drug. When alcohol is taken in combination with prescribed or over-the-counter medications, there can be undesirable and quite possibly dangerous alcohol-drug interactions. Though these interactions can vary from individual to individual, they depend primarily on the amount of alcohol and type of medication consumed, as well as the person's drinking history. The moderate drinker who has not developed tolerance will have a very different response than the habitual heavier drinker. In fact, the consequences may be far more serious.

The basis of alcohol-drug interactions   Two basic mechanisms can explain virtually all alcohol-drug interactions. One is that the presence of alcohol alters the liver's ability to metabolize other drugs. In the moderate drinker, the MEOS system, which metabolizes a variety of other drugs as well as alcohol (see Chapter 2), may be significantly inhibited, or slowed down, in the presence of alcohol. Therefore drugs ordinarily metabolized by the liver's MEOS system will not be removed as rapidly or as completely as usual. The result is that these medications will then be present in the body in higher-than-expected levels. This can result in unexpected toxic effects.

On the other hand, for those with a long history of heavy drinking, alcohol has the opposite effect on the MEOS system. The activation of the MEOS system is enhanced, or speeded up, through a process known as enzyme induction. Thus certain drugs will be removed, or metabolized, more quickly. The medication is removed more rapidly, so its levels in the body will be lower than expected or desired. The net effect is that the individual will very likely not be receiving the intended therapeutic effects of a given dose of the drug. To compensate for this, it may be necessary to increase the dose of the drug administered to achieve the intended therapeutic effect at doses where it wouldn't ordinarily be expected.

The other major source of difficulty results from so-called additive effects. Alcohol is a CNS depressant. Other medications may also depress CNS functions. When two depressant drugs are present simultaneously, their combined effects often may be far greater than would be expected with the sum of the two. It is important to be aware that drugs and alcohol are not metabolized instantaneously. Recall that it takes the body approximately 1 hour to handle one drink (whether the drink is a 12-ounce bottle of beer or one mixed drink with a shot of 80-proof liquor). Therefore if someone has had several drinks, an hour or two later alcohol will still be in the system. As long as alcohol remains in the body, the potential exists for significant additive effects, even though the other depressant drugs are taken several hours later, or vice versa.

Common interactions of medications and alcohol   Many of the potential interactions of alcohol with some commonly prescribed medications are outlined in Appendix C. These include the general types of interactions described here and a variety of others not specifically discussed. Please note that the table is not all-inclusive. If a drug is not listed, don't assume that it has no interaction with alcohol. Anyone who uses alcohol and is taking other medications is advised to ask his or her physician or pharmacist specifically about potential alcohol-drug and drug-drug interactions.

Problems associated with drinking and intoxication

Accidents and injury   Along with alcohol-drug interactions the other common medical problem associated with alcohol use is accidents and injuries. These are more likely to occur during an intoxicated state because of the nature of alcohol-induced impairment. Judgment is impaired, placing individuals in situations that invite danger. Diminished judgment, along with decreased reaction and response time and poorer coordination and motor skills, leads to a lessened ability to cope with whatever occurs. In addition to injuries being more common with intoxication, their severity has also been found to rise with the level of impairment. Similarly, other psychoactive substances that affect judgment and motor skills can be a contributing factor in accidents.

AIDS   In the minds of the general public as well as health care and substance abuse professionals, AIDS is clearly linked with those who use drugs intravenously, a group for whom AIDS is becoming virtually endemic. The dramatic rise of AIDS among intravenous drug users is not based primarily on the pharmacological properties of the drugs but rather on the route of administration. Among intravenous drug users, HIV infection is readily transmitted by the common and dangerous practice of sharing needles. Given the multiple problems associated with chronic drug use, this group is not easily influenced by informational and preventative efforts.

Within the ever-growing body of research on AIDS, the relationship of alcohol use and AIDS has also being examined. The ability of chronic alcohol use to suppress the immune system (as described later) has been clearly established. Even the effects of acute use among those who drink moderately have more recently become evident. Pilot experiments with healthy volunteers suggest that a single administration equivalent to 0.7 to 3.1 liters of beer (that converts to the range of two to eight 12-ounce cans) can have an impact on the immune system. Furthermore, these effects may extend for up to 4 days after ingestion. The question this raises is whether casual alcohol consumption can increase either the vulnerability to infection or enhance the progression of latent HIV infection. On behavioral grounds alone, there is a link between intoxication and an increased risk of HIV infection. With intoxication, sexual activity is likely to be more casual and less considered, involve sexual partners determined by their "availability" rather than their being associated with an ongoing close emotional relationship, and be less likely to involve contraception or safer sex practices to reduce the risk of sexually transmitted disease, including HIV infection.

Unexpected and sudden natural deaths   The association between intoxication and unnatural causes of death such as accident, suicide, and homicide has been described in Chapter 1. Equally as significant is the recent finding of the high prevalence of positive BACs among people who have died suddenly and unexpectedly from natural causes. This finding is based upon the determination of the blood alcohol concentration as part of medicolegal autopsies conducted for all natural out-of-hospital deaths occurring during a 1-year period in a large Finnish metropolitan area. For this group of sudden and unexpected deaths, 36% of males and 15% of females had positive blood alcohol levels. The blood alcohol concentration for approximately half of these men and women was 0.15 or greater. Acute consumption of alcohol in nonalcoholics was certified as being a significant contributor in 23% of male and 8% of female sudden, unexpected deaths. For men, acute alcohol use was a contributing factor for 11% of deaths from coronary artery disease, 40% of other heart disease, and 7% for all other diseases. For both sexes the most vulnerable people are those in middle age.

Alcohol use and exercise

With the increasing interest in fitness and exercise, what are the recommendations for drinking in relation to sports and exercise? Alcohol can affect performance and be the source of potential problems if used immediately before, during, or immediately after exercise. Athletes who release pregame tension with a "few beers" before competition to take care of the jitters may slow reaction time and impair coordination, thus reducing their optimal performance. Before competition, endurance athletes sometimes "carbohydrate load," i.e., eat extra carbohydrates to increase the glycogen stored in muscles that serves as a source of energy. They may include beer as part of their pregame meal. However, beer is a poor source of carbohydrates compared to juices or soda. As for calories, two thirds of the calories in beer come from the alcohol. These calories are therefore used as heat and are not available for energy. Besides being a poor source of carbohydrates, the alcohol can affect heat tolerance and lead to dehydration because of alcohol's inhibition of antidiuretic hormone. Athletes who consume alcohol before a performance are at risk for significant fluid loss. Hence the recommendation of sports physicians is not to consume alcohol for 24 hours before performance.

Other drug use

As has been discussed previously, despite its illegal status, marijuana is the only other widely available psychoactive drug used in which the phenomenon of "moderate" use occurs. The abuse and addiction potential of virtually all other substances are so high that any use at all quickly escalates to abuse and addiction when use continues over time. The potential severity of problems associated with these other drugs should make us caution against *any* use. For the "moderate" marijuana user the cautions cited in respect to alcohol and accidents and injury clearly apply. Another major contraindication is respiratory problems, due to marijuana's intake via smoking. This applies to those with acute as well as chronic respiratory conditions.

Part II
Medical complications of chronic heavy alcohol use

Alcoholism is one of the most common chronic diseases. The prevalence is 7% in the population at large. Untreated, its natural history is a predictable, gradually progressive downhill course. The observable early symptoms and manifestations of the primary disease alcoholism are largely behavioral and nonphysical. Later in its course, alcoholism causes a wide variety of secondary medical complications in a multitude of different organ systems. These are associated with a host of different physical signs and symptoms.

It is important to emphasize the distinction between the primary disease alcoholism and its later secondary medical complications. Alcoholism, the disease, is one of the most highly treatable of chronic illnesses. If recognized and treated early—that means before major medical complications have occurred—it may be entirely arrested. Treated individuals can function quite normally. Their only long-term limitation is that they cannot use alcohol. Its complications, on the other hand, may be irreversible and may have a fatal outcome if the underlying alcoholism is untreated.

This section focuses on the later secondary medical complications of alcoholism. Because virtually every organ system is affected, an acquaintance with the medical complications of chronic heavy alcohol use is equivalent to familiarity with an exceedingly broad array of disease. In the past, in view of the protean and multi-system manifestations of both tuberculosis and syphilis, it was often said that, "to know TB or

There is this to be said in favor of drinking, that it takes the drunkard first out of society, then out of the world.
EMERSON, 1866

There are more old drunkards than old physicians.
RABELAIS

syphilis is to know medicine." The same could be said of alcoholism, "to know alcoholism is to know medicine."

We will now touch briefly, in a systems-oriented fashion, on many of the major alcohol-related problems. First, however, let us examine a composite picture of a person manifesting the visible signs of chronic alcoholism.

Visible signs and symptoms of chronic heavy drinking

Statistically, the typical alcoholic is male; thus we will use "he" in our examples. However, women alcoholics can and do show virtually all the same signs of chronic heavy alcohol use except those involving the reproductive organs. Bearing in mind that any given alcoholic may have many or only a few of these visible manifestations, let us examine a hypothetical chronic drinker who has most of them.

He is typically a thin, but occasionally somewhat bloated-appearing, middle-aged individual. Hyperpigmented, sallow, or jaundiced skin accentuates his wasted, chronically fatigued, and weakened overall appearance. He walks haltingly and unsteadily with a broad-based gait (ataxia). Multiple bruises are evident. He perspires heavily. His voice is hoarse and croaking, punctuated by occasional hiccups, and he carries an odor of alcohol on his breath.

His abdomen protrudes, and closer examination of it reveals the *caput medusae*—a prominent superficial abdominal vein pattern. There is marked ankle swelling, and he has hemorrhoids. His breasts may be enlarged; his testicles may be shrunken; and his chest, axillary, and/or pubic hair is entirely lost or thinned. Inspection of the skin reveals dilated capillaries and acne-like lesions. His nose is enlarged and bulbous. There is scabbing and crusting secondary to generalized itching. On the upper half of his body he has "spider angiomas." These are small red skin lesions that blanch with light pressure applied to their centers and spread into a spidery pattern with release of pressure. His palms may be a fiery red (liver palms). He may have "paper money" skin, so called because tiny capillaries, appearing much like the tiny red-colored fibers in a new dollar bill, are distinctly visible. In colder climates, there may be evidence of repeated frostbite. The fingernails are likely to be affected. They may have either transverse white-colored bands (*Muehrcke's lines*) or transverse furrows, or they may be totally opaque without half-moons showing at the base of the nail. He may have difficulty fully extending the third, fourth, and fifth fingers on either or both hands because of a flexion deformity called *Dupuytren's contracture*. A swelling of the parotid glands in the cheeks, giving him the appearance of having the mumps, is known as "chipmunk facies." Finally, a close look at the whites of his eyes reveals small blood vessels with a corkscrew shape.

Now, with this as an external picture, let us look inside the body at the underlying diseased organ systems that account for these visible changes.

It's not the fluid that bothers me, Doc. It's the two live goldfish I swallowed last time I was drunk.

GASTROINTESTINAL SYSTEM

Alcohol affects the gastrointestinal (GI) system in a variety of ways. This system is the route by which alcohol enters the body and is absorbed. It is where the first steps of metabolism take place. Moderate amounts of alcohol can disturb and alter the normal functioning of this system. Moreover, chronic heavy use of alcohol can raise havoc. Alcohol can have both direct and indirect effects. Direct effects are any changes that occur in response to the presence of alcohol. Indirect effects would be whatever occurs next, as a consequence of the initial, direct impact.

Many a man keeps on drinking till he hasn't a coat to either his back or his stomach.

GEORGE PRENTICE

Irritation, bleeding, and malabsorption

Chronic use of alcohol, as does any alcohol use, stimulates the stomach lining's secretion of hydrochloric acid and irritates the gut's lining. It also inhibits the muscular contractions called peristalsis that move food through the intestines. In combination, these effects can lead to a generalized irritation of the mucous membranes lining the gut, especially in the stomach. Chronic heavy drinkers may also complain of frequent belching, loss of appetite, alternating diarrhea and constipation, morning nausea, and vomiting.

Alcohol-induced irritation, rather than being found throughout the GI system, more often is localized to particular portions of it. For instance, if the esophagus is irritated, esophagitis results—experienced as midchest pain and pain when swallowing. Acute and chronic stomach irritation by alcohol result in gastritis, which involves inflammation, abdominal pain, and maybe even bleeding. Chronic alcohol use can certainly aggravate, if not indeed cause, ulcers of the stomach or duodenum (the first section of the small intestine). Bleeding can occur at any of the irritated sites. This represents a potentially serious medical problem. Bleeding from the GI tract can be either slow or massive. Either way, it is serious. Frequently, for reasons to be discussed later in this chapter, the alcoholic's blood clots less rapidly, so the body's built-in defenses to reduce bleeding are weakened. Surgery may even be required to stop the bleeding in some cases.

In addition to the causes of GI bleeding just mentioned, there are several other causes. The irritation of the stomach lining, not unexpectedly, upsets the stomach. With that can come prolonged nausea, violent vomiting, and retching. This may be so severe as to cause mechanical tears in the esophageal lining and bring on massive bleeding. Another cause of massive and often fatal upper GI bleeding is ruptured, dilated veins along the esophagus (esophageal varices). The distention and dilation of these veins occurs as a result of chronic liver disease and cirrhosis.

Chronic irritation of the esophagus by a combination of long-standing heavy alcohol consumption and cigarette smoking significantly increases the risk of developing esophageal cancer. The result of chronic excessive use of alcohol on small intestinal function can lead to

Pouring to achieve a large "head" on the beer enhances the bouquet and allows less carbonation to reach the stomach.

THE DOCTOR SAID
Alcohol was making
my blood too thin—
so now I add a little
CORN STARCH to each
drink to help thicken
it up.

abnormal absorption of a variety of foods, vitamins, and other nutrients. Although no specific diseases of the large intestine are caused by alcohol use, diarrhea frequently occurs in alcoholics. Hemorrhoids, also a by-product of liver disease and cirrhosis, are also common in alcoholics.

Pancreatitis

A drunkard is like a whiskey bottle, all neck and belly and no head.

AUSTIN O'MALLERY

Alcohol is frequently the culprit in acute inflammation of the pancreas. This is known as *acute pancreatitis*. The pancreas is a gland tucked away behind the stomach and small intestine. It makes digestive juices that are needed to break down starches, fat, and proteins. These juices are secreted into the duodenum through the pancreatic duct, in response to alcohol as well as other foodstuffs. They are alkaline and thus are important in neutralizing the acid contents of the stomach, thereby helping to protect the intestinal lining. The pancreas also houses the islets of Langerhans, which secrete the hormone insulin, needed to regulate sugar levels in the blood.

Currently there are two major theories as to how alcohol causes acute pancreatitis. The first, which is less favored, suggests that the pancreatic duct opening into the duodenum, the first part of the small intestine, can become swollen if the small intestine is irritated by alcohol. As it swells, pancreatic digestive juices cannot pass through it freely; they are obstructed or "stopped up." In addition, it has been suggested that bile from the bile duct, which opens into the pancreatic duct, may "back up" into the pancreatic duct and enter the pancreas itself. The pancreas then becomes inflamed. Because the bile and digestive juices cannot freely escape, in effect, autodigestion of the pancreas occurs.

The second theory holds that some of the excess fats in the bloodstream caused by excessive drinking are deposited in the pancreas. These fats are then digested by pancreatic enzymes, whose usual task is breaking down dietary fats. In turn the products of this process, free fatty acids, cause cell injury in the pancreas, which results in further release of fat-digesting enzymes, thus creating a vicious cycle.

The symptoms of acute pancreatitis include nausea, vomiting, diarrhea, and severe upper abdominal pain radiating straight through the back. Chronic inflammation of the pancreas can lead to calcifications, visible on abdominal x-ray films. This is chronic pancreatitis, a relapsing illness almost always associated with long-standing alcohol use. Diabetes can result from decreased capacity of the pancreas to produce and release insulin as a result of chronic cell damage.

Liver disease

The liver is a fascinating organ. You recall that it is the liver enzyme alcohol dehydrogenase (ADH) that begins the process of breaking down alcohol. The liver is also responsible for a host of other tasks. It breaks down wastes and toxic substances. It manufactures essential blood components, including clotting factors. It stores certain vitamins such as

B$_{12}$, which is essential for red blood cells. It helps regulate blood sugar (glucose) level, a very critical task because glucose is the only food the brain can use. Liver disease occurs because the presence of alcohol disturbs the metabolic machinery of the liver. Metabolizing alcohol is always a very high priority function of the liver. Therefore whenever alcohol is present, the liver is "distracted" from other normal and necessary functions. For the heavy drinker, this can be a good part of the time.

As you may know, liver disease is one of the physical illnesses most commonly associated with alcoholism. Three major forms of liver disease are associated with heavy alcohol use. The first is acute fatty liver. This condition may develop in anyone who has been drinking heavily, even for relatively brief periods of time. Fatty liver gets its name from the deposits of fat that build up in normal liver cells. This occurs because of a decrease in breakdown of fatty acids and an increase in the manufacture of fats by the liver. The latter is a result of the "distracting" metabolic effects of alcohol (see Chapter 2). Acute fatty liver occurs whenever 30% to 50% or more of the dietary calories are in the form of alcohol. This is true even if the diet is otherwise adequate. Acute fatty liver is a reversible condition if alcohol use is stopped.

Alcoholic hepatitis is a more serious form of liver disease that often follows a severe or prolonged bout of heavy drinking. [Alcoholic hepatitis is not related to infectious hepatitis (hepatitis A) or serum hepatitis (hepatitis B) or non-A, non-B known as hepatitis C.] Although more commonly seen in alcoholics, hepatitis, like acute fatty liver, may occur in nonalcoholics as well. In hepatitis, there is actual inflammation of the liver and variable damage to liver cells. One may also find associated evidence of acute fatty liver changes. Frequently, liver metabolism is seriously disturbed. Jaundice is a usual sign of hepatitis. Jaundice refers to the yellowish cast of the skin and the whites of the eyes. The yellow color comes from the pigment found in bile, a digestive juice made by the liver. The bile is being handled improperly in the liver, and therefore excessive amounts circulate in the bloodstream. Other symptoms of alcoholic hepatitis may include weakness, itching or welts that are a variety of hives, tiring easily, loss of appetite, nausea and vomiting, low-grade fever, weight loss, increasing ascites (fluid collecting in the abdomen), dark urine, and light stools.

In some patients, alcohol-induced hepatitis is completely reversible with abstinence from alcohol. In others, alcoholic hepatitis may be fatal or go on to become a smoldering chronic form of liver disease. Among patients with alcoholic hepatitis who stop drinking, only one in five will go on to develop alcoholic cirrhosis. For those who to continue to drink, 50% to 80% develop cirrhosis. For many, alcoholic hepatitis is clearly a forerunner of alcoholic cirrhosis, but it is thought that alcoholic cirrhosis can also develop without the prior occurrence of alcoholic hepatitis.

The liver has a remarkable ability to heal and regenerate, but there are limits. Cirrhosis of the liver is a condition in which there is widespread destruction of liver cells. These cells are replaced by nonfunctioning

scar tissue. In fact, the word *cirrhosis* simply means scarring. There are many different types and causes of cirrhosis. However, in the United States, long-term heavy alcohol use is the cause in the majority (80%) of cases. It is estimated that about one in ten long-term heavy drinkers will eventually develop alcoholic cirrhosis. Given the nature of the disease, it is accompanied by very serious and often relatively irreversible metabolic and physiological abnormalities, which is very bad news. In fact, more than half of the patients who continue to drink after a diagnosis of alcoholic cirrhosis are dead within 5 years.

In alcoholic cirrhosis the liver is simply unable to perform its work properly. Toxic substances, normally removed by the liver, accumulate and circulate in the bloodstream, creating problems elsewhere in the body. This is particularly true of the brain, as we shall see later. The liver normally handles the majority of the blood from the intestinal tract as it returns to the heart. The cirrhotic liver, now a mass of scar tissue, is unable to handle the usual blood flow. The blood, unable to move through the portal vein (the route from the blood vessels around the intestines to the liver), is forced to seek alternative return routes to the heart. This leads to pressure and "backup" in these alternative vessels. This condition is call portal hypertension. It is this pressure that causes the veins in the esophagus, which are part of this "alternative return route" to become enlarged, producing esophageal varices and inviting hemorrhaging. The same pressure accounts for hemorrhoids and the *caput medusae*.

Another phenomenon associated with cirrhosis is *ascites*. As a result of back pressure, the fluid in the tissues of the liver "weeps" directly from the liver into the abdominal cavity. This fluid would normally be taken up and transported back to the heart by the hepatic veins and lymph system. Large amounts of fluid can collect and distend the abdomen; a woman with ascites, for example, can look very pregnant. If you were to gently tap the side of a person with ascites, you would see a wave-like motion in response, as fluid sloshes around.

Another result of alcoholic liver disease is diminished ability of the liver to store glycogen, the body's usual storage form of sugar. There is also less ability to produce glucose from other nutrients such as proteins. This can lead to low blood sugar levels (see Chapter 2). This is an important fact when it comes to treating an alcoholic diabetic, since insulin also lowers the blood sugar. Another situation in which this is important is in treating coma in any alcoholic. Insufficient amounts of blood sugar may cause coma, essentially because the brain does not have enough of its usual fuel supply to function normally. Intravenous glucose may be necessary to prevent irreversible brain damage. On the other hand, alcohol and alcoholic liver damage may also lead to states of diabetes-like, higher than normal blood glucose levels. This occurs in large part both because of the effects of liver disease and the effects of alcohol on the range of hormones that regulate glucose.

Hepatic coma can be one result of cirrhosis. In this case, the damage comes from toxins circulating in the bloodstream. In essence, the brain

is "poisoned" by these wastes and its ability to function is seriously impaired, leading to coma. Cancer of the liver is also a complication of long-standing cirrhosis. Another source of bad news is that as many of 50% of those with cirrhosis will also have pancreatitis. These persons have two serious medical conditions. Still other complications may include GI bleeding, salt and water retention, and kidney failure. The main elements of treatment for cirrhosis are abstinence from alcohol, multivitamins, a nutritionally balanced diet, and bed rest. Even with such treatment, the prognosis for cirrhosis is not good, and many of the complications just described may occur.

The different forms of alcohol-related liver disease result from specific alcohol-induced changes in liver cells. Unfortunately, there is no neat and consistent relationship between a specific liver abnormality and the particular constellation of symptoms that develops. Although laboratory tests indicate liver damage, they cannot pinpoint the specific kind of alcohol-related liver disease. Therefore some authorities believe a liver biopsy, which involves direct examination of a liver tissue sample, is essential to evaluate the situation properly.

Until the early-to-mid-1970s it was not recognized that the liver damage common in alcoholism was a direct result of the alcohol. Rather, it was believed that the damage was caused by poor nutrition. It has since become clear that alcohol itself plays a major, direct role. Even in the presence of adequate nutrition, liver damage can occur when excessive amounts of alcohol are consumed.

HEMATOLOGICAL SYSTEM

The blood, known as the hematological system, is the body's major transportation network. The blood carries oxygen to tissues. It takes up waste products of cell metabolism and carts them off to the lungs and kidneys for removal. It carries nutrients, minerals, and hormones to the cells. The blood also protects the body through the anti-infection agents it carries. Although the blood looks like a liquid, it also contains "formed elements" (solid components). These formed elements include red blood cells, white blood cells, and platelets. They are all suspended in the serum, the fluid or liquid part of the blood. Each of the formed elements of the blood is profoundly affected by alcohol abuse. Whenever there is a disturbance of these essential blood components, problems arise.

Red blood cells

Let us begin with the red blood cells. The most common problem here is anemia—too few red blood cells. *Anemia* is a general term like fever. It simply means insufficient function or number of red blood cells. Logically, one can imagine this coming about in a number of ways. Too few red blood cells can be manufactured if there is a shortage of

nutrients to produce them or toxins interfere with production. Even if they are produced in adequate amounts, they can be defective. Or they can be lost, for example, through bleeding. Or they actually can be destroyed. Alcohol contributes to anemia in each of these ways.

How does alcohol abuse relate to the first situation, inadequate production? The most likely culprit here is inadequate nutrition. Red blood cells cannot be manufactured if the bone marrow does not have the necessary ingredients. Iron is a key ingredient. Alcohol, or some of its metabolic products like acetaldehyde, are thought to interfere with the bone marrow's ability to use iron in making hemoglobin, which is the oxygen-carrying part of the blood. Even if there is enough iron in the system, it "just passes on by." On the other hand, a poor diet, not uncommon among alcoholics, may mean an insufficient iron intake. Chronic GI bleeding may also result from chronic alcohol abuse. If so, the iron in the red blood cells is lost and not available for recycling. This type of anemia is called *iron deficiency anemia.* Another variety, *sideroblastic anemia,* is also related to nutritional deficiencies. This comes from too little pyridoxal phosphate (a substance that facilitates the production of vitamin B_6 related cofactor). This substance is also needed by the bone marrow cells to produce hemoglobin.

These first two varieties of anemia account for the inadequate production of red blood cells. Another variety, *megaloblastic anemia,* is also related to nutritional deficiencies. There is too little folate. This happens because folate is not in the diet in sufficient quantities, and/or the small intestine is unable to absorb it properly because of other effects of chronic alcohol abuse. What results then is defective red blood cell production. Without folic acid, red blood cells cannot mature. They are released from the bone marrow in primitive, less functional forms that are larger than normal. Chronic loss of blood from the gut—GI bleeding—can also lead to anemia. Here the bone marrow simply cannot make enough new cells to keep up with those that are lost. The body normally destroys and "recycles" old red blood cells through a process called *hemolysis.* Abnormally rapid hemolysis may occur in alcoholics. The life span of red cells can be shortened by up to 50%. One abnormal cause of hemolysis is hypersplenism, which results from chronic liver disease. The spleen, enlarged and not working properly, destroys perfectly good red blood cells as well as the old worn-out ones. Toxic factors in the blood serum are also thought to be responsible for three other varieties of accelerated hemolysis. *Stomatocytosis* is a transient, relatively benign form of anemia related to binge drinking and unrelated to severe alcoholic liver disease. *Spur cell anemia,* on the other hand, is associated with severe, often end-stage, chronic alcoholic liver disease. The name comes from the shape of the red cell, which, when looked at under the microscope, has jagged protrusions. *Zieve's syndrome* is the simultaneous occurrence in an alcoholic patient of jaundice, transient hemolytic anemia, elevated cholesterol levels, and acute fatty liver disease without enlargement of the spleen.

In France, other changes in red blood cells have on occasion been reported in those who drink at least 2 to 3 quarts of wine each day. These have been changes typically seen with lead poisoning. (Lead, even in low concentrations, can mean trouble.) Excessive intake of wine in France is thought to be a significant source of dietary lead. In the United States, there are periodic reports of lead poisoning connected with alcohol use, but the circumstances are different. The beverage has not been wine but moonshine. In these cases, old car radiators were being used in the distilling process.

White blood cells

On to the effects of alcohol on white blood cells. These cells are one of the body's main defenses against infection. The chronic use of alcohol affects white cells. This contributes to the increased susceptibility to and frequency of severe infections, especially respiratory tract infections, in alcoholics. Alcohol has a direct toxic effect on the white blood cell reserves. This leads to a reduced number of two types of white cells that fight infection (granulocytes and T lymphocytes). *Chemotaxis,* or white cell mobilization, is diminished by alcohol. In other words, although the white cells' ability to kill the bacteria is not affected, they have difficulty reaching the site of infection in adequate numbers. Alcohol also interferes with white cell adherence to bacteria, which is one of the body's defensive inflammatory reactions. As a result, under the influence of alcohol, white cells may have a diminished ability to ingest bacteria.

Platelets

Alcoholics are frequently subject to bleeding disorders. Bleeding can occur in the GI tract, the nose, and the gums. They bruise easily. This is largely explained by the effect of alcohol on decreasing the number of platelets. Platelets are a major component of the body's clotting system and act like a patch on a leak. Alcohol has a direct toxic effect on bone marrow's production of platelets. Thus, 1 out of every 4 alcoholic patients will have abnormally low platelet counts. Within 1 to 3 days of stopping drinking, the count will begin to rise. Recall that severe liver disease can cause hypersplenism. This can cause abnormally rapid destruction of platelets, as well as red blood cells, thereby contributing to the low platelet counts seen in alcoholics.

Clotting factors and DIC

When the liver's metabolic processes are disrupted by the effects of chronic alcohol use, there is often a decrease in the production of some of the necessary serum-clotting factors. One thing to bear in mind is that there are 13 to 15 such substances needed to make a normal clot. Of these, five are liver produced; hence liver disease may in this way also contribute to bleeding problems in alcoholics.

Severe liver damage can also contribute to the occurrence of *disseminated intravascular coagulation* (DIC). This is a life-threatening state of diffuse, abnormally accelerated coagulation. It consumes large quantities of clotting factors, as well as platelets, and leads to dangerously lowered amounts of both, which can, in turn, result in excessive and uncontrolled bleeding and eventual death.

Alcohol and the immune system

Another area of research is examining ways in which the immune system may be altered by alcohol. Actually, there are two different immune systems. One includes immune factors, such as antibodies, complement, and immunoglobulins, circulating freely in the blood system. The other is associated with antibodies attached to individual cells. Changes in both systems can occur with chronic alcohol use. The ability of serum (the unformed elements of the blood) to kill gram-negative bacteria is impaired by alcohol. This may be related to the diseased liver's lowered ability to produce complement, an important agent in the body's inflammatory response. Many immune and defensive responses depend on adequate levels of complement.

Although not clearly established, the effects of alcohol on certain kind of lymphocytes (B-cells) may lead to decreased production of circulating antibodies, which normally fight bacterial infections. Alcohol has also been shown to decrease the numbers of the other major type of lymphocytes (T-cells) which mediate cellular immunity. Moreover, it inhibits their responsiveness to stimuli that ordinarily activate their functioning. These changes are a major contributor to increased susceptibility to infection among alcoholics.

Research has suggested that alcohol-induced changes in other types of white cells, together with changes in the cell-based immune system, may lead to an increased production of certain types of fibrous tissues. It is just such fibrous tissues that are characteristic of cirrhosis. A current question is whether the scar tissue of cirrhosis may at least in part be due to white cell changes and alterations in immune response that are induced by chronic alcohol use.

Even though the hematological complications of chronic heavy alcohol use are many and potentially quite serious, they are in general totally reversible with abstinence. But the liver disease that caused some of them may be so severe as to preclude this. The speed with which they improve is often dependent upon improvement in the underlying liver disease. Reversal can be enhanced in many instances by administering essential vitamins and minerals, such as folate, pyridoxine, and iron, that are deficient, in addition to restoring a fully adequate diet. Still, cessation of alcohol is the main factor.

CARDIOVASCULAR SYSTEM

A specific form of heart muscle disease is thought to result from long-term heavy alcohol use. Known in the past as alcoholic cardiomyopathy, it is now referred to as *alcoholic heart muscle disease* (AHMD). This occurs in a clinically apparent form in 2% of alcoholics. However, it is estimated that 80% have similar, though less severe, and therefore sub-clinical forms of alcohol-related heart muscle disease. When clinically apparent, AHMD is a severe condition with low-output heart failure, marked by shortness of breath with the least exertion and dramatic enlargement of the heart. This is due to weakness of the pumping action of the heart muscle. Low-output failure refers to the heart's inability to pump the volume of blood necessary to meet the body's usual, normal demands. Most commonly, AHMD occurs in middle-aged men who have been drinking heavily for 10 or more years. It often responds well to discontinuing alcohol, plus long-term bed rest. As some have noted, "Abstinence makes the heart grow stronger." Other standard medical treatments for congestive heart failure may also be helpful as adjuncts in the treatment of AHMD.

Another form of alcoholic heart disease, high-output congestive heart failure, is known as *beriberi heart disease*. High-output heart failure is a form of secondary heart failure. It occurs when an otherwise normal heart fails because it can't keep up with the abnormally high metabolic needs of the body. For reasons that are unclear, it results from a deficiency of vitamin B_1, thiamine. It may respond dramatically to correction of the thiamine deficiency and replacement of thiamine in the diet. As an aside, a rather unusual and specific type of severe cardiac disease occurred a few years ago among drinkers of a particular type of Canadian beer. It was found to be caused not by alcohol per se but rather by the noxious effects of small amounts of cobalt. The cobalt had been added to the beer to maintain its "head." These cases occurred in the mid to late 1960s and had a mortality rate of 50% to 60%. Fortunately, the cause was identified, and presumably cobalt-induced heart disease no longer occurs. An earlier similar epidemic of congestive heart failure because of arsenic-contaminated beer occurred around the turn of the century in England.

A variety of abnormalities in cardiac rhythm have been associated with alcohol. In fact, nearly the entire spectrum of such abnormalities may be caused by acute and chronic alcohol intake. *Arrhythmias,* as they are called, may affect either the upper (atrial) or lower (ventricular) portions of the heart. The upper chambers of the heart are like the primers to the lower part, which acts as the pump. Thus ventricular rhythm irregularities that interfere with the heart's pumping action tend to be more serious. Atrial fibrillation and atrial flutter occur in the upper heart muscles and produce ineffective atrial beat that diminishes the priming of the ventricular beats that follow. Another alcohol-induced irregular rhythm involving the upper part of the heart is *paroxysmal atrial tachycardia*. This involves a different and more rapid than usual kind of heartbeat. Alcohol also causes an increase in the frequency of premature ventricular contractions. These, along with atrial flutter and fibrillation, are the most common alcohol-induced arrhythmias. There are also abnormal heartbeats involving the lower part of the heart. These can be dangerous. If these irregular heartbeats occur in a particular pattern, which may be induced by alcohol, they can cause sudden death. In fact, studies have shown an increased incidence of sudden death in alcoholic populations. Another speeding up of the normal heartbeats is *sinus tachycardia with palpitations*. This is thought to occur because of the effects of alcohol and its metabolite, acetaldehyde, in releasing norepinephrine. The sinus node is the normal pacemaker of the heart. Its rate of firing can be speeded up by increasing the amount of circulating epinephrine and norepinephrine.

Recently there have been reports of a new alcohol-induced, arrhythmia-related syndrome. It goes by the name *holiday heart syndrome*. As you might expect from the name, arrhythmias occur after heavy alcohol intake, around holidays and on Mondays after weekend binges. The syndrome involves palpitations and arrhythmias but no evidence of cardiomyopathy or congestive heart failure. The signs and symptoms clear completely after a few days of abstinence.

Even in moderate amounts, alcohol exacerbates certain abnormalities of blood fats in individuals with Type IV hyperlipoproteinemia but not in normal persons who don't have this condition. In such patients, alcohol elevates fat levels of a particular kind believed to increase the rate of development of arteriosclerosis (hardening of the arteries). As a result, the coronary arteries become increasingly narrowed and eventually blocked, leading to premature heart attacks. Even small amounts of alcohol can significantly affect this disorder in individuals at risk.

Alcohol is also well known for causing dilation of superficial skin blood vessels and capillaries. It does not seem to have a similarly predictable effect on the coronary arterial blood vessels and the blood flow through them. Therefore, despite its past use in treating angina, alcohol is not currently considered helpful. In fact, recent studies indicate that in persons with angina, alcohol decreases exercise tolerance. In conjunction with vigorous exercise or physical activity, alcohol use by persons with angina may be especially dangerous.

Perhaps somewhat surprisingly, other findings of recent research suggest that moderate amounts of alcohol (two or fewer drinks per day) may provide a protective effect against the occurrence of heart attacks in people without blood fat abnormalities. Such reports suggest that one cocktail per day may have roughly the same effect on serum cholesterol as the average lipid-lowering diet or regular vigorous exercise. Moderate alcohol intake is known to increase levels of HDL cholesterol and decrease levels of LDL cholesterol. Higher and lower levels of these substances, respectively, are associated with lower risks of heart attacks, so moderate daily use of alcohol may be desirable from your heart's point of view.

Research has shown a definite link between heavy drinking and hypertension. Heavy drinkers had both elevated systolic and diastolic blood pressures. This was true even when weight, age, serum cholesterol level, and smoking were controlled. Although this relationship seems well established, the specific role alcohol plays in the development of atheresclerosis (the process by which hardening of the arteries occurs) is much less clear, especially in view of the multiple and complex interaction of factors causing this condition. More recently the potential importance of alcohol in causing strokes has been recognized, probably as a result of alcohol's effects on blood pressure. (See the section on the Central Nervous System.)

GENITOURINARY SYSTEM

Urinary tract

Almost uniquely, the kidneys are not directly affected by alcohol to any great extent. What happens in the kidneys generally is the result of disordered function elsewhere in the body. For example, alcohol promotes the production of urine through its ability to inhibit the production and output of antidiuretic hormone by the hypothalamic-pituitary region of the brain. Normally blood goes to the kidney for filtering, and water and wastes are separated from it and excreted through the bladder. Usually during this process, antidiuretic hormone causes water to be reabsorbed by the kidney to maintain the body's fluid balance. When the hormone levels are suppressed, the kidney's capacity to reabsorb water is diminished. Instead, it is excreted from the body. Alcohol inhibits this hormone's production when the blood alcohol level is rising. This is so after as little as 2 ounces of pure alcohol. When the blood alcohol level is steady, or falling, there is no such effect. In fact, the opposite may be true; body fluids may be retained. Alcohol can also lead to acute urinary retention and recurrence and exacerbation of urinary tract infections and/or prostatitis. This is due to its ability to cause spasm and congestion in diseased prostate glands as well as in the tissues surrounding previously existing urethral strictures.

It has recently been found that patients with alcoholic cirrhosis occasionally have abnormalities involving the glomeruli in their kidneys. The glomeruli are tiny structures at the extreme "upstream end" of the kidney's major functional unit, the nephron. They act somewhat like a sieve filtering excess fluid and wastes from red and white blood cells, serum proteins, and other elements that are to be returned to the general circulation. There are two main types of glomerular abnormalities that are related to alcohol use. The first, a variety of *glomerulosclerosis,* is more common and rarely causes significant problems. The second, *cirrhotic glomerulonephritis,* fortunately far less common, interferes with the filtration process and elimination of the wastes produced by the kidney. Cirrhosis may also cause other troubles. It can cause retention of sodium, which may play a significant role in the ascites and edema seen with cirrhosis, abnormal handling of other ions, and an inability to excrete excess water normally. The complex causes of all these functional renal abnormalities are not fully understood, and are very likely caused by a number of factors in combination.

A nearly always fatal but fortunately uncommon consequence of chronic alcohol use is the *hepatorenal syndrome*. This is thought to be caused by a toxic serum factor or factors produced by severe alcoholic liver disease. These factors cause shifts in kidney blood flow and impede effective filtration of the blood by the kidney. Unless the underlying liver disease is somehow reversed, irreversible kidney failure can occur. Interestingly, there appears to be nothing intrinsically wrong with the kidneys themselves. They can be transplanted into a patient without underlying liver disease and perform normally. Likewise, liver transplantation in such patients will restore normal kidney function. Thus the kidney failure is thought to be due to some circulating toxic factor or factors presumably resulting from the associated liver disease.

Reproductive system

Chronic heavy alcohol use adversely affects the reproductive system in both men and women. In women, there may be decreased fertility and skipped menstrual periods; in men, diminished libido, impotence, and occasionally sterility may result. In addition to its many other functions, the liver plays an important role in the balance of sex hormones, so when the liver is impaired, an imbalance of sex hormones results. This can play havoc with the normal reproductive function in both men and women.

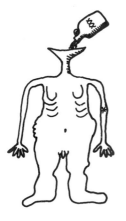

Both male and female sex hormones are normally present in both sexes, only in different proportions. Increased levels of female hormones in alcoholic men, caused by decreased liver metabolism of these hormones, can lead to "feminization" of features. Breasts can enlarge, testicles shrink, and a loss or thinning of body hair can occur. Sex-hormone alterations in males can also result from alcohol's direct inhibitory action on the testes, decreasing the production of testosterone, a male sex hormone. Ingestion of alcohol also may speed up the liver's metabolism of testosterone, thereby even further decreasing its levels. Testosterone levels may be lowered in other ways, such as by alcohol's direct inhibiting effect on the brain centers involved in the production and release of luteinizing hormone (LH), which in turn prompts the release of testosterone by the testicles. When alcohol diminishes LH levels, the net effect is decreased testosterone levels. This brain-mediated inhibitory effect of alcohol is a direct one, independent of any liver or nutritional factors.

Sex-hormone alterations in women are not as completely understood. In part, this is because the female reproductive system, located within the body, is less accessible to study and research. However, it is also because the effects of the use of alcohol by women as a distinct area of inquiry is a fairly recent development. Nonetheless, there is some evidence that alcohol, paralleling its effects on men, may have direct toxic effects on the ovaries and the pituitary. These effects play an important role in the menstrual and fertility changes in female alcoholics.

Finally, although sexual interests and pursuits may be heightened by alcohol's relaxation of inhibitions, ability to perform sexually can be impaired. For example, in men there may be either relative or absolute impotency, despite alcohol-fueled increased desire. Centuries ago, Shakespeare in *Macbeth* (Act II, Scene 1) described these paradoxical effects of alcohol:

> *Macduff:* What three things does drink especially provoke?
>
> *Porter:* Merry sir, nose-painting, sleep, and urine. Lechery, sir, it provokes, and unprovokes; it provokes the desire, but it takes away the performance.

Wine prepares the heart for love, unless you take too much.

OVID

Abstinence from alcohol, improvement in liver disease, and an adequate diet will significantly improve, though often not reverse completely, the alcohol-induced changes in sexual and reproductive functions. Some males who are testosterone deficient may benefit from testosterone replacement.

ALCOHOL AND PREGNANCY

Fetal alcohol syndrome

Since the 1970s, considerable attention has been directed toward the effects of chronic alcohol use during pregnancy. It was in 1971 that a researcher first reported his observations of infants born to alcoholic mothers. The constellation of features observed has since been termed *fetal alcohol syndrome* (FAS). Alcohol can pass through the placenta to affect the developing fetus and interfere with normal prenatal development. At birth, infants with FAS are smaller than normal, both in weight and length. The head size is smaller, probably as a result of arrested brain growth. These infants also have a "dysmorphic facial appearance," that is, they appear "different," although the differences are not easily described. The differences include an overall small head, flat cheeks, small eyes, and a thin upper lip. At birth these infants are jittery and tremulous. Whether this jitteriness is the result of nervous system impairment from the long-term exposure to alcohol and/or mini-withdrawal is unclear. There have been reports of newborn infants having the odor of alcohol on their breath. Cardiac problems and retardation are also associated with FAS in almost half of the cases (46%). In recent reports, FAS, in combination with fetal alcohol effects (FAE), has been established as the leading cause of retardation in the United States—and the most preventable one. (See Chapter 6 for further discussion of the effects of maternal alcoholism on children.)

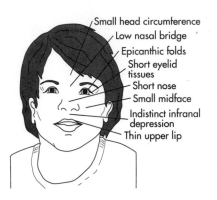

- Small head circumference
- Low nasal bridge
- Epicanthic folds
- Short eyelid tissues
- Short nose
- Small midface
- Indistinct infranal depression
- Thin upper lip

Facial appearance in FAS.

Fetal alcohol effects

It is now well established that a mother does not have to be an alcoholic to expose her unborn baby to the harmful effects of alcohol during pregnancy. Nor do alcohol's effects on the fetus have to occur as the full-blown fetal alcohol syndrome. They can occur with variable degrees of severity. When less severe, they are referred to as *fetal alcohol effects*.

Perhaps even more worrisome than the classical FAS are the reports documenting the potential adverse effects on the unborn babies of any pregnant women drinking more than 1 drink (1/2 ounce of pure alcohol) on even single occasions. Drinking more than one drink per day invites increased risk of abnormalities. These figures are not a numerical average but refer to the amount of alcohol consumed on any single day. As the amount of alcohol consumed on any given day rises, the risk also increases:

Less than one drink	Very little risk
Two drinks	Threshold for risk
Two to four drinks	10% risk of abnormalities
Ten drinks	50% risk of abnormalities
Over ten drinks	75% risk of abnormalities

Clearly, FAE is not restricted to the children of women who are alcoholics. Not unexpectedly, given similar findings with other drugs, the teratogenic effects of alcohol are greater in the first three months of pregnancy than they are in the fourth through ninth months. Based on this information, in the summer of 1977, the NIAAA issued a health warning advising expectant mothers not to have more than two drinks a day. In 1981 a much stronger warning was issued. The U.S. Surgeon General (the nation's highest public health official) advised that women wishing to become pregnant, as well as women who are pregnant, consume no alcohol. More recent research confirms that this advisory was well placed. Current research, suggests that there are both dose-related and threshold effects. "Dose-related" means that the more alcohol consumed the greater the likelihood of damage to the unborn child. Threshold refers to a particular level when the effects of drinking "kick in." Amounts below the threshold seemingly have no impact, but when drinking exceeds the threshold amount, there is a risk of alcohol-induced problems. The current research suggests that the threshold is around 1 drink per day, during the second trimester. Drinking 1 to 2 drinks per day, for a total of one ounce of alcohol per day, doubles the risk of spontaneous abortions during the second trimester. Also, the age of the mother may play a role. One study found that even with the same levels and patterns of drinking, older mothers, those over age 30, were 2 to 5 times more likely to have children with functional impairment.

How alcohol interferes with normal prenatal growth is not fully understood. Research with animals suggests that alcohol crosses the placenta freely and diffuses throughout fetal tissues in much the same fashion as it does in adults. As a toxin, alcohol seems to disrupt the normal growth sequence; the developing fetus cannot later "make up" for these disruptions. The particular abnormalities seen are directly related to the critical development that were occurring when alcohol was present.

Preliminary research suggests, too, that the alcohol level of some of the fetal tissues may be higher than that of the mother. If this is in fact the case, the reason has not been clearly identified. One would predict that the alcohol, because it can pass freely through the placenta to the fetus, should be able to exit just as easily. Therefore both mother and fetus would be expected to have equivalent blood alcohol levels. Case reports of women who drank alcohol during labor, and in whom blood alcohol level studies were done, indicate that the newborn baby's blood alcohol and tissue alcohol levels do not drop as fast as the mother's. The reason presumably is that the infant has an immature liver. Newborns do not have the fully developed enzyme systems (alcohol dehydrogenase) necessary to metabolize and eliminate alcohol as rapidly as their mothers do. Thus for a given maternal blood alcohol level, the fetus may have a somewhat higher blood and tissue alcohol concentration for a longer period of time than the mother.

With the passage of time since FAS and FAE were first recognized, there has been the opportunity to follow affected individuals into adolescence and young adulthood. The nature and extent of impairments found to be associated with FAS and FAE can only be characterized as devastating. Retardation is a common part of the picture. In a large group of FAS/FAE individuals, it was found that the average IQs of FAS and FAE patients were 68 and 73, respectively. (Typically an IQ of 100 is considered average.) In the study group, the range of IQs extended from 20 (severely retarded) to 105 (the normal range). No FAS patient had an IQ of 90 or greater at follow-up. Thus there is some variation, and it is impossible to predict the severity of intellectual deficits, but what is evident is that both FAE as well as FAS individuals are at very high risk for diminished intellectual and adaptive functioning. In the study the average chronological age was 16.5 years, but in terms of general functioning and ability to get along in the world, the general level of functioning in these individuals was estimated to be equivalent to normal children of 7.5 years. Impulsiveness, lack of social inhibition, and social naiveté are often problems as well. Attention deficit hyperactivity disorder (ADHD) is one of the more common behavioral deficits found in children with FAS. Also, ADHD in these individuals is less responsive to treatment with stimulant medications than is true for others with this condition.

People with FAS often behave in ways that cause them problems because their behavior is inappropriate and potentially dangerous or invites being exploited by others. Inappropriate sexual behavior is common. Behavior that as children or preteens may have been seen by others as being very "friendly," involving touching and being physically close to others, becomes socially less acceptable as they grow older. Among adolescents and in adulthood, such behavior can invite considerable social problems and legal encounters. Of all those studied, 95% had been in special education classes at some point during their school experience.

Most significantly, there is no improvement with age—in IQ, achievement, or ability to cope with everyday tasks. Within one large study of adults with FAS, only 5% lived alone and none were fully self-sufficient. The special needs of children with FAS/FAE persist through life. This means that some kind of protective services and special structure are necessary for such children throughout their lives. Clinical research has been directed to identifying what kinds or supportive services within schools and the community, as well as behavioral therapies, can best assist these children as they enter school and move into adulthood.

RESPIRATORY SYSTEM

Alcohol affects the respiratory rate. Low to moderate doses of alcohol increase the respiration rate; presumably this is due to the direct action of alcohol on the respiration center in the brain. In larger, anesthetic, and/or toxic doses, the respiration rate is decreased. This latter effect may contribute to respiratory insufficiency in persons with chronic obstructive pulmonary disease or cause death in cases of acute alcohol poisoning.

In the past, it was thought that for the most part alcohol spared the lungs as far as the direct harmful effects were concerned. This is apparently not the case. Recently such effects have been recognized and investigated. Alcohol can interfere with a variety of important pulmonary cellular defenses, both mechanical and metabolic. These can contribute importantly to chronic airflow obstruction and possibly produce bronchospasm in some individuals. The direct effects of alcohol on the lungs may have significant consequences for individuals with emphysema, chronic obstructive pulmonary disease, chronic bronchitis, and asthma. With the high association of smoking with heavy drinking, lung cancer is also more common among alcoholics.

There also are a number of noxious effects of alcohol that can occur in an indirect fashion. The combination of stuporousness, or unconsciousness, and vomiting as the results of alcohol use can lead to aspiration of mouth and nose secretions or gastric contents. This can lead to bacterial infections and/or aspiration pneumonia. Because of alcohol-induced diminished defenses against infection, pulmonary infections, especially with pneumococci and gram-negative bacteria, seem to occur more frequently and severely in alcoholics than in nonalcoholics. Also because of the alcoholic's diminished defenses against infection, there is a higher incidence of tuberculosis. Thus any alcoholic with a newly positive skin test for tuberculosis should be considered for treatment to prevent possible active tuberculosis.

Normal cilia pushing dust out bronchial tree

drunk cilia with hangovers

ENDOCRINE SYSTEM

The endocrine system is composed of the glands of the body and their secretions, the hormones. Hormones can be thought of as chemical messengers, released by the glands into the bloodstream. They are vital in regulating countless body processes. There is a very complex and involved interaction between hormonal activity and body functioning.

Although there are many glands in the body, the pituitary gland, located in the brain, can be thought of as the "master gland." Many of its hormonal secretions are involved in regulating the other glands. Alcohol can affect the endocrine system in three major ways. One is by altering the function of the pituitary. If this happens, other glands are unable to function properly because they are not receiving the proper "hormonal instructions." Alcohol can affect other glands directly. Despite their receiving the correct instructions from the pituitary, alcohol can impede their ability to respond. Finally, interference with the endocrine system can develop as a result of liver damage. One of the functions of the liver is to break down and metabolize hormones, thereby removing them from the system. Liver disease diminishes this capacity and hormonal imbalances can result.

Several hormonal changes have already been mentioned. As previously described, the level of testosterone, the male sex hormone, is lowered by alcohol in a number of different ways. First, it is lowered by the direct action of alcohol on the testes, and second, through alcohol's action on the pituitary and its subsequent failure to secrete LH, the hormone that stimulates the testes' secretion of testosterone. Another factor is that the liver's clearance of testosterone may be decreased in the alcoholic. Finally, malnutrition, which frequently occurs in alcoholics, may inhibit the function of the hypothalamic-pituitary-adrenal axis at all levels.

Serious liver disease reduces the liver's ability to break down another of the pituitary's hormones, melanocyte-stimulating hormone (MSH). This may result in increased levels of MSH, which leads to a deepening of skin pigmentation and frequently a "dirty tan" skin color. With increased levels of other hormones that stimulate activity of other cells, the question arises about their potential role in cancers (more on this on the next page).

The adrenal glands are also affected by alcohol. The adrenal glands produce several hormones and thus serve multiple functions. One function known to us all comes from the release of adrenaline (epinephrine) when we are frightened or fearful. This charge of adrenaline, with its associated rapid heartbeat and sweating, makes up the "fight-or-flight" response. Heavy intake of or withdrawal from alcohol prompts increased discharge of catecholamines, like epinephrine, by the adrenals. This may be partly responsible for the rapid heartbeat and hypertension during withdrawal. Another adrenal hormone, aldosterone, which plays a major role in regulating the body's salt and water levels, increases both with heavy use as well as during alcohol withdrawal. Increased aldosterone levels often lead to significant and potentially serious salt and water imbalances, visible clinically as swelling (edema). Increased aldosterone levels are frequently seen in patients with cirrhosis with ascites. This is thought to be, in part, the cause of the peripheral edema that is also seen with this condition. In some alcoholics the adrenals secrete excess cortisol. The excess cortisol causes a condition clinically indistinguishable from Cushing's disease, except that it clears rapidly with abstinence from alcohol.

Animal research is raising several interesting questions about alcohol's effects on the endocrine system. In animals, heavy drinking increases the levels of norepinephrine in the heart. This raises the question of whether increased levels of norepinephrine might contribute to the development of alcoholic heart muscle disease.

As noted earlier, carbohydrate metabolism, ordinarily regulated by the hormone insulin, can be adversely affected by chronic alcohol intake. Heavy drinking may lead to abnormally high levels of glucose similar to those seen in diabetics. This condition is referred to as *hyperglycemia.* Usually all that is needed to correct this is abstinence from alcohol and an improved, well-balanced diet. Long-term excessive alcohol intake as well as short-term heavy drinking binges can, on the other hand, lead to low blood sugar levels, known as *hypoglycemia.* This abnormality has two endocrine-system-related causes. First, because of poor diet and liver dysfunction, there is decreased glycogen present, the body's stored form of glucose that is usually available for conversion into circulating glucose. Second, there is a diminished ability by the liver to produce glucose on its own by converting proteins and amino acids into glucose. Hypoglycemia can cause coma. If severe and prolonged, irreversible brain damage can result. This is a medical emergency and must be treated as rapidly as possible.

The increased NADH to NAD^+ ratio is also a major function in causing two dangerous forms of metabolic acidosis frequently seen in alcoholics. The first is known as *alcoholic ketoacidosis,* which occurs when the altered cofactor ratio leads to the production not of carbon dioxide and water, as alcohol is metabolized, but ketones, which are organic acids. The second, *lactic acidosis,* also occurs because of the altered ratio of NADH to NAD^+. In this case, there is an increased production of lactate. Both types of acidosis are dangerous and must be treated with intravenous fluids and sodium bicarbonate.

Cancer

Research is being conducted to explore whether alcohol's effect on the endocrine system might contribute to the development of different types of cancer. Heavy drinkers are known to have a higher incidence of skin, thyroid, head and neck, esophageal, stomach, liver, lung, and breast cancers. Recall that the pituitary gland is the master control gland. It influences the activity of various other glandular tissues through the hormones it secretes. Alcohol inhibits the breakdown of pituitary MSH, as mentioned above. It may also play a role in the release of hormones that promote thyroid activity and milk production by the breast. These three hormones have one thing in common: they affect their target tissues—the skin, thyroid gland, and breast—by causing these tissues to *increase* their metabolic activity. So, the pieces may be falling into place. Cancer, simply put, occurs when there is uncontrolled or abnormal cellular metabolic activity and growth and inadequate immune defenses that normally eliminate any cancerous cells that might develop. It is possible that alcohol's presence over long periods of time produces so many hormonal messages to the skin, thyroid, and breast tissues that in certain patients, in some as yet undetermined fashion, malignant cells may be produced at these sites. Because alcohol may also have impaired the function of the body's protective immune surveillance system, these are not eliminated by the body.

SKIN

Chronic alcohol use affects the skin both directly and indirectly. Its most pronounced direct effect is dilation of the vessels of the skin. A variety of pathological effects on other systems are reflected by the appearance of the skin. For example, a chronic flushed appearance, itching, jaundice, thinning of the skin, changes in hair distribution, the presence of spider angiomas, a grayish cast to the skin, and fingernail changes all may reflect significant liver dysfunction. Bruising, paleness, and skin infections may reflect major abnormalities in the hematological and immune systems.

Skin changes may suggest the presence of nutritional deficiencies in alcoholism. These include vitamin B deficiency, especially of niacin, which causes pellagra, and vitamin C and zinc deficiencies. Skin manifestations often may reflect the chaotic life situations of many alcoholics. There may be evidence of accidents, such as bruises, abrasions, lacerations, and multiple old scars. In colder climates, there may be evidence of frostbite. Nicotine stains and/or cigarette burns may be present. Heavy and chronic alcohol use, among other causes, will precipitate or aggravate a skin condition known as rosacea in predisposed persons. This condition includes flushing and inflammation, especially of the nose and middle portion of the face. Particularly striking is the excessive growth of the subcutaneous tissue of the nose, a condition called *rhinophyma* or "rum nose." Another skin condition associated with chronic alcoholism and alcoholic liver disease is *porphyria cutanea tarda*. This includes increased pigmentation, hair growth, and blistering in sun-exposed areas. It has been thought by some that there may be a causal link between other important skin diseases, such as psoriasis, eczema, and scleroderma, and heavy alcohol use. Others feel that it is more likely that these conditions are simply much harder to manage and therefore seem to be more severe in alcoholics because of concurrent multiple medical problems, nutritional inadequacy, and generally poor treatment compliance often seen.

MUSCULOSKELETAL SYSTEM

Chronic alcohol use affects the skeletal system in three significant ways. First, there are at least four different types of arthritis that are linked to heavy alcohol use. *Gouty arthritis* results from increased uric acid levels, which can occur in two ways. One is as a result of the increased levels of organic acids that accompany the altered ratio of NADH to NAD$^+$. In this instance the kidneys try unsuccessfully to secrete both uric acid and as well as these other acids, so, excess amounts of uric acid accumulate. Another comes from lead-contaminated "moonshine." The lead can damage the kidneys which leads to increased uric acid levels. In both cases, abstinence and specific treatment for gouty arthritis may prove beneficial. Arthritis occurs too in conjunction with alcoholic pancreatitis. This is believed to be caused by the direct or indirect damage to joints by the enzymes that are circulating in the bloodstream as the result of damage to the pancreas. *Degenerative arthritis,* also known as "old age" arthritis or osteoarthritis, occurs more frequently with chronic heavy alcohol use. This probably comes from the higher frequency of falls, injuries, and fractures in alcoholics. *Septic arthritis* (infection in a joint space) also is seen more frequently in those who drink heavily. This is probably a result of several factors in combination. Osteoarthritis, as mentioned, is more common in alcoholics and involves roughened joint surfaces where bloodborne infectious agents may be more likely to settle. Alcoholics too are likely to have a higher incidence of blood-borne bacterial infections for a number of reasons, including more frequent infections of all types, more frequent injuries, and less attention to personal hygiene. Again as noted, the alcoholic's defenses against such infections are diminished.

Osteoporosis, a generalized thinning or demineralization of the bones most typically occurring in the elderly, is accelerated by heavy alcohol use. This condition can lead to a 25% decrease in bone mass, which in turn can frequently lead to fractures. Fractures of the hip (especially the neck of the femur), the wrist, the upper arm bone or humerus, and the vertebral bodies in the spinal column are the most common. Rib fractures are also quite common in heavy drinkers, but they are probably caused by an increased frequency of falls and trauma rather than the result of changes in the bone. There are many factors that contribute to the occurrence of osteoporosis in alcoholics. They include alcohol-induced loss of calcium and/or magnesium due to excess excretion by the kidneys, decreased absorption of calcium and/or vitamin D by the small intestine with a diminished capacity for absorption, and the demineralizing effects of excessive adrenal corticosteroid hormones, due to the stimulating effects of alcohol on the adrenal glands.

Aseptic necrosis, a form of bone death, especially of the head of the femur, caused by inadequate blood supply to that region, is another condition especially frequent in alcoholic men. In fact, as many as 50% of those with this condition (of whom two-thirds are men) have a history of heavy alcohol use. Deformity of the hip joint often results in and can lead to severe arthritis, which can be disabling and may eventually require total hip joint replacement. The cause is unknown but is postulated to be related to fat deposits, which are thought to be caused by pancreatitis or alcohol-induced abnormalities in the liver's metabolism of fats (see Chapter 2). These fatty deposits are believed to lodge in the small arterial vessels supplying the femoral head and cut off essential nutrition and oxygen to that area, resulting in bone death.

NERVOUS SYSTEM

The central nervous system (CNS), of all the major organ systems, is perhaps most widely and profoundly affected by the effects of acute and chronic alcohol use. Over time, with sufficient quantities of alcohol, the CNS becomes adapted or accustomed to its presence. This adaptation is what addictive states are all about. Drinking a quart of liquor daily for as little as 1 week can create a state of physical dependence.

Dependence, tolerance, craving, and withdrawal

Physical dependence is defined by the presence of *tolerance*. Tolerance refers to changes that occur as a result of repeated exposure to alcohol. Tolerance represents the nervous system's ability to adapt and function more or less normally despite the presence of alcohol. These changes include alterations in how the body handles the alcohol (metabolic tolerance) as well as changes in alcohol's effects on the nervous system (functional or behavioral tolerance). After repeated exposures, there is both an increased rate of metabolism of alcohol and a decrease in behavioral impairment at a particular blood alcohol level. Consequently, the person requires increasing amounts of alcohol to get the effects previously produced by lower doses and to ward off withdrawal symptoms.

After physical dependence has been established, if consumption is curtailed there will be characteristic symptoms. These symptoms constitute the so-called *abstinence* or *withdrawal syndrome*. One sure way to terminate an abstinence syndrome is to administer more of the addictive drug. The withdrawal symptoms for any drug are generally the reverse of the effects induced by the drug itself. Alcohol belongs to the depressant class of drugs. Therefore the alcohol abstinence syndrome is characterized by symptoms that are indicative of an activated state. A hangover, a kind of mini-withdrawal, testifies to this. The well-known symptoms of jumpiness, edginess, irritability, and hyperactivity are the exact opposite of alcohol's depressant qualities.

As classically considered, the individual who has regularly abused alcohol—that is, he or she has developed tolerance to it—will have withdrawal symptoms whenever there is a relative absence of alcohol. This means that although the person may still be drinking, withdrawal

symptoms appear if the amount consumed is less than usual and therefore the blood alcohol level is lowered. The symptoms can include intention tremors (the shakes when trying to do something), which are rapid and coarse, involving the head, tongue, and limbs. The is the basis of the morning shakes, in a heavy drinker whose last drink was the night before. These symptoms result from a drop in the blood alcohol level.

If the chronic heavy drinker does not consume more alcohol, he or she is likely to develop more serious symptoms of withdrawal. These are thought to represent a sort of rebound effect. In the absence of alcohol and its chronic suppressant effects, certain regions of the brain become overactive. The severity of the symptoms of withdrawal can vary widely, depending on the length of time of heavy drinking and the amount of alcohol consumed during that period, plus individual differences in people. Symptoms of withdrawal can include tremulousness, agitation, seizures, and hallucinations. These will be discussed in detail later in this chapter.

Craving is also associated with addiction and results from changes in the central nervous system. With alcohol, craving is that deep desire, that virtually irresistible impulse, that strong "need" to have a drink. When it strikes it is difficult to "just say no" or to ignore it. Craving is discrete from withdrawal, although the state of abstinence may well trigger it. In fact multiple factors may prove to be triggers—the situation, a song on the radio played at your favorite bar, certain foods, particular friends, or your mood. These urges arise from physical changes in the brain, particularly the neurotransmitter systems.

Alcohol idiosyncratic intoxication (pathological intoxication)

Aside from withdrawal symptoms, other important CNS disorders are related to alcohol use. A relatively unusual manifestation is a condition previously called *pathological intoxication,* which was later classified as alcoholic *idiosyncratic intoxication.* (This condition is no longer included in the Diagnostic and Statistical Manual of the American Psychiatric Association referred to the DSM.) Some susceptible persons, for reasons unknown, have a dramatic change of personality when they drink even small amounts of alcohol. It is a transient psychotic state with a very rapid onset. The individual becomes confused and disoriented; may have visual hallucinations; and may be very aggressive, anxious, impulsive, and enraged. In this state the person may carry out senseless, violent acts against others or himself. The state can last for only a few minutes or for several hours; then the person lapses into a profound sleep and has amnesia for the episode. Were he to be interviewed later, he might be very docile, not at all the madman he appeared to be during the episode. Most likely the person would report, "I don't know what happened; I just went bananas." It is unclear whether there is a relationship between this syndrome and other organic impulse disorders.

Organic brain disease

Chronic alcohol use can also lead to varying degrees of dementia or organic brain disease. The particular type of brain disease, its name and associated impairment, is determined by the portion of the brain involved. *Wernicke's syndrome* and *Korsakoff's psychosis* are two such syndromes closely tied to alcoholism. Sometimes they are discussed as two separate disorders; other times people lump them together as the Wernicke-Korsakoff syndrome. Both are caused by nutritional deficiencies, especially thiamine, a B vitamin, in combination with whatever direct toxic effects alcohol has on nerve tissue. In addition, recent evidence suggests that a genetic factor in the form of an inherited lack of an enzyme (transketolase) may play an important role in the development of Wernicke-Korsakoff syndrome.

The difference in terms of pathology is that Wernicke's syndrome involves injury to the midbrain, cerebellum, and areas near the third and fourth ventricles of the brain, whereas Korsakoff's psychosis results from damage to areas of the brain important to memory function (the diencephalon, hypothalamus, and hippocampal formation) and is often associated with damage to peripheral nerve tissue as well. Prognostically, Wernicke's syndrome has a brighter picture. When recognized and treated early, it often responds very rapidly to thiamine therapy. Korsakoff's psychosis is much slower to respond and less likely to improve. Patients with Korsakoff's psychosis often require nursing home or custodial care.

Clinically, a person with Wernicke's syndrome is apt to be confused, delirious, and apprehensive. There is a characteristic dysfunction called *nystagmus* and/or paralysis of the eye muscles that control eye movements. Nystagmus and other eye signs are among the first symptoms to appear and, following treatment, the first to disappear. Difficulty with walking (ataxia) and balance are a typical part of Wernicke's syndrome. This can lead to unsteadiness and gait disturbances. Both are caused by peripheral nerve damage in conjunction with cerebellar damage.

Korsakoff's psychosis presents a somewhat different picture. There is severe memory loss and confabulation. *Confabulation*—that is, making up tales, talking fluently without regard to facts—is the hallmark. It occurs in an individual who is otherwise alert, responsive, and able to attend to and comprehend the written and spoken word. In other words, the memory impairment is greatly out of proportion to other cognitive dysfunctions. Because of the severe damage to areas of the brain crucial to memory, the person simply cannot process and store new information. In order to fill in the memory gaps, he makes up stories. These are not deliberate lies: trickery would require more memory and intent than someone with Korsakoff's psychosis could muster. For example, were you to ask someone with this disorder if he had met you before, the response might be a long, involved story about the last time the two of you had been together. It would be pure fantasy having no basis in reality. This is the phenomenon of confabulation. Memory for things that happened both recently as well as long ago is variably but usually severely impaired. Things simply are not stored for recall, and the person cannot remember events even 5 minutes after they occur. With Korsakoff's psychosis, ataxia may also be present. Ataxia causes a characteristic awkward manner of walking, with feet spread apart to assist. Korsakoff's psychosis and Wernicke's syndrome can both have a sudden, rapid onset. Frequently Korsakoff's psychosis follows a bout of delirium tremens (the DTs).

Cerebral atrophy (generalized loss of brain tissue) often can occur in chronic alcoholism. Most typically this is seen in people in their 50s and 60s. Another name for this disorder is *alcoholic dementia*. A variety of factors common in alcoholics seemingly combine to cause this condition. Treatment of these diseases includes administration of thiamine, a well-balanced diet. Discontinuation of alcohol is imperative. This treatment is more successful in reversing the signs and symptoms of Wernicke's syndrome. Only about 20% of persons with Korsakoff's psychosis recover completely. The recovery process is slow, taking as much as 6 to 12 months. The mortality rate of the combined disorder is approximately 15%. The dementia associated with cerebral atrophy is irreversible. However, with abstinence and adequate nutrition it may stabilize and not progress further.

Alcoholic cerebellar degeneration is a late complication of chronic heavy alcohol use combined with nutritional deficiencies. It is more likely to occur in men, typically only after 10 to 20 years of heavy drinking. Patients gradually develop a slow, broad-based, lurching gait, as if they were about to fall over. This results from the fact that the cerebellum, the area of the brain that is damaged, is what coordinates complex motor activity such as walking. There is no associated cognitive or mental dysfunction because the portions of the brain governing such activities are not usually affected, but signs of peripheral neuropathy and malnutrition may be present.

Two forms of organic brain dysfunction are a direct result of severe alcoholic liver disease. These are acute and chronic *portosystemic encephalopathy* (PSE). They are caused by the diseased liver's diminished ability to prevent naturally occurring toxic substances from getting into the general body circulation. (These toxins include ammonia and glutamine, for example, which are normally confined to the blood vessels flowing from the small intestines into the liver, where they are metabolized.) This raises havoc with the central nervous system. In both acute and chronic forms of PSE there may be cognitive and memory disturbances, changes in levels of consciousness—the extreme being so-called *hepatic coma*—a flapping-like tremor, and a foul, musty odor to the breath. In the acute form, which is much less common, there is no evidence of chronic liver disease that is typically present in the chronic form. Along with abstinence from alcohol to allow the liver to recover as much normal function as possible, aggressive, multipronged medical management must be instituted. The goal is to

In some cases a flap-like Tremor and a foul breath does not indicate Porto systemic encephalopathy. It indicates you are examining a seal.

reduce the body's production of toxic nitrogen-containing substances. A particularly severe variant of chronic PSE is known as *chronic hepatocerebral disease*. This is a complication of long-standing liver disease in which the brain has been harmed by toxins chronically circulating in the bloodstream. As a result, the brain has areas of cell death and proliferation of scarlike CNS cells. Mirroring these, there is a corresponding loss of brain function, with dementia, ataxia, speech impairment (dysarthria), and sometimes bizarre movements. Scarred or damaged brain tissue cannot be repaired, so any such losses are permanent. Patients with this condition often require chronic care facilities.

Two other organic brain diseases, which are quite obscure but serious if they occur, are also related to alcohol abuse and nutritional deficiencies. First, *central pontine myelinolysis* involves a part of the brainstem known as the pons. This disease can vary in intensity from very mild to fatal over a 2- to 3-week period. The pons controls respiration, among other things. As it degenerates, coma and finally death occur from respiratory failure. Second, *Marchiafava-Bignami disease,* also exceedingly uncommon, involves the nerve tracts connecting the frontal areas on the two sides of the brain. Their degeneration leads to diminished language and motor skills, gait disorders, incontinence, seizures, dementia, hallucinations, and frequently eventual death.

Finally, a term one sometimes hears in discussion of alcohol's chronic effects on the central nervous system is "wet brain." There is no specific medical condition that goes by this name. Probably it developed colloquially among lay people to encompass the variety of nonreversible organic brain syndromes that cause significant mental impairment and diminished physical capacity such that those affected require nursing home care.

Nerve and muscle tissue damage

Nerve tissue in other parts of the body can also be damaged by chronic alcohol use. The most common disturbance is *alcoholic polyneuropathy* from nutritional deficiencies. This has a gradual onset and progresses slowly. Recovery is equally slow and generally incomplete, taking weeks to months after the discontinuation of alcohol, plus administering appropriate vitamins. Most commonly the distal nerves (those farthest from the body trunk) are affected first. The damage to these nerves seems to be caused primarily by nutritional deficiencies, though direct toxic effects of alcohol may also be involved. Typically, someone with polyneuropathy will have a painful burning feeling in the soles of the feet, yet an absence of normal sensation. Because there is sensory impairment, the individual doesn't have the necessary feedback to the brain to tell him or her how the body is positioned in space. This loss of position sense may lead to an unsteady, slapping style of walking because the person is uncertain where the feet and legs are in relation to the ground.

Muscle damage often accompanies such nerve damage. In turn, muscle tissue is usually wasted in the same areas that have been affected by nerve damage. Other forms of muscle damage and degeneration have been reported even in the absence of neuropathy. One form involves acute muscle pain, swelling, and destruction of muscle tissue in the aftermath of acute binges and is referred to as *acute alcoholic myopathy*. Another form seen in chronic heavy drinkers is chronic alcoholic myopathy, which involves the proximal muscles (those nearer the body trunk). Yet another type of muscle damage may result when a person is intoxicated, passes out, and lies in the same position for a long time. With the constant pressure of body weight on the same muscles, pressure necrosis can result, leading to muscle degeneration. Like any other myopathy, this means that certain muscle proteins (myoglobins) are released into the bloodstream. If these muscle protein levels are too high, kidney failure can occur. Potassium is also a product of such muscle tissue breakdown. An increase in the level of potassium can disturb mineral balance throughout the body. For reasons that are currently unclear, alcoholics are known to be very prone to muscle cramps.

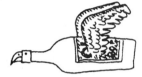

Finally, an entity known as *alcohol-tobacco amblyopia* (diminished vision) is another nervous system disorder. As the name implies, it is associated with chronic, excessive drinking and smoking. It is characterized by the slow onset of blurred, dim vision with pain behind the eyes. There is difficulty reading, intolerance of bright light, and loss of central color vision. Although blind spots can occur, total blindness is uncommon. The cause is again thought to be a vitamin deficiency coupled with the direct neuro-toxic effects of alcohol. Treatment includes B-complex vitamins, plus abstinence, which are usually effective in reversing the eye symptoms. Typically, recovery is slow and unfortunately only partial.

Subdural hematoma

An indirect result of chronic alcoholism is the increased frequency of *subdural hematomas*. These can be the result of falling down and striking the head, being assaulted, or being in an auto accident, all of which are more likely to occur when intoxicated. Any such injury to the head can cause tearing of the vessels of the brain lining, the dura, with bleeding as a result. The skull is a rigid box, so any bleeding inside this closed space exerts pressure on the brain. This type of bleeding can be very serious, even life threatening, and often is not recognized. Signs and symptoms can vary widely, although fluctuating states of consciousness (i.e., drifting in and out of consciousness) are often associated with this. Treatment involves surgical removal of the blood clot.

Miscellaneous CNS disturbances

Other neurological conditions occur with increased frequency in alcoholics. These include bacterial meningitis, seizures following head trauma, and concussive syndromes. Strokes (cerebrovascular accidents) and brain hemorrhages seem to occur with increased frequency during acute alcohol intoxication. Whether this is also true in cases of chronic alcoholism has yet to be proven. These are thought to be due to the acute hypertensive effect of alcohol and may be aggravated by alcohol's interfering with the normal clotting mechanisms discussed earlier.

NEUROPSYCHOLOGICAL IMPAIRMENT

Personality changes have long been regarded as a prominent feature of chronic alcohol use. Historically this was chalked up to serious underlying psychological problems. Then the emphasis shifted to viewing the "alcoholic personality" as an adaptive behavior style the alcoholic developed to rationalize his alcoholic problems and to justify the continuation of drinking. There was little systematic research to explore a physiological basis, if any, for these behaviors. This is now changing. Neuropsychological research, using formal psychometric testing, has uncovered specific impairments associated with alcohol abuse.

Overall intellectual deterioration is not seen until very late in the course of alcoholism. The IQ of most alcoholics, especially verbal IQ, remains relatively intact and in the normal range. Nonetheless, there are other specific deficits, including the diminished ability to solve problems, less ability to perform complex psychomotor tasks, decreased ability to use abstract concepts, and memory impairment. The drinking history is the major factor determining severity of impairments. How much alcohol has been consumed and for how long are the questions to be asked. These deficits tend to improve with abstinence. The first 2 to 3 weeks after stopping alcohol bring the most dramatic improvement. After that, further improvement occurs gradually over the next 6 to 12 months. It is important to realize that the improvement, though considerable, is not necessarily complete.

The areas of the brain that seem to be the most affected are the frontal lobes and the right hemisphere. This may help to explain the profound personality changes associated with chronic alcohol use. In fact, some of the behaviors accompanying alcoholism, such as "inability to abstain" and "loss of control," may partially be a product of organic brain dysfunctions. Most of the impairments in functioning are subtle and not readily apparent to the casual observer. In fact, many of those in the clinical studies documenting neuropsychological impairment appeared "normal." They were often described as "young, intelligent, and looking much like any other citizen." That should alert us to the possibility that such alcohol-related brain damage may be more widespread than previously thought.

MISCELLANEOUS EFFECTS

Chronic alcohol use is also related to a variety of other signs, symptoms, and conditions that do not fit neatly into a discussion of any particular organ system.

Hodgkin's disease is a form of lymphatic cancer that, although certainly very serious, is becoming more and more treatable. Many persons with Hodgkin's disease who drink may experience pain in the lymph nodes that are affected by the disease. Alcohol abuse may also be associated with Dercum's disease, which is characterized by symmetrical and painful deposits of fat around the body and limbs. Painless parotid gland enlargement which looks very much like mumps may be seen in as many as 25% of patients with cirrhosis.

An interesting property of alcohol is its ability to alleviate dramatically the tremor in persons with *familial tremor.* As suggested by the name, this condition runs in families. It may occur in relatively young persons, through it is more common in the elderly. The cause is unknown. To account for the heavier-than-expected drinking seen in many patients with this condition, it has been hypothesized that they might be medicating themselves by drinking, thereby inviting alcoholism. Fortunately, other drugs are as effective as alcohol for this condition and are much safer.

Alcohol abuse is associated with a variety of metabolic disorders, including the following:

• *Hyperuricemia,* that is, elevated uric acid levels in the blood, causing a number of medical complications. (See the section on the musculoskeletal system.)

• *Diminished potassium levels* (hypokalemia) caused by excess mineral-regulating hormone (aldosterone), associated with cirrhosis and ascites.

• *Decreased magnesium* levels in the blood, probably from alcohol's enhancement of the kidney's excretion of magnesium along with decreased oral intake and increased loss through the GI system.

• *Metabolic acidosis,* an increase of hydrogen ion concentration in the blood from altered liver metabolic functioning.

• *Decreased levels of calcium and phosphate,* for which neither the cause nor the clinical significance is well understood.

What has been described are the many medical complications frequently associated with chronic heavy drinking and/or alcoholism. It is important, however, to realize that health problems can arise from any alcohol use. One does not have to be an alcoholic or problem drinker. Increasingly, alcohol use is being considered a risk factor for the development of a variety of common illnesses. The earlier general notion that alcohol poses a health hazard "only if you really drink a lot" is going by the wayside.

SLEEP AND SLEEP DISTURBANCES IN ALCOHOLICS

Many people say they can't sleep unless they have a drink or two before bedtime "to relax." Actually, alcohol interferes with sound sleep. To understand this, let's look at how people sleep, how alcohol affects normal sleep, and what can be done for clients who cannot sleep after they have stopped drinking.

Scientists have studied sleep by recording brain waves of sleeping subjects on an EEG. Everyone sleeps in basically the same way. There are four stages of sleep: stage 1, stage 2, delta, and rapid eye movement (REM). Each stage has characteristic brain-wave patterns. These stages occur in a fairly predictable sequence throughout the night.

Sleep patterns

Before we can fall asleep, we need to relax. This is a fairly individualized affair—what might relax one person would stimulate someone else. Some relax best in a dark, quiet bedroom; others need a loudspeaker blasting rock music before they can let go. In either case, as soon as one becomes drowsy, the brain will show alpha waves. Next comes the transition period, a time when one is half asleep and half awake. This is called stage 1. One still feels awake but does not attend to input from the environment. Brief dream fragments or images may occur at this time. Stage 1 sleep lasts anywhere from 2 to 10 minutes in normal sleepers, but it can last all night in some recovering alcoholics. Finally, there comes the real thing—sleep. The average, nondreaming sleep is called stage 2, and we spend about 50% to 60% of our sleep in this stage. Stage 2 is a medium deep and restful sleep, and the first episode of it will last about 20 to 45 minutes.

Gradually, sleep deepens until we are in the most sound sleep of the night—delta sleep. The length of time one spends in delta sleep depends on age, ranging from up to several hours in children to little or none in older age groups. Delta sleep is mainly concentrated in the early part of the night and rarely occurs after approximately the first 3 hours of sleep. After delta sleep, we return to stage 2 sleep for awhile. Then, about 60 to 90 minutes after falling asleep, the most exciting sleep begins. This is rapid eye movement, or REM, sleep. The brain waves now resemble a waking pattern. The eyes are moving rapidly under closed eyelids, but the body is completely relaxed (in fact, paralyzed) and asleep. During REM sleep we dream. The first dream of the night lasts about 5 minutes. Following it, there is a return to stage 2, possibly some delta sleep again, but it is not quite as deep as the first time. The second dream sleep of the night occurs about 3 hours after sleep onset and lasts about 10 minutes.

The cycle of alternating nondreaming (stage 2) and dreaming (REM) sleep continues throughout the night. Dreams occur about every 90 minutes. As the night goes on, nondreaming sleep becomes shorter, and dreaming (REM) sleep becomes longer. You can see that we are guaranteed about four dreams in 6 hours of sleep. In fact, you dream for about 20% of an average night. During dreaming, part of the brain is awake, part is not. For example, the long-range memory part of the brain does not function during dreaming. So, to remember a dream, you have to

wake up from it and think about the dream immediately after you awaken. (Because dreaming is a light state of sleep, one often wakes up from it.) Someone who reports dreaming a lot either is not sleeping very well, and therefore wakes up a lot, or thinks about the dreams a lot just after waking. Someone who claims never to dream is probably a reasonably sound sleeper, with few awakenings. That person probably also jumps right out of bed upon waking and therefore forgets the dreams. Someone who claims to be dreaming "more" lately has either become more interested in himself and thinks more about his dreams or is waking up more because he has developed poorer sleep.

Sleep seems to be good for both body and mind. Stage 2 and especially delta sleep are thought to be mainly body-recovery sleep. When this sleep functions well, the body feels refreshed on awakening in the morning. Dreaming sleep, on the other hand, has something to do with our psychological recovery. People do not go crazy if they are deprived of dreams, as was originally believed, but they lose some psychological stability. Someone who is usually very reliable, stable, and punctual may become irresponsible, irritable, and impulsive if deprived of REM sleep. As to the amount of sleep someone needs, the old 7 to 8 hours rule is useless. It depends on the individual. Some people do perfectly well with only 2 or 3 hours; 12 hours are necessary for others.

Sleep disturbances

Why do we need sleep? Take it away and see what happens! Despite what most of us think, an occasional sleepless night is not all that devastating. Although you might feel awful and irritable, total loss of sleep for one or two nights has surprisingly little effect on normal performance and functioning. Two exceptions are very boring tasks, such as watching radar blips or driving long distances, and very creative tasks, such as writing an essay. These are affected by even one night of very little sleep. On the other hand, for most jobs of average interest and difficulty, if one really tries to do so, one can draw on one's reserves and "rally" to the task even after two to four totally sleepless nights.

Three brain systems regulate the state of our existence: the awake or arousal system (the reticular activating system), the sleep system, and the REM (dreaming) system. There is a continual struggle among the three, each trying to dominate the other two. The three different systems have different anatomical bases in the brain and apparently run on different neurochemicals. If you influence these neurochemicals, you disturb the balance among the three systems. Alcohol does disturb these neurochemicals.

It is not too difficult to disturb the balance between the waking and the sleeping systems for a few days. Stress and stimulants, such as coffee and Dexedrine, will strengthen the waking system; sleeping pills will help the sleeping system. However, after just a few days or weeks, the brain chemistry compensates for the imbalance, and the chemicals become ineffective. Therefore after just 1 month on sleeping pills, an insomniac's sleep will be as poor as ever. There is even some evidence that the continued use of sleeping pills in itself causes poor sleep. Furthermore, when the sleeping pill is withdrawn, sleep will become extremely poor for a few days or weeks because the brain's chemical balance is now disturbed in the opposite direction. Many people stay on sleeping pills for decades even though the pills do not really help them because of this "rebound insomnia" when they try to sleep without drugs. Because one sleeps so poorly for awhile when withdrawing from the chronic use of sleeping pills, caution should be used. Go slowly, cutting down on the use of sleeping pills in very gradual doses over a period of weeks. Abrupt withdrawal from some sleeping pills can be dangerous and even cause seizures. In addition, practically all sleeping pills, contrary to advertising, suppress dreaming sleep. After stopping the pills, the dreaming sleep increases in proportion to its former suppression. It then can occupy from 40% to 50% of the night. Dreaming sleep, too, takes 10 days or so to get back to normal. During these days there is very little time for deep sleep because dreaming takes up most of the night. You feel exhausted in the morning because you had very little time for body recovery. Nonetheless, people who have taken heavy doses of sleeping pills for a long time often sleep better after being withdrawn than they did while taking them. It is all right to take a sleeping pill on rare occasions, say before an important interview, or after three to four nights of very poor sleep. However, it rarely makes any sense to take sleeping pills regularly for more than a week or two.

Insomnia

Insomnia can be based on either an overly active waking system or a weak sleeping system. On rare occasions insomnia can have an organic or genetic basis. Some people have a defective sleep system from birth; however, most insomnias are based on psychological factors. Any stress, depression, or tension will naturally arouse the waking system. When this is the case, the cure obviously involves helping the person deal with the psychological stress.

Surprisingly, poor sleep is often little more than a bad habit! Say you went through a stressful life situation a few years back and, quite naturally, couldn't sleep for a few nights because of it. Being very tired during the day after a few bad nights, you needed sleep more and more. So you tried harder and harder to get to sleep, but the harder you tried, the less you could fall asleep. Soon a vicious cycle developed. Everything surrounding sleep became emotionally charged with immense frustration, and the frustration alone kept you awake.

How can this cycle be broken? The treatment is simple and effective, provided you stick with it. The first step is to recognize you are misusing the bed by lying in it awake and frustrated. The specific rules for treatment are as follows:

1 Whenever you can't fall asleep relatively quickly, get up, because you are misusing the bed. You can do your "frustrating" somewhere else, but not in the bedroom.

2 As soon as you are tired enough and think you might fall asleep quickly, go to bed. If you can't fall asleep quickly, get up again. This step is to be repeated as often as necessary, until you fall asleep quickly.

3 No matter how little sleep you get on a given night, you have to get up in the morning at the usual time.

4 No daytime naps!

If you stick to this regimen for a few weeks, the body again becomes used to falling asleep quickly. Therapists trained in this type of behavioral treatment may be of considerable help and support.

Shortening the time spent in bed is also crucial to many insomniacs. Because they haven't slept during the night, many insomniacs stay in bed for half the morning. They want to catch a few daytime naps, or they feel too tired and sick after not sleeping to get up. Pretty soon they lie in bed routinely for 12, 14, even 20 hours. They sleep their days away while complaining of insomnia. It is important that one maintain a regular day/night rhythm, with at least 14 to 16 hours out of bed, even if the nights are marred by insomnia. In some individuals, undiagnosed medical disorders or physical disturbances during sleep may give rise to insomnia. If insomnia problems persist for months or years, it is a good idea to consult with a doctor or a specialist in sleep disorders.

Alcohol's effects on sleep

How does alcohol affect sleep? Many find that a nightcap "fogs up" an overly active waking system. No question, some people can fall asleep faster with a drink. However, alcohol depresses REM (dreaming) sleep and causes more awakenings later at night. The drinker frequently wakes many times throughout the night, which results in a lack of recovery during sleep. These effects continue in chronic drinkers. In addition, the pressure to dream becomes stronger the longer it is suppressed. The dreaming sleep system will finally demand its due. Thus after a binge there is a tremendous recovery need for dreaming. It is thought that part of the DTs and the hallucinations of alcohol withdrawal can be explained by a lack of sleep (many awakenings) and a pressure to dream (lack of REM). The great fragmentation of sleep and lack of delta and REM sleep in chronic alcoholics is a serious problem. Even though they think they sleep well, there is little or no recovery value in it. This very poor sleep makes people want to sleep longer in the morning and during the day, which adds to the usual problem of coping.

Another sleep problem of real concern to alcoholics is that of *sleep apnea*. This is a relatively common breathing disturbance in which a person's air passages become obstructed during sleep. It is especially common in older individuals and those who are overweight. Alcohol

markedly worsens sleep apnea and puts the affected individual at serious risk for medical complications that can be life-threatening. Frequent, loud snoring is often a good indicator of this problem.

What happens to sleep when the booze is taken away from a chronic alcoholic? First, there is the rebound of dreaming. Increased dreaming can last up to 10 days before subsiding. Often there are nightmares because dreaming is so intense. The sleep fragmentation lasts longer. A loss of delta sleep can go on for as long as 2 years after drinking ceases. Sober alcoholics, as a group, still have more sleep disturbances than nonalcoholics. We don't know why. It could be due to some chronic damage to the nervous system during binges, as has been produced in alcoholic rats, or it could be that some alcoholics were poor sleepers to start with. In any case, it appears that the longer one can refrain from drinking, the more sleep will improve.

BLACKOUTS

Having covered a multitude of physical disorders associated with alcohol abuse, it would seem that there is nothing left to go wrong! Yet there remains one more phenomenon associated with alcohol use that is highly distinctive: the blackout. Contrary to what the name may imply, it does not mean passing out or losing consciousness. Nor does it mean psychological blocking out of events, or repression. A blackout is an amnesia-like period that is often associated with heavy drinking. Someone who is or has been drinking may appear to be perfectly normal. He or she seems to function quite normally with the task at hand. Yet later, the person has no memory of what transpired. A better term might be blank out. The blank spaces in the memory may be total or partial. A person who has been drinking and who experiences a "blank out" will not be able to recall how the party ended, how he got home, how he landed the 747, how he did open-heart surgery, or how the important decisions were made at a business lunch. As you can imagine, this spotty memory can cause severe distress and anxiety, to say nothing of being dangerous in certain circumstances.

What causes blackouts? The exact mechanisms are not fully understood, but, apparently, during a blackout, memory function is severely and selectively impaired by alcohol, while virtually all other spheres of affect—cognition, behavior, and brain function—remain relatively intact. Up to one-third of alcoholics report never having had a blackout. Some alcoholics have blackouts frequently, whereas others only have them occasionally. Recent research indicates that blackouts occur in nonalcoholics who have drunk more heavily than they usually do and to the point of intoxication. However, blackouts have usually been associated with alcoholism that is at a fairly advanced stage, and thus they are thought to be generally, although nonspecifically, dose-dependent and dose-related. As a general rule, the greater the severity of the alcoholism (the heavier the drinking and the greater the number of years over which

We were to do more business after dinner; but after dinner is after dinner—an old saying and a true, 'much drinking, little thinking.'

JONATHAN SWIFT, 1768

it has occurred), the more likely the occurrence of blackouts. There is also a positive relationship between the occurrence of blackouts and the extent and duration of alcohol consumption during any given drinking episode. Several other factors correlate with the occurrence of blackouts in alcoholics: poor diet, high tolerance, a previous head injury, and the tendency to gulp drinks.

The current research findings on blackouts differ in significant respects from the frequently quoted early alcohol research, done in the 1950s, by EM Jellinek, which will be described more fully in the next chapter. In considering the progression of alcoholism, he focused on blackouts as being an early manifestation of the disease or as a warning sign for those at risk for developing it. He felt that blackouts had a high degree of specificity in predicting eventual alcoholism. Thinking has now changed. Studies done more recently have found that 30% to 40% of young- to middle-aged, light-to-moderate (social) drinkers have had at least one alcohol-induced blackout. Typically, it occurred on one of the few occasions when they were truly inebriated. In fact, among these individuals, blackouts seem to be most frequent among those who generally are light drinkers.

How are the disparities between the old and new research findings reconciled? One possibility is that individuals vary in their "susceptibility" to blackouts. Accordingly, those people who experience the blackout-producing effect of alcohol may find it so frightening and unpleasant that they will be strongly motivated to drink in moderation in the future. Others, possibly with a genetic predisposition to alcoholism, may have a naturally high "tolerance" to blackouts. Consequently, they will not experience them until relatively late in their drinking careers, after the disease of alcoholism has been established. In effect, those who become alcoholics, not having experienced blackouts earlier, may have been deprived of an important physiological warning signal.

What is evident, despite the still limited research, is that for some reason, in some people, alcohol selectively interferes with the mechanisms of memory. Memory is one of the many functions of the brain, a complex process that in general is still not fully understood. We can recall and report what happened to us 5 minutes ago. Similarly, many events of yesterday or a week ago can be recalled. In many cases, our memories can extend back many years, indeed decades. Psychological and neuropsychological research has identified different types of memory, categorizing them into immediate, short-term (recent), and long-term memory. Memory of whatever type involves the brain's capacity to receive, process, and store information. According to one popular theory of memory function, the brain has at least two different kinds of "filing systems" for information. Immediate memory is stored for very short periods electrochemically. Long-term memory involves a biochemical storage system that is relatively stable over long periods. Short-term, or recent, memory is a way station somewhere between these two that is thought to involve the process of conversion of electrochemical brain activity into stable neuronal, probably protein macromolecular changes. It is hypothesized that this is the point at which alcohol exerts its influence to impair memory function. It is suspected that this occurs because alcohol interferes with the metabolic production of proteins by certain neuronal cells. This in turn inhibits the brain's ability to move short-term memory into longer-term storage. Although alcohol interferes with the "conversion process," it does not seem to interfere directly with the electrochemical basis of immediate memory (events occurring during the blackout itself) or for events from before the blackout (those already stored in long-term memory banks as stable protein macromolecules). This could account for the seemingly normal appearance and function of the person in a blackout, even with respect to relatively complicated tasks.

The amnesia that occurs during a blackout is typically one of two types. It may be sudden in onset, complete, and permanent, or it can lack a definite onset and be something that the person is unaware of until he is reminded of or spontaneously recalls the forgotten event. In the latter instance, recall is usually dim and incomplete. Interestingly, in such cases recall may be enhanced by the use of alcohol. This facilitation of recall by alcohol is thought to reflect the phenomenon of state-dependent learning, in which whatever has been learned is best recalled when the person is in the same state or condition that existed at the time of the original learning.

Interestingly, there has been discussion of blackouts being employed as a defense in criminal proceedings. Although a novel approach, it would appear that there is no evidence to support the contention that a blackout alters judgment or behavior at the time of its occurrence. The only deficiency appears to be in later recalling what occurred during the blackout. Of course, having no memory of an event would make it difficult to prepare a case or decide from one's own knowledge whether to plead guilty or innocent. It is hoped that more will be learned about blackouts. Research is difficult because it depends almost entirely on anecdotal self-report. Thus far, no one has found a predictable way to produce blackouts experimentally. Nor can one know for sure when a spontaneous blackout is occurring. Thus to date it has not been possible to use new, highly sophisticated noninvasive, neurodiagnostic imaging techniques that might help us better understand the neurophysiological basis of blackouts.

WITHDRAWAL SYNDROMES

The physiological basis of withdrawal is hypothesized to be related to alcohol's depressant effects on the CNS. With regular heavy use of alcohol, the activity of the CNS is chronically depressed. With abstinence, this chronic depressant effect is removed. There follows a "rebound" hyperactivity. An area of the CNS particularly affected is the *reticular activating system,* which modulates or regulates the general level of CNS arousal and activity. The duration of the withdrawal syndrome is

determined by the time required for this "rebound" overactivity to be played out and a normal baseline level of neurophysiological functioning to be reestablished. Studies of CNS activity with EEGs during heavy drinking, abstinence, and withdrawal support this.

Not everyone physically dependent on alcohol who stops drinking has the same symptoms. In part, the severity of the withdrawal state will be a function of how long someone has been drinking and how much. Another big factor is the drinker's physical health plus his or her unique physiological characteristics. Therefore accurately predicting the difficulties with withdrawal is impossible. Despite the phrase *abstinence syndrome,* withdrawal can occur even while someone continues to drink. The key factor is a relative lowering of the blood alcohol level. Thus *relative abstinence* is the condition that triggers withdrawal. This phenomenon often prompts the alcoholic's morning drink. He is treating his withdrawal symptoms.

Four different major withdrawal syndromes have been described in conjunction with alcohol. Although they can be distinguished for the purpose of discussion, clinically the distinctions are not so neat. In reality, these syndromes often blend together.

The earliest and most common sign of acute alcohol withdrawal is a generalized state of hyperarousal. This can include anxiety, irritability, insomnia, loss of appetite, rapid heartbeat (tachycardia), and tremulousness (the "shakes"). Avoiding this state often is what motivates the actively drinking alcoholic to have a morning or midday drink. Recall that with increasing tolerance, increasing amounts of an addictive drug are necessary to ward off withdrawal symptoms, and only a relatively lowered blood alcohol concentration (BAC) is necessary to induce withdrawal. An alcoholic who is used to drinking heavily in the evenings is eventually going to find himself feeling shaky the next morning. The BAC will have fallen from the level of the night before. A drink, by raising the BAC, will take this discomfort and edginess away. With time, further boosts of booze during the course of the day may be necessary to maintain a BAC sufficient to prevent the shakes. As tends to be the case with all addicting drugs, progressively increasing amounts of alcohol will be consumed, not for their positive effects but as a means of dealing with withdrawal symptoms.

If the physically dependent person abstains completely, there will be a marked increase of symptoms. The appearance is one of stimulation. The alcoholic will startle easily, feel irritable, and in general be "revved up" in a very unpleasant way. He will have a fast pulse, increased temperature, elevated blood pressure, sweating, dilated pupils, a flushed face, and trouble sleeping. Usually these symptoms subside over 2 or 3 days. The shakes will disappear, and the vital signs will return to normal. However, feeling awful, being irritable, and having difficulty sleeping can persist for 2 to 3 weeks or even longer. Although the judicious use of medication (benzodiazepines) may make the withdrawal process more tolerable by lessening the severity of symptoms, this acute withdrawal syndrome by itself often does not require medical treatment. But it is important that the person not be left alone and be carefully observed for signs of incipient DTs. When the acute stage passes, the probability of developing DTs is greatly lowered. However, if the acute symptoms do not resolve or if they should worsen, beware. Be sure the person is evaluated by a physician because such symptoms indicate that the progression to DTs is likely.

Another syndrome of alcoholic withdrawal is *alcoholic hallucinosis.* This condition occurs in some 25% of those withdrawing from alcohol. It is usually seen early, within the first 24 hours of withdrawal. It includes true hallucinations, both auditory and visual. It also includes illusions, the misperception or misinterpretation of real environmental stimuli. However, the individual with hallucinosis is oriented to person, place, and time. Very bad nightmares often accompany this withdrawal syndrome. It is believed that the nightmares may be due to REM rebound following the release from alcohol's long suppression of dreaming sleep. This rebound effect usually clears by the end of the first week of withdrawal. In a small number of cases, however, a chronic and persistent form of the syndrome may develop and continue for weeks to months. Acute alcoholic hallucinosis is not dangerous in itself and does not necessarily require specific medical treatment. It is important, however, to recognize it as a common withdrawal phenomenon and not be misled into thinking that the hallucinations are necessarily indicative of an underlying primary psychiatric disorder.

The chronic form of alcoholic hallucinosis accompanying alcohol withdrawal is often thought of as a separate syndrome. It is characterized primarily by persistent, frightening auditory hallucinations. Usually the hallucinations have a distinctly paranoid flavor and are of voices familiar to the patient, often of relatives or acquaintances. In the early stages they are threatening or demeaning or arouse guilt. Because they are true hallucinations, the person believes they are real and acts on them as if they were. This can lead to the person harming himself or others. When the hallucinations persist over time, they become less frightening and may be tolerated with greater equanimity. Some patients with chronic hallucinosis may develop a schizophrenia-like condition and require treatment with antipsychotic medications. However, in most instances alcoholic hallucinosis does not indicate an underlying psychiatric problem but simply represents the CNS's response to the absence of alcohol. Appropriate treatment entails observing someone in an environment in which he will be safe, plus possible use of mild sedation. Alcoholic hallucinosis, unless very severe, probably should not be treated with antipsychotic medications during the first 2 to 4 days of withdrawal. During that period there is an increased risk for seizures, and such drugs are known to lower the seizure threshold.

Convulsive seizures, sometimes referred to as "rum fits," also occur in association with acute alcohol withdrawal. These seizures are almost

Epilepsy. This fearful disease is one of the maladies to which the excessive drinker is subject. It is most frequent among absinthe drinkers. In its early stages alcoholic epilepsy is comparatively easy of cure. It is cured spontaneously sometimes by simple total abstinence from alcohol.

SPOONER WATLER W.
The Cyclopaedia of Temperance and Prohibition, 1891.

always generalized, grand mal, major motor seizures, in which the eyes roll back in the head, the body muscles contract and relax and extend rhythmically and violently, and there is loss of consciousness. In fact, these seizures are so common that the occurrence of any other type of seizure should raise concern about causes other than simply alcohol withdrawal. After the seizure, which typically lasts a minute or two, the person may be stuporous and groggy for as long as 6 to 8 hours. Although very frightening to watch, convulsive seizures in and of themselves are not usually dangerous. Any treatment during a seizure is limited to protecting the person's airway and to preventing injury from the seizure-induced muscle activity. A serious complication of a single, isolated seizure is the development of *status epilepticus,* in which seizures follow one another with virtually no intervening seizure-free periods. Usually only one or two seizures occur with acute alcohol withdrawal. Status epilepticus is very uncommon with alcohol withdrawal and, if present, suggests causes other than withdrawal. The only long-term treatment of alcohol withdrawal seizures is to prevent them through abstinence. Unless a person in withdrawal has a history of prior seizures, anticonvulsant drugs are not routinely prescribed. If they are used for seizures clearly attributable to acute alcohol withdrawal, they should be discontinued before discharge, because further seizures would not be expected after withdrawal. It is critical, though, to rule out any other possible cause of the seizures and not merely to assume that alcohol withdrawal is responsible. Infections, electrolyte disturbances, and falls with associated head trauma or subdural hematoma, to which the alcoholic is prone, can be causes. Seizures are most likely to occur between 12 and 48 hours after stopping alcohol use, but they can occur up to 1 week after the last drink. Alcohol withdrawal seizures indicate a moderate to severe withdrawal problem. Up to one-third of persons who have withdrawal go on to develop DTs.

Withdrawal seizures are also thought to be caused by "rebound" CNS hyperexcitability. Alcohol has an anticonvulsant effect acutely in that it raises the seizure threshold. With abstinence, however, the seizure threshold is correspondingly lowered. (This has been postulated as the basis for the increased seizures in epileptics who drink, because these seizures tend to occur the morning after, when the blood alcohol level has fallen.)

Delirium tremens (DTs) is the most serious form of alcohol withdrawal syndrome. In the past, mortality rates as high as 15% to 20% were reported. As many as 1 of every 5 persons who went into DTs died. Even with modern treatment, there is a 1% to 2% mortality rate. The name indicates the two major components of this withdrawal state, and either of these components can predominate. Delirium refers to hallucinations, confusion, and disorientation. Tremens refers to the heightened autonomic nervous activity, marked tremulousness and agitation, fast pulse, elevated blood pressure, and fever. Someone who eventually goes on to develop the DTs will initially have all the symptoms first described with early withdrawal. However, instead of clearing by the second or third day, the symptoms continue and, in fact, get worse. In addition to increased shakiness, profuse sweating, fast pulse, hypertension, and fever, there are mounting periods of confusion and anxiety attacks. In full-blown DTs, there are delusions and hallucinations, generally visual and tactile. The terrifying nature of the hallucinations and delusions is captured by the slang phrase for DTs, "the horrors." Seeing bugs on the walls and feeling insects crawling all over the body naturally heighten the anxiety and emotional responses. In this physical and emotional state of heightened agitation, infections, respiratory problems, fluid loss, and physical exhaustion create further difficulties. These complications contribute substantially to the mortality rate. The acute phase of DTs can last from 1 day to 1 week. In 15% of cases it is over in 25 hours; in 80%, within 3 days. The person will then often fall into a profound sleep and, on awakening, feel better though still weak. Usually he or she will have little memory of what has happened.

Since there is no specific cure for DTs, treatment is aimed at providing supportive medical care while it runs its course. Vital signs are monitored closely to spot any developing problems. Efforts are made to reduce the agitation, conserve energy, and prevent exhaustion. This involves administering sedatives. Despite arguments to the contrary, there is no clear-cut single regimen that is obviously superior. Amounts and type of medications will be determined by the patient's physical condition. One of the concerns will be liver function. The liver, possibly damaged by alcohol, is the organ needed to metabolize virtually any drug given. If the liver is not up to the task, drugs will not be as speedily removed from the body, a situation that can lead to further problems. The benzodiazepines (Ativan, Librium, Valium, Serax) are often the first choice. They have been shown to be as effective as other agents, have a wider margin of safety and less toxicity than some of the alternative drugs, and contribute a significant anticonvulsant effect as well. The specific benzodiazepine chosen will depend upon a number of pharmacological considerations. As symptoms abate, the dose is decreased gradually over time to avoid cumulative unwanted sedation. Paraldehyde, an old, time-tested, and effective agent, has over time become less popular. Paraldehyde is metabolized by the liver and consequently must be used with care when significant liver disease is present. It also must be carefully stored in sealed brown bottles to prevent its breakdown into acetaldehyde. Last, it imparts an objectionable odor to the breath that is unavoidable because it is extensively excreted by the lungs. The major tranquilizers, or antipsychotic agents, are also somewhat less desirable. Although they have sedative and tranquilizing properties, they also lower the seizure threshold, which is already a problem for withdrawing alcoholics. Whatever medication is used, the purpose is to diminish the severity of the acute symptoms accompanying the DTs, not to introduce long-term drug treatment for the alcoholism.

Although predictions cannot be made about who will go into DTs, those who fit the following description are the most likely candidates.

Don't worry, Mr. White; we'll give you some pills to make the bugs disappear.

A daily drinker who has consumed over a fifth a day or more for at least a week prior to abstinence and who has been a heavy drinker for 10 years or more is statistically very susceptible. The occurrence of withdrawal seizures, or the persistence and worsening rather than improving over time of the acute early withdrawal symptoms, should indicate that the DTs are more likely to occur. If in a prior period of acute abstinence the person had convulsions, extreme agitation, marked confusion, disorientation, or DTs, he or she is also more likely to have them again. Another ominous sign is recent abuse of other sedatives, especially barbiturates, which also have serious withdrawal syndromes much like those seen with alcohol. Abuse of multiple drugs complicates withdrawal management. If there is evidence of physical dependence on more than one drug, generally simultaneous withdrawal will not be attempted. Serial withdrawal is the preferred approach.

Late withdrawal phenomena

Late withdrawal phenomenon is a less than tidy concept. It refers to withdrawal-like symptoms that occur after the period normally associated with withdrawal. There are two different situations covered by this phrase. One is the seemingly unexpected "reemergence" of symptoms of withdrawal, or that is what is thought is happening. While not common this situation is more likely to occur in instances of dependence on several different drugs. Thus, different withdrawal syndromes may be occurring simultaneously, each of which has a different timetable. If high doses of benzodiazepines are used to treat the symptoms of acute alcohol withdrawal, and these are abruptly discontinued, there may be a reemergence of withdrawal symptoms. But this is the appearance of sedative-hypnotic withdrawal syndrome caused by discontinuing the benzodiazepines and is not a delayed alcohol withdrawal. It can be treated by reintroducing the benzodiazepines and then discontinuing them more gradually.

Protracted abstinence syndrome is characterized by persistence over a variable but prolonged period (several weeks to months) of symptoms suggestive of the acute stages of alcohol withdrawal. These can include variable cognitive and memory disturbances, anxiety and irritability, insomnia, tremulousness, depressive symptoms, and an intense desire to drink. Neither the basis for this syndrome nor the frequency of occurrence is known. The suspicion is that comorbid psychiatric conditions may play a role, and what is now apparent would be symptoms of depression or anxiety disorders, or panic disorders that alcohol may have previously masked. Unfortunately alcohol provides prompt relief for this often intensely uncomfortable state.

Some cautions

Often those who experience withdrawal symptoms certainly don't intend to! Withdrawal will occur by itself in a physically dependent person whenever a drug is reduced or terminated, so circumstances may play

Delirium Tremens. Delirium tremens, or mania a potu, is a nervous disorder caused by the habitual use of alcoholic stimulants, and in regard to its pathological tendency may be defined as nature's ultimate protest against the continuance of the alcohol vice. The first remonstrance comes in the form of nausea, langor and sick headache—symptoms familiar in the experience of every incipient toper. Loss of appetite and general disinclination to active exercise are the penalties of intemperance in its more advanced stages of development, and those injunctions remaining unheeded, nature's ultimatum is expressed in the incomparable distress of nervous delirium.

SPOONER WATLER W.
The Cyclopaedia of Temperance and Prohibition, 1891.

their part and catch some people unaware. Addicted individuals who enter hospitals for surgery, thereby having to curtail their usual consumption, may, to their surgeon's (and even their own) amazement, develop acute withdrawal symptoms. Another possibility is the family vacation. When the secretly drinking housewife, who has been denying a problem, intends to just "sweat it out," she can wind up with more than she bargained for.

Any clinician working with active alcoholics is going to work with people who do want to loosen their grip. Giving up alcohol can be tough on the body as well as the emotions. In making any assessment, the therapist will have to be concerned about the real possibility of physical dependence and the likelihood of withdrawal. In all cases, medical evaluation is essential. Withdrawal needs to be medically supervised and carefully monitored. Not every withdrawing patient requires hospitalization. In fact, the vast majority of patients— in some studies 90% or more—who do not have serious medical complications can be safely and effectively withdrawn on an outpatient basis.

Planning has to include arrangements for care during the process of physical withdrawal. No person should be alone. Family members need to know what to be alert for so that the necessary medical treatment can be sought when and if indicated. A simple rule of thumb is that if there is any significant likelihood of serious withdrawal, seek hospitalization. Virtually every alcoholic has stopped drinking for a day or so at some point, so he or she has some sense of what happened then. Any client with a history of previous difficulty during withdrawal is at increased risk in the future. Even when there is no history of prior difficulty during withdrawal, if current symptoms are worse, one should seek medical treatment immediately. At every step along the way it is imperative that alcohol-dependent persons receive lots of TLC. They need repeated reassurance and support. They need their questions answered and all procedures explained. Anything that can be done to reduce anxiety and fear is vitally important. Surprisingly such support may often help clients through alcohol withdrawal without the use of sedative-hypnotic medications.

Part III
Other drug use

CHRONIC EFFECTS OF OTHER DRUG USE

The chronic effects of other drugs are summarized in Table 3.1. These are organized by drug class. For each drug class, there is a summary of the common problems associated with use, the signs and symptoms of withdrawal, the medical use(s) if any, the doses used in clinical medicine, the risk of abuse potential, and the classification of the drug within the Drug Enforcement Agency (DEA) schedule.

Note: In the table that follows there are a number of abbreviations from Latin terms that are used in writing prescriptions to indicate dose and frequency, amount, and how administered.

- mg means 'milligrams.'
- q means 'every.'
- kg refers to 'kilograms of body weight.' For some drugs, the appropriate amount is dependent upon the size of the person.
- PO does not mean post office box, but 'by mouth.'
- tab is short for 'tablet.'
- IM, 'intramuscular,' means to inject into a muscle.
- IV, 'intravenous,' is to inject into a vein.

TABLE 3.1   OTHER DRUG USE: CHRONIC EFFECTS

Note: In the following tables, amounts used significantly in excess of recommended use should be considered abuse. Patients with substance abuse history may be at increased risk. The usual therapeutic daily dose is for adults unless otherwise noted.

Sedative-Hypnotics

Common problems:	Tolerance, physical dependence, addiction, risk of falls in the elderly, respiratory depression (more common with substances other than benzodiazepines).
Withdrawal symptoms:	Similar to those of alcohol withdrawal, but may have slower onset. Severity and time of onset vary with half-life of drug.
	Mild: anxiety, restlessness, nausea, vomiting, insomnia, hypertension, tachycardia, agitation, tremors, sensory hypersensitivity, dizziness, confusion, fatigue.
	Severe: autonomic hyperactivity, vital sign instability, elevated temperature, delusions, hallucinations, mania, delirium, catatonia, seizures, tremulousness, altered perceptions, withdrawal seizures possibly leading to death (barbiturates).
Category includes:	Benzodiazepines, barbiturates, meprobamate, chloral hydrate.
Medical uses:	Sleep, anxiety disorders, muscle relaxation, alcohol and sedative/hypnotic withdrawal, control of seizures.

Sedative-Hypnotic Drugs	Usual Therapeutic Dose/Day (Adults)	Addiction Risk	DEA Schedule
Benzodiazepines			
Alprazolam (Xanax®)	0.25–6 mg	High	IV
Chlordiazepoxide (Librium®)	5–100 mg	Low	IV
Clonazepam (Klonopin®)	0.5–4 mg	Low	IV
Diazepam (Valium®)	2–40 mg	Moderate/High	IV
Flurazepam (Dalmane®)	15–30 mg	Low	IV
Lorazepam (Ativan®)	1–10 mg	Moderate/High	IV
Oxazepam (Serax®)	10–120 mg	Low	IV
Temazepam (Restoril®)	15–30 mg	Low	IV
Triazolam (Halcion®)	0.125–0.5 mg	Moderate/High	IV
Estazolzm (Prosom®)	0.5 mg–2.0 mg	Low	IV
Flunitrazepam (Rohypnol®)	not approved for use in U.S.	High	
Barbiturates			
Butabarbital (Butisol sodium)	15–120 mg	Moderate	III

TABLE 3.1   (*continued*)

Butalbital (Fiornal®)	1–6 tabs	Moderate	III
Pentobarbital (Nembutal®)	100 mg	High	II
Phenobarbital	30–400 mg	Low	IV
Secobarbital (Seconal®)	100 mg	High	II
Other Compounds			
Chloral Hydrate	250–500 mg	Low	IV
Meprobamate (Miltown/Equanil®)	200–2400 mg	Moderate/High	IV

Stimulants

Withdrawal symptoms:	Depression (possibly with suicide potential), excessive need for sleep, increased appetite, fatigue, anhedonia (absence of pleasure), and (especially with cocaine) craving for the drug. Usually not life-threatening except for suicide potential resulting from depression.
Common problems:	Anxiety, confusion, irritability, loss of appetite and weight loss, psychosis, psychological and physical dependence, social withdrawal, multiple medical problems (cardiac, central nervous system, respiratory) with potential death. With intranasal cocaine use, sinusitis, nosebleeds, and perforation of the nasal septum can occur.
Category includes:	Cocaine, amphetamines, methylphenidate.
Medical uses:	Cocaine for local (ear, nose, throat) anesthesia.
	Amphetamines and methylphenidate and pemoline: attention deficit disorder with or without hyperactivity (especially in children).
	Narcolepsy.
	Rarely used for depression unresponsive to other treatments.

Stimulant Drugs	Usual Therapeutic Dose/Day (includes child's ADD dosage)	Addiction Risk	DEA Schedule
Cocaine	Only medical use is for local anesthesia	High	II
Dextro-amphetamine (Dexedrine)	2.5–60 mg	High	II
Methamphetamine (Desoxyn)	5–25 mg	High	II
Methylphenidate (Ritalin)	10–60 mg	High	II
Pemoline (Cylert)	33.5–112.5 mg	Undetermined	IV

Opioids

Withdrawal symptoms:	Drug craving, dysphoria, anxiety, yawning, perspiration, sleep difficulties, fever, chills, gooseflesh, abdominal cramps, nausea, diarrhea, muscle cramps, bone pain, tears.
Common problems:	Rapidly acquired tolerance, physical dependence, respiratory depression with accidental overdose, cellulitis and sepsis (infections at site of injection), endocarditis, increased likelihood of exposure to HIV infection and hepatitis by sharing of needles in intravenous use; risk to sexual partners of IV opiate users who have acquired HIV; legal problems related to acquiring opiates illegally.
Category includes:	Heroin, morphine meperidine, oxycodone, opium, codeine, hydrocodone fentanyl, methadone.

(*continued*)

TABLE 3.1   (*continued*)

Medical uses:	Pain: morphine, meperidine, hydromorphone, methadone, oxycodone, hydocodone. Cough suppression: codeine. Anesthesia: fentanyl. Addiction treatment: methadone, buprenorphine, LAAM (Levo-alpha acetyl methadol). Diarrhea: opium.

Opiates and Opioid Drugs	Usual Therapeutic Dose (Adults)	Addiction Risk	DEA Schedule
Opiates			
Codeine (multiple products)	Cough: 5–15 mg q 4 hr. Pain: 15–60 mg q 4 hr	High	II
Heroin	No U.S. medical uses	High	I
Morphine	5–20 mg q 4 hr	High	II
Opium (Paregoric®)	6 mg or 6 ml q 4 hr	High	II
Opioids			
Fentanyl	2–50 micrograms/kg	High	II
Hydrocodone (Vicodan®)	5–10 mg q 4 hr Limit 8/day	Moderate	III
Hydromorphone (Dilaudid®)	1–4 mg q 4–6 hr	High	II
Levorphanol (Levo-Dromoran®)	2–3 mg q 6–8 hr	High	II
Meperidine (Demerol®)	55–150 mg q 3–4 hr	High	II
Methadone (Dolophine®)	Pain: 2.5–10 mg q 3–4 hr Maintenance: 5–120 mg/day	High	II
Levo-acetyl-acetylmethadol (LAAM)	Maintenance: 80 mg three times weekly		
Oxycodone (Percodan®) (Percocet, Tylox®)	One tab q 6 hr	High	II
Propoxyphene (Darvon®) (Darvocet, Darvon-N)	One tab q 4 hr	Low	IV
Tramadol (Ultram®)	50–100 mg PO q 4–6 hr	Low	N/A
Partial Opioid Agonists			
Buprenorphine (Buprenex®)	Pain: 0.3–0.6 mg IM or IV Maintenance: 8–16 mg/day	Low	V
Butorphanol (Stadol®)	Pain: IM or IV 1–2 mg q 3–4 hr Intranasal spray: 1–2 mg q 3–4 hr	High	IV
Nalbuphine (Nubain®)	Pain: 10 mg IM, IV, or subcutaneously q 3–4 hr	Low	N/A
Pentazozine (Talwin®)	Pain: 30 mg IM, IV, or subcutaneously q 3–4 hr	Moderate	IV

TABLE 3.1   (*continued*)

Cannabis

Common problems:	Impairment of ability to learn. Medical effects with prolonged use include respiratory problems, possible impaired immune function and possible reproductive problems including low birth weight infants. Tolerance and withdrawal symptoms.
Withdrawal symptoms:	Rare. Appear limited to some heavy users.
	Possible irritability, restlessness, craving, loss of appetite, nausea, diarrhea, muscle twitching, overt aggression, and depression.
Medical uses:	Used to reduces nausea and stimulate appetite in cancer patients; possible treatment of glaucoma.

Drug	Average Amount Taken	Addiction Risk	DEA Schedule
Marijuana	4–40 mg	Moderate	I
Hashish	of THC per	Moderate	I
THC	cigarette	Moderate	II
Medications Dronabinol (Marinol®)	Appetite: 2.5–20 mg per day Nausea: 5–15 mg 4–6 times daily	Moderate	II

Hallucinogens

Common or potential problems:

LSD group:	Flashbacks long after use has terminated that can lead to depression, hallucinogenic mood disorder, psychotic (delusional) disorders with varying courses.
MDMA group:	Coagulopathy, possible degeneration of serotonergic nerve terminals (not clinically observed).
Withdrawal symptoms:	There is no clinical evidence of withdrawal effects when use is terminated.
Category includes:	LSD, Mescaline, Psilocybin, Ecstasy, STP.

As there is no accepted medical use of hallucinogens, dosages listed below are the average amount taken.

Hallucinogenic Drugs	Average Amount Taken	Addiction Risk	DEA Schedule
LSD Group			
LSD (Acid)	10–400 micrograms	Low	I
Mescaline (mescal button)	100–200 mg	Low	I
Psilocybin	4–10 mg	Low	I
DOM (STP)	3–5 mg	Low	I
DMT	3.3–5 mg	Low	I
MDMA Group			
MDMA (Ecstasy)	110–150 mg	Low	I
MDA		Low	I

(*continued*)

TABLE 3.1   (*continued*)

Phencyclidine (PCP)

Common problems:	Psychotic reactions; bizarre behavior; outbursts of hostility and violence; feelings of severe anxiety, doom, or impending death; gross impairment of coordination; nystagmus; hypersalivation, vomiting; fever.
	With longer-term use: persistent cognitive and memory problems, speech difficulties, mood disorders, loss of purposive activities, and weight loss.
Withdrawal symptoms:	Limited reports of withdrawal effects in humans (depression, drug craving, increased appetite, and increased need for sleep). In other primates, symptoms include poor feeding, weight loss, irritability, bruxism, vocalizations, goose flesh, preconvulsive activity, tremors, and impaired motor coordination.
Medical uses:	Possible prevention of neurological damage due to ischemia (suggested by early research findings).

Drug	Average Amount Taken	Addiction risk	DEA Sehedule
Phencyclidine (PCP)	1–100 mg (street dose)	Low	II

Inhalants

Common Problems:

Hydrocarbons:	Encephalopathy; peripheral, cranial and optic neuropathy, Parkinson atrophy of various areas of brain with attendant behavioral symptoms (with chronic use); renal complications; upper respiratory symptoms.
Nitrous Oxide:	Paranoid psychosis with confusion (chronic use). Appears to inactivate actions of Vitamin B12, resulting in neurologic damage and symptoms.
Nitrites:	Minimal
Withdrawal symptoms:	Psychological symptoms documented. Physical symptoms not well established.
Examples:	Paints, other aerosols, organic solvents and cleaning agents, gasoline and other petrochemicals, glue, vasodilators (amyl and butyl nitrite), anesthetics (nitrous oxide).
Medical uses:	None except for use of nitrous oxide for anesthesia.

Drug	Average Amount Taken	Addiction Risk	DEA Schedule
Industrial & commercial solvents, paints, glues, other hydrocarbons and aerosols	Variable	Moderate	N/A
Amyl Nitrite	Variable	Unknown	N/A
Butyl Nitrite	Variable	Unknown	N/A
Nitrous Oxide	Variable	Unknown	N/A

Nicotine

Common problems:	Many problems are not directly the effect of nicotine, but of smoking. Cough, bronchitis, increased respiratory infections, chronic obstructive pulmonary disease, lung cancer, oral cancers, likely increase of many other cancers with use, death or injury by fire, low birth weight babies. Wrinkling.

TABLE 3.1 (*continued*)

Withdrawal symptoms: Craving, irritability, anxiety, possible depression.

Examples: Cigarettes, cigars, pipes, chewing tobacco, snuff.

Drug	Average Amount Taken	Addiction Risk	DEA Schedule
Nicotine	15–20 mg/cigarette	High	N/A

Anabolic Androgenic Steroids

Common problems: Virilizing side effects (vary by gender) including increased facial hair, deepening of voice, male pattern of baldness, acne. Feminizing effects in men (e.g., gynecomastia); reduction in HDL cholesterol; jaundice, hepatitis, liver cancer; psychiatric side effects (hypomania, mania, depression, panic, and aggressive symptoms all reported). In women, clitoral enlargement and menstrual irregularities.

Withdrawal symptoms: Depression, fatigue, decreased libido, muscle pain, headache, and craving.

Examples: Testosterone, compounds, 19-nortestosterone derivatives, orally active androgen.

Medical uses: Replacement of endogenous testosterone; increase of red blood cells and complement factor; treatment of endometriosis and fibrocystic breast disease.

Anabolic Androgenic Steroid Drugs	Average Amount Taken	Addiction Risk	DEA Schedule
Testosterone Esters			
Testosterone cypionate		Moderate	III
Testosterone enanthate		Moderate	III
19-Nortestosterone	Daily doses		
Derivatives	range from		
Nandrolone decanoate	20 to 2000 mg[1]	Moderate	III
Nandrolone (phenylpropionate)		Moderate	III
Orally Active Androgens			
Adanazol		Moderate	NS[2]
Fluoxymesterone		Moderate	III
Methyltestosterone		Moderate	III
Oxandrolone		Moderate	III
Stanzolol		Moderate	III
Testosterone (transdermal patch)	2.5–5.0 mg/day	Low	III

[1]Equivalent of testosterone per day of 20–2,000 mg times testosterone the usual pharmacologic dose of androgens
[2]NS = Not Scheduled

SIGNS AND SYMPTOMS OF ACUTE INTOXICATION AND OVERDOSE

Table 3.2 summarizes the signs and symptoms that occur with intoxication and overdoses. Not all of the signs and symptoms noted will be present with individual patients.

TABLE 3.2   SIGNS AND SYMPTOMS OF ACUTE INTOXICATION AND OVERDOSE

Sedative Hypnotics

Includes:	benzodiazepines; barbiturates, and others such as chloral hydrate and meprobamate.
Intoxication and overdose:	
Vital signs:	minimal changes except for decreased respiration rate with nonbenzodiazepines.
Physical exam:	slurred speech, ataxia (unable to walk a straight line), stupor, coma, and for the nonbenzodiazepines, respiratory depression.
Mental status:	slurred speech, confusion, impaired judgement, delirium, coma.

Stimulants

Includes:	cocaine, crack, amphetamines, methylphenidate (Ritalin®)
Intoxication and overdose:	
Vital signs:	increased heart rate, respiration decreased, blood pressure elevated, and temperature elevated.
Physical exam:	pupils dilated, dry mouth, cardiac arrhythmias, twitching, tremors, convulsions, stroke, coma.
Mental status:	confusion, disinhibited behavior, paranoid thoughts, hallucinations, hypervigilance, elation and/or depression, suicidal behavior, impaired judgment.

Opiates

Includes:	heroin, morphine, codeine, opium, fentanyl, methadone, oxycodone (Percocet®), hydrocodone (Vicodan®), propoxyphene (Darvon®), or meperidine (Demerol®)
Intoxication and overdose:	
Vital signs:	respiration decreased, blood pressure decreased, temperature decreased.
Physical exam:	pupils constricted, reflexes absent or diminished, pulmonary edema, consulsions with propoxyphene or meperidine.
Mental status:	euphoria, sedation, possible normal mood, possible stupor.

Cannabis

Includes:	marijuana, hashish, THC, Droabinal® (prescription).
Intoxication and overdose:	
Vital signs:	increased respiration rate, increased heart rate, mild increase in temperature.
Physical exam:	red eyes (conjunctival injection), mild dilation of pupils, mild tremor, decreased coordination, decreased strength, less ability to perform complex motor tasks, dry mouth.
Mental status:	feelings of depersonalization, anxiety, panic, memory problems, alteration in mood, disorganization, hallucinations, paranoid thoughts.

Hallucinogens

LSD group includes:	LSD, psilocybin, mescaline.
Intoxication and overdose:	
Vital signs:	elevated blood pressure, increased heart rate, elevated temperature with possible hyperthermia.
Physical exam:	increased reflexes, tremors, weakness, flushing and chills, seizures.
Mental status:	inappropriate mood, elation, hallucinations, bizarre behavior, disorientation, confusion, delusions, impaired judgement.
MDMA (ecstasy)	
Intoxication and overdose:	
Vital signs:	elevated heart rate, high blood pressure progressing to low blood pressure, possible hyperthermia.

TABLE 3.2   (*continued*)

Physical exam:	tremor, hypertonicity of muscles, nausea, decreased appetite, sweating.
Mental status:	elation, inappropriate affect, poor judgement.
PCP (phencyclidine)	
Intoxication and overdose:	
Vital signs:	initially increased respiration but later decreased, and possible apnea (stopping breathing), mild to severe blood pressure elevation, and possible hyperthermia.
Physical exam:	red eyes, muscle rigidity, increased reflexes, repetitive movements, flushing, salivation, sweating, nausea, vomiting, possible coma, seizures, stroke.
Mental status:	abnormal appearance and behavior, disorientation, inappropriate affect, memory problems, depression, elation, suicidal or homicidal behavior, impaired judgement.
Inhalants	
Intoxication and overdose:	
Hydrocarbons	
Vital signs:	possible irregular heartbeat.
Physical exam:	ataxia, muscle weakness, dysarthria, nystagmus, diminished reflexes.
Mental status:	euphoria, giddiness, fatigue, confusion, disorientation.
Nitrous Oxide	
Vital signs:	increased respiration rate.
Physical exam:	possible asphyxiation and frostbite of nose, lips, or larynx if inhaled from tank; loss of motor control, nausea, ataxia, muscle weakness, dysarthria, nystagmus, diminished reflexes.
Mental status:	laughter, giddiness, confusion.
Nitrites ("poppers")	
Vital signs:	decreased blood pressure, increased pulse.
Physical exam:	minimal findings.
Mental status:	minimal changes.
Anabolic Androgenic Steroids	
Most of the negative effects are from regular and prolonged use, rather than from intoxication and overdose.	
Nicotine	
Most of the negative effects are from regular and prolonged use, rather than from intoxication and overdose.	

PREGNANCY AND OTHER DRUG USE

Epidemiology

In addition to alcohol there is also concern about the effects of other drug use on the fetus. The first national survey on the prevalence of drug use during pregnancy found that in 4 million women who had given birth there were the following levels of reported drug use: nicotine, 20.4%, alcohol, 18.8%, marijuana 2.9%, cocaine, 1.1%, and other illicit drug use including opiates, less than 1.1%. The total for any illicit drug use among pregnant women was 5.5%.

In terms of numbers, the largest group of pregnant women using other drugs are white women. There are differences between the rates of drug use for different racial/ethnic groups. The rate of any illicit drug use during pregnancy was 11.3% for African Americans, 4.5% for Hispanics, and 4.4% among white women. However, these differences are not a product of race/ethnicity per se. When one takes into account age, level of education, and household income the differences in terms of race and ethnicity disappear. The underlying factors are socioeconomic.

Cocaine-exposed infants

Cocaine is highly soluble in both water and fat tissue; therefore, it can easily cross the placenta from mother to fetus. When cocaine is used intravenously or as a free base (crack), passage from mother to fetus is enhanced. The fetus has a limited ability to metabolize cocaine, which may lead to its accumulation in the fetus. A "binge" pattern commonly associated with cocaine use may also contribute to even higher levels of cocaine in the fetus. Transfer of cocaine appears to be greater in the first and third trimesters of pregnancy. One of cocaine's most potent effects is to constrict blood vessels. Therefore, the constriction of blood vessels in the uterus, placenta, and umbilical cord can retard the transfer of cocaine from mother to fetus. However, this constriction of blood vessels is far from being a totally protective device for the unborn baby. This constriction also means that there is less passage of everything else, including essential nutrients, and less ability to exchange the waste products from the fetus to the mother. It is thought that this decreased blood flow may be as important as the cocaine itself in causing whatever abnormalities occur in fetal development.

Many reports have expounded on the detrimental effects of prenatal exposure to cocaine. This is a subject that has received considerable coverage in the media. However, the effects are not as clear-cut as such reports imply. In any consideration of the effects of cocaine on pregnancy, keep in mind that women who use cocaine throughout pregnancy also have many other risk factors. These include cigarette smoking, alcohol consumption, a tendency to stay among lower socioeconomic classes, less education, poor prenatal/medical care, use of other drugs of abuse, younger age, being a single parent, and having sexually transmitted diseases. In addition, problems can arise from toxic products that may be mixed with the cocaine.

The following have consistently been reported as accompanying maternal cocaine use: a greater likelihood of maternal health problems that can have an impact on the neonate (e.g., infections), impaired growth, smaller head circumference, premature birth, and an increased risk of still-births. Cocaine use also affects labor; it appears to be involved with the onset of premature labor. Higher rates of early pregnancy losses and third trimester placental abortions appear to be major complications of maternal cocaine use. The highly publicized behavioral problems that were supposedly to be characteristic of "crack babies" do not seem to be at all universal among children that have been exposed to cocaine prenatally.

Animal studies have helped to provide some answers regarding cocaine's effects by controlling for many of the other factors that complicate studies with humans. These provide evidence of growth retardation, separation of the placenta, as well as suggesting cerebral infarctions (strokes), increased general pre- and postnatal mortality, as well as limb/digit reductions and eye anomalies. But the risk of such abnormalities seems low in animal models and seems to require high doses. Analysis of all available studies conducted with this population suggests that cocaine is not a major human source of birth defects and that most children are likely to be normal in terms of body structure and later neurological developmental. The problems that are seen may well be the result of other factors that are present in the lives of the addicted women, not necessarily attributable to the cocaine per se, again these being poverty, inadequate pre- and postnatal care, inadequate nutrition, other drug use, and other medical problems of the mother.

Opiate-exposed infants

The physical problems encountered by the pregnant opiate-dependent mother are enormous. For one, medical complications abound due to the frequent use of dirty needles. Moreover, many opiate-dependent women tend to be extremely sexually active and have a history of sexually transmitted diseases. Their living conditions are often poor, and many infections are transmitted within these settings. Because these women are poorly nourished, they frequently have vitamin deficiencies such as vitamin C (associated with nicotine and smoking) and the B vitamins (associated with cocaine use). In addition, iron deficiency anemia and folic acid deficiency anemia occur during pregnancy. Due to the frequent use of needles, the women have abscesses, ulcers, bacterial infections, and hepatitis. Sexually transmitted diseases such as gonorrhea, syphilis, herpes, and AIDS are common.

The most common obstetrical complication in opiate-dependent women who have had no prenatal care is preterm birth. These infants have the expected complications seen in infants born prematurely. If the infants are born at full term, they may have pneumonia or meconium aspiration syndrome.

The extremely high risk environment from which the pregnant drug-dependent woman comes predisposes them to a host of neonatal problems. In heroin-dependent women, a significant part of the medical complications seen in their babies is due to low birth weight and prematurity. The incidence of low birth weight may approach 50%. There are a number of conditions known to be associated with low birth weight, regardless of its cause. Medical complications generally reflect: (a) the amount of prenatal care that the mother has received; (b) whether she has suffered any particular obstetrical or medical complications, including toxemia of pregnancy, hypertension, or infection; and, most importantly, (c) multiple drug use that may produce an unstable intrauterine milieu complicated by withdrawal and overdose. This last situation is extremely hazardous, since it predisposes the neonate to meconium staining and subsequent aspiration pneumonia, which may cause significant problems and increase risk of death.

In both premature and term infants, withdrawal from opiates can occur. Appropriate assessment and rapid treatment is essential to treat withdrawal in these infants so that the infants may recover without incident. Narcotic abstinence contributes considerably to problems after birth. However, not all infants born to drug-dependent mothers experience withdrawal. Estimates of the number who have some withdrawal symptoms range between 60% and 90%. The neonatal narcotic abstinence syndrome is characterized by signs and symptoms of central nervous system hyper-irritability, gastrointestinal problems, respiratory distress, and vague autonomic symptoms that include yawning, sneezing, mottling, and fever. The infants initially develop tremors ("the shakes") that are mild at first but progress in severity. A high-pitched cry, increased muscle tone, irritability, increased deep tendon reflexes, and an exaggerated Moro reflex are all characteristic of opiate withdrawal among newborns.

In infants experiencing withdrawal, the rooting reflex—the impulse to snuggle in and nurse—is increased, and sucking either fists or thumbs is common, yet feedings are difficult and the babies regurgitate frequently. These feeding difficulties occur because of an uncoordinated and ineffectual sucking reflex. The infants may develop loose stools; therefore they are susceptible to dehydration and electrolyte imbalance. The time of onset of symptoms is variable. Following delivery, serum and tissue levels of the drug(s) used by the mother begin to fall. The newborn infant continues to metabolize and excrete the drug. Withdrawal occurs when the level of opiates in the tissues reach a critically low level. Because of the variation in time of onset and in degree of severity, a spectrum of abstinence patterns may be observed. Withdrawal may be mild and wax and wane, or it can be delayed in onset, or there can be a stepwise pattern, with gradual continuing increases in severity.

More severe withdrawal seems to occur in babies whose mothers have taken large amounts of drugs over a longer period. Generally, the closer to delivery a mother takes a narcotic, the greater the delay in the onset of withdrawal and the more severe the eventual symptoms in the baby. The maturity of the infant's own systems to metabolize and excrete the drug plays an important role after delivery. Due to the variable severity of the withdrawal, the duration of symptoms may be anywhere from 6 days to 8 weeks. Drug therapies may be used to accomplish neonatal detoxification. Although the babies may be discharged from the hospital after drug therapy is stopped, their symptoms or irritability may persist for more than three to four months.

RESOURCES AND FURTHER READINGS

Adler RA: Clinically important effects of alcohol on endocrine function (review), *Journal of Clinical Endocrinology and Metabolism* 74(5): 957–960, 1992.
The purpose of this review is to highlight those effects of alcohol use and abuse that cause clinical abnormalities of endocrine function. Many other effects of ethanol are of interest but are beyond the scope of this review. There are both direct and indirect effects of alcohol. Acute and chronic alcohol ingestion may have separate effects, and alcohol withdrawal may change endocrine function. Secondary complications such as liver disease, malnutrition, and other medical illnesses commonly found in alcoholics may also have endocrine consequences. (Author abstract.)

Al-Jarallah KF, Shehab DK, Buchanan WW: Rheumatic complications of alcohol abuse (review), *Seminars in Arthritis and Rheumatism* 22(3): 162–171, 1992.
The purpose of this report is to review rheumatic complications associated with alcoholism. Alcoholism is associated with many rheumatic problems, including neuropathic arthropathy, hyperuricemia with gouty arthritis, septic arthritis, and joint hypermobility. Osteoporosis, osteonecrosis, and myopathy also are common. Several other rare musculoskeletal complications have been described. Early recognition of these problems is important for management. (Author abstract.)

Alcohol Health and Research World 21(2): entire issue, 1997.
This thematic issue deals with neurobiology and the impact of alcohol on the brain. Specific articles include

Dichara G. Alcohol and dopamine. pp 108–114.

Dohrman DP; Diamond I; Gordon AS. Role of the neuromodulator adenosine in alcohol's actions. pp 136–143.

Finn DA; Crabbe JC. Exploring alcohol withdrawal syndrome. pp 149–156.

Froehlich JC. Opioid peptides. pp 132–136.

Lovinger DM. Serotonin's role in alcohol's effects on the brain (review). pp 114–120.

Gonzales RA; Jaworski JN. Alcohol and glutamate (review). pp 120–127.

Mihic SJ; Harris RA. GABA and the GABA(A) receptor (review). pp 127–131.

Roberts AJ; Koob GF. The neurobiology of addiction. pp 101–106.

Alcohol Health and Research World 21(1): entire issue, 1997.
Apte MV; Wilson JS; Korsten MA. Alcohol-related pancreatic damage: Mechanisms and treatment. pp 13–20.

Ballard HS. The hematological complications of alcoholism. pp 42–49.

Bode C; Bode JC. Alcohol's role in gastrointestinal tract disorders. pp 76–83.

Emanuele N; Menauele MA. Endocrine system: Alcohol alters critical hormonal balance. pp 53–64.

Epstein M. Alcohol's impact on kidney function. pp 84–91.

Maher JJ. Exploring alcohol's effects on liver function. pp 5–12.

Oscar-Berman M; Shagrin B; Evert DL; Epstein C. Impairments of brain and behavior: The neurological effects of alcohol. pp 65–75.

Szabo G. Alcohol's contribution to compromised immunity. pp 30–38.

Boghdadi MS, Henning RJ: Cocaine: Pathophysiology and clinical toxicology, *Heart and Lung* 26(6):466–483, 1997. (200 refs.)
This article reviews the medical complications of cocaine abuse and the mechanisms of action that contribute to them.

Brust JCM: Acute neurologic complications of drug and alcohol abuse, *Neurologic Clinics* 16(2):503–519, 1998. (79 refs.)
Recreationally abused substances include both legal and illegal agents, broadly classified as opioids, psychostimulants, sedatives, cannabis (marijuana), hallucinogens, inhalants, dissociative anesthetics (phencyclidine), anticholinergics, ethanol, and tobacco. These substances are associated with an array of neurological emergencies resulting from overdose, withdrawal, and other medical and neurological complications. (Author abstract.)

Connor PD, Streissguth AP: Effects of prenatal exposure to alcohol across the life span, *Alcohol Health and Research World* 20(3):170–174, 1996. (36 refs.)
Prenatal exposure to alcohol can have many detrimental effects throughout the life span. Of primary concern are changes in the brain that lead to deficiencies in cognitive functioning, including memory and learning problems, attention deficits, poor motor coordination, and difficulties with problem-solving. These cognitive deficiencies create long-standing problems in many spheres of life, including disturbances in work, school, and social functioning. Treatment strategies that have been used with other cognitively impaired populations may be adapted to assist patients who display the various cognitive symptoms associated with prenatal alcohol exposure.

Deitz DK, Williams GD, Dufour MC: Alcohol consumption and dietary practices in the US population: 1987 and 1992, *Alcohol Health and Research World* 20(2):128–140, 1996. (24 refs.)
Research indicates that the link between alcohol and poor nutrition is highly complex, Alcohol consumption is known to disrupt nutritional status via several mechanisms, including inducing changes in dietary practices. Findings are presented based on 2 years of data from a national survey of health-related activities. The relationship between alcohol consumption and dietary practices—such as types of food consumed or whether vitamins were taken, or belief that diet influences health, and frequency of eating out—is examined. The results show that associations exist between alcohol and diet. These findings have important implications for understanding the interaction between alcohol intake and nutritional status and the effect of this interaction on overall health.

Griffiths HJ, Parantainen H, Olson P: Alcohol and bone disorders, *Alcohol Health and Research World* 17(4):299–304, 1993.
The effects of alcohol consumption on bone often go unrecognized. Several specific bone disorders may accompany alcoholism. Alcohol also causes fractures indirectly as a result of an increased number of motor vehicle crashes and falls. A complex combination of alcohol-related metabolic bone disorders can result in loss of bone mineral. The factors

that promote this combination of disorders in alcoholics include dietary deficiencies, impaired vitamin D metabolism, and hormonal imbalances. Death of bone tissue in alcoholics is caused by factors that decrease the blood supply to a portion of a bone.

Higgins EM, du Vivier AWP: Alcohol and the skin, *Alcohol and Alcoholism* 27(6):595–602, 1992.
The cutaneous stigmata of chronic alcoholic liver disease have been well recognized since the nineteenth century. However, it is now clear that the skin may be affected as an early feature of alcohol misuse. In particular, psoriasis, discoid eczema, and superficial infections are more common in heavy drinkers. Awareness of these early associations can alert physicians to patients at risk of future complications of alcoholism. Great advances have been made in the understanding of the physiological and pathological effects of ethanol. The implications of these changes in the skin are discussed with reference to both the new and established cutaneous signs of alcohol misuse. (Author abstract.)

Lange WR, White N, Robinson N: Medical complications of substance abuse, *Postgraduate Medicine* 92(3):2051, 1992.
Substance abuse is involved in many instances of intentional and unintentional injury. It can also cause medical complications that affect various organ systems, among them the cardiac, vascular, neurologic, pulmonary, gastrointestinal, immunological, and reproductive systems. Alcoholism and drug abuse, with their associated psychosocial and clinical ramifications and complications, cut across all specialty fields. Consequently, all physicians need to be familiar with the spectrum of clinical problems associated with substance abuse and comfortable with addressing these problems prudently and promptly.

Lehman LB, Pilich A, Andrews N: Neurological disorders resulting from alcoholism, *Alcohol Health and Research World* 17(4):305–309, 1993.
Severe neurological disorders, from chronic memory and muscle control to acute blackouts and seizures, have been associated with chronic heavy drinking. The authors review both chronic and acute effects of alcohol on the nervous system, the cause of such effects, and the resulting symptoms.

Lieber CS: *Medical and nutritional complications of alcoholism: Mechanisms and management*, New York: Plenum Publishing Corporation, 1992.
This work, with 18 chapters and 17 different contributors in addition to the author, provides a review of the major medical complications associated with alcoholism, as well as the pathophysiological basis and approaches to clinical management. Individual chapters deal with metabolism; acetaldehyde and acetate; hormonal influences on metabolism; lipid disorders including fatty liver, hyperlipemia, and atherosclerosis; effects of ethanol on amino acid and protein metabolism; interactions of alcohol and other drugs; the liver; immunological reactions resulting from liver disease; the hematological system; the digestive system; the pancreas; the cardiovascular system; effects on skeletal muscle, the central nervous system, the kidney. It also discusses carcinogenic effects, fetal alcohol syndrome; nutritional problems associated with alcoholism, and biological markers of alcoholism.

Marsano A: Alcohol and malnutrition, *Alcohol Health and Research World* 17(4):284–291, 1993.

The human body uses alcohol as a source of calories. At high blood alcohol levels and in alcoholics, however, the body uses the calories from alcohol less efficiently than it does those from food sources. The author describes alcohol's relationship with malnutrition and the use of such nutrients as carbohydrates, proteins, lipids, and vitamins. The author also discusses alcohol's deleterious effects on portions of the digestive system and gives a summary of clinical methods for assessing a person's nutritional status.

Meadows R, Verghese A: Medical complications of glue sniffing (review), *Southern Medical Journal* 89(5):455–462, 1996. (93 refs.)

Glue sniffing refers to the deliberate inhalation of volatile solvents, commonly found in adhesives, for the purpose of intoxication. This review of sources is intended to aid clinicians in the recognition of glue-sniffing patients and in the diagnosis of acute and chronic medical complications associated with the abuse of glues, solvents, and related substances. Glue sniffing has been linked to sudden death and chronic damage to the heart, lungs, kidneys, liver, peripheral nerves, and brain. Inhalant abuse in general is associated with mortality and morbidity, including social, educational, and economic deprivations in adolescents and young adults. (Author abstract.)

Mendenhall CL: Immunity, malnutrition, and alcohol, *Alcohol Health and Research World* 16(1):23–28, 1992.

Nutrition influences all aspects of the immune system, and malnutrition—in particular, protein energy malnutrition—has been found both to suppress and to stimulate certain immune responses. Alcoholism is associated with poor nutrition and, in severe cases, with malnutrition. The author discusses the complex and poorly understood relationships among nutrition, alcoholism, and functioning of the immune system.

Murray JB: Psychophysiological aspects of amphetamine-methamphetamine abuse, *Journal of Psychology* 132(2):227–237, 1998. (41 refs.)

Abuse of amphetamines-methamphetamines has increased worldwide. Profiles of abusers, effects of different methods of administration, and research on amphetamine psychosis are reviewed, along with research on psychophysiological mechanisms, addictive potential, and psychotherapeutic strategies. (Author abstract.)

Nathan KI, Bresnick WH, Batki SL: Cocaine abuse and dependence: Approaches to management, *CNS Drugs* 10(1):43–59, 1998. (94 refs.)

Cocaine abuse and dependence constitute major health and social problems in the United States and elsewhere. They are associated with a wide range of psychiatric and medical morbidity, including an increased risk of transmission of HIV. The paper is organized into 6 main sections: (1) overview of cocaine as a drug of abuse, pharmacologic effects, routes of administration, patterns of use, and clinical symptomatology; (2) epidemiology; (3) medical and psychiatric comorbidity; (4) management, assessment, and treatment; (5) drug therapies, by drug type; and (6) conclusions. (Author abstract.)

National Institute on Alcohol Abuse and Alcoholism: *Ninth special report to the U.S. Congress on alcohol and health*, Rockville MD: National Institute on Alcohol Abuse and Alcoholism, 1997.

This most recent in a series of reports by NIAAA, first published in 1971, provides current documentation of progress in understanding the effects of alcohol on health. A valuable reference tool, the report contains a wealth of current data, statistical information displayed in numerous tables and charts, and summaries of the major topics of current interest: epidemiology, genetics and environmental influences, neurosciences, medical consequences, fetal alcohol syndrome and other effects on pregnancy outcome, social consequences, diagnosis and assessment, prevention, early and minimal intervention, and treatment. Each chapter has an extensive bibliography.

Roehrs T, Roth T: Alcohol-induced sleepiness and memory function, *Alcohol Health and Research World* 19(2): 130–135, 1995. (37 refs.)
Alcohol has sedative, as well as performance and memory-impairing effects. Several independent lines of research indicate that alcohol-induced sleepiness may contribute to the observed memory and performance impairment. Such a link would imply that alcohol consumption in combination with other drugs or conditions that enhance sleepiness could increase the risk for alcohol-related impairment.

Streissguth A, Kanter J, eds: *The challenge of fetal alcohol syndrome: Overcoming secondary disabilities*, Seattle WA: University of Washington Press, 1997. (208 refs.)
The volume contains 22 selected papers summarizing the research to date as well as the most innovative approaches to assessment and treatment by health-care professionals and community-based agencies. Individual chapters address neurobehavioral and neuroanatomical effects of heavy prenatal exposure to alcohol, primary and secondary disabilities of fetal alcohol syndrome and fetal alcohol effects, as well as a range of clinical issues.

4

ALCOHOL DEPENDENCE

DEFINITIONS

The social problems associated with alcohol use were described earlier. Even if there were no such phenomenon as alcohol dependence, the mere presence of the beverage, alcohol, would lead to social disruption and considerable social costs. This is now being recognized. For too long the statistics on dented fenders caused by impaired drivers, or the dollars lost by industry, or even the percentage of alcohol-related hospital admissions were ignored. Seen merely as the product of many people's single, uninformed encounters with alcohol, they were dismissed as the cost a drinking culture has to pay.

Attitudes, however, have changed dramatically. Those who choose to drink are no longer seen as potentially endangering only themselves. Drinkers no longer are accepted as having a right to "get smashed" to celebrate, to "unwind," or to indiscriminately "tie one on" or "get wiped" from time to time. Drinkers no longer are viewed as not accountable for things that occur while they are under the influence. Having come to recognize the impact of these individual decisions upon the public safety, society has significantly changed its attitudes as to what constitutes acceptable and unacceptable drinking. Though still not universally true, in more and more quarters individuals are not considered free to drink in a manner that endangers others. Increasingly, intoxicated behavior is not overlooked, is far less tolerated, and is likely to be met with direct expressions of disapproval.

There are, however, those whose drinking behavior will not be touched by admonitions to "Drink responsibly." There are those whose behavior will not be altered by TV ads that urge friends to select a designated driver to see that all return home safely after an evening that includes drinking. There are those whose behavior will not respond to friends' suggestions to "take it easy" or friends' expressions of disapproval. The special problem that besets these 26 million individuals is that for them alcohol is no longer the servant, but the master. The chances are quite good that this concern is individualized with the faces of people we know or have known. There are also the estimated 100 million family members who live directly in the shadow of someone's dependence on alcohol.

What is alcohol dependence? Who has alcoholism? These questions will confront the substance abuse clinician daily. A physician may request assistance in determining if an alcohol problem exists. A client or a spouse may challenge, "Why, she can't be an alcoholic because . . ." Even in nonworking hours the question crops up during conversation with good friends or casual acquaintances. A number of definitions have been provided. As a starting point, consider the word *alcoholic*. This continues to be the term most commonly used for those with alcohol dependence. The word itself provides some clues. The suffix -*ic* has a special meaning, according to Webster's *New Collegiate Dictionary:*

-*ic* n suffix: One having the character or nature of; one belonging to or associated with; one exhibiting or affected by.

Drunkenness is nothing but voluntary madness.

SENECA

One drink is plenty
Two drinks too many
And three not half enough.

W. Knox Haynes

Attaching *-ic* to alcohol, we form a word that denotes the person linked with alcohol. Okay, that's a start. Clearly, not all drinkers are linked with alcohol, just as all baseball players are not linked with the Boston Red Sox. Why the link or association? The basis is probably frequency of alcohol use, pattern of use, quantity used, or frequency of indications that the person has been drinking. "Belonging to" has several connotations, including "an individual being possessed by or under the control of." The Chinese have a saying that goes: "The man takes a drink, the drink takes a drink, and then the drink takes the man." This final step closely approximates what the word "alcoholic" means. It offers a good picture of the progression of alcoholism, or alcohol dependence.

It is worth noting that the discussion or debate on who is an alcoholic and what is alcoholism is relatively recent. This doesn't mean that society before had not noticed those we now think of as suffering from alcoholism. Certainly, those deeply in trouble with alcohol have been recognized for centuries, but their existence was accepted as a fact, without question or any particular thought about the matter. To the extent that there was debate, it centered on why, as well as how the person should be handled. Essentially two basic approaches prevailed. One was that "obviously" these individuals were morally inferior. The evidence cited was that of the vast majority of people who drank moderately without presenting problems for themselves or their communities. The other view has been that "obviously" such individuals were possessed: would those in their right mind drink like that of their own volition?

With increasing scientific study and understanding of the "drink taking the man" phenomenon, the more complicated the task of definition became. In addition to the awareness that some people are distinctly different from many who drink moderately, the other clear discovery was that those with alcoholism are not alike. Not all develop DTs (delirium tremens) upon cessation of drinking. There are big differences in the quantity of alcohol consumed or the number of years of drinking before family problems arise. Many chronic heavy drinkers develop cirrhosis but more do not. Given the range of differences among those with alcoholism, what is the basic core, the essential features that are common to all cases of alcoholism? An answer to this question is fundamental to any attempt to define the condition.

Early definitions

Over the past half century, as alcoholism increasingly was viewed as a disease, a number of attempts were made to define the condition. What follows is a cross section of the early definitions that were put forth.

1940s, Alcoholics Anonymous. AA has never had an "official" definition. The concept of Dr. William Silkworth, one of AA's early friends, is sometimes cited by AA members: . . . an obsession of the mind and an allergy of the body. The obsession or compulsion guarantees that the sufferer will drink against his own will and interest. The allergy guarantees that the sufferer will either die or go insane.

Another operative definition frequently heard among AA members is: "An alcoholic is a person who cannot predict with accuracy what will happen when he takes a drink."

1946, E.M. Jellinek, a pioneer in modern alcohol studies. "Alcoholism is any use of alcoholic beverages that causes any damage to the individual or to society or both."

1950s, Marty Mann, a founding member of the National Council on Alcoholism (now known as the National Council on Alcoholism and Drug Dependence). "An alcoholic is a very sick person, victim of an insidious, progressive disease, which all too often ends fatally. An alcoholic can be recognized, diagnosed, and treated successfully."

1950, World Health Organization. The Alcoholism Subcommittee defined alcoholism as: "Any form of drinking which in extent goes beyond the tradition and customary 'dietary' use, or the ordinary compliance with the social drinking customs of the community concerned, irrespective of etiological factors leading to such behavior, and irrespective also of the extent to which such etiological factors are dependent upon heredity, constitution, or acquired physiopathological and metabolic influences." This initial formulation has since substantially been revised.

1960, Mark Keller, former editor of the *Journal of Studies on Alcohol.* "Alcoholism is a chronic disease manifested by repeated implicative drinking so as to cause injury to the drinker's health or to his social or economic functioning."

1968, American Psychiatric Association. According to the Committee on Nomenclature and Statistics: "Alcoholism: this category is for patients whose alcohol intake is great enough to damage their physical health, or their personal or social functioning, or when it has become a prerequisite to normal functioning." Three types of alcoholism were further identified: episodic excessive drinking, habitual excessive drinking, and alcohol addiction.

1977, American Medical Association. From the *Manual on Alcoholism,* edited by the AMA Panel on Alcoholism: "Alcoholism is an illness characterized by significant impairment that is directly associated with persistent and excessive use of alcohol. Impairment may involve physiological, psychological, or social dysfunction."

In examining the early definitions, we find that each, although not necessarily conflicting, tended to have a different focus or emphasis. Some were purely descriptive. Others attempted to speak to the origins of the condition. Several concentrated on the unfortunate consequences associated with alcohol use. Others zeroed in on hallmark signs or symptoms, especially loss of control or frequency of intoxication.

Add to these expert definitions all of the definitions that have been used casually by each of us and our neighbors. These have varied from

One swallow doesn't make a summer but too many swallows make a fall.

G.D. PRENTICE

"alcoholism is an illness," to "it's the number one drug problem," to "when someone's drunk all the time," to "someone who panhandles," to "those who can't hold their liquor." Note that generally, lay people have had far more permissive criteria and have adopted definitions that would exclude themselves and most they know as candidates for the condition!

Actions taken by the World Health Organization (WHO) in 1977 and the American Psychiatric Association (APA) three years later were important in clarifying and promoting greater consensus as to the definition of alcoholism. The changes instituted by these groups were important in introducing more consistency between identifying alcoholism and conditions related to other psychoactive substance use. (The WHO prepares and publishes the *International Classification of Diseases,* known as the ICD. It provides a comprehensive list of all injuries, diseases, and disorders and is used worldwide. The APA publishes a manual restricted to mental disorders, known as the *Diagnostic and Statistical Manual.*) Ironically, for the sake of clarification both groups abandoned use of the term "alcoholism." Neither group disputed the existence of the phenomenon of alcoholism. For medical and scientific purposes, however, both the WHO and the APA substituted *alcohol dependence syndrome* for what heretofore had been discussed as alcoholism. This was done because of the multiple definitions abounding in the professional community. This change also was necessitated by the general public's widespread everyday use of "alcoholic" and the variants that were being coined, such as "workaholic." When the same term is shared by lay people and medical scientists, but used differently, confusion is likely. So, paradoxically, it was in part the very success in educating the public about alcoholism as a disease that necessitated the change in terminology.

Uniform terminology is essential. When it comes to clinical interactions with colleagues and other professionals, the day is past when each clinician has the luxury of defining the disease according to individual biases and preferences. In the United States, the APA's *Diagnostic and Statistical Manual* provides the approved terminology. The 1980 version of the *Diagnostic and Statistical Manual,* the third edition (DSM-III), distinguished between two separate alcohol-related syndromes: alcohol abuse and alcohol dependence. Both conditions entailed impairment in social and occupational functioning. The essential distinguishing feature of dependence was the presence of tolerance and withdrawal. There is always room to quibble with definitions, and that particular operational definition did have its critics. The major criticism of the definition had been that physical dependence was required to make the diagnosis of dependence. This is never a black-and-white situation. There are those who may not show marked physical dependence but whose lives are in utter chaos because of alcohol use. However, this was an instance when living with imperfections was preferable to the alternative, which would have been everyone's continuing to feel free to define the condition for themselves. In subsequent revisions of the Manual, the DSM-III-R in 1987 and the DSM-IV in 1994, changes were made in response to these concerns.

With the growing acceptance of alcoholism as a disease, there was a corresponding drop-off in the number of formal definitions. Attention had turned to efforts to specify the conditions which need to be met to make a diagnosis of the condition. Then suddenly, what seemingly had been settled—that alcohol dependence was a disease and ought to be treated as such—was called into question. The prospect of health-care reform and the need to make decisions about what would and would not be covered by any mandated health insurance rekindled the debate. Within this context, a policy statement defining alcoholism was issued by the American Society of Addiction Medicine (ASAM), a professional association of physician specialists in the alcohol and drug field.

1993, American Society of Addiction Medicine. "Alcoholism is a *primary,* chronic *disease* with genetic, psychological and environmental factors influencing its development and manifestations. The disease is often *progressive* and *fatal.* It is characterized by continuous or periodic *impaired control* over drinking, preoccupation with the drug alcohol, use of alcohol despite adverse consequences, and distortions in thinking, most notably *denial* . . ."

The statement then proceeds to elaborate on each of the words in italics. Interestingly, the society makes an explicit statement about the meaning of the word "disease." It emphasizes that a disease represents an "involuntary disability."

'Tis not the drinking that is to be blamed, but the excess.

JOHN SELDON, 1689

A DISEASE?

The remainder of this chapter will be devoted to the evolution of the understanding of alcoholism as a disease and the major pieces of work that have led to our present formulation of what alcohol dependence is, its complexity, and how to recognize it. First, we turn to the work of E.M. Jellinek, who has been called the father of alcohol studies not only in the United States but internationally. Next discussed are the guidelines established by a Committee of the National Council on Alcoholism and published in 1972. The guidelines represented the first effort to set forth explicit signs and symptoms to be used in diagnosing alcoholism. Following this, in 1980, there was the publication of the APA's first diagnostic criteria for alcohol dependence. Then, in 1983, a landmark study by George Vaillant was published outlining the natural history of alcoholism and its recovery. Finally, there are the most recent revisions to the APA's Diagnostic and Statistic Manual, and the research and thinking that shaped them.

Anyone who is sufficiently interested in alcohol problems to have read this far is probably accustomed to hearing alcoholism referred to as an illness, disease, or sickness. As noted repeatedly, this has not always been the case. Alcoholism—alcohol dependence—has not always been distinguished from drunkenness. Alternatively, it has been seen as a lot of drunkenness and categorized as a sin or character defect. The work of E.M. Jellinek was largely responsible for the shift from a defect to an illness model. In essence, through his research and writings he said, "Hey, world, you folks mislabeled this thing. You put it in the sin bin, and it really belongs in the disease pile."

Implications of disease classification

How we label something is very important. It provides clues to how to feel and think, what to expect, and how to act. Whether a particular bulb is tagged as a tulip or garlic will make a big difference. Depending on which I think it is, I'll either chop and sauté or plant and water. Very different behaviors are associated with each. An error may lead to strangely flavored spaghetti sauce and a less colorful flower bed next spring.

For both lay people and professionals the recognition that alcoholism belongs properly in the category of disease has had a dramatic impact. Sick people generally are awarded sympathy. The accepted notion is that sick people do not choose to be sick. Being sick is not pleasant. It is agreed that care should be provided to restore health. During the period of sickness, people are not expected to fill their usual roles or meet their responsibilities. A special designation is given to them—that of patient. Furthermore, sick people are not to be criticized for manifesting the symptoms of their illness. To demand that a person with flu stop running a fever would be pointless and unkind. Accompanying the perception of alcoholism as an illness, the individual with the disease—the alcoholic—came to be viewed as a sufferer and victim. Much of the bizarre behavior displayed came to be recognized as unwillful and symptomatic. No longer the object of scorn, the individual with alcoholism was seen as requiring care. The logical place to send the alcoholic was a hospital or some type of rehabilitation facility instead of jail. Since the 1940s there has been a gradual shift in public perceptions. Nationwide polls now find that over 80% of the respondents say they believe alcoholism to be an illness.

Although Jellinek's efforts may have triggered this shift, a number of other events added impetus. The National Council on Alcoholism put its efforts into lobbying and public education. The American Medical Association and American Hospital Association published various committee reports. State agencies created treatment programs. Medical societies and other professional associations assumed responsibility for their members' education and addressed the ethical responsibility to treat alcohol problems. We suspect that the single biggest push has come from recovering alcoholics, especially through the work of AA. Virtually everyone today has personal knowledge of an apparently hopeless alcoholic who has stopped drinking and now seems a new, different person.

The formulation of alcoholism as a disease opened up possibilities for treatment that were formerly nonexistent. It brought into the helping arena the resources of medicine, nursing, social work, and other professions that before had no mandate to be involved. Also it is gradually removing the stigma associated with the condition of alcoholism. This

improved the likelihood that individuals and families would seek help rather than be encumbered by shame or burdened by a sense of hopelessness trying to keep the condition a family secret. Finally, the resources of the federal government were focused on alcohol problems as a major public health issue, and a host of treatment and educational programs were created.

Criticisms of the disease concept

The disease concept of alcoholism has had its critics. One criticism arose in academic circles. Over a decade ago, a rash of articles were published setting forth different models or frameworks for viewing alcoholism. The different models were described as the moral model, disease model, AA model, learning model, self-medication model, and social model. The writers described these different models as if they were mutually exclusive, conflicting, and as if an either/or choice were required. Such narrow thinking is now discredited. The current view is that models representing differing approaches are not in opposition; they might be compared to the "blind-men-describing-the-elephant" phenomenon. They complement one another and highlight differing points of emphasis. To view alcoholism as a disease does not mean that one discounts the role of learning, disregards the influence of society, or fails to recognize that some drinking is self-medication. Similarly the views of AA on alcoholism don't require that one discount alcoholism as a disease. Certainly its members don't!

Other objections to the disease concept used to be heard from the treatment community. One is that it possibly can put too much emphasis on the physician as the major helper. While doctors certainly have a role to play in diagnosis and physical treatment, medical training has not necessarily prepared them for counseling. Even if it has, a physician alone does not have available all the time needed to offer counseling, support, and education to both patient and family. This requires a team of professionals. Yet the disease concept may imply that the doctor alone is qualified to provide or direct treatment. Criticism frequently has been leveled at MDs for being uninterested in or unconcerned with the problem of alcohol dependence. Possibly the misuse of the disease concept also may foster unrealistic expectations of, and place undue burdens on, doctors.

Another criticism with some merit is that the disease label implies the possibility of a cure through the wonders of modern medicine worked on a passive patient. Emphasis on alcoholism as a chronic illness requiring the active participation of the patient in rehabilitation should remove this reservation. Characteristically the management of chronic disease involves five elements. There is treatment of acute flare-ups. Emotional support is a necessity; after all, no one likes having a chronic illness! Education is needed, so that the individual can be well informed about the illness and assist in self-care. Rehabilitative measures are initiated to prompt the life changes necessary to live with the limitations imposed

by the illness. Family involvement is critical so the family can be informed and can deal with the impact that the chronic illness has on their lives, which is a prerequisite for their being supportive.

A noteworthy characteristic of a chronic illness is that it tends to develop slowly. Quite conceivably, with an acute illness such as flu, one can go to bed feeling chipper and wake up the next morning sick. It literally happens overnight. However, one does not become diabetic, arthritic, or drug dependent overnight. The disease state develops slowly. There will be warning signs and symptoms before the point at which it is unequivocally present. We have E.M. Jellinek to thank for beginning to sketch out this progression in alcoholism.

Another criticism levied at the disease concept is that it can be used as an excuse. "Don't look at me, I'm not responsible. I'm sick. Poor me (sigh, sigh)." But this criticism overlooks a significant point. A drinking alcoholic is expected to try shooting holes into any definition. Some who would criticize the disease concept on this basis are possibly those who have run headlong into the denial that characterizes alcohol dependence. If denial goes unrecognized as a symptom of the disease, it can only cause frustration. And, even then, alcohol-dependent individuals are very sensitive to what will immobilize those around them so that their drinking can continue undisturbed. As you acquire more information about alcohol dependence, you will begin to recognize these maneuvers—the first step in gaining skill to effectively counter disarming tactics. A one-liner that seems to cover the situation fairly well comes from a once-prominent billboard on the Boston skyline: *There's nothing wrong with being an alcoholic, if you're doing something about it.*

Another recent variant of this criticism is less concerned with the particular individual who is alcohol-dependent than with the larger social trend. People have questioned whether or not, as a society, we have become too accepting of the notion of "disease" or "victim" and too willing to excuse behaviors for which people do need to be held accountable. One piece of evidence cited is the proliferation of "recovery literature." In it everyone is seemingly a victim of some sort, as witnessed by the burgeoning information on codependency, adult children of alcoholics, and dysfunctional families. Many of the terms and constructs were borrowed from the addictions field and applied to other areas. Upon first hearing of the notion of sexual addiction, someone commented, "Whatever happened to bad judgment, immorality, sin, and the notion of personal responsibility for choices?" Indeed, that question does need to be asked. Although we are probably more sympathetic to self-help efforts generally than others may be, and appreciative of their contributions—especially the traditional 12-step programs—there is a danger of not drawing lines where they need to be drawn. In overextending concepts such as the disease model to areas further afield, there is the danger of trivializing and diminishing the usefulness of the model when it is very much needed.

NATURAL HISTORY

The natural history of an illness refers to the typical progression of signs and symptoms as the disease unfolds if it goes untreated. Jellinek was one of the first to speak of alcoholism as a disease and of its progression. Thus he was seeing the condition in what was wholly a new light and considering it from a perspective that was quite different from the views that then prevailed. An appreciation of this early work is important. Those in any profession need to be knowledgeable about its history. As in our personal lives our family history casts a long shadow and partially determines how we see the world, so history molds the thought and theory of our professions and occupations. We may not always be fully aware of the influences in our personal lives; the same is true of our professional practice. Much of how we view alcohol dependence today is clearly derived from the work of Jellinek. Those involved in substance abuse counseling need to be familiar with the work that marked the evolution of the field.

Jellinek's phases of alcoholism

How did Jellinek arrive at his disease formulation of alcoholism? A trained biostatistician, he was understandably fascinated by statistics, the pictures they portray, and the questions they raise. Much of his work was descriptive, defining the turf of alcoholism: who, when, where. One of his first studies, published in 1952, charted the signs and symptoms associated with alcohol addiction. This work was based on a survey of over two thousand members of AA. Although differences certainly existed between persons, the similarities were, to him, striking. There was a definite pattern to the appearance of the symptoms. Also there was a progression of the disease in terms of increasing dysfunction. The symptoms and signs tended to go together in clusters. On the basis of these observations, Jellinek developed the idea of four different phases of alcohol addiction: prealcoholic, prodromal, crucial, and chronic. Although many may not be aware of the origins, these phases have been widely used in alcohol treatment circles. The four phases are portrayed graphically on p. 140.

In the *prealcoholic phase,* according to Jellinek's formulation, the individual's use of alcohol is socially motivated. However, the prospective alcoholic soon experiences psychological relief in the drinking situation. Possibly his or her tensions are greater than other people's, or possibly the individual has no other way of handling tensions that arise. It does not matter. Either way, the individual learns to seek out occasions at which drinking will occur. At some point the connection is perceived. Drinking then becomes the standard means of handling stress. But the drinking behavior will not look different to the outsider. This phase can extend from several months to 2 or more years. An increase in tolerance gradually develops.

Suddenly the prealcoholic will enter the *prodromal phase.* Prodromal means warning or signaling disease. According to Jellinek, the behavior

Prealcoholic

Signs of Developing Alcoholism

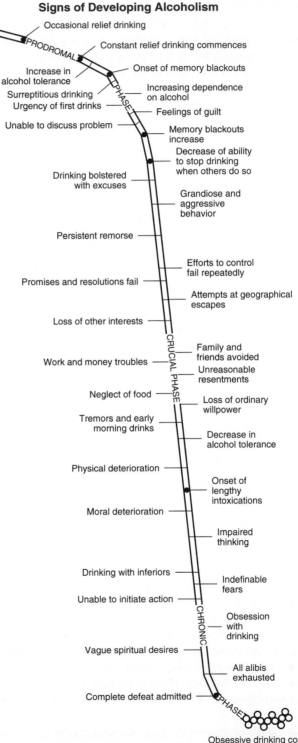

Occasional relief drinking

PRODROMAL

Constant relief drinking commences

Increase in alcohol tolerance

Onset of memory blackouts

Surreptitious drinking

Increasing dependence on alcohol

Urgency of first drinks

PHASE

Feelings of guilt

Unable to discuss problem

Memory blackouts increase

Decrease of ability to stop drinking when others do so

Drinking bolstered with excuses

Grandiose and aggressive behavior

Persistent remorse

Efforts to control fail repeatedly

Promises and resolutions fail

Attempts at geographical escapes

Loss of other interests

CRUCIAL PHASE

Family and friends avoided

Work and money troubles

Unreasonable resentments

Neglect of food

Loss of ordinary willpower

Tremors and early morning drinks

Decrease in alcohol tolerance

Physical deterioration

Onset of lengthy intoxications

Moral deterioration

Impaired thinking

Drinking with inferiors

Indefinable fears

Unable to initiate action

CHRONIC

Obsession with drinking

Vague spiritual desires

All alibis exhausted

Complete defeat admitted

PHASE

Obsessive drinking continues in vicious circles

that heralds the change is the occurrence of "alcoholic palimpsests" or blackouts.* Blackouts are amnesia-like periods during drinking. The person seems to be functioning normally but later has no memory of what happened. Other behaviors emerge during this phase that testify to alcohol's no longer being just "a beverage," but a "need." Among these warning signs are: sneaking extra drinks before or during parties, gulping the first drink or two, and guilt about the drinking behavior. At this point consumption is heavy, yet not necessarily conspicuous. To look "okay" requires conscious effort by the drinker. This period can last from 6 months to 4 or 5 years, depending on the drinker's circumstances.

The third phase is the *crucial phase*. The key symptom that ushers in this phase is loss of control. Now taking a drink sets up a chain reaction. The drinker can no longer control the amount consumed after taking the first drink. Yet the drinker can control whether or not to take a drink. So, it is possible to go on the wagon for a time. With loss of control, the drinker's cover-up is blown. The drinking is now clearly different. It requires explanation, so rationalizations begin. Simultaneously, the alcoholic attempts a sequence of strategies to regain control. The thinking of the alcoholic goes as follows: "If I just _____, then it will be okay." Solutions commonly adopted by the alcoholic are: "going on the wagon," i.e., deliberate periods of abstinence; changing drinking patterns; or geographical changes to escape/avoid/be relieved of _____; similarly, job changes occur. All these attempted solutions are doomed to failure. The alcoholic responds to these failures by being alternately resentful, remorseful, and aggressive. Life has become alcohol-centered. Family life and friendships deteriorate. The first alcohol-related hospitalization is now likely to occur. Morning drinking may begin to creep in, foreshadowing the next stage.

The final stage in the process as outlined by Jellinek is the *chronic phase*. In the preceding crucial phase, drinkers may have been somewhat successful in maintaining a job and their social footing. Now, as drinking begins earlier in the day, intoxication is an almost daily, day-long phenomenon. "Benders" are more frequent. The individual may also go to dives and drink with persons outside his normal peer group. Not unexpectedly, the alcoholic finds himself on the fringes of society. When ethanol is unavailable, poisonous substitutes are the alternative. During this phase, marked physical changes occur. Tolerance for alcohol drops sharply. No longer able to hold the liquor, the alcoholic becomes stuporous after a few drinks. Tremors develop. Many simple tasks are impossible in the sober state. The individual is beset by indefinable fears. Finally, the rationalization system fails. The long-used excuses are revealed as just that—excuses. The alcoholic is seen as spontaneously open to treatment. Often, however, drinking is likely to continue because the alcoholic can imagine no way out of these circumstances. Jellinek

Prodromal

Crucial

Chronic

*This is a description of Jellinek's work. A discussion of blackouts and the more recent findings about them is covered in the preceeding chapter.

did emphasize that alcoholics do not have to go through all four stages before successful treatment can occur.

Types of alcoholism: Jellinek's species

The pattern described above refers to the stages of alcohol addiction. Jellinek continued his study of alcoholism, focusing on alcohol problems in other countries. The differences he found could not be accounted for simply by the phases of alcohol addiction. They seemed to be differences of kind rather than simply of degree of addiction. This led to his formulation of species, or categories, of alcoholism. Each of these types he named after a Greek letter.

Alpha alcoholism This type represents a purely psychological dependence on alcohol. There is neither loss of control nor an inability to abstain. What is evident is the reliance on alcohol to weather any or all discomforts or problems in life, which may lead to interpersonal, family, or work problems. A progression is not inevitable. Jellinek noted that other writers may call this species *problem drinking.*

Beta alcoholism This is present when physical problems such as cirrhosis or gastritis develop from alcohol use but the individual is not psychologically or physically dependent. Beta alcoholism is likely to occur in persons from cultures where there is widespread heavy drinking and inadequate diet.

Gamma alcoholism This variant is marked by a change in tolerance, physiological changes leading to withdrawal symptoms, and a loss of control. In this species there is a progression from psychological to physical dependence. It is the most devastating species in terms of physical health and social disruption. This is the species Jellinek originally studied. It progresses in the four phases discussed: prealcoholic, prodromal, crucial, and chronic. The gamma alcoholic appeared to be the most prominent type in the United States. This species was the type most common among the members of AA that Jellinek studied. Characteristics of this species alone are often seen as synonymous with alcoholism.

Delta alcoholism Delta alcoholism is very similar to the gamma variety of alcoholism. There is psychological and physical dependence, but there is no loss of control. Therefore on any particular occasion the drinker can control the amount consumed. The individual, however, cannot go on the wagon for even a day without suffering withdrawal.

Epsilon alcoholism While not studied in depth, this type appeared to be significantly different from the others. Jellinek called this *periodic alcoholism,* a type marked by binge drinking. Though not elaborating, he felt this was a species by itself, not to be confused with relapses of gamma alcoholics.

Having described these various species in *The Disease Concept of Alcoholism,* Jellinek concluded that possibly not all of the species identified are properly categorized as diseases. There was no question in his mind that gamma and delta varieties, each involving physiological changes and a progression of symptoms, were diseases. He speculated that maybe alpha and epsilon varieties are, however, symptoms of other disorders. By more adequately classifying and categorizing the phenomena of alcoholism, he brought scientific order to a field that formerly had been dominated by beliefs. That was no modest contribution.

Species reexamined

In many respects a considerable portion of the research now being undertaken is addressing the same question that concerned Jellinek. As noted earlier, although there are common features in alcoholism, there are differences too. Because of this, alcohol dependence is sometimes described as a "heterogeneous" disease. Differences need to be explained. They represent factors that may have important implications for treatment, prevention, or early diagnosis. By way of comparison, it is recognized that there are different types of pneumonia or different types of diabetes. Distinguishing between them is necessary to determine appropriate treatment; in the case of pneumonia the type dictates the type of antibiotic that will be prescribed.

With respect to types of alcoholism, several possible subgroups are now being suggested. People involved with genetics research believe it is possible and useful to distinguish between familial and nonfamilial alcoholism. Familial alcoholism is marked by a positive family history of alcoholism, has an earlier age of onset, has no increased presence of other psychiatric disorders, and has more severe symptoms that necessitate early treatment. Jellinek too had recognized a possible subgroup of alcoholics. In 1940, he had proposed a diagnostic category termed *familial alcoholism.*

Another set of distinctions sometimes made is between primary alcoholism and secondary or reactive alcoholism. The *secondary* or reactive type is seen as alcoholism that grows out of or is superimposed on a psychiatric illness or major psychological problem. This is not to imply that such researchers think that this alcoholism need not be treated in its own right. It does mean that in such cases the individual probably requires active treatment for more than alcoholism, i.e., treatment for the condition(s) that spawned or facilitated its development.

GUIDES FOR DIAGNOSIS
NCA criteria

Having introduced the perspective of alcoholism as a disease, the next major task was to establish guidelines for diagnosis. This step was taken in 1972 with the publication of a paper entitled "Criteria for the

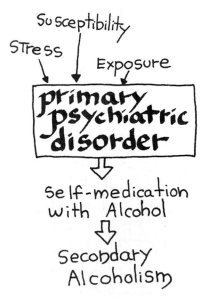

Alcoholic: Arrested

Alcoholism: Arrested

Diagnosis of Alcoholism." The article was prepared by a special committee of the National Council on Alcoholism (NCA) and published in two different medical journals. The committee's charge was to set forth guidelines to be used by physicians in diagnosing alcoholism. Physicians were provided thereby with an explicit, firm set of standards to use in making a diagnosis. In undertaking this endeavor the committee collected all the signs and symptoms of alcoholism that could be ascertained through physical examination, medical history, social history, laboratory tests, and clinical observations. These signs and symptoms were then organized into two categories, or "tracks," of data. The first track was called the Physiological and Clinical Data. Included within that track were the facts a physician can discover either through physical examination, laboratory tests, or medical history. The second track was termed the Behavioral, Psychological, and Attitudinal Data. It was composed of information that the patient or family might report about the patient's life situation, the social history, and those things the physician can observe directly about the patient's involvement with alcohol.

Within each of the two data tracks, the criteria were further divided into subgroups of major or minor criteria. That means exactly what you would expect: major criteria were the "biggies"; the presence of only one was sufficient to make the diagnosis. However, several minor criteria, from both tracks, were needed to support a diagnosis. Finally, each of the potential signposts was weighted as to whether or not it "definitely," "probably," or "possibly" indicated alcoholism.

Table 4.1 summarizes some of the key criteria set forth by the NCA's criteria committee.

Many similarities existed between the symptoms of alcohol addiction developed by Jellinek in 1952 and the criteria published 20 years later. However, Jellinek composed his list based on the self-reports of recovering alcoholics, so the signs were from their point of view. A good number of the symptoms Jellinek included involved efforts to deceive and the attempts of the alcoholic individuals to appear normal. This provided little assistance to the physician or helper interviewing an active alcoholic. In those situations, the physician is unable to rely on his or her usual instincts to believe the client. To further complicate the process of making a diagnosis based on Jellinek's list, many of the behaviors included are not the kinds of things a physician can easily detect, so the NCA criteria were a marked improvement.

The committee that developed the criteria for diagnosis also addressed the nature of alcoholism and commented on its treatment. Alcoholism was characterized as a chronic progressive disease. It was noted that although it is incurable, it is highly treatable. Because it is a chronic disease, the diagnosis once made never can be dropped. Therefore an individual successfully involved in a treatment program would have his or her diagnosis amended to "alcoholism: arrested" or "alcoholism: in remission." Criteria were set forth to determine when this change in diagnosis was appropriate. The committee recommended that factors other

TABLE 4.1 CRITERIA FOR DIAGNOSIS OF ALCOHOLISM

Physiological data	Diagnostic significance*	Behavioral data	Diagnostic significance*
Major criteria		**Major criteria**	
Physiological dependence evidenced by withdrawal syndromes when alcohol is interrupted or decreased	1	Continued drinking, despite strong medical indications known to patient	1
		Drinking despite serious social problems	1
Evidence of tolerance, by blood alcohol level of 0.15 without gross evidence of intoxication or consumption of equivalent of fifth of whiskey for more than one day by 180-lb man	1	Patient's complaint of loss of control	2
Alcoholic blackouts	2		
Major alcohol-related illnesses in person who drinks regularly			
Fatty Liver	2		
Alcoholic hepatitis	1		
Cirrhosis	2		
Pancreatitis	2		
Chronic gastritis	3		
Minor criteria		**Minor criteria** (very similar to Jellinek's symptoms of phases of alcohol addiction)	
Laboratory tests			
Blood alcohol level of 0.3 or more at any time	1†	Repeated attempts at abstinence	2
		Unexplained changes in family, social, or business relationships	3
Blood alcohol level of 0.1 in routine examination	1†	Spouse's complaints about drinking	2
Odor of alcohol on breath at time of medical appointment	2		

Modified from Criteria Committee, National Council on Alcoholism. Criteria for the diagnosis of alcoholism, American Journal of Psychiatry, August 1979, pp. 41–49.

*1 Must diagnose alcoholism; 2, probably indicates alcoholism; 3, possibly due to alcoholism.

†1 There seems to be some discrepancy between 1 meaning a must diagnose alcoholism and the committee's statement that more than one must be in evidence. We note this out, have no explanation.

than the length of sobriety be taken into account. Among the items listed as signs of recovery were full, active participation in AA, active use of other treatments, use of Antabuse-like preparations, no substitution of other drugs, and returning to work. The committee was primarily interested in diagnosis, not treatment. Yet implicit in the standards suggested for diagnosing "alcoholism: arrested" is a view that alcoholism requires a variety of treatment and rehabilitative efforts.

DSM-III criteria

Although definitely on the right track and more useful to clinicians than Jellinek's formulations, the NCA criteria were nonetheless very cumbersome. With the publication in 1980 of the *APA's Diagnostic and Statistical Manual,* Edition 3, these criteria were taken a step forward. Known

as DSM-III, the *Diagnostic and Statistical Manual* was a milestone not only for alcoholism, but for other psychiatric conditions as well. It provided a major departure from previous diagnostic schemes in several ways. For one, it set forth very specific diagnostic criteria, explicitly stating what signs and symptoms must be present to make a diagnosis for a specific condition. The purpose for this was to make diagnosis of psychiatric conditions more uniform. Thus diagnosis was no longer based on what the clinician thought was the underlying reason for the condition, for example, whether it was psychological maladjustment or a physiological abnormality.

In this third edition of the Manual there was also significant revision, reorganization, and renaming of major groups of psychiatric illnesses. Thus for the first time substance use disorders, which includes alcohol dependence and alcohol abuse, became a separate major diagnostic category. Previously these different addictions had been assigned to the category of personality disorders. This earlier assignment reflected the common notion that substance abuse was the result of psychological problems. With the creation of the new category, the manual no longer implied any particular etiology.

The diagnostic manual and its counterpart, the *International Classification of Diseases* (ICD), are routinely updated and revised to reflect new knowledge. In response to clinicians' concerns, in 1987 when the third edition was revised—resulting in the version known as DSM-III-R—changes were made in the way alcohol dependence was defined.

One of the criticisms of the third edition had been that alcohol dependence was tied to the presence of physical evidence of addiction. The third edition required the presence of tolerance and/or withdrawal symptoms. Thus in the DSM-III formulation, those whose lives were in utter disarray as the result of their drinking, but who were without these physical manifestations, could not be diagnosed as alcohol-dependent. This was the case even though their drinking pattern was not that of a "social drinker" and included those for whom the consequences of use were clearly destructive. In response to this concern modifications were introduced in the DSM-III-R. In that edition, nine symptoms were listed. A diagnosis was to be made when any three were positive for a period of at least one month. This revised version of the third edition was intended to be exactly what its title suggested: a revision, an interim document until the fourth edition was prepared. The fourth edition was published in 1994.

DSM-IV criteria

Revision of the diagnostic manual is a complex process. It entails convening study groups of experts who not only review the literature but also conduct pilot tests to determine the impact of any changes being considered. In developing the fourth edition there were several issues of particular importance to those involved in preparing the section on substance use. The group felt it was important to devise a single set of criteria that would be applicable to all psychoactive substances. For example, evidence of withdrawal might be such a common feature of dependence, even though the particular symptoms would depend on the particular substance. Another area of concern was the relationship of any proposed criteria to the World Health Organization's classification system, *ICD-10*. Indeed, pilot research showed that there was a high degree of overlap between the two classification systems. If a person is diagnosed as alcohol-dependent by one standard, there is very high likelihood that he or she will be diagnosed as dependent by the other criteria.

One of the biggest issues with which the task force drafting the Substance-Related Disorders section struggled was whether to keep or drop the category of abuse. There were those who questioned whether abuse really was a separate condition, or whether it was really just "early" dependence. Because some of the same criteria are used to diagnose either condition, e.g., "use despite negative social consequences," the issue was further confused. In making diagnoses, the idea is to find the features that distinguish between illnesses, not the features that are common among them. Here research findings were able to offer some guidance. A follow-up study was conducted of individuals who had been diagnosed with alcohol abuse four years previously. The results showed that alcohol abuse did not inevitably blossom into dependence. That was true of only 30% of those reexamined. For the remaining 70%, either their problems remitted, or a pattern of abuse continued without escalating. Thus the natural history of alcohol abuse appears to differ from that of alcohol dependence. For the latter, the likelihood that dependence will "go away" without treatment is very low. The more common pattern is continued and worsening symptoms. The task force decided to retain abuse as a distinct category from dependence. The counterpart to abuse in the ICD-10 schema is "harmful use."

Finally, the task force also was aware that in some sections the DSM-III-R was not as specific as was desirable. For example, severity for dependence was to be noted as mild, moderate, or severe, with the latter being when "many criteria" beyond the minimum number required were positive.

Thus in the DSM-IV edition, the number of criteria for dependence has been reduced from nine to seven, not by deletions but by combining previously separate items. Beyond the diagnosis, there is other information that clinicians are requested to note in a medical or clinical record. They are asked to indicate if dependence occurs with or without physiological dependence. For those who are alcohol-dependent but no longer actively drinking, and in recovery, some description of their current status is important. Several options are provided to denote the extent of recovery, whether there is full or partial remission, and the duration, either early or sustained. The time interval suggested for determining that someone has achieved full sustained remission is a 12-month period. Other information to be noted in a medical or clinical record is whether the patient is living in a controlled environment, be it a half-way house or a correctional facility, and whether the patient is using specific medications that interfere with or deter intoxication. Such medications are more common in the treatment of narcotics addiction. However, disulfiram (Antabuse) would apply for those with alcohol dependence. Both of these latter situations are important because they may well have implications for the patient's ability to maintain sobriety independently.

DSM-IV DIAGNOSTIC CRITERIA

DSM-IV CRITERIA FOR ALCOHOL DEPENDENCE

The *DSM-IV* describes *alcohol dependence* as a maladaptive pattern of use leading to significant impairment or distress, when three or more of the following seven items occur in the same 12-month period:

1 Tolerance can be evidenced either as (a) a need for increased amounts of alcohol to achieve intoxication or the desired effect, or (b) diminished effect with continued use of the same amount
2 Withdrawal is the presence of characteristic signs of alcohol withdrawal, or the use of the same or closely related substance to relieve or avoid withdrawal
3 Drinking in larger amounts or over a longer period than was intended
4 A persistent desire or unsuccessful efforts to cut down or control drinking
5 Considerable time spent in activities related to drinking, or recovering from drinking episodes
6 Important social, occupational, or recreational activities given up or reduced due to drinking
7 Drinking continues even when it is known that physical or psychological problems are caused by or aggravated by continued use

DSM-IV CRITERIA FOR ALCOHOL ABUSE

The *DSM-IV* describes *alcohol abuse* as a maladaptive pattern of use leading to significant impairment or distress, when one or more of the following have occurred in a 12-month period:

1 Recurrent drinking that results in a failure to fulfill major role obligations at work, school, or home
2 Recurrent drinking when it is physically hazardous, such as while driving, or when involved with risky recreational activities
3 Recurrent alcohol-related legal problems
4 Continued drinking despite persistent social or interpersonal problems caused or aggravated by use

The criteria selected for the diagnosis of abuse do not overlap those for dependence. However, it may seem a fine line to distinguish between continued use that causes physical or psychological problems (dependence) and continued use that leads to social or interpersonal problems (abuse). But there is a difference: Drinking qualifies as abuse if it leads to problems with other people, even if there is no particular distress for the drinking person.

In addition to standards for diagnosing substance abuse and substance dependence, other substance-related conditions are addressed. These include intoxication and withdrawal, as well as several conditions that are substance-induced, such as sleep disorders and delirium (mental confusion), which are handled in other sections of the diagnostic manual.

NATURAL HISTORY OF ALCOHOLISM: JELLINEK REVISITED

In 1983 George Vaillant published *The Natural History of Alcoholism*. This book set forth the results of several studies that have been invaluable in confirming, and in many instances amplifying, our understanding of alcoholism as a disease. This work can be seen as representing an update of the work initiated more than 30 years earlier by Jellinek, when he outlined the stages of alcohol addiction. Vaillant's work is based upon two groups of men who had been followed for approximately 50 years, from their adolescence into their sixties. The major goal of the research was to study adult development through the life cycle. There was an interesting side benefit for the alcohol field, however. Not unexpectedly, during the course of the study, members from both groups developed alcoholism. Thus for the first time it became possible to begin to separate "the chicken from the egg." The question could be asked, "What are the factors that distinguish those who develop alcoholism from those who do not?"

A HARVARD ALCOHOLIC

A CORE CITY ALCOHOLIC

One group in the study, the college sample, has been officially described as "students from an Eastern university." In fact it is composed of Harvard undergraduates from the classes of 1942 to 1944. The other group, referred to as "the core city sample," is comprised of men who were from high-crime, inner-city neighborhoods. They were initially selected to participate in the study when they were about 14 years old, primarily because they were not known to be seriously delinquent. At the beginning of these studies, members of both groups were extensively interviewed. A variety of psychological tests were administered, detailed family histories were obtained, and measures of the subjects' personal functioning were made. Since that time these men have been periodically recontacted to collect detailed information on the progress of their lives.

In brief, Vaillant determined that those who became alcoholic were not more likely to have had impoverished childhoods or to have had preexisting personality or psychological problems. Therefore it was his conclusion that such problems, which are often cited as evidence of an "alcoholic personality," do not predate the emergence of the disease. On the contrary, they are the symptoms or consequences of alcohol dependence. As for predictors of alcoholism, the significant determinants were found to be a family history of alcoholism or having been raised in a culture with a high rate of alcoholism.

Several other findings are worth noting. Vaillant compared the various diagnostic classifications or diagnostic approaches. He discovered a high overlap between those people diagnosed as alcoholic (using

DSM-III criteria) and those identified as "problem drinkers" with a high "problem index"—a sociological classification system. The specific negative consequences seemed to be of little importance. However, by the time the individual had experienced four or more negative consequences as the result of drinking, it was almost assured that a formal diagnosis of alcohol dependence could be made. Virtually no one had four or more alcohol-related problems through mere "bad luck."

Also, as alcoholism progressed over time, the number of problems tended to increase and the overall life situation—psychological adjustment, economic functioning, social and family relationships—deteriorated. Vaillant observed that studies that have pointed to the contrary usually were reporting on persons who went for treatment and were recontacted at a single point. He speculates that these studies have not followed up the individuals for a sufficient length of time. While active alcoholism has a downward course, there will be, during the slide, both ups and downs. Presumably, people who enter treatment facilities do so at a low point. Therefore at follow-up, even if they continue as active alcoholics, it should not be surprising to find their situation somewhat improved. However, if follow-up were conducted at several times, the full ravages of untreated alcoholism would become apparent. As Vaillant notes, paraphrasing an AA saying, "Alcoholism is baffling, cunning, powerful, . . . and patient."

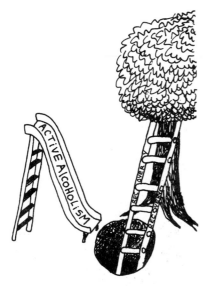

Vaillant concluded that there is indeed a progression in alcoholism (however, there is not the orderliness in symptoms' emergence that Jellinek had described). As a result of the progression, there are only two likely outcomes. The men in the study either died or recovered through abstinence. The proportion who either returned to nonproblematic drinking or whose alcoholism stabilized was very small. Again, over time, with increasing incidence of follow-up, this small middle ground continued to shrink.

In his book *The Disease Concept of Alcoholism*, Jellinek had noted that a disease is "simply anything the medical profession agrees to call a disease." By that standard, alcohol dependence has been a disease for some time. However, with the refinement of diagnostic criteria there is now far clearer guidance in identifying those who suffer from it.

OTHER DRUGS OF ABUSE

The above discussion has focused on the emergence of the current definition of alcohol dependence. There are some differences with respect to the evolution of our understanding of other drug dependence, and there are also similarities. The most striking difference in terms of other drugs of abuse is the point at which their addictive properties and the problems associated with use became evident. For the most part narcotics—such as morphine—and also cocaine were recognized as problematic before the turn of the last century. This recognition in part was prompted by the involvement of physicians in providing these drugs to patients and then being faced by the emergence of addiction. The "typical" narcotic addict at the end of the 1800s was a white female who had been prescribed narcotics for the treatment of a wide variety of "female problems." Beyond physician prescription were the hosts of patent medicines available, many of which contained narcotics.

The sad irony is that drugs believed to be medically useful and nonproblematic turned out otherwise. For example, cocaine was initially touted as being very useful in weaning people from the opiates; thus it was seen as a good means of treating opiate addicts. However, it quickly became apparent that it too created dependence and that one was simply substituting one addictive drug for another. Then there was the introduction of heroin by the Bayer Laboratory in 1898. (This centennial event was not celebrated by Bayer.) The same pharmaceutical research team that produced aspirin, synthesized heroin in the same month. It was marketed as a cough suppressant. Heroin was believed—erroneously—to be superior to other available products because it was thought not merely to suppress coughs but also to improve lung function. Had this mistake not been made, in all probability heroin would never have been manufactured. Within a decade it was recognized that heroin did not promote lung function. However, by then it had taken on a life of its own.

The societally felt indiscriminate use of such drugs by medical practitioners, popularly called "dope doctors," as well as their ready availability in over-the-counter preparations, sparked the passage of two key pieces of legislation in the United States. One was the legislation that created the Food and Drug Administration in 1906. It contained what were the earliest federal provisions affecting narcotics. Any over-the-counter preparations containing opiates, cannabis (marijuana), cocaine, or chloral hydrate needed to have a label identifying these and the relative percentage(s). The other was the passage of the Harrison Act in 1914, which classified certain drugs as "controlled substances." This meant that they could no longer be sold over-the-counter, but had to be dispensed only by physicians and for medical purposes. In the earliest days of the Harrison Act, a legitimate purpose was to provide the drugs to addicted people. However this understanding of "proper" use was rather quickly eliminated. Along with that there was the closing of the small number of clinics that had been established to provide drugs to existing addicts.

RESOURCES AND FURTHER READING

The recommended readings on this resource list might appear sorely out of date. But when assembling this list, we deliberately chose the primary, original sources for the major historical pieces of work discussed. Because this chapter reviews the evolution of the disease framework as well as approaches to diagnosis, there is considerable value in examining the original articles. Beyond allowing the authors to speak for themselves, these older classic works offer instructive insights into the views of alcoholism that then prevailed.

American Psychiatric Association: *Diagnostic and statistical manual, edition 3,* Washington DC: APA, 1980.

American Psychiatric Association: *Diagnostic and statistical manual, edition 3 (revised),* Washington DC: APA, 1987.

American Psychiatric Association: *Diagnostic and statistical manual, edition 4,* Washington DC: APA, 1994.

Brower KJ, Blow FC, Beresford TP: Treatment implications of chemical dependency models: An integrative approach, *Journal of Substance Abuse Treatment* 6(3):147–157, 1989.

Five basic models of chemical dependency and their treatment implications are described. The moral model, although disdained by most treatment professionals, actually finds expression in over half the steps of Alcoholics Anonymous. The learning model, albeit the center of the controlled-drinking controversy, is also utilized by most abstinence-oriented programs. The disease model, which enjoys current popularity, sometimes ignores the presence of coexisting disorders. The self-medication model, which tends to regard chemical dependency as a symptom, can draw needed attention to coexisting disorders. The social model emphasizes the importance of environmental and interpersonal influences in treatment, although the substance abuser may endorse it as a justification to adopt a victim's role. A sixth model, the dual diagnosis model, is presented as an example of how two of the basic models can be integrated both to expand the treatment focus and to increase treatment leverage. Whereas the five basic models are characterized by a singular, organizing treatment focus, the dual diagnosis model is viewed as an example of a multifocused, integrative model. It is concluded that effective therapy requires (1) flexibility in combining elements of different models in order to individualize treatment plans for substance abusers, and (2) careful assessment of both the therapist's and the substance abuser's beliefs about treatment models in order to ensure a treatment match based on a healthy alliance.

Criteria Committee, National Council on Alcoholism: Criteria for the diagnosis of alcoholism, *American Journal of Psychiatry* 129(2):41–49, 1972.

Hasin DS, Grant B, Endicott J: The natural history of alcohol abuse: Implications for definitions of alcohol use disorders, *American Journal of Psychiatry* 147(11):1537–1541, 1990.

Is the DSM-III-R category of alcohol abuse validly differentiated from the DSM-III-R category of alcohol dependence, or is abuse primarily a mild, prodromal condition that typically deteriorates into dependence? A 4 year longitudinal epidemiologic study of male drinkers provided data to answer this question. The study used identical questions at baseline and follow-up. At follow-up, 70% of the subjects who were initially classified as alcohol abusers were still abusers or were classified as remitted. This contrasted significantly with outcome in the subjects who initially reported alcohol dependence. Although additional research is needed, these results indicate that alcohol abuse often has a course distinct from that of alcohol dependence. (Author abstract.)

Jellinek EM: Phases of alcohol addiction, *Quarterly Journal of Studies on Alcohol* 13:673–684, 1952.

This work sets forth the natural history and the progression of the disease of alcoholism, based upon a survey of 2,000 early AA members, each of whom identified the order of symptom appearance. This study has continued to influence current views of the course of alcoholism.

Jellinek EM: *The disease concept of alcoholism*, New Haven CT: Hill House Press, 1960.

This work synthesizes research conducted by E.M. Jellinek, including his discussion of the conditions under which alcoholism might be viewed as a disease.

Rinaldi RC, Steindler EM, Wilford BB, Goodwin D: Clarification and standardization of substance abuse terminology, *Journal of the American Medical Association* 259(4):555–557, 1988.

A four-stage Delphi survey of substance abuse experts was conducted to help achieve greater clarity and uniformity in terminology associated with alcohol and other drug-related problems. This multidisciplinary group of experts was asked to reach a consensus on alcohol and other drug-related terms and definitions. Results produced a list of 50 substance abuse terms deemed important, along with the most agreed-on definition for each term. (Author abstract.)

Stepney R: The concept of addiction: Its use and abuse in the media and science, *Human Psychopharmacology* 11(Supplement 1): S15–S20, 1996. (18 refs.)

Since it relates to common and frequently troublesome aspects of human behaviour, the concept of addiction is of considerable interest to the media, as it is to the health sciences and medicine. With some exceptions, the problems that emerge from the media's use of the concept are similar to those evident in the scientific literature. The term is sometimes used simply to draw attention to a behaviour which evokes disapproval, and the concept may be applied so broadly that sight of its core meaning is lost. However, the fact that there are problems in the way we employ the concept of addiction does not mean that there is no problem of addiction. Important aspects of human experience are well captured by much lay and scientific usage of the term. These experiences involve a range of appetitive behaviours (frequently but not exclusively drug-related) which the person concerned finds genuinely difficult to control and which are the source of conflict both within and between individuals. Among drug-related behaviours, opiate use can be considered the paradigm of addiction; and it is meaningful, even if not always appropriate, to consider the addictive potential of other psychoactive drugs in relation to this standard. (Author abstract.)

Vaillant GE: *The natural history of alcoholism, revisited,* Cambridge MA: Harvard University Press, 1996.

This volume represents both a reprinting and an up-dating and reflection on a now classic work in the alcohol field, originally published fifteen year earlier. This seminal study entails a longitudinal prospective study of adult development involving two cohorts that provided the opportunity to examine the natural history of alcoholism. The significant findings were as follows: (1) There was a lack of support for the theory of an "alcoholic personality." The presumed "predisposing personality factors," or emotional problems, result from drinking in actuality. (2) The major predictors of alcoholism are a positive family history, that is, being raised in a culture whose norms proscribe childhood alcohol use, prescribe

Four Factors Associated with Recovery
(see Vaillant, G.E.)

1. A Vital Interest

How would you like to see my collection of Campbell Soup labels.

2. External Reminders

It looks lousy on the lawn— but it reminds me that I can't drink.

3. Unambivalent Social Support

We all like you even though you're wierd.

4. A Source of Hope and Inspiration

HiGHER POWER

heavy adult alcohol use, and accept intoxication. (3) With respect to diagnosis, by the time individuals have experienced four lifetime problems from use, typically they will meet any diagnostic criteria for alcoholism. (4) Treatment was not usually initiated until the occurrence of 8 to 11 lifetime problems. (5) After alcohol dependence is established, the two most common eventual outcomes are recovery or death: over the 30-year follow-up, nonproblematic drinking continually declined. (6) Successful recovery is associated with four factors: developing a vital interest that can replace the role of drinking; external reminders that drinking is painful; increased sources of unambivalently offered social support; and the presence of a source of inspiration, hope, and enhanced self-esteem.

Woody G, Schuckit M, Weinrieb R, Yu E: A review of the substance use disorder section of the DSM-IV, *Psychiatric Clinics of North America* 16(1):21–32, 1993.

In 1988 the Board of Trustees of the APA appointed a Task Force on DSM-IV to revise the *Diagnostic and Statistical Manual* to be compatible with the WHO's ICD-10. The Substance Use Disorders work group was formed to assist in the effort. A three-step process included literature reviews on selected topics, re-analysis of several preexisting data sets, and conducting of field trials in America and Europe to determine the best way to diagnose abuse and dependence. Reports from the work group suggested significant alterations to DSM-IV in several areas: the optimal criteria for abuse, modifications in the criteria for dependence, diagnostic guidelines for dealing with psychiatric syndromes in individuals with substance use disorders, further scrutiny for diagnostic criteria for remission, the need to define severity more clearly, reorganization in the notation of some substance use disorders, handling of nicotine withdrawal, and inclusion/exclusion of alcohol idiosyncratic intoxication. In addition, other reports suggested no change for DSM-IV with regard to inclusion of caffeine abuse and dependence, highlighting anabolic steroid dependence, relevance of protracted abstinence syndromes (withdrawal), a new subtype of dependence based on familial pattern of the disorder, and combination of amphetamines and cocaine into a large category, "Stimulants." (Author abstract.)

ETIOLOGY OF ALCOHOL DEPENDENCE

What is man, when you come to think upon him, but a minutely set, ingenious machine for turning, with infinite artfulness, the red wine of Shiraz into urine?

ISAK DINESEN, 1934

What are the causes of alcohol dependence? As more knowledge is gained, the answers become more complex. It may be useful to make a comparison to the common cold. Once you have "it," there isn't much question. The sneezing, the runny nose, the stuffed-up feeling that the cold tablet manufacturers describe so well leave little doubt. But why you? Because "it" was going around. Your resistance was down. Others in the family have "it." You became chilled when caught in the rain. You forgot your vitamin C. Everyone has a pet theory and usually chalks it up to a number of factors working in combination against you. Some chance factor does seem to be involved. There are times when we do not catch colds that are going around. Explaining the phenomenon cannot be done with precision. It is more a matter of figuring out the odds and probabilities as the possible contributing factors are considered.

The public health field has developed a systematic way of tackling this problem of disease, its causes, and the risks of contracting it. First, they look at the agent, the "thing" that causes the disease. Next, they consider the host, the person who has the illness, to find characteristics that may have made him or her a likely target. Finally, the environment is examined, the setting in which the agent and host come together. A thorough look at these three aspects ensures that no major influences are overlooked. With respect to alcohol and other drug problems, each of these areas is significant. Accordingly, alcohol dependence is often termed a bio-psycho-social illness, reflecting the fact that causality is seen as an interplay of *bio*logical, *psycho*logical, and *social* factors.

PUBLIC HEALTH MODEL

Alcohol dependence qualifies as a public health problem. It is among the leading causes of death in the United States. It afflicts one out of every ten adults. It touches the lives of one out of every eight children. The response to alcohol dependence is unfortunately pale compared to its impact.

From the public health viewpoint, the first sphere to be examined as a possible cause is the agent. For alcohol dependence the agent is the substance, alcohol. This is such an obvious fact that it might seem silly to dwell on it. No one can be alcohol dependent without an exposure to alcohol. The substance must be used before the possibility of dependence exists. Alcohol is an addictive substance. With sufficient quantities over long enough time, the body undergoes physical changes. When this has occurred and the substance is withdrawn, there is a physiological response, withdrawal. For alcohol there is a well-defined set of symptoms that accompanies cessation of drinking in an addicted person. Any person can be addicted to alcohol, but to use this fact alone to explain alcohol dependence represents untidy thinking. That alcohol is addicting does not explain why anyone would drink enough to reach the point of addiction. Temperance literature tried to paint a picture of an evil demon in the bottle. Take a sip, and he's got you. This is no longer a very convincing metaphor. It is obvious that drinking need not lead inevitably to a life of drunkenness. Let us look at the action of the drug itself. What invites its use and makes it a candidate for use sufficient to cause addiction?

THE AGENT

We take any number of substances into our bodies, from meats to sweets, as solids or liquids. Although everyone overeats occasionally, to consider habitual overeating as a form of "substance" abuse, or the associated craving as just as powerful as that associated with drugs, is a very recent concept. A physiological basis for this has not been identified. However, in the case of alcohol, the physiological effects themselves suggest some of the reasons it is such a likely candidate for heavy chronic use. First, alcohol is a depressant drug. One of its first effects is on the central nervous system, the "higher" centers related to judgment, inhibition, and the like. What is more important is what this feels like, how it is experienced. With mild intoxication comes relaxation, a more carefree feeling. It is generally experienced as pleasant, a high. Preexisting tensions are relieved. A good mood can be accentuated. Alcohol is experienced as changing mood for the better. This capacity of alcohol is one factor to remember in trying to understand use sufficient for dependence.

A common expression is "I sure could use a drink now." It may be said after a hard day at work, after a round of good physical exercise, or after a period of chaos and emotional stress. This expression certainly includes the awareness that alcohol can influence our emotional state. Equally as important is the word *now*. There is a recognition that the effects are immediate. Not only does alcohol make a difference, it does so very rapidly. If alcohol had a delayed reaction time, say 3 days, or 3 weeks, or even 3 hours, it wouldn't be a useful method to alter our feelings. The unpredictability of people's lives makes drinking now for what may happen later seem quite pointless. So its speed in altering emotional states is another characteristic of the drug alcohol that enhances its likelihood for overuse.

Alcohol has another characteristic common to all depressant drugs. With mild inebriation, behavior is less inhibited; there are feelings of relaxation. However, at the same time there is a gradual increase of psychomotor activity. While feeling the initial glow, the drinker is unaware of this. As the warm glow subsides, the increased psychomotor activity will become apparent, often experienced as a wound-up and edgy feeling similar to that caused by too many cups of coffee or caffeinated soft drinks. The increase in psychomotor activity builds up gradually. Since it is delayed and its onset masked, the drinker is not very likely to recognize the feeling as a product of the alcohol use. This phenomenon is akin to a mini-hangover. Possibly some people, including those not

Candy is dandy
But liquor is quicker.
OGDEN NASH

The peculiar charm of alcohol lies in the sense of careless well-being and bodily comfort which it creates. It unburdens the individual of his cares and fears. Under such conditions it is easy to laugh or to weep, to love or to hate, not wisely but too well.

DR. HAVEN EMERSON, Alcohol and Man.

dependent upon alcohol, have a second or third drink "to relax" and in fact to get rid of the very feelings created by the earlier ones.

What is being discussed here is the abuse potential of the drug alcohol. *Abuse potential* refers to the likelihood that individuals will chose to readminister the drug. There are ways of studying the abuse potential of a drug in a laboratory setting. For example, given a choice of two substances, both of which have been sampled, which one will people choose if given a choice of one over the other? If there is a marked preference for drug A, rather than drug B, then A is the one with more likelihood of being abused. Another approach is to compare a new drug to one with a known level of abuse. Here the question is, "Which will people choose?" If people are given two choices, with one being a drug, and the other a placebo—meaning it is inert without any psychoactive properties —is there any preference? If the drug is not selected more frequently than the "nondrug" it has a very low abuse potential. In essence people don't feel different than if they'd taken nothing. Another method is to ask people to rate the effects of a drug: "How does it make you feel? Is it pleasant? Would you want to take it again? In addition, they can be asked to rate the drug in comparison to other substances. If someone's eyes light up, and a smile comes to the face as the person describes his or her response to the drug, watch out—the drug has a greater likelihood of abuse than if they are unimpressed by its effects or find it unpleasant.

Beyond the immediate effects of the drug there are other related factors that influence abuse potential. As a general rule, the quicker the effects are felt the greater the likelihood of abuse. And at the same time, the more rapidly the drug effects disappear, the greater its abuse potential. Typically the drugs with the highest abuse potential are those that you take and almost immediately it's "wow!" The desired effects are immediate. It's truly magic. This occurs most often with inhaling or injecting, which deliver the drug to the brain quickly. But the speed of delivery is only part of the story. The other factor that influences abuse potential is how rapidly these desired effects fade. If drugs have a dramatic impact but with a short duration, this invites re-administration. What further increases the odds of re-administration and increases the likelihood of abuse is when the drug has unpleasant effects as it wears off. By way of example, in terms of abuse potential, cocaine ranks right up there on all counts. Forget the hour or so that may be needed for one to feel alcohol; with the ingestion of cocaine it is literally seconds. This is clearly captured by the language used to describe cocaine's effects. It is described as a "rush," not as a "warm glow" or a "buzz," the phrases heard with alcohol. However, the euphoria fades quickly. The effects dissipate within 10 to 30 minutes depending on whether the cocaine was snorted or injected. As the effects wane there is the inevitable "crash," characterized as feelings of dysphoria, a general negative-feeling state. Among drinkers the vast majority are properly described as social drinkers; of those who use cocaine regularly, there are far, far fewer "social snorters."

THE HOST—GENETIC FACTORS

The belief that alcoholism runs in families has long been a part of the folk wisdom. If not in your childhood then certainly in your parent's, a great-aunt may well have explained away the town drunk with "He's his father's son." No further comment was presumed necessary. The obvious truth was clear: many of life's misfortunes are the result of "bad" genes. Historically, just such an understanding of genetics, supported by warped theological views, led to statutes that authorized the sterilization of the feebleminded, the hopelessly insane, as well as the chronically drunk.

Such an approach has fallen into disrepute. It is now clear that heredity is not as simple as it seemed. Each individual, at the point of conception, receives a unique set of genetic material. This material is like a set of internal "instructions" that guide the individual's growth and development. In many instances, the genetic endowment simply sets down limits, or predispositions. The final outcome will depend on the life situation and environment in which the person finds, or places, him- or herself. Thus some people tend to be slim and some tend to put on weight easily. Such a tendency is probably genetic. In large measure, however, whether people are fat, thin, or just right depends on them.

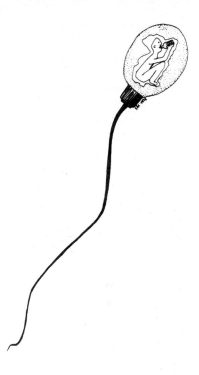

Nature versus nurture

What are the facts about the role of heredity in alcohol dependence? Actually, alcohol dependence does run in families. The child of an alcohol dependent parent is more likely to become similarly alcohol troubled. One study tracing family trees found that 50% of the descendants of alcoholics were themselves also alcoholic. Though that figure is a bit higher than other similar studies, it is a dramatic example of the typical finding that suggests that the offspring of those who are alcohol-dependent have a four-times-greater risk of developing the disease.

The observations of those working in the area of alcohol rehabilitation and treatment lend anecdotal support to the view of a constitutional vulnerability. Some clients encountered will report a major alcohol problem very early in life, often by the time of adolescence, that progressed rapidly in the absence of any unique identifiable psychological stress. Similarly, at AA meetings the remark may be heard, "I was an alcoholic from my first drink." Usually this means that for seemingly idiosyncratic reasons the speaker never drank "normally" as did peers, but used, and was affected by, alcohol differently. Interestingly, back in 1940, Jellinek recognized a possible hereditary factor and suggested a distinguishable "familial" type of alcoholism. (This is described in Chapter 4.)

Yet something running in families is not proof that it is inherited. After all, speaking French runs in families—in France. Separating nature from nurture is a complex but necessary job. Certainly, an alcohol-dependent, actively drinking parent would be expected to have an impact on a growing child. It is not unreasonable to expect that

Drunkards beget drunkards.
PLUTARCH

Heredity. The heredity of form and the heredity of mental traits and character are unquestioned. Inebriety belongs to the same class, and has been recognized as hereditary for all ages. On one of the monuments of Egypt there is a drawing of a drunkard father and several drunken children, and the grouping conveys the idea that the inebriety of the parent was the direct cause of the children's disgrace.

SPOONER WALTER W.
The Cyclopaedia of Temperance and Prohibition, 1891.

inherent in the family lies the soil of addiction. Yet again, the simple fact that this sounds reasonable does not make it true.

The current understanding is that heredity plays a significant role in the development of alcohol dependence in some people. Research to determine which people, and by which mechanisms, is exploding, and much has been learned since the early 1970s. There are different types of research which shed light on this question from different angles. These different types of studies are described below. Ultimately, if heredity is a factor, there must be some basic biochemical differences between those who are prone to develop alcohol dependence and those who are not. But the initial task was simply to establish the extent to which alcohol dependence does or does not run in families.

Twin and adoption studies

Methods of scientific investigation using an experimental model are not possible in the task of separating human nature and nurture. We can't ask some families to raise children one way and other families to raise their children differently so that the differences might be determined! Human research requires locating individuals with particular life experiences or characteristics and then comparing them to those with other backgrounds. Twin studies and adoption studies are the two classical methods for doing this. Donald Goodwin is a clinician-researcher who conducted some of the important initial work on the topic of alcoholism and the role of genetics. Many of his (and others') studies have used data from Scandinavia, because these countries keep very complete records of marriages, births, and so on. This makes tracing families easier.

One early study was based on a large sample of twins. In each set, one twin was alcoholic. The researchers determined whether the twins were identical or fraternal. Then they interviewed the twin of the known alcoholic. The prediction: if alcoholism has a hereditary basis, the other twin of identical sets would be more likely also to be alcoholic than if he were a fraternal twin. This assumption was made because identical twins share the same genetic material. That proved to be the case. However, the hereditary endowment does not act to totally dictate the development of alcoholism, because not all the identical twins were both alcoholic. It was further discovered that an apparent predisposition exists toward having, or being spared, the social deterioration associated with alcoholism. If both twins were alcoholic, the best predictor of the other twin's life situation was not how much or how long he had been drinking. The life situation of the first twin was more reliable. So there appears to be a hereditary predisposition both to alcoholism and the social problems associated with it.

An adoption study conducted by Goodwin, using Danish subjects, further supported the influence of heredity. He traced children born to an alcoholic parent. These children had been adopted by the age of 6 weeks. He compared them to adopted children of nonalcoholic biological parents. The adoptive families of both groups were essentially the same. He discovered that those who had a biological parent who was alcoholic were themselves more likely to develop alcoholism in adulthood. Thus alcoholism cannot be attributed simply to the home environment. While these earliest studies involved only males, subsequent research suggests that there is a similar genetic predisposition among women.

Further studies have helped separate the relative influence of genetic makeup and home environment. These studies have used half-siblings. Of the half-siblings, one had an alcoholic parent, the other did not. Thus one of the children had a biological predisposition while the other did not. These half-brothers and half-sisters were raised together in the same home. In some cases both were reared in a nonalcoholic family. In other cases, both grew up in a home with an alcoholic parent. As expected, those with a genetic background positive for alcoholism were themselves more likely to develop alcoholism as adults. Of equal significance was the finding that being reared in a home with an active alcoholic did not further increase the chances of developing alcoholism. This was true for both the biologically at-risk children and their half-brothers and half-sisters who did not have a biological predisposition. This finding has been confirmed by other studies. Growing up in a home with an alcoholic parent does not add to the risk of developing alcoholism. Such findings provided strong support for the importance of the genetic predisposition in some cases of alcoholism.

Studies of nonalcoholic blood relatives

With the presence of a genetic factor established, the next step was to understand the nature of this genetic predisposition. The National Institute on Alcohol Abuse and Alcoholism established a major research effort, the Collaborative Study on the Genetics of Alcoholism, to undertake such study. As noted above, any genetic difference between those biologically prone to alcohol dependence and those who are not will be manifested in some biochemical differences. Efforts are underway to explore what biochemical differences distinguish between these two groups. The major hypotheses are that there are differences in the way our bodies handle alcohol and how our brains experience its effects. The differences could conceivably be differences of metabolism, or differences in response to chronic exposure to ethanol, or possibly a unique response to a single dose. For example, those at high risk may experience greater pleasure and those at low risk more discomfort.

What does the research to date show?

• One group of studies has looked at how alcohol's effects are experienced. These have used young men who exhibit no symptoms of alcohol dependence but who have an alcoholic blood relative. Those having an alcohol dependent family member typically describe a lesser response to a single dose of alcohol than do those with no alcoholic blood relative. To translate this—those with a family history of alcoholism didn't feel as "high" as did those who had no family history of alcohol dependence. So think about it: if feeling alcohol's effects is a significant part of drinking, then those with a family history will need to drink more than their peers. This may increase their risks for dependence.

This difference in response to alcohol proved to be important. Follow-up studies eight years later indicates that those who had a markedly less-ened response to alcohol were 4 times more likely to themselves be alcohol dependent. 56% of the subjects with a low alcohol response had developed alcoholism, versus only 14% of those with high levels of sensitivity. Notice here the comparison was no longer on the basis of having or not having an alcohol dependent relative. The comparison was the response to alcohol's effects. But having alcoholism in the family stacked the deck in terms of the chances of being a high or low responder.

• In a similar vein, other studies have explored other responses to alcohol. One such study determined that those with a family history of alcoholism have greater muscle relaxation with a single dose of alcohol than those without such a family background. After drinking, those at high risk are more likely to have brain alpha-wave activity, as measured by electroencephalogram (EEG). Such brain waves are associated with feelings of relaxation.

• High-risk subjects, those with a family history of alcohol dependence, perform less well on portions of standard neuropsychological tests. Such tests measure a variety of different cognitive functions. This finding is noteworthy because it long has been recognized that those who are alcohol dependent do poorly on some of these tests, such as a test for abstracting ability. However, their diminished performance had always been presumed to be the result of brain damage from heavy drinking. Now the question has to be whether or not this condition predates the dependence.

• Finally, there also appears to be a difference in metabolism. In one study, a group of presently nonalcoholic young men with an alcoholic father or brother showed greater acetaldehyde levels during alcohol metabolism than another similar group who did not have an alcoholic family member. Much higher levels of acetaldehyde often accompany drinking in many Asians. These higher levels produce a disulfiram-like reaction, which discourages alcohol consumption and thereby provides protection against the development of alcoholism. Paradoxically though, with a modest increase of acetaldehyde, the addiction process may be facilitated.

The differences described above have often been considered as deficiencies, as something "missing" or "lacking." It is now being recognized that what is inherited may not necessarily be a deficiency but might, paradoxically, be a "strength." In other words, some people might inherit an ability to handle alcohol "too well." They may be more immune to negative physical consequences of drinking such as nausea and hangovers, or be able to function better than the average person when alcohol is ingested. If so, those who are alcoholism-prone are deprived of the very cues that may keep drinking in check for others.

Genetic markers

Genetics research is growing increasingly sophisticated. It is now possible not only to examine genes directly but also to manipulate them. A massive national research program is underway called the "Human Genome Project." The goal is to create a map of all genetic material. For the field of biology, this is a challenge similar to that of space exploration and landing a person on Mars. The task of identifying the function of individual genes is especially important in light of other related advances. Techniques have been developed that allow the altering of defective portions of genes. People now speak of "gene therapy" or "genetic engineering." This provides the potential for treating illnesses that are known to be caused by a specific genetic abnormality. It is more than treatment as we usually think about it, because the source of the disease is totally removed.

The earliest genetic marker studies, pre-molecular biology, were relatively straightforward. They attempted to link alcohol dependence to other traits that were known to be inherited. If such associations could be identified, this would indicate the gene responsible. Some of the characteristics examined for an association with alcoholism were blood type, an inherited type of color blindness, and the ability to taste or not to taste particular chemicals. This work continues.

Animal studies too have offered valuable insights. The findings cannot be directly generalized to humans; however, work with chimps, baboons, and rats can shed light on the promising areas for human investigation and provide clues. Among the more interesting early animal studies was the discovery of "drinking rats." Different strains of rats were given a choice of water or water spiked with alcohol of differing concentrations. Inevitably, they sampled each and usually opted for plain water. They would drink the alcohol-water solution only when it was the sole liquid available. However, several strains of rats were important exceptions. They preferred alcohol and water solutions of around 5%, which translates to 10 proof. These "drinking rats" could be inbred to produce offspring that preferred even higher alcohol concentrations.

But do these rats develop a condition that would appear to resemble alcohol dependence? Seemingly they do—there are some strains that consistently chose to drink alcohol and reach a BAC of .5 to .20. These rats will "work" (press a bar) to obtain alcohol. In addition, the alcohol's attraction is not merely its taste or smell. They select it over other favorite foods or drinks; they will even self-administer alcohol directly into the stomach. These rats seek alcohol for its pharmacological properties. Furthermore there is evidence of tolerance, as well as differences in initial sensitivity to alcohol.

The studies of drinking rats have offered some other insights. Other behaviors were noticed amongst the drinking rats that distinguished them from their nondrinking counterparts. As several of the observed differences have parallels to human behaviors, they may shed some light on factors that give impetus to drinking. For example, the drinking rats were described as having an innately higher level of activity when presented with a new or novel environment. They are more inclined to explore. They are also described as more anxious.

But the basic question remains, what is the inherited "something?" The speculation is that the difference lies somewhere in the brain chemistry. This brings to light one area in which alcohol is different than other drugs. There is no one single receptor in the brain that has been identified as uniquely linked to alcohol. By contrast, we know that there are special sites in the brain, such as opiate receptors, or nicotine receptors, or benzodiazepine receptors, which are responsible for at least a significant part of those drugs' effects. So in the absence of a special alcohol receptor, the assumption is that alcohol must affect or alter the function of a wide range of the usual, "everyday" receptors and neurotransmitters that serve as the communications system for the central nervous system. The area of particular interest is the neurotransmitters—dopamine, serotonin, GABA, and the naturally occurring internal opioid systems.

Here too animal studies have been helpful. The drinking and nondrinking rats differ with respect to their brain chemistry. In some instances there are more or lesser amounts of a particular enzyme. Or, there can be more or fewer receptors that are available to respond to these chemicals. Also, differences exist in the concentration of these receptors in different parts of the brain. The range of possible factors in combination can boggle the mind. By current count, for serotonin, just one of the many different neurotransmitters, there are seven different receptor cells. Quite conceivably, each could respond to the presence of alcohol differently.

What about human studies? A study published in 1990, involving human subjects, at the time seemed a major breakthrough in the understanding of alcoholism's genetic basis. The excitement proved to be a bit premature. In hindsight it is recognized that possibly we were a bit naive in thinking it could be so easy. The particular research involved examination of genetic material in the brain tissue of persons with alcoholism and comparing it to genes in the brain tissue of nonalcoholics. Of particular interest was a gene, known as D_2, that is associated with the brain's receptors for dopamine, a neurotransmitter. Dopamine is one of the neurochemicals in the brain that is involved with the sensation of pleasure. The receptor is the site where this neurochemical acts. It was found that there are two different forms of this gene. Different forms of a gene are called alleles. As a point for comparison, think of the gene for eye color as having different alleles. One allele corresponds to brown eyes, another to blue eyes, and so on. The researchers discovered that there were two forms of the dopamine receptor gene. In the shorthand that geneticists use, these gene variations are referred to as A_1 and A_2. Of special interest was whether or not alcoholism was associated with a particular form of the gene. Indeed that was found to be so. Among those with alcoholism, 69% had the A1 allele. Only 20% of those without alcoholism had that version. This kind of association suggested that the A1 gene may act to increase the susceptibility to alcoholism. Its presence does not make alcohol dependence inevitable, or one would expect a 100% association. Likewise, the absence was not seen as providing immunity.

Other researchers had difficulty in reproducing the findings of the 1990 study, which raised the question of whether the first results were just a fluke, a matter of chance. (Sort of like winning the lottery, statistically improbable but it does happen.) Well, almost ten years later, the answer seems to be, "No it wasn't, but. . ." The initial study comprised its alcoholic group from those who had "very severe" alcoholism. This is the variety of alcohol dependence that is now seen as most likely to have a genetic component. Equally important, the comparison group was carefully selected for the absence of alcoholism. This control population is described as being "super normal." (Because alcohol dependence is *so* common, unless one makes a clear point of excluding alcoholics, the chances are that within a random assortment of people some will be alcoholic.) Further research that similarly restricted their samples also found associations between the A1 gene and alcohol dependence.

Other research on the D_2 gene has suggested other relationships. It has been found that D_2 plays a role in how alcohol is metabolized. One form of the D_2 gene is associated with the flushing that is common in some Asians in its promotion of faster metabolism of aldehyde dehydrogenase (see Chapter 2). The D_2 gene also seems to be implicated in the differences in cognitive style and neuropsychological functioning that were found in looking at people at risk for alcohol dependence.

The current wisdom is that no single gene will prove to be *the* genetic basis for alcohol dependence. What is presumed is that there are a number of genes that may function both independently as well as in concert. Our genetic makeup may well determine our susceptibility not simply to alcohol dependence but also to organ damage associated with heavy drinking, or the severity of withdrawal, as well as our susceptibility to other drug dependencies and some co-occurring psychiatric disorders.

Research indicates that other substance dependence too is influenced by genetic factors, in a similar fashion.

Familial versus nonfamilial alcoholism: So what?

Given the strong evidence for the role of a genetic factor in some cases of alcohol dependence, it is being suggested that we routinely begin to think in terms of at least two types of alcoholism: familial and nonfamilial. The familial form is believed to be characterized by a positive family history of alcohol dependence, an earlier age of onset, and more "destructive" symptoms. This necessitates and leads to treatment at a relatively young age. This form involves no increased likelihood of other psychiatric illness. On the other hand, the nonfamilial type is seen as having a later onset. It is also characterized by less virulent symptoms.

With a genetic vulnerability clearly established, how might this information be used clinically? Certainly, the issue is relevant to prevention efforts. But how might it also be useful in treating alcohol dependence? In what is clearly a very preliminary and pilot effort, there has been some exploration of the impact of medications that effect dopamine activity. In one study the alcoholics with the D_2 gene associated with dopamine deficiency who received such medication reported less craving, less anxiety, and less depression. They were less likely to drop out of treatment. This medication certainly does not cure alcohol dependence. It would seem to address biochemical problems that may allow people to participate in treatment and decrease the likelihood of relapse.

THE HOST—PERSONALITY AND PSYCHOLOGICAL MAKEUP

It is important to note at the outset of this section that in the not-too-distant past, psychological factors were seen as *the* single most important predictors and/or precursors of future alcoholism. The "bio" and the "social" elements in what we now see as a biopsychosocial illness received far less attention. There are probably several reasons for this. Research on alcoholism stopped during prohibition. "No alcohol—no problem" was the short-lived attitude. Much of what we now take for "fact" was established only recently. Until 1953, the DTs were thought to be caused by malnutrition, not by alcohol withdrawal. It was only in 1973 that fetal alcohol syndrome was described in the scientific literature in the United States. Until 1976, it was thought that cirrhosis of the liver was due wholly to malnutrition. Molecular biology, a field that can help identify the basic mechanisms for a genetic predisposition, is a very new medical science. It wasn't that long ago that cloning sheep was in the realm of science fiction.

Given how little was known about the basic medical facts, it is not surprising that people looked to psychological explanations to understand the origins of alcoholism. Particular attention was directed to defining the nature and origins of what was presumed to be the "alcoholic personality."

Psychological needs

It is now generally recognized that our behavior is at least partially determined by factors of which we are unaware. What are these factors? Our grade school social studies classes usually focused on food, clothing, and shelter as the three basic human needs. But there are emotional needs, just as real and important, if people are to survive healthy and happily. What do we need in this realm? Baruch, in her book *New Ways of Discipline: You and Your Child Today* (published in 1949, so now hardly new!), put it this way:

> What are the emotional foods that every human being must have regardless of age? What are the basic emotional requirements that must come to every small infant, to every growing child, to every adult?
>
> In the first place, there must be affection and a lot of it. Real, down-to-earth, sincere loving. The kind that carries the conviction through body warmth, through touch, through the good mellow ring of the voice, through the fond look that says as clearly as words, "I love you because you are you."
>
> Closely allied with being loved should come the sure knowledge of belonging, of being wanted, the glow of knowing oneself to be a part of some bigger whole. Our town, our school, our work, our family—all bring the sound of togetherness, of being united with others, not isolated or alone.
>
> Every human being also needs to have the nourishment of pleasure that comes through the senses. Color, balanced form and beauty to meet the eye, harmonious sounds to meet the ear. The heady enjoyment of touch and taste and smell. And finally, the realization that the pleasurable sensations of sex can be right and fine and a part of the spirit as well as the body.
>
> Everyone must feel that he is capable of achievement. He needs to develop the ultimate conviction, strong within him, that he can do things, that he is adequate to meet life's demands. He needs also the satisfaction of knowing that he can gain from others recognition for what he does.
>
> And most important, each and every one of us must have acceptance and understanding. We need desperately to be able to share our thoughts and feelings with some other person, or several, who really understand. . . . We yearn for the deep relief of knowing that we can be ourselves with honest freedom, secure in the knowledge that says, "This person is with me. He accepts how I feel!"*

If these needs are not satisfactorily met, the adult is not whole. A useful notion in assessing what has happened is to think of the unmet needs as "holes." Everybody has some holes. They vary in number, size, and pattern. And too, some holes may prove to be more debilitating than others. What is true for all is that holes are painful. Attempts are made to cover up, patch over, or camouflage our holes so we can feel more whole, less vulnerable, and more presentable.

Early psychological approaches

Historically, through the 1960s a variety of personality theories were applied to the problem of alcoholism. Each represented an attempt to categorize the nature of the "holes," their origins, and why alcohol is used to

*Baruch D. *New Ways of Discipline: You and Your Child Today.* New York: McGraw-Hill, 1949.

cover them up. Although seemingly logical enough at the time, there were several major flaws in these studies. One was that the people being studied were already alcoholics. The idea that an "alcoholic personality" might be a result of the disorder rather than an underlying cause was overlooked. One of the strengths of George Vaillant's work in the 1980s was that he began not with alcoholics, but with individuals before their development of alcoholism. In effect, he studied large samples of people over time, beginning in late adolescence. Some of these people later developed alcoholism, and others did not. Thus he was able to see what actually were the predictors of the disease.

Personality theories applied to alcoholism

Among the theories of personality that shaped early thinking, the first was the psychoanalytical, based on the work of Sigmund Freud. Freud himself never devoted attention to alcoholism. However, his followers did apply aspects of his theory to the disease. It is impossible to present briefly the whole of Freud's work. He recognized that psychological development is related to physical growth. He identified stages of development, each with its particular, peculiar hurdles that a child must overcome on the way to being a healthy adult. Tripping over one of the hurdles, he felt, led to difficulties in adulthood.

Some of the events of childhood are especially painful, difficult, and anxiety-producing. They may persist unrelieved by the environment. This makes the child feel incompetent, resulting in a "hole." The child seeks unique ways to patch over the holes. However, the existence of the hole shapes future behavior. It may grow larger, requiring more patchwork. The hole may render the child more vulnerable to future stress and lead to new holes.

The concept of oral fixation was used in applying psychoanalytic theory to alcoholism. This meant the holes began in earliest childhood. Observe infants and see how very pleasurable and satisfying nursing and sucking are. Almost any "disease" or discomfort can be soothed this way. Individuals whose most secure life experiences were associated with this period will tend to resort to similar behaviors in times of stress. These people will also, as adults, tend to have the psychological characteristics of that life period. The major psychological characteristics of the oral period are infants' egocentricity and inability to delay having their needs met. They're hungry when they're hungry, be it a convenient time from mother's viewpoint or not. And they're oblivious to other people except as they fit into their world. Thus alcoholics, according to this theory, were likely to be individuals who never fully matured beyond infancy. They were stuck with childlike views of the world and childlike ways of dealing with it. They were easily frustrated, impatient, demanding, wanting what they wanted when they wanted it. They had little trust that people could help meet their needs. They were anxious and felt very vulnerable to the world. According to this theory, nursing a drink seemed an appropriate way of handling discomforts. Alcohol was doubly attractive because it worked quickly: bottled magic.

Another psychoanalytic concept, applied to male alcoholics, was that of latent homosexuality. (It needs to be pointed out that homosexuality, like alcoholism, is far better understood today. It is no longer considered a "disease." Being gay or lesbian is no longer seen as caused by psychological problems. Sexual identification is seen as genetically established. One does not choose to be homosexual any more than one chooses to be six feet tall.) The earlier thinking was that the origins of alcoholism were rooted in the oedipal period, which corresponds to the preschool and kindergarten age. According to Freud, an inevitable part of every little boy's growing up is a fantasy love affair with his mother. There is an accompanying desire to get Dad out of the picture. Given the reality of Dad's size, he has a clear advantage in the situation. The little boy eventually gives up and settles on being like Dad, rather than taking his place. Through this identification process, the little boy assumes a male role. Several possible hitches can occur. Maybe the father is absent, or the father is not a very attractive model. In such instances, the child will not grow to manhood with a sense of himself as a healthy, whole male. As an adult he may turn to alcohol to instill a sense of masculinity. Or he may like drinking because it provides a socially acceptable format for male companionship.

Other personality theorists focused on different characteristics. Adler latched onto the feelings of dependency. He saw the roots of alcoholism as being planted in the first 5 years of life and tied to feelings of inferiority and pessimism. The feelings of inferiority, or the longing for a sense of power, may require strong proofs of superiority for satisfaction. If continuing into adulthood, as new problems arise and create anxiety, the person may seek a sense of feeling superior rather than really overcoming difficulties. So theoretically, drinking as a solution is, to the alcoholic, intelligent. Alcohol does temporarily reduce the awareness of anxiety and gives relief from feelings of inferiority.

In 1960, William and Joan McCord published *Origins of Alcoholism.* Their studies used extensive data collected on 255 boys throughout their childhoods. What they found negated many of the psychoanalytic theories. Oral tendencies, latent homosexuality, and strong maternal encouragement of dependency were not, in fact, predictors of alcoholism. The McCords' work highlighted the complexity of the social and psychological interactions.

On the heels of this research was the emergence in the 1960s of what was called the human potential, or personal growth movement. In essence it was devoted not to "curing" mental illness but to applying the expertise of psychology and psychiatry to assist "normal" people to function better (whatever that meant to them). Tied in with this was the emergence of new personality theories. Two of these, Transactional Analysis and Reality Therapy, were applied to the problem of alcoholism.

Learning theories

Another branch of psychology provided a very different orientation to the etiology of alcoholism. These arise from the learning theorists, who see behavior as being a result of learning, motivated by an individual's attempt to minimize unpleasantness and maximize pleasure. What is pleasant is a very individual thing. A child might misbehave and be "punished," but the punishment, for that child, might be a reward and more pleasant than being ignored. Thus what is pleasant or rewarding is very much a factor of the environment.

In applying learning theory to alcoholism, the idea was that alcoholic drinking has a reward system. Alcohol, or its effects, are sufficiently reinforcing to cause continuation of drinking by the individual. Behavior most easily learned is that with immediate, positive results. The warm glow and feeling of well-being associated with the first sips are more reinforcing than the negative morning-after hangover. This theory would hold that anyone could become alcoholic if the drinking were sufficiently reinforced. Vernon Johnson, founder of a highly successful treatment program and author of the book *I'll Quit Tomorrow* gave great emphasis to the importance of learning in explaining drinking. He noted that those who use alcohol have learned from their first drink that alcohol is exceedingly trustworthy. It works every time and it does good things. This learning is highly successful, being sufficient to set up a lifetime relationship with alcohol. The relationship may alter gradually over time, finally becoming a destructive one, but the original positive reinforcement keeps the person seeking the "good old days" and minimizing the destructive elements. Seen in this light, alcoholic people are not so far distant from people who remain in what are now unsatisfactory marriages, jobs, or living situations out of habit or some hope that the original zest will return.

Current thinking

There is no longer an effort to explain alcoholism exclusively on the basis of individual personality. However, it is recognized that individual factors can and do play a role. The issue now is to better understand how individuals, given their particular genetic and physical makeup, interact with their environment. Probably the field of psychology is one area that is most sensitive to the different contributing factors from these domains. In an earlier edition of this book we referred to this as "the slot machine approach." To be alcoholic requires getting three cherries. An individual may be born with one cherry thanks to his or her genetic makeup. The culture in which the individual is raised may provide a second or sociological cherry. And the psychological makeup may confer a third cherry. Or there may be some variation: say two-thirds genetic and one-third psychological. But one lone cherry is not an accurate predictor of who becomes alcoholic.

There are a number of areas of psychological inquiry with particular relevance to alcohol dependence. One is the role of expectancies. How does what we believe about alcohol, our expectation, determine our response? What are the different sources of information that give rise to our beliefs, and how do these change? What is the relative influence of peers versus family? How does the relative weight of these shift as children move from pre-adolescence through young adulthood? The research suggests that expectancies of alcohol's effects are important in drinking behavior. There are multiple sources of these beliefs. Some come from the larger cultural landscape, including everything from alcohol advertising to the depiction of alcohol use in TV and movies. There is also the culture of the family, how we see alcohol being used, the kinds of occasions, the kinds of behavior that occur in the presence of drinking, and the related attitudes.

The field of psychology has also been examining the issue of temperament—similar to but different than personality. Temperament is not thought to be merely or purely the product of life experiences or parenting styles. Rather, temperament represents an innate predisposition that influences one's ways of tackling the world. People seem to have some innate tendency to be risk-takers or to avoid risk taking, to welcome novelty or like things to be more predictable. Whether one is shy or outgoing, adventuresome or cautious, in part seems to be a biological given. Also there seem to be predispositions toward different cognitive styles. These have some bearing on how we tackle problem solving, as well as the degree to which we consider future consequences of actions.

The following traits and behavior patterns have been identified as risk factors for future alcohol or other drug problems. Some of these are seemingly interrelated. It is important to consider each of the following traits as existing on a continuum rather than as their being present or absent.

- *Cognitive structure.* Those who dislike ambiguity and desire to make decisions based on definite knowledge are at reduced risk.
- *Harm avoidance.* Those who dislike "exciting activities," especially involving potential physical dangers, are at reduced risk.
- *Impulsivity.* Those who are more willing to act on the spur of the moment, or speak their mind freely, or not hide their emotions, are at higher risk.
- *Playfulness.* Those who describe themselves as liking to do things "just for fun," or spend substantial time in games, sports, and social activity, are at higher risk.
- *Disinhibition/sensation seeking.* Those who are extroverts and like to take both social and even physical risks just for the sake of having the experience, and like spontaneous unplanned activities are at higher risk.
- *Stressful life events.* The presence of painful, stressful experiences increase the risk of future substance use problems. Such events can include the divorce of parents or other serious life disruption such as a parent's loss of a job, or serious illness, death in the family, domestic violence, or physical or sexual abuse.

Such traits are considered lifelong predispositions. They are seen as predispositions that can be and are modified by experience and learning, however. For example "liking novelty" at age 63 probably looks far different than what it looked like when the same person was 17 years old. The same with impulsivity.

In addition, there are some psychiatric disorders that are recognized to be correlated with substance abuse problems in adulthood. These include conduct disorders, antisocial personality disorders, and attention deficit hyperactivity disorder. (See Chapter 11 for further discussion.) If or how these might contribute to substance abuse problems is not clear, but what is evident is that they are risk factors, meaning they signal the greater likelihood of a later substance abuse problem.

The other side of the coin from risk factors is protective factors. It is important to be alert not only to things that might signal a potential problem but also those that will reduce the likelihood of this. What traits and life experiences serve to shield someone from developing alcohol problems and alcoholism? If one were to boil them all down, it might be said that the basic psychological needs outlined above were met and in some abundance. In brief, those who have positive social bonds to family, to community, to school, to a religious community are less likely to develop problems later.

THE ENVIRONMENT—SOCIOLOGICAL FACTORS

Cultural orientation

Statistically, the odds of becoming an alcoholic have in the past varied significantly from country to country. This is *not* a matter of genetic differences. The genetic differences *within* racial and ethnic groups are greater than the differences *between* groups. Alcohol consumption varies widely from country to country. See Table 5.1. Equally important is the differences in attitudes and customs that prevail.

Studies in epidemiology once showed that the Irish, French, Chileans, and Americans had a high incidence of alcoholism. The Italians, Chinese, and Portuguese had substantially lower rates. The difference seemed to lie with the country's habits and customs. Indeed whether someone drinks at all depends as much on culture as it does on individual characteristics. With television, jet travel, etc., differences between cultural groups are less clear-cut than they once were. However, historically the differences in rates of alcoholism from culture to culture were substantial enough to provoke study and research. Just as genetic and psychological approaches fall short of fully explaining the phenomenon of alcoholism, so do cultural differences. But a review of past studies is useful in considering the ways in which broad cultural attitudes seemingly contribute to high rates of alcoholism, or, conversely, to identify those attitudes that promote moderate use.

Culture includes the unwritten rules and beliefs by which a group of people live. Social customs set the ground rules for behavior. The rules

TABLE 5.1   THE TOP 10 CHART: INTERNATIONAL COMPARISONS OF PER CAPITA ALCOHOL CONSUMPTION*

			Per capita Consumption (liters of alcohol, total population 1995)						
			Beverage Type						
Ranking	Country	Total	Spirits		Beer		Wine		
1.	Luxembourg	11.6L	1. Russia	4.60L	1. Czech Rep.	160.0L	1. France	63.5L
2.	France	11.5	2. Romania	3.96	2. Ireland	141.3	2. Italy	60.4
3.	Portugal	11.0	3. China	†	3. Germany	137.7	3. Portugal	58.4
4.	Hungary	10.2	4. Poland	3.8	4. Denmark	120.1	4. Luxemb'g	58.2
5.	Spain	10.2	5. Cyprus	3.6	5. Austria	115.6	5. Argentina	43.8
6.	Czech Republic	10.1	6. Slovak Rep	2.8	6. Belgium	104.0	6. Switzerland	43.6
7.	Denmark	10.0	7. Hungary	2.77	7. UK	102.7	7. Spain	36.3
8.	Germany	9.9	8. Bulgaria	2.75	8. Hungary	102.4	8. Hungary	34.7
9.	Austria	9.8	9. Greece	2.70	9. Luxemb'g	99.4	9. Greece	34.5
10.	Switzerland	9.4	10. France	2.52	10. New Zeal'd	98.8	10. Austria	32.8
26.	United States	6.6	15. United States	1.97	12. United States	87.9	23. United States	<15.0

*Keep in mind, when reviewing this or any similar chart, that international comparisons are always approximations. National consumption data may not reflect actual consumption due to factors accounted for, such as home and illicit production, black markets, and smuggling. Generally any information on consumption is derived from tax revenue, so home-brewed beer or spirits distilled at home, or any alcohol smuggled into a country, thus escaping taxation, are not included. The northern Scandinavian countries are aware that the official statistics underrepresent actual consumption. Sweden estimates that actual consumption may be as much as 40%–50% higher than official data indicate. This is seen as a result of their high taxes on alcohol which set the price far above other European countries, along with the tradition of home-made vodka, and very long unpatrolled coast lines.

Also, as in this case, the per capita consumption is based on the entire population, rather than those 15 and older, which is sometimes termed the "drinking population." So if a country has a larger proportion of children than another, that leads to greater underestimates of adult consumption.

†Data not available, based on prior year's ranking.

Source: Alcohol Advisory Council of New Zealand, February 1998. www.alcohol.org.nzChart 2

are learned from earliest childhood and are followed later, often without a thought. Many times such social customs account for the things we do "just because. . . ." The specific expectations for behavior differ from nation to nation, and between separate groups within a nation. Differences can be tied to religion, sex, age, or social class. The ground rules apply to drinking habits as much as to other customs. Cultures vary in attitudes toward alcohol use as they differ in the sports they like or what they eat for breakfast.

Virtually all societies have alcohol. At the same time, there are some dramatic differences among societies in terms of attitudes, and drinking patterns, and the kinds of problems associated with alcohol use. Several distinctive drinking patterns and related attitudes toward alcohol have been identified. Which orientation predominates in a culture or a cultural subgroup was, and in certain cases still is, thought to be influential in determining that group's rate of alcoholism. One such attitude toward drinking is total *abstinence,* as with the Muslims or Mormons. With drinking forbidden, the chances of alcoholism are almost nil. Expectedly, the group as a whole has a very low rate of alcoholism. There is an interesting twist we'll get to later about what happens when members leave the group.

Another cultural attitude toward alcohol promotes *ritual use*. Drinking is primarily connected to religious practice, ceremonies, and special occasions. Any heavy drinking in other contexts would be frowned on. When drinking is tied to social occasions, with the emphasis on social solidarity and camaraderie, it is termed *convivial use*. Finally, there is *utilitarian use*. The society "allows" people to drink for their own personal reasons—to meet their own needs, for example, to relax, to forget, or to chase a hangover. Rates of alcoholism are highest where utilitarian use is dominant.

Differences among nations are growing less marked. Italy has adopted the cocktail party; America is on France's wine kick. Nonetheless, a look at some of the differences between the traditional French and Italian drinking habits shows that cultural attitudes toward the use of alcohol can influence the rate of alcoholism. Both France and Italy are wine-producing countries—France first in the world, Italy second. Both earn a substantial part of their revenue from the production and distribution of wine. Yet the incidence of alcohol dependence in Italy a generation ago was less than one-fifth that of France.

Traditionally in France there were no controls on excessive drinking. Indeed there was no such thing as excessive drinking. Wine was publicly advertised as good for the health—credited with promoting gaiety, optimism, and self-assurance. It was seen as a useful or indispensable part of daily life. Drinking in France was a matter of social obligation; a refusal to drink was met with ridicule, suspicion, and contempt. It was not uncommon for a Frenchman to have a little wine with breakfast, to drink small amounts all morning, to have half a bottle with lunch, to sip all afternoon, to have another half bottle with dinner, and to nip until bedtime, consuming 2 liters or more a day. Frenchmen did get drunk. On this schedule, drunkenness would not always show up in drunken behavior. The body, however, was never entirely free of alcohol. Even people who never showed open drunkenness could have withdrawal symptoms and even DTs when they abstained. The "habit," and the social atmosphere that permitted it, seemed to be facilitating factors in the high rate of alcoholism in France.

Italy, on the other hand, which had the second-highest wine consumption in the world, consumed only half of what was consumed in France. Italy had a low rate of alcoholism on a world scale. The average Italian didn't drink all day but only with noon and evening meals. One liter a day was the accepted amount, and anything over that was considered excessive. There was no social pressure for drinking as in France. As Jellinek said, "In France, drinking is a must. In Italy it is a matter of choice."

Drunkenness, even mild intoxication, was considered a terrible thing, unacceptable even on holidays or festive occasions. A guy with a reputation for boozing would have had a hard time getting along in Italy. He would have had trouble finding a wife. Both she and her parents would have hesitated to consent to a marriage with such a man. His social life would have been hindered, his business put in jeopardy; he would have been cut off from the social interaction necessary for advancement.

Jews historically have had a low rate of alcoholism. Jewish drinking patterns were similar to the Italians, bolstered by the restraint of religion. The Irish were more like the French and had a high incidence of alcoholism for many of the same reasons. The Irish had ambivalent feelings toward alcohol and drunkenness, which tended to produce tension and uneasiness. Drinking among the Irish (and other groups with high rates) was largely convivial on the surface; yet purely utilitarian drinking—often lonely, quick, and sneaky—was a tolerated pattern.

What, then, are the specific factors that account for the differences? These are obviously not based on abstinence. Among the Italians and Jews, many used alcohol abundantly and yet they had a low incidence of alcoholism. While the attitudes in these cultures have changed over the years, some factors that do affect the rates of alcoholism still seem to be found in certain groups. Low rates of alcoholism are found in cultures in which the children are gradually introduced to alcohol in diluted small amounts, on special occasions, within a strong, well-integrated family group. Parents who drink a small or moderate amount with meals, who are consistent in their behavior and their attitudes, set a healthy example. There is strong disapproval of intoxication. It is neither socially acceptable, stylish, funny, nor tolerated. A positive acceptance of moderate, nondisruptive drinking and a well-established consensus on when, where, and how to drink create freedom from anxiety. Drinking is not viewed as a sign of manhood and virility, and abstinence is socially acceptable. It is no more rude to say no to liquor than to coffee. Liquor is viewed as an ordinary thing. No moral importance is attached to drinking or not drinking; it is neither a virtue nor a sin. In addition, alcohol is not seen as the primary focus for an activity; it accompanies rather than dominates or controls.

High rates of alcoholism tend to be associated with the reverse of the above patterns. Wherever there has been little agreement on how to drink and how not to drink, alcoholism rates go up. In the absence of clear, widely agreed upon rules, whether one is behaving or misbehaving is uncertain. Ambivalence, confusion, and guilt easily can be associated with drinking. Those feelings further compound the problem. Individuals who move from one culture to another are especially vulnerable. Their guidelines may be conflicting, and they are caught without standards to follow. For this reason, individuals who belong to groups that promote abstinence similarly run a very high risk of alcoholism if they do drink. Thus, while Mormons as a group have a low rate of alcoholism, among those who were raised as Mormons who do drink, there is a much higher rate.

Again, the above studies provide insights into what the broad determinants are for differing rates of alcoholism. In many cases they describe traditional practices of specific groups that have changed in the intervening years. For example, French drinking patterns have changed dramatically. Many changes are being attributed to automation and television. The workers in a Renault factory are not going to be sipping wine throughout the day as was the custom of their grandfathers who were manual laborers.

"Man comes from dust and ends in dust" (Holy Day Musaf prayer)—and in between, let's have a drink.

YIDDISH PROBERB

The bistro no longer serves as the hub of social life, and the practice of stopping by after work has declined with television. The French, just like their American counterparts, head home to an evening with the tube—the news, the Monday-night soccer match, the late movies.

Just as cultural differences between groups are becoming less marked, so too it cannot be assumed that every member of a specific group follows the group norms. Being Jewish is no protection against alcoholism. The historically low rates of alcoholism among Jews may lead to under-recognition and greater stigmatization of those who are alcoholic.

Drinking styles and alcohol problems

The focus thus far has centered on the effects of culture on alcohol dependence. In addition there are attitudes, norms, and drinking patterns that are predictive of the occurrence of *problems,* that is, the occurrence of negative consequences, arising from alcohol use. These include

1 solitary drinking;
2 overpermissive norms of drinking;
3 lack of specific drinking norms;
4 tolerance of drunkenness;
5 adverse social behavior tolerated when drinking;
6 utilitarian use of alcohol to reduce tension with anxiety;
7 lack of ritualized and/or ceremonial use of alcohol;
8 alcohol use apart from family and social functions with close friends;
9 alcohol use separated from overall eating patterns;
10 lack of child socialization into drinking patterns;
11 drinking with strangers, which increases violence;
12 drinking pursued as recreation;
13 drinking concentrated in young males; and
14 a cultural milieu that stresses individualism, self-reliance, and high achievement.

The influence of cultural subgroups

Beyond the influence of broad-based cultural factors, there has been recent interest in the relative influence of cultural subgroups such as family or peers, as well as the characteristics of the immediate drinking situation. Not surprisingly, much of this research has focused upon adolescents and the factors that promote or protect against alcohol use and abuse. Some of these studies have resulted in some interesting findings. However, although considerable research is being conducted, each study is fairly circumscribed and specific. This body of research has yet to be integrated into a theoretical approach to the influences of the smaller social systems in which we live.

For example, among the research findings of interest, in a group of people drinking, the heaviest drinker sets the pace for the others. Thus, how much an individual drinks on a particular occasion is likely to be influenced by the amount consumed by others in the group. Another is that adolescent alcohol use increases with perceived access to alcohol and the perceived lack of degree of adult supervision. If one were to extrapolate from the broad cultural norms, one might reasonably suspect that when alcohol use is introduced in the home, this would provide a protective factor. However some research has not supported that assumption. To the contrary, adolescents who are introduced to alcohol in the home are more likely than other adolescents to use alcohol in unsupervised settings. The authors note that further research is required to examine whether later unsupervised use is an across-the-board phenomenon or associated with different ways in which alcohol use is introduced. Having a glass of wine with a family meal may be quite different than a father and son both having a beer while watching a televised football game, or an adolescent being allowed to help himself to the cold beer in the fridge.

Legal sanctions and approaches

The focus thus far has been on the unwritten rules that govern drinking behavior and influence the rates of alcoholism. How about the rules incorporated into law that govern use and availability? What impact do they have on the rates of alcoholism? Though their impact is less than the factors just discussed, which permeate all of daily life, they do make a considerable difference. Think back to this nation's experience of Prohibition. On one level Prohibition can only be described as a fiasco. It did little to abolish problems associated with alcohol use, and it is credited with introducing other social problems that resulted from bootlegging and the illegal market for alcohol. On the other hand, with the lowering of consumption there was a marked reduction in the prevalence of alcoholism. Death from cirrhosis during Prohibition declined.

Short of prohibition, there are significant ways society can influence the use of alcohol. The common denominator involves laws that limit access to alcohol. A major factor influencing access is price. As the price of alcoholic beverages increases, people drink less. The group that is most responsive to price changes are moderate drinkers, as opposed to "light" or "heavy" drinkers. Presumably "light" drinkers use alcohol so infrequently that it is not a significant part of the individual's or household budget. Also, drinking tends to be tied to special occasions, such as the anniversary dinner, the retirement party, the family reunion. For example, if you only drink once a month, even if the price doubles that isn't going to have a big impact on your pocketbook. However, for the moderate drinker, as the price of alcohol increases there are occasions when a soda will do just as well, or a cup of coffee becomes a substitute for the beer. Even heavy drinkers, who will tend to give up almost anything before sacrificing the alcohol, are not wholly indifferent to price. A significant relationship has been found between the rate of cirrhosis and the level of liquor taxes. The level of taxation has also been found to

The Last Straw
New Hampshire's budget woes have not yet set the masses marching in the streets. Warnings that our schoolchildren will be deprived have not done it. Warnings that a student's costs for attending the University of New Hampshire will rise have not done it. Warnings that there will be less treatment for the mentally ill have not done it. Warnings that there will be reduced counseling services for the troubled have not done it. Warnings that there will not be enough manpower to ensure pure water supplies have not done it. Warnings that law enforcement officials may not be able to hold down the crime rate have not done it. But now you better batten down the hatches and keep your riot shields handy. This week there was a headline that said, "LIQUOR STORES THREATENED BY BUDGET." That'll do it.

Editorial that appeared in *The Valley News,* Lebanon, New Hampshire, in September 1977, after the New Hampshire legislature and governor had failed to adopt a budget for the state.

have a small but significant impact on rates of violent crime. As consumption declines, the rates of rape, assault, and robbery go down. Despite the fact that taxation can be a potent means of influencing alcohol use, and despite the fact that there is seemingly a growing concern about the problems associated with alcohol, since the early 1950s the tax rate on alcohol has been declining. In 1954, the average tax—the total of federal, state, and local taxes—was about 50% of the cost of the alcohol, before taxes were added. By the early 1980s that tax rate had been halved. (The tax rate was a set amount rather than being tied to inflation.) Subsequent increases in taxes have only served to stop the downward trend. By way of contest, in Sweden taxes are imposed according to alcohol content. The tax on vodka is 90% of the retail price.

Another legal measure that can have an impact on alcohol use is related to regulations on advertising, as well as legislation on when and where alcohol may be sold. The party line of the alcohol beverage industry is that advertising does not influence whether or not people drink. Rather the impact of advertising is seen as influencing the selection of a particular beverage or brand. To use advertising jargon, the goal of advertising is to increase "market share." Well, research suggests that this is not quite the case. As advertising increases so does the level of consumption. One question of public policy is how to restrict advertising. It has been suggested that a complete ban will simply lead to other avenues to promote sales. Counteradvertising is suggested as one potential step. This too raises some interesting policy questions. The United States has just committed $1 billion for a 5-year media blitz that will be orchestrated by the "Partnership for a Drug-Free America." The Partnership, largely funded by the advertising revenues of the alcohol and the tobacco industries, has ignored the drugs of choice among American teens—alcohol and nicotine. The question needs to be considered whether this "oversight" is sending an unintended and unfortunate message—drinking and smoking is no big deal. For the same period, the fact that the alcohol industry's own advertising budgets is three times the amount being committed to fight illicit drug abuse should not go unnoticed.

Cross-cultural comparisons

Ofttimes questions are raised about what lessons might be learned from the experience of other countries with different laws and drinking practices. Frequently queries deal with adolescents, e.g., the impact of legal drinking age. The implication is that knowing the answer will give some guidance as to steps that we might take in our country. But we aren't that lucky. Things are just not that simple. The drinking age, in this example, is embedded in a context of cultural attitudes about what represents appropriate and inappropriate use, as well as being only one of many laws that influence drinking, such as limits set on the numbers and locations of alcohol outlets, or the taxes levied that thereby influence price, or laws that govern drinking and driving.

In Europe the legal age to purchase alcoholic beverages is lower than in the United States, typically between ages 16 and 18. Also, in many countries there is no single legal drinking age. It may vary by the setting, e.g., stores versus restaurants, as well as for types of beverages, or by the alcohol content. See Table 5.2 for a list of legal drinking ages in various countries.

Even when we know the legal drinking age in a given place we need to beware of quick comparisons. Having a legal age for purchase on the books doesn't mean that it is enforced with the same rigor as occurs in America. We also need to appreciate that the legal drinking age simply isn't the big deal elsewhere that it is in the United States. The differences

TABLE 5.2   LEGAL AGES FOR PURCHASE OF ALCOHOL

Country	Purchasing Age

Austria	age for drinking in public varies by state
	    spirits, age 18 (9 states)
	    wine/beer, age 16 (8 states)
	    age 15 (other states)

Belgium	age 16
Denmark	age 15 in shops age 18 in restaurants and bars
Finland	age 20; over 2.2% alcohol content age 18, ≤ 2.2% alcohol
France	age 16
Germany	age 16, beer and wine age 18, spirits
Greece	age 18 for purchase in public places
Ireland	age 18
Italy	age 16
Luxembourg	age 16
Netherlands	age 16, beer and wine age 18, spirits
Norway	age 18, wine and beer age 20, spirits
Portugal	age 16

Spain	varies by region
	    age 16 for most areas,
	    age 18 Basque region

Sweden	age 18 in restaurants
	    and grocery stores ("medium strength")
	    age 20 state-run liquor stores
	    no age restriction for light beer,
	    2.25% alcohol content

United Kingdom	age 16 pubs and restaurants with meals age 18 other purchase

Source: EuroCare, an organization comprised of members of the European Union directed to alcohol issues and problems. Compiled by data provided by member nations. See EuroCare's website, which provides alcohol-related data, reports, and policy statements. The website address is www.eurocare.org.

in language indicate this. In the United States we refer to the "legal drinking age"; in Europe the reference is to the "legal age for purchase." Other countries are a bit befuddled at times by the extent to which we in the United States are so caught up with drinking age. While our mind-set may be a mystery to them, the reverse is equally true. The following is a good example. A study was conducted in Switzerland on adolescents' ability to purchase alcoholic beverages in bars and restaurants. In four out of five attempts, 13- and 15-year-old boys were able to purchase beer or "pastis," an aniseed-flavored aperitif. In Switzerland, the minimum age to purchase beer is 16 years and to purchase pastis, it's age 18. Researchers who were observing these transactions noted that "the time needed to refuse orders appeared to be a big factor in making these sales." This seemed to them a reasonable explanation, which demonstrates how our culture influences how we understand the data we do have. In the United States, there would be few researchers and even fewer state liquor control board investigators who would consider "being busy" an acceptable reason not to card people. Of further interest for this discussion is that follow-up interviews with the bar and tavern owners and personnel found that only 17% knew the correct minimum legal ages for purchasing and consuming alcoholic beverages! Living in a country where seemingly every teen, every parent, and every bartender knows the legal drinking age, the more casual (from our point of view) attitude of the Swiss is difficult to imagine.

Any perceived casual attitude of the people in European countries regarding age for purchase is offset by very strict laws in other areas. The most dramatic difference is around drinking and driving. In most European countries a BAC of .05 is the cut-off for driving while intoxicated; and penalties tend to be more harsh than in the United States. Take Sweden, for example. In 1990 Sweden lowered its level for impaired driving from .05 to .02. (This is the same level as is being promoted in the United States for those under age 21, a level referred to as "zero tolerance," i.e., no alcohol use if driving.) The penalties for drinking and driving in Sweden are linked to the BAC. Lesser offenses are for BACs of between .02 and .10; more serious offences are for BACs above .10. Lesser offenses lead to fines and license suspensions lasting anywhere from 6 months to 1 year. The driver also has to see a physician and have a liver enzyme test, which provides some indication of a history of heavy use. A physician visit and laboratory tests are required when a driver applies for license restoration. Restoration of the license is conditional, with further medical evaluations required, in 6 and 12 months. Any evidence of heavy drinking results in continued or re-revocation of driving privileges. For more serious offences, a BAC above .10, there are prison terms as well as fines in about half of all cases. (Prior to 1990, prison terms were virtually routine for all serious offences. The changes in the law were made in part to reduce prison costs.) For serious offenders, regaining one's driving license is likely to be accompanied by a number of restrictions, as well as the required medical evaluation.

Driving may be limited to "essential" purposes such as transportation to work, or may only be allowed on weekdays, or no driving may be allowed after 9 o'clock at night.

Do these laws have an impact? In 1996, Sweden, with a population of slightly over 8 million, had a total of 30 alcohol-related fatalities. Alcohol is implicated in only 4.8% of all driving fatalities, a rate 10 times less than in the United States. But again there are other differences that may help make a difference. For young Swedes, beer is the most popular alcoholic beverage, as is true in the United States; however, it is estimated that in the vicinity of 60% of beer is consumed as part of meals, rather than at parties, or outings, or to use the American phrase, when "going out drinking."

There are a few natural occasions when it is possible to gain some insights into the impact of a particular legal approach. These occur at a time when there is an important shift in public policy or social circumstances. In our country, such opportunities were provided with the advent of the rise in drinking age. One can compare the differences in drinking among different age groups, and differences in associated problems, such as DWI, before and after the law change. Yes, there was less drinking and there were fewer accidents when the legal age was raised. Even here other factors are at work, however; for example, changes in laws are generally accompanied by publicity, stricter enforcement, and more visible law enforcement. As a consequence there is less inclination to think that one might "get away with it."

Another such opportunity to examine the role of laws arises in the wake of dramatic social changes, such as those in the former Soviet Union and Soviet-block countries during the 1980s and 1990s. For example, in the early 1980s when martial law was established in Poland, vodka was rationed, leading to a decline in drinking and alcohol problems. Not many years later, between 1988 and 1991, the import taxes were abolished and millions of litres of very cheap alcohol were imported in what was known in Poland as "the schnapps-gate affair." Consumption quickly matched earlier levels. Similarly, in the Soviet Union in the mid-1980s, Gorbachov implemented a far-ranging anti-alcohol campaign. Almost overnight breweries were converted into manufacturing plants for fruit juices. One innovation was the introduction of replaceable caps for vodka bottles. Previous to that, fifths of vodka produced for domestic consumption had only a foil cover that was peeled off. Why would one need a cap that could be replaced on a bottle? Typically, a fifth of vodka would be consumed at one sitting. With this array of legal reforms, indeed there was a marked decline in drinking and its related problems. Later, upon the breakup of the Soviet Union, alcohol production increased, both legally and through black-market/private initiatives. This was accompanied by a corresponding rise in alcohol problems. With an almost overproduction of alcohol, there were even more new developments, such as the sale of vodka in paper cups from kiosks on the street.

An examination of the Soviet-Russian anti-alcohol initiates also demonstrates the potential for unintended and unanticipated consequences. When alcohol availability was limited by Gorbachov, there was a sudden shortage of sugar, presumably arising from the home production of distilled spirits. This is certainly consistent with the American experiment with Prohibition. But there were also reforms with unforeseen consequences. One strategy to reduce the consumption of vodka—the most popular drink—was to introduce wines and other beverages with a lower alcohol content. Vodka had never been a woman's drink. With the introduction of other alcoholic beverages, drinking among women rose markedly. Along with that, there was a corresponding sharp rise in fetal alcohol syndrome. Women had tended not to drink vodka, and certainly not in the traditional Russian drinking style. The common drinking pattern in all of Eastern Europe, including Russia and Finland, is very heavy drinking at one sitting. We would term it "binge drinking." There it has no special name, it is simply "drinking." To the extent that women not only increased consumption but also adopted the standard drinking patterns, the risk of FAS rose accordingly. Recall that the risks to the fetus increase with the number of incidents of heavy drinking. So even with the same level of total consumption, more moderate drinking on more occasions poses less danger to the fetus than fewer drinking occasions but with greater intake per occasion.

Another perspective on cultural influence

An essay published in 1972, "The Cybernetics of 'Self': A Theory of Alcoholism," while not addressing the causes of alcoholism per se, provides an interesting hypothesis on the impact of cultural orientation on recovery. It provides a possible insight as to why abandoning alcohol is so difficult for the alcohol dependent.

The author Gregory Bateson points out that Western and Eastern cultures differ significantly in the way they view the world. Western societies focus on the individual. The tendency of Eastern cultures is to consider the individual in terms of the group or in terms of one's relationships. To point out this difference, consider how you might respond to the question "Who is that?" The "Western" way to answer is to respond with the person's name, "That's Joe Doe." The "Eastern" response might be "That's my neighbor's oldest son." The latter answer highlights the relationship of several persons.

One of the results of Westerners' zeroing in on the individual is an inflation of the sense of "I." We think of ourselves as wholly separable and independent. Also we may not recognize the relationships of ourselves to other persons and things and the effects of our interactions. According to Bateson, this can lead to problems. One example he cites is our relationship to the physical environment. If nothing else, the ecology movement has taught us that the old rallying cry of "man against nature" does not make sense. We cannot beat nature. We only win—that is,

survive—if we allow nature to win some rounds too. To put it differently, we are now starting to see ourselves as a part of nature.

How does this fit in with alcohol? The same kind of thinking is evident. The individual who drinks expects, and is expected, to be the master of alcohol. If problems develop, the individual can count on hearing
"control your drinking" or "use willpower." The person is supposed to
fight the booze and win. Now there's a challenge. Who can stand losing
to a "thing?" So the person tries different tactics to gain the upper hand.
Even if the individual quits drinking for a while, the competition is on:
me versus it. To prove who's in charge, sooner or later the drinker will
have "just one." If disaster doesn't strike then, the challenge continues to
have "just one more." Sooner or later. . . .

Bateson asserted that successful recovery requires a change of world
view by the person in trouble with alcohol. The Western tendency to see
the self (the I) as separate and distinct from, and often in combat with,
alcohol (or anything else) has to be abandoned. The alcoholic must learn
the paradox of winning through losing, the limitations of the I and its interdependence with the rest of the world. He continues with examples of
the numerous ways in which AA fosters just this change of orientation.

The 1990s: A decade of change

In terms of social policy, in our country, we cannot expect to have all of
the approaches just described implemented as one piece of legislation.
American society tackles public concerns in a more incremental fashion.
A variety of steps have been taken that reflect efforts to moderate drinking patterns.

In the United States, for the most part, the laws regulating alcohol use
are set by the states. This includes defining by law what constitutes intoxication, as well as setting the legal drinking age. States vary as well
on when, where, and what a citizen may drink within its borders. And
some states even vary from county to county—Texas, for example.
Laws range from dry, to beer only, to anything at all but only in private
clubs, to sitting down but not walking with drink in hand, ad infinitum.
States also provide a role for communities in establishing local ordi-
nances, such as those governing the location and number of alcohol
retail outlets and bars, or their hours of operation.

The gap between states is beginning to close in response to federal
actions, and its use of financial incentives, as well as changes in public
perceptions. The uniform increase of the drinking age to 21 years was
championed by many, in the hope that it would be an effective measure
to reduce alcohol-related highway fatalities among young people, but it
was also resisted on several grounds. Some cited the fact that the age of
majority is 18 years; college administrators, despite the recognition
of problem drinking on campus, were concerned about living with a
law that was so out of sync with the behavior of college students. Ultimately the states' passage was in no small part prompted by a federal

"incentive"—the tying of federal highway funds to a state's enactment of a 21-year-old drinking age. States are similarly being encouraged to lower the standard for legal intoxication to a BAC of .08. Sixteen states have already done so. Those states, plus any others that adopt the lower standard, split $55 million in federal funding in 1999.

There have been other governmental initiatives that would have been highly improbable a decade ago, such as the requirement that alcohol beverages have warning labels. This was accomplished despite the presence of a highly organized and well-financed alcohol beverage industry lobby. Such steps require broad public support rather than advocacy by a small, highly vocal minority. Regulatory agencies at the state level are having a major influence. Again, sparked by receipt of federal monies, efforts to monitor the ability of underage people to purchase alcohol and cigarettes are being monitored. Both the failure to ask for proof of legal age and the sale of products to minors has consequences ranging from fines to suspension of licenses. We are far beyond not bothering to even check for infractions, or simply providing a slap on the wrist if a violation occurs.

During the 1990s there were dramatic changes in how health care is organized, how it is provided, and how it is paid for. The catch-all phrase "health care reform" is often used to denote these changes. With respect to alcohol and other drug problems, many of these changes may have been reforms, but they have not felt like improvements. Of particular concern has been the limitations and exclusions placed on care, limitations which do not apply to other illnesses. States have begun to take action to address this, passing laws that assure both substance abuse and psychiatric illness are treated in a fashion comparable to other medical concerns. These laws are referred to as "parity bills."

With respect to drinking and driving, the changes are being maintained. The efforts of community- and state-level organizations such as MADD (Mothers against Drunk Driving) and its derivative SADD (Students . . .) continue. Lobbying for stricter penalties for drinking and driving offenses has continued. The concept of the "designated driver" clearly has taken hold. Advertising campaigns to combat drinking and driving are now commonplace, at least at holiday times. All of this has had an impact. Driving fatalities attributable to alcohol continue to decline. Accompanying this are the growth in efforts directed toward prevention.

The legal system also has both spurred and reflected changes in society. One major influence has been the issue of legal liability and the suits that can be filed for compensation when death or injury occur as a result of drinking. There long have been Dram Shop laws, which hold a tavern owner or barkeeper liable for serving an obviously intoxicated customer. Until several years ago these were rarely invoked, but this is no longer the case. Liability also has been extended to hosts or to those who might allow an intoxicated person to use their car. The issue of liability, particularly in light of higher legal drinking ages, has prompted college campuses to pay attention to issues of alcohol use.

Concern about liability also has touched the workplace. It has prompted business establishments largely to abandon parties where the alcohol flows freely, particularly on company time. If drinking takes place at work-sponsored activities, during the time for which an employee is being paid, any alcohol-impaired employee injured on the way home is a candidate for worker's compensation. In addition the company can anticipate a lawsuit. Other changes in business practices resulted from a "small" change in the Internal Revenue Code. The three-martini lunch went by the boards when the IRS no longer allowed companies to write off the purchase of alcohol as a legitimate business cost. This is a good example of how social change occurs. Small changes such as alteration of the tax code affect behavior, which in turn modifies perceptions or allows alternative views to be expressed. The three-martini lunch not only does not qualify as a business expense; it no longer is viewed as a requisite for doing business and, in many quarters, is considered inappropriate.

As changes have been prompted by governmental action, they have been reinforced and mirrored by the actions of private groups who also have the capacity to influence patterns of alcohol use. For example, in professional and collegiate sports, drunken fans were long seen as an inevitable part of the game! At professional sports events, drinking in the stands was spurred by beer sales at the concession stand, a not-insignificant source of revenue for professional teams. Over the past several years, professional teams have begun to sharply curtail drinking. In some instances drinking has been entirely banned. In both professional and college stadiums there are now blocks of "family" seats, where no alcohol consumption is allowed. In collegiate sports in 1990, the NCAA limited the amount of advertising by beer companies during television broadcasts of its games.

ALE-GATOR

Less clear is the extent of a relationship, if any, between the changes in attitudes and policies toward alcohol use and the intensive efforts in the arena of illicit drug problems. In 1988, the federal government passed legislation, The Omnibus Anti-Drug Abuse Act, which became the foundation of the "war on drugs." The Anti-Drug Abuse Act incorporated steps to decrease the availability of drugs. This, borrowing from economic jargon, is the "supply side"; and efforts directed toward reducing the use of drugs, thus reducing the markets, is the "demand side." It was in the context of this initiative that then-First Lady Nancy Reagan launched a public drug prevention campaign with the slogan, "Just say No." The prime target of these initiatives was illicit substances, particularly cocaine; alcohol and tobacco were ignored in the attendant discussions.

With the above legislation as the backdrop for social policy, the federal government has also used its regulatory powers to promote changes in society. The federal goals of the "drug-free campus" and the "drug-free workplace" (by the year 1995) were encouraged through education and also through linking institutions' receipt of federal funds to their

mounting prevention programs. Though questioned by unions and those concerned about civil liberties and intrusion on privacy, as part of these initiatives drug screening in the workplace became more common for both current employees and job applicants.

An ongoing concern about anti-drug initiatives is that they largely continue to ignore the substances most widely associated with addiction in our society—alcohol, nicotine, and prescription drugs. Many in the alcohol and public health fields are appalled by the lack of attention alcohol is receiving despite the fact that its associated problems dramatically overshadow those associated with illicit drug use. There are those too who remember the public's response to the "counterculture" of the '60s, when psychoactive drug use and experimentation was accepted by a large segment of the adolescent and young adult population. Alcohol was then viewed as far more benign than other drugs. The refrain of parents when confronted with an adolescent's drinking was purportedly a relieved, "Well at least he isn't on drugs." As a means of reminding everyone that alcohol is a drug, the federal Center for Substance Abuse Prevention (CSAP) adopted the terminology of "alcohol and other drug use" rather than the phrase "alcohol and substance abuse." That was later changed to "alcohol, tobacco, and other drug use," or the acronymn ATOD.

We're drinking my friend,
To the end of a brief episode,
Make it one for my baby
And one more for the road.
JOHNNY MERCER, "One For My Baby"

Attitudes toward alcohol use continue to be varied. In some quarters, it remains masculine or sophisticated to drink. In others, drinking is felt to be unnecessary. In some, it is seen as outright decadence. Despite the considerable changes in laws and public policy, our contradictory and ambiguous views toward alcohol remain embodied in our liquor laws. Regardless of concern about adolescent use, the law implies that on that magical twenty-first birthday, individuals are treated as if they suddenly know how to handle alcohol appropriately. As the rhetoric of "Just say No" is applied to alcohol, as it has been in federally funded campus prevention efforts and the growing prevention efforts among teens, it skirts the issue of alcohol's legal status for those 21 and over. There's no mention of when or under what circumstances it is okay to "say Yes."

A perspective now well established in other countries has barely taken hold in the United States. This is the concept of harm reduction as a basis of public policy. With this orientation the issue is less about whether individuals use or do not use than it is focused upon reducing problems associated with use. Thus for example, with respect to intravenous drug use, the emphasis is on taking steps to reduce needle sharing or other activities that will increase the risk of AIDS. Or in working with adolescents, the focus would be on steps that can be taken to reduce drunk driving, or to provide pointers about recognizing and responding to an alcohol medical emergency. Such efforts are not to be seen as condoning IV drug use or as condoning drinking by adolescents. What such policies try to reflect is the reality that such behavior does occur. And in light of that reality, this view maintains that efforts must be undertaken to reduce associated risks even as one simultaneously tries to curb the behavior.

As a society, we long have attempted to "have our alcohol and drink it too." We want alcohol without the associated problems. Because that is not possible, the question has been, what compromises are we willing to make? As individuals, what inconveniences and costs are we willing to assume? Will we accept further steps to limit access to alcohol? Would we, for example, accept a ban on package sales after 10:00 PM on the assumption that folks who want to buy alcohol at that hour don't need it? Or how willing are each of us to intervene if confronted by a possible substance abuse problem that presents a threat to public safety? If driving on the highway and witnessing an erratic driver, does it even occur to me to telephone the police from my car phone? If the thought even arises, would I make such a call if it requires my pulling to a rest area to use a pay phone? How likely am I to do if it requires exiting the highway to locate a public telephone? I suspect not very.

Collectively, will we allocate a reasonable share of the alcohol tax dollar to help the inevitable percentage who get into trouble with the drug? Will treatment of alcohol and other drug problems in fact be covered by health insurance in the same fashion as other medical conditions? Comments that have arisen in the discussion of mandating alcohol and other drug treatment as part of a basic health-care plan have been instructive. In light of concern about cost, the question has been raised as to why those who don't need such benefits should be forced to purchase the coverage and be required through their insurance payments to subsidize treatment of others. Can we resist the "we" versus "they" attitude such discussion implies? It suggests a belief that those with alcohol and/or other drug problems brought their difficulties on themselves. For all the discussion of addictions representing a disease, seemingly just below the surface continues to lurk the perception of addictions as immoral, "bad" behavior. How addiction treatment is covered by health insurance may be the most telling statement of how far we have or have not come in our national understanding of this public health issue.

America is moving towards a consensus, at least about the behaviors deemed unacceptable with respect to drinking. But, with alcohol widely available everywhere, until agreement emerges on appropriate as well as inappropriate use, and until America really comes to grips with alcohol as a drug as well as a beverage, American society will continue to be a fertile breeding ground for alcohol problems.

A closing comment on other drugs   In considering the factors that influence the risk for other drug dependence, the genetic and psychological factors discussed here are relevant. The most significant differences between alcohol and tobacco and other drugs lie in the social attitudes toward use and their illicit status, the implications for those who use these drugs. An adequate discussion of these differences is beyond the scope of this handbook.

RESOURCES AND FURTHER READING

Several of these references may appear dated. However, we have selected original primary sources for inclusion, that is, the articles in which the ideas or findings set forth were first introduced in the scientific literature.

Bales R: Cultural differences in rates of alcoholism, *Quarterly Journal of Studies on Alcohol* 6:489–499, 1946.

It has long been recognized that in considering the origins of alcohol problems and alcoholism, one must look not only at the individual but also at society. Countries were recognized as having different rates of alcoholism. Bales describes four different cultural orientations toward drinking and their role in influencing the culture's rate of alcoholism. The effects of a cultural orientation toward alcohol or other drug use continue to influence the understanding of the origins of alcohol and other drug problems, and thereby influence public policy and program development.

Bates ME, Labouvie EW: Adolescent risk factors and the prediction of persistent alcohol and drug use into adulthood, *Alcoholism: Clinical and Experimental Research* 21(5):944–950, 1997. (60 refs.)

Adolescence is a time of heightened risk for relatively intensive alcohol and other drug use behaviors. However, heavy use is often "adolescence-limited," giving way to moderation or cessation in adulthood. The authors examine individual differences in risk factors at age 18 that are predictive of alternative alcohol and drug use trajectories from adolescence to adulthood. Data were collected prospectively on four occasions from participants in the Rutgers Health and Human Development Project. Subsets of individuals representing three prototypical trajectories of (1) consistently low alcohol and drug use during adolescence and early adulthood; (2) heavier alcohol or drug use during adolescence, but not during adulthood; and (3) persistent heavier alcohol or drug use from adolescence into adulthood were found to differ significantly on a number of intrapersonal, behavioral, and environmental risk factors, with the adolescence-limited group consistently scoring between the other two groups. Based on these results, a composite risk index was constructed. In the total sample, however, when the effect of alcohol and drug use behaviors at age 18 was controlled, the composite risk index was unrelated to adult (age 28 to 31) levels of alcohol and drug use and consequences. Thus, in this community sample, well-documented risk factors assessed in adolescence did not exhibit any direct, long-term effects on use intensity and problems in adulthood. The authors concluded that the assessed risk factors (disinhibition, cognitive structure, pity, deviant coping, friends' deviance, and stressful life events) are not immutable, but subject to individual and normative changes during the transition from adolescence to adulthood. More research is needed to determine the long-term stability of risk factors, and how changes in risk factors over time, discontinuities in what constitutes risk in adolescence versus adulthood, and proximal adult protective factors that compensate for early risk contribute to developmental patterns of use. (Copyright 1997, Research Society on Alcoholism.)

Bateson G: The cybernetics of "self": A theory of alcoholism, *American Journal of Psychiatry* 34:1–18, 1971.

DiCarlo ST, Powers AS: Propylthiouracil tasting as a possible genetic association marker for two types of alcoholism, *Physiology & Behavior* 64(2):147–152, 1998. (40 refs.)

The ability to taste 6-n-propylthiouracil (PROP) as bitter is determined genetically. The present study investigated whether this genetic ability was correlated with alcoholism and/or depression. Four groups of community college students (n = 25 each) were constituted based on the presence or absence of alcoholism and/or depression in themselves or their parents. Family history was assessed using the Family History-Research Diagnostic Criteria. Each subject was given a taste test using paper saturated with PROP. The results showed that subjects who had only alcoholism in their family were more likely to be nontasters of PROP than the control group, whereas subjects with both alcoholism and depression in their family were more likely to be so-called supertasters of PROP; that is, they found it extremely bitter. These findings suggest that PROP tasting might function as a genetic marker for two types of alcoholism. (Author abstract.)

Doria JJ: Gene variability and vulnerability to alcoholism, *Alcohol Health and Research World* 19(3):245–247, 1995. (10 refs.)

Variability within genes may explain why so many differences in alcoholism exist between individuals and among populations. Researchers studying this phenomenon have focused on genes that may affect both the way the body metabolizes alcohol and the way the brain responds to alcohol, thereby increasing or decreasing the likelihood of addiction. Gene variants may ultimately be used as markers of alcoholism vulnerability and as guides to help match patients to the most appropriate alcoholism therapies.

Ferguson RA, Goldberg DM: Genetic markers of alcohol abuse (review), *Clinical Chimica Acta* 257(2):199–250, 1997. (232 refs.)

In this paper, the authors review the current status of genetic markers for the development of alcohol abuse. Family, twin, half-sibling, and adoption studies of alcoholic subjects suggest that the inheritability of liability to alcoholism is at least 50%. These findings have fuelled intensive investigation in the fields of neurology, biochemistry, genetics, and molecular biology aimed at the identification of markers for the risk of alcoholism. The most promising of these are discussed in detail. Alcohol dehydrogenase (ADH) and aldehyde dehydrogenase (ALDH) polymorphisms, specifically the ADH3*1, ADH2*2, and ALDH2*2 genotypes, appear to confer a protective effect against alcoholism, most notably in Asian subjects. Caucasian alcohol abusers and their first-degree relatives exhibit depressed platelet monoamine oxidase activity, the degree of which is greater in Type II than Type I alcoholics. Electrophysiological characteristics of alcoholics and those at risk for developing alcoholism have also been identified, including the reduced amplitude of the event-related brain potential and, after ethanol ingestion, characteristic EEG alpha-wave activity. Lower platelet adenylate cyclase activity is seen in alcoholics compared to controls, presumably as a result of overexpression of an inhibitory G-protein. Markers related to other signal transduction pathways of the central nervous system, including the serotoninergic, muscarinic, and dopaminergic systems, are also discussed. In this group of markers, the putative association between the inheritance of the A1 allele of the D_2 dopamine receptor and the susceptibility to alcoholism provides the most dramatic illustration of the challenges presently existing in this field of scientific investigation. Current limitations in the definition, diagnosis, and classification of alcoholism, the confounding influences of race and gender on association studies, as well as the statistical approach of linkage studies are discussed as they relate to the endeavor to uncover valid genetic markers for the risk of alcoholism. (Author abstract.)

Finn PR, Justus A: Physiological responses in sons of alcoholics, *Alcohol Health and Research World* 21(3): 227–231, 1997. (15 refs.)
Researchers have differentiated sons of alcoholics (SOAs) from sons of nonalcoholics (non-SOAs) on various measures of physiological activity that appear to be related to the SOAs' increased vulnerability to developing alcohol problems. This article summarizes major findings in the literature and discusses the implications of risk-related physiological characteristics for the future development of alcohol problems. SOAs tend to show signs of physiological activity associated with anxiety states, such as increased heart rate in response to stressful stimuli. Studies also demonstrate that SOAs differ greatly from non-SOAs in their response to alcohol. Drinking alcohol dramatically reduces SOAs' reactivity to both stressful and nonstressful stimuli. Additionally, SOAs appear to be less sensitive to alcohol's intoxicating and impairing effects. However, studies also suggest that some SOAs may experience more of alcohol's rewarding effects for a brief period after drinking. Increased stress-dampening and reduced responsiveness to alcohol's negative effects also appear to predict the development of future alcohol problems and may reflect important vulnerabilities in SOAs.

Fraser M, Kohlert N: Substance abuse and public policy, *Social Services Review* 62(1):103–126, 1988.
This article assesses the American effort to control and eradicate substance abuse and drug trafficking. Five drug control strategies—foreign crop eradication, border interdiction, deterrence, treatment, and prevention—are evaluated. In each area the basic programs and their effectiveness are described. The authors conclude that U.S. policy is misdirected and dominated by long-standing and insupportable beliefs about the effectiveness of supply-side intervention such as eradication and interdiction.

Goodwin DW: Is alcoholism hereditary? *Archives of General Psychiatry* 25:545–549, 1971.
This article presents the first studies that demonstrated the role of heredity in some cases of alcohol dependence. Although it has been observed for a long time that alcoholism runs in families, the task of separating the influences of nature vs. nurture is still difficult.

Helzer JE, Canino GJ, eds: *Alcoholism in North America, Europe, and Asia,* New York: Oxford University Press, 1992. (Chapter refs.)
This volume deals with the epidemiology of alcohol dependence and associated problems in 10 different cultural regions. The work reported developed out of the Epidemiologic Catchment Area survey and the WHO/ADAMHA Cooperative project. Thus this work represents a cross-national comparison. It addresses the methodology, as well as the findings in the 10 different countries surveyed.

Johnson V: *I'll quit tomorrow* (rev ed), New York: Harper & Row, 1980.
This work introduced the technique of "the intervention," a method to initiate treatment. The use of 'interventions' promoted earlier treatment and prompted care for those previously seen as either 'unready' or 'inaccessible.' The adoption of this clinical approach dispelled the myth that a patient's apparent motivation to cease use is a significant factor in determining treatment outcome, thus revolutionizing alcohol treatment and, by example, drug abuse treatment as well. This work also introduced the concept of "enabling," i.e., the interactions of the family of the alcoholic that unwittingly support the continuation of drinking or drug use. Efforts to counter these behaviors, tied to the framework of the intervention, offer the family a constructive role beyond "detachment with love," the primary orientation of Al-Anon, the self-help group for family members.

Li T-K, McBride WJ: Pharmacogenetic models of alcoholism (review), *Clinical Neuroscience* 3(3):182–188, 1995. (81 refs.)
This article reviews recent efforts in developing laboratory animal models for the study of alcoholism and abnormal alcohol-seeking behavior. Through selective breeding, stable lines of rats that reliably exhibit high and low voluntary alcohol consumption have been raised. The high-preference animals self-administer ethanol by free-choice drinking, and operantly for intragastric infusion, in amounts that produce intoxication. With chronic free-choice drinking, the preferring rats develop tolerance and physical dependence. Low to moderate concentrations (50–150 mg%) of ethanol are reinforcing to the preferring rat, as evidenced by intracranial self-administration studies. Compared with non-preferring animals, they are less affected and develop tolerance more quickly to the sedative-hypnotic effects of ethanol. Neurochemical, neuroanatomical, and neuropharmacological studies indicate that innate differences exist between the alcohol-preferring and -nonpreferring lines in the brain limbic structures. Depending on the animal model under study, a change in the main dopaminergic pathway and/or the serotonergic, opioid, and GABAergic systems that regulate this pathway may underlie the vulnerability to the abnormal alcohol-seeking behavior in these pharmacogenetic animal models of alcoholism. (Author abstract.)

McCord W, McCord J: Some current theories of alcoholism: A longitudinal evaluation, *Quarterly Journal of Studies on Alcohol* 20:727–749, 1959.
A significant research dilemma in efforts to ascertain the influence of emotional and personality factors on the origins of alcohol or other drug dependence is that the individuals most easily studied are already alcohol or drug dependent. In that case the research requires efforts to define retrospectively the premorbid personality. The preferred methodology is a longitudinal prospective study to allow comparisons between those who do and those who do not become alcoholic or drug dependent and to allow a clear assessment of personality before the emergence of symptoms. The McCords' study was the first to use such a longitudinal, prospective research design. The subjects had been closely studied many years earlier and initially recruited as part of a research project to explore the origins and precursors of juvenile delinquency.

NIAAA: The genetics of alcoholism. *Alcohol Alert No. 18,* October, 1992.

The Genetics of Alcoholism. *Alcohol Health and Research World.* 19(3): 161–256 (entire issue) 1995.

This issue is devoted to an examination of genetic factors related to alcoholism. Individual articles are directed to reviews of the major areas of research—adoption studies, the longitudinal study of sons of alcoholics, biochemical markers. There are also brief articles that explain the approaches used in these studies.

Noble EP. The D-2 receptor gene: A review of association studies in alcoholism and phenotypes. *Alcohol* 16(1):33–45, 1998. (119 refs.)

The role of the D_2 dopamine receptor (DRD2) gene in alcoholism and other substance use disorders has come under intense investigation since the minor TaqI A (Al) allele of the DRD2 gene was first reported to be associated with alcoholism. In a meta-analysis of 15 U.S. and international studies of European (non-Hispanic) Caucasians, consisting of 1015 alcoholics (more severe and less severe) and 898 controls (unassessed and assessed for alcoholism), alcoholics had a higher prevalence (p < 10(−7), and frequency (p < 10(−5)) of the Al allele than did controls. The prevalence of the Al allele was 1.5-fold higher in more severe than less severe alcoholics (p < 10(−4)), whereas unassessed controls had a twofold higher prevalence of the Al allele than did assessed controls (p < 10(−4)). Whereas more severe alcoholics had a threefold higher Al allelic prevalence than did assessed controls (p < 10(−10)), Al allelic prevalence was virtually identical in less severe alcoholics and in unassessed controls. The Al allele has also been associated with other drug problems, including cocaine, nicotine, and polysubstance abuse. Furthermore, the minor TaqI B (B1) allele of the DRD2 gene has been associated with alcoholism and psychostimulant (cocaine, amphetamine) abuse. Beyond association studies, phenotypic differences exist between genotypes containing the TaqI A minor (A1A1 and A1A2) and major (A2A2) alleles of the DRD2. These different phenotypes have been identified through a number of approaches, including pharmacological, neurophysiological, neuropsychological, stress, personality, metabolic, and treatment studies. In conclusion, the present review suggests that the type of alcoholics and the nature of controls used are among critical factors in DRD2 association studies in alcoholism. Intronic mutations in both the 3′(TaqI A) and 5′(TaqI B) regions of the DRD2 associate with alcoholism and other drug use disorders. The identification of phenotypes of DRD2 genotypes suggests that the observed intronic DRD2 mutations may have functional consequences that predispose individuals to a variety of substance use disorders. (Author abstract.)

Pittman DJ, White HR, eds: *Society, culture, and drinking patterns reexamined,* New Brunswick NJ: Rutgers Center of Alcohol Studies, 1991.

This volume represents a revision or sequel to the classic work "Society, Culture and Drinking Patterns," by Pittman and Snyder, which was first published in 1962. It is a compilation of primary materials, and chapters prepared especially for this volume, by those whose work has defined the field. Thus it has assembled the thinking on use and abuse of alcohol, from the range of social science research. The book is intended to consider the social and cultural influences that shape drinking practices, and that alongside individualistic and genetic based factors contribute to alcoholism. There are forty chapters organized into five major sections. The first section sets forth an anthropological approach to drinking. The second provides current observations of alcohol use, both patterns of use and socialization processes related to use. The third focuses upon social structure, subcultures, and drinking patterns, considered by age, religion, race and ethnicity, and drinking institutions. The fourth section deals with the genesis and patterns of alcohol problems. This includes definitions, concepts of the phenomena, the pro- and anti-disease positions, the natural history, etiology, and relation of alcohol problems to social institutions—the family, economic and legal structures. The final section is directed to social movements that have arisen in response to these phenomena and the systems of control. This section considers the AA group, the adult children of alcoholics movement, medicalization of alcohol-related problems, and societal values, including the rise of what has been described as the "new" temperance movement.

Schuckit MA: Reaction to alcohol as a predictor of alcoholism, *Clinical Neuropharmacology* 15(1):305–306, 1992.

Alcoholism is a genetically influenced disorder. However, unlike Huntington's disease, the development of alcohol dependence requires the interaction between relatively strong environmental influences and genetic factors. The hereditary forces in this disorder are complex, probably representing either polygenic forces and/or incomplete penetrance of a dominant inheritance pattern. Thus, it is not likely that there is a single major gene that is a potent contributor to the alcoholism risk in the great majority of alcoholics. As a consequence of these complex factors, a search is under way for more easily identified trait markers of an alcoholism vulnerability. Ideally, these traits will be relatively easily measured attributes of an individual which are linked to specific genes that contribute to the alcoholism vulnerability which would always be expressed, even if environmental events such as lifelong abstinence preclude the expression of alcoholism itself. To date, several potentially important markers of risk have been studied, with most efforts focusing on children of alcoholics. One important lead relates to a lower amplitude of the P3 wave of the Event-Related Potential (ERP) in the substantial minority of sons of alcoholic fathers. Other investigations are evaluating the pattern of lower frequency waves (e.g., alpha and beta) on the background cortical EEG. Several other more preliminary studies point to the potential relevance of a number of blood proteins as potential trait markers of the alcoholism risk, including activity level of adenylate cyclase and monoamine oxidase. (Author abstract.)

Vaillant G: *The natural history of alcoholism,* Revisited. Cambridge MA: Harvard University Press, 1995.

This volume represents both a reprinting as well an updating and reflection on a now classic work in the alcohol field, published fifteen years ago. Drawing upon the analysis of two major longitudinal studies, that work described the natural history of alcoholism (alcohol dependence). The significant findings of this study were as follows: (1) There was a lack of support for the theory of an "alcoholic personality." The presumed "predisposing personality factors" or emotional problems in actuality result from drinking. (2) The major predictors of alcoholism are a positive family history and being raised in a culture whose norms prescribe childhood alcohol use, prescribe heavy adult alcohol use, and accept intoxication. (3) With respect to diagnosis, by the time individuals have experienced 4 lifetime problems from use, typically they will meet any diagnostic criteria for alcoholism. (4) Treatment is not initiated until the occurrence of 8 to 11 lifetime problems. (5) After alcohol dependence is established, the two most common eventual outcomes are recovery or death: over the 30-year follow-up, nonproblematic drinking continually declined. (6) Successful recovery is associated with four factors: developing a vital interest that can replace the role of drinking, external reminders that drinking is painful, increased sources of unambivalently offered social support, and the presence of a source of inspiration, hope, and enhanced self-esteem. This edition clearly denotes the new sections interspersed that offer a commentary on the earlier work, drawing upon new research in the field, further follow-up of subjects, and the author's reflections.

6

THE BEHAVIOR OF DEPENDENCE

There are some striking similarities in the behavioral "look" of those who are alcohol or drug dependent. This is true whether the person is male or female, age 17 or 70. From these similarities a general profile can be drawn, although it will not totally apply to all. This profile will cause signal bells to ring when seen by someone familiar with substance use disorders. Indeed, it was the recognition of these similarities among alcoholics that in part prompted the futile pursuit for "the alcoholic personality."

A BEHAVIORAL COMPOSITE

Those who are dependent on alcohol or other drugs create confusion for those around them. They are constantly sending out mixed messages. "Come closer, understand. Don't you dare question me!" The moods and behaviors can be very volatile: jubilant and expansive, then secretive, angry, suspicious, laughing, or crying. Tense, worried, and confused, she quickly changes to a relaxed, "Everything's fine." Anxious over unpaid bills one day, the alcoholic is financially irresponsible the next. He buys expensive toys for the kids while the rent goes unpaid. She may be easy-going or fight like a caged tiger over a "slight." His telling unnecessary lies and having them come to light is not uncommon.

A considerable amount of time is spent justifying and explaining why she does things. She is constantly minimizing any unpleasant consequences of drinking. He is hard to keep on track. There is always a list of complaints about any number of people, places, and things. "If only. . . ." She considers herself the victim of fate and of a large number of people who are "out to get her." He has thousands of reasons why he *really* needs and deserves a drink or a joint. She will be exuberant over a minor success only to decline rapidly into an "I'm a failure because of . . ." routine. He's elusive and is almost never where he says he'll be when he says he'll be there. She's absolutely *rigid* about her schedule, especially her drinking times.

The mood swings are phenomenal! The circular arguments never quite make sense to others. The denial can cause a lot of exasperation. Now and then the thought surfaces in the drinker's awareness that he or she might have a psychiatric problem. Those around the drinker also can wonder if that is where the problem lies. She is a perfectionist at some times and a slob at others. Though occasionally cooperative, he's often a stone wall. Her life is full of broken commitments, promises, and dates that she often doesn't remember making.

Most of all, the behavior denotes guilt. Extreme defensiveness accompanies alcohol dependent drinking or other drug use. This seems to be one of the key behaviors that is picked up on early and seen, but not understood, by others. "Wonder why Andy's so touchy? What a short fuse!" Certainly sometimes behavior that can only be described as that of a drunken slob is obvious, but often the really heavy drinking is secretive and carefully hidden.

Woe unto them that rise up early in the morning, that they may follow strong drink.

ISAIAH 5:11

With alcohol it would be easier to pin down the problem if the behaviors described only occurred with a drink in hand. This is rarely the case. The behaviors are sometimes more pronounced when the individual is "on the wagon," or working very hard at controlling the drinking. The confusion, anger, frustration, and depression are omnipresent until a radical change occurs in the relationship with alcohol.

Comparing alcohol and other drug use, there are clear similarities and some significant differences. The differences are related in large measure to the levels of social acceptance of a substance's use, its legal status, and also the associated acute effects. Take nicotine, for example. It is legally available, as is alcohol. Given the rapidity with which dependence develops, there is no such phenomenon as "social smoking" that would be tobacco's counterpart to social drinking. Smokers and others have long acknowledged that someone who smokes regularly is "hooked." And in light of this, until relatively recently, smokers more or less smoked whenever and wherever they wanted. While now inconceivable, it was little more than 20 years ago when one major medical center removed the cigarette vending machines *and* the ashtrays from its conference rooms where hospital staff meetings were held! While nonsmokers may not have welcomed basking in a cloud of others' cigarette smoke, they put up with it. While there were probably occasional pangs of guilt or some self-censure on the smoker's part, there were no particular efforts to hide or control smoking.

This has now changed dramatically. Given the diminished public acceptance and tolerance of smoking, those who do smoke are forced to control their smoking. More and more places are "off-limits." This even includes many smoker's own homes, thanks to the objections of spouses, children, or roommates, so smokers have become more similar to alcoholics or those dependent on some illicit drugs. They too are now forced to spend more time orchestrating their drug use. The smoker certainly has the advantage over someone dependent on heroin. He or she can go to any number of convenient locations from the local jiffy mart to, ironically, the neighborhood drug store to buy cigarettes. The smoker doesn't have to cultivate a dealer or worry about supply. However, the smoker certainly is sensitive to the need for and seeks the opportunity for cigarette breaks.

There are some drugs whose acute effects alter behavior in a fashion that may make their use more noticeable to others. For example, there are the hallucinogens. Or there are the drugs commonly used with the clear intent of getting high. In both instances, the use of these drugs requires expending energy to create circumstances in which use will be undetected. This may mean some kind of "time out" or "time away." This pattern of use is not that dissimilar to that of teenagers who descend on the home of a friend whose parents are out of town, or those who live in rural areas and find an out-of-the-way spot for a beer party. Or there is the twenty-something professional who uses cocaine at weekend parties. These gatherings are far removed from the corporate world of conservative three-piece suits that he or she inhabits Monday through Friday.

Wine in excess keeps neither secrets nor promises.

CERVANTES, *Don Quixote*

In any of these instances, if or when use no longer is just "recreational," when it is no longer separate from day-to-day lives but spills over into them, the resemblance to alcohol dependence becomes more marked.

HOW, IF NOT WHY

The profile in the previous section is a fair description of the behavior that accompanies alcohol and other drug dependence. This behavior is part of the disease syndrome, which develops slowly. The many changes in personality occur gradually, making them less discernible either to the individual or those around him or her. So the slow, insidious personality change is almost immune to recognition as it occurs.

Despite the fact that a host of physical problems have long been known to accompany long-term heavy drinking, medical researchers are only beginning to get clues to the physiological basis for the behavior seen (see Chapter 3). Current neurological and physiological research does not yet come close to providing an adequate explanation for this well-known behavioral phenomenon. Despite the inability to provide the exact cause of personality changes, one can describe how the transformation occurs. Vernon Johnson, in *I'll Quit Tomorrow,* developed a four-step process that accurately captures the personality changes occurring in the alcohol dependent person. They apply also to other drug dependence. His explanation in effect describes what emerging alcohol dependence feels like from "the inside out." Becoming familiar with these stages will be helpful in dealing with those with alcohol dependence or alcohol abuse, as well as those whose use of any drug is becoming a problem.

Alcohol or other drug dependence requires the use of alcohol or other drugs—an obvious fact. Another obvious fact: for whatever reasons, drinking or drug taking becomes an important activity in the life of the problem drinker or drug user. The individual develops a relationship with alcohol or another drug of choice. The relationship, with all that word implies, is as real and important a bond as the bond with friends, a spouse, or the long-time family pet. Accordingly, energy is expended to maintain the relationship. The bond may be thought of as a love affair. Long after the good times, the pleasure, and the thrill are gone, all kinds of mental gymnastics are used to maintain the myth that it's still great.

How does this progression occur? The first step is quite simple. The individual destined for later trouble is seemingly no different than anyone else. In this example, we use alcohol. This is the prototypic drug in our culture. For anyone who uses alcohol, the first important experience is to *learn the mood swing.* This learning has a physiological basis. Alcohol is a drug with acute effects. It makes us feel good. At any time, our moods could be plotted on a graph representing a continuum. One end represents pain and the other end represents euphoria. Before drinking, if our mood falls in the middle or normal range, the effect of the drink is to shift our mood toward the euphoric end. When the effects of the alcohol wear off, we're back where we started.

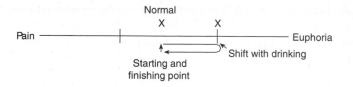

Anyone who drinks learns this pharmacological effect of alcohol. As importantly, we learn that it happens consistently. Alcohol the drug can be depended upon. If you reflect back on the discussion of alcohol's acute effects in Chapter 2, you'll recall that a number of things make this learning potent. You do not have to wait very long to experience what alcohol does. The effects of the drug can be felt almost immediately. For the new drinker, who has not acquired any tolerance to alcohol's effects, the change can be dramatic.

The primary "payoff" for drug use is generally thought of as the physiological effects. But there are other factors at work. For example, the first-time smoker does not find smoking very pleasant. There is dizziness, feelings of nausea, and the unpleasant taste. One would have a hard time explaining smoking on the basis of the initial physiological effects. Rather, the positive-feeling state that accompanies smoking is what smoking *means* to the person, not what the nicotine does. The attraction may be that smoking is considered to be "cool," sophisticated, denoting independence from parental/social norms, whatever. In the beginning, smoking occurs *despite* the immediate physical experience. However, the nicotine that accompanies the smoke quickly plays a role in perpetuating use.

The second stage in the developmental process is termed *seeking the mood swing*. This happens after someone learns that alcohol can be counted on to enhance or improve mood. Now drinking can have a particular purpose. Anyone who drinks occasionally does so to make things better. Whatever the occasion—an especially hard day at work, a family reunion, celebrating a promotion, or recovery from a trying day of hassling kids—the expectation is that alcohol will do something nice. In essence, the person has a contract with alcohol. True to its promise, alcohol keeps its side of the bargain. Furthermore, by altering the dose, the person can control the degree of mood change. Still there are no problems. Nothing up to this point suggests that alcohol use can be anything but pleasurable.

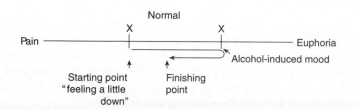

Who hath woe?
Who hath sorrow?
Who hath contentions?
Who hath babbling?
Who hath wounds without cause?
Who hath redness of eyes? They that
tarry long at the wine.

PROVERBS 28:31–32

One of the disadvantages of wine is
that it makes a man mistake words for
thoughts.

SAMUEL JOHNSON

Somewhere along the line, predictably, most people who use alcohol will have a negative drinking experience. This may happen early in someone's drinking career. The unpleasant event can be the discomfort of a hangover, "the morning after," or it can be the sensation of closing one's eyes and feeling the world begin to spin. It also may not be the physical aftermath of intoxication but the behavior that took place then. What occurred when drinking can make the person squirm at its recollection. At any rate, most people are quite clear that alcohol was the significant factor. They tell themselves, "Never again," and that's that. Possibly described as "sadder but wiser" as a result of what has happened, they alter their pattern of use in the future and markedly reduce the risk of future problems resulting from alcohol use.*

For a significant minority of drinkers, the above scenario has a different outcome. These are the people for whom alcohol use becomes an emerging problem. In Johnson's schema, these people have crossed a thin and still undefined line that separates the second and third stages. The third phase is *harmful dependence.* (The term dependence is not used in the physiological sense.) Suddenly alcohol's use has a boomerang effect. Alcohol, which previously had only a beneficial, positive effect, now has some negative consequences. Sketched out on the pain-euphoria continuum: initially the mood changes in the desired direction and achieves the drinker's purpose. But then something new occurs: the mood swings back, "dropping off" the person with less comfortable feelings than prior to the drinking. The same phenomenon can be seen with other drug use.

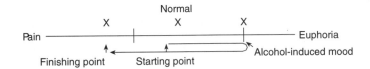

Reaching the stage of harmful dependence has important consequences. From this point, to continue drinking or using drugs in the same fashion will exact *emotional costs.* For whatever reasons, unwilling to abandon the use of alcohol as a means of altering their moods, some are willing to pay the price and accept whatever the negative consequences may be. This decision to accept the consequences isn't a conscious one. Emotionally, they remain "loyal" to their relationship with the drug. It is here that denial enters the picture and there is an altering of priorities which is needed to maintain the relationship with alcohol.

*Here too there is a difference between nicotine and alcohol worth noting. Despite its clearly greater addiction potential, nicotine does not alter behavior to the extent that alcohol does. There is no equivalent to drunkenness, intoxication, or equivalent alteration of consciousness that accompanies smoking. Thus, nicotine does not have the same capacity to create behavioral problems as does alcohol. The problems associated with nicotine are medical and the result of long-term use. The smoker is therefore unlikely to have the same kind of experience that will lead to a change in the pattern of use.

The most significant costs are psychological. Drinking and other drug-induced behavior and its consequences are inconsistent with fundamental values and self-image. To deal with this contradiction, continued use requires the individual to make personality adjustments. The normal, run-of-the-mill psychological devices will be used to distort reality just enough to explain away the costs. These psychological defenses are the same ones each of us uses virtually daily to some degree. If I'm walking down the street, say hello to a friend, and get no response, my feelings are momentarily hurt. Almost automatically I tell myself, "She must not have seen or heard me." So I shut off the hurt feelings with an explanation that may or may not be true. I seize an explanation that allows me to turn off the unpleasant feelings the situation has evoked. Another time, if I'm ill-tempered, a complete grouch, and behaving in a fashion that I don't really like, I become uncomfortable with myself. In such circumstances I could say, "Yep, I sure am being a real pain in the neck to anyone near me." More likely the internal conversation will come out: "I've not been myself. The pressure of work must have gotten to me." In this way, we all attempt to control our discomfort and maintain psychic harmony. In doing so, we often overlook the obvious and adjust our experience just enough to take off the painful, rough emotional edges.

The person with a budding alcohol or drug problem uses these kinds of defenses to maintain harmony and equilibrium in the relationship with their drug of choice. One way to accomplish this and "explain away" the costs is to suppress emotions. As negative emotions arise, the individual strives to keep them at bay: "I just won't think about it." So the fellow who made a fool of himself at last night's party tries to ignore the whole thing. "Heavens, these things happen sometimes. There's no sense in worrying about it." However, pretending emotions aren't there doesn't make them disappear. They simply crop up somewhere else. Because suppression doesn't work totally, other psychological devices need to be used. Rationalization is a common device—seizing an explanation that inevitably stays clear of alcohol itself. "I really got bombed last night because Sean was pouring such stiff ones." Here projection is at work as well. The reason for whatever occurred and the accompanying emotional discomfort was that the drinks were stiff, and it's Sean's fault! No responsibility is accepted by the drinker or blame laid on alcohol.

A number of rationalizations are so frequently used that they might almost qualify as warning signals of alcohol dependence. For example: "I can't be alcoholic because I never drink in the morning. *I'm* too young, too old, too smart, etc. I can quit *whenever* I want to. *Everyone* I know drinks the same way I do. I *only* drink beer. I *only* drink wine spritzers. I *never* miss work." Casual drinkers would never consider such explanations necessary.

Several factors allow such distortions to go unchallenged. One is attributable to the action of the drug. Alcohol warps perceptions. The only firsthand memory anyone will have of a drinking event is the one that was laid down in a drugged state. So if someone under a haze of alcohol

perceives herself as being clever and witty, sobering up in the morning is not going to be sufficient to make her realize that she was loud, coarse, and vulgar. This "rosy memory" is termed by Johnson as "euphoric recall." Until recently, with the advent of greater public awareness of alcohol problems, it was unlikely that other people would take it upon themselves to let the drinker know what really transpired. There might not be any problems if these distortions were only occasional, but they aren't. And what proves to be even more destructive is that with continued heavy drinking, the discrepancy becomes greater and greater between what the individual *expects* to happen and what *does* happen. Proportionately, the need for further distortion to explain this discrepancy grows.

Drinking is supposed to improve the mood, but as dependence emerges, more and more frequently the opposite proves to be the case. To illustrate this on the mood continuum, after a drinking occasion the emotional state is one of greater discomfort than it was before the drinking. As alcohol's effects wear off, the individual is finding himself being dropped off further down toward the pain end of the spectrum. The result of alcohol use is not an enhanced but a diminished sense of well-being.

A vicious cycle is developing. The psychological mechanisms used to minimize the discomfort simultaneously prevent a recognition of what is really happening. None of the defenses, even in combination, are completely foolproof. At times, individuals feel remorse about their behavior. At those times it doesn't matter where the blame lies—on Sean, on oneself, on alcohol—any way you cut it, the drinker regrets what's happening. So a negative self-image develops.

For the most part, the drinker truly believes the reality created by his or her projections and rationalizations. Understandably, this begins to erode relationships with others. There are continual hassles over whose version of an event is accurate. This introduces additional tensions, and problems arise with friends, family, and coworkers. Self-esteem shrinks. The load of negative feelings expands. Ironically, there is more and more reliance on the old relationship with alcohol. Drinking is deliberately structured into life patterns. Drinking is anticipated. The possibilities of drinking may well determine which invitations are accepted, where business meetings are held, and other activities. Gradually, *all* leisure time is set up to include drinking.

The stage is set for the last developmental phase in the emergence of clear-cut dependence. The individual now *drinks to feel normal.* This is often wholly unappreciated by those for whom drinking is not a

Boundless intemperance
In nature is a tyranny; it hath been
Th'untimely emptying of the happy throne
And fall of many kings.

SHAKESPEARE, *Macbeth*

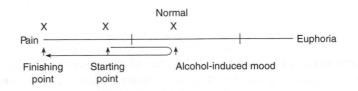

problem. Others assume, erroneously, that the alcohol dependent person is drinking to feel "good" and have "fun." By this point the idea of drinking to feel euphoric has long since gone. Alcohol has become essential *just* to achieve a normal feeling state.

In addition to offering a normal feeling state, alcohol may assist "normal" functioning in other respects. Psychologists have documented the phenomenon of "state-dependent learning." Things learned in a particular context are most readily recalled under similar circumstances. Thus things learned when sober are best recalled later in a sober state. Similarly, information learned while drinking will also be more available for recall later when the person is again (or still) consuming alcohol. Thus the heavy drinker may have a repertoire of behavior, coping mechanisms, social skills, even information that, if learned during drinking, is less accessible when sober. In fact, drinking may be necessary to tap a reservoir of knowledge. This fact is what sometimes explains the inability to find liquor stashes that were hidden when drinking. Another way in which alcohol may be essential to "normalize" function is to ward off withdrawal symptoms if the drinker has become physically dependent.

Memory distortions are not uncommon at this point. Blackouts may mean the absence of memory for some events. Repression is a psychological mechanism that also blocks out memory. Further havoc continues to be raised by "euphoric recall." The memories are only of the good times and the sense of relief associated with drinking. The problems and difficulties seemingly don't penetrate.

The same kind of progression can be seen in the use of other drugs. With illegal substances there are also the extra problems of cost and assuring a steady supply, as well as the ever-present danger of contaminants and varying levels of potency. These factors exacerbate deterioration and may make the problems more apparent. Some drugs are more quickly addicting than others, and in some cases the progression is less gradual. Here again, nicotine is the best example. Dependence is established very quickly. One study of the natural history of smoking had the very arresting title of "The addiction trap: A forty-year sentence for four cigarettes." Basically, there are exceedingly few individuals who have had four or more cigarettes who did not become regular, long-term (addicted) smokers.

DETERIORATING FUNCTIONING

Because of the transformation of thinking, distorted view of reality, and ebbing self-esteem, the alcohol or drug dependent person's functioning deteriorates. Each of us is expected to fulfill various roles in life. For each slot in which we find ourselves, there is an accompanying set of expectations about appropriate behavior. Some of the typical roles are parent, spouse, employee, citizen, friend. Others may be more transient, such as scout leader, committee chair, patient, or Sunday school teacher. No matter what the role, with alcohol or drug dependence performance usually suffers. There are expectations that others

If God wanted us high, He would have given us wings.
ARSENIO HALL

have of us in a particular role. The alcohol or drug dependent individual does not reliably meet them. Behavior is inconsistent. The individual is undependable—sometimes doing what is expected and doing it beautifully; the next time, "no show" followed by the flimsiest excuse. To add insult to injury, he or she gets furious at others for being disappointed or annoyed or for not understanding.

This unreliable behavior has a profound impact on the people around the alcohol or drug dependent person. Since these people have the normal insecurities of all humans, they think it might or must be their fault. Unwittingly, they accept the rationalizations and projections. Some find themselves confused and often feel left out. They sense and fear the loss of an important relationship, one that has been nourishing to them. In turn, their usual behavior becomes distorted. Now, in addition to whatever problems are directly attributable to alcohol or drug use, interpersonal relationships are impaired. This fuels the tension.

FAMILY AND FRIENDS

Wine makes a man better pleased with himself;
I do not say that it makes him more pleasing to others.

SAMUEL JOHNSON

Let us focus briefly on the family, close relationships, and friends. Applying behavioral learning terms, the dependent person has those people in his or her life on a variable interval-reinforcement schedule. There they are, busily trying to accommodate. Everyone feels that somehow if they behave differently, do the "right thing," the alcohol or drug dependent person will respond. One time they're harsh, the next time they try an "understanding" approach. Then another time they might try to ignore the situation. But nothing works. The dependent person does not respond in any predictable way to their behavior. If he happens to be a "good boy" or she's been a "perfect lady" on occasion, it really has no connection to what the family has or has not done. The others, in fact, are accommodating themselves to the alcohol or drug dependent individual. Never sure why some times go better, they persist in trying—and trying some more. Meanwhile, the inconsistency and unpredictability remain.

Eventually the family or partner, as well as close friends, give up and try to live around the situation. Alternately the drinker is ignored or driving them crazy. Yet, out of love and loyalty, for all too long others provide protection from the consequences of the drinking or drug use. This dynamic has been described as "enabling behavior" and will be elaborated on in Chapter 7. In a marriage or relationship, if one partner has a major substance use problem, the other gradually assumes the accustomed functions of the impaired partner. If a wife is alcoholic, the husband may develop contingency plans for supper in case it isn't ready that night. If a husband is alcoholic, the wife may be the one who definitely plans to attend Little League games or school conferences. If the husband is up to it, fine, if not, a ready excuse is hauled out. This leads to resentments in both partners. The spouse carrying the load feels burdened; the drinker feels deprived and ashamed.

With alcohol dependence present, you can count on sexual problems in the primary relationship. In American society, concern over sexual performance seems to be the national pastime. Sexual functioning is not merely a physical activity, it also has strong psychological components. How someone feels about himself or herself and a partner is bound to show up in the bedroom. Any alcohol use can disturb physiological capacity for sex. Shakespeare said it most succinctly: "alcohol provokes the desire but takes away the performance." In the male, alcohol interferes with erection—popularly referred to as "brewer's droop." The psychological realm has as strong an impact. Satisfying sexual relationships require an emotional relationship, a bond of love and affection. In a relationship with alcohol as the third member, neither partner is able to trust that bond. There are doubts on both sides. Problems result in many ways. Intoxication invites revulsion and rejection. Any qualities of love have, for the moment, been washed away by booze. Intercourse also can become a weapon. One of the partners can try the old tactic of emotional blackmail used in the ancient Greek play *Lysistrata:* refusing sex unless the partner changes his or her behavior. On the other hand, both partners can approach intercourse as the magic panacea. If they can still make love, they can minimize the importance of everything else lacking in the relationship. Sexual fears and anxiety, which are rampant in the total population, are compounded in the alcoholic relationship.

In the earlier stages of substance use problems, friends, especially close ones, make the same kind of excuses for the individual that family members make. But as time goes on, and problems mount as behavior deteriorates, friendships disappear in inverse relationship to their closeness. In the later stages of alcohol dependence there may be "drinking buddies" but few true friends. The reasons are fairly obvious. Casual acquaintances are unlikely to be interested in becoming friends after a few examples of erratic behavior. It's simply not worth it. Close friends who have begun to see a problem emerging will probably try to help by talking to the drinker. In the early stages of an alcohol problem this may well be effective in prompting treatment. However, the defenses grow in magnitude to the problem. Later in the development of dependence, the common response is telling the friend to mind her or his own business, thus immobilizing the friend. The relationship to the bottle or another drug takes precedence over all others.

The exceptions only highlight the problem. One type of friend who may remain a companion is one who also drinks as the drinker does and can be counted on to share the sherry luncheons or the six-packs on the way home from work. Another kind of friend will remain in loose touch, ready to lend a hand when needed. This person may be recovering and have gone through much the same process. She knows the friendship cannot be maintained or profitably cultivated while the drinking or drug use continues, but she will often stay in touch, poised to be of assistance and support should the drinker show evidence of wishing to face the problem and stop. When faced with an alcohol problem in someone close to them, recovering individuals, or treatment professionals for that matter, often don't have an edge on anyone else, however. Their special expertise or personal experience matters little given the dynamics of the family or friendships. Maybe because they are more aware than others of the dangers associated with abusive or alcoholic drinking, their desire to have things be "anything but" may be very strong.

WORK

Often, although alcohol or drug dependent people are deeply mired in deteriorating social and family relationships and suffering physical problems, they still may be able to function at work. The work arena seems to be the last part of the drinker's or user's life to be affected. The job is often the status symbol for both the dependent employee and the partner. With families counting more and more upon two paychecks for economic stability, maintaining the income of both members is necessary. He or she might think or say: "There's nothing wrong with me. I'm still bringing in a good paycheck!" The partner is likely to make excuses to the other's boss to protect the family livelihood.

Intervention at the workplace is, of course, possible at even the earliest signs. Much effort is being made to alert employers to the early signs of alcohol and other drug-use problems and to acquaint them with rehabilitation possibilities. The employer is in a unique position to affect treatment at a relatively early stage. A recommendation that someone go for treatment may well be a precipitating factor in a recovery. The fact that the employer sees the problem and calls a spade a spade can go far in breaking down the denial system. Keeping a job may be sufficient motivation for an employee to face the problem. Employee assistance programs and their impact on earlier intervention and treatment are described further in Chapter 10.

Those in serious trouble with alcohol generally believe that their public cover-up is successful. The behavior of those about them often does little to challenge this misconception. Too often their deteriorating functioning is covered up by other workers. Absences with the "flu" are ignored, and a gradual decline in their work is put down to "problems at home" or some other such excuse. Most people, finding that it is not easy to confront someone with a drinking problem, wait until ignoring it is no longer possible. Over 20 years ago a study found that persons other than family members had noticed drinking problems on an average of 7 years before the alcoholics first sought help. Vaillant's work confirmed this too. Although 4 or more alcohol-related problems were virtually sufficient to guarantee a diagnosis of alcohol dependence, it wasn't, in fact, until 11 separate such incidents had occurred that people entered treatment.

Often alcohol impaired persons have no idea how obvious their difficulties are to so many other people. When they are finally confronted, it can be a great shock to find out how much of their behavior that they thought was hidden was, in fact, observed. The rationalization and denial systems actually convinced the active alcoholic that *no one* on the job or in the community knew about the drinking problem.

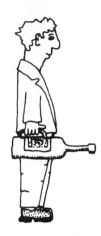

The behavior that accompanies alcohol or drug dependence causes pain and confusion for all—the individual and those around him or her. Unfortunately, most of the family's and friends' efforts to alter the situation don't work. Regardless of good will, alcohol/drug dependence rarely responds to the more common maneuvers of concerned people. Affecting these destructive patterns takes a special knowledge of the dynamics of the disease, its effects on others, and treatment approaches, with the clinical skills of a disinterested, but not an uninterested, participant.

RESOURCES AND FURTHER READING

In this chapter the attempt has been to convey what dependence feels like for the individual with the disease and for those whose lives are closely touched by it.

Tackling the scientific writings, with their reports of controlled studies, tables of data, and reams of footnotes, is unlikely to be a useful avenue for further exploration. Instead we suggest you turn to literature. An autobiography of someone with alcoholism or drug dependence might provide more insight into and understanding of the behavior and feelings that characterize the disease. Consider the plays of Eugene O'Neill: *Long Day's Journey into Night* powerfully captures the family beset by addiction.

Identify a recovering individual with whom you can just talk. Don't consider this a formal interview; consider it a conversation initiated by an interested person who wants to know what another's life was like. Take as a guide the conversation you might have with a close friend who has returned from that long-anticipated trip of a lifetime. Through your questioning and listening, by asking her to "relive" the trip, you imagine being a companion on the adventure.

Attend open meetings of AA, NA, or other self-help groups. As members tell their "stories," as they speak about "what it was like," the behavior and the emotional life of active alcoholism are powerfully conveyed.

Johnson V: *I'll Quit Tomorrow,* revised edition. New York: Harper & Row, 1983.

Russell MAH: The nicotine addiction trap: A 40-year sentence for four cigarettes, *British Journal of Addiction* 85(2):293–300, 1990. (34 refs.)
It is generally recognized that smoking causes more preventable illness than any other form of drug addiction. Despite this, and unlike the case with other addictions, few services are provided to help people to give it up. Yet nicotine is highly addictive. Its role in the recruitment process, in the development of dependence, and as a block to smoking cessation are discussed within the context of the typical smoking career. Over 90% of teenagers who smoke 3–4 cigarettes are trapped into a career of regular smoking which typically lasts for some 30 to 40 years. Only 35% of regular smokers succeed in stopping permanently before the age of 60, although the large majority want to stop and try to stop. (Author abstract.)

Schuckit MA, Smith TL, Anthenelli R, and others: Clinical course of alcoholism in 636 male inpatients, *American Journal of Psychiatry* 150(5):786–792, 1993.

This study was undertaken to determine the relative order of appearance of symptoms in alcohol dependence. The age at which 21 alcohol-related major life events first occurred was investigated in 636 male alcohol dependent inpatients through a standardized, structured personal interview with each subject and at least one resource person. A general pattern of first occurrence of these events was observed. Heavy drinking escalated further when the subjects were in their late 20s, followed by evidence of interference with functioning in multiple life areas in the early 30s, a subsequent perception of loss of control, and then an intensification of social and job-related problems, along with evidence of deterioration in body systems, in the mid to late 30s. Similar patterns of problems emerged when the alcoholic subjects were divided into subgroups based on onset of alcohol dependence before or after age 30, presence or absence of a family history of alcoholism, and presence or absence of additional psychiatric disorders. These data indicate that there is a typical progression of events related to alcohol dependence. This information can be useful for clinicians in their work with patients and for teachers and researchers as well. (Author abstract.)

7

EFFECTS OF ALCOHOL PROBLEMS ON THE FAMILY

THE "FAMILY ILLNESS"

In the early 1980s a review of two books purporting to be comprehensive works on alcoholism noted the scanty attention paid to the impact of alcoholism on the family. The reviewer plaintively asked, "Why is so much written about the effects of alcoholism upon a patient's liver enzymes and so little written about the effects of parental alcoholism on the children?" Fortunately that question no longer has the same ring of truth to it.

One of the major developments in the alcohol field during the 1980s was the vastly increased attention to the plight of the family. This is evidenced particularly by the involvement of families in alcohol treatment. In addition, there were efforts to reach out to family members, even if the alcohol dependent person was not in treatment. As part of the attention to the family, one began to hear alcoholism described as a "family illness." This refers to the tremendous impact those with active alcohol dependence have upon those around them. There is no way the family members can escape or ignore the alcoholic member. The majority of the impairments symptomatic of alcohol dependence are behavioral. So in the day-to-day interactions of family life, the family members are confronted with the behaviors symptomatic of alcoholism, although the behaviors initially may appear to have little connection to the drinking. Over time, the family can become as functionally impaired as the member with alcoholism.

While no family member ever caused alcoholism, despite what the alcoholic may have claimed, the family can, despite its best intentions, behave in a way that allows the drinking to continue. They may protect the alcoholic member, make excuses or accept the explanations of the alcoholic, and endeavor in a variety of ways to cover up. They might call the employer, pretending the absenteeism is due to "the flu." Or they may cover a bad check or retain a good lawyer to beat a DWI charge. The alcoholic's actions are bound to create stresses and increase the family's anxiety level. This in turn may provoke more alcoholic drinking to relieve the alcoholic's own anxiety, which raises the family's anxiety even higher, and the family members react by simply doing more of what they were already doing. The pattern escalates on both sides until some crisis occurs. The family is no better able to cope with the disease in its midst than is the impaired member, and thus involvement in treatment is essential.

The issues of the family also caught the attention of the alcohol research community. However, there is always a lag time between an issue gaining the attention of the research community and the point at which the research is conducted, findings analyzed, the results published, and the findings translated into practice. In the meantime, clinicians are forced to "do the best they can," drawing upon their clinical observations and using the information that is available.

Inevitably, the approaches during such transitional periods will later be recognized as a combination of fact and fiction. As research findings become available, the challenge is to refine our practice to incorporate new knowledge, and, as required, lay aside our earlier formulations. That in many respects is where we are now. We can no longer continue discussing the problems of alcohol and the family simply by drawing upon the best guesses of yesterday. We too are being forced to recognize there is far more variety in family life today than there was several generations ago. Families today come in many forms. They range from the 'traditional' family, statistically described as husband, wife, 2.2 children, and a dog, to single-parent families, to unmarried couples, to same-sex couples, as well as "blended" families that include children from prior marriages or relationships. Variations on the traditional theme inevitably introduce new twists for families. While there may be common issues, there may be differences posed by the particular family structure.

The family's response

The earliest attention to alcohol and the family can be traced to a classic monograph published by Joan Jackson in 1954, "Alcoholism and the Family." It endeavored to describe the stages that occur as a family comes to grips with alcoholism. Her work paralleled that of E.M. Jellinek, who only 8 years before had studied members of AA to identify the stages of alcohol addiction (see Chapter 4). Jackson's work was conducted through her attending meetings and speaking with members of a group known as the AA Auxiliary. Later, the Auxiliary became what we know as Al-Anon Family Groups. Given the era in which her research was conducted, the stages she identified are based upon the family in which the husband and father was the alcoholic, and also when alcoholism was considered a disease of "middle age," taking hold between the ages of 35 and 50. The six stages Jackson sketched out are described below in the order in which, in her sample, they typically unfold.

Denial   Occasional episodes of excessive drinking at first are explained away by both partners. Early in the emergence of alcoholism, drinking because of tiredness, worry, nervousness, or a bad day is not unbelievable. The assumption is that the episode is an isolated instance and therefore no problem. If the couple is part of a group in which heavy drinking is acceptable, this provides a handy cover for developing dependency. A cocktail before dinner easily becomes two or three, and wine with the meal and brandy afterward also pass without much notice.

Attempts to eliminate the problem   Here the alcoholic's partner recognizes that the drinking is not normal and tries to pressure him or her to quit, be more careful, or cut down. "If you only pulled yourself together," or "If you only used a little willpower," or "If you really love me, you won't do this any more." Simultaneously, the alcoholic's

partner tries to hide the problem from the outside and keep up a good front. At the same time the alcoholic probably sneaks drinks, or drinks outside the home, in an attempt to hide the amount he or she is drinking. Children in the family may start having problems in response to the family stress.

Note: years after Jackson's article, Vernon Johnson pointed out, in *I'll Quit Tomorrow,* that these early attempts to eliminate the problem may be successful. In such cases, formal treatment or AA involvement is unlikely. Indeed, it may not be needed. Historically, the danger for families at this point was that they might enter some general counseling—whether with clergy, psychologist, or social worker—that failed to address the problem drinking head on. In such cases, couples or individual therapy easily became a part of the denial. It could be a way for the alcoholic to continue drinking and for both partners to pretend to be doing something about it. Helping professionals are far more knowledgeable about substance abuse today, so the chances of alcohol problems going undetected are less likely.

I get no kick from champagne,
Mere alcohol doesn't thrill me at all,
So tell me why should it be true
that I get a kick out of you?

COLE PORTER (1934) *I Get a Kick Out of You*

Disorganization and chaos   The family equilibrium has now broken down. The alcoholic's spouse can no longer pretend everything is okay and spends most of the time going from crisis to crisis. Financial troubles are common. Under real stress, possibly questioning her own emotional health, the spouse may seek outside help. In general, women are more likely than men to use outside assistance. Too often spouses may seek help from friends who know no more than they do about what to do. Similarly, they may seek out a member of the clergy who has no training in dealing with alcoholism. Or they may turn to the family physician, who in the past may have prescribed some "nerve" pills when confronted by their distraught condition. If at this stage the nonalcoholic partner seeks assistance from alcohol professionals and/or becomes involved with Al-Anon, the process will probably take a different course altogether.

Reorganization in spite of the problem   The spouse's coping abilities have been strengthened. He or she gradually assumes the larger share of responsibility for the family unit. This may mean getting a job or taking over the finances. The major focus of energy is no longer directed toward getting the alcoholic partner to "shape up." Instead, the spouse takes charge. The spouse fosters family life, despite the alcoholism. It has since been recognized that the degree to which a stable family life can be established and maintained, even if the alcoholic remains in the home, can have important implications for the welfare of children in the family. Children fare far better in families in which the family rituals are maintained, whether these are celebrations such as Christmas or birthdays, or continuing regular family meal times, or going on the family vacation, or any of the other things, large or small, that "we always do."

Efforts to escape   Separation or divorce may be attempted. If the family unit remains intact, the family continues living around the alcoholic member.

Family reorganization   In the case of separation, family reorganization occurs without the alcoholic partner and parent. If the alcoholic achieves sobriety, a reconciliation may take place. Either path will require both partners to realign roles and make new adjustments.

Further thoughts   As mentioned, Jackson's formulations are focused on the family in which the husband is alcoholic. An important difference is found in marriage outcomes depending on which partner has the alcohol problem. Among alcoholics, the female alcoholic is much more likely to be divorced than is the male alcoholic. In the past, those trying to account for this difference speculated that women who marry alcoholics have unconscious, neurotic needs to be married to weak, inadequate males. The implication was that because of this need, they stayed married and got psychological strokes for doing so. That view no longer has much credence. Given economic realities, it is not unexpected that the nonalcoholic wife stays in her marriage longer than the nonalcoholic husband. She may well feel a need for the husband's financial support to maintain the family. Indeed, following a divorce, the economic situation for the majority of women and their children declines. On the other side, men in general are less likely to seek outside help for any kind of problem—no matter what kind. Therefore the husband of a female alcoholic may see no alternative to divorce to save himself, as well as the children.

Research on marriage has identified some reasons why partners choose each other. For all persons, it is generally recognized that finding one's "true love" and the choice of a marriage partner is not a random event. People tend to select marriage partners with similarities to their parents. Many women who marry alcoholic men are daughters of alcoholics. For them, a situation that appears to us as stressful and painful may simply be what they expect in a marriage. Those involved in alcohol treatment are struck by the fact that some women marry or live with a succession of alcoholics.

Jackson's formulations may be useful in considering the situation of a family and its efforts to cope. While providing a useful general framework, do not expect all families to experience these stages in the textbook fashion. Some families might get bogged down in different stages. Some never move beyond denial. Some may seem trapped in an endless cycle of chaos and crisis. And some go through a painful succession of attempts to escape from the situation, reconciliations, followed by later attempts again to escape. Our understanding of the factors that account for these differences is limited. One factor that may make a difference is when the problem drinking emerges. Those who have studied alcoholic marriages suggest that wives most able to help themselves and their families are those who were married before their husbands became problem drinkers.

THE FAMILY SYSTEM

A common dimension of virtually all approaches to the alcoholic family is viewing the family as a system. This is a very common perspective within the larger field of family therapy. Central to this is the belief that changes in any part of the system (any family member) affect all of the others. The other members, in response, also make changes in an attempt to maintain the family equilibrium. The metaphor that captures this close interdependence is that of a circus family specializing in a high-wire balancing act. All members of the act climb up to the top of the tent. In turn, they step out on to the thin wire to begin an intricate set of maneuvers to build a human pyramid high above the audience. Timing and balance are critical; the mutual interdependence is obvious. Each is sensitive to even the tiniest movement of the others. All of the family members in the performance continually adjust and readjust their balance, which is necessary to maintain the routine. If only one fails to do the expected, the entire routine fails.

In essence, families with an impaired member function in a very similar fashion. The alcoholic's behavior begins to invade the family routine. Everyone attempts to compensate, with the goal of restoring the equilibrium to the family. Most families make precarious, and usually unhealthy, adjustments to the presence of drinking. They expend energy to maintain the status quo, "the familiar and known." The family's behavior is designed to avoid doing anything that might further upset the delicate balance that prevails, which to their minds would prompt further deterioration of the family's situation. And, after having adjusted to a problem, the family would be required to make significant readjustments if the impaired member were to seek treatment.

In terms of the kinds of accommodations that families make, there can be a range of responses. At one extreme, the drinking alcoholic is almost like a boarder in the family's household. The family isolates and walls off the alcoholic. They expect little. They give little. In this way, they maintain some stability and continuity for themselves. At the other extreme, the entire family life is constantly alcohol-centered, responding to the crisis of the moment. In addition, families can vacillate between patterns of accommodating the alcoholic, depending on whether the alcoholic is drinking or on the wagon.

Recent research has identified three different approaches family members use in living with an alcoholic: (1) keeping out of the way of the drinker and managing one's own life; (2) care-giving, counseling, and controlling; and (3) resigning and maintaining a facade. While all are used at various times, there may be a "usual approach," and the approach most commonly chosen differs by gender and between spouse and children. Most commonly the spouse is involved with care-giving, counseling, and controlling. Children of problem drinkers, on the other hand, are more likely to opt for keeping out of the way of the drinker and managing their own lives. Men more than women are more likely to adopt "resignation" while women are likely to selectively "keep out of the way" while also engaged in care-giving.

Enabling

Vernon Johnson introduced the idea of the "intervention" as a means of moving alcoholics into treatment. A basic component is working with family members to identify the ways they may help protect the alcoholic member.   He noted that many behaviors of family members have an unanticipated result. While attempting to live with and around the alcoholism and to reduce the level of pain for themselves, the family's behavior often unwittingly "allows" the drinking to continue. This is occurring whenever the family's actions protect the alcoholic member from the consequences of drinking. By removing the costs that result from drinking, the family takes away the major impetus for change. This phenomenon Johnson termed *enabling*. Enabling behavior can be "white lies," the explanations provided to others that take the alcoholic off the hook. Enabling can consist of "overlooking," or not commenting upon, the most outrageous behavior. Often it entails active intervention on the alcoholic's behalf. It is happening whenever the spouse scurries around to raise bail money and then follows up with a call to the local newspaper requesting that the arrest be kept out of the paper. It is happening when parents cover the cost of an adolescent son's car repairs plus the added insurance premiums resulting from a DWI. Enabling can be cleaning up your college roommate when she comes in drunk and throws up on herself, the rug, the bed, and your sweater that she was wearing.

Ironically, while sparing the alcoholic from experiencing the consequences and thus the associated pain, the family members absorb the pain themselves. The behavior considered as enabling may be viewed as necessary because: "I care," "At least it buys peace," "I just can't take any more," "I'm afraid of what will happen to me (to the children) if I don't," "Someone has to assume some responsibility," and on and on. Nonetheless, it often involves actions that are distasteful or feel wrong. Enabling behaviors can evoke twinges of guilt, anger, despair, frustration, and shame. To draw upon a metaphor from a family systems approach commonly used in psychotherapy, the enabler and alcoholic are in an "escalating equilibrium." This means the behavior of each reinforces and maintains the other, while also raising the costs and the emotional consequences for both.

Co-dependency

A term commonly used to describe the effects of alcohol problems on family members is *co-dependency,* and *co-dependent* is the term used for the affected family member(s). There has never been a single consistent definition for these terms. In some instances, these are used as a label—a shorthand means to refer to affected family members. At the other end of the spectrum, co-dependence has been proposed as a Personality Disorder, a distinct psychiatric condition warranting inclusion in the American Psychiatric Association's *Diagnostic and Statistical Manual.* This view has received little support.

Timmen Cermak, M.D., one of the major advocates for naming co-dependency as a new psychiatric disorder, suggested the following criteria for making the diagnosis: (1) Continued investment of one's self-esteem in the ability to control oneself and others in the face of serious adverse consequences. (2) Assumption of responsibility for meeting others' needs to the exclusion of one's own. (3) Anxiety and boundary distortions with respect to intimacy and separation. (4) Enmeshment in relationships with personality disordered, chemically dependent, other co-dependent, and/or impulse-disordered individuals. (5) Three or more of the following: excessive reliance on denial; constriction of emotions; repression; hypervigilance; compulsions; anxiety; substance abuse; being the victim of past or current physical or sexual abuse; stress-related medical illnesses; remaining in a primary relationship with an active substance abuser for at least 2 years without seeking help. Research has not provided support for the notion of family member's sharing a set of symptoms that represent a discrete psychiatric condition.

The widespread adoption of the terms "co-dependency" and "co-dependent" has been the source of considerable discomfort for many in the alcohol and substance abuse fields. Since its initial introduction the concept has been widely adopted by self-help groups and has spread into the popular culture. Witness the book *Co-Dependent No More,* which topped the New York Times best-seller list for nearly a year.

Such a widespread popular acceptance of an idea that is without scientific support represents a dilemma for clinicians. The notion of co-dependency *has* hit a responsive chord. This fact should remind us of the pain that family members experience in response to problems in their midst, the sense of impotence these can evoke, and their felt need for assistance in making changes. However, in discussions with clients, it is important to draw upon its utility as a *metaphor,* without implying, or acting as if, it is a proven scientific concept. If we treat it as more than a metaphor, we are in danger of providing poor clinical care. No one would dispute the effects of alcohol dependence on family members, nor the fact that these family members are statistically more likely to encounter many problems and in greater numbers than their counterparts in the general population. However, to award labels indiscriminately and to presume that every family member shares the constellation of symptoms is a grave disservice to clients. Assumptions based simply on family status cannot substitute for a careful assessment and evaluation. There is the danger too that the strengths of families and family members are overlooked when one assumes pathology.

Current thinking

The research on families touched by substance abuse is growing. What has become clear is that all families are not affected by alcohol dependence in a uniform manner. Thus, there are few universal statements that can be made about families facing substance abuse or alcoholism.

Furthermore, it is now recognized that the features originally seen as distinctive to the alcoholic family are also seen in other families confronted by stress. The response to stress seemingly is the common denominator. It doesn't matter whether it is the result of substance abuse, or serious mental illness, or family disruptions due to job loss or death.

Among the questions being considered now are the factors that are associated with differing levels of family dysfunction, the factors that are associated with stable recoveries in families following treatment, and the indications for different types of family treatment. Attention is also being directed to a family's protective factors, those family attributes that seem to reduce the disruption that can accompany substance abuse. Interestingly, much of the current research is directed to the types of factors in the family that may promote or protect children from later alcohol problems, rather than looking for some general psychological profile. For children with an alcoholic parent, *the* single major problem associated with parental alcoholism is their own increased risk of alcoholism, due to genetic endowment.

Earliest examination of the impact of alcoholism on the family zeroed in on its psychological impact and the impact on personality, self-esteem, and identity. Attention has now turned to other factors and their costs to family members. Domestic violence is more common in the home with alcoholism. Psychiatric illness may also be present. Members of the family themselves have greater levels of physical illness, especially of stress-related illnesses. Family members are more vulnerable to gastrointestinal disease, migraine headaches, hypertension, anxiety, and depression. A comparison of health-care costs for family units both before and after alcoholism treatment of a family member bears this out. Before treatment of the alcoholic member, others in the family have significantly more medical problems than do the general population. After treatment, this difference disappears.

CHILDREN OF ALCOHOLICS

Children in the home

It is estimated that in the United States, 11% of children under the age of 18 are living in a family with a parent in need of alcohol or substance abuse treatment. These children deserve special attention. In an atmosphere of conflict, tension, and uncertainty, their needs for warmth, security, and even physical care may be inadequately met. In a family where adult roles are inconsistently and inadequately filled, children lack good models to form their own identities. It is more likely that such children will have a harder time than do their peers as they enter into relationships outside the home, at school, or with playmates. A troubled child may be the signal of an alcohol problem in a family. Although alcoholics represent only 7% of the American population, their children have been estimated to account for approximately 20% of all referrals to child guidance clinics.

It cannot be emphasized too strongly how much remains unknown about the impact of alcoholism on children. In the following discussion of children's coping styles and the impact that continues into adulthood, it must be emphasized that these formulations are *not* based on unbiased scientific research. Much of what has been attributed to children of alcoholics originated in self-help groups of adults who grew up in alcoholic homes. Or the information has come from children of alcoholics who have sought treatment. Although their wounds are real, one must ask how far one can safely generalize from their experiences. They may represent a minority of children of alcoholics. Or they may be speaking primarily for another generation—when alcoholism treatment was less common, when family treatment was unheard of, and when alcoholism was more of a stigma. In any case, it must be remembered that being a child in an alcoholic family does *not* confer an automatic sentence of lifelong problems.

Without question, growing up with an alcoholic parent is far from ideal. At the same time, the experiences of children in alcoholic families vary greatly. There are different patterns of drinking and different behaviors associated with drinking. Children are various ages, as are their parents, when the drinking problem becomes apparent, or when loss of control occurs. Furthermore, there are differences in the coping styles of the nonalcoholic parent, which can moderate the impact of the drinking on family life. All these factors influence how a parent's drinking affects the child. The specific problems of particular children will vary. Furthermore, a child's own natural resilience may be buttressed by the nurturing of extended family, scout leaders, coaches, teachers and neighbors, or parents of peers. Thus a child's experience may be less impoverished than it might appear. Furthermore, many of the problems encountered are not exclusive to the alcoholic home. Many of the characteristics attributed to alcoholic families may be generally true of any dysfunctional family. Nonetheless, in thinking of children it is hard not to think in terms of the dramatic.

Take 5 minutes to imagine what life might be like for a child with an alcoholic parent.

As a preschooler   What is it like to lie in bed listening to your parents fight? Or to have Daddy disappear for periods of time unexpectedly? Or to be spanked really hard and sent away from dinner just because your milk spilled? Or to have a succession of sitters because Mommy works two jobs? Or to get lots of attention one moment and be in the way the next instant?

As an elementary schoolchild   What is it like when your mom forgets to pack a lunch? Or to wait and wait after soccer practice for a ride, long after the other kids have been picked up? Or for Dad to cancel out on the cub scout hike because he is sick? Or not to be allowed to bring friends home to play? Or to have your friends' moms not let them ride in your car? Or to be scared to tell your mom you need a white shirt to be a pilgrim in the class Thanksgiving play?

As an adolescent   What is it like if you can't participate in school functions because you must get home to care for your younger brothers and sisters? Or if the money you made mowing lawns is missing from your room? Or if your dad's name is regularly featured in the court column? Or if your mother asks you to telephone her boss because she has a black eye from falling down? Or if there's no one from your family to come to the athletic awards banquet?

In considering the impact of such behaviors, it is helpful to consider the normal developmental tasks that confront children of different ages and consider how these may be impeded by a parental alcohol problem. Those who have studied the process of emotional development see very early childhood as the period in life in which the major emotional tasks center on developing a sense of security and an ability to trust the environment. At the same time a sense of one's ability to interact with others to have basic needs met should be learned. For the child of an alcohol dependent parent, these basic conditions may not be met. For preadolescent children a major emotional task is developing a sense of autonomy and an ability to use rules to cope with life events. For adolescents, the emotional tasks center around separation from the family and developing the ability to function independently in the world.

The problems may have begun before birth   As discussed in Chapter 3, maternal alcohol use can influence fetal development. At its most extreme, this is expressed as fetal alcohol syndrome. In addition to the direct impact of the drug, behaviors associated with alcoholism may affect fetal development. Physical trauma, including falls, malnutrition, or abnormalities of glucose metabolism, are not uncommon in alcoholics. Any of these could have an impact on a developing baby.

The emotional state of the expectant mother probably influences fetal development. It certainly has an influence on the course of labor and delivery. The emotional state of the alcoholic expectant mother might differ dramatically from that of a normal, healthy, nonalcoholic expectant mother and may be a source of problems. An alcoholic expectant father may exert some indirect prenatal influences. If he is abusive or provides little emotional and financial support, this could cause anxiety in the mother. Lack of support and consequent anxiety during pregnancy are associated with more difficult deliveries. In turn, these difficulties are related to developmental disorders in children. In a similar vein, stress at certain times during pregnancy increases fetal activity. This, in turn, is linked to colicky babies. No specific data are available on labor and delivery for either female alcoholics or wives of male alcoholics.

Another crucial time in any infant's life comes shortly after delivery. The very early interactions between mother and infant are important influences in the mother-child relationship. Medications that may be

required for a difficult delivery can make the bonding more difficult. Both the mother and the infant, under the effects of the medication, are less able to respond to each other.

A new mother needs emotional and physical support to help her deal with the presence of the baby in her life. At a minimum, the baby requires food, warmth, physical comfort, and consistency of response from the mother. In the case of a family with an active alcoholic, one cannot automatically assume that everything is going smoothly.

Children's coping styles

Some children of alcoholics may be having quite apparent and obvious problems. Yet, given the potential for a chaotic environment in the alcoholic family, it is sometimes striking how well children cope with alcoholism. Over 15 years ago, drawing on a family systems approach to the alcoholic family, clinicians working in the alcohol field postulated several distinctive coping styles that children adopt in response to parental alcoholism. These are described below. These coping styles were seen as well to be tied to problems in later life.

Children's alleged coping styles are mentioned here because they are so widely discussed. Efforts to verify these behavior patterns have generally been unsuccessful. At best they can only be used as a metaphor, as a way of outlining the *kinds* of adjustments children *might* make. To encourage a family or for you yourself to put a family under a microscope to identify a child's role in the alcoholic family is unwarranted.

What are these supposed coping styles? One formulation includes three different roles that children may adopt. One is to be the *responsible one*. This role is seen as usually falling to the only child or the oldest child, especially the oldest daughter. The child may assume considerable responsibility not only for himself or herself but also for younger brothers and sisters—taking over chores and keeping track of what needs to be done. In general, this child compensates as much as possible for the instability and inconsistency introduced by the parental alcoholism. A second coping response is that of the *adjuster*. This child doesn't take on the responsibilities of managing. Instead the child follows directions and easily accommodates to whatever comes along. This child is remarkable for how much he or she takes in stride. The third proposed style is to be the *placater*. This role involves managing not the physical affairs, as the responsible one does, but the emotional affairs. This child is ever attuned to being concerned and sensitive to others. It may include being sympathetic to the alcoholic and alternately to the nonalcoholic parent, always trying to soothe ruffled feathers.

The common denominator to these roles is that each in its own way is an attempt to survive, a coping strategy. These roles are seen as providing the child with support and approval from persons outside the home. For example, the responsible one probably is a good student, Mommy's little helper, and gets praise for both. The danger to a child is becoming frozen in these roles. These roles can become a lifetime pattern. What is helpful in childhood can be detrimental for an adult. Thus the responsible one can become an adult who needs always to be on top of things, in control, destined to experience the stress of attempting to be a lifetime superachiever. The flexible one (the adjuster) may be so tentative, so unable to trust, as to be unable to make the long-term commitments that are required to succeed in a career or intimate adult personal relationships, such as that of spouse or parent. Likely as not, the adjuster adults, so attuned to accommodating others, allow themselves to be manipulated. An ever-present option for the adult adjuster would be to marry someone with a problem, such as an alcoholic, which allows the continuation of the adjuster role. The adult placaters are seen as continually caring for others, often at the price of being unaware of their own needs or being unable to meet them. This can lead to large measures of guilt and anger, neither of which a placater can handle easily.

A different but similar typology of the roles that children adopt includes the *family hero,* the *lost child,* the *family mascot,* and the *scapegoat.* The first three have much in common with the three styles just discussed: the responsible one, the adapter, and the placater. Most of these coping styles would not elicit external attention or invite intervention. The exception is the scapegoat, who is the one most likely to be in trouble in school or with the authorities. This is the one who, usually acting angry and deviant, may be the only child clearly seen as having a problem. If the child is a teenager, the trouble may take the form of drug or alcohol abuse. (This is discussed in the section on adolescents in Chapter 10.) Frequently, through the attention focused on this child by outsiders or the family, the family alcohol problem may first surface. Of course, initially the family will see the child as the central problem. And the scapegoat's behavior takes the focus off the parental alcohol problem. Having a common problem to tackle may help keep a fragile family intact. Often the family may create the myth that the drinking is the parent's coping response to the child's behavior. Alternately, the child may be held responsible for aggravating the parent's drinking.

It is suggested that in adulthood, these coping styles could be translated into skills. The placater's sensitivity and ability to be sympathetic and understanding may be assets in helping professions such as social work, psychiatry, and counseling. So, too, the responsible ones may have acquired skills that can serve them in good stead, through their diligence as students and their continued sense of responsibility. The challenge for both is to appreciate the origins and be attuned to the pitfalls.

Adult children of alcoholics

Another aspect of the attention directed to the issues of the family was the emergence of the adult children of alcoholics as a group warranting special attention. The acronym is ACoA. Self-help groups sprouted up, and on the heels of this, treatment programs began to pay more attention

THe family Scapegoat

to this group. However, in hindsight, this therapeutic interest might be considered a passing fad. Presumably because attention and help for the alcoholic was such a recent phenomenon, the now adult children reared in homes with parental alcoholism received no help as children in dealing with this, no matter what the fate of the alcoholic parent. Whether the alcoholic parent died from the disease, or left the home, or recovered, these children, in adult life, see themselves as experiencing difficulties that developed from their experiences in an alcoholic family.

Again the most widely cited writings were not based on research data. Instead they were based on anecdotal evidence and observations of those involved in self-help, who viewed their problems in adulthood as related to their childhood experiences in a home with alcoholism. This literature has set forth a set of characteristics seen as common to adult children of alcoholics. The characteristics include fear of losing control, fear of feelings, fear of conflict, an overdeveloped sense of responsibility, feelings of guilt when standing up for oneself, an inability to relax, let go, or have fun, harsh self-criticism, living in a world of denial, difficulties with intimate relationships, living life from the stance of a victim, the tendency to be more comfortable with chaos than with security, the tendency to confuse love and pity, the tendency under pressure to assume a black-and-white perspective, suffering under a backlog of delayed grief, a tendency to react rather than to act, and an ability to survive.

The current thinking is that the problems adult children of alcoholics may experience are not unique to the alcoholic family but may pertain to families who have had other major problems. As has been pointed out, children of alcoholics may also be children of those with psychiatric illness, or children raised in poverty, or children in a home with domestic violence.

An insight from PT Barnum

If there is no scientific support for these childhood roles, nor for the symptoms ascribed to adult children of alcoholics, why have they not faded from discussion? Note how these characteristics are dependent upon a lot of "coulds," "mights," "possiblys," and "tends to." In effect a logical sequence is postulated that "could" be true. But there is more to it. An article entitled "Psychological characteristics of children of alcoholics," authored by Ken Sher in a 1997 issue of *Alcohol and Research World,* addressed this question. He reported that over 40 years ago it was recognized that people are likely to accept a personality description as valid merely because it is "so vague, double-headed, socially desirable, or widely occurring in the general population that it is difficult to refute." These types of descriptions were termed "Barnum" statements. This is in honor of the noted showman P.T. Barnum whose recipe for a successful circus was "making sure there's a little something for everyone."

Sher points out how many of the descriptors of children of alcoholics have all of the features of classic Barnum statements. For example:

Barnum Characteristic	Statement
vague	Children of alcoholics have difficulty in determining what normal is.
double-header	Children of alcoholics are either super responsible or super irresponsible.
socially desirable traits	Children of alcoholics are sensitive to others' needs.
common in general population	Children of alcoholics are uncomfortable when they are the center of attention.

Indeed, two researchers tested the idea that many of the traits attributed to children of alcoholics are such Barnum statements. They administered a supposed personality inventory that people were told would generate a profile for them based upon their individual responses. The profile actually presented, which was identical for all individuals, consisted of generalizations drawn from the literature on adult children of alcoholics. How did people respond to "their" profiles? All of the subjects rated the adult child of alcoholics profile as highly descriptive of themselves. This was equally true of those from nonalcohol or nonproblem families as it was of actual children of alcoholics. In addition, people saw these descriptions as particular to themselves, and more accurate for them, than for "people in general."

Someone has used another analogy for this phenomenon, making a comparison to the daily newspaper's astrology horoscopes. Most of the statements that are given in such columns are the kind of things that a large number of people can identify with. After all, if they only applied to a handful of people, who would read them? So, you read, "You often are not as tidy as you would like to be," or, "You like to have your accomplishments recognized, but hate to be the center of attention." These statements work because they sound familiar to all of us.

It cannot be assumed that all children who grew up or are now growing up in an alcoholic home share a single set of personality characteristics. Nor can it be assumed that all problems encountered in adult life can be attributed to being a child of an alcoholic. But the adult-children-of-alcoholics framework may well be useful to those suffering from problems, of whatever origins, who need to find some way out of an impasse and make needed changes.

Resiliency

Unfortunately, with the attention directed to the problems that the alcoholic family poses children, what was too long overlooked was the fact that children are not inevitably destined to problems in later life. An important piece of research that did not get the attention it deserved examined this very question. The research was conducted by Emily Werner. It compared the offspring of alcoholics who did and those who did not develop serious coping problems by age 18. The study examined the characteristics of the children and the care-giving environment in which they were raised. Those studied were members of a multiracial cohort of approximately 700 children born in 1955 on the Hawaiian island of Kauai. Follow-up studies were conducted at ages 1, 2, 10, and 18. Of this entire group, approximately 14% had either a mother or father who had alcoholism. Children of alcoholics who did not develop serious coping problems by age 18 were distinguished from those who did, in terms of their personal characteristics and their early environment. Those without serious problems had a belief in taking care of themselves, an orientation toward achievement, a positive self-concept, and an internal locus of control (meaning their behavior was prompted more by their own feelings and beliefs than its being a response to others). In terms of the environment, in the first 2 years of life they received a high level of attention from the primary care-giver and experienced fewer stressful events that disrupted the family unit. Thus Werner found it was not the presence or absence of alcoholism per se that predicted difficulties, but the interaction of the child and the environment. Werner also identified some differences depending upon the sex of the alcoholic parent and the child. Boys had higher rates of psychosocial problems in childhood and adolescence than did girls. Also, the children of alcoholic mothers had higher rates of problems in childhood and adolescence than did offspring of alcoholic fathers.

Genetic vulnerability

Possibly the single most important way in which the child of an alcoholic is vulnerable to alcoholism is in terms of genetic endowment. Children of alcoholics are considered at risk for development of the disease in an approximate 4:1 ratio to those without an alcoholic parent. Research has suggested that the gender too can be a significant factor influencing later life problems. Boys of alcoholic parents are more likely to suffer from attention deficit disorders with hyperactivity than are children of nonalcoholic parents. On the other hands, girls are more likely than their brothers to encounter eating disorders or depression in later life.

ALCOHOLISM IN OTHER FAMILY MEMBERS

Alcoholism is obviously not limited only to the parental generation. It may occur in adolescents, or it may occur in grandparents. The effects on the family are still powerful, though possibly less dramatic. Adolescent substance abuse problems and alcohol/substance abuse among the elderly are discussed in Chapter 10. However, it is important to realize that regardless of the particular family member affected, the effects of alcoholism are not limited to the alcoholic alone. The problems of the family are now seen as requiring intervention. Also, they are increasingly the focus of prevention efforts. In addition, family issues are now a central part of any alcohol treatment. Treatment approaches to the alcoholic family are discussed in Chapter 9.

PROBLEMS OF OTHER DRUG ABUSE AND THE FAMILY

This chapter has focused on the issues of alcohol and the family. The thinking on the family in respect to other drug use is quite different. Undoubtedly much of the thinking of the alcohol field— in terms of family stages of adaptation, or family roles, or children's coping styles— has to some degree crossed into the substance abuse field generally. However, it never took hold in the same way.

Accordingly the major attention to family issues and drug use has been research based. The focus of attention represents many of the same issues now being considered in terms of alcohol. These include risk and protective factors, parenting styles, issues of domestic violence, child abuse and neglect, and the role of psychiatric illness. Much of the discussion of the family in the context of other drug use, primarily the opiates and cocaine/crack, is concern about the prenatal effects, providing access to treatment for substance abusing mothers, and providing the full array of services during treatment and recovery.

RESOURCES AND FURTHER READING

Alcohol Health and Research World, Special issue on children of alcoholics 21(3): entire issue, 1997.

This issue devoted to children of alcoholics examines issues of prenatal alcohol exposure, the influence of parenting, the role of family influences in development and risk, prevention approaches, and psychological characteristics of children of alcoholics.

Barber JG, Gilbertson R: Evaluation of a self-help manual for the female partners of heavy drinkers, *Research on Social Work Practice* 8(2): 141–151, 1998. (31 refs.)

This article reports on a controlled field trial testing the effectiveness of a self-help manual based on the Pressures to Change procedure for the female partners of heavy drinkers. Thirty-eight female partners of heavy drinkers were randomly assigned either to counseling, self-help, or a waiting list control group. Clients were pre- and post-tested using two self-report measures of distress, and the drinking behavior of the male partner was also monitored. Both self-help and counseling were superior to no treatment in producing behavior change in the drinker and in relieving the female partner's level of depression. There was no difference between the counseling and self-help modalities. Self-help therapy is now a realistic option for female partners who either cannot or will not present for treatment. Similarly, a self-help manual for partners provides generalist social workers in secondary settings with a new intervention option in their work with resistant drinkers. (Author abstract.)

Barber JG, Gilbertson R: Unilateral interventions for women living with heavy drinkers, *Social Work* 42(1):69–78, 1997. (35 refs.)

Despite the fact that unilateral therapy is often the only treatment option for women living with heavy drinkers, very few structured programs have been developed for this client group. Moreover, the programs that do exist lack empirical support (as in the case of Al-Anon) or have as their highest priority promoting change in the drinker. This article looks at unilateral therapy for women partners of heavy drinkers and concludes that although a number of promising developments have occurred in recent years, more research is needed on the benefits to the women themselves. (Author abstract.)

Barber JG, Gilbertson R: Coping with a partner who drinks too much: Does anything work? *Substance Use & Misuse* 32(4):485–494, 1997. (26 refs.)

This paper reports on a multiple-regression study in which the efficacy of positive and negative coping responses adopted by the partners of heavy drinkers were compared under conditions of drinker intoxication and sobriety. Results indicated that only one combination of response type and drinker state was associated with higher levels of partner well-being: positive responses when the drinker is sober. Moreover, even this coping pattern accounted for relatively little variance in partner well-being scores. It is concluded that programs which aim to improve the quality of partner's lives should not generalize about desirable coping behaviors but should take account of situational and individual difference variables.

Beidler RJ: Adult children of alcoholics: Is it really a separate field of study? *Drugs and Society* 3(3/4):133–141, 1989.

This article reviews the nature of the literature on children of alcoholics, comparing and contrasting that which is research based and that which is intuitive and largely anecdotal. The central question addressed by this review is whether there is a discrete set of characteristics that warrant the consideration of adult children of alcoholics as a separate field of study.

Cermak TL: *Diagnosing and treating co-dependence: A guide for professionals who work with chemical dependents, their spouses and children,* Minneapolis MN: Johnson Institute Books, 1986.

The author, a clinician involved early in the treatment of those living with an alcoholic spouse or parent, describes these dysfunctions as a syndrome, which he terms "co-dependency" and conceptualizes as a disease entity consistent with DSM-III diagnostic criteria. Using a DSM-III-like schema, criteria for diagnosis of codependency are presented and treatment approaches described.

Denton RE, Kampfe CM: The relationship between family variables and adolescent substance abuse: A literature review, *Adolescence* 29(114):475–495, 1994. (27 refs.)

Adolescent substance abuse has been the focus of nationwide attention, and researchers have examined an assortment of variables relating to this disease. One area of interest has been the relationship between adolescent chemical dependency and family factors. A review of the current literature yields two broad categories: (1) family drug usage patterns, and (2) family atmosphere. In general, there seems to be a significant relationship between family variables and teenage substance abuse; however, the strength of the relationship differs with the substance used.

Specifically, research has shown a strong relationship between adolescent substance abuse and family drug usage, family composition, family interaction patterns, and discrepancies in family perceptions. Findings and their implications for practitioners are discussed. (Author abstract.)

Harrington CM, Metzler AE: Are adult children of dysfunctional families with alcoholism different from adult children of dysfunctional families without alcoholism? A look at committed, intimate relationships, *Journal of Counseling Psychology* 44(1):102–107, 1997.

Investigating the validity of classifying adult children of dysfunctional families with alcoholism as a unique population, this study compared dysfunctional families with alcoholism to adult children of dysfunctional families without alcoholism, and also to adult children in functional families. Results indicated that dysfunction in the family of origin is significantly related to global distress and difficulties with problem-solving communication in intimate relationships later in life. Results do not support the idea that there is a difference between dysfunctional families with alcoholism versus dysfunctional families without alcoholism.

Holmila M: Family roles and being a problem drinker's intimate other, *European Addiction Research* 3(1):37–42, 1997. (13 refs.)

This article presents empirical data from a Finnish study of the roles, life situations, coping, and other behaviors of family members and significant others of problem drinkers. The following were the major approaches to coping: (1) keeping out of the way of the drinker and managing one's own life; (2) care-giving, counseling, and controlling; and (3) resigning and maintaining a facade. Family role was related to how the respondent related to the problem drinker, in that the more distant relatives tended to adopt the attitude of resigning and maintaining a facade. Children of problem drinkers, on the other hand, rated highest on the component of keeping out of the way of the drinker and managing one's own life, in an attempt to minimize harm. Spouses of the drinkers had high scores on the component of care-giving, counseling, and controlling. Differences in gender were evident in that men had higher scores on the third component and women had higher scores on the first two components. Results indicate that the nuclear family carries the main load of dealing with a problem-drinking significant other, even when other family members and friends have roles as well. (Author abstract.)

Jackson JK: The adjustment of the family to the crisis of alcoholism, *Quarterly Journal of Studies on Alcohol* 15(4):562–586, 1954.

Through a study of members of the "AA Auxiliary," the predecessor for what became Al-Anon, the author identifies a seven-step progression in a family's adjustment to the presence of an alcoholic member. This progression continues to inform discussions of alcoholism's effects on the family. The stages are denial, efforts to eliminate the problem, disorganization, efforts to reorganize despite the problem, efforts to escape the problem, which may entail a dissolution of the marriage, leading either to reorganization of part of the family or recovery and reorganization of the whole family.

Johnson V: *I'll quit tomorrow,* rev. ed. New York: Harper & Row, 1980.

This work introduces the technique of the intervention, a method to initiate treatment. The use of interventions promotes earlier treatment and prompts care for those previously seen as either unready or inaccessible. The adoption of this clinical approach dispelled the myth that a patient's apparent motivation to cease use is a significant factor in determining treatment outcome, thus revolutionizing alcohol treatment and, by example, drug abuse treatment as well. This work also introduces the concept of enabling, i.e., the interactions of the family and the alcoholic that unwittingly support the continuation of drinking or drug use. Efforts to counter these behaviors, tied to the framework of the intervention, offer the family a constructive role beyond "detachment with love," the primary orientation of Al-Anon, the self-help group for family members.

Rotunda RJ, Scherer DG, Imm PS: Family systems and alcohol misuse: Research on the effects of alcoholism on family functioning and effective family interventions (review), *Professional Psychology: Research and Practice* 26(1):95–104, 1995. (106 refs.)
This article reviews the most prominent research at the interface between studies of alcohol addiction and family systems psychology. The review addresses the general effects of alcohol misuse on family functioning as determined in empirical studies comparing healthy families, alcohol-afflicted families, and otherwise troubled families. Three factors ("dry" versus "wet" families, family development and the progression of alcoholism, and family structure) are identified as particularly relevant to understanding the treatment needs of families affected by alcohol misuse. Research examining the general efficacy of family interventions in the treatment of alcoholism and specific treatment considerations unique to treating families coping with alcohol misuse are reviewed.

Walker JP, Lee RE: Uncovering strengths of children of alcoholic parents (review), *Contemporary Family Therapy* 20(4):521–538, 1998.
Being a child of an alcoholic (COA) is neither a diagnosis nor a psychosocial death sentence. Neither alcoholic families nor COAs are monolithic. A variety of factors converge in developmental trajectories resulting in diverse individual outcomes. Supportive relationships with non-substance-using parents and siblings and appropriate levels of parentification all may enable a significant proportion of COAs to enjoy high self-esteem, lack of problematic substance use, and good adaptive capability. Therapists and clients should refrain from looking at COAs through a deficit framework and instead should look for evidence of relational resilience in alcoholic families of origin. Such strengths-based assessments will increase therapeutic leverage with COAs seeking treatment for a range of presenting problems. (Author abstract.)

Werner EE: Resilient offspring of alcoholics: A longitudinal study from birth to age 18, *Journal of Studies on Alcohol* 47(1):34–40, 1986.
This study focuses on child characteristics and on the qualities of the care-giving environment that differentiated between offspring of alcoholics who did and those who did not develop serious coping problems by age 18. The 49 subjects (22 male) are members of a multiracial cohort of 698 children, born in 1955, on the Hawaiian island of Kauai. Follow-up studies were conducted at ages 1, 2, 10, and 18. In this group, males and the offspring of alcoholic mothers had higher rates of psychosocial problems in childhood and adolescence than did females and the offspring of alcoholic fathers. Children of alcoholics who developed no

serious coping problems by age 18 differed from those who did in characteristics of temperament, communication skills, self-concept, and locus of control. They also had experienced fewer stressful life events disrupting their family unit in the first 2 years of life. Results of the study support a transactional model of human development and demonstrate bidirectionality of child care-giver effects. (Author abstract.)

Note: There is concern that the dysfunctions associated with being a child of an alcoholic are being overdiagnosed and too often are ascribed on the basis of family history rather than upon clinical evaluation. Another trend of concern is the tendency to generalize from the body of work on children of alcoholics, much based upon lay efforts, to the larger field of children of dysfunctional families. This study provides an invaluable context for any consideration of the effects of alcohol problems upon children, and the study from which it was derived (Werner EE, Smith RS. *Vulnerable but invincible: A longitudinal study of resilient children and youth,* New York: McGraw-Hill, 1982) similarly offers a context for consideration of the impact of dysfunctional families upon child development.

Woititz J: *Adult children of alcoholics,* Hollywood FL: Health Communications, Inc., 1983.
One of the first popular handbooks on the topic and widely read in both the counselor and lay communities, it has been the source of many of the precepts that have influenced both professional treatment and self-help approaches.

Wolstein J, Rosinger C, Gastpar M: Children and families in substance misuse, *Current Opinion in Psychiatry* 11(3):279–283, 1998. (45 refs.)
The consequences of parental substance misuse on children of all age groups is discussed in this review. Current issues related to substance misuse in children and adolescents are also presented. Several interesting, mainly longitudinal studies offer new insights into both fields. (Author abstract.)

8

EVALUATION AND TREATMENT OVERVIEW

When one is acutely aware of alcohol or other drug problems, the question arises, "How can they be treated?" Perhaps your question is more personal, "How can I help?" As a prelude to this, it is essential to consider how people recover and what treatment or intervention is about.

At this juncture in earlier editions the focus was almost exclusively on alcohol. In that context we (1) made a principled plea for early intervention, (2) backed that up with the reminder that this approach is indicated for any chronic disease process, then (3) acknowledged that this represented an ideal, which unfortunately was infrequently reflected in actual practice, and (4) proceeded to zero in on treatment of alcoholism. There was virtually no mention of evaluation, diagnostic assessment, or treatment approaches to problems associated with alcohol use. Indeed, even 10 years ago many substance abuse clinicians had very little need for or opportunity to use those skills. The diagnosis of dependence, for all practical purposes, had occurred before a client's arrival in the clinician's office. Very few individuals came into contact with alcohol or drug treatment facilities by mistake. The chief practical use for informing substance abuse professionals of diagnostic criteria was to enable them to educate other human service professionals, thereby facilitating identification and referrals of those whose problems were going undetected. This information was also helpful in providing client education. Similarly, the major role of the substance use history was in developing treatment plans, rather than its being a prerequisite for diagnosis.

In days past, those who would now be diagnosed as having alcohol abuse were treated as "early-stage" alcoholics. Accordingly, they were provided the standard treatment for alcoholism. Their life situations often were reminiscent of the typical alcoholism client's circumstances 10 to 20 years before treatment. Remember, an average of 7 years elapsed from the point of the disease being clearly present to the point of entering treatment. That fact was used to "sell" the diagnosis and attempt to have the client accept it, hopefully with gratitude! Treatment professionals obviously recognized that such individuals were different from the usual client. It was recognized that providing full-blown treatment for dependence might be a bit drastic. However, it was viewed as the prudent, cautious approach. Even if the diagnosis of alcoholism were incorrect, initiating treatment seemed preferable to the alternative, which would be allowing the condition to go unaddressed and presumably progress. The two choices were then perceived as either loss of drinking "privileges" or potential loss of life. Equally important was the fact that, back then, the clinician could offer the problem drinker no other treatment options.

Another pitfall occurs when conceptualizing all alcohol problems in terms of the progression of the disease of alcoholism. It is related to the temptation to treat all alcohol problems as emerging dependence, and offering alcoholism treatment. This can cause clients to balk or bolt. This can also set up barriers when dealing with other professionals. Such

As muse or creative companion, alcohol can be devastating. In memoriam to some of those who did battle with this two-faced spirit:

JOHN BARRYMORE
MICKEY MANTLE
TRUMAN CAPOTE
TENESSE WILLIAMS
JOHN BERRYMAN
ROBERT YOUNG
JOHN CHEEVER
LILLIAN ROTH
U.S. GRANT
O. HENRY (William Sydney Porter)
EUGENE O'NEILL
STEPHEN CRANE
HART CRANE
F. SCOTT FITZGERALD
EDNA ST. VINCENT MILLAY
JACK LONDON
ERNEST HEMINGWAY
DYLAN THOMAS
DIANA BARRYMORE
ISADORA DUNCAN
SINCLAIR LEWIS
KENNETH ROBERTS
JUDY GARLAND
JOSEPH McCARTHY
ROBERT BENCHLEY
EDGAR ALLEN POE
JIM THORPE
CHARLES JACKSON
DAME MAY WHITTY
SARAH CHURCHILL
JACKSON POLLOCK
W.C. FIELDS
AUDIE MURPHY
HENRI DE TOULOUSE-LAUTREC
JANIS JOPLIN
BAUDELAIRE
BRENDAN BEHAN
RING LARDNER
ROBERT LOWELL
JIMI HENDRIX
ALEXANDER the Great

an approach can give the impression of clinicians, not as therapists, but as "technicians," always ready to apply their treatment formula indiscriminately.

The situation now is dramatically different. Along with alcohol use, other drug use is common. Those with alcohol dependency undoubtedly continue to represent the majority of those who come into contact with treatment programs, but at the same time, there is an ever-increasing proportion of referrals for other kinds of alcohol-related problems. One can no longer assume that any alcohol problem is synonymous with dependence. The problem may be abuse. The referral may have followed on the heels of a drinking incident. There are self-referrals of individuals who are concerned about a family member, a friend, or their own alcohol use. Similarly, treatment personnel are called upon more and more by other helping professionals—school counselors, social workers, physicians, clergy—to provide consultation.

With clients now reflecting the spectrum of substance use problems, there is increasing demand upon therapists to provide a thoughtful assessment and to match clients to appropriate treatment. In this era of managed care, assessment, evaluation, and diagnostic skills have become more central. It has been a long time since insurance companies, state regulatory agencies, HMOs, or for that matter clients, their families, or employers unquestioningly accepted 28 days of residential treatment—once the norm—as the treatment of choice.

THEORETICAL PERSPECTIVES

It may have been far simpler when the major and exclusive concern for the clinician was alcohol and alcoholism. Knowing how to treat the person sitting in the office was rarely a difficulty. The real challenge and major frustration was in getting those who needed care across the threshold. As the clinical concerns broaden to encompass a range of substance use problems, life becomes more complicated for the clinician. The remarks presented here are intended to provide a framework and offer orientation.

In terms of alcohol, if treatment programs are oriented primarily toward treating alcoholism, ironically that orientation serves as a set of blinders preventing recognition of other kinds of substance use problems. This is reminiscent of the old adage, "If the only tool you have is a hammer, every problem tends to look like a nail!" In thinking about alcoholism, we have tended to think of a progression, moving from alcohol use, to alcohol problems, to alcohol abuse, to alcoholism. In such a framework, severity depends upon where the client falls on that continuum. This thinking contains some pitfalls. The necessity for action or intervention is understandably associated with what is perceived as the seriousness of the situation. Thus the person with the alcohol problem may be seen as being in less danger. This is not necessarily the case.

PROBLEMS OF USE

Alcohol problems are not restricted to alcoholism. Nor are they restricted to alcohol use at intoxicating levels. For example, the danger of alcohol use by the individual who is depressed is not alcoholism—it is suicidal thoughts being "loosened" by the person's impaired state and diminished capacity. Therefore, those who are in treatment for depression should be counseled to abstain from alcohol.

Adolescents provide some of the most dramatic examples of the dangers of alcohol use. For teenagers, the primary danger of alcohol use isn't dependence, although it certainly does occur. The leading causes of death in this age group are accidents, suicide, and homicide, all of which are clearly linked to alcohol use. The net and tragic result is that the age group from 16 to 24 years has all too recently been the only group in our country with a declining life expectancy. Alcohol use may also have more subtle dangers for adolescents, such as impeding emotional and social maturation. In addition, there are the problems related to sexuality, unwanted pregnancies, and HIV infection.

Any drinker is at some risk for alcohol problems. Alcohol is a potent pharmacological agent. Negative consequences can follow on the heels of a single drinking episode. These would represent problems of acute use. Negative consequences can also result from the pattern of use. This represents a chronic problem. Evaluation and assessment need to explore both possibilities.

What is a "safe" dose of alcohol or a low-risk pattern of alcohol use? This varies from individual to individual. What is judicious use similarly varies for a single individual throughout his or her life span. For the pregnant woman, no alcohol is the safest alternative. Alcohol use is a health issue in the broadest sense. Treatment professionals are unlikely to see an individual until some problem becomes evident. Therefore much of the burden of prevention and identification of individuals at risk falls to those outside the clinical arena.

Chronic disease framework

In considering the spectrum of substance use problems, the model for managing chronic disease is very useful. It offers an approach that ensures that acute problems are effectively addressed. At the same time, it ensures that dependence will not develop unnoticed. All acute problems are seen as requiring attention in their own right, as well as being a potential warning of a possible long-term problem. The following example may help.

In the general medical management of any chronic disease, among the most significant actions are those taken before the clear onset of the full-blown disease process. Take heart disease, for example. A young man comes into his physician's office. He is overweight, both smokes and drinks, consumes a cholesterol-laden diet, never exercises, and has a family history of men who die before the age of 50 of coronary disease.

From his physician's perspective, he is a walking time bomb. To feel comfortable intervening, the physician does not have to be convinced that this individual will be true to his genes. It is sufficient to know that statistically this individual is at risk. Even if the client is wholly asymptomatic, that is, has no elevation of blood pressure, the physician will feel perfectly comfortable urging rather drastic changes to reduce risk. (These changes for our hypothetical young man are equivalent to the changes associated with abstinence.) If the physician were really on top of it, she or he would refer this client to several groups, load him down with pamphlets, and through continuing contacts monitor compliance and provide encouragement and support. This model is the optimal approach to the management of alcohol problems. In this framework, with respect to alcohol problems, the most relevant question is no longer, "Is this person alcoholic?" The central question instead becomes, "If this person continues with the current alcohol use pattern, is he or she at risk for developing alcoholism or other alcohol-related problems?"

Using the framework of chronic disease, many of the questions that now plague care-givers are circumvented. In the discussion that follows, we are going to act as if alcohol dependence is a condition like heart disease. As a chronic disease, alcohol dependence has well-demonstrated warning signs. It develops slowly over time. For this reason, it would probably be impossible ever to pinpoint an exact time at which a nonalcoholic "turns" alcoholic. No one wakes up in the morning having come down with a case of alcoholism overnight! Remember, the time when it is most critical to act is before the disease process is firmly established, when the individual is in that "gray" area. So it is useful to think in terms of whether someone is *developing* dependence. If so, then intervention is appropriate.

Such an approach makes it clear that any alcohol problem is sufficiently serious to warrant continuing attention. It has become widely recognized that alcoholism isn't "cured" and that ongoing efforts will be needed to maintain abstinence. Similarly, an alcohol problem shouldn't be assumed to be "fixed" by a single encounter with a clinician or participation in an alcohol education class. An ongoing relationship is appropriately established to monitor the client's status. Over time, there needs to be the opportunity to assess the efforts to moderate risks and alter dangerous drinking patterns. If these efforts prove to be unsuccessful, then further intervention is going to be required.

Consider the changes that have occurred over the last 25 years regarding tobacco use. Questions about smoking are now a standard part of any medical history. Probably very few smokers are unaware that smoking may cause or aggravate medical problems. A smoker who sees a physician expects to be asked questions about smoking and awaits the associated comments that smoking is ill-advised. Beyond that there is the increasing likelihood that a referral will be made to a smoking cessation program. Also the attitudes of the general public have changed. There is now a vocal anti-smoking lobby that does not wish to put up

Give me a Perrier-on-the-rocks with a double of scotch on the side.

with secondhand smoke. There are concerned family members and friends of smokers, who are more frequently expressing their concerns directly to the smoker. The regulation of smoking in public places has become the norm. Restaurants generally must provide nonsmoking accommodations and more and more are smoke-free. The White House is a nonsmoking building, not to mention hospitals. Beyond protecting nonsmokers, these regulations certainly cramp a smoker's style and prompt him or her to consider the inconvenience as well as the problems that result from smoking. We may well be on the brink of a similar revolution with alcohol use.

Now alcohol is more commonly viewed as a drug. Drunkenness is far less tolerated. Intoxication is becoming less socially acceptable in more and more circles and circumstances. The possibility that an intoxicated person puts others in jeopardy is an issue of public concern. Reinforcing this is the general public's heightened interest in a variety of efforts to promote health—diet, exercise, and other self-care measures. This has provided a moderating influence upon alcohol use. So along with less red meat, fewer animal fats, jogging, and personal trainers, there's more Perrier water. Coupled with all these changes are the improvements that have taken place in the professional training of physicians, clergy, nurses, social workers, and teachers about alcohol, alcohol problems, and alcoholism, compared to the previous generation.

At the same time, there is still some way to go. In the abstract, a person can be well informed about alcohol or other drug problems, but when they pop up in real life, it can be a different matter. All too often, along with the realization that there is a possible alcohol problem comes a lot of hand-wringing and waiting. The family, friends, physician, clergy—all those involved—can be immobilized. They can often wait until the possible problem has progressed to the point where it is unequivocally and unquestionably the real thing.

Also problematic is the fact that the professional treatment community has not yet reached a clear consensus as to what constitutes appropriate treatment for those who are in trouble with alcohol but who are not alcohol dependent. This should not be a surprise. The substance abuse field has not had the similar collective experience in approaching alcohol problems that it has had with alcoholism. The legacy of some of the nontraditional approaches to treatment of alcohol dependence may continue to cast a shadow. We refer to efforts many years ago to institute controlled drinking among clients with alcoholism, an approach that has been discarded. However, what was ineffective with that population in many instances is exactly the approach called for in the treatment of alcohol abuse, when abstinence is not an essential goal in treatment. There are those in specialized niches of the alcohol field who are acquiring considerable experience in dealing with alcohol problems. This is true particularly of the drinking and driving programs and of efforts on the college campus. Such programs can be looked to as a guide for the future.

Other drug use and drug problems   Many of the issues outlined with respect to alcohol apply to other drug use, but there are some important differences. As with alcohol, use per se cannot be taken as evidence of full-blown dependence. Similarly, the pharmacological effects of a given drug can lead to acute problems in the absence of dependence. However, even in the absence of dependence, trying to help someone achieve moderate use of other drugs is not typically considered an appropriate treatment goal. (The potential exception is marijuana, which is discussed later.) In part this is related to a drug's illicit status. This alone raises the ante considerably. As a culture we do not condone recreational cocaine use, nor consider 'a little' steroid use okay, nor view "chasing the dragon" (snorting heroin) as no big deal. These judgments for the most part are not simply arbitrary social conventions. In many the concern about any use reflects a drug's addiction potential. The pharmacological properties of the drug determine the abuse potential and likelihood of dependence. For example, with cocaine or nicotine, the risk is considerable. Consequently, establishing and maintaining a moderate, low-risk pattern of use is unlikely. Another concern is related to the route of administration. Intravenous use as a means of drug administration has special problems, namely infection from nonsterile techniques and from sharing of syringes. As an individual's drug career takes hold, for some drugs there is increasing likelihood that people will go from sniffing, or oral routes of administration, to intravenous use. Also, it is recognized that there are significant health consequences that can accompany long-term use, for example, steroids. Or use can have serious medical consequences even over the short haul, e.g., inhalants. In such instances, any use is considered to be risky. Accordingly, clinical efforts would be directed to helping someone stop using. Period. Most would consider it clinically inappropriate if not downright unethical to work with someone to achieve a moderate level of cocaine use.

SCREENING AND EVALUATION

A few words about screening for any health-care problem. Screening efforts can be undertaken at different levels. They can be applied routinely to everyone. Or, they can be targeted, administered only to those in higher-risk groups. Broad-based screening efforts, meaning routine use of a screening tool in a range of settings, is desirable when the condition is common. Otherwise checking everyone would make no sense. But to justify doing so it is also important that a condition be treatable. The common cold may warrant routine screening on the basis of its being commonplace. But inasmuch as there is very little to be done to alter its course, and the serious long-term consequences are rare, screening would be a waste of time. It is necessary that screening efforts be practical—that the available tools are both inexpensive and easily administered. Finally, the instrument used has to be well "tuned." It needs to cast a sufficiently broad net so as to not miss many people, but at the same time not falsely include too many who don't have the condition. Using these criteria, screening for alcohol problems is certainly warranted. It is common, it is treatable, a failure to treat it carries serious consequences, and it can be done easily and inexpensively in any setting. Compared to screening that requires a laboratory test, alcohol screening is very inexpensive. Screening for alcohol problems should be routine in any counseling or health-care setting. In the process of screening for alcohol use, there is also the possibility to screen for other drug use as well.

Several screening tests have proven to be effective in identifying those with a high likelihood of having alcoholism or other alcohol problems. As their name indicates, they are screening instruments, not diagnostic instruments. Screening instruments do not provide sufficient information to allow formulation of a treatment plan, although there are other standardized instruments to assist with that. But these screening tests if routinely administered can assist in identifying those for whom a closer examination is appropriate. In this instance, the goal is to identify those whose alcohol or drug use warrants closer scrutiny. These tests may have less utility in a setting that deals exclusively with alcohol and/or drug problems, where already something has occurred to suggest a problem exists. But they are basic tools for any human service worker's repertoire. They should be kept in mind by substance abuse professionals for use in training others who may be less comfortable in discussing and less experienced in dealing with substance abuse issues. Several screening tests are described below. The alcohol instruments are described first.

A word to those who are suspicious of screening instruments and their ability to detect a problem, especially given that prominent symptoms of dependence include minimizing, denial, repression, and distortions of memory and perception. Part of developing such instruments is to compare the results obtained by the test to the results of an assessment by a trained substance abuse clinician. The purpose of such screening instruments is, after all, to approximate the judgment that would be made by professionals were they to undertake a systematic evaluation. Indeed, for the instruments described below, those who answered the indicated number of questions positively were those whom the clinicians agreed had the syndrome (dependence or abuse) that the instruments were designed to detect.

If you remain leery, reflect back to the description of the behavior that is symptomatic of alcohol dependence in Chapter 6. The candor or absence of distortion is possibly not so unexpected. What the alcoholic client often strongly disagrees with is not the "facts," but their interpretation. Thus the alcohol dependent individual might very readily acknowledge that a family member has expressed concern about drinking. What he or she would be likely to dispute is whether the concern is justified. The client may well provide the interviewer a very lengthy and unsolicited rebuttal of the family's concern and offer justifications for

the drinking. In such situations, the interviewer needs to note the initial response to the question despite the explanation.

Screening instruments

CAGE   Since its introduction in 1970, the CAGE, developed by Ewing and Rouse, has become recognized as one of the most efficient and effective screening devices for alcohol dependence. The CAGE is both easy to administer as well as less intimidating than some of the other screening instruments. It consists of the following four questions:

"Have you ever felt you should	**C**ut down on your drinking?"
"Have people	**A**nnoyed you by criticizing your drinking?"
"Have you ever felt bad or	**G**uilty about your drinking?"
"Have you ever had an	**E**ye-Opener first thing in the morning to steady nerves or get rid of a hangover?"

Scoring two or three affirmative answers should create a high index of suspicion of the presence of alcoholism. Four positive responses are seen as equivalent to a diagnosis of alcohol dependence. The CAGE is not an instrument that is intended for use in screening for other alcohol problems (that is, a score of a one or two does not indicate alcohol abuse).

For those concerned about being overly inclusive and thus falsely identifying as possibly alcoholic those who are not, the CAGE holds little danger. It is very reliable in providing an initial way of sorting those who may be alcoholic from those who are not. Of those with a CAGE score of 1, only 20% are nonalcoholics. As the number of positive responses increases, the nonalcoholic individuals who would be incorrectly labeled drops markedly. Only 11% of those who score 2 are in fact nonalcoholics. For 3 positive responses, the proportion of nonalcoholics drops to 1%. For four responses, the percentage is 0.

Michigan Alcohol Screening Test (MAST)   The MAST is another of the most widely used screening tools. The original MAST, first published in 1971 by Selzer and associates, was a 25-item yes or no questionnaire. It was designed for use either within a structured interview or for self-administration. The questions touch on medical, interpersonal, and legal problems resulting from alcohol use. Since its introduction, the reliability and validity of the MAST have been established in multiple populations. Several variations have since been developed. The Brief MAST uses ten of the MAST items. The Short MAST (SMAST) was specifically created to be self-administered and uses 13 items found to be as effective as the entire MAST for screening.

MAST (Michigan Alcoholism Screening Test)

Points		
2	(*1.)	Do you feel you are a normal drinker?
2	2.	Have you ever awakened the morning after some drinking the night before and found that you could not remember part of the evening before?
1	3.	Does your wife, husband (or parents) ever worry or complain about your drinking?
2	*4.	Can you stop drinking without a struggle after one or two drinks?
1	5.	Do you ever feel bad about your drinking?
2	(*6.)	Do friends or relatives think you are a normal drinker?
0	7.	Do you ever try to limit your drinking to certain times of the day or to certain places?
2	*8.	Are you always able to stop drinking when you want to?
5	(9.)	Have you ever attended a meeting of Alcoholics Anonymous (AA)?
1	10.	Have you gotten into fights when drinking?
2	11.	Has drinking ever created problems with you and your wife, husband?
2	12.	Has your wife, husband (or other family member) ever gone to anyone for help about your drinking?
2	(13.)	Have you ever lost friends or girlfriends/boyfriends because of your drinking?
2	(14.)	Have you ever gotten into trouble at work because of drinking?
2	15.	Have you ever lost a job because of drinking?
2	(16.)	Have you ever neglected your obligations, your family, or your work for 2 or more days in a row because you were drinking?
1	17.	Do you ever drink before noon?
2	18.	Have you ever been told you have liver trouble? Cirrhosis?
2	(19.)	Have you ever had delirium tremens (DTs), severe shaking, after heavy drinking?
5	(20.)	Have you ever gone to anyone for help about your drinking?
5	(21.)	Have you ever been in a hospital because of your drinking?
2	22.	Have you ever been a patient in a psychiatric hospital or on a psychiatric ward of a general hospital where drinking was part of the problem?
2	23.	Have you ever been seen at a psychiatric or mental health clinic, or gone to a doctor, social worker, or clergyman for help with an emotional problem in which drinking has played a part?
2	24.	Have you ever been arrested, even for a few hours, because of drunk behavior?
2	(25.)	Have you ever been arrested for drunk driving or driving after drinking?

*Negative responses are alcoholic responses.
Note: Parentheses indicate questions included in the Brief MAST. Parentheses and underlines indicate questions included in the SMAST.
Scoring: A score of three points or less is considered nonalcoholic, four points is suggestive of alcoholism, and a score of five points or more indicates alcoholism.

Drug Abuse Screening Test (DAST)   The DAST is essentially an adaptation of the MAST used to identify other possible drug problems.

1 Have you used drugs other than those required for medical reasons?

2 Have you abused prescription drugs?

3 Do you use more than one drug at a time?

4 *Can you get through the week without using drugs (other than those required for medical reasons)?

5 *Are you always able to stop using drugs when you want to?

6 Do you use drugs on a continuous basis?

7 *Do you try to limit your drug use to certain situations?

8 Have you had "blackouts" or "flashbacks" as a result of drug use?

9 Do you ever feel bad about your drug use?

10 Does your spouse (or parents) ever complain about your involvement with drugs?

11 Do your friends or relatives know or suspect you use drugs?

12 Has drug use ever created problems between you and your spouse?

13 Has any family member ever sought help for problems related to your drug use?

14 Have you ever lost friends because of your use of drugs?

15 Have you ever neglected your family or missed work because of your use of drugs?

16 Have you ever been in trouble at work because of drug use?

17 Have you ever lost a job because of drug use?

18 Have you gotten into fights when under the influence of drugs?

19 Have you ever been arrested because of unusual behavior while under the influence of drugs?

20 Have you ever been arrested for driving while under the influence of drugs?

21 Have you engaged in illegal activities to obtain drugs?

22 Have you ever been arrested for possession of illegal drugs?

23 Have you ever experienced withdrawal symptoms as a result of heavy drug intake?

24 Have you had medical problems as a result of your drug use (e.g., memory loss, hepatitis, convulsions, or bleeding)?

25 Have you ever gone to anyone for help for a drug problem?

26 Have you ever been in hospital for medical problems related to your drug use?

27 Have you ever been involved in a treatment program specifically related to drug use?

28 Have you been treated as an outpatient for problems related to drug abuse?

Scoring: Each positive response yields 1 point, except for questions denoted with an asterisk. *Items 4, 5, and 7 are scored in the "no" or false direction. A score of greater than five requires further evaluation for substance abuse problems.

Trauma index   Recognizing how commonly trauma is associated with excessive alcohol use, several Canadian researchers developed a five-question scale to identify early-stage problem drinkers, among both men and women, in an outpatient setting. The questions are as follows:

Since your 18th birthday, have you

1 had any fractures or dislocations to bones or joints?
2 been injured in a traffic accident?
3 had a head injury?
4 been injured in an assault or fight?
5 bccn injured after drinking?

Two or more positive responses are indicative of excessive drinking or alcohol abuse. Though not as sensitive as the CAGE or the MAST, it will identify slightly over two-thirds of problem drinkers.

The previous tests have several limitations. One is that they look at lifetime problems. Typically the wording is "have you ever. . ." Thus, someone in middle age who hasn't had a problem for a decade could still come out with a positive score. Presumably, a few follow-up questions could pick this up rather quickly, so although this is a possible nuisance it isn't an insurmountable problem. A more serious concern is how effective these instruments are in identifying alcohol problems among women and members of racial/ethnic minority groups. Almost universally these tests were developed using white, middle-aged males. As a general rule, these tests have performed less well with women. Where this was a particular issue was in obstetric settings, where alcohol use is a special concern, and the need to intervene is so important.

TWEAK   This five-item scale was initially developed to meet the need for a sensitive, easy to administer screening test for pregnant women. It draws upon existing tools, with the researchers eliminating or rewording questions that didn't seem to work as well with women, while retaining those that did. While designed for women it has since been examined for use in other populations as well. TWEAK is an acronym that stands for *T*olerance, *W*orry about drinking, *E*ye-opener, *A*mnesia (blackouts), and *K*/Cut down. The questions and scoring are as follows:

1A. How many drinks does it take before you begin to feel the first effect of alcohol? (Tolerance)	3 or more drinks = 2 points
or	
1B. How many drinks does it take before the alcohol makes you fall asleep or pass out? Or, if you never pass out, what is the largest number of drinks that you have? (Tolerance)	5 or more drinks = 2 points
2. Have your friends or relatives *worried* about your drinking in the past year?	Yes = 1 point
3. Do you sometimes take a drink in the morning when you fist get up? (*E*ye-opener)	Yes = 1 point

4. Are there times when you drink and afterwards
   can't remember what you said or did? (<u>A</u>mnesia)   Yes = 1 point

5. Do you sometimes feel the need to <u>C</u>ut down
   on your drinking. (K or C, Cut down)   Yes = 1 point

A total score of three or more is considered positive for either version of the TWEAK.

Alcohol Use Disorders Identification Test (AUDIT)   Finally, there is the AUDIT, which was developed to serve as a screening tool that would be effective in different cultures. In 1982 the World Health Organization assembled an international work group to develop a simple screening instrument to identify persons who are at risk of developing alcohol problems. The goal was to create a tool that could be used by an array of health-care workers in both developing and developed countries. The Alcohol Use Disorders Identification Test (AUDIT) is the result. It consists of 10 questions. The AUDIT has been tested with a variety of populations.

AUDIT
Alcohol Use Disorders Identification Test

1. How often do you have a drink containing alcohol?
   - Never   (0)
   - Monthly or less   (1)
   - Two to four times a month   (2)
   - Two to three times a week   (3)
   - Four or more times a week   (4)

2. How many drinks containing alcohol do you have on a typical day when you are drinking?
   - 1 or 2   (0)
   - 3 or 4   (1)
   - 5 or 6   (2)
   - 7 to 9   (3)
   - 10 or more   (4)

3. How often do you have six or more drinks on one occasion?
   - Never   (0)
   - Less than monthly   (1)
   - Monthly   (2)
   - Weekly   (3)
   - Daily or almost daily   (4)

4. How often during the last year have you found that you were not able to stop drinking once you had started?
   - Never   (0)
   - Less than monthly   (1)
   - Monthly   (2)
   - Weekly   (3)
   - Daily or almost daily   (4)

5. How often during the last year have you failed to do what was normally expected from you because of drinking?
   - Never   (0)
   - Less than monthly   (1)
   - Monthly   (2)
   - Weekly   (3)
   - Daily or almost daily   (4)

6. How often during the last year have you needed a first drink in the morning to get yourself going after after a heavy drinking session?
   - Never   (0)
   - Less than monthly   (1)
   - Monthly   (2)
   - Weekly   (3)
   - Daily or almost daily   (4)

7. How often during the last year have you had a feeling of guilt or remorse after drink?
   - Never   (0)
   - Less than monthly   (1)
   - Monthly   (2)
   - Weekly   (3)
   - Daily or almost daily   (4)

AUDIT (*continued*)

8. How often during the last year have you been unable to remember what happened the night before because you had been drinking?

    Never   (0)
    Less than monthly   (1)
    Monthly   (2)
    Weekly   (3)
    Daily or almost daily   (4)

9. Have you or someone else been injured as a result of your drinking?

    No   (0)

    Yes, but not in the last year (2)
    Yes, during the last year   (4)

10. Has a relative or friend, or a doctor or other health worker been concerned about your drinking or suggested you cut down?

    No   (0)
    Yes, but not in the last year (2)
    Yes, during the last year   (4)

SCORING: Questions 1–8 are scored 0,1, 2, 3, or 4.
              Questions 9 & 10 are scored 0, 2, or 4 only.
              The minimum score (for nondrinkers) is 0 and the maximum possible score is 40. A score of 8 or more indicates a strong likelihood of hazardous or harmful alcohol consumption.

FROM: Saunders JB, Aasland OG, Babor TF, de la Fuente JR, Grant M. Development of the Alcohol Use Disorders Identification Test (AUDIT): WHO Collaborative Project on Early Detection of Persons with Harmful Alcohol Consumption. II. *Addiction* 88(6):791–804, 1993.

Dartmouth Assessment of Lifestyle Instrument (DALI) Most screening instruments do not work very well for those with serious mental illness. These existing instruments rely on questions that tap into physical dependence, e.g., the need for an "eye-opener" (both the CAGE and TWEAK). For those with serious mental illness, problems may be present far before physical signs and symptoms are present. The life situations among those with serious mental illness are often tenuous. Problems can occur in the presence of alcohol or other drug use far before there is the appearance of tolerance or withdrawal. Alcohol or other drug use can also make management of the psychiatric condition more difficult. This new instrument was developed for this population. This questionnaire, with 18 questions, four of which are lead-ins and unscored, screens for both alcohol and drug problems. It was developed to be administered by computer and thus is scored automatically. (Hand scoring is a bit cumbersome, but do-able.) Interestingly, virtually all patients are able to complete a computer version and enjoy doing so, and the information elicited is as reliable as that secured through an interview.

The DALI consists of questions to assess both alcohol and drug use problems among those with chronic mental illness. It was designed to be computer administered and scored. Hand scoring at first glance may seem a bit complicated, but it really isn't. Notice that several of the initial questions are unscored and are included to set the tone for the inventory, also some of the points are *minus* numbers.

DALI (Dartmouth Assessment of Lifestyle Instrument)

Question		Scoring	
	Values	Alcohol Score	Drug Score
1. Do you wear seatbelts while riding in a car?	Yes = 0 No = 1 refused or don't know = .4	_____	
2. How many cigarettes do you smoke?	not scored		
3. Have your tried to stop smoking cigarettes?	not scored		
4. Do you control your diet for total calories?	not scored		
5. How much would you say you spent during the past six months on alcohol?	$0–$49 = 0 >$49 = 1 ref/DK = 1 >$49 = −1*	_____	
6. How many drinks can you hold without passing out? If patient does not know, "how many do you think it would take?"	0 = 0 1–5 = 1 ref/DK = 1.6	_____	
7. Have friends or relatives worried or complained about your drinking in the past 6 months?	Yes = 0 No = −1 ref/DK = .5	_____	
8. Have you ever attended a meeting of AA because of your drinking?	Yes = 0 No = −1 ref/DK = −.8	_____	
9. Do you sometimes take a drink in the morning when you first get up?	Yes = 0 No = −1* ref/DK = −.8*	_____	
10. How long was your last period of voluntary abstinence? or Most recent period when you chose not to drink? NB. 2 or more wks = a month; exclude periods of incarceration or hospitalization.	> or = 60 mo = 0 0–59 months = 1 ref/DK = .4	_____	

DALI   *(continued)*

Question	Scoring		
	Values	Alcohol Score	Drug Score
11. How many months ago did this abstinence end? or When did you start drinking again?	0 months = 0 >0 months = 1 ref/DK = .4	_____	
12. Have you used marijuana in the past 6 months?	Yes = 0 No = −1* ref/DK = .7		_____
13. Have you lost a job because of marijuana use?	Yes = 0 No = −1 ref/DK = .9		_____
14. How much would you say you spent in the past 6 months on marijuana?	0$ = 0 >0$ = 1 ref/DK = 1		_____
15. How troubled or bothered have you been in the past 6 months by marijuana problems?	not at all = 1 slightly = 2 moderately = 3 considerably = 4 extremely = 5 ref/DK = 1		_____
16. Has cocaine abuse created problems between you and your spouse or parents?	Yes = 0 No = −1* ref/DK = −.8		_____
17. How long was your longest period or voluntary period when you chose not to use cocaine? NB. 2 or more wks = a month; exclude periods of incarceration or hospitalization.	0–59 months = 1 > 59 months = 0 not applicable = 0		_____
18. Do you ever use cocaine when you're in a bad mood?	Yes = 0 No = 1 ref/DK = 0		_____

Total_____ + _____   = _____
                    alcohol   drug   alcohol & drug

Scoring: The total score can range from −4 to +6. Alcohol scale: Scores between +2 and +6 indicate a high risk of a current alcohol use problem. Drug scale: A score above −1 indicates a high risk for cocaine or marijuana problems.

*a minus value

Initial follow-up questions

When screening is positive, what next? William Clark of Harvard Medical School, and formerly the Chief of Medicine at Cambridge City Hospital, has authored some of the best material on alcoholism diagnosis directed to physicians. Although his comments are concerned with the medical interview, they would be useful in any counseling situation. He has three basic rules: (1) Ask about the person, not about the alcohol. He is a firm believer in routinely using the CAGE questions. (2) Use the laboratory sparingly. That's easy for nonphysicians to follow! (3) Be prepared with some follow-up questions for use when the CAGE is positive. He suggests a series of follow-up questions to get at the client's preoccupation with alcohol. To help remember them he has two mnemonics, HALT and BUMP.

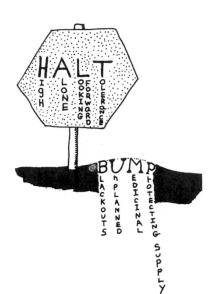

Do you usually drink to get	**High?**
Do you sometimes drink	**Alone?**
Have you found yourself	**Looking forward to drinking?**
Have you noticed an increased	**Tolerance for alcohol?**
Do you have	**Blackouts?**
Have you found yourself using alcohol in an	**Unplanned way?**
Do you drink for	**Medicinal reasons?**
Do you work at	**Protecting your supply of alcohol?**

To get at the common problems associated with alcohol use, Clark suggests another series of questions. The device for remembering this is FATAL DTs:

Family history of alcohol problems
Alcoholics Anonymous attendance
Thoughts of having alcoholism
Attempts or thoughts of suicide
Legal problems
Driving while intoxicated
Tranquilizer or disulfiram use

Identifying situations requiring medical attention

While there is no suggestion that a counselor attempt to deliver medical care, there are situations in which being informed about medical issues is important. When screening is positive, medical information is part of the additional information required. Counselors need to evaluate withdrawal risks and to be aware of situations where medical attention is indicated. Every counselor needs to have someone to turn to as a medical backup.

Some general questions about health status that should be asked include:

- Have you ever been hospitalized and for what?
- Do you have a history of accidents or injuries, or have you been in any fights that required medical attention?

- Did any of these occur when you were drinking or using drugs?
- Have you been seeing a doctor recently or thought that you should have seen one?
- When was the last time you were seen by a physician?

Assessing withdrawal risk   For clients who are drinking or using other drugs, or who have recently stopped, there is the potential for withdrawal. To assess withdrawal risks, the following information should be secured for any patient for whom there has been a decrease in regular use or recent cessation of use.

- The type and amounts of drugs used during the past week.

Try to elicit specific details and quantifiable amounts. When the amount is essentially unknown to the individual, make efforts to infer levels of use. The following questions may be necessary: "How often do you go to the liquor store? How much do you purchase? How long does this amount last?"

For prescription drug abuse, ask, "How long does a prescription last? How many sources do you have for the prescription?"

For illicit drugs, the key parameters are, "How often do you use cocaine or crack? Daily? Weekends? How often do you purchase drugs?"

- Level of tolerance. "What is the amount of the alcohol/drug you require to feel the effects?"
- The interval since the last alcohol or drug use and the current physical status.

This information provides a valuable means of assessing tolerance. It indicates the symptoms of withdrawal with a declining blood level. In response to this, what objective signs are there of the presence of withdrawal? Tremulousness? Agitation? Sweating? Confusion? Hypervigilance? Rapid pulse?

- Current or past medical problems, allergies.
- Prior experience of either decreasing or stopping drinking or drug use.

Prior clinical status during withdrawal is significant, especially when prior withdrawal was problematic. This is not to be limited to formal detoxification. Many individuals have had periods of relative or absolute abstinence dictated by circumstances such as conscious efforts to curtail or limit use, or hospitalizations or vacation periods, which disrupt their usual source of drugs.

When it comes to drugs other than alcohol, regardless of training no clinician will ever be as knowledgeable as some of their clients regarding various drug actions and the desired effects. Do not trip yourself up as a result of your lack of knowledge by pretending to be informed. Sometimes clients may refer to drugs by their street names, which you may not recognize, or talk about drug effects using street slang. Ask the client to define these terms. Ask what a drug does for him or her;

ask how it is administered, the duration of effects, and what it feels like as the effects wear off. There may be some disbelief about your naiveté, but generally there will be an appreciation that you bothered to ask and were well-informed enough about drug use to ask the right questions.

Indications for immediate medical evaluation Many medical emergencies will be clearly recognizable. In these situations, use emergency transportation, police, or rescue squads. This is especially important if the client needs life support. This is evidenced by shallow, uneven breathing, rapid pulse, fluctuating levels of consciousness, or when there is the threat of danger to others or harm to self. When an individual is transported for emergency care, inform the emergency department of the patient's imminent arrival. Any information that can be provided to emergency staff is helpful, including current status; names of family or friends who may be with the patient and can provide information; diagnostic impressions; and relevant past medical history.

The following may not appear to be immediately life-threatening, however, prompt medical attention should be arranged. Without an adequate evaluation, serious problems could occur.

- Recent substance intake at levels that risk developing toxicity, poisoning, or organ damage even if patient is asymptomatic.
- Ingestion of unknown quantities and substances.
- Hallucinations, marked paranoia.
- Confusion or delirium.
- Severe agitation; efforts to quiet the patient are unsuccessful.
- Severe tremors.
- Tachycardia (heart rate >110 per minute).
- Fever (>38.0° C).
- History or evidence of trauma, especially head trauma.
- Patient is semi-conscious and able to be aroused briefly, but falls asleep when stimulus is removed.

For individuals who have recently stopped drinking or have reduced their consumption significantly or intend to, the following items would suggest a significant risk for serious withdrawal:

- Past history of a difficult withdrawal.
- Seizures or history of seizures.
- Dependence on multiple substances.

There are also situations that, while not medical emergencies, still warrant a patient's arranging for a check-up. These include all clients with heavy extended alcohol or drug use who have not had a recent check-up, anyone reporting a history of bleeding, and those who have a history of chronic medical illness such as high blood pressure, who are not under a doctor's care.

SUBSTANCE USE HISTORY

Beyond attending to possible immediate medical problems, when routine screening provides evidence of an alcohol or other drug problem, then a more detailed use history is always indicated. Similarly, an alcohol/drug use history should be an integral part of an interview with any troubled person, whether the person has come to a physician or hospital with a physical problem, or to a social worker, psychiatrist, psychologist, or clergy member concerning an emotional or life adjustment problem. The reasons for this should now be clear. As we have previously noted, this is a drinking society; most people drink at least some alcohol. We have also noted that alcohol is a chemical and not as benign as previously thought. It simply cannot be ignored as a possible factor in whatever brings a person to a care-giver of any kind. Again, do not limit your attention to alcoholism alone. The purpose of the alcohol use history is simply to get as clear a picture of alcohol use as you would of other medical aspects, family situation, job difficulties, feelings, or whatever. It is part of the information-gathering process, which is later added up to give you an idea of what is going on in the person's life and how best to proceed.

Clinical style

Many sample drinking history forms are floating around—for physicians, nurses, and others. Our bias has long been that the attitude of the questioner is as important, if not more important, than the actual list of questions. If asking about drinking strikes you as an invasion of privacy, a waste of time, or of little use because the presenting problem is clearly not alcohol- or drug-related, then you are going to be uncomfortable asking and will probably get less reliable answers from a now uncomfortable client. If your bias is the opposite and you see alcohol or drugs lurking in the corner of every problem, again discomfort and unreliable answers will probably be your lot. Somehow you need to begin with an objective stance. Alcohol might or might not be a factor, just as any other aspect of the client's life might or might not be of concern.

Motivation

A word about motivation is also needed at this point. For all too long the tendency has been to lay the blame for treatment failure on the shoulder of the client. He or she was "in denial," wasn't ready to change, was unmotivated, hadn't "hit bottom." A growing body of research shows that clinical style can make a difference in terms of treatment outcome. Tied to this is the recognition that there is a series of discrete stages that accompany any behavioral change. A significant contribution of learning psychologists active in the alcohol and substance abuse fields has been in clarifying the concept of motivation. In the past, motivation was seen as a characteristic of a client, as a "something" that was either absent or present. "Motivated" clients were perceived as having good outcomes;

conversely, treatment failures were often chalked up to a client's "lack of motivation." William Miller, drawing upon work done in other fields, has introduced into the alcohol and substance abuse treatment a very different view of motivation. In his formulation, motivation is a dynamic process with discrete stages that parallel the stages occurring whenever anyone makes significant life changes. Specific clinical interventions are either well suited or to be avoided, depending upon where the client is in the change process. The stages outlined by Miller are as follows:

• *Precontemplation.* This is the point when the individual is not even considering change. There is no perceived need to. Instead, a problem is recognized by someone else, such as family member, physician, clergy, or coworker. In this stage, the important clinical task is to help the individual gain awareness of the dangers involved in his or her present behaviors.

• *Contemplation.* Now the individual is more ambivalent. There is a mixture of favoring and resisting change. As change is considered, the person perceives both pluses and minuses. In this stage if confronted with arguments on one side, the client's likely response is to defend the opposite side. So it is helpful for the clinician to address both the negative effects of the alcohol use, the features the client considers pluses, and the potential benefits of change.

• *Determination.* In this phase, there is less ambivalence. The client often "sounds" different and can acknowledge a situation warranting change. Efforts are actively being made to consider alternatives. For the patient at this stage, rapid, immediate intervention is important. If too much time passes, the individual reverts to the stage of contemplation. Thus a potential opportunity for change has been lost. In this stage the client needs the professional's assistance in selecting an optimal strategy for making changes, plus the client needs lots of support for the resolve to follow through.

• *Action.* At this point the client is engaged in implementing a plan, which often may be formal treatment. At this point, the clinical task is providing assistance and direction as the client carries out the plan.

• *Maintenance.* When significant changes in behavior have been made, then maintenance of the change is what becomes important. The individual can't simply rest on his or her laurels. Maintenance of change is seen as being sustained by continuing action. Interestingly, the process of making change is in and of itself reinforcing. It encourages the desire to make other needed changes and demonstrates that change is possible.

• *Relapse.* Here the individual reverts back to the previous behavioral pattern. If relapse occurs, then it is necessary to once again go through the stage of initiating change, again starting with contemplation.

Rather than motivation being considered a "thing" that you have or don't have, this formulation considers motivation as a process. It is a process that can be helped or hindered by the clinician's efforts. Different clinical approaches are considered to be particularly helpful at particular stages in prompting change. These are outlined in Table 8.1. Tailoring the clinical approaches to the stage of change is a process that

TABLE 8.1   STAGES OF MOTIVATION

Stages of Change	Clinician efforts to promote motivation
Precontemplation	Raise doubts. Prompt the client to consider the risks and problems with the current situation.
Contemplation	Here the client is ambivalent; try to tip the balance. Have the client consider the benefits of change and risks of the situation continuing as is.
Determination	Focus on specific actions the individual can take.
Action	Facilitate the steps outlined above.
Maintenance	Identify factors that may prompt a relapse and develop strategies to counter this.

has been termed *motivational interviewing*. William Miller, a psychologist, is one of the people who has been involved in articulating this approach.

When to ask

It takes practice to take a reliable alcohol-drug history. It also takes recognition of timing and a good look at what is in front of you. It may seem redundant to say, but an intoxicated or withdrawing client cannot give you good information. You wouldn't expect accurate information from someone going under or coming out of anesthesia. Unfortunately, some of the forms we have seen are designed to be filled out on admission or intake with no recognition of this factor. Again, use your common sense. Try to ask the questions you need to at a time when the person is at least relatively comfortable both emotionally and physically. Ask them matter-of-factly. Remember that your own drinking pattern is no yardstick for others. For example, when someone responds to the question, "How much do you usually drink on a typical occasion?" with "About four or five drinks or so," don't stare open-mouthed.

What to ask

The information needed about alcohol consumption includes what does the client drink, how much, how often, when, where, and is it causing, or has it caused, a problem in any area of life, including physical problems. These questions can be phrased in different ways. In general, however, we lean to a more informal approach than sitting there filling out a form as you ask the questions in order. Another issue that we consider to be as important as the above information, but that is not included on most forms, is the question of what the drinking does for the client. Questions such as, "How do you feel when you drink?" "What does alcohol do for you?" and "When do you most often want a drink?" can supply a lot of information.

How to ask

If the questions are asked conversationally along with other questions regarding general health, social aspects, and other use of prescribed drugs or medications, most people will answer them. The less threatened you are by the process, the more comfortable the individual being questioned will be.

Other drug use   Following questions about alcohol use, queries can also be directed to other drug use. You could ask a question such as, "Have you used drugs other than those required for medical reasons?" If the answer is positive, the follow-up questions would be similar to those suggested above—what substances, under what circumstances, with what kinds of accompanying problems, and is there concern by either the individual or others.

Recording the data in the record

Alcohol use should be adequately described in the agency chart or medical record so that changes in drinking practices can be detected over time. If there is no evidence of alcohol being a problem, that, too, should be noted. Notes in the chart should include sufficient objective detail to provide meaningful data to other clinicians. Avoid one-word descriptions such as "socially" or "occasionally." If the agency does not have a prescribed format, it is suggested that the following be included for all clients: drinking pattern, problems related to alcohol use, expression of concern by family or friends, the MAST or CAGE score, and the presence or absence of other drug use.

Additional information may be desired for the counselor's own records. The following worksheet is one means of summarizing the data elicited.

WHAT NEXT?

Making a referral

Having identified an alcohol or drug problem, the clinician who isn't primarily a substance abuse professional is faced with referring the client to a substance abuse program. This may be either for further evaluation or for treatment. Drawing upon motivational interviewing, the following are key: removing barriers, practical as well as attitudinal; giving clear direction; actively helping; providing feedback; reinforcing and supporting the client's efforts to effect change.

To make this concrete, keep several things in mind. First, you cannot enthusiastically recommend the unfamiliar. Therefore you need to know about various facilities, their programs, and personnel. Second, in making any referral, there's always a danger of clients falling through the cracks. Therefore you need to be actively involved in the referral. Don't

DSM-IV DIAGNOSTIC WORK SHEET

Client Name _____

SYMPTOMS | DIAGNOSTIC CRITERIA

SYMPTOMS	DIAGNOSTIC CRITERIA	YES	NO
	ALCOHOL ABUSE: A definite diagnosis of abuse is made when <u>one</u> of A is 'yes', and both B & C are also 'yes'.	☐	☐
A.1 __ Missing school/work __ Lost job	__ Lost time from work __ Child care neglected	A)1 Recurring failure to meet social, family, work responsibilities due to use.	—	—
2 __ Driving under the influence __ Reckless driving __ Serious injury	__ Intoxicated at home __ Use at work or school __ Other _____	2 Recurrent use when this is physically hazardous.	—	—
3 __ DWI __ Domestic disputes	__ Arrests __ Physical fights or property damage	3 Recurring legal problems.	—	—
4 __ Friends/family express concern __ Guilty about use __ Arguments about drinking	__ Arrests __ License suspension	4 Continued use despite negative consequences or recurring problems due to use.	—	—
	__ Alcohol related arrests			
	__ Unpaid child support __ Other _____	B) These symptoms have occurred repeatedly during a 12 month period.	—	—
	Drinking causes life problems: __ relationship __ legal __ job __ Other _____	C) Never having met the criteria for Dependence. The pattern is consistent with a diagnosis of abuse.	—	—
	__ Increased tolerance __ Past heavy drinking pattern __ Other _____			
	__ Blackouts __ Physical health harmed by use			

(continued)

253

DSM-IV DIAGNOSTIC WORK SHEET (*continued*)

ALCOHOL DEPENDENCE:

A definite diagnosis of dependence is made when any three of A and B are 'yes'

	YES	NO

A)1 Marked tolerance (50% increase) to achieve effect. ___

2 Withdrawal symptoms or use to avoid withdrawal symptoms. ___

3 Drinking more or for longer periods than intended. ___

4 A persistent desire, or one or more unsuccessful efforts to control use. ___

5 Considerable time spent obtaining alcohol, or drinking it, or recovering from its effects. ___

6 Important activities (social, occupational, recreational) given up or reduced because of drinking. ___

7 Continued drinking despite knowledge of persistent social, psychological, or physical problems due to use. ___

B) These symptoms have occurred repeatedly during a 12 month period. The pattern is consistent with a diagnosis of dependence. If Substance Dependence: with___ or without___ physiological dependence

---

1 ___ Consumed as much as one case beer, 1 gallon wine, 1/5 hard liquor at one time ___ Less use required to achieve intoxication ___ Other
   ___ 4+ drinks/sitting

2 ___ Morning hand tremor   ___ Hallucinations
   ___ Night sweats   ___ Other
   ___ Morning drinking   ___ Use of substitutes to self-medicate withdrawal symptoms
   ___ Drinking before work

3 ___ Not a social drinker   ___ Experiences difficulty cutting down
   ___ Drinks more than intended ___ Other

4 ___ Thoughts about cutting down   ___ Periods of abstinence
   ___ Guilty about use   ___ Sees self as problem drinker
   ___ Annoyed with concerns of others   ___ Relief drinking ___ Other

5 ___ Daily drinking   ___ Hidden alcohol
   ___ Binge drinking   ___ Preoccupation with alcohol
   ___ Drinking alone   ___ Needs drink ___ Other

6 ___ Lost friends   ___ Physical fights or property damage under the influence
   ___ Arguments about drinking   ___ Increased isolation ___ Other

7 ___ Prior DWI   ___ Told drinking harming liver   After drinking:
   ___ Other arrests   ___ Told by MD to decrease use   ___ rowdy/noisy
   ___ Lost job due to alcohol ___ Blackouts   ___ courage/self-confidence
   ___ Other   ___ Health would be better without alcohol/drug use   ___ angry/quarrelsome

just give an agency name and phone number with instructions for the client to call. You make the appointment with a specific individual, at a specific time. With this active helping, the likelihood of the individual following through virtually doubles, jumping from under 40% if the client was only given a phone number and told to call, to over 80% when the counselor sets up the appointment. Inform the family or significant others of the actions being taken and why. Third, if you've had an ongoing relationship with the client, a referral may feel like abandonment. If appropriate, continue the contact and let the client know that you are in this together.

In large measure the ability to effect a successful referral lies in your conveying a sense of concern and hope. It also depends upon assisting the client to see the difficulties in a new light, that there may be a disease causing these difficulties, and that it's not a question of who is at fault. In presenting the need for referral, remember that someone can absorb only so much information at one time. Consider for a moment the woman whose physician discovers a lump in her breast. The physician's next step is making a referral to a surgeon for a biopsy and possibly to an oncologist. This is not the time to discuss the relative merits of radical mastectomy and/or chemotherapy in terms of 5-year survival. Nor is it the time to talk of side effects from chemotherapy. Such presentations would be likely to cause the woman to run because she abandons hope, or it might cause her to retreat into denial. The important messages to convey initially are (1) the situation is serious enough to warrant further investigation, (2) I'm referring you to someone I can trust, and (3) I'm in this with you. That same concern is what one is attempting to convey when making a referral for substance abuse problems.

Evaluation in a substance abuse treatment setting

For those working in a designated substance abuse program, the situation is a bit different. Here, the person may be referred or come in with a good idea that alcohol or drug use is a problem. The person may, however, want to prove that it isn't. Because of the alcohol or drug treatment designation, the questions about substance use can be more forthright and in depth. Consequently the responses may be more guarded—particularly responses to how much and how often. However, those are not the most helpful questions anyway. Remember the maxim, "Ask about the person, not about their drinking (or drug use)." Indeed, some suggest never asking these questions, at least in an initial encounter. The reason is that they are the questions most likely to trigger the client's defenses. It is probably the topic that has caused the most friction with family. If asked, the responses around alcohol can range all the way from a gruff "a few and just socially" to a bragging "a whole case of beer whenever I feel like it." The prospective client will usually need to feel somewhat comfortable about seeing you before more candor is possible. And there is always the real possibility that the client doesn't know exactly how much or how often. The key thing for the clinician is to get as much reasonably reliable information as possible to develop appropriate treatment plans or initiate an appropriate referral. Information about quantity and frequency is not necessary to diagnose alcoholism. It can be useful in gauging the level of physical dependence and assessing possible withdrawal problems; however, tolerance can be gleaned indirectly by other means, such as "How many drinks does it take to feel the effect?"

Another point to consider is that you do not always have to get all the history at one sitting. If a client comes to a treatment facility smelling of alcohol, clearly uncomfortable, and somewhat shaky, you need to know immediately how much alcohol has been consumed, for how long, and when the last drink was taken. You also need to know about other physical problems and what happened on other occasions when drinking was stopped. These questions are necessary to determine if the client needs immediate attention from a physician. If the client is not in crisis, the evaluation may occur over several outpatient visits.

Initial interview   The initial interview is intended to get a general picture. As a result of the initial interview, the alcohol clinician will want to be able to answer the following questions:

1 What is the problem the client sees?
2 What does the client want?
3 What brings the client for help now?
4 What is going on in the individual's life, i.e., the "facts" of the family situation, social problems, medical problems, alcohol use— how much, for how long—and other drug use?
5 Is there a medical or psychiatric emergency?
6 What are the recommendations?

Certainly, much other information could be elicited. But the answers to the foregoing questions make up the essential core for making decisions about how to proceed.

Counseling is an art, not a science. No series of rules can be mechanically followed. However, one guideline is in order for an initial interview. It is especially apt in situations in which someone is first reaching out for help. Don't let the interview end without adopting a definite plan for the next step. Why? People with alcohol or other problems are ambivalent. They run hot and cold. They approach and back off from help. Remember the stages of change. The contemplation stage is probably the most common at this point, and what precedes determination and adopting a plan of action. The person who comes in saying, "I'm an alcoholic or an addict and want help" is very, very rare. You are more likely to meet the following: "I think I may have a problem with alcohol, sort of, but it's really my _____ that's getting to me." The concrete plan adopted at the close of the interview may be very

Counseling is an art NOT A SCIENCE

simple. The plan may be nothing more than agreeing to meet a couple more times so that you can get a better idea of what's going on. Set a definite time. Leaving future meetings up in the air is like waving good-bye. It is not uncommon for the individual to try to get off the hook by flattering the therapist. "Gee you've really helped me. Why don't I call you if things don't improve? Why, I feel better already, just talking to you."

Despite your title of substance abuse therapist, clients first coming to an agency are not coming to you to have you "do your treatment routine" on them. Possibly what they really want is a clean bill of health. They want to figure out why their drinking isn't "working" anymore. The only thing that may be clear is the presence of drinking or other drug use. Clients are often unaware of its relationship to their problems in life. As they paint a picture of what is going on in their lives, the therapist will certainly see things the clients are missing or ignoring.

You can see, for example, that the client is alcohol dependent. In your opinion, the client may unquestionably need some intensive treatment. However, at the moment, the client is unable to use the treatment. First, it is necessary to make a few critical connections—that is, get the arrows pointed in the right direction.

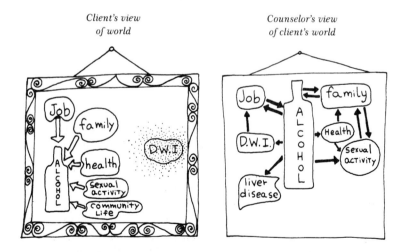

*Client's view
of world* *Counselor's view
of client's world*

Standardized assessment tools   The substance abuse field is increasingly using standardized instruments to promote treatment planning as well as to provide a yardstick for measuring treatment effectiveness. The most widely used tool for both of these purposes is the Addiction Severity Index (ASI). It was first introduced in the early 1980s and has been widely used. The ASI is a semistructured interview that collects data from substance abusers in seven problem areas: medical, employment, legal, alcohol, other drug use, family-social functioning, and psychological status. For each of these areas, there is a score indicating the severity of the problems in that area. Everyone in the substance use field should acquire skill in using the Addiction Severity Index. Training programs to introduce the ASI to clinicians have been developed, some including some videotape vignettes, that help you learn to use the Index smoothly.

Family involvement   Participation of family in the evaluation is very desirable and becoming the norm. This is so vital that it's hard to imagine why family involvement was not always the case. In some instances family members may be the more reliable historians. Even if not, their perspective on the problem is essential. By including family members, the clinician can assess firsthand their needs and their ability to provide support, as well as engage them as partners in treatment.

Treatment planning and treatment settings

An evaluation may take several sessions. The Addiction Severity Index can be a useful tool. In essence, the goal of the evaluation is to understand the client's situation and based on that develop a "recipe" or plan that will offer the client the optimal chance of acquiring the skills and resources needed to maintain abstinence, and in the process get those arrows pointed in the proper direction. The essential tasks of treatment will be discussed shortly. The treatment plan may use many of the treatment techniques discussed in Chapter 9.

What is the appropriate treatment setting? One wants to avoid either under-treatment or over-treatment. The American Society of Addiction Medicine (ASAM) has developed patient placement criteria to guide decisions about the appropriate treatment setting. Six different factors, or using ASAM terminology, "dimensions," have been identified as germane to determining the type of care required. These dimensions are outlined below, along with some of the key questions to consider for each.

• Dimension 1. *Acute intoxication and/or likelihood of withdrawal syndromes*. Is the patient currently intoxicated? Does the level of intoxication represent a potential life-threatening situation? Is there evidence of physical dependence? Is withdrawal likely? If so, are there factors that may complicate detoxification, e.g., the presence of other medical problems or a history of serious past withdrawal? If withdrawal could be accomplished without medical supervision, are there family or friends available to provide support and identify any emerging problems were these to arise?

• Dimension 2. *Biomedical conditions and complications*. Are there any serious medical problems that may complicate treatment or chronic conditions that need to be monitored?

• Dimension 3. *Emotional-behavioral conditions*. Are there apparent psychiatric issues? Are they an expected part of the addictive disorder or do they appear to be a separate disorder?

- Dimension 4. *Acceptance of need for treatment.* Does the patient recognize the need for treatment? Is the patient indicating a desire for treatment versus resisting treatment? Is the patient feeling pressured or coerced to enter treatment? To what extent is entry into treatment prompted by internal motivation, and to what degree is it the result of external pressures?
- Dimension 5. *Relapse or likelihood of continued use.* What are the apparent immediate risks if the patient does not enter treatment at this time? What are the longer-term risks associated with continuing to drink or use drugs? What kind of skills and supports does the patient have both to stop alcohol or drug use, as well as to maintain this abstinence?
- Dimension 6. *Recovery environment.* This refers to the client's social situation. What kind of family and social supports are present? What is the employment status, educational status, financial situation? What community resources are needed *and* available—vocational counseling, social service agencies, etc. Is the client confronted by a situation where family members' or friends' drug or alcohol use would invite relapse or threaten participation in treatment?

Taking into account the results of the assessments of these domains, different levels of patient care have been identified. These specify the kind of care that is required given the client's status. These levels of care are:

Level 0.5	Early Intervention.
	[This level of care was added when the criteria were reviewed and subsequently revised. So as not to introduce confusion by renumbering the existing levels, this was made .5 (one-half), to place it before Level I.]
Level I	Outpatient Services
Level II	Intensive Outpatient and Partial Hospitalization Services
Level III	Inpatient /Residential Services
Level IV	Medically Managed Intensive Inpatient Services

To help clinicians incorporate the data, ASAM has devised a table, set forth in the form of a grid. For each type or level of care, the relevant factors are reviewed from the different domains. In some instances, there is a single dimension that is *the* deciding factor in specifying what kind of care should be provided. For example, if there is apt to be serious withdrawal in a medically ill patient, medically managed intensive inpatient care is indicated. No ifs, ands, or buts. At that particular moment, other domains, such as the recovery environment or degree of family support, are irrelevant. When these will come into play is after the medical status has stabilized. Those factors will then be considered to determine whether the client is discharged to outpatient care or a residential program. Not only do the criteria state what kind of care is required given the patient's status in each of the six areas, but they also indicate when discharge from a particular level of care is appropriate.

Treatment planning for those previously treated   A few comments are warranted with respect to treatment planning for the client who has been in treatment previously. A portion of the evaluation needs to focus on prior treatment. What was the treatment? Did the client have a period of stable sobriety? If so, what contributed to its maintenance? To what do the family and the client attribute the resumption of drinking or drug use? These perceptions may be insightful or way off base. However, they are important beliefs that will either need to be supported or challenged. If a stable sobriety or abstinence was never achieved, what are their hypotheses as to what went wrong? Is there evidence to suggest a psychiatric disorder that has gone undiagnosed? Is there multiple drug use? In light of what is now known about matching patients to particular treatments, is there a particular treatment approach that might be indicated? Also, is this individual a possible good candidate for drug therapies?

The client who has been through treatment a number of times and has not achieved abstinence is often termed a "treatment failure." This is unfortunate. This categorization fails to recognize that relapse is not uncommon. Also, this is obviously a very loaded label for the client and the family (if they still are on the scene), as well as the treatment staff. It is never possible to predict when treatment will "take." Nonetheless, simply one more exposure to the same treatment is possibly not the best clinical decision. The comparison might be made to someone with an infection that does not respond to a particular drug. Simply increasing the dose probably won't work. One of the things treatment repeaters do have going for them is a knowledge of what doesn't work. To the extent possible, the client should be actively engaged in treatment planning and committing to it, for example, agreeing ahead of time to attend more AA meetings, seeking an AA sponsor, entering a halfway house after inpatient care, and continuing in aftercare. A sense of self-efficacy is an important factor, too. This refers to the individual's belief in their ability to do things, to effect change. Efforts to help clients focus on what they have learned, and how this can be useful, are important.

Another difficulty commonly encountered with these clients is that they show up in the midst of a serious crisis, for example, a medical illness requiring hospitalization or family turmoil or legal problems. This can lead to a situation in which the person, willing to comply (or at least not to resist), in essence finds himself or herself entered into a program. Although one may need to respond to the crisis, it is imperative to engage the client as soon as possible in planning treatment after the crisis is stabilized.

If someone comes to an agency with a history of multiple unsuccessful treatment attempts in that agency's program, the question needs to be asked whether a referral to another facility might now be indicated. It is important this not be done as "punishment." Instead it should be a clinical decision based on the possibility that entry into treatment elsewhere may increase the odds in favor of a different outcome because that staff will not have been involved in the previous efforts and see the client as a "failure."

TREATMENT

Within the professional community there is reasonable consensus upon what constitutes the standard of treatment for alcohol dependence. However, as noted above, there are no universally accepted standards of care for the treatment of other types of alcohol problems. Nonetheless we are presenting some guidelines for your consideration. These we think can serve as a conservative approach until the time when a body of clinical experience with treatment of alcohol problems emerges, similar to that which has been acquired around alcoholism.

If it is a small sacrifice to discontinue the use of wine, do it for the sake of others; if it is a great sacrifice, do it for your own sake.

S.J. MAY

Alcohol incidents

By alcohol incidents, we refer to the negative consequences that result from an individual's drinking. This may be an accident, an altercation, or whatever. However, a thorough evaluation indicates no pattern of recurring problems to indicate abuse or alcoholism.

The "Thou shall nots"   Don't presume that the incident has been enough to teach someone a lesson and guarantee that there will be no future difficulties. It's easy to assume that the embarrassment, guilt, discomfort, or anxiety that resulted was sufficient. It may even seem almost cruel to discuss it further. Others may mistakenly think the polite, kind thing to do is "just not mention it." Especially with younger people, who may be those most likely to experience an alcohol-related problem, the incident may be treated by peers as a joke. What is required? All those who may have contact—be it emergency room personnel, a school counselor, the police, or the family—all need to acknowledge the role of alcohol in what occurred. The actual or potential seriousness needs to be made clear. If you recall the progression of alcoholism in the framework set forth by Johnson (described in Chapter 6), the absence of feedback by others in the face of alcohol-related incidents is, in part, what allows a chronic alcohol problem to blossom. In fact, a second such incident should be a clear tip-off that a problem is emerging. One DWI "might" just happen, but a second should sound the warning signal that the person is continuing in a destructive pattern, despite prior negative consequences.

In the face of an incident involving alcohol, basic education is essential. This should not be cursory and superficial, but detailed and personalized. Alcohol has to be explained as a drug to the individual in light of what has occurred. What does BAC mean? How is it that alcohol can induce poor choices? What happens when someone chugs drinks? What are the mechanisms for alcohol-drug interactions?

The underlying message is that if people are going to use the drug alcohol, they need to be fully informed about it. Don't assume that people, however bright and sophisticated, are sufficiently knowledgeable about alcohol and its actions to figure out what the risks are. So the evaluation should also include an inventory of drinking practices, a review of settings in which drinking takes place, behaviors associated with drinking, plus family history of alcoholism or medical conditions that may be adversely influenced by alcohol use. The question to be answered is this: "Are there circumstances that are likely to place the individual at risk?" If so, specific steps should be discussed to address these. What might the person who is faced with being a passenger in a car with an intoxicated driver do? For the person who takes allergy medications, what are the implications for drinking? Identify potential problems and help the client think through—ahead of time—what should be done. One finding from the substance abuse prevention research is pertinent. One of the techniques in reducing teenage drug use is literally to have the kids practice how to say no. Adequate information alone isn't enough, nor were exhortations to "just say NO." They needed some practice doing it. What is required are tips for applying this knowledge. What is being suggested here is an extension of that. This is very important, too, in the event that future problems with alcohol use occur. If a problem were handled in the fashion suggested here, later it could be safely assumed that the individual, from that point on, was fully informed! A subsequent problem would indicate that a serious ongoing problem with alcohol is emerging and that alcohol dependence may be unfolding.

It is important that an alcohol incident not be treated as a "secret." It is suggested that the client's consent be secured to bring the situation to the attention of the client's family, friends, or spouse. The family needs to be informed in order to be aware and supportive of what is recommended. Although in an ideal world at least one follow-up visit might be scheduled just to check in with the individual, it is more likely that this will not happen. The family physician, often an untapped ally, is in a position to monitor how things are going in the future. The family physician is in a position to routinely inquire about alcohol use and therefore may be in the best position to spot any future difficulties. Because one of the most useful factors in spotting an alcohol problem early is detecting changes that occur over time, getting the occurrence of an alcohol problem into the individual's medical record is important. A brief communication with the physician will accomplish that. For the person at risk for developing alcohol dependence, the signs and symptoms that should trigger a need for further evaluation should be understood by all.

Other drug incidents

For any incident involving drugs other than alcohol, many of the same actions are required. Information, information, information. But again, there is an important caveat. There is an assumption made with alcohol that does not apply to other drugs, which is that with information, future drinking can be educated, informed, and involve less risk. For most other drugs, the "informed" stance is that low-risk use is a contradiction in terms. Indeed, nonuse is the reasonable, educated stance. This isn't just a matter of addiction potential, or risks down the road of more dangerous routes of administration. Any drug incident that brings someone to clinical and often medical attention demonstrates that problems are equally risky in the short run. Any street drugs involve risks of contaminants, adulterants, of being of unknown strength as well as unknown purity, or not being the substance it is purported to be—all of which invite medical emergencies. Or prescription drugs may be ingested without regard for their effects, side effects, or dosage. It is possible to address these issues in a way that isn't judgmental or moralizing. If educational efforts are educational and not sermons, the facts themselves can speak volumes.

Alcohol abuse

Unlike an alcohol incident that represents an acute problem, alcohol abuse is a chronic problem. It is defined as a pattern of use that is physically hazardous or that interferes with the ability to fill major obligations, be it at home, work, or school, or that causes major problems with others. Practically speaking, alcohol abuse can be considered to be present when there is a pattern of alcohol problems and the sense that alcoholism is "just around the corner." Alcohol abuse may be present in an individual even if loss of control is unclear, because there may have been no efforts to control or moderate alcohol use. If physical dependence and loss of control have not occurred, then moderation of drinking practices from a physiological standpoint is possible. However, depending upon the person's social situation and life circumstances, this may still represent a monumental feat. Consider the college student who is into the party scene. Changing drinking patterns will require marked changes in the student's circle of friends, daily routine, and choices of recreational activities. To achieve this magnitude of change will require that the client be engaged in more than a supportive chat.

To the author's mind, to do this requires that the individual be engaged in some formal treatment, involving education, individual counseling, and possibly participation in a group with others in the same situation. Monitoring efforts to moderate alcohol use and avoid future problems is imperative. Through this process, in a number of cases, evidence may mount that there is loss of control or preoccupation with drinking indicating that abstinence and alcoholism treatment are now needed. In essence, if efforts to address alcohol abuse are unsuccessful, the diagnosis of alcoholism can now be made.

This kind of approach is very similar to what is known as a "harm reduction" model. A harm reduction perspective is one that is just now taking hold in the United States, although it has become a cornerstone of public health policy in many other countries. This model grew out of the prevention efforts to stem the spread of HIV infection. This approach has implications for alcohol use as well. Within a harm reduction model, the emphasis is not really directed to use versus nonuse. The primary goal is to decrease possible harm if/when there is use. Unquestionably in terms of intravenous drug users and AIDS transmission, the purest form of harm reduction would be drug treatment thereby eliminating IV drug use. However, not every individual is ready to accept treatment. And, in many locations, those who want treatment find that there are waiting lists for treatment programs. Short of this ideal approach, there are a number of other steps that can be taken to reduce risk. These can range from educational initiatives around the dangers of sharing needles, to promoting the use of bleach to sterilize needles, to mounting needle exchange programs, to allowing the purchase of syringes at pharmacies. Even if the levels of IV use were to remain the same, any one of these steps could make an important difference in lowering the risk of AIDS transmission via shared needles.

Harm reduction is particularly relevant in terms of adolescent alcohol use. Drinking by adolescents need not be condoned to face the reality that it does occur. Accordingly, attention needs to be directed to reducing the likelihood of acute problems. This is the kind of thinking that is part of the promotion of designated drivers.

Marijuana: incidents and abuse

Despite its being an illicit drug, there are those who distinguish marijuana from other drugs. The fact is that in some social circles, marijuana use is tolerated or accepted, if used with discretion. This is a bit like the "don't ask, don't tell" rule regarding gays and lesbians in the military. Many consider marijuana use a private matter, and no one else's business if not used in situations that invite physical risk or endanger others, such as driving. It is noted that the problems that can occur with marijuana use simply are not in the same league as those associated with other drugs, including alcohol. Dependence can occur with marijuana, but in a much smaller proportion of those who use it than is true for many other drugs. Nor is there a clear-cut withdrawal syndrome associated with dependence. Infrequent or moderate use is not associated with significant medical sequelae. Even the problems associated with long-term heavier use are less dramatic than those that accompany heavy long-term drinking. On the basis of this, there are those who feel strongly that the criminal sanctions that can be brought to bear are disproportionately harsh. Given the levels of social problems that are related to use, there is discussion in some quarters to decriminalize if not actually legalize use. Those who hold that marijuana should remain an illicit drug cannot point to its drug properties to make the case. While a case certainly can be made, it has to be made on other grounds. Generally, these arguments boil down to the position that as a society we have enough problems with the drugs that are licit, so why add to our problems?

The person who comes to a clinician's attention around marijuana use may represent a situation containing the same issues as those posed by alcohol abuse. Clearly some problems have resulted from use, otherwise the individual wouldn't be in a clinician's office. But there may not be dependence. As clinicians our job is not to be police officers. Nonetheless, this is where the legal status begins to cast a shadow over the issue. By the fact that someone comes to professional attention, use has clearly become somewhat public. In light of someone's being seen by a clinician, one may question if "moderate" marijuana use is a reasonable clinical goal. Marijuana use can also be problematic in the context of other drug use. Just as marijuana is notorious for causing the "munchies," it is also true that when someone is stoned, the decision to drink or not to drink is hardly an informed, thoughtful one. The client needs to be engaged in the same process of self-examination that is required in the presence of alcohol abuse. Again, follow-up is required to see whether efforts to reduce risk are being effective.

ALCOHOL DEPENDENCE

Alcoholism treatment is nothing more (or less) than the interventions designed to short circuit the alcoholic process and provide an introduction to a sober, drug-free existence. Alcoholism is among the leading causes of death in the United States. It shouldn't be. In comparison to other chronic diseases, it is significantly more treatable. Virtually any alcoholic person who seeks assistance and is willing to actively participate in rehabilitation efforts can realistically expect to lead a happy, productive life. Sadly, the same may not be true for a victim of cancer, heart disease, or emphysema. The realization that alcoholism is treatable is becoming more widespread. The public efforts of prominent individuals who are recovering has contributed to this acceptance. Both professional treatment programs and AA are discovering that clients today are often younger and in the early or middle stages of alcoholism when they seek help. It is imperative for the helping professions to keep firmly in mind the hope that surrounds treatment.

Just as people initially become involved with alcohol for a variety of reasons, so is there similar variety in what prompts treatment. For every person who wends his or her way into alcoholism, there is also an exit route. This exit is most easily accomplished with professional help. The role of the professional is to serve as a guide, to share knowledge of the terrain, to be a support as the alcoholic regains footing, and to provide encouragement. The therapist cannot make the trip for the alcoholic but can only point the way. The therapist's goal for treatment, the destination of the journey, is to assist the alcoholic individual in becoming comfortable and at ease in the world, able to handle life situations. This will require the alcoholic to stop drinking. In our experience, drinking alcoholics cannot be healthy, at peace with themselves, or alive in any way that makes sense to them. The question for the professional is never, "How can I make him or her stop?" The only productive focus for the therapist is, "How can I create an atmosphere in which he or she is better able to choose abstinence for himself or herself and gain the tools to accomplish this?"

In this discussion, abstinence is presumed to be required for the treatment of alcohol dependence. Vaillant, when questioned as to an alcoholic's ability to resume social drinking, uses the example of a motorist who decides to remove the spare tire from the car trunk. Disaster may not strike the next day, or the next week, or even within the month. But sooner or later. . . . In addition, the seriousness of the consequences cannot be predicted. It may be only a flat tire in one's driveway, or it may be a blowout on a busy freeway during rush hour. It may represent an inconvenience, or it may entail serious consequences.

Abstinence as a requisite for recovery is viewed as having a solid physiological basis. Tolerance, once established, is maintained, even in the absence of further alcohol use. Were someone who has been abstinent for a considerable period to resume drinking, the person would very quickly be physically capable of drinking amounts consistent with the highest levels previously consumed. Drinking isn't resumed with a physiologically "clean slate." It may have taken a drinking career of 10 or more years for the alcohol dependent person to reach consumption levels of a fifth a day. However, after tolerance has been established, that level of drinking can be reinstated literally within days, even after a decade of sobriety. This "rapid reinstatement of tolerance" is recognized in medical circles as one of the hallmark signs of dependence, or what was formerly described as addiction. For those clients who ask, "Is total abstinence really necessary?" one stock response is, "Your body will always remember you have alcoholism, even if you forget!"

Obstacles to treatment

If alcoholism is so highly treatable, what has been going wrong? Why aren't more people receiving help? The obstacles do require examination. Historically, one big handicap has been society's attitude toward alcohol and its use. Unfortunately, until recently, the chances of being treated for alcoholism were far too slim. Oh, you could count upon treatment for depression, gastritis, or even cirrhosis, but not for alcoholism. Despite all the public information and education, the notion remains lurking that talking about someone's drinking is in bad taste. It seems too private somehow, none of anyone's business. Most of us have a good feel for the taboo topics—sexual behavior or people's way of handling their children. The way someone drinks has long been a strong taboo. Ironically, as we have collectively become better informed, our reticence may be chalked up less to the topic's being in bad taste than to the fact that we feel as if we are making an accusation! If the behavior that evokes disapproval is not viewed as a symptom of alcoholism, it is perceived as wholly volitional. We have not yet reached the point where to comment on what is perceived as unwise, dangerous, or inappropriate alcohol use is a wholly neutral topic, much less a topic upon which we can universally assume anyone would welcome another's observations. The notion of alcoholism as a moral issue still remains a situation for which "willpower" is the presumed solution. The person with the alcohol problem believes that as firmly as anyone and expends considerable energy at trying not to drink so much.

Of course, an alcoholic has a stake in keeping the drinking and its associated problems off-limits. Should the drinking behavior be discussed, the symptomatic rationalization combined with our cultural tendency to "psychologize" or analyze would spring another trap. The notion that someone drinks alcoholically only because he is an alcoholic sounds circular and simpleminded. Thus everyone scurries around to find the "real" cause. Alcoholism as a phenomenon, a fact of life, gets pushed aside and forgotten in the uproar.

Another obstacle is the confusion introduced for alcoholic individuals and their families by the behavioral symptoms of alcoholism. One common characteristic of alcoholic behavior is the extreme variation, the lack of consistency—sometimes good mood, sometimes foul mood, sometimes sloshed, sometimes sober. This inconsistency prompts a host of explanations. Further, this very inconsistency allows the alcoholic, family, and friends to hope things will get better if left alone. It permits them to delay seeking assistance. It almost seems to be human nature to want—and wait—for things to improve on their own. Consider for a moment the simple toothache. If the toothache comes and goes, you probably will delay a trip to the dentist. After all, maybe it was something hot you ate. Maybe it was caused by something cold. On the other hand, if the pain is constant, if it is clearly getting worse, if you can remember wicked toothaches in the past, you'll probably call immediately for an emergency appointment with your dentist. The total time you are actually in pain in the latter case may be much less than what you would have put up with in the former example, but you are spurred into action because it doesn't appear it will improve by itself.

Another obstacle can be the lack of treatment resources. Some populations are particularly hard hit, such as women and adolescents. In the wake of managed care, treatment is less accessible to many. Too often providing the "least restrictive" treatment turns into offering no treatment. Residential stays are largely limited to detoxification. However, the length of time one is in detox is often not sufficient to help patients understand the need for ongoing treatment and get them engaged in the process of rehabilitation. It is not merely a matter of time. Even though physically present, the patient is little able to absorb information or engage in much reflective thought given the disturbances of cognitive function while in the midst of withdrawal.

Factors in successful treatment

Having alluded to failure and some sense of what to avoid, let us proceed to success. The likelihood of success is greatly enhanced if treatment is tailored to the characteristics of the disease being treated. The

There are two things that will be believed of any man whosoever, and one of them is that he has taken to drink.

BOOTH TARKINGTON

following factors, always present, should guide both the planning and process of treatment.

1 *Dysfunctional life patterns.* The individual's life has been centered around alcohol or drugs. If this is not immediately evident, it is because the particular client has done a better-than-average job of disguising the fact. Thus the clinician cannot expect a repertoire of healthy behaviors that come automatically. Treatment will help the individual build new behaviors, as well as rediscover and dust off behaviors from the past to replace the warped "alcoholic" or "drug" responses. This at times is what makes intensive treatment, whether inpatient or outpatient, desirable. Besides cutting down the number of easy drinking or drug use opportunities, it provides some room to make a new, fresh beginning.

2 *Alcohol or drugs as a constant companion.* Alcohol or drugs are used to anticipate, get through, and then get over stressful times. These individuals, to their knowledge, do not have effective tools for handling problems. In planning treatment, be alert to what may be stressful for a particular client and provide supports. In the process, the therapist can tap skills the client can turn to instead of the bottle or the drug of choice.

3 *Psychological wounds.* Any drug, including alcohol, can be both a best friend and a worst enemy. The prospect of life without the drug seems either impossible or so unattractive as to be unworthwhile. The dependent individual feels lost, fragile, vulnerable, fearful. No matter how well put together the client can appear or how much strength or potential the professional can see, the client by and large is unable to get beyond those feelings of impotence, nakedness, nothingness. Even when being firm and directive, the therapist has to have an awareness of this.

4 *Physical dysfunctions.* Chronic alcohol or drug use often takes its toll on the body. Even if spared the more obvious physical illnesses, other subtle disturbances of physical functioning are often present. For example, with alcohol, sleep disturbance can last up to 2 years. Similarly, a thought impairment would not be unusual on cessation of drinking. In the initial stage of recovery, difficulty in maintaining attention is commonplace. There will be diminution of adaptive abilities. During treatment, education about the drug, in this case, alcohol and its effects, can help allay fears, remembering always that the most important ingredient in treatment is time away from the drug. Reminding the client of this and helping him or her see that improvement will come with more drug-free time is an important factor.

5 *Chronic nature of dependence.* A chronic disease requires continuing treatment and vigilance regarding the conditions that can prompt a relapse. This continued self-monitoring is essential to success in treatment.

6 *Deterioration in family function.* As described in Chapter 7, the family needs as much help as the family member who is the identified patient. Better outcomes result when they have a treatment program independent of the addicted member's treatment.

Recovery process

Recall how the progression of alcoholism or drug dependence can be sketched out. Similarly, recovery is a process that does not happen all at once. Gradually, in steps, the client becomes better able to manage his or her life. For the purpose of our discussion, we have distinguished three different phases: the preliminary or introductory phase, active initial treatment, and the continuing maintenance of recovery. There is no clearcut beginning or end point, yet each phase has its observable hallmarks.

Others, too, have sketched out the stages or progression of recovery. Stephanie Brown has titled these stages of recovery as (1) drinking, (2) the transition from drinking to abstinence, (3) the early stages of recovery, and (4) ongoing recovery. The terminology may differ slightly, but the common denominators of these perspectives is to approach recovery as a dynamic process. It occurs over time and has the client address different tasks at different stages. The clinician needs to have a repertoire of skills to be able to intervene appropriately. In the discussion below we have used alcohol and alcoholism as the example, but the same process applies as well to other drug use.

But you're a doctor! Why can't you help my father stop drinking?

Preliminary or introductory phase   The preliminary or introductory phase begins when the problem of alcoholism comes to the foreground. This happens when those nagging suspicions that there is something wrong with the drinking are permitted to surface. On personal initiative, there might be some initial inquiries, which may be directed to friends and associates. "You know, Jane was really mad at me for getting a bit tipsy when we went out last Friday night. You were there. I don't see anything wrong with letting go after a long hard week, do you? She's always on my back about something these days." Often others may not recognize these queries as a disguised or tentative "cry for help." This is equivalent to precontemplation and contemplation in the stages of change framework.

Ideally the friend, coworker, or colleague who is the recipient of these initial queries listens carefully and avoids the trap of offering false reassurance or reinforcing denial with a comment like, "Oh, you're just imagining it." Ideally they will share the information that people can get in trouble with alcohol and that alcohol use can be a significant health problem. They will then urge the seeking of a professional opinion and do whatever they can to see that the person gets there. The first overture may instead be made by a member of the clergy, a family member, a friend, or a perceptive physician—someone who is sufficiently concerned to speak up and take the risk of being accused of meddling. Suspecting an alcohol problem, any one of them might request that an alcohol expert be sought to explore the possibility. On the other hand, a court

may sentence an individual convicted of DWI to treatment. Increasingly common, too, is that the spouse may seek assistance as a result of the chaos of living with an alcoholic; or the employer may notice developing problems and attempt to intervene.

At this point the alcoholic is nibbling at the bait. He moves close and backs off. He wants to know, but he doesn't. Sharing the societal view of the stigma against those with alcohol problems, he or she will do or say anything to avoid being labeled as one of "them." Of course the drinking causes problems, but he or she doesn't want or is scared to stop. What someone in this state really wants to learn is how to drink well. The hope is to drink without the accompanying problems. In getting in touch with a substance abuse professional, the chances are pretty good the individual wants the professional to teach him or her how to drink without the negative consequences. (This represents an impossible request, so avoid getting sucked into trying.)

What can the therapist do? The first step is to carefully evaluate the problem to assess its nature and severity. Following that, a tentative treatment plan will be devised, possibly using outside expert opinions. These treatment recommendations will then be discussed with the client. This discussion will explain the recommendations, including any possible "risks" of treatment contrasted with the dangers of not initiating care. The assessment process for an alcohol problem or alcoholism, just like any other evaluation process, is intended initially to collect data. The clinician in a very general way will endeavor simply to get a clear picture of what is going on in the client's life.

In terms of the specifics, keep in mind that it is of the utmost importance to avoid getting into a defensive position. You need not be defensive as to the reason you can't be helpful in teaching the alcoholic how to drink successfully, since that might provoke the client to run away. There is, however, a mutual goal "to have things be okay." The therapist can buy into this without accepting the client's means of achieving it. The task of the therapy will be to assist the individual to see his or her behavior and its consequences accurately. As this occurs, the client will be confronted with the impossible nature of his or her request. The therapist will be most successful by being open, candid, and patient. Treatment is doomed if you are seduced into playing the "patsy" or if you try to seduce the client by being the "good guy, rescuer." Having a coworker with whom to discuss cases and their frustrations can help keep the objectives in sight.

For a long time it was thought that alcoholism was a disease that required the client to make a "self-diagnosis" for successful treatment to occur. Treatment, full steam ahead, was considered impossible until the alcoholic client, inside himself or herself, attached that label to cover all that is transpiring. A head, or intellectual, understanding could not suffice; it must come from the heart. The whole thing can be confusing. He or she certainly doesn't have to be happy about the diagnosis, he simply needs to know it's true. Then without hope of his own, he borrows the therapist's belief that things can change. This thinking has now been brought into question. Within the stages of change model, the critical moment is when the client comes to see that the balance has been tipped in favor of the need to change versus going with the status quo. When this occurs, the client goes from contemplation to determination. Whatever words one uses to describe this, there seemingly is a moment when the client decides to go for it. There is a leap of faith, when the risk of the unknown and the possibility of something better is preferable to what is.

Active treatment phase   At the point of acknowledging a desire to change, the clients by themselves often are at a dead end. If they knew what to do, they would have done it. In essence, they turn the steering of their life over to the therapist. The clinician, in turn, must respond by providing clear, concrete, and simple stage directions. A rehabilitative regimen needs to be set forth. The environment must be simplified. The number of decisions to be confronted must be pared down. There is little ability to deal with anything more than, "How am I going to get through this day (or hour) without a drink?" Effort needs to be centered on doing whatever is necessary to buy sober time. To quote the old maxim, "Nothing succeeds like success." A day sober turns on the light a little. It has become something that is possible. For the alcoholic this is an achievement. It does not guarantee continued sobriety, but it demonstrates the possibility. In the sober and straight time, the individual in treatment is gaining skills. Behavior is discovered that can be of assistance in handling those events that previously would have prompted drinking or drug use.

Although we are not attempting to discuss specific techniques of treatment here, drawing upon motivational interviewing, William Miller has provided some very practical tips about how to build motivation as well as how to follow through when a commitment to change has occurred. A mention of AA and other 12-step programs is appropriate. Professionals in the substance abuse field have long believed that clients who become involved in AA or other 12-step programs have a much better chance of recovery. This is not accidental. These programs combine key ingredients essential for recovery. They provide support, and they embody hope. They provide concrete suggestions without cajoling. They provide a haven, a place which ensures contact with other sober alcoholics or straight addicts. Their slogans are the simple guideposts needed to reorder a life. And their purpose is never lost.

George Vaillant, in summarizing the four factors that his research identified as associated with recovery from alcoholism, noted that all four are embodied in AA affiliation. AA offers a source of hope. Attendance at meetings and associations with members provides the needed external reminders to prevent the fading from memory of one's being alcoholic. It offers the opportunity for new relationships, where a clean slate is possible, relationships that aren't encumbered by the emotional baggage of the period of alcoholic drinking. AA also offers support.

The necessity for a direct and uncluttered approach cannot be over-stressed. In early treatment, clients are not capable of handling anything else. This is one of several reasons for the belief that substance abuse has to be the priority item on any treatment agenda. The only exceptions are life-threatening or serious medical problems. To work actively and successfully on a list of difficulties is overwhelming. Interestingly enough, when treatment is undertaken, the other life problems often fade. Furthermore, waiting to treat the alcoholism or addiction until some other matter is settled invites ambivalence. This waiting feeds the voice that says, "Well, maybe it isn't so bad after all," or "I'll wait and see how it goes." In essence one allows the client to move from the stage of action and determination back to precontemplation. Generally the matters are unsolvable because an actively drinking alcoholic or person using drugs has no inner resources to tackle anything. He or she is drugged.

Focusing on alcoholism as a priority, achieving the client's acceptance of this, and providing room and skills to experience sobriety make up the meat of therapy. As this takes place, the individual is able to assume responsibility for managing his or her life, using the tools acquired. With this, the working relationship between clinician and client shifts. They collaborate in a different way. The clinician may be alert to potential problematic situations, but the client increasingly takes responsibility for identifying them and selecting ways to deal with them. Rather than being a guide, the therapist is a resource, someone with whom the client can check things out. At this point, continuing treatment has begun.

Continuing treatment phase The alcohol dependent person learns, as do others with a chronic disease, the importance of being able to identify situations and their responses to them that may signal a flare-up. With alcoholism, this entails maintaining a continuing awareness of the alcoholic status if abstinence is to continue. The individual certainly will not continue to see the therapist for a lifetime as a reminder of the need to be vigilant. However, each alcoholic will need to develop other alternatives to succeed in staying sober. Within treatment programs explicit attention is directed to relapse prevention. This may involve stress reduction efforts, focusing on specific things to be used when faced with craving or the urge to drink, or efforts directed to enhancing general coping strategies. The thinking is that the skills that are needed to maintain sobriety may be different from those needed earlier in treatment. Relapse is seen as being triggered by things going on within the individual, internal events, as well as external events. Important internal factors boil down to thoughts, attitudes, and feelings. Negative feelings can include anger, feelings of frustration, guilt, or helplessness. The thoughts and feelings that can get people in trouble are the little phrases that seem so often to just play across the mind's screen automatically: "Just one toke or drink wouldn't matter." "I won't be able to _____, without a drink or drug." The fill-in-the blank can include everything from "have fun" to "relax" to "concentrate" to "survive the stress of this weekend." Coupled with this is the expectation that using a drug or having a drink will have been a positive thing in the short run. The long-term effects don't make it into the equation.

Why do I drink?   This is the recurrent theme of many active alcoholics and those beginning active treatment. In our experience, focusing on this question, even when it seems most pressing to the client, is of little value. It takes the client off the hot seat. It looks to the past and to causes "out there." The more important question addresses the present moment: "What can be done now?"

If there is a time to deal with the "whys," it comes during the continuing treatment phase. Don't misunderstand. Even then, long hours spent studying what went wrong, way back, are never helpful. On the other hand, the "whens" can be very instructive. The question "When do I want a drink or a joint?" points out the areas in which work can be done to prevent relapse. Typically, some clues can be discerned from the present, daily-life events, on those occasions when taking a drink is most tempting, as well as looking back over the last six months or year of active use. Examining such situations can provide clients with a wealth of practical information about themselves for their immediate use, and allow them to develop strategies to address these situations in other ways. Dealing with the present is of vital importance. Newly recovering individuals, who have spent their recent lives in a drugged state, have had less experience than most of us in attending to the present. The automatic tendency is to analyze the past, way back when, or worry about the future. The only part of life that any of us can hope to handle effectively is the present.

A client's hope for change often must be sparked by the clinician's belief in that possibility. Your attitudes about your clients and their potential for health exerts a powerful influence. This doesn't mean you cannot and will not become frustrated, impatient, or angry at times. Whether therapy can proceed depends on what you do with these feelings. You can only carry them so long before the discomfort becomes unbearable. Then you will either pretend they aren't there or unload them on the client. Either way your thinking can become "she can never change," "this guy is hopeless," or "she's just not ready." When that happens, therapy is not possible even if the people continue meeting. A better approach is to have a coworker with whom you can discuss these feelings of impotence and frustration. Another aid for a therapist is involvement in Al-Anon. Either or both of these together makes it easier to say, "I know this person can change, even if I can't imagine how it will happen. Certainly, stranger things have happened in the history of the world." At this point therapy can proceed. However, if an impasse in working with a particular client isn't broken through, the client should be referred to a coworker.

Treatment is a process involving people. People have their ups and downs, good days, bad days. Some that you think will make it, won't.

Some that you are sure don't have a chance will surprise you. There will be days when you will wonder why you ever got into this line of work. On others it will seem a pretty good thing to be doing. Remembering that it is an unpredictable process may help you keep your balance.

Common themes in treatment

Early in the recovery process, many clients have a tendency to become quite upset over very small matters. They look well, feel well, and sound well—but they really aren't quite there yet. This can be very trying for the clinician, the client, and the family as well. Remembering and reminding them of how sick they have recently been makes their upsets less threatening. The steps after any major illness seem slow and tedious. There are occasional setbacks; yet eventually all is well. It works that way with substance abuse, too. It is simply harder to accept because there are no bandages to remove, scars to point to, or clear signs of healing to check on. It cannot be emphasized enough that it takes time.

During the early phase of treatment, one point often overlooked is the client's inability to function on a simple daily basis. It is almost inconceivable to therapists (or anyone else for that matter) that a person who seems reasonably intelligent, looks fairly healthy after detoxification, and is over 21 can have problems with when to get up in the morning or what to do when he is up! Along with family, work, and social deterioration caused by alcohol dependence, the simple things have gotten messed up, too. He may have gargled, brushed his teeth, and chewed mints continually while drinking in an effort to cover up the smell of alcohol. He may, on the other hand, have skipped most mealtimes and eaten only sporadically with no thought to his nutritional needs. He may have thrown up with some regularity. Also, as we have seen in Chapter 3, his sleep is not likely to be normal. Getting dressed without trying to choke down some alcohol to quell the shakes may be a novel experience. It may have been years since he has performed the standard daily tasks in a totally drug-free state.

Clients are rather like Rip Van Winkle during the early weeks of their recovery. Everything they do is likely to feel strange. The face looking back at them from the mirror may even seem like a stranger's. They became used to the blurred perceptions they experienced while drinking. It is terribly disconcerting to find virtually every task one faces as a whole new thing. Whereas it used to take 2 very careful days to prepare Thanksgiving dinner, it now requires only a few hours. The accompanying wine for the cook, trips back to the store for forgotten items (and by the way, a little more booze), the self-pity over having to do it, the naps necessary to combat the fatigue of the ordeal, the incredible energy devoted to controlling the drinking enough to get everything done—all these steps are eliminated.

The newly sober individual is continually being faced with the novelty of time—either having too much time or not having enough time. He or she also may panic over the problem of what to do next. Many clients will need help scheduling their time. After years of getting by on the bottle, they have to regain a sense of how much time it really takes to accomplish some tasks. The individual may plan to paint the entire house in 2 days or, conversely, decide that he or she can't possibly fit a dental appointment, a luncheon engagement, and a sales call into one day. She may believe that it is all she can manage to stop by the bank on the way to work and pick up a loaf of bread and the dry cleaning on the way home. Tomorrow she intends to make new living room drapes in time for that evening's dinner party! The perception of time is as distorted as other areas of perception. Reassurance that this is a common state of affairs, along with assistance in setting realistic daily goals, is greatly needed. This is one reason newcomers to 12-step programs find the slogans "Keep it simple" and "First things first" so helpful.

Clients may not mention their dilemmas over time and schedules to you. They may feel ashamed about such helplessness over simple things. However, a gentle question from you may open the floodgates. This provides the opportunity to help bring order out of chaos. You can offer some much-needed guidance in remastering the details of daily living. All too often they wail, "I don't know! The house was a mess. . . . The kids were a mess. . . . I was a mess. . . . I just couldn't handle it, so I drank!"

Another aspect of reorienting the client to reality involves the misperception of events. The faulty memories caused by the drugged state will have to be reexamined. One cannot always wait for some sudden insight to clear things up. For example, he is talking to you about difficulties he has had with his wife. He remembers her as a nagging bitch, on his back about a "few little drinks." You might remind him that on the occasion in question, he was picked up for driving while impaired with a blood alcohol content of 0.20—clearly not just a few drinks. Then go on to point out that because he has misperceived the amount he was drinking to such an extent, he may have misperceived his wife's behavior. The opportunity is there, if indicated, to educate the client briefly on the distortions produced by the drug or alcohol and to suggest that sober observations of his wife's behavior are more valid. You might instead suggest a couples' meeting, but keep clearly in front the issue of the alcohol use.

Different strokes for different folks   Another easy trap to fall into is to expect the same course of recovery to occur for most clients. They don't get sick at the same rate, and neither do they get well at the same rate. One will be up and at 'em and lookin' good in very short order; another will seem to be stuck, barely hanging on, forever; and there will be those in between. What is difficult for one is a breeze for another. Don't assume that you know what is going to be a problem for any one particular person. We have tried to point out some of the more common difficulties, but there are lots of surprises around still. There are simply no formulas or easy prescriptions that will work every time. There is no substitute for knowing a particular alcoholic individual and dealing with the one sitting before you. Treatment matching efforts are based on the recognition that clients do differ, and some clients and some clinical approaches may represent better fits than others.

Still later   After about 3 months, upon achieving some level of comfort with the new state of affairs, the focus of treatment can shift. Until then attention is mainly on the mechanics of daily living. With that out of the way, or reasonably under control, the focus can become sorting out the client's stance in the world, feelings, and relationships. Though 3 months is a somewhat arbitrary designation, it is not wholly so. Recall the subacute withdrawal syndrome (see Chapter 3). With alcohol, the acute withdrawal period may pass within 5 days, but a longer period is required to regain the ability to concentrate, for example. Thus there is a physical basis for what the alcoholic client in early recovery can work on productively. This does not mean that all the problems previously discussed are totally overcome or that work is not proceeding along some of the above paths. It simply means that other problems may now be surfacing. It is also at this point that some assessment should be made as to whether to refer the client to other professionals if the present care-giver is not equipped to handle this work. Some problems are fairly common, and one must be alert to them. Most basically require finding a balance between two extremes of behavior that are equally dangerous. John Wallace, a psychologist with long experience in the field, has compared these extremes to rocks and whirlpools that must be avoided in the recovery "voyage."

Denial   One of the first difficulties entails denial. The tendency for clinicians new to alcohol treatment, when faced with a massive rejection of reality, is to want to force these clients to face all the facts right now. The trouble with this approach is that self-knowledge is often bought at the price of anxiety, and anxiety is a drinking trigger. What to do? Provide lots of support to counteract the initial anxiety caused by the acceptance of the reality of the drinking itself. Then, gradually, keep supporting the small increments in awareness that occur in the sober experience.

It is always the temptation to take denial personally, to think the client is "lying." Remind yourself that the person has adopted this defense as protection against the massive pain that would accompany facing the 'cold, hard facts.' Its function is to deceive or protect the self, not others. It is difficult, but very necessary, to remember that the denial of some particular issue is serving a useful purpose at the time, keeping overwhelming pain and anxiety at bay until more strength is available. The therapist must decide how much of either the client can tolerate. The therapeutic issue is whether the denial is still necessary or whether it has become counterproductive, blocking further progress.

Guilt   The presence of denial, the function of which is to protect against emotional pain, is evidence that the behavior is not congruent with the individual's core values and internal image. (The phrase used in psychotherapy for this phenomenon is ego dystonic, i.e., being out of harmony with one's "real" self.) So where there is denial, the issues of guilt and its fraternal twin, self-blame, cannot be far behind. It is clearly desirable to mitigate the degree of both. It is simultaneously necessary to avoid the pitfalls of their opposites, the rejection of social values and blaming others. Although excessive guilt leads to the guilt-drinking spiral, some degree of conscience and sense of responsibility is necessary to function in society. The therapist needs to be clear on this issue. The clinician must be able to point out unnecessary burdensome guilt on the one hand and yet allow honest guilt to be expressed. Dealing with both kinds of guilt appropriately is essential. On the blame issue, help is needed in accepting personal responsibility where necessary. Often, it can be helpful to point out that the disease itself, rather than oneself or others, may be the true cause of some of the difficulties, while gently reminding them that they are responsible for what happens now.

Compliance versus rebellion   Two other unhealthy extremes are often seen, particularly early in treatment: compliance and rebellion. In either case, strong confrontation is not a good strategy to choose. It seems simply to produce more of either. The compliant client becomes a more "model" client; the rebellious one says: "Aha! I was right. You are all against me," and then drinks. Moderation is again the key. The aim is to help clients to acknowledge their alcoholism and accept the facts of their situation.

Emotions   Emotions, and what to do about them, are another obstacle to be faced. Newly sober persons are likely to repress their feelings entirely. They do this to counteract their all-too-uncontrolled expression during the drinking experiences. Respect for this need to repress the emotions should prevail in the initial stages of recovery. But the eventual goal is to assist the client to recognize emotions and deal with them appropriately. Clients need to learn (or relearn) that feelings need not be repressed altogether, or conversely, wildly acted out. Instead, a recognition and acceptance of them can lead to better solutions. These are by no means the only examples of extremes for which you need to be alert. The therapist needs to be wary when dealing with any extreme behavior or reaction to avoid having the client plunge into the opposite danger. Some of these problems are continuing ones and may require different tactics at different stages in the recovery process.

Dependency and intimacy Many articles, and indeed whole books, have been written about dependency and alcoholism. Historically, the alcoholic individual was depicted as a particularly dependent type emotionally who had resolved conflicts inappropriately by using alcohol. This is basically another variant of the earlier mistake of confusing the symptoms of alcoholism with the individual's personality before the onset of alcoholism. Nonetheless, it is crucial to address issues of dependency throughout treatment. One long-term worker in the field, Dr. LeClair Bissel, has summed up the whole of treatment as "the task of helping people to become dependent upon people rather than booze." Be alert during treatment of the client's characteristic "all or none" approach. There is the vacillation between stubborn independence and indiscriminate dependence. During the early months of recovery the individual may need to poll everyone he or she knows to make a decision on some seemingly inconsequential matter; but when a major decision comes along, no advice is solicited. As individuals discover their need for others, this can lead to discomfort and confusion. On one hand, there is the potentially mistaken notion that turning to others is evidence of some weakness, and a voice within says, "I should be able to do this myself." On the other hand, with little recent history of good judgment and having little reason to trust one's own capacities, and feeling there may not be much margin for error, one can see a tendency to turn to others for almost everything. One of the long-term tasks of recovery is not only to recognize the need for dependence, but to become more discriminating in handling it. The basic questions the client will be addressing in this process are, "Whom should I and can I be dependent on? For what? At what cost? For what gain?"

Closely tied to the issue of dependency is that of intimacy. Intimacy is the capacity for closeness, for allowing oneself to be vulnerable to another. One of the tasks in early recovery is becoming reacquainted with oneself while simultaneously growing emotionally. To be rediscovering oneself while also establishing relationships with others is not an insignificant undertaking. One of the features of AA that contributes to recovery is that it provides a community in which the traditions of the fellowship provide safeguards and limits for all its members as the issues of dependency and intimacy in relationships get sorted out. It is also a setting in which one discovers that people are all interdependent to some degree.

Left to their own devices, recovering alcoholics seem to have an uncanny capacity for finding persons with whom they forge destructive relationships. There are always those around who would rescue them and be willing to assume the role of their perpetual caretakers.

Another issue may be encountered by single persons or those caught in unhappy marriages. It is not uncommon for them to find themselves "suddenly" involved in an affair or an extramarital relationship. With a little bit of sobriety, they are very ripe to fall in love. This may have several roots. They may be questioning their sexuality, and the attentions of another may well provide some affirmation of attractiveness. Also possible is that with sobriety comes a sense of being alive again. There is the reawakening of a host of feelings that have long been dormant, including sexual feelings. In this sense, it may be like the bloom and intensity of adolescence. A romantic involvement may follow very naturally. Unfortunately, it can lead to disaster if followed with abandonment. A counselor needs to be alert to this general possibility, as well as the possibility of being the object of the crush.

Getting stuck   Speaking of dependency, anyone working with alcohol troubled people is bound to hear this remark some time: "Sending someone to AA just creates another dependency." The implication of this is that you are simply moving the dependency from the bottle to AA and ducking the 'real' issue. That the dependency shifts from alcohol to AA or a clinician or treatment program for the newcomer is probably true. This should be viewed as a plus. Also, no one should get stuck there. By "there," we mean in a life that is just as alcohol-centered as before. The only difference is that the focus is on "not drinking" instead of "how to continue drinking." Granted, physical health is less threatened, traumatic events are less frequent, and maybe even job and family stability have been established. Nonetheless, it is a recovery rut (maybe even a trench!).

The fact that some do get stuck is unfortunately true. Many factors probably account for the "stuckness." One might be an "I never had it so good, so I won't rock the boat" feeling, a real fear of letting go of the life preserver even when safely ashore. Another factor is that some people in recovery, particularly those who began drinking as teenagers, have spent the bulk of their adult lives as active alcoholics. Therefore they have no baseline of adult healthy behaviors to return to. They are confronted with gaining sobriety, growing up, and functioning as adults simultaneously. This is a tall order that can be overwhelming. To make the task more manageable, it may well be tempting for these people to keep their world narrowed down to recovery. The only thing they now feel really competent to do, the only area where they have had support and a positive sense of self, is in getting sober. Giving up the status of "newcomer" to be replaced by that of "sober, responsible adult" may be scary, so a relapse or drinking episode may ensue. They then can justify and ensure that they can keep doing the only thing they feel they do well, which is being a client, an AA newcomer, and a recovering alcoholic.

Another factor that may cause the newcomer to get stuck could be that some clinicians (and some 12-step members) are better equipped to deal with the crisis period of getting sober than with the later issues of growth. Time constraints are too often the cause of the clinician's inability to encourage the "letting go," or stretching, phase. They are often overwhelmed with the numbers of clients truly in crisis. They simply have no time or energy to put out for the clients who are "getting along okay." Those who are not content with their clients' just getting by could aid the process by referring them to different types of therapy and groups that deal with specific and related issues. The adjunctive treatments are not substitutes for alcoholism therapy. Instead they supplement whatever has worked thus far, whether it is AA, individual therapy, or some other regimen.

The professional who works with clients on a long-term basis should beware of getting stuck in back-patting behavior. The phrase, "Well, I didn't do much today, but at least I stayed sober," is okay once in awhile. When it becomes a client's standard refrain over a long period, it should be questioned as a satisfactory lifestyle. Those who work around treatment programs affiliated with larger agencies are all too aware of groups of alcohol clients who hang around endlessly, drinking coffee, talking to others in similar circumstances, and clearly going nowhere. For instance, for some who may have suffered brain damage and thus have serious limitations, this may be the best that can be hoped for. However, we suspect that many are there simply because they are not being helped and encouraged to proceed any further. These are the recovering individuals most clearly visible to the health-care professionals; thus they may be one reason for the low expectations professionals have for the recovery process. They don't see the ones who are busy, involved, highly functioning individuals. Our contention is that professionals can increase the number of the latter and "unstick" more and more if they are sensitive to this issue.

Relapse   Any individual with a chronic disease is subject to relapse. For those with alcohol dependence, relapse means the resumption of drinking. Why? The reasons are numerous. For the newly sober person it may boil down to a gross underestimation of the seriousness and severity of the disease. For these individuals, there has been a failure to really come to grips with their own impotence to deal with it single-handedly. Hence, while perhaps going through the motions of treatment, there may be a lingering notion that although others in recovery may need to do this or that, somehow they are exempt. This may show up in very simple ways, such as the failure to address the little things that are likely to make drinking easier than not drinking: "Hell, I've always ridden home in the bar car; after 20 years that's where my friends are." "What would people say if _____ " "There's a lot going on in my life; getting to the couples group simply isn't possible on a regular basis." If families and close friends are not well informed about treatment and are not willing themselves to make adjustments, they can unwittingly support and even invite this dangerous behavior.

For the recovering individual with more substantial sobriety, relapse is commonly tied to two things. Relapse may be triggered by the recovery rut already described. On the other hand, if things have been going well in the recovering alcoholic's life, there is the trap of considering alcohol dependence to be a closed chapter.

As an aside, probably to counter this danger, there is preference for the phrase "recovering alcoholic" rather than "recovered." The use of *recovering* serves as a reminder that one is not cured of alcohol dependence. From a medical standpoint, as discussed earlier, this is quite accurate. The evidence points strongly to biological changes that occur during the course of heavy drinking. Even with long-term abstinence, in this respect there is no return to the "normal" or pre-alcoholic state. The body's biological memory of alcoholism remains intact, even if the recovering individual has "forgotten." The addiction can be rapidly reinstated. The alcohol dependent individual who resumes drinking may very quickly, in weeks or even days, be drinking quantities equal to amounts prior to abstinence.

An observation frequently made when considering the treatment of addictions is reminiscent of Mark Twain's comment about having stopped smoking—"I've done it many times." The more difficult task for clients is not necessarily stopping the drinking or substance use, but maintaining abstinence. Treatment programs are focusing on this issue in a more formal fashion. In the past the temptation for treatment professionals, as they contemplated relapse, was simply to add more and more components to the original treatment regimen, as if engaged in a search for the missing ingredient. The popular view now is that the maintenance of sobriety entails different tasks for the client than those necessary for ceasing initial use and that one can teach skills that will enhance a client's ability to maintain sobriety.

It is recommended that management of a relapse, should one occur, be discussed and incorporated into the continuing treatment plan. After all, relapse is not an unheard-of occurrence. It is far better for the client, family, and clinician to openly discuss how it shall be handled ahead of time. In the midst of the crisis of relapse, neither the family nor the client can do their most creative and clear-headed problem solving. Also, having gotten this taboo subject out in the open, it may be easier for all to attend to the work at hand, rather than worry about "what if." Any plan for responding to a relapse should be very explicit and concrete; for example, the family will contact the therapist, the client will agree to do A, B, and C.

Although one can look ahead in the abstract, it is during ongoing therapy that the clinician needs to be alert to possible signals of impending relapse. This can then be dealt with in individual sessions. Of course, part of the real meat of educational efforts is teaching clients to become aware of danger signals. If a drinking episode occurs, it does not have to be the end of the world, but neither should it be taken lightly. Whether it is one drink or an evening, a weekend, or a month of drinking, the individual needs to be immediately reinvolved with a treatment center, a clinician, or—if active or previously active in AA—become re-involved with AA. The important thing is not to sit back and do nothing. It is critical that a drinking cycle not be allowed to develop. Active intervention is needed to prevent this. If the client is still involved in treatment with you at the time of

It would take 14,931,430 six-packs of 12-oz cans to float a battleship.

NATHAN COBB, *Boston Globe*

relapse, it is a clear sign that more help is needed. If treatment is being provided on an outpatient basis while the individual continues to hold down a job and handle all the usual obligations, the drinking episode clearly shows that this approach is not working. A residential inpatient experience that allows, and indeed forces, the client to direct his or her full attention and energy to treatment may well be what is needed.

Some may instead have "played" at treatment, seen a therapist a few times, and decided things were under control. Fully resolved not to drink again, they then terminated formal treatment. However, willpower and determination, even with a dash of counseling, did not accomplish what they had intended; so the answer is to make a commitment and become engaged in more substantive care.

Seasoned clinicians often say that the most dangerous thing for a recovering alcoholic is a "successful drink." By this they refer to the recovering individual who has a drink, does not mention it to anyone, and suffers no apparent ill effects. It wasn't such a big deal. A couple of evenings later it isn't a big deal either. Almost inevitably, if this continues, the individual is drinking regularly, drinking more, and on the threshold of being reunited with all the problems and consequences of active alcoholism. The danger, of course, is that the longer the drinking continues, the less able the alcoholic is to recognize the need for help or to reach out for it. Someone who has had a difficult withdrawal in the past may also be terrified of the prospect of stopping again. It may be wise for you to make an agreement with the client that if he or she has a drink—or a near encounter—this has to be discussed.

With some substantial sobriety, reentry into treatment after relapse may be especially difficult. Among a host of other feelings there is embarrassment, remorse, guilt, and a sense of letting others down. Recognition that alcoholism is a chronic disease and that it can involve relapses may ease this. However, refrain from giving the impression that relapse is inevitable. Following a relapse, it is necessary to look closely at what led up to it, what facilitated its occurrence. The client can gain some valuable information about what is critical to maintaining his or her own sobriety. That is another reason it is so important to deal with a relapse openly. The clinician must also be sensitive to the issues that a relapse may evoke in the family.

For the moment—and we emphasize the moment—the family also may be thrown back into functioning just as it did during the old days of active drinking. The old emotions of hurt, anger, righteous indignation, and the attitude of "to hell with it all" may spring up as strongly as before. This is true even if—or especially if—the family's functioning has vastly changed and improved. All of that progress suddenly evaporates. There also may be the old embarrassment, guilt, and wish to pretend it isn't so.

Longer-term change   It is important that you maintain contact with your clients for an extended period to help reduce the likelihood of relapse. The client's best insurance against relapse is continuing to make changes and addressing the inevitable rough spots. So don't be casual with follow-up care. Concluding sessions are as important as all the earlier ones. By taking it seriously, you communicate this to your clients as well. Although your contacts may be less frequent, and possibly appointment times will be less than a full hour, don't allow the follow-up visits to become an empty ritual. Greeting clients with a "Hi, how are you?" and "You're looking great," and then escorting them to the door is not a very therapeutic style. If things are not going well, the client hasn't been given much opportunity to tell you! Be alert to the fact that clients may be reluctant to talk about difficult times. They may feel they should be able to handle it alone, or they may feel they are letting you down. But the opportunity provided by follow-up sessions may allow continuing therapeutic work to be done.

It isn't as if you don't know the person you are seeing! Be sure to bring up issues that have been problematic in the past, such as work or family issues. Find out how things are going now. If there were particular concerns the last time you met, be sure to find out how things turned out. Identifying successes is every bit as important as identifying difficulties. Notes made in the clinical record may be especially important to help you keep track of what has been discussed and to identify any recurrent themes. Be sure to review your notes before seeing a client; it's easy to lose track of what happened, when, and sometimes even with whom.

Pay attention to the things that are known to be stress points for the client. These may include job changes, even when it's a promotion; entrances and exits from the family, whether it's a birth, death, divorce, or the children leaving home for the military, college, or even kindergarten; illness in the family; changes in economic circumstances, from retirement, a family member's entering or leaving the work force or taking a second job, or even winning the lottery. Don't forget holidays. These supposedly joyous occasions are also stressful for most individuals. Preholiday tension is often followed by postholiday blues.

The reason for emphasizing considerable treatment over a fairly long period is simple. The people most successful in treating alcoholism are those who recognize that anywhere from 18 to 36 months are necessary to be well launched in a stable and functional recovery pattern. It might be said that recovery requires becoming "weller than well." To maintain sobriety and avoid developing alternate harmful dependencies, the client needs to learn a range of healthy alternative behaviors to deal with tensions arising from problems that accompany living. Nonaddicted members of society may quite safely from time to time alleviate such tensions with a drink or two. Because living, problems, and tensions go hand in hand, being truly helpful implies efforts to assist the client to become healthier than might be necessary for the general population.

RESOURCES AND FURTHER READING

Screening

Allen JP, Litten RZ, Fertig JB, Babor T: A review of research on the Alcohol Use Disorders Identification Test (AUDIT), *Alcoholism: Clinical and Experimental Research* 21(4):613–619, 1997.

Bradley KA, Boyd-Wickizer J, Powell SH, Burman ML: Alcohol screening questionnaires in women: A critical review, *Journal of the American Medical Association* 280(2):166–171, 1998.

Ewing JA: Detecting alcoholism, the CAGE questionnaire, *Journal of the American Medical Association* 252(14):1905–1907, 1984.

Rosenberg SD, Drake RE, Wolford GL, Mueser KT, Oxman TE, Vidaver RM et al: Dartmouth Assessment of Lifestyle Instrument (DALI): A substance use disorder screen for people with severe mental illness, *American Journal of Psychiatry* 155(2):232–238, 1998. (48 refs.)

Schorling JB, Buchsbaum DG: Screening for alcohol and drug abuse (review), *Medical Clinics of North America* 81(4):845–865, 1997. (97 refs.)

Selzer M: The Michigan Alcoholism Screening Test: The quest for a new diagnostic instrument, *American Journal of Psychiatry* 127(12): 1653–1658, 1971.

Skinner HA: The drug abuse screening test, *Addictive Behavior* 7(4):363–371, 1982.

Skinner HA, Holt S, Schuller R, Roy J, Israel Y: Identification of alcohol abuse using laboratory tests and a history of trauma, *Annals of Internal Medicine* 101(6):847–851, 1984.

Steinbauer JR, Cantor SB, Holzer CE III, Volk RJ: Ethnic and sex bias in primary care screening tests for alcohol use disorders, *Annals of Internal Medicine* 129(5):353–362, 1998. (55 refs.)

Assessment

Clark WD: Alcoholism: Blocks to diagnosis and treatment, *American Journal of Medicine* (71):275, 1981.

Clark WD: The medical interview: Focus on alcohol problems, *Hospital Practice* 20(11):59–68, 1985.

McLellan TA: *Guide to the Addiction Severity Index: Background, administration and field testing results,* Rockville MD: National Institute on Drug Abuse, 1988.
This monograph reviews the Addiction Severity Index (ASI), which is a structured interview designed for administration by a trained technician and takes approximately 45 minutes to administer. It is suitable for clients who abuse alcohol or other substances and is designed for both male and female clients. The interview collects objective and subjective information in seven problem areas—alcohol use, medical condition, drug use, employment support, illegal activity, family/social relations, and psychiatric function. From this, a 10-point rating of severity is obtained for each problem area. The ASI is suited for research purposes, diagnostic screening, and/or assessing changes at intervals of a month or longer. The monograph describes the background of the ASI and the impetus for its development. Also, it describes the design of the ASI and the studies to establish reliability and validity, reviews its strengths and

limitations, and provides instructions for administration. Appendixes include a copy of the ASI, instructions for scoring, plus instructions for computer coding and data entry.

O'Connor PG: Engaging the patient in treatment. Chapter 3. In Kinney J, ed: *Clinical manual of substance abuse,* 2d edition, St. Louis MO: Mosby-Year Book, 1996, pp. 57–73. (58 refs.)

This chapter deals with the issues related to the clinical work of moving the patient identified as having a substance use problem into treatment. It deals with the concept of motivation, what it is and is not; clinician attitudes and behaviors that can sabotage treatment; treatment planning; and the management strategies and clinical skills to deal with the patient's resistance to entering treatment.

O'Connor PG: Routine screening and initial assessment. Chapter 2. In Kinney J, ed: *Clinical manual of substance abuse,* 2d edition, St. Louis MO: Mosby-Year Book, 1996, pp. 40–56. (66 refs.)

Directed to primary care providers, particularly physicians and nurses, this chapter deals with instruments and techniques to conduct routine screening, contains steps for further assessment when screening is positive, describes approaches to patients at risk, and also offers general guidelines for interviewing. There is also discussion of interview approaches that facilitate data collection and foster a therapeutic relationship.

Motivation

Krampen G: Motivation in the treatment of alcoholism, *Addictive Behaviors* 14(2):197–200, 1989.

The study replicates work conducted 30 years ago on alcoholics' motivations for going into treatment and their relationship to treatment outcome. The results confirmed earlier findings that "threatened" loss of job, spouse, or driver's license, plus a subjective discomfort, are positively related to treatment outcome. However, if the person has already sustained such a loss, the alcoholic's prognosis is not favorable. (Author abstract.)

Miller WR: Why do people change addictive behavior? The 1996 H. David Archibald lecture, *Addiction* 93(2):163–172, 1998. (66 refs.)

The reasons why people change addictive behaviors are still not well understood. Many people who recover do so without formal treatment. Even relatively brief interventions seem to trigger change, and the dose of treatment delivered is surprisingly unrelated to outcomes. Client outcomes also vary depending upon the therapist who delivers treatment. Various models are briefly considered that may help in understanding this intriguing puzzle of change. (Author abstract.)

Miller WR, Benefield RG, Tonigan JS: Enhancing motivation for change in problem drinking: A controlled comparison of two therapist styles, *Journal of Consulting and Clinical Psychology* 61(3):455–461, 1993.

To investigate the impact of counselor style, a two-session motivational check-up was offered to 42 problem drinkers (18 women and 24 men) who were randomly assigned to three groups: (A) immediate check-up with directive-confrontational counseling, (B) immediate check-up with client-centered counseling, or (C) delayed check-up (waiting-list control). Overall, the intervention resulted in a 57% reduction in drinking within 6 weeks, which was maintained at 1 year. Clients receiving immediate check-up showed significant reduction in drinking relative to controls. The two counseling styles were discriminable on therapist behaviors coded from audiotapes. The directive-confrontational style yielded significantly more resistance from clients, which in turn predicted poorer outcomes at 1 year. Therapist styles did not differ in overall impact on drinking, but a single therapist behavior was predictive ($r = .65$) of 1-year outcome such that the more the therapist confronted, the more the client drank. (Author abstract.)

Miller WR, Rollnick S: *Motivational interviewing: Preparing people to change addictive behavior,* New York: The Guilford Press, 1991. (299 refs.)

Client ambivalence is a key stumbling block to therapeutic efforts toward constructive change. Motivational interviewing, a nonauthoritarian clinical approach, is a clinical technique for overcoming ambivalence and helping clients to get "unstuck." This book represents the first full presentation of this technique for practitioners, written by the psychologists who introduced and have been developing motivational interviewing since the early 1980s. The book reviews the conceptual and research background from which motivational interviewing is derived; provides a practical introduction to the what, when, why, and how of the approach; and brings together contributions from international experts describing their work with motivational interviewing in a broad range of populations.

Clinical Care

O'Connor PG, Schottenfeld RS: Patients with alcohol problems (review), *New England Journal of Medicine* 338(9):592–602, 1998. (112 refs.)

This article reviews major clinical features and recent developments in the identification and treatment of patients with alcohol problems from the perspective of generalist physicians. Topics covered include patterns of alcohol use and diagnostic criteria (abstention, moderate and risky drinking, and alcohol abuse and dependence); epidemiology of alcohol abuse and dependence (general population, medical settings); screening and diagnosis of alcohol problems (barriers to effective screening and diagnosis, screening approaches in medical settings including general history and screening questionnaires, physical examination and laboratory studies, and assessment of patients for alcohol-related problems); treatment approaches for problem drinkers (discussing alcohol problems with patients and assessing their readiness for treatment, use of brief interventions, treatment approaches for alcohol dependence, management of the alcohol withdrawal syndrome, referral of patients to self-help groups, referral to treatment programs, and pharmacological treatments to prevent relapse); and the role of physicians in caring for patients with alcohol problems. (Author abstract.)

Rohrer GE, Thomas M, and Yasenchak AB: Client perceptions of the ideal addictions counselor, *International Journal of the Addictions* 27(6): 727–733, 1992.

Addicted persons in a residential treatment center rated the traits that they felt were the most positive and negative in a counselor. Lists of traits were developed by having one group of clients make a list, in their own words, of positive and negative traits. These traits were compiled into lists from which other groups of clients rated the top 10 positive and the top 10 negative counselor traits. Profiles were developed for eight subgroups (Males, Females, Black Clients, White Clients, Alcoholics, Cocaine Addicts, Younger Clients: 18–23 years old, and Older Clients: 43+ years). Significant differences were found in the type of counselor preferred by various groups within the sample. The data suggest that addicted persons, while using colorful and imprecise language, have definite preferences and aversions toward certain counselor traits. These findings should be useful to counselors, as well as those involved in training programs. (Author abstract.)

9

TREATMENT TECHNIQUES AND APPROACHES

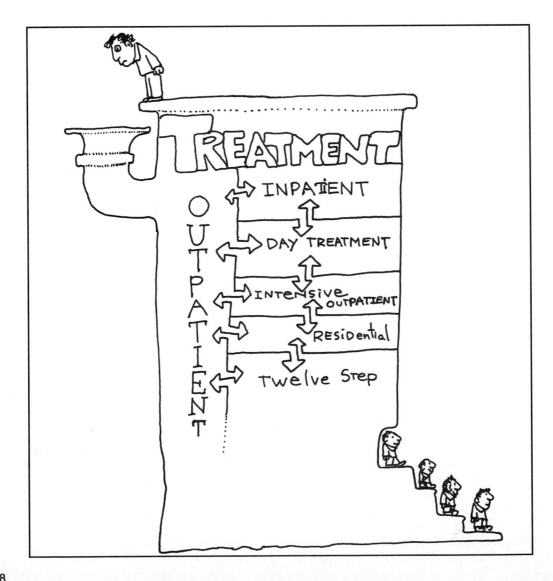

INDIVIDUAL COUNSELING

Earlier we defined treatment as all the interventions intended to short-circuit the process of abuse or dependence and to introduce the individual to effective sobriety. This could be put in equation form as follows:

Treatment = individual counseling +/or family therapy
+/or family education +/or client education
+/or group therapy +/or medical care +/or self-help
+/or pharmacotherapy +/or vocational counseling
+/or activities therapy +/or spiritual counseling. . . .

As can be seen, individual counseling is only a small part of the many things that treatment can involve. So what is it? A very simple way to think of individual counseling is as the time, place, and space in which the rest of the treatment is organized, planned, and processed. One-to-one counseling is a series of interviews. During these sessions the therapist and client work together to define problems, explore possible solutions, and identify resources, with the therapist providing support, encouragement, and feedback to the client as he or she takes action.

One of the difficulties in thinking about, discussing, or writing about counseling is knowing where to begin. It can seem a bit overwhelming. One of the problems is that most of us have never seen a real counselor at work. We have all seen police officers, telephone line workers, carpenters, or teachers busy on the job. So we have some sense of what is involved in those lines of work and can imagine what such work entails. The clinician's job is different. It is private and not readily observable. Unfortunately, most of our ideas come from books or television. It doesn't take too much television viewing to get some notion that a good counselor is almost a magician, relying on uncanny instincts to divine the darkest, deepest secrets of the client's mind. You can't help thinking the therapist must have a T-shirt with a big letter **S** underneath the button-down collar. Television does an excellent job of teaching us that things are not always as they seem. Yet, remember, in real life they often—indeed, usually—are. Everyone is quite adept at figuring out what is going on.

Observation

Each day we process vast amounts of information without much thought. Our behavior is almost automatic. Without the benefit of a clock, we can make a reasonable estimate of the time. When shopping, we can, without too much trouble, distinguish the clerk from fellow customers. Sometimes, though, we cannot find a person who seems to be the clerk. Take a couple of minutes to think about the clues you use in separating the clerk from the customer. One of the clues might be dress. Clerks may wear a special outfit, such as a smock, apron, or shirt with the store's logo. In colder weather, customers off the street will be wearing or carrying their coats. Another clue is behavior. The clerks stand

behind counters and cash registers, the customers in front. Customers stroll about casually looking at merchandise, whereas clerks systematically arrange displays. Another clue might be the person's companions. Clerks are usually alone, not hauling their children or browsing with a friend. Although we have all had some experience with guessing incorrectly, it rarely happens. In essence, this is "the good guys wear white hats" principle. A person's appearance provides us with useful, reliable information about them. Before a word of conversation is spoken, our observations provide us with some basic data to guide our interactions.

We hope that you are convinced everyone has observational powers. Usually, people simply do not think about these skills. The only difference between the clinician and others is that the therapist will cultivate these observational capacities, listen carefully, and attend to "how" something is said and not merely "what" is said. The counselor will ask himself or herself: "What is the client's mood? Is the mood appropriate to what is being said? What kinds of shifts take place during the interview? What nonverbal clues, or signs, does the client give to portray how she feels?" So, in a counseling session, from time to time, momentarily tune out the words and take a good look. What do you "see"? Reverse that. Turn off the picture and focus on the sound.

One important thing to note is that the questions you ask yourself (or the client) are not "why" questions. They are "what" and "how" questions that attempt to determine what is going on. Strangely enough, in substance abuse treatment, successful outcomes can occur without ever tackling a "why." Ignoring what or how issues, however, may mean you'll never even get into the ball park.

So what is the importance of observation? It provides data for making hypotheses. A question continually before the therapist is: "What's going on with this person?" What you see provides clues. You do not pretend to be a mind reader. Despite occasional lapses, you do not equate observations, or hunches, with ultimate truth. Your observations, coupled with your knowledge of alcohol and drugs and their impact upon people, suggest where attention might be focused. An example: a client whose coloring is poor and who has a distended abdomen and a number of bruises will alert the counselor to the possibility of serious medical problems. The client may try to explain this all away by "just having tripped over the phone cord," but the therapist will urge the client to see a physician.

You do your work by observing, listening, and asking the client (and yourself) questions to gain a picture of the client's situation. The image of a picture being sketched and painted is quite apt to capture the therapeutic process. The space above is the canvas. The total area includes everything that is going on in the individual's life. As the client speaks with the therapist, this space is filled in. Now the therapist is getting a picture of the client's situation. Not only do you have the "facts" as the client sees them, but also you can see the client, and his or her mood and

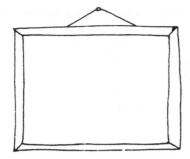

feelings, and get a sense of what the world and picture feels like to the client as well. As this happens, the space gets filled in and begins to look like this:

You have a notion of the various areas that make up the client's life: family, physical health, work, economic situation, community life, how the person feels about himself/herself, and so on. You are also aware of how substance use may affect these areas. As you find it necessary, you will guide the conversation to ensure that you have a total picture of the client's life. You are also aware that if the client is having a problem, it means that the pieces are not fitting together in a way that feels comfortable. Maybe some parts have very rough edges. Maybe one part is exerting undue influence on the others. So you must also attempt to see the relationship and interaction between the parts.

Feedback

In assisting the client to "see" what is going on, the therapist's observation skills pay off. A common feature of alcohol dependence, for example, is a markedly warped perception of reality. The ability of the therapist to provide accurate feedback to the client, giving specific descriptions of behavior and of what the client is doing, is very valuable. The alcohol dependent person has lost the ability for self-assessment. It is quite likely that any feedback from family members or friends has also been warped and laced with threats so that it has become useless. In the counseling session, it may go like this: "Well, you say things are

going fine. Yet as I look at you, I see you fidgeting in your chair, your voice is quivering, and your eyes are cast down toward the floor. For me, that doesn't go along with someone who's feeling fine." Period. The therapist simply reports the observations. There is no deep interpretation. There is no attempt to ferret out unconscious dynamics. The client is not labeled a "liar." Your willingness and ability to simply describe what you see is a potent therapeutic weapon. The client can begin to learn how he or she comes across, how others see him. Thus your use of observation serves to educate the client about himself.

Another related technique, earlier termed "confrontation," can be used by the therapist to help the client make the essential connections. Unfortunately this term has taken on very different meaning from when it was first introduced by Vernon Johnson. Now it too often can be an aggressive, even hostile, form of "tough love," with the emphasis on the tough not the love. Earlier confrontation did not equal attack. According to Webster's, to confront means "to cause to meet: bring face to face." Several examples of what therapists may do to bring clients face to face with the consequences of their behavior are to have a family meeting so that the family's concerns can be presented; to make a referral to a physician for treatment and consultation about the "stomach problems"; or to make a referral to an alcohol discussion and educational group. The therapist endeavors to structure situations in which the client is brought face to face with facts.

Education

Clients also need education about alcohol as a drug, about other drugs, and about the disease of addiction. Provide facts and data. A host of pamphlets are available from state alcohol agencies, medical societies, the federal alcohol and drug institutes, insurance companies, and self-help groups. Everybody likes to understand what is happening to them. This is becoming increasingly apparent in all areas of medicine. Some institutions have hired patient educators. Patient education sessions on diabetes, heart disease, cancer, and care of newborns are commonplace. Education about alcohol and drug problems is important for two reasons. The first is to help instill new attitudes toward alcoholism and other drug addictions—that they are a treatable disease, with recognizable signs. The hope is to elicit the client's support in helping to manage and treat the problem.

The other reason for education is to help the client handle feelings of guilt and low self-esteem. The chances are pretty good that the client's behavior has been looked at as downright crazy—and not just to others; it has also been inexplicable to the alcoholic individual. The fact that he or she has been denying a problem confirms this. There is no need to deny something unless it is so painful and so inconsistent with values that it cannot be tolerated. Learning facts about alcohol, other drugs, and addiction can be a big relief. Suddenly, things make sense. All the

bizarre behavior becomes understandable, at least for an active alcoholic. That makes a significant difference. Successful recovery appears
to be related to a client's acceptance of this framework of disease as the
basis for what has been occurring. Energy now can be applied to figuring out how one can live successfully around the illness. The individual
is relieved of the need to hash around back there, in the past, to uncover
causes, to figure out what went wrong. There is no need to dwell on the
pattern of harmful, senseless behavior; it becomes merely a symptom,
one that the individual isn't doomed to reexperience if efforts are made
to maintain sobriety and to live drug-free.

Self-disclosure

At this juncture it seems appropriate to add some cautionary word about
the technique of self-disclosure. And make no mistake about it, we consider this to be a counseling technique. As such, it requires the same
thoughtful evaluation of its usefulness as any other counseling tool. It is
important to recognize that "self-disclosure" is not limited to sharing information of one's own problems with alcoholism. Self-disclosure in
counseling or therapy refers to sharing not only the facts of one's life but
also one's feelings and values as well. This is in contrast to the style of
the early psychoanalyst, who never revealed information about himself
nor in any way presented himself as an individual to his clients. Counselors are self-disclosing when they express empathy or when they note
that the client's concerns are those with which other clients have also
struggled.

The concept of self-disclosures, however, has special meaning in the
alcohol and substance abuse field. The clinician may be a recovering
alcoholic or addict and may be involved in AA or NA where self-
disclosure is appropriate. In professional individual counseling or
group therapy sessions the need for self-disclosure may not always be
clear-cut.

Particularly at the early stages of the client's treatment or in the assessment process, it may seem only natural to allay some of the client's
nervousness or resistance with the news that you, as a clinician, have
"been there," know just how he or she feels, and furthermore can testify
to the possibility of a successful recovery. What seems natural may, however, be totally inappropriate or even countertherapeutic. Therapists need
to remember that their professionalism is important to the client, particularly in the early days of treatment. That professionalism is comforting!
The patient in an intensive cardiac care unit is interested in the physician's medical assessment of his condition, the physician's treatment recommendations, and the probable outcome. That patient is not interested
in hearing the physician's personal story of her own heart attack.

This is not to imply that self-disclosure shouldn't ever be used or that
it is ineffective. But we see the technique too often used as a matter of
course without proper thought given to the possible ramifications of it in

a particular instance. Because we do see it as a very powerful clinical tool, we recommend that great care be taken to see that it is used at the best possible time for the best possible reason—the benefit of the client. It should never be used to make the therapist feel more comfortable by getting "everything out in the open" or as a substitute for professional skills.

When is self-disclosure therapeutic? There may be times when the behavior that has resulted from alcoholism or drug use creates an overwhelming sense of worthlessness, isolation, and pervasive hopelessness. In such circumstances, self-disclosure may be useful. It may provide a desperately needed human connection, helping to relieve feelings of utter despair, spark just a glimmer of hope and a recognition that maybe, just maybe, things can be different. In a group setting, it may be preferable that such efforts to reach out come from group members. But there are times, certainly in individual sessions, when this falls to the clinician.

Client responsibility

The therapist expects the client to assume responsibility for his or her actions. You do not accept the client's view of himself as either a pawn of fate or a helpless victim. An ironic twist is present. You make it clear that you see the client as an adult who is accountable for his or her choices. Simultaneously, you are aware that those dependent upon alcohol, for example, when drinking, abdicate control to a drug. By definition, an alcoholic cannot be responsible for what transpires after even one or two drinks. Therefore being responsible ultimately means that the attempt to manage alcohol use must be abandoned. Here again, facts about the drug, alcohol, and the disease of alcohol dependence are important. A large chunk of the client's work will be to examine the facts of his or her own life in light of this information.

The client's need to have an alibi, to rationalize, and to otherwise explain away the obvious varies. But the therapist consistently holds up the mirror of reality, playing the client's story back to him. The therapist shares his or her observations, and in this way the client is enabled to move toward the first step of recovery—acknowledging the inability to control alcohol.

A word of caution

One word of caution to newcomers to the field: active alcoholics are sometimes described as manipulative or "con artists." Appreciate that they've had to be. To continue drinking alcoholically, in spite of the consequences, has required their adopting behaviors and perceptions of the world that could make their drinking feel and appear rational. These patterns do not disappear with the first prod, push, or pull toward treatment. Old habits die hard. With alcohol dependence, the habit of protecting the right to drink (even to death) is a long-standing one. When a client

I've heard him renounce wine a hundred times a day, but then it has been between as many glasses.
DOUGLAS JERROLD

discovers that you are probably not going to hand out a simple "three-step way to drink socially" and thus allow the drinking to continue, all considerable cunning can rise up in defense.

"Gee, you've really helped me to see exactly what I have to do. I'll do _____ and _____ and everything will be just fine. Thanks so much. You've made my life so much better already."

"Both my parents were alcoholics. I even had a grandfather who was. But you know, I really don't drink like that at all! It only started when Jake had that awful operation, and I spent hours at the hospital, and then my husband was called away to South America, and I needed something to help me over those awful times. But my husband's due home next week, and I'm just sure that now that I know all the facts you've given me, I'll just stop by myself, and everything will be just fine! Thank you so much."

"I can't imagine why my wife says what she does about my drinking. She must really be down on me, or jealous, or something. After all, I only have a couple of beers with the guys after work."

"Did you hear about that new research they've been doing? You know, the stuff that talks about how having a dog helps. I bet if I just get a dog and take something for my nerves (after all, my nerves are the real problem), I'll be just fine!"

Many individuals can be far more inventive than these examples show. Add tears, or a charming smile, or bruises from a beating. If they're not at the moment falling down, slobbering, throwing up, or slurring their words, it is hard not to believe them. There they sit, full of confidence, hopeful, and very friendly. After all, this isn't a charade for your benefit. The active alcoholic is desperately trying to hold on to the picture they paint. Experience has shown that at some point, you will either see, hear from, or hear about these people, and their situations will have gone downhill. They don't know how familiar their stories are—to themselves, the stories are unique. These people are not lying; they are simply trying to hang on to the only help they feel they have—the bottle.

Also, always keep in mind that the purpose of the "con" is not to deceive you. The client is trying above all to maintain his or her own self-deception. You may be able to help him or her loosen the grip by not allowing these pat replies to go unchallenged.

Problem identification and problem solving

In therapy, problem identification and problem solving constitute a recurring process. No matter what the problem, two kinds of forces are always at work: some factors help perpetuate the problem; other factors encourage change. These can be sketched out in a diagram, as shown on the next page. Suppose the problem is: "I don't like my job." The line going across represents the current situation. The arrows pointing upward stand for the factors that ease or lighten the problem. The arrows pointing downward represent the factors aggravating the problem.

If the individual's goal is to be more content at work, this might happen in several ways. The positive forces can be strengthened or others added, or attempts can be made to diminish the negative ones. A similar sketch might be made for alcoholic drinking. This kind of chart can help you decide what factors might be tackled to disturb the present equilibrium.

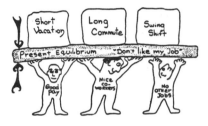

Left to his or her own devices, the alcoholic individual would piddle along for years. The fact that he is sitting in front of you indicates that something has happened to jiggle the equilibrium. This can be a force for change. Take advantage of it. Jiggle the equilibrium further. In the illustration just given, to take away the family denial or coworker cover-up would blow the whole act. It is becoming widely acknowledged that for the clinician to precipitate such a crisis can be the most helpful thing to do.

The therapeutic relationship

Whole volumes have been written on the nature and components of the therapeutic relationship. This book cannot even begin to summarize what has been set forth. Some of the attributes of the helping relationship were alluded to at the beginning of the previous chapter on treatment. The therapist is a guide. The therapist cannot do the work but can only attempt to bring the client's attention to the work that needs to be done. The therapist may provide some "how to" suggestions but will proportionally provide more support as the client does the actual work.

Although an exposition of the therapeutic relationship is beyond the scope of this book, several items are common points of confusion for newcomers. First, whatever the peculiar thing is that is the client-clinician relationship, it is not a friendship. It is not based on liking one another. The value of the therapist to the client is paradoxically that he is not a friend; the therapist does not need or exact anything from the client. Indeed, if that sneaks into the equation, then the potential value of the therapist has accordingly been diminished. Beyond being someone with a

knowledge of alcohol/drugs and their effects, the therapist is someone who can be trusted to be candid and open and who strives for objectivity. She or he can be counted upon to say what needs to be said and trusted to hear the difficult things a client must say without scolding or judging. Although it may initially sound demeaning, in point of fact the therapist is most effective with clients when the relationship is "just part of the job."

With the client-therapist relationship outside the realm of friendship, several potentially difficult situations for the clinician are more easily avoided. Some predictably difficult situations are what to do when the client becomes angry, threatens to drop out of counseling, claims you are taking someone else's side, or insists that you don't care or understand. It's very tempting and ever so easy to experience such situations as personally (and undeservedly) directed toward you. So first, take a deep breath. Second, remind yourself it isn't you who's being attacked. This is not an occasion for either reminding the client of "everything you've done for him," or just how experienced you are, even if the client doesn't appreciate it. As quietly and calmly as possible, discuss what's going on, which includes acknowledging the feelings the client is experiencing. Resist trying to make the patient feel "better" or talk him or her out of those feelings. Expression of negative emotion is something to be anticipated. Indeed, if it never occurs, it may mean that the therapist is sending signals that it is not permitted. Allowing negative feelings to be expressed doesn't mean being a sponge for everything, or not setting limits, or not stating a different perspective if you have one. One of the most important lessons the client may need to learn during treatment is that negative emotions can be expressed and the world doesn't fall apart. Nor will others immediately try to placate or run away.

The other side of the "emotions coin" can present a different trap. It is difficult not to respond to: "You are so wonderful," "You are the only person who really understands," or "You are the only person I can say this to." Beyond the danger of inflating the therapist's ego, there is the danger for the client that all the power is invested in the therapist. In the process of treatment, it is important that the client experience, and take credit for, the therapeutic work that is being done. So, for example, in responding to "You are the only person who really understands," a gentle reminder of the client's share of the work is appropriate. You might ask if there are other relationships, too, in which the client wishes to be able to share more and then help decide how to attempt to do that.

Case management and administrative tasks

Now to sound a very different note. An inevitable and necessary part of a therapist's work is administrative—writing notes in the chart, contacting agencies or counselors for previous records, dictating discharge summaries, contacting the referring party or others to whom a client will be referred. This is often perceived as a pain in the neck and the portion of one's job most likely to get short shrift. However, attending to these

I like writing chart notes, but I'd never admit it in public.

details is an important part of good clinical care. Treatment is almost never a solo act, but a team effort. How effectively the team functions often depends on the clinical personnel who orchestrate and coordinate the various efforts.

The client's chart or medical record is one very important vehicle for communicating information. This is especially true in a residential facility, with multiple staff working different shifts. There are often questions as to what should and shouldn't go in a chart. To handle things that should be noted but are particularly sensitive, some agencies have adopted the practice of keeping a set of confidential files, separate from the main record. Although not wishing to take lightly the concern for confidentiality, it can be a red herring. In thinking about what to include in the chart, ask yourself "What do others need to know to respond therapeutically?" Rarely does this have anything to do with "deep dark secrets." More often it has to do with the everyday nuts and bolts—worrying over a date for discharge, preoccupation with an upcoming court appearance, or a strained family meeting. The chart is not the place for verbatim accounts of individual sessions. But notation of any general themes, plus any modification of treatment plans, is needed. It also falls to the client's primary therapist or case mangers to present cases at team planning meetings. On such occasions, a little preliminary thought helps: Are there special questions you have that you'd like to discuss with others? Along with these formal routes of communication, there are also informal channels. Take the opportunity to brief others.

Beyond orchestrating the activities of an agency treatment team, it falls to the case manager to be a liaison, and often an advocate, with external groups such as employers, or vocational counselors, or social service workers, or the courts. Many clients have a wide range of need for supportive services. In these situations, you always must have the client's permission before acting. Also, it is important not to do for clients what they can do for themselves. Generally, it is more therapeutic to do a lot of hand holding as clients take care of business, rather than doing it yourself in the interest of efficiency. This can be very time-consuming, but this work should never be dismissed as less important than other aspects of treatment.

GROUP WORK

Group therapy has become an increasingly popular form of treatment for a range of problems, including alcohol and drug issues. (Of course, with AA dating back to 1935, recovering has been occurring in groups long before group therapy became popular or alcohol/drug treatment was even known.) Why the popularity of group treatment methods? The first response often is: "It's cheaper," or "It's more efficient; more people can be seen." These statements may be true, but a more fundamental reason exists. Group therapy works, and it works very well with alcoholics.

Some of the reasons for this can be found in the characteristics of the illness, plus normal human nature.

For better or worse, people find themselves part of a group. And whatever being human means, it does involve other people. We think in terms of our family, our neighborhood, our school, our club, our town, or our church. On the job, at home, on the playground, wherever, it is in group experiences where we feel left out or, conversely, experience a sense of belonging. Through our contacts with others, we feel okay or not okay. As we interact, we find ourselves sharing our successes or hiding our supposed failures. Through groups we get pats on the head or a kick in the pants. There is no avoiding the reality that other people play a big part in our lives. Just as politicians take opinion polls to see how they're doing with the populace, so do each of us run our own surveys. The kinds of questions we ask ourselves about our relationships are: "Do I belong? Do I matter to others? Can I trust them? Am I liked? Do I like them?" To be at ease and comfortable in the world, the answers have to come up more ayes than nays. The active alcoholic or drug dependent person doesn't fare so well when taking this poll. For the myriad reasons already discussed, relationships with other people are poor. Isolated and isolating, rejecting and rejected, helpless and refusing aid—with such a warped view of the world, they are oblivious to the fact that their drinking or drug use has been causing the trouble. When one is tied to drugs or wed to the bottle, other bonds cannot be formed. Attempts to make it in the world sober or straight will require reestablishing real human contacts. Thus groups, the setting in which life must be lived, become an ideal setting for treatment.

Group as therapy

Being part of a group can promote some powerful therapeutic work. The active alcohol or drug addicted person is afraid of people "out there." The phrase "tiger land" has been used by alcoholics to describe the world. That's a fairly telling phrase! Through group treatment, ideally the client will reexperience the world differently. The whole thing need not be a jungle—other people can be a source of safety and strength.

Another bonus from a group experience is derived from individuals' opportunities to become reacquainted with themselves. A group provides a chance to learn who they are, their capabilities, their impact on and importance to others. Interacting candidly and openly provides an opportunity to adjust and correct their mental pictures of themselves. They get feedback. Group treatment of those in a similar situation reduces the sense of isolation. Those with active alcohol or drug dependence tend to view themselves very negatively and have an overwhelming sense of shame over their behavior. Coming together with others proves that one is not uniquely awful.

Yet mere confession is not therapeutic. Something else must happen for healing to occur. Just as absolution occurs in the context of a church, in a group that functions therapeutically, the members act as priests to

one another. Members hear one another's confession and say, in essence: "You are forgiven, go and sin no more." That is to say, group members can see one another apart from the behavior that accompanies alcoholism. They can also often see a potential that is unknown to the individual. This is readily verified in our own lives. Solutions to other people's problems are so obvious, but not so solutions to our own. Members of the group can see that people need not be destined to continue their old behaviors. Old "sins" need not be repeated. Thus they instill hope in one another.

Interestingly enough, one often finds that people are more gentle with others than they are with themselves. In this regard, the group experience has a beneficial boomerang effect. In the process of being kind and understanding of others, the members are in turn forced to accord themselves similar treatment.

What has been discussed is the potential benefit that can be gleaned from a group exposure. How this group experience takes place can vary widely. Group therapy comes in many styles and can occur in many contexts. Being a resident in a halfway house puts one in a group, just as the person who participates in outpatient group therapy. Group therapy means the use of any group experience to promote change in the members. Under the direction of a skilled leader, the power of the group process is harnessed for therapeutic purposes.

When you ask one friend to dine,
Give him your best wine!
When you ask two,
The second best will do!

LONGFELLOW

Group work with those with alcohol problems

In contemplating group work for those with alcohol/drug problems, the leader will need to consider several basic issues. What is the purpose of the group? What are the goals for the individual members? Where will the group meet? How often? What will the rules be? The first question is the key. The purpose of the group should be clear in the leader's mind. There are many possible legitimate purposes. Experience shows that not all can be met simultaneously. It is far better to have different types of groups available, with members participating in several, than to lump everything into one group and accomplish nothing. Some of the most common types of groups are education, self-awareness, problem-solving, and activity or resocialization.

Educational groups attempt to impart factual information about alcohol and other drugs and their effects, including dependence. There is a complex relationship between knowledge, feelings, and behavior. Correct facts and information do not stop serious problematic drinking, but they can be important in breaking down denial, which protects the drinking or drug use. Information provides an invaluable framework for understanding what has happened and what treatment is about. In an educational group, clients acquire some cognitive tools to participate more successfully in their own treatment. Educational groups may be organized around a lecture, film, or presentation by a specialist in the substance use field, followed by a group discussion. Topics such as a description of self-help groups and how they work, alcohol's effects on the body, and the recovery process may be included.

Self-awareness and support groups are intended to assist their members to grapple seriously with the role of alcohol in their lives. The group function is to support abstinence and to identify the characteristic ways in which people sabotage themselves. In these groups, the emphasis is on the here and now. The participants are expected to deal with feelings as well as facts. The goal is not for members to achieve an intellectual understanding of why things have or are occurring. Rather, the goal is to have members discover how they feel and learn how feelings are translated into behavior. Then they can choose how they would prefer to behave and try it on for size.

A problem-solving group is directed at tackling specific problems or stressful areas in the group members' lives. Either discussion, role play, or a combination may be used. For example, how to say no to an offer to have a beer, how to handle an upcoming job interview, or how to get through the upcoming holidays could be appropriate subjects. The goal is to develop an awareness of potential stressful situations, identify the old habitual response patterns, recognize how these patterns have created problems, and then try new behaviors. These sessions thus provide practice for more effective coping behaviors.

Activity groups are those least likely to resemble the stereotype of group therapy. In these groups an activity or project is undertaken, such as a ward or client government meeting or a planning session for a picnic. The emphasis is on more than the apparent task. The task is also a sample of real life. Thus it provides an arena for the clients to identify areas of strength and weakness in interpersonal relationships. Here, too, is a safe place to practice new behaviors.

That is a treacherous friend against whom you must always be on your guard. Such a friend is wine.

C. N. BOVEE

Group functions

No matter what the kind of group, a number of functions will have to be performed. For any group to work effectively, there are some essential tasks, regardless of the goal. Initially the leader may have to be primarily responsible for filling these roles:

- Initiating—suggesting ideas for the group to consider, getting the ball rolling
- Elaborating or clarifying—clearing up confusions, giving examples, expanding on contributions of group members
- Summarizing—pulling together loose ends, restating ideas
- Facilitating—encouraging others' participation by asking questions, showing interest
- Expressing group feelings—recognizing moods and relationships within the group

- Giving feedback—sharing responses to what is happening in the group
- Seeking feedback—asking for others' responses about what you are doing

As time goes on, the leader does need to teach the group members to share the responsibility for these functions.

Different types of group therapy can be useful at different times during recovery. During the course of a residential stay, a client might well attend an educational group, a relapse prevention group, and a couples group. In addition, the person could attend outside self-help meetings. In this example, the client would be participating in four different types of groups. On discharge the person may return for weekly group sessions as part of follow-up, with his or her spouse, and they might continue in a couples group. None of these group experiences is intended to substitute for 12-step groups. The most effective treatment plans will prescribe self-help plus substance abuse-related group therapy. They are no more mutually exclusive than is AA/NA or group therapy occurring simultaneously with medical treatment of diabetes.

Groups as a diversion

Sunday night I go to a parent support group. Monday night I have my NA meeting. Tuesday night is my Overeaters Anonymous meeting. Wednesday night is my children of alcoholics group. Thusday there's a single mother's support group. Friday is my emotions anonymous group. And Saturday nights I stay home and watch television. I love Saturday nights.

For a while group experiences, for the general population, became something of a fad. There was a bandwagon phenomenon, with all sorts of groups available—marathon, encounter, TA, gestalt, sensitivity, EST. These and many other forms were seemingly offered everywhere: schools, churches, on the job, by women's clubs, at community centers. There was a whirlwind of activity around the use of groups for "personal growth." While these variants of groups directed to personal growth may sound a bit dated and passée, the group phenomena remains, having simply changed focus. Groups directed at personal growth have seemingly been supplanted by an ever-burgeoning number of self-help groups. The earliest self-help groups were modeled after AA—Narcotics Anonymous (NA), Cocaine Anonymous (CA), Gamblers Anonymous, Overeaters Anonymous. They have been supplanted by adult children of alcoholics; victims of incest, rape, and child abuse; codependency; those with sexual addictions; plus those who have been batterers or have engaged in or are concerned about their potential for child abuse.

The emphasis placed on groups here does not imply that those with a serious drinking or drug problem should ride the group therapy circuit. On the contrary, those seeking and requiring substance abuse treatment in a group not restricted to those with alcohol or drug problems are likely to waste their own and other people's time. As was stated earlier, until one has taken some step to combat the substance use, there is little likelihood of working on other problems successfully. Inevitably, the still drinking or using member will raise havoc in a non-alcohol/drug focused group. Our prediction is that the alcoholic group member will have others running in circles figuring out the whys, get gobs of sympathy, and remain unchanged. Eventually others in the group will wear out, end up treating the alcoholic member just as the family does, and experience all the same frustrations as the family. However, in a group with others in trouble with alcohol and a leader familiar with the dynamics of alcohol dependence or alcohol abuse, it's a different story. The opportunity to divert others' attention from the role of alcohol is diminished to virtually zero because everyone knows the game thoroughly. The agenda, in this latter instance, clearly is how to break out of that pattern.

WORKING WITH FAMILIES

Historically, and for too long, family members of those being treated for drug/alcohol problems were shortchanged. In the past, if a family member contacted a treatment agency about an alcohol problem in the family, what was likely to happen? He or she may have been told to have the troubled person call on his or her own behalf, or have heard a sympathetic "Yes, it's awful" and be told to call Al-Anon. It was unusual that families or family members were invited to come in as clients in their own right. In instances in which the alcohol-troubled person was seeking help, the family may have been called in by a clinician only to provide some background information and was then subsequently ignored. Any further attention family members got came only if a problem arose or if the counselor believed that the family wasn't being supportive. Treatment efforts did not routinely take into account the problems the family faced and their own, independent need for treatment. Although these events described above may still occur, nonetheless very few in the field would claim that the approach is adequate. By definition, treatment that ignores the family has come to be seen as second-rate care! Although larger treatment programs now have staff whose specialty is family work, every clinician needs to have some basic understanding of the issues that confront families, of whatever composition, and develop some basic skills for working with family members.

Too often, any family that didn't match the traditional mold was invisible. The importance of the extended family as a support system went unrecognized. The special problems of single mothers, the difficulties that confront blended families were not acknowledged, intergenerational households didn't count as a "real" family. In this discussion, by families we include not only the traditional family, but the many new forms of family life. "Home" was described by the poet Robert Frost as the place where, "when you have to go there, they have to take you in." Calling upon this definition, "family" includes all those in the "home."

Members of the family may need treatment as much as the dependent person. More and more often they are coming to this conclusion themselves and seeking help. Clinicians are likely to find that more and more of their clients are, in fact, family members. The most important thing the clinician needs to keep in mind is that the client being treated is the person in the office—in this case, the family. The big temptation, and

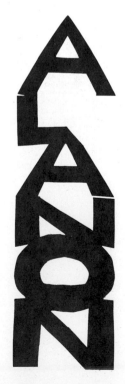

what was once seen as the appropriate stance, was to try treating the alcoholic family member in absentia. This may be the family member's wish, too, but it would be futile to attempt it.

What does the family or support system need? One important need is for education about the nature of alcohol and other drugs and the problems that evolve with chronic heavy use and dependence. The family also needs education on how the symptoms of the disease affect the family. Another area in which assistance is required is in sorting out the family's behavior to see how it fits into or even perpetuates the substance use. They need also to sort out their feelings and realistically come to grips with the true dimensions of the problem and the toll being exacted from them. Accompanying all this is the need to examine their options for problem solving. Most importantly the family members require support to live their own lives despite the alcoholism in their midst. Paradoxically, by doing this, the actual chances of short-circuiting the process of addiction are enhanced.

Family assessment

Just as all those with dependence do not display the identical symptoms or have the same degree of chronicity and extent of impairment, so is the same true of family members. In the assessment process, many of the same questions the therapist asks in dealing with the individual should be considered. What has caused the family member to seek help now? What is the family's understanding of the problem? What supports do they have? What is the economic, social, and family situation like? What coping devices do they use? What are their fears? What do they want from you? Where the clinician goes in working with the family will depend on the answers to these questions. Treatment plans for family members might include individual counseling, support groups, or being seen in a general social service agency.

You will notice that we have been speaking interchangeably about families and family members. Contact with a helping person is typically made by a single individual. Efforts to include the other members of the family or the alcohol- or drug-troubled member often fall to the clinician. In some cases, all it takes is the suggestion. In other cases the family member who made the contact may resist. This resistance may result from a sense of isolation or that no one else in the family cares, or it may instead be fear of the other family members' disapproval for having "spilled the beans" about the family's secret. Although the ideal might be having the family member approach the others, as the therapist, you (with the client's permission) can contact other family members to ask them to come in for at least one session. Almost universally others will come in at least once (and this includes the drug-using or alcoholic member), if you tell them you are interested in their views of what is happening.

Family intervention

The initial focus has to be working with the family members on their own problems. Nonetheless, the indisputable fact is that the dependence is a central problem and that the family would like to see the alcohol or drug dependent member receive help. It is important to recognize that, ineffective as their efforts may have been, still much of a family's energy has gone into "helping." Now, as a result of education about the disease, and after assistance with sorting out their own situation, they in essence have become equipped to act more effectively in relation to the alcohol or drug dependent family member. At the very least the family has been helped to abandon its protective and, though unintended, its nonetheless enabling behavior.

However, more is possible. In the early 1970s, a time when it was believed in the alcohol field that treatment could not be successful unless the alcoholic individual had "hit bottom" and was requesting help, a clinical technique was introduced by the Johnson Institute in Minneapolis that proved otherwise. This clinical approach, mentioned earlier, is intervention. It consists of involving the family and other significant people in the person's life to promote the alcohol dependent member's entry into treatment. This intervention technique and its supporting rationale were first described in *I'll Quit Tomorrow*.

The introduction of the intervention dramatically changed the treatment field. It forced clinicians, the recovering community—all concerned about those with alcoholism—to rethink some of the earlier assumptions about what was necessary for successful outcomes. Family and clinicians no longer had to sit around helplessly, waiting and praying for some magic insight to promote the request for help. Whether described as "raising the bottom," "early intervention," or "confrontation," clinicians now had a therapeutic tool that could help move sick people into care.

Since the introduction of intervention, it has become increasingly apparent that successful treatment can occur in a number of situations in which the entry into treatment might be considered "coercive." Among the programs with the best treatment outcomes are those in which the stakes are quite clear, such as EAP (employee assistance programs), programs conducted by the military, court-mandated treatment, or treatment offered to professionals where there is close monitoring of posttreatment, such as airline pilots, physicians, and nurses. In such instances, while the individual may not be highly motivated to enter treatment, entry into care is clearly preferable to the alternative. To use the framework for motivation described earlier, external circumstances often play a role in sparking change. With hindsight we now can see that the treatment field's historical mistake was in not recognizing that ambivalence is a part of the change process and, thus, expecting alcoholic individuals to be further along in the process of making change before we were ready (or knew how) to extend professional assistance.

The ingredients of intervention

The intervention process involves a meeting of family, other concerned persons, and the alcoholic individual, conducted under the direction of a trained clinician. The scenario entails each individual present, in turn, presenting to the alcoholic person a list of specific incidents related to drinking that have caused concern. Each person also expresses the hope that the person will enter treatment. To be effective, these facts must be conveyed in an atmosphere of genuine concern for the alcohol or drug dependent person. The intended effect of this is that the alcoholic person can more accurately see the fundamental nature of the problem and why external assistance is needed. By providing the painful facts, the intervention process attempts to cut through the denial and can be viewed as precipitating a crisis.

The therapist who is involved in family work is well advised to become skilled in conducting interventions, either by attending workshops or by "apprenticing" to someone trained in this technique. We should be clear that conducting an intervention is not something you do on the spur of the moment. It is not something to be done impromptu, just because you happen to have the family together. Nor is it something you describe to the family and suggest they do on their own after supper some evening.

The effectiveness of intervention depends on the participants' ability to voice a genuine concern and describe incidents that have caused concern in an objective, straightforward manner. This takes briefing and preparation. Typically, this will entail several meetings with the family. The family members must become knowledgeable about the disease that confronts them so that the behaviors that previously were seen as designed to "get them" can be seen for what they are, symptoms. The preparation will usually involve a rehearsal during which each participant goes through the things he or she would like to convey to the alcoholic family member. The participants also need to discuss what treatment options are to be presented, and the actions they will take if the person does not seek help. Is the spouse ready to ask for a separation? Is the grown daughter ready to say she will not be comfortable allowing Mom to baby-sit for the grandchildren anymore? Are the parents ready to make continuation of college tuition payments contingent upon their son's entering treatment? Beyond preparing the participants, a successful intervention also requires that the therapist be supportive to all present, equally, and deflect the alcoholic member's anxiety and fears, which may surface as anger.

Family treatment in conjunction with alcohol treatment

By whatever process and point at which individuals enter formal treatment, involvement of the family is critical. The family should be included as early as possible. Family involvement is far from being elective or a nice touch; it is vital to securing an adequate database for treatment planning.

Say alcohol or drug dependence is clearly evident, having for example progressed to the stage it is diagnosable even by the parking lot attendant. In such circumstances, the family may be the only reliable source of even the most basic information, such as how much alcohol is being consumed, past medical history, and prior alcohol treatment. The individual's judgment may be so severely impaired that realistically others will need to make the decision about admission for treatment.

The family members' views of what the problem is, their understanding of alcoholism as a disease, their ability to provide support, and their willingness to engage in the treatment will have a bearing on the treatment plans for the individual. The family may be in pure chaos, at a point at which concern for the alcohol dependent member is lost under feelings of anger and frustration. In this case inpatient care may be far preferable to outpatient treatment. On the other hand, the family may have already been involved in treatment for themselves and thus be able to be supportive and to marshal its collective resources.

Many substance abuse clinicians find themselves with clients referred from other sources. To point out the obvious, for them the individual and his or her family are new patients. Even the best crafted letter of referral or prior telephone contact only imparts basic information. This initial database will need to be supplemented by working with the patient and family to develop treatment plans. Even more importantly, while a medical record or chart can be used to pass along a client from one clinician to another, therapists cannot pass along or be the recipient of a therapeutic relationship. Each clinician needs to establish this for himself or herself.

For these reasons a family meeting is becoming a routine part of the intake and assessment process. At this time, the clinician will seek the family members' view of what is happening. In initial contacts with the family you don't go into a family therapy routine. It is data collecting time. For a newly involved clinician, the task is to understand how the family sees and deals with the substance abuse in its midst. In joint meetings, be prepared to provide the structure and lay the ground rules. For example, explain that people often see things differently and that you want to know from each of those present what has been going on. If need be, reassure them that everyone gets equal time, but no interruptions, please.

During the individual's treatment the family may become involved in regularly scheduled family counseling sessions or participate in a special group for family members or couples, in addition to attending Al-Anon. Some residential treatment programs are beginning to hold "family weekends." In these programs the families of patients are in residence and participate in a specially structured program of education, group discussion, and family counseling.

Family issues

Entry into treatment may impose very real immediate problems for a family. The spouse may be concerned about even more unpaid bills, problems of child care, fears of yet more broken promises, and so on. In the face of these immediate concerns, the possibility of long-range benefits may offer little consolation. Attention must be paid to helping the family deal with the nitty-gritty details of everyday living. Just as the alcoholic individual in early treatment requires a lot of structure and guidance, so does the family.

Another issue for the family will be to develop realistic expectations for treatment. On one hand, they may think everything will be rosy, that their troubles are over. On the other, they may be exceedingly pessimistic. Probably they will initially bounce back and forth between these two extremes.

The family at some point will need to have the alcoholic member "really hear" what it has been like for them at the emotional level. If there has been an intervention, it stressed objective factual recounting of events and being sympathetic to the alcoholic member. Although a presentation of the family's emotional reality may not be apropos at the time of the intervention, it must take place at some point. If the family is to be reintegrated into a functioning unit, it is going to require that both "sides" gain some appreciation of what the disease has felt like for the other. How this occurs will vary. Within a series of family sessions there may be a session specifically devoted to "feelings," led by skilled family therapists. These can be highly charged, "tell-it-like-it-is" cathartic sessions. To do this successfully requires considerable skill on the therapist's part, as well as a structure that provides a lot of support for the family members. For the individual, the pain and remorse and shame of his or her drinking or drug use can be devastating. For the family, witnessing the remorse and shame can, in turn, invoke guilt and remorse in themselves. These responses must be addressed; a session cannot be stopped with the participants left in those emotional states. More commonly this material will be dealt with over time, in "smaller doses." It may occur within family sessions and frequently also within the context of working in the 12-step program.[1] Again, the important issue is that you recognize this as a family task that must be dealt with in some way at some time. Otherwise, the family has a closet full of "secrets" or "skeletons" that will haunt them, come between them, and interfere with their regaining a healthy new balance.

Suggestions for working with families during treatment

The data gathering completed, the task turns to helping the family make the readjustments necessary to establish a new balance. Here are some

---

[1]For the alcoholic, dealing with the effects of the alcoholic's drinking on the family may be part of taking an inventory (step 4) and part of making amends (step 8). See the Twelve Steps of AA later on in this chapter.

concrete suggestions for dealing with families at this treatment stage. You are the most objective person present; therefore it is up to you to evaluate and guide the process.

Concentrate on the interaction, not on the content Don't become the referee in a family digression.

Teach them how to check things out People tend to guess at other peoples' meanings and motivations. They then respond as though the guesses were accurate. This causes all kinds of confusion and misunderstandings and can lead to mutual recriminations. The therapist needs to put a stop to these mind reading games and point out what is going on.

Be alert to "scapegoating" A common human tendency is to lay it all on George. This is true whatever the problem. The alcoholic family tends to blame the drinker for all the family's troubles, thereby neatly avoiding any responsibility for their own actions. Help them see this as a no-no.

Stress acceptance of each person's right to his or her own feelings Any good therapy stresses acceptance of each person's right to his or her own feelings. One reason for this is that good feelings get blocked by unexpressed bad feelings. One of the tasks of a therapist is to bring out the family's strengths. The focus has been on the problems for so long that they have lost sight of the good points.

Be alert to avoidance transactions Avoidance transactions include such things as digressing to Christmas 3 years ago in the midst of a heated discussion of Dad's drinking. It is up to you to point this out to the family and get them back on the track. In a similar vein, it may fall to you to "speak the unspeakable," to bring out in the open the obvious, but unmentioned, facts.

Guide them into problem-solving techniques as options You can do this by making these patterns clear to the family. You can help them begin to use these techniques in therapy, with an eye to teaching them to use them on their own.

After some success, when things seem to be going better, there may be some resistance to continuing therapy. The family fears a setback and wants to stop while they're ahead. Simply point this out to them. They can try for something better or terminate. If they terminate, leave the door open for a return later.

Things to keep in mind when working with families

Pregnancy You may recall some of the particular family problems that relate to pregnancy and the presence of young children in the family. A few specific words should be said about these potential problematic

areas. The first is contraceptive counseling. Pregnancy is not a cure for alcohol problems in either partner. In a couple in which one or both partners are actively drinking, they should be advised to make provisions for the prevention of pregnancy until abstinence is well established. It is important to remember that birth control methods adequate for a sober couple may be inadequate when alcoholism is present. Methods that require planning or delay of gratification are likely to fail. Rhythm, foam, diaphragms, or prophylactics are not wise choices if one partner is actively drinking. A woman who is actively drinking is not advised to use the pill. So the alternatives are few: the pill for the partner of an active male alcoholic, a condom for the partner of a sexually active female alcoholic. In the event of an unwanted pregnancy, the possibilities of placement or therapeutic abortion represent two difficult options that may need to be considered. At the moment, no amniotic fluid assay test exists that can establish the presence of fetal alcohol syndrome.

Should pregnancy occur and a decision be made to have the baby, intensive intervention is required. If the expectant mother has alcoholism, every effort should be made to initiate treatment and get her to stop drinking. Regular prenatal care is also important. Counseling and supporting both parents if alcohol is present is essential to handle the stresses that accompany any pregnancy. If the prospective father is alcohol dependent, it is important to provide additional supports for the mother.

Pregnancy is always a stress for any couple or family system. Contraceptive counseling should also be considered for persons in early recovery. At that point, the family unit is busy coping with sobriety and establishing a solid recovery.

Children in the family   A few words on behalf of older children in the family are in order. In many cases, children's problems are related to their parents' stress. Children may easily become weapons in parental battles. With alcohol or drug dependence, children may think their behavior is causing the problem. A child needs to be told that this is not the case. In instances where the clinician knows that physical or significant emotional abuse has occurred, child welfare authorities must be notified. In working with the family, additional parenting persons may be brought into the picture. Going to a nursery school or day-care center may help the child from a chaotic home.

What cannot be emphasized too strongly is that children must not be "forgotten" or left out of treatment. Sometimes parents consider a child too young to understand or feel the children need to be "protected." What this can easily lead to is the child's feeling even more isolated, vulnerable, and frightened. Children in family sessions tend to define an appropriate level of participation for themselves. Sometimes the presence of children is problematic for adults not because they won't understand, but because of their uncanny ability to see things exactly as they are. For example, without self-consciousness the child may say what the rest are only

hinting at or may ask the most provocative questions. Along the same line, while a parent is actively drinking or using, the inevitable concerns and questions of the child must be addressed. Children may not need all the details, but the pretense effected by adults that everything is okay is destructive. Another area in which it is critically important to address children's concerns is when the parent or caretaker has HIV/AIDS or Hepatitis C with a clear medical problem, including possible hospital stays and a poor prognosis. Often information is withheld from the children, in the interest of preventing worry. What is going on does not escape them. Big questions for them are "What will become of me?" and "Who will take care of me?" Making arrangements for children may be very hard for the sick parent; discussing them with a child can be even harder. Research suggests the absence of this information and the uncertainty is far more troubling than the facts, including an open discussion of plans for custody.

When initially involving the family, consider the children's needs in building a treatment plan. Many child welfare agencies or mental health centers conduct group sessions for children around issues of concern to children, such as a death in the family, divorce, or substance abuse problems. Usually these groups are set up for children of roughly the same age and run for a set period, such as 6 weeks. The goal is to provide basic information, support, and the chance to express feelings the child is uncomfortable with or cannot bring up at home. The subliminal message of such groups is that the parents' problems are not the child's fault, and talking about it is okay. In family sessions, you can make the message clear too. You can provide time for the child to ask questions and also provide children with pamphlets that may be helpful for them.

Occasionally a child may seem to be "doing well." In fact, the child may reject efforts by others to be involved in discussion groups or treatment efforts. If the parent who is alcohol dependent is actively drinking, the child's resistance may be part of the child's way of coping. Seeing you may be perceived by the child as taking sides; it may force the child to look at things he or she is trying to pretend are not there. Resistance also may surface to joining the family treatment during early sobriety for many of the same reasons. Listen to the child's objections for clues to his or her concerns. What is important here is not to let a child's assertion that "everything is fine" pass without some additional questioning.

On the other hand, beware of embarking on a witch hunt to ferret out the unspoken problems of children. Children cannot be expected to function as adults. While they can be amazingly insightful at times, don't presume that those who do not voice "the unspeakable" are therefore "hiding" something. It is important to appreciate the defenses that children do have. Defenses are never to be viewed as "good" or "bad" but as fostering or impeding functioning. Children's defenses may be quite important for them. In dealing with children, if you have any questions or are concerned you are in danger of getting in over your head, feel free to seek advice from a child therapist.

Recovery and the family   A common mistake when working with the family is to assume that once the drinking stops, things will get better. Yet with abstinence, the family again faces a crisis and time of transition. Such crises can lead to growth and positive changes, but not automatically or inevitably. For the family who has lived with alcoholism, for example, there has been a long period of storing up anger and of mistrust and miscommunication. This may have been the children's only experience of family life. At times children who previously were well behaved may begin acting out when a parent becomes sober. Children may feel that earlier their parent loved alcohol more than them and that now their parent loves AA more. The parent may have stopped drinking, but in the children's eyes they're still in second place.

Recovering families have a number of tasks to accomplish before they return to healthy functioning. They must strengthen generational boundaries. They must resume age- and sex-appropriate roles in the family. They must learn to communicate in direct and forthright ways with one another. They must learn to trust one another. And finally they must learn to express both anger and love appropriately. It might be expected, if one considers the family as a unit, that there are stages or patterns of a family's recovery. This has not yet been adequately studied. No one has developed a "valley chart" that plots family disintegration and recovery. Those professionals who have had considerable involvement with families of recovering alcoholics have noticed and are now beginning to discuss some common themes of the family's recovery.

It has been suggested that the family unit may experience some of the same kinds of issues that confront the alcohol or drug dependent individual. It has long been a part of folk wisdom in the alcohol field that the alcoholic individual's psychological and emotional growth ceases when the heavy drinking begins. So when sobriety comes, the individual is going to have to face some issues that the drinking prevented attending to. In the family system, what may be the equivalent of this Rip Van Winkle experience? Consider an example of a family in which the father is the alcohol dependent individual whose heavy drinking occurred during his children's adolescence and whose recovery begins just as the children are entering adulthood. If he was basically "out of it" during their teenage years, they grew up as best they could, without very much fathering from him. When he "comes to," they are no longer children but adults. In effect, he was deprived of an important chunk of family life. There may be regrets. There may be unrealistic expectations on the father's part about his present relationship with his children. There may be inappropriate attempts by him to "make it up" and regain the missing part. Depending on the situation, his therapist may need to help him grieve. There may be the need to help him recognize that his expectations are not in keeping with his children's adult status. He may be able to find other outlets to experience a parenting role or reestablish and enjoy appropriate contacts with his children.

Divorce or separation   Vaillant, in examining the course of recovery from alcoholism, found that quite commonly those men who recovered "acquired a new love object." Among several other factors, one that differentiated those who recovered from those who did not was having found someone to love and be loved by. This "someone" had not been part of his life during the period of active alcoholism. This cannot be used as evidence that family treatment is not warranted because there has been too much water over the dam, too much pain, and too much guilt. The men in Vailliant's study were those who were treated before the time in which family involvement in treatment was commonplace. So who knows what the outcome would have been had attention been directed to family members as well. Early intervention was not the rule then either. His sample consisted of men with long-established cases of alcoholism. However, it does serve to remind us of an important fact. Not all families will come through alcohol treatment intact. Divorce is not uncommon in our society. Even if alcoholic individuals had a divorce rate similar to that of nonalcoholics, it would still mean a substantial number of divorces during or following treatment. Therefore, for some families, the work of family counseling will be to achieve a separation with the least pain possible and in the least destructive manner for both partners and their children.

Issues of family relationships are not important for only the client whose family is intact. For those who enter treatment divorced and/or estranged from their families, the task during the early treatment phase will be to help them make it without family supports. Their family members may well have come to the conclusion long ago that cutting off contact was necessary for their own welfare. Even if contacted at the point of treatment, they may refuse to have anything to do with the client and his or her treatment. However, with many months or years of sobriety, the issue of broken family ties may emerge. Recovering individuals may desire a restoration of family contacts and have the emotional and personal stability to attempt it, be it with parents, siblings, or their own children. If the client remains in follow-up treatment at this point, the clinician ought to be alert to his or her attempts to reconcile with the family. If the individual is successful, it will still involve stress; very likely many old wounds will be opened. If the attempt is unsuccessful, the therapist will be able to provide support and help the person adjust to the reality of those unfulfilled hopes. As family treatment becomes an integral part of treatment for alcoholism, the hope is that fewer families will experience a total disruption of communications in the face of alcoholism. It is hoped that a more widespread knowledge of the symptoms of alcoholism may facilitate reconciliation of previously estranged families.

Self-help for families

Al-Anon   Long before alcoholism was widely accepted as a disease, much less one that also affected family members, wives of the early members of AA recognized disturbances in their own behavior. They also encountered problems living with their alcoholic spouses whether they were sober or still drinking. They saw that a structured program based on self-knowledge, reparation of wrongs, and growth in a supportive group helped promote the alcoholic's recovery, so why not a similar program for spouses and other family members?

In its earliest days, what became Al-Anon was known instead as the AA Auxiliary. Then in the mid-1950s, Al-Anon was officially formed and soon became a thriving program in its own right. The founders were quick to recognize that patterns of scapegoating the alcoholic person and trying to manipulate the drinking were nonproductive. Instead, they based their program on the premise that the only person you can change or control is yourself. Family members in Al-Anon are encouraged to explore and adopt patterns of living that can nourish them, regardless of the actions of the alcoholic.

Using the twelve steps of AA (described in detail on pp. 317 and 318) as a starting point, the program also incorporated the AA slogans and meeting formats. The major difference is in Al-Anon members' powerlessness being over others' alcohol use rather than over their own personal alcohol use. Effort is directed at gaining an understanding of their habitual responses to situations that are dysfunctional and evoke pain and substituting behaviors that will promote health and well-being. They are encouraged to accept responsibility for themselves by abandoning their focus upon the alcoholic family member as "the problem." Instead, they can see by shared example the effectiveness of changing themselves, of "detaching with love" from the drinker.

Although no promises are made that this will have an impact on a still-drinking alcoholic, there are many examples of just such an outcome. At the very least, when family members stop the behaviors that tend to perpetuate the drinking, not only will their lives be better, but the odds are increased for a breakthrough in the pervasive denial characteristic of alcohol dependence.

Many people have found support and hope in the Al-Anon program. It can promote personal change and growth. This occurs through education about the disease and its impact on families, and sharing experiences with others who have also lived with the shame and grief that are a part of living with the disease of alcoholism.

Alateen   Alateen is an outgrowth of Al-Anon set up for teenagers with an alcoholic parent. Their problems are different from those of the partner of the alcoholic, and they need a group specifically to deal with these problems. Under the sponsorship of an adult Al-Anon or AA member, they are taught to deal with their problems in much the same manner as the other programs teach.

Even with the currently more widespread information about alcoholism, alcoholics and their families still feel stigmatized. Most of them feel completely alone. It is such a hush-hush issue that anyone experiencing it thinks they are unique in their suffering. The statistics mean little if your friends and neighbors never mention it and seem "normal" to you. It is very painful to have a problem about which you are afraid to talk because of the shame of being "different." One of the greatest benefits of both Al-Anon and Alateen is the lessening of this shame and isolation. Hard as it may be to attend the first meeting, once there, people find many others who share their problems and pain. This can begin a healing process.

Although Al-Anon or Alateen can be a tremendous assistance to the family, you need to point out what they are not designed to do. Frequently confusion is introduced because all family treatment efforts may be erroneously referred to as "Al-Anon." Al-Anon is a self-help group. It is not a professional therapeutic program whose members are trained family therapists, any more than AA members are professional clinicians. However, Al-Anon participation can nicely complement other family treatment efforts. Referral to Al-Anon or Alateen is widely recommended as a part of the treatment regimen for families.

SELF-HELP

Alcoholics Anonymous

Alcoholics Anonymous is the best known and largest self-help program and has been the model for other 12-step programs. Volumes have been written about the phenomenon of AA. It has been investigated, explained, challenged, and defended by lay people, newspapers, writers, magazines, psychologists, psychiatrists, physicians, sociologists, anthropologists, and clergy. Each has brought a set of underlying assumptions and a particular vocabulary and professional or lay framework to the task. The variety of material on the subject reminds one of trying to force mercury into a certain-sized, perfectly round ball.

In this brief discussion, we certainly have a few underlying assumptions. One is that "experience is the best teacher." This text will be relatively unhelpful compared to attending some AA meetings and watching and talking with people in the process of recovery actively using the AA program. Another assumption is that AA works for a variety of people caught up in the disease and for this reason deserves attention. Alcoholics Anonymous has been described as "the single most effective treatment for alcoholism." The exact whys and hows of its workings are not of paramount importance, but some understanding of it is necessary to genuinely recommend it. Presenting AA with such statements as "AA worked for me; it's the only way," or, conversely, "I've done all I can for you, you might as well try AA," may not be the most helpful approaches.

History   Alcoholics Anonymous began in 1935 in Akron, Ohio, with the meeting of two alcoholics. One, Bill W., had a spiritual experience that was the major precipitating event in beginning his abstinence.

On a business trip to Akron after about a year of sobriety, he was overtaken by a strong desire to drink. He hit upon the idea of seeking out and talking with another suffering alcoholic as an alternative to taking that first drink. He made contact with some people who led him to Dr. Bob, and the whole thing began with their first meeting. The fascinating story of AA's origins and early history is told in the book *AA Comes of Age.* The idea of alcoholics helping each other spread slowly in geometric fashion until 1939. At that point, a group of about a hundred sober members realized they had something to offer the thus far "hopeless alcoholics." They wrote and published *Alcoholics Anonymous,* generally known as the *Big Book.* It was based on a retrospective view of what they had done that had kept them sober. The past tense is used almost entirely in the Big Book. It was compiled by a group of people who, over time, working together, had found something that worked. Their task was to present this in a useful framework to others who might try it for themselves. This story is also covered in *AA Comes of Age.* However, it was in 1941 that AA became widely known as the result of an article published in a widely read national magazine, *The Saturday Evening Post.*[2] The geometric growth rapidly advanced, and in 1999 there were an estimated 1,900,000 active members worldwide.

Goals Alcoholics Anonymous stresses abstinence and contends that nothing can really happen until "the cork is in the bottle." Many other helping professionals tend to agree. A drugged person—and an alcoholic person is drugged—simply cannot comprehend, or use successfully, other forms of treatment. First, the drug has to go. The goals of each individual within AA vary widely: simple abstinence to adopting a whole new way of life are the ends of the continuum. Individuals' personal goals may also change over time. That any one organization can accommodate such diversity is in itself something of a miracle. AA now includes many people with multiple addictions, to alcohol and other drugs. With more younger people entering the program, drug use of some kind often accompanies the alcohol. References to alcohol in the following sections do not exclude the use of other substances.

In AA, the words *sober* and *dry* denote quite different states. A dry person is simply not drinking at the moment. Sobriety means a more basic, all-pervasive change in the person. Sobriety does not come as quickly as dryness and requires a desire for, and an attempt to work toward, a contented, productive life without reliance on mood-altering drugs. The twelve steps provide a framework for achieving this state.

Here we wish to mention the important advice the newcomer receives about getting a sponsor. The sponsor is a person with substantial sobriety

I drink when I have occasion, and sometimes when I have no occasion.
—Cervantes

---

[2]Reading this article by Jack Alexander is highly recommended. Its graphic depiction of what confronted the early members of AA and what the disease of alcoholism was like in that era, when it was viewed paradoxically as the result of human failing and a terminal condition, is a useful point of reference for anyone in the field.

and one with whom the newcomer feels comfortable. "Comfortable" does not mean primarily being of similar backgrounds, social class, or ethnic membership, although that may be important. It refers to someone the newcomer respects and therefore can speak with and most importantly listen to and hear. The role of the sponsor is to be a mentor and a guide and assist the newcomer in working the program. Much of this occurs outside of the context of meetings. The sponsor is a person who will keep a close eye on the newcomer, leading him or her through difficult times and helping out in situations that are best dealt with outside the context of meetings. Sponsors can also help the newcomer focus on the basic principles and not get sidetracked by extraneous, secondary issues. The sponsor is one of the most valuable resources a newcomer can have.

The twelve steps   The twelve steps function as the therapeutic framework of AA. They were not devised by a group of social scientists, nor are they derived from a theoretical view of alcoholism. Rather the twelve steps of AA grew out of the practical experience of the earliest members, based on what they had done to gain sobriety. They do, indeed, require action. AA is not a passive process.

The initial undrugged view of the devastation can, and often does, drive the dry alcoholic back to the bottle. However, the twelve steps of AA, as experienced by its sober members, offer hope for another road out of the maze.

Step 1, "We admitted we were powerless over alcohol—that our lives had become unmanageable," acknowledges the true culprit, alcohol, and the scope of the problem, the whole life. *Step 2,* "Came to believe that a Power greater than ourselves could restore us to sanity," recognizes the insanity of the drinking behavior and allows for the gradual reliance on some external agent (e.g., God, some other spiritual concept, the AA group, the therapist, or a combination) to aid an about-face. *Step 3,* "Made a decision to turn our will and our lives over to the care of God as we understood Him," enables the person to let go of the previous life preserver, the bottle, and accept an outside influence to provide direction. It has now become clear that as a life preserver, the bottle was a dud, but free floating cannot go on forever either. The search outside the self for direction has now begun.

Step 4, "Made a searching and fearless moral inventory of ourselves," allows a close look at the basic errors in perceiving the world and at behaviors that were part of the drinking debacle. This is the step that begins the process of teaching alcohol dependent people about their own responsibility during the drinking days. This step also includes space for the positive attributes that can be enhanced in the sober state. An inventory is, after all, a balance sheet. *Step 5,* "Admitted to God, to ourselves, and to another human being the exact nature of our wrongs," provides a method of cleaning the slate, admitting just how painful and destructive

it all was, and getting the guilt-provoking behavior out in the open instead of destructively "bottled up."

Steps 6 and 7, "Were entirely ready to have God remove all these defects of character," and "Humbly asked Him to remove our shortcomings," continue the "mopping-up" process. Step 6 makes the alcoholic individual aware of his or her tendency to cling to old behaviors, even unhealthy ones. Step 7 takes care of the fear of repeated errors, again instilling hope that personality change is possible. (Remember, at this stage in the process, the recently sober person is likely to be very short on self-esteem.)

Steps 8 and 9 are a clear guide to sorting out actual injury done to others and deciding how best to deal with it. Step 8 is "Made a list of all persons we had harmed and became willing to make amends to them all." Step 9 is "Made direct amends to such people wherever possible, except when to do so would injure them or others." They serve other purposes, too. First, they get the person out of the "bag" of blaming others for life's difficulties. To make an amend, that is, to attempt to atone for a wrong committed, does not require the forgiveness of the receiver. The recovering person's part is to make the effort to apologize, pay back money, or do whatever is necessary to try to balance the scales, whatever the response of the person to whom the amend is being made. This attempt offers a possibility for repairing presently strained relationships and hope of alleviating some of the overwhelming guilt that is common with initial sobriety. These steps clearly relate to the importance of acknowledging and owning up to events that have occurred, whether they took place in an impaired state or as part of the disease.

Steps 10 to 12 promote the maintenance of sobriety and the continuation of the change process that has already begun. Step 10, "Continued to take personal inventory and when we were wrong promptly admitted it," ensures that the alcoholic person need not slip back from the hard-won gains. Diligence in focusing on one's own behavior and not excusing it keeps the record straight. Step 11, "Sought through prayer and meditation to improve our conscious contact with God as we understood Him, praying only for knowledge of His will for us and the power to carry that out," fosters continued spiritual development. Finally, Step 12, "Having had a spiritual awakening as a result of these Steps, we tried to carry this message to alcoholics and to practice these principles in all our affairs," points the way to sharing the process with others. This is one of the vital keys Bill W. discovered to maintain his sobriety. It also implies that a continued practice of the new principles is vital to the sober life.

A word must be said here about "Two Steppers." This phrase is used to describe a few individuals in AA who come in, admit they are alcoholics, dry out, and set out to rescue others. However, it is often said in AA that "you can't give away what you don't have." This refers to a quality of sobriety that comes after some long and serious effort applying all the twelve steps to one's life. It is interesting to note that "carrying the message" is not mentioned until Step 12. Once that point is reached, however, it is important that the member reach out to others, repaying a debt so to speak, and also in the process experience feelings of being of use again.

No AA member who is serious about the program and sober for some time would ever imply that the steps are a one-shot deal. They are an ongoing process that evolves over time—a great deal of it—into ever-widening applications. When approached with serious intent, the steps enable a great change in the individual. That they are effective is testified to not only by great numbers of recovering alcoholics, but also by their adoption as a basis for such organizations as Overeaters Anonymous, Narcotics Anonymous, and Gamblers Anonymous. These other fellowships simply substitute their own addiction for the word *alcohol* in step 1.

A therapist, counselor, or friend should be alert to the balance required in this process of "working the Program." The newcomer who wants to tackle all twelve steps the first week should be counseled with one of AA's slogans: "Easy does it." The member hopelessly anguished by step 4, for instance, could be advised that perfection is not the goal and a stab at it the first time through is quite sufficient. The agnostic having difficulty with "the God bit" can be told about using the group or anything else suitable for the time being as the external agent to rely upon. After all, the spiritual awakening doesn't turn up until step 12 either.

The twelve traditions   *Organization*   AA has very little structure as an organization. It describes itself as a fellowship and functions around the twelve steps and twelve traditions. The twelve traditions cover the organization as a whole, setting forth the purpose of the fellowship, which is to carry its message to the still-suffering alcoholic. They also define principles of conduct; for example, that AA does not affiliate with other groups, nor lend its name; that it should not be organized and should remain forever nonprofessional. Individual AA groups are autonomous and decline outside contributions. Thus all care has been taken not to obscure or lose sight of the organization's purpose. The individual groups function in accord with these principles. Their focus is on sobriety, anonymity, and individual application of "the program," which includes meetings, attempting to work the twelve steps, and service to other alcoholics.

Anonymity   Before discussing the meetings, a special word about anonymity. Alcoholics Anonymous' tradition 12 reads as follows: "Anonymity is the spiritual foundation of all our traditions, ever reminding us to place principles before personalities." This concept evolved out of the growth pains of the organization. Early members admit candidly that fear of exposure of their problem was their original motivation for remaining anonymous: the need "to hide from public distrust and contempt." However, the principle of anonymity, which was introduced into the fellowship on the basis of fear, soon demonstrated evidence of its value on a totally different level.

This same evolutionary process tends to occur for most individual members of AA. At first, the promise of anonymity is viewed as a safeguard against exposure. The stigma attached to alcoholism has not yet disappeared. Added to this are the alcohol dependent person's own guilt, sense of failure, and low self-esteem. It is vital to maintain this promise to encourage fearful newcomers to try out the program while assuring them of complete confidentiality. As individuals gain sobriety, fear gives way to the deeper understanding revealed in the practice. To be simply Joe or Mary, one alcoholic among many, has a therapeutic value.

In practice, anonymity takes the form of first names only during the meetings, not identifying oneself through the media as a member of AA, and being careful not to reveal anyone else's attendance at meetings. Some meetings end with the reminder that who you see here and what is said here, stays here. It is important that this principle of anonymity be respected for AA to be able to continue its healing mission to suffering alcoholics.

Meetings plus   There are open meetings, open to any spouses, friends, interested parties, etc., and closed meetings, with only professed alcoholics attending. Both types can be speaker or discussion meetings. Speaker meetings have one to three speakers who tell what it was like drinking (for the purpose of allowing newcomers to identify), what happened to change this, and what their sober life is now like. A discussion meeting is usually smaller. The leader may or may not tell his story briefly as just described (or "qualify" in AA jargon). The focus of the meeting is a discussion of a particular step, topic, or problem with alcohol, with the leader taking the role of facilitator.

Attendance at meetings is not all there is to AA. The AA meeting might be like a patient's visit to a doctor's office. The office visit doesn't constitute the whole of therapy. It is a good start, but how closely the patient follows the advice and recommendations and acts on what is prescribed makes the difference. Sitting in the doctor's office doesn't do it. So too with AA. The person who is seriously trying to use AA as a means of achieving sobriety will be doing a lot more than attending meetings. Those successful in AA will spend time talking to and being with other more experienced members. Part of this time will be spent getting practical tips on how to maintain sobriety. Time and effort go into learning and substituting other behaviors for the all-pervasive drinking behavior. Alcoholics Anonymous contacts will also be a valuable resource for relaxation. It is a place a newly recovering alcoholic will feel accepted. It is also a space in which the drinking possibilities are greatly minimized. A new member of AA may spend a couple of hours a day phoning, having coffee with, or being in the company of other AA members. Although it is strongly recommended that new members seek sponsors, they will be in touch with a larger circle of people. Frequent contact with AA members is encouraged, not only to pass on useful information but also to make it easier for the new members to reach out in times of stress, when picking up a drink would be so easy and instinctive. The new member's contacting a fellow AA member when a crunch time comes makes the difference in many cases between recovery and relapse.

Slogans   Slowly the new member's life is being restructured around not drinking, and usually the slogans are the basis for this: "One day at a time," "Easy does it," "Keep it simple," "Live and let live," "Let go and let God" are just a few. Although they can sound trite and somewhat corny, remember the description of the confused, guilt-ridden, anxious product of alcohol dependence. Anyone in such a condition can greatly benefit from a simple, organized, easily understood schedule of priorities. A kind of behavior modification is taking place so that changes may begin. Some new members feel so overwhelmed by the idea of a day without a drink that their sponsor and/or others will help them literally plan every step of the first few weeks. They keep in almost hourly touch with older members. Phone calls at any hour of the day or night are encouraged as a way to relieve anxiety.

Resistances   Some alcoholic individuals and their families may be quite resistant to AA. A therapist often finds they may agree to anything, as long as it isn't AA. This resistance probably has a number of sources. It may be based on erroneous information and myths about AA. Quite likely it is embarrassment, plain and simple. The client may have been notorious at office parties, a regular in the newspaper column for drinking and driving offenses, or almost single-handedly keeping the neighborhood general store solvent with beer purchases, but heaven forbid that the individual should be seen entering a building where an AA meeting is held! Also, going to an AA meeting represents, if not a public admission, at least a private one that alcohol is a problem. Seeing a therapist, even one clearly specializing in alcohol and substance abuse, may allow the alcoholic client multiple interpretations, at least for a while. Going to AA is clear-cut, not open to ambiguity, and in that respect it is a big step. In dealing with this resistance, education is useful. Also required is a certain quiet insistence that going at least for a reasonable "experimental" period is expected of the client, so he or she can get firsthand knowledge.

Sometimes clients will have had some limited prior exposure to AA, which they use as the basis for their objections. Commonly this is coupled with the similarly "negative" experiences of their best drinking buddies, who also agree AA doesn't work. Usually these clients say they "tried it once," but it wasn't for them, and they didn't like it. Any examination of what was going on in their lives often reveals, at best, a very halfhearted "try." More importantly, liking or not liking AA is not an issue. Usually we care little if people like any other prescribed treatments as long as the treatment produces positive results. No one likes braces or casts on broken limbs or hospital stays for any reason, but they are accepted as necessary to produce a desired result. Feel free to point out that it is the results that are important.

The alcoholic may have found some professionals who will support his or her resistance. If the alcoholic remains in treatment with such a person, consider getting in touch with that professional. Possibly the alcoholic is misinterpreting what has been said. If not, you need to do a bit of informal education, explaining why you think AA is indicated and dispelling misconceptions.

Professional resistance toward AA is certainly far less than it once was, but it has not wholly disappeared. Some professionals both in the general helping professions as well as in the alcohol-substance abuse field do, at times, show resistance to expecting their clients to use AA. At times one gets the sense that AA is not considered to be "real" treatment, or it is considered less sophisticated. Why these feelings? Although we're not sure, our suspicion is that a number of reasons lie behind such attitudes. One reason is that anyone who deals with alcohol troubled people will periodically lose touch with what the disease of alcoholism is really like. The literal hell that is the life of the active alcoholic is forgotten. Those people are who AA is for. Yet at times, we forget that the primary purpose of AA is to help people to escape their hell. Then we begin to act as if AA were supposed to do other things, for example, be a psychologically oriented therapy group or handle marital problems.

Another point of possible professional resistance is that we sometimes take our resistive clients' objections too seriously. We unwittingly buy their criticisms of AA. We accept their not "liking" AA as a valid reason for their not going. But we do not expect them to "like" to see their physicians or "like" to use other forms of treatment! With alcohol problems being addressed at earlier and earlier stages, there may be the tendency for those helping professionals outside of the substance abuse field to consider that AA involvement is only for those whose disease has been long-standing, and who have many highly visible problems that resulted from drinking. In other words, some people's alcohol dependence isn't yet "bad enough" to warrant prescribing AA.

Another point of friction seems to be that AA does not build termination into the program. Although more could be said about this, for now it is sufficient to remember that any chronic disease is terminated only by death. For chronic illnesses, even when the disease is under control, regular checkups are routine practice. Finally, professionals sometimes have mistakenly gotten the impression that AA, as an organization, holds AA to be incompatible with other therapies. This is not true. Nothing in the AA program would support this premise. Certainly, an occasional client will give this impression, in which case as a therapist, you can help clear up this misconception.

View of recovery   One thing assumed in AA is that recovery is a serious, lifelong venture. Safety does not exist, and some kind of long-term support is necessary. This seems to be the case, and a lot of experience supports the assumption. Alcoholics, like all of us, have selective memories and are inclined, after varying periods of dryness, to remember only the relief of drinking and not its consequent problems. Some kind of reminder of reality seems to be necessary. Any alcoholic with long-term sobriety will be able to tell about the sudden desire to drink popping up out of nowhere. Those who do not succumb are grateful, for the most part, to some aspect of their AA life as the key to their stability returning. No one knows exactly why these moments occur, but one thing is certain: they are personally frightening and upsetting. They can reduce the reasonably well-adjusted recovering alcoholic to a state very like that first panic-ridden dryness. The feelings could be compared to the feelings after a particularly vivid nightmare. Whatever the reason for the phenomenon, these unexpected urges to drink do spring up. This is one reason continued participation in AA is suggested. Another is the emphasis (somewhat underplayed from time to time) on a continued growth in sobriety. Certainly, groups will rally around newcomers with a beginner's focus and help them learn the basics. In discussion meetings with a group of veterans, however, the focus will be on personal growth within the context of the twelve steps. Alcoholics Anonymous may advertise itself as a "simple program for complicated people," but an understanding of it is far from a simple matter. It involves people, and people are multifaceted. Its simplicity is deceptive and on the order of "Love thy neighbor as thyself." Simple, and yet learning to do so could easily take a lifetime. In closing, we again strongly urge you to attend a variety of AA meetings; also speak at some length with veteran members. So much has been written about AA—in some respects it is so understandable an approach—that people assume they know what it's about without firsthand knowledge. Just as you would visit treatment programs or community agencies to see personally what they are about, so, too, go to AA.

Referral   A few words are in order about making an effective referral to AA. In most cases simply telling someone to go probably won't work. The clinician needs to play a more active role in the referral. Alcoholics Anonymous is a self-help group. What AA can do and offer is by far best explained and demonstrated by its members. The clinician can assist by making arrangements for a client to speak to a member of AA or can arrange for the client to be taken to a meeting. Helping professionals, whether dealing exclusively with addiction or not, often have a list of AA members who have agreed to do this. Even if the clinician is an AA member, a separate AA contact is advisable. It is less confusing to the client if AA is seen as distinct from, although compatible with, other therapy. The therapist need not defend, proselytize, or try to sell AA. Alcoholics Anonymous speaks eloquently for itself. You do your part well when you persuade clients to attend, listen with an open mind, and stay long enough to make their own assessments.

A standard part of many treatment programs is an introduction and orientation to AA or other 12-step programs. This would seem to be very important because treatment programs are an ever-growing source of referrals. Many residential treatment programs include AA and/or NA meetings on the grounds or transport clients to outside meetings. It is not unusual for presentations to be included in an educational series or references made to them in individual counseling or group therapy. Some programs encourage, indeed some push, clients to work on steps 1 through 5 while they are actively involved in treatment. The hope is that this will give clients added insight into AA and increase the chances of their continuing involvement.

As a growing source of referrals to AA, treatment programs are challenged in several respects. Although wishing to be supportive of AA, treatment programs need to respect the boundaries between AA and treatment. One challenge to treatment programs is to help clients distinguish between formal treatment and AA. Nowhere may this be more important than in terms of aftercare. It must be pointed out that attending a treatment program's alumni group is not the same as going to AA. Nor for that matter is a chat with a sponsor necessarily a substitute for an aftercare session. Conversely, having a therapist should not be allowed to be seen as a substitute for having an AA sponsor. Another challenge to programs is not to appropriate AA through overly lengthy intellectual presentations on the nature of AA or using the language of AA and its slogans to mislead clients into thinking such discussions and their treatment is the same as AA involvement. There is a danger of clients becoming pseudosophisticates with respect to AA. They can use the jargon properly, make reference to the slogans and the steps, but have very limited firsthand experience of the AA fellowship.

AA membership   Since 1968 the General Service Office of AA has conducted a triennial survey of its members. The most recent survey, conducted in 1996, provides a profile of the members. Ages run the gamut; the prior survey indicated the age range is from 12 to 85. Presently, 1% of members are under 21 and 3% are over age 70. Men in AA outnumber women by about a 2-to-1 ratio: of all members, 67% are men and 33% women. However, 40% of those under age 30 are women and 60% are men. In terms of marital status, 39% are married, 28% single, 24% divorced, 6% widowed, and 3% separated. The composition by racial and ethnic groups shows that 86% are white, 5% black, 4% Hispanic, 4% Native American, and 1% Asian and other. The average length of sobriety of members is more than six years.

AA members clearly do not find counseling incompatible with AA involvement. Sixty percent of the members report some professional assistance before their joining AA. Of those, 78% said this played a part in directing them to AA. Furthermore, after their joining AA over half of the members (62%) report having received some other type of counseling help of these people, 85% credit this with playing an important role in their recovery. Of all those coming into AA, about 40% acknowledge a treatment program as a significant factor. That is twice the number since 1977.

In terms of length of sobriety, 45% of members have been sober over 5 years, 28% have been sober between 1 and 5 years, and 27% represent newcomers, those sober less than 1 year. The prior triennial survey (1992) focused on multiple substance use, with 38% of all members reporting a history of abuse of other substances. This was particularly true of younger members where it was the usual pattern, for 79% of those under age 21 and 60% of those under age 31.

Other self-help groups

In addition to AA, there are a wide variety of other self-help groups. Many are 12-step programs modeled after AA. These include, for example, Narcotics Anonymous, Cocaine Anonymous, Nicotine Anonymous, and Overeaters Anonymous, and Gamblers Anonymous. There are also a number of programs that have emerged that are not modifications of AA, but that were created as different from the 12-step approach. These include Rational Recovery, Women for Sobriety, Men for Sobriety, Secular Organizations for Sobriety, and S.M.A.R.T. (Self Management And Recovery Training) Recovery. Typically these groups reject what are seen as the spiritual and religious overtones of the 12-step programs. Similarly, they each see themselves as addressing issues of importance that are not a focus of AA, or as reframing some of the AA tenets, such as the first step, which focuses upon recognizing one is "helpless" over alcohol, to espouse beliefs in competence and the ability to successfully grapple with the addiction.

By way of example, Rational Recovery was founded in 1985 as an alternative to AA. While AA members refer to *Alcoholics Anonymous,* one of its key publications, as the "Big Book," as a point of contrast, Rational Recovery has dubbed its counterpart publication "The Little Book." It is directed to those who are turned off by AA. Another self-help group, Women for Sobriety, obviously directed to women, was founded in 1976. It is based upon 13 principles that, according to its literature, "encourage personal and emotional growth."

For the counselor, deciding whether to refer a client to a traditional self-help group such as AA or NA versus Rational Recovery or Women for Sobriety may not be the big issue it might appear at first glance. Setting aside whatever biases the clinician may have, there are several practical matters. One is the presence of these groups in the community in which you practice. AA, for example, and NA to a lesser degree, are available in virtually every community, and thereby the fellowship can assure a client access to a group no matter what. On the other hand, if a client tries AA and even after a reasonable exposure vigorously resists and is having problems making a connection, then a referral to an alternative is warranted. Whatever the biases of the counselor, if it works, it works. Remember, what is important is the destination, not necessarily the route!

OTHER APPROACHES

Spiritual Counseling

There is increasing effort to educate and inform clergy members about alcohol abuse, alcoholism, and other drug problems. The focus of the effort is to equip pastors, priests, rabbis, ministers, and chaplains who come into contact with alcoholic individuals or their families to assist in early identification of the disease and to facilitate the entry into appropriate treatment.

Against diseases the strongest fence is the defensive virtue, abstinence.

ROBERT HERRICK

Presumably the merits of this effort are self-evident. There is plenty of room in the alcohol field for many different kinds of care providers. This section on spiritual counseling is not about the educational outreach to clergy members. Instead, we wish to discuss the contribution that clergy members, priests, or rabbis may make to the recovery process in their pastoral roles. Those with alcoholism may have a need for pastoring, "shepherding," or spiritual counseling, as do other members of the population. In fact, their needs in this area may be especially acute. Attention to these needs is a critical part of recovery.

It is not easy to discuss spiritual matters. Medical, social work, psychology, or rehabilitation textbooks do not include chapters on spiritual issues as they affect prospective clients and patients. The split between spirituality and the "rest of life" in America has been virtually total. In our society, that means for many it has become an either/or choice. Because defining crisply what we mean by spiritual issues is not easy, let us begin by stating what it is not. By spiritual we do not mean the organized religions and churches. Religions can be thought of as organized groups and institutions that have arisen to meet spiritual needs. The spiritual concern is more basic than religion, however. That civilizations have developed religions throughout history can be evidence of a spiritual side to human beings. There are also experiences, difficult to describe, that hint at another dimension different from but as real as our physical nature. They might be called "intimations of immortality," and they occur among sufficient numbers of people to give more evidence for the spiritual nature of humankind.

Over the past decade there was a renewed interest in spiritual concerns in contemporary America. Whether it has been transcendental meditation, the teaching of Eastern gurus, fundamentalism, mysticism, the golden era of television evangelists, or the more traditional Judeo-Christian Western religions, Buddhist, or Muslim traditions, people have been flocking in. They are attempting to follow these teachings and precepts in the hope of filling a void in their lives. It is being recognized that "the bottom line" may not be adequately calculated in terms of status, education, career, or material wealth. The culturally defined evidence of achievement and having "made it" can still leave someone feeling that there is something missing. This "something" is thought by many to be of a spiritual nature. This missing piece has even been described as a "God-shaped hole."

Sociologists have observed that the apparent renewed interest in religion and increased church attendance in the mainline denominations can be explained by sheer demographics. It may not be attributable to a societal perception of a spiritual vacuum. Church attendance historically is always lowest among adolescents and young adults. Consequently with the "baby boomers" marching through middle age, this large segment of the population has reached the age where religious interests have always arisen. These two viewpoints are not mutually exclusive. With maturity and some life experiences, a part of adult development is to reassess values, reexamine one's priorities in life, and redefine what is important. An offhand comment seems to capture this well: "No one on a death bed ever expressed regret that he or she hadn't spent more time on work!"

Alcoholism as a spiritual search   How do spiritual concerns fit in with alcohol use and the disease of alcoholism? First, it is worth reflecting on the fact that the word most commonly used for alcohol is "spirits." This is surely no accident. Indeed, consider how alcohol is used. It is often used in the hope it will provide that missing something or at least turn off a gnawing ache. From bottled spirits, a drinker may seek a solution to life's problems, a release from pain, an escape from circumstances. For awhile it may do the job, but eventually it fails. To use spiritual language, you can even think of alcoholism as a pilgrimage that dead-ends. Alcohol can be thought of as a false god, or, to paraphrase the New Testament, as not being "living water."

If this is the case and alcohol use has been prompted in part by spiritual thirst, the thirst remains even though alcoholic drinking ceases. Part of the recovery process must be aimed at quenching the thirst. Alcoholics Anonymous has recognized this fact. It speaks of alcoholism as a threefold disease with physical, mental, and spiritual components. Part of the AA program is intended to help members by focusing on their spiritual needs. It is also worth noting that AA makes a clear distinction between spiritual growth and religion.

Assistance from the clergy   How can the clergy be of assistance? Ideally, the clergy are society's designated "experts" on spiritual matters. Notice we say "ideally." In real life, clergy are human beings, too. The realities of religious institutions may have forced some to be fund raisers, social directors, community consciences, almost everything but spiritual mentors. Yet there are those out there who do, and maybe many more who long to, act as spiritual counselors and advisors. One way the clergy may be of potential assistance is to help those seeking recovery deal with "sin" and feelings of guilt, worthlessness, and hopelessness. Many of those with alcoholism, along with the public at large, are walking around as adults with virtually the same notions of God they had as 5-year-olds. He has a white beard, sits on a throne on a cloud, checks up on everything you do, keeps a ledger of your behavior,

It is hard to believe in God, but it is far harder to disbelieve in Him.

EMERSON

and punishes you if you aren't "good." This is certainly a caricature but also probably very close to the way a lot of people really feel if they think about it.

Those just getting sober feel remorseful, guilt-ridden, worthless, endowed with a host of negative qualities, and devoid of good. In their minds, they certainly do not fit the picture of someone God would like to befriend or hang around with. On the contrary, they probably believe that if God isn't punishing them He ought to be! So these persons may need some real assistance in updating their concept of God. There's a good chance some of their ideas will have to be revised. There's the idea that the church, and therefore (to them) God, is only for the "good" people. A glance at the New Testament and Christian traditions doesn't support this view, even if some parishes or congregations may act that way. Jesus of Nazareth didn't exactly travel with the "in crowd." He was found in the company of fishermen, prostitutes, lepers, and tax collectors. Or consider the Judaic tradition as reflected in the Torah or Old Testament. The chosen of God were constantly whining, complaining, going astray, and breaking as much of the Law as they followed. Nonetheless, God refused to give up on them. Virtually all spiritual traditions have taken human frailty as the given. Whether a new perspective on God or a Higher Power leads to reinvolvement with a church, assists in affiliation with AA, or helps lessen the burden of guilt doesn't matter. Whichever it does, it is a key factor in recovery.

Again, to use spiritual language, recovery from alcoholism involves a "conversion experience." The meaning of conversion is very simple, "to turn around" or "to transform." Comparing the sober life with the previous drinking certainly testifies to such a transformation. A conversion experience doesn't necessarily imply blinding lights, visions, or a dramatic turning point—although it might. Indeed, if it does involve a startling experience of some nature, the newly sober individual will need some substantial aid in understanding and assimilating this experience.

Carl Jung   It is interesting to note that an eminent psychiatrist recognized this spiritual dimension of alcoholism and recovery almost 60 years ago, in the days when alcoholism was considered hopeless by the medical profession. The physician was Carl Jung. A man named Roland H. had been through the treatment route for alcoholism before seeking out Jung in 1931. He admired Jung greatly, saw him as the court of last resort, and remained in therapy with him for about a year. Shortly after terminating therapy, Roland lapsed back into drinking. Because of this unfortunate development, he returned to Jung. On his return, Jung told Roland his condition was hopeless as far as psychiatry and medicine of that day were concerned. Very desperate and willing to grab at any straw, Roland asked if there was any hope at all. Jung replied that there might be, provided Roland could have a spiritual or religious experience—a genuine conversion experience. Although comparatively rare, this had been known to lead to recovery from alcoholism. So Jung advised Roland to place himself in a religious atmosphere and hope (pray) for the best. The "best" in fact occurred. The details of the story can be found in an exchange of letters between Bill W. and Jung, published in the AA magazine, *The Grapevine*.

In recounting this story many years later, Jung observed that unrecognized spiritual needs can lead people into great difficulty and distress. He wrote that either "real religious insight or the protective wall of human community is essential to protect man from this." In talking specifically of Roland H., Jung wrote: "His craving for alcohol was the equivalent, on a low level, of the spiritual thirst of our being for wholeness, expressed in medieval language; the union with God."

Such concepts are foreign in contemporary American society; we no longer have even the vocabulary to consider such a matter. You would be hard pressed to find drinkers who would equate the use of alcohol with a search for God! Heaven only knows they are too sophisticated, too contemporary, too scientific for that. Yet an objective examination of their use of alcohol may reveal otherwise. Alcohol is viewed as a magical potion, with the drinker expecting it to do the miraculous. The problem is that for a time indeed it does, by alleviating shyness or awkwardness, or simply by turning off painful feelings. The backlash occurs later, as we have seen.

Clinician's role   If convinced that a spiritual dimension may be touched by both alcoholism and recovery, what do you as a therapist do? First, we recommend cultivating some members of the clergy in your area. It seems that many communities have at least one member of the clergy who has stumbled into the alcohol field—and we do mean stumbled. It was often not a deliberate, intellectual decision. It may have occurred through a troubled parishioner who has gotten well or one whom the clergy member couldn't tolerate watching drink himself or herself to death any longer and so blundered through an intervention. The pastor may have aided a parishioner with alcoholism and then found more and more people with alcoholism showing up on his/her doorstep for help. Or the clergy may themselves be in recovery and thus drawn into helping others. At any rate, this is the one you want. If you cannot find him or her, find one with whom you are comfortable talking about spiritual or religious issues. That means one with whom you don't feel silly or awkward and, equally important, who doesn't squirm in his or her seat either at talk of spiritual issues. (Mention of God and religion can make people, including some clergy, as uncomfortable as talk of drinking can!)

Once you find a resource person, it is an easy matter to provide your client with an opportunity to talk with that person. One way to make the contact is simply to suggest that the client sit down and talk with Joe Smith, who happens to be a Catholic priest, or a rabbi, or something else. It may also be worth pointing out to the client that the topic of concern is important and that the individual mentioned may be helpful in sorting it out. Set up the appointment, and let the clergy member take it from there. Some residential programs include a clergy member as a resource person. This person may simply be available to counsel with clients or may take part in the formal program, for example, by providing a lecture in the educational series. What is important is that the presence and availability of this person gives the message to clients that matters of the spirit are indeed important and not silly.

How do you recognize the person for whom spiritual counseling may be useful? First, let us assume you have found a clergy member who doesn't wag a finger, deliver hellfire and brimstone lectures, or pass out religious tracts at the drop of a hat. Rather, you have found a warm, caring, accepting, and supportive individual. A chat with someone like that isn't going to hurt anyone. So don't worry about inappropriate referrals. Nonetheless, for some clients the contact may be particularly meaningful. Among these are individuals who have a spiritual or religious background and are not experiencing it as a source of support, but rather as a condemnation. Others may, in their course of sobriety, be conscientiously attempting to 'work the program' but have some problem that is hanging them up. Another group who may experience difficulty are Jewish alcoholics. The belief that "Everyone knows Jews don't become alcoholics" presents a problem for those who do. It has been said that there is double the amount of denial and consequent guilt for them. Because the Jewish religion is practiced within the context of a community, there may also be a doubled sense of estrangement. A contact with a rabbi may be very important. It is worth pointing out that someone can be culturally or ethnically Jewish but not have been religiously Jewish. The intrusion of an alcohol problem may well provide the push to the Jewish alcoholic to explore his or her spiritual heritage. Other groups for whom spiritual issues may be of particular importance are, for example, Native Americans, as spiritual issues are integral to traditional culture. They too may need special help in reconnecting with their spiritual heritage and incorporating it into their recovery. The clinician is advised to be sensitive to this as well as supportive.

There is interest in the substance abuse field as well as in medicine in general to consider the role of spiritual involvement in healing and health. The clinician, as an individual, may or may not consider spiritual issues personally important. What the care-giver needs is an awareness of the possibility (even probability) of this dimension's importance to a client, as well as a willingness to provide the client with a referral to an appropriate individual. Current research findings indicate that an active spiritual or religious involvement reduces the risk of alcohol or drug abuse. The risk for alcohol dependency is 60% higher among drinkers with no religious affiliation compared to members of conservative Protestant denominations. Religiously involved individuals are consistently less likely to use alcohol and other drugs and when they do so are less likely to engage in heavy use and suffer its adverse consequences. Research has shown that recovering individuals involved in working the 12 steps of Alcoholics Anonymous are more likely to remain abstinent, showing significantly better outcomes than alcoholics treated with two other types of psychological therapy devoid of spiritual components.

Activities therapy

Activities therapy has been a mainstay of inpatient psychiatric treatment for a long time. It includes recreational and occupational therapy. To those unfamiliar with this field, the activities that are encompassed may look like "recreation" or "free time" or diversionary activities, not real treatment. For the activities therapist, the event, such as a picnic—with the associated menu planning, food preparation, setup and clean up afterwards—is of far less importance than the process.

Recall that the alcohol dependent person's repertoire of social skills has been depleted. Plus, it may have been a long time since there have been social interactions without alcohol, or tasks completed, or responsibilities assumed and fulfilled. In addition, many clients have come to think of drinking not only as part of relaxation or leisure time, but also as necessary to get some "time out" from responsibilities, to let them "turn off" tensions, or to "get into" some diversions. Then, too, during treatment, the client can spend only so many hours a day in individual counseling, or group therapy sessions, or listening to lectures and films. Activities therapy programs can be the forum in which the client has the opportunity, with support and guidance, to try out some of the new behaviors that may have been discussed elsewhere and will be necessary in sobriety. Activities therapy may be the portion of the therapeutic program that will most closely approximate real life.

A common dilemma for those in recovery is how to fill the time that they used to spend drinking. A part of the activity therapist's task will be to identify past interests or activities that can be reawakened and resumed, not only to fill time but also to provide a sense of accomplishment and belonging. The activities therapist will be sensitive to the client's limitations. The person who used to have a half-acre garden and is now going to make up for lost time by plowing up another half acre can be cautioned to take it easy. One or two tomato plants plus a few lettuce and radish plants may be the place to start.

One of the more imaginative adaptations of activities therapy in alcohol treatment has been the use of Outward Bound programs. Outward Bound grew out of the British Merchant Navy in World War II. It was discovered that among the merchant marines who were stranded at sea, those who survived were not the youngest and most physically fit but their older "life-seasoned" comrades. From that observation, an attempt was made to provide a training experience that incorporated physically challenging and psychologically demanding tasks to demonstrate to people their capacities.

Outward Bound was introduced in the United States in 1961. Since that time, its programs have been conducted in a range of settings from rehabilitation programs for the physically handicapped to training for corporate executives. The programs can be a day, several days, or a week in length.

Typically, an Outward Bound experience combines group exercises, such as a group being given the task of getting all of its members over a 10-foot wall, with individual activities, such as rock climbing. Within alcohol treatment programs, Outward Bound has been made available to individual clients and clients with their families, and it has been used particularly with adolescents. The staff often includes a professional alcohol clinician, as well as the Outward Bound instructors. Integral to Outward Bound is discussing and processing what transpires during a particular exercise. Alcoholics Anonymous adages such as "One step (day) at a time" or "Easy does it" might be the topic of a group meeting. These take on a new meaning to someone who has been involved in scaling a cliff or negotiating a ropes course 20 feet off the ground.

A few words about fun   A family beset by alcoholism usually has lived a lopsided life. There's probably been little time, energy, or capacity for anything except crisis management or holding one's breath waiting for the next incident. Any sense of fun or true recreation has long since disappeared in a sea of alcohol. Despite what they may claim, being drunk is not fun for active alcoholics and neither are the clenched-teeth efforts to control drinking. Witnessing either of these behaviors is no fun either. Even small children in the home where alcoholism is present may have become so inhibited by the tension or so hypervigilant that there is too little opportunity for true play.

A common complaint from an alcoholic nearing or entering treatment is "Everyone drinks! How can I have any fun if I'm the only one who isn't!" Lots of others in recovery seem to manage, however. Despite the fact that this is often a last gasp effort to discount the need for treatment, it does point to a real problem down the line—how to have fun without alcohol, or for some, how to have fun at all. What is the clinician to say? There may be little to be said at the point the question is raised, when the more significant question is "Is life fun now?" But it is an issue that has to be taken seriously.

In planning treatment, whether an inpatient program or outpatient care, the issue of fun needs to be addressed. "Fun" ultimately is not what we do but how we experience what we do. It is not an event but an experience. The word *recreation* thus may be more apt to capture the phenomena. It flows from the activities in life that refresh us, renew us, and offer us the sorely needed counterpoint to the hectic, busy lives we live. One person's recreation is another's work. Recreation can encompass active pursuits, such as swimming, a brisk walk, or a pick-up game of softball on the empty neighborhood lot. Recreation can be individual, a private activity with some solitary time for reading a book, writing a letter, gardening, or puttering in the basement workshop. Recreation may be group activity. It can be spontaneous or it may be planned. Were one to attempt to define an essential characteristic of recreation, it is being wholly engaged. When we are living in the present, we can neither worry about tomorrow nor relive yesterday.

Initial treatment, whether in a residential or an outpatient setting, is going to be highly regimented and entail a well-structured schedule. The idea is not to schedule assigned time slots in which clients are instructed to "have fun." They would be at a total loss. To relax or "have fun" does not usually occur on command either. For those in recovery, it is a capacity that will need to be evoked and rediscovered. For many, the initial moments of relaxation may go unrecognized. They may be quite unspectacular moments. A game of cards, a conversation, or going to a movie—recreation can encompass anything that pushes alcohol from the foreground and turns off preoccupation with oneself and one's plight. It is important to assist clients to recognize these moments and not discount the enjoyment. It is more important too, to incorporate events that up the odds of these moments occurring. During later recovery, recreation is no less an issue. At this point it may be considered as a part of the task that confronts us all. It can be put under the rubric of "taking care of ourselves." Recreation is a necessary self-indulgence.

Promoting well-being   Activities that center around fitness and sports are becoming a more important element in many individuals' efforts to take care of themselves. Within treatment programs, efforts to address general fitness and well-being are now more common. In residential settings, without conscious effort to have it be otherwise, the day would be filled almost exclusively with sedentary activities. The link between emotional well-being and physical well-being is being appreciated. The treatment of alcohol or substance abuse can simultaneously address larger issues of general well-being, without diverting attention from the focus of alcohol or substance abuse as the paramount concern. Regular exercise and good nutrition do have a significant impact on how we feel. This in turn can set in motion a positive cycle—one of change promoting further change. Feeling better and being proud of efforts that contributed to this leads to an improved sense of competence, reinforces expectations that things can improve, and opens up new possibilities for activities that are rewarding and that enhance self-worth.

The self-care focus prompted many alcohol treatment programs to be "smoke free," to not allow smoking, and to promote or require smoking cessation as well as abstinence from alcohol use. The case for not allowing nicotine use can be made on many grounds—(1) smoking is viewed as a health issue and medical concern, as serious as chronic alcohol use, (2) smoking is seen as a behavior that often accompanies drinking so that if not discontinued it will be a ready cue to take a drink, (3) nicotine is viewed as a drug that is as, or more, addictive than alcohol or other substances, or (4) all of the above. As a practical point, the physical and emotional discomfort of withdrawal from alcohol is not compounded by the simultaneous withdrawal of nicotine. Residential programs that have initiated such policies have reported a relatively infrequent number of client complaints in respect to also giving up nicotine.

Behavioral approaches

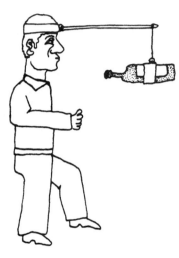

Behavioral therapy and *behavior modification* have long been a part of substance abuse treatment. For a long time, the terms were used so casually and so imprecisely that what was being discussed was often unclear. Historically several treatment approaches were based on behavioral therapy and techniques were introduced that went against the grain of the treatment field and aroused considerable controversy. One unfortunate result was to make clinicians skeptical of any mention of behavioral approaches. As the substance abuse field has matured, so has the use of behavioral techniques. It is not an exaggeration to now say that they have the most useful tools available to us. Here we would like to give you a brief rundown of the pertinent factors and to point out some things that have muddied the waters.

Early approaches   Obviously, any therapy has behavior modification as its goal. However, behavioral therapy is the clinical application of the principles psychologists have discovered about how people learn. The basic idea is that if a behavior can be learned, it can also be unlearned, or changed. This can be done in several ways. To put it very simply, one way is to introduce new and competing behavior in place of the old or unwanted behavior. By using learning principles, the new behavior is reinforced, meaning the person experiences positive results and the old behavior is in effect "squeezed out." Another technique is to negatively reinforce, or punish, the unwanted behavior; therefore it becomes less frequent. Recall the discussion of Johnson's model for the development of drinking behavior in Chapter 6. That explanation was based on learning principles. People learn what alcohol can do; alcohol can be counted on in anyone's early drinking career to have dependable consequences. Therefore drinking is reinforced and the behavior continues.

Behavioral therapy is a field of psychology that rose to prominence in the early 1950s. Its techniques were then applied to the treatment of alcoholism. However, the early behavioral approaches fared no better than did other psychological approaches, which also were unable to offer, by themselves, a complete guide to treatment. Historically, one of the first behavioral methods to be used in alcohol treatment was *aversion therapy*. Electric shock and chemicals were the primary tools. The alcoholic person would be given something to drink, and as he swallowed the alcohol, a shock would be applied. Alternatively, a drug similar to disulfiram (Antabuse® is the trade name) would induce sickness when one drank alcohol. The procedure was repeated periodically until it was felt that the drinking was so thoroughly associated with unpleasantness in the subject's mind that the person would be unlikely to continue drinking alcohol. Although short-term success was ensured, those results were not maintained over the long haul. As one author noted in reviewing the early behavioral approaches toward alcoholism treatment, "Historically there have been many fads in the treatment of alcoholism. Behavioral therapists have also been guilty of this faddism in the form of aversion therapy. There has been an awareness on the part of behavioral therapists that this rather naive approach to a complex clinical problem such as alcoholism is unwarranted." Aversion therapy of this form is now very rarely used.

As the field became more sophisticated, it became clear that an effective behavioral treatment program could not be based on a single behavioral technique. One cannot expect all clients to be successfully treated by the routine application of the same procedure. Just as not all clients are given the same kind and dose of a medication, neither can they be given the same behavioral treatment. Thus efforts were then made to devise total alcohol treatment programs based on a variety of behavioral techniques. One such behaviorally oriented program received considerable attention and generated much controversy. It centered on efforts by behavioral psychologists in the early 1970s to teach controlled drinking as the treatment for alcohol dependence. Linda and Mark Sobell are the researchers most closely identified with this. The initial reports were quite positive. Controlled drinking as an alternative to abstinence seemed to be further supported by several studies that followed up on individuals who had been similarly treated for alcoholism. Though the programs the clients had been involved in were generally abstinence oriented, a portion of these clients (although nowhere near a majority) were reported to have returned to moderate drinking without problems.

The optimism about controlled drinking as an alternative to abstinence could not be sustained. A group of researchers very painstakingly tracked down the subjects of the Sobells' study to see how they had fared over the long haul. Of the original group, only one was described as continuing as a moderate drinker. All of the others had serious problems and relapses, and four had died of alcohol-related problems. (Similarly, Vaillant's work suggested that once an addictive state has been established, a return to moderate, controlled drinking is very rare. If one follows people over time as he did, the proportion who can maintain a controlled drinking pattern declines.) It must also be noted that "controlled" drinking is not to be confused with "social" drinking. Most social drinkers do not need to invest considerable attention and energy to maintain a moderate level of alcohol use.

Ironically, while controlled drinking did not prove to have been a viable goal for treatment of alcohol dependence, many of the approaches used have subsequently been successfully adopted in treating a different population of persons, those whose diagnosis is alcohol abuse. In this instance, abstinence may not be a requisite treatment goal, although those diagnosed with alcohol abuse need to moderate their drinking practices, to reduce the likelihood of acute problems that arise with intoxication and to reduce the risk of future dependence. Such approaches have been used, for example, with the college-age population, to reduce dangerous drinking practices. In this context, the phrase "controlled drinking" is less often used than the phrase "moderate use" or "efforts to reduce harm associated with drinking."

Few treatment programs are any longer totally designed along behavioral methods. What is now far more common is the use of behavioral methods to treat particular aspects of an alcohol or drug problem in the context of a multipronged clinical approach.

Relaxation therapy   In recovery, the client is likely to face a multitude of problems. One of these may be a high level of anxiety. It can be of a temporary nature, the initial discomfort with the nondrinking or nonusing life, or more chronic if one is the "nervous" type. Whether temporary or chronic, it is a darned uncomfortable state, and the client has a very low tolerance for it. Those dependent upon alcohol, for example, have become accustomed to using alcohol for the quick, if temporary, relief of anxiety. What is later remembered (and longed for) is the almost instant relief of a large swig of booze. When alcohol or drugs are no longer an option, the recovering individual has the problem of how to deal with anxiety. Many simply "sweat it out"; others relapse.

Some positive things can be done to alleviate recovering persons' anxiety. One is relaxation therapy. It is based on the fact that if the body and breathing are relaxed, it is impossible to feel anxious. The mind rejects the paradox of a relaxed body and a "tense" mind. Working with this fact, some techniques have evolved to counter anxiety with relaxation. Generally, the therapist vocally guides a person through a progressive tensing and relaxing of the various body parts. The relaxing can start with the toes and work up or with the scalp and work down. The process involves first tensing the muscles, then relaxing them at the direction of the therapist. These directions are generally given in a modulated, soft voice. When the client is quite relaxed, it is suggested that a soothing picture be held in his or her mind. The client is then given a tape of the process to take home, with instructions on its use, as an aid in learning the relaxation. With practice, the relaxed state is achieved more easily and quickly. In some cases, the client may finally learn to totally relax with just the thought of the "picture." Once thoroughly learned, the relaxation response can be substituted for anxiety at will. This response can be used by the recovering alcoholic to deal with those situations in which taking a drink might be almost second nature.

Systematic desensitization   Another behavioral approach to deal with anxiety, *systematic desensitization,* builds upon the relaxation response. This technique has been found quite useful in treating people with phobias. This is an appropriate approach for recovering alcoholics who may feel panic at the mere thought of a particular situation. We mean real panic, such that even the idea gets them so tense that the temptation to drink may be overwhelming.

In this process, with the aid of a therapist the individual in his imagination approaches the situation that leads to anxiety. As the anxiety builds up, the person is directed to use relaxation techniques that have been taught. Gradually, going step by step, relaxation is used to turn off the anxiety, and eventually the situation itself becomes much less anxiety provoking. In alcohol treatment, this approach has been used for persons whose drinking has been partially prompted by stressful, anxiety-producing situations. Given another option, they are better equipped to avoid drinking when such situations arise.

Life skills training   This is another technique that is based upon behavioral methods. One very simple example of its application is helping people practice how to say "no" to things that might threaten sobriety.

Record keeping   This is another tool that builds upon behavioral psychology. Not uncommonly, in recovery, some clients report finding themselves, with some regularity, "suddenly" in the midst of some kind of troubling situation (e.g., an argument with a spouse), with no idea of what led up to it. There may instead be periods of inexplicable despondency. Often there is a pattern, but the key elements may not be apparent. Keeping a personal log or diary of one's daily routine sometimes is used to help identify the precursors that lead up to difficult moments. Recovery requires all kinds of readjustments to routines. By keeping a daily log, over time, one may have a far better sense of what areas need attention.

Relapse prevention   Many of the various techniques being described are the mainstays of relapse prevention. Relapse prevention efforts are increasingly a standard component of care. Alan Marlatt and colleagues from the University of Washington were among the first to tackle this issue in a systematic fashion and sketch ways in which this could be incorporated into care. A variety of relapse prevention curriculam have been developed. These consist of defining the content and approaches to use in a series of counseling sessions. They can include homework assignments, worksheets, skills training, role play, interactive videotapes, as well as lifestyle interventions, such as exercise, stress management, and relaxation techniques. Prior to that, the substance abuse field tended to avoid any mention of relapse in working with clients. The topic was taboo, as if in acknowledging relapse as a possibility, one was either giving permission to clients to resume drinking or drug use or that it was inevitable.

Common elements of relapse prevention involve the following:

• Identifying high-risk relapse situations and developing strategies to deal with them.

Beyond providing people with essential skills, such efforts also increase the sense of competency. Having been provided a set of tools, there are things that a client can do. They aren't left feeling vulnerable with nothing to do but "keep a stiff upper lip" when problematic situations arise. In this as well as all of the instances below, the effort is not for the counselor to identify the high-risk situation, but for the client to do so.

• Seeing relapse as a process, not as an event.

Relapse doesn't just come out of the blue. Often one can see a series of things, a chain of events that generally proceed a relapse, be it stress, negative feelings, or finding oneself (or placing oneself) in a vulnerable situation, such as going to a favorite old haunt, "just for the music." From this perspective there are any number of steps that can be taken to avoid the accumulation of things that lead to relapse.

• Dealing with drug and alcohol cues and cravings.

Cues are the little things that can trigger craving. There are any number of possible cues, or reminders. Clients need to identify their own special package of things that set the ball rolling. It may be a morning cup of coffee for those hooked on cigarettes. It may be a particular setting or social situation, such as the Friday night after-work stop at a tavern with coworkers. It may be after a period of stress, or hard work, that the cocaine addict had often rewarded himself.

• Facing social pressures.

Social pressures can include situations in which someone can feel that not drinking or using will make them feel conspicuous, or out of place. This is as, if not more common than outright comments of others, or offers of a drink, or a line of cocaine. When such offers occur, they often are not motivated by someone out "to get" the client, but may be offered quite innocently. The waiter at the restaurant does not know that the customer is a nondrinker, or trying to be.

• Creating and nurturing a supportive social network.

Clients need to be able to recognize the supports that are available to them, and in turn consider ways to use them. This includes families, friends, and self-help programs.

• Developing skills to handle negative emotional states.

One of the most common triggers for resuming use is, simply put, "feeling bad." A variety of very different techniques may be used depending on the nature of the bad feeling. If there is someone who is very passive, never stating his or her views, assertiveness training may be useful. Or if the demon is frustration, finding alternative means of handling this are required.

- Correcting errors in thinking.

Cognitive distortions, that is, automatic ways of thinking that don't really mesh with reality, can be a real problem. For example, there is the person who sees disaster around every corner, or the one who jumps to conclusions. Efforts to correct these erroneous assumptions are sometimes termed cognitive therapy, closely linked to behavioral therapy. At times the two terms are combined, referred to as cognitive-behavioral approaches. There are a variety of exercises that have been devised to identify what these little voices say, to examine the errors in the message and to draft a new script to replace that old tape.

- Developing a healthy and balanced lifestyle.

Much of the emphasis needs to be on balance. Working hard, accumulating stresses, needs to be balanced by relaxation, time-outs, and activities undertaken for no better reason than that they are enjoyable. It is also important to consider the role of exercise in providing a sense of well-being. The above discussion is not an exhaustive list of behavioral approaches being used. For example, there are also contingency contracts. These are most common in drug treatment programs. Part of the treatment involves a contract, with the client "earning" either money or vouchers that can be redeemed at a local store, for achieving specific treatment goals. Thus, the client may receive $2 for each negative drug screen. The amount earned may increase the longer the client is drug-free.

Meditation

Meditation is frequently suggested as an aid in achieving and maintaining sobriety. It is increasingly being used in many areas of medicine. Any number of approaches are available to those wishing to try it, and many treatment centers include an introduction to one or more of these methods. Although meditation has different results depending on the type practiced, the process of reaching a meditative state is somewhat similar to practicing relaxation. A fairly relaxed state is necessary before meditation can begin. Some schools of meditation use techniques quite similar to relaxation methods as a lead-in to the meditation period. In yoga, physical exercises are coupled with suggested ideas as a precursor. Studies have shown that altered physiological states accompany meditation or deep relaxation. Altered breathing patterns and different brainwave patterns are examples. These changes are independent of the type of meditation practiced. The real physical response in part accounts for the feelings of well-being after meditation periods. Those who practice meditation find it, on the whole, a rewarding experience. Many also find in the experience some form of inspiration or spiritual help. Several highly advertised schools of meditation are receiving attention these days. You might investigate those that are available for clients who express an interest in meditation.

A word of caution is needed here. Alcoholics tend to go overboard. Meditation should never be a substitute for their other prescribed treatment. Also, there are extremists in every area of life, and meditation is no exception to exploitation. That is why some personal knowledge of what is available, who is using it, and how it affects those who do use it is necessary before advising your alcoholic client to try it. Meditation is only helpful if it alleviates anxiety and stress, and allows the recovering client to continue learning how to function better in the world.

In conclusion, all of the aforementioned therapies can be used together or in almost any combination that is deemed by the counselor to suit the situation of the client. They can be considered as a set of tools, which the therapist and other treatment staff use as appropriate to the circumstances in any particular combination, to get the job done.

PHARMACOTHERAPY

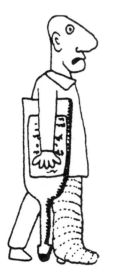

Our increasing knowledge about the biological factors that are a part of abuse and dependence—namely our understanding about the changes in the central nervous system that accompany abuse and dependence—has opened the doors for the development of drug therapies that may be useful in the treatment of addictive disorders. Interestingly, the substance abuse field has shown some resistance to the introduction to drug therapies. While possibly oversimplifying the resistance, the common denominators seem to be relatively clear. There apparently is the fear, at least in some quarters, that pharmacological intervention may offer alcoholics or addicts an easy way out. Closely aligned with this is the notion that the use of drugs to treat addiction may be a "slippery slope," erroneously encouraging the impression that drugs can be used to solve problems. There is the fear among some that even the therapeutic use of drugs may send a mixed message, and inadvertently suggest that sobriety or a drug-free life isn't really necessary. Thus, alcoholics are seen as able to indulge their dependence and at the last minute use drug therapies to avoid the long-term cost. Some too have described drug therapy as a crutch. This doesn't seem really out of place when one's legs are impaired. Instead, one might think of drug therapies as vital aids. For the alcohol dependent person, for example, drug therapy can buy sober time until the "legs" are steadier and other healthy supports are developed. The supports may be available already, but the individual has to be able to use them successfully.

Drugs used in alcohol treatment

Disulfiram (Antabuse®)   Disulfiram has been available for almost fifty years. It was discovered in the late 1940s, through a series of accidents. A group of Danish scientists found that the drug disulfiram, which they were testing for other purposes, led to a marked reaction when alcohol was ingested by a person exposed to it. Disulfiram alters the metabolism of alcohol by blocking out an enzyme necessary for the breakdown of acetaldehyde, an intermediate product of alcohol metabolism. Acetaldehyde is normally present in the body in small amounts, in somewhat larger ones when alcohol is ingested, and in toxic amounts when alcohol is taken into the body after disulfiram medication. Thus, the basis for disulfiram's effects are based on the alteration of the process of metabolism, not upon its influence in the brain.

This adverse physical reaction is characterized by throbbing in the head and neck, flushing, breathing difficulty, nausea, vomiting, sweating, tachycardia (rapid heartbeat), weakness, and vertigo. The intensity of the reaction can vary from person to person and varies also with the amount of disulfiram present and the amount of alcohol taken in. Disulfiram is excreted slowly from the body, so the possibility of a reaction is present for 4 to 5 days after the last dose and in some cases longer. Because of this reaction, Antabuse® (the trade name for disulfiram) has been widely used in the treatment of alcoholism.

Prescription, administration, and use   Over the years since disulfiram's discovery, trial and error and research have led to some suggestions for its prescription, administration, and use in alcohol treatment. Disulfiram is not a cure for alcoholism. At best, it can postpone the drink. If the recovering client chooses to use disulfiram as an adjunct to AA, psychotherapy, group therapy, and so forth, it can be most useful in helping someone not take the impulsive drink. Because disulfiram stays in the system for such a long time, whatever caused the impulsive desire for a drink can be examined and possibly worked through during the 5-day grace period to forestall the need for the drink entirely.

Anyone who wishes to use disulfiram should be allowed to do so, provided they are physically and mentally able. The client should first be thoroughly examined by a physician to determine physical status. Some conditions contraindicate disulfiram usage. There is still some debate about the need for such caution with lower doses, but only the client's physician can decide this point. In some cases, physicians consider the risks of a disulfiram reaction not as dire as continued drinking certainly would be. There are those who suggest that administration should usually be supervised for at least a short time. Preferably the spouse should not be the one expected to do this. Rather this can be done through a visit to an outpatient clinic or an employee health clinic. Disulfiram should be used in combination with other supportive therapies.

The client taking disulfiram must be thoroughly informed of the dangers of a possible reaction. A variety of substances (such as cough syrup, wine sauces, paint fumes) that contain some alcohol can cause a reaction. Clients taking disulfiram should be provided a list of such substances. Carrying a card or wearing a "Med-Alert disk" stating they are taking disulfiram may be wise. Some medications given to accident victims or in emergency situations could cause a disulfiram reaction compounding whatever else is wrong. There is no way to tell if an unconscious person has been taking disulfiram without such a warning.

A client who wishes to use disulfiram often begins taking the drug in a hospital setting after primary detoxification. Generally, one tablet (0.5 gm) daily for 5 days is given, then half a tablet daily thereafter. During the initial 5 days the client is carefully monitored for side effects. Once the client is receiving the maintenance dose, the client can continue for as long as it is beneficial.

Disulfiram can free the client from the constant battle against the bottle. When someone decides to take the pill on a given day, that person has made one choice that will postpone that drink for at least 4 or 5 days. If continuing to take it daily, that fourth or fifth day is always well out ahead. This allows time to begin acquiring or relearning behaviors other than drinking behaviors, and the habits of sobriety can take hold.

Medications containing alcohol   Alcohol, in one or another of its many forms, was for centuries virtually the only pharmacological agent available to physicians. In the twentieth century, alcohol has had rather limited medicinal uses. Now, in addition to being used externally as an antiseptic (e.g., to wash the skin before giving an injection or taking a blood sample, except when this sample is being obtained to measure blood alcohol levels), its only other major use is as an "inert" medium or carrier for liquid medications. Alcohol is an almost universal ingredient of cough medicines and liquid cold preparations sold over the counter or by prescription (see Table 9.1). Furthermore, the percentage of alcohol in such preparations can be substantial. NyQuil, for example, contains 25% alcohol. That's 50 proof! Alcohol is also an ingredient in a variety of other kinds of commonly used liquid medications (see Table 9.2). Recovering alcoholics in general are well advised to avoid alcohol-containing preparations. For those taking disulfiram, it is imperative. Increasingly there are preparations available for coughs and colds that do not contain alcohol (see Table 9.3). A pharmacist is always the most knowledgeable person to provide information on alcohol content of over-the-counter drugs and the availability of alternative preparations.

Anticraving agents   While potentially triggered by events, and feelings, and situations, craving has a physiological basis. The increased knowledge of brain chemistry and the various neurotransmitter systems that play a role in dependence opens a large array of possibilities for development of drugs that can aid treatment. One drug, *naltrexone,* first used in the treatment of opiate addiction, was discovered to be helpful as well in the treatment of drug dependence. Among alcoholics, naltrexone, marketed as *ReVia®*, has been shown to reduce craving. In the earliest studies using naltrexone with alcoholics, the alcoholics who used it reported fewer episodes of craving, as well as a diminished response to alcohol and consumption of smaller amounts if drinking did occur. These early reports were particularly encouraging because the patients being

TABLE 9.1   SOME ALCOHOL-CONTAINING PREPARATIONS FOR COUGHS, COLDS, AND CONGESTION

Drug	Manufacturer	Percentage of alcohol
Actol Expectorant	Beecham Labs	12.5
Ambenyl Expectorant	Parke-Davis	5.0
Calcidrine Syrup	Abbott	6.0
Chlor-Trimeton Syrup	Schering	7.0
Citra Forte Syrup	Boyle	2.0
Coryban-D Syrup	Pfipharmecs	7.5
Demazin Syrup	Schering	7.5
Dilaudid Cough Syrup	Knoll	5.0
Dimetane Elixir	Robins	3.0
Dimetane Expectorant	Robins	3.5
Dimetane Expectorant-DC	Robins	3.5
Dimetapp Elixir	Robins	2.3
Hycotuss Expectorant and Syrup	Endo	10.0
Lufylin-GG	Mallinckrodt	17.0
Novahistine DH	Dow Pharmaceuticals	5.0
Novahistine DMX	Dow Pharmaceuticals	10.0
Novahistine Elixir	Dow Pharmaceuticals	5.0
Novahistine Expectorant	Dow Pharmaceuticals	7.5
NyQuil Cough Syrup	Vicks	25.0
Ornacol Liquid	Smith Kline & French	8.0
Periactin Syrup	Merck Sharp & Dohme	5.0
Pertussin 8-Hour Syrup	Cheeseborough-Ponds	9.5
Phenergan Expectorant, Plain	Wyeth	7.0
Phenergan Expectorant, Codeine	Wyeth	7.0
Phenergan Expectorant VC, Plain	Wyeth	7.0
Phenergan Expectorant VC, Codeine	Wyeth	7.0
Phenergan Expectorant, Pediatric	Wyeth	7.0
Phenergan Syrup Fortis (25 mg)	Wyeth	1.5
Polaramine Expectorant	Schering	7.2
Quibron Elixir	Mead Johnson	15.0
Robitussin	Robins	3.5
Robitussin A-C	Robins	3.5
Robitussin-PE and DM	Robins	1.4
Robitussin-CF	Robins	4.75
Rondec-DM	Ross	0.6
Theo-Organidin Elixir	Wampole	15.0
Triaminic Expectorant	Dorsey	5.0
Triaminic Expectorant DH	Dorsey	5.0
Tussar-2 Syrup	Armour	5.0
Tussar SF Syrup	Armour	12.0
Tussi-Organidin	Wampole	15.0
Tuss-Ornade	Smith Kline & French	7.5
Tylenol Elixir	McNeil	7.0
Tylenol Elixir with Codeine	McNeil	7.0
Tylenol Drops	McNeil	7.0
Vicks Formula 44	Vicks	10.0

TABLE 9.2   OTHER COMMONLY USED DRUGS CONTAINING ALCOHOL

Drug	Manufacturer	Percentage of alcohol
Alurate Elixir	Roche	20.0
Anaspaz-PB Liquid	Ascher	15.0
Aromatic Elixir	Circle	22.0
Asbron Elixir	Dorsey	15.0
Atarax Syrup	Roerig	0.5
Belladonna, Tincture of	Purepac	67.0
Benadryl Elixir	Parke-Davis	14.0
Bentyl-Phenobarbital Syrup	Merrell-National	19.0
Carbrital Elixir	Parke-Davis	18.0
Cas-Evac	Parke-Davis	18.0
Choledyl Elixir	Warner/Chilcott	20.0
Decadron Elixir	Merck Sharp & Dohme	5.0
Dexedrine Elixir	Smith Kline & French	10.0
Donnagel	Robins	3.8
Donnagel-PG	Robins	5.0
Donnatal Elixir	Robins	23.0
Dramamine Liquid	Searle Labs	5.0
Elixophylin	Cooper	20.0
Elixophyllin-KI	Cooper	10.0
Feosol Elixir	Smith Kline & French	5.0
Gevrabon	Lederle	18.0
Ipecac Syrup	Lilly	2.0
Isuprel Comp. Elixir	Winthrop	19.0
Kaochlor S-F	Warren-Teed	5.0
Kaon Elixir	Warren-Teed	5.0
Kay Ciel	Cooper	4.0
Kay Ciel Elixir	Cooper	4.0
Marax Syrup	Roerig	5.0
Mellaril Concentrate	Sandoz	3.0
Minocin Syrup	Lederle	5.0
Modane Liquid	Warren-Teed	5.0
Nembutal Elixir	Abbott	18.0
Paregoric Tincture		45.0
Parelixir	Purdue Frederick	18.0
Parepectolin	Rorer	0.69
Propadrine Elixir	Merck Sharp & Dohme	16.0
Serpasil Elixir	CIBA	12.0
Tedral Elixir	Warner/Chilcott	15.0
Temaril Syrup	Smith Kline & French	5.7
Theolixir (Elixir Theophylline)	Ulmer	20.0
Valadol	Squibb	9.0
Vita-Metrazol Elixir	Knoll	15.0

TABLE 9.3 SOME NONALCOHOLIC PREPARATIONS FOR COUGHS, COLDS, AND CONGESTION

Drug	Manufacturer
Actifed-C Expectorant	Burroughs Wellcome
Actifed Syrup	Burroughs Wellcome
Hycodan Syrup	Eaton Labs.
Ipsatol Syrup	Key
Omni-Tuss	Pennwalt
Orthoxicol Syrup	Upjohn
Sudafed Syrup	Burroughs Wellcome
Triaminic Syrup	Dorsey
Triaminicol Syrup	Dorsey
Tussionex Suspension	Pennwalt

prescribed naltrexone were the "treatment failures"—those who had been in treatment several times and had never achieved sustained sobriety. ReVia® was approved for alcoholism treatment in the early 1990s. (*Acamprosate* is a drug used in Europe that also has been reported to reduce craving. It has not been approved for use in the United States.) Naltrexone, like disulfiram, can be useful in opening a window of opportunity for clients, by "buying time." By addressing the acute, short-term pressures to resume use, there is the chance to gain the tools needed to maintain sobriety and make the needed long-term changes.

Pharmacologic treatment of other drug dependence

Again, given our increasing knowledge of the changes in the brain that accompany long-term drug use, there is the possibility of that which was previously only a dream, that is, the potential to develop drugs with specific properties that may be helpful in treatment. The discussion here does not do justice to the topic but only highlights the main issues. Please see the suggested reading and further resources at the conclusion of this chapter. In brief there are three major approaches to drug therapies.

Drug replacement In some instances drug replacement means substitution of a different drug; in other instances it involves actually prescribing the drug of abuse. The goals of drug replacement are twofold. One is harm reduction. The other is to promote an environment in which rehabilitation efforts can get a foothold, in which there is time to engage people in treatment, thereby creating the possibility for long-term, including abstinence-oriented, treatment. Nicotine replacement is a prime example of drug replacement. Whether the nicotine is delivered by patch or an inhaler or a nasal spray, the delivery route is much safer than smoking. When combined with other smoking cessation strategies there is a better chance of quitting smoking. Another example is the use of methadone. Methadone is a pharmacological substitute for heroin. Many of the risks of heroin are related to the route of administration. With a street drug, neither dealers nor manufacturers abide by FDA standards! Thus there is the ever-present risk of contaminants or unintentional overdose. Also, compared to methadone, heroin has a shorter length of action which requires more frequent administration. On several counts methadone is a far safer alternative to heroin. Furthermore, methadone, while pharmacologically similar to heroin, does not provide the "rush" that accompanies heroin use, though it does stave off withdrawal. A newer drug has become available that is an alternative to methadone, LAAM (levo-alpha acetyl methadol). It too blocks the effects of other opiates and prevents withdrawal, and it does not produce a subjective high. One of its advantages over methadone is that it only has to be taken 3 times a week, so daily trips to a clinic are not necessary. For any of these medications, what is required is that an adequate dose be given. If patients are being undermedicated, they are far more likely to leave treatment.

Anticraving drugs   Craving seems to be reported as a more prominent feature of some drugs of dependence than others. Most notable are nicotine, cocaine, heroin, and alcohol. Thus, a priority in exploring new medications are those that may be effective with these substances in which craving is a prominent feature. One does not typically associate a similar kind of craving with inhalants, or the hallucinogens, or even marijuana. At present, the major successes have been with the craving accompanying alcohol dependence. There is an antidepressant medication, wellbutrin, known as Zyban® when marketed as a smoking cessation drug to assist smoking cessation efforts.

Research is also suggesting that some patients having particular symptoms, particularly anxiety or depression, may respond to psychotropic medications.

Blocking agents   Blocking agents are the pharmacological equivalent of football's linemen. They interfere with abused drugs' ability to make contacts needed in the brain to have the hoped-for effect. Disulfiram, while not acting on the brain, could still be considered a "blocker" as it interferes with metabolism.

RESOURCES AND FURTHER READING

The special reports and treatment-related series available from various federal institutes are valuable tools. In addition to the NIAAA's *Alcohol Alert* and *Alcohol Health and Research World,* there are also the publications of NIDA, such as *NIDA Notes.* In addition, there are two series worth mentioning: The "TAP series" (Technical Assistance Protocols) and the "TIP Series" (Treatment Improvement Protocols).

Technical assistance protocols

TAP 1. Fleisch B: *Approaches in the treatment of adolescents with emotional and substance abuse problems, Technical Assistance Publication (TAP) Series 1,* Rockville MD: Office for Treatment Improvement, 1991. (42 refs.)

TAP 4. Baker F: *Coordination of alcohol, drug abuse, and mental health services, Technical Assistance Publication (TAP) Series 4,* Rockville MD: Office for Treatment Improvement, 1991. (95 refs.)

TAP 5. Molloy JP: *Self-run, self-supported houses for more effective recovery from alcohol and drug addiction, Technical Assistance Publication (TAP) Series 5,* Rockville MD: Office for Treatment Improvement, 1992. (0 refs.)

TAP 7. McCann MJ, Rawson RA, Obert JL, Hasson AJ: *Treatment of opiate addiction with methadone: A counselor manual, Technical Assistance Publication (TAP) Series 7,* Rockville MD: Center for Substance Abuse Treatment, 1994. (Chapter refs.)

TAP 9. Center for Substance Abuse Treatment: *Funding resource guide for substance abuse programs, Technical Assistance Publication (TAP) Series 9,* Rockville MD: Center for Substance Abuse Treatment, 1994. (13 refs.)

TAP 10. Center for Substance Abuse Treatment: *Rural issues in alcohol and other drug abuse treatment: Award for excellence papers, Technical Assistance Publication (TAP) Series 10,* Rockville MD: Center for Substance Abuse Treatment, 1994. (Chapter refs.)

TAP 12. McArthur LC, Goldsberry Y: *Approval and monitoring of narcotic treatment programs: A guide on the roles of federal and state agencies, Technical Assistance Publication (TAP) Series 12,* Rockville MD: Center for Substance Abuse Treatment, 1994. (0 refs.)

TAP 14. Weber EM, Cowie R, eds: *Siting drug and alcohol treatment programs: Legal challenges to the NIMBY syndrome, Technical Assistance Publication (TAP) Series 14,* Rockville MD: Substance Abuse and Mental Health Services Administration, 1995. (Chapter refs.)

TAP 16. Kushner JN, Moss S, eds: *Purchasing managed care services for alcohol and other drug treatment: Essential elements and policy issues, Technical Assistance Publication (TAP) Series 16,* Rockville MD: Center for Substance Abuse Treatment, 1995. (21 refs.)

TAP 17. Center for Substance Abuse Treatment: *Treating alcohol and other drug abusers in rural and frontier areas, Technical Assistance Publication (TAP) Series 17,* Rockville MD: Center for Substance Abuse Treatment, 1995. (Chapter refs.)

TAP 18. Legal Action Center: *Checklist for monitoring alcohol and other drug confidentiality compliance, Technical Assistance Publication (TAP) Series 18,* Rockville MD: Substance Abuse and Mental Health Services Administration, 1996. (0 refs.)

TAP 19. Gorski TT, Kelley JM: *Counselor's manual for relapse prevention with chemically dependent criminal offenders, Technical Assistance Publication (TAP) Series 19, Criminal Justice Subseries, Volume II.* Rockville MD: Office for Treatment Improvement, 1996. (0 refs.)

TAP 20. Center for Substance Abuse Treatment, ed: *Bringing excellence to substance abuse services in rural and frontier America, Technical Assistance Publication (TAP) Series 20,* Rockville MD: Center for Substance Abuse Treatment, 1997. (Chapter refs.)

TAP 21. Center for Substance Abuse Treatment, Addiction Technology Transfer Centers Curriculum Committee, Deitch DA: *Addiction counseling competencies: The knowledge, skills, and attitudes of professional practice, Technical Assistance Publication (TAP) Series 21.* Rockville MD: Center for Substance Abuse Treatment, 1997. (Chapter refs.)

Treatment improvement protocols

TIP (draft). Center for Substance Abuse Treatment, Kandall SR, eds: *Improving treatment for drug-exposed infants: The recommendations of a consensus panel, Treatment Improvement Protocol (TIP) Series (Draft),* Rockville MD: Center for Substance Abuse Treatment, undated. (208 refs.)

TIP 1. Parrino MW: *State methadone treatment guidelines, Treatment Improvement Protocol (TIP) Series 1,* Rockville MD: Center for Substance Abuse Treatment, 1993. (Chapter refs.)

TIP 2. Mitchell JL: *Pregnant, substance-using women, Treatment Improvement Protocol (TIP) Series 2,* Rockville MD: Center for Substance Abuse Treatment, 1993. (92 refs.)

TIP 3. McLellan AT, Dembo R: *Screening and assessment of alcohol- and other drug-abusing adolescents, Treatment Improvement Protocol (TIP) Series 3,* Rockville MD: Center for Substance Abuse Treatment, 1993. (Chapter refs.)

TIP 4. Schonberg SK: *Guidelines for the treatment of alcohol- and other drug-abusing adolescents, Treatment Improvement Protocol (TIP) Series 4,* Rockville MD: Center for Substance Abuse Treatment, 1993. (70 refs.)

TIP 5. Kandall SR: *Improving treatment for drug-exposed infants, Treatment Improvement Protocol (TIP) Series 5,* Rockville MD: Center for Substance Abuse Treatment, 1993. (210 refs.)

TIP 6. Barthwell AG, Gibert CL: *Screening for infectious diseases among substance abusers, Treatment Improvement Protocol (TIP) Series 6,* Rockville MD: Center for Substance Abuse Treatment, 1993. (Chapter refs.)

TIP 7. Center for Substance Abuse Treatment: *Screening and assessment for alcohol and other drug abuse among adults in the criminal justice system, Treatment Improvement Protocol (TIP) Series 7,* Rockville MD: Center for Substance Abuse Treatment, 1994. (41 refs.)

TIP 8. Nagy PD. *Intensive outpatient treatment for alcohol and other drug abuse, Treatment Improvement Protocol (TIP) Series 8,* Rockville MD: Center for Substance Abuse Treatment, 1994. (39 refs.)

TIP 9. Center for Substance Abuse Treatment: *Assessment and treatment of patients with coexisting mental illness and alcohol and other drug abuse, Treatment Improvement Protocol (TIP) Series 9,* Rockville MD: Center for Substance Abuse Treatment, 1994. (105 refs.)

TIP 10. Center for Substance Abuse Treatment: *Assessment and treatment of cocaine-abusing methadone-maintained patients, Treatment Improvement Protocol (TIP) Series 10,* Rockville MD: Center for Substance Abuse Treatment, 1994. (158 refs.)

TIP 11. Center for Substance Abuse Treatment: *Simple screening instruments for outreach for alcohol and other drug abuse and infectious diseases, Treatment Improvement Protocol Series (TIP) Series 11,* Rockville MD: Center for Substance Abuse Treatment, 1994. (7 refs.)

TIP 12. Davis C, Henderson R: *Combining substance abuse treatment with intermediate sanctions for adults in the criminal justice system, Treatment Improvement Protocol (TIP) Series 12,* Rockville MD: Center for Substance Abuse Treatment, 1994. (16 refs.).

TIP 13. Gartner L, Mee-Lee D: *The role and current status of patient placement criteria in the treatment of substance use disorders, Treatment Improvement Protocol (TIP) Series 13,* Rockville MD: Center for Substance Abuse Treatment, 1995. (35 refs.)

TIP 14. Harrison PA, ed: *Developing state outcomes monitoring systems for alcohol and other drug abuse treatment, Treatment Improvement Protocol (TIP) Series 14,* Rockville MD: Center for Substance Abuse Treatment, 1995. (90 refs.)

TIP 15. Selwyn PA, Batki SL, ed: *Treatment for HIV-infected alcohol and other drug abusers, Treatment Improvement Protocol (TIP) Series 15,* Rockville MD: Center for Substance Abuse Treatment, 1995. (84 refs.)

TIP 16. Rostenberg PO: *Alcohol and other drug screening of hospitalized trauma patients. Treatment Improvement Protocol (TIP) Series 16,* Rockville MD: Center for Substance Abuse Treatment, 1995. (165 refs.)

TIP 17. Vigdal GL, ed: *Planning for alcohol and other drug abuse treatment for adults in the criminal justice system, Treatment Improvement Protocol (TIP) Series 17,* Rockville MD: Center for Substance Abuse Treatment, 1995. (171 refs.)

TIP 19. Wesson DR, ed: *Detoxification from alcohol and other drugs, Treatment Improvement Protocol (TIP) Series 19,* Rockville MD: Substance Abuse and Mental Health Services Administration, 1995. (151 refs.)

TIP 20. Kauffmann JF, Woody GE, eds: *Matching treatment to patient needs in opioid substitution therapy, Treatment Improvement Protocol (TIP) Series 20,* Rockville MD: Substance Abuse and Mental Health Services Administration, 1995. (205 refs.)

TIP 22. Marion IJ, ed: *LAAM in the Treatment of opiate addiction, Treatment Improvement Protocol (TIP) Series 22,* Rockville MD: Substance Abuse and Mental Health Services Administration, 1995. (101 refs.)

TIP 23. Center for Substance Abuse Treatment, Shuman D, Henderson R, Shilton M, Sevick JR, Davis C, Heard J, Vitzthum V: *Treatment drug courts: Integrating substance abuse treatment with legal case processing, Treatment Improvement Protocol (TIP) Series 23,* Rockville MD: Center for Substance Abuse Treatment, 1996. (0 refs.)

TIP 24. Sullivan E, Fleming M: *A guide to substance abuse services for primary care clinicians, Treatment Improvement Protocol (TIP) Series 24,* Rockville MD: Substance Abuse and Mental Health Services Administration, 1997. (198 refs.)

TIP 25. Fazzone PA, Hotlin JK, Reed BG: *Substance abuse treatment and domestic violence, Treatment Improvement Protocol (TIP) Series 25,* Rockville MD: Substance Abuse and Mental Health Services Administration, 1997. (208 refs.)

Aguilar TE, Munson WW: Leisure education and counseling as intervention components in drug and alcohol treatment for adolescents, *Journal of Alcohol and Drug Education* 37(3):23–34, 1992.
The purpose of this paper is to illustrate the association between substance abuse and leisure experiences and to present a rationale for leisure

interventions designed to remediate this social and behavioral problem. Leisure education and counseling is suggested for inclusion in broad-based prevention or intervention strategies for substance abuse. Recommendations are provided for strengthening leisure education and counseling programs by including suggestions for theory, content, format, and duration. (Author abstract.)

Carroll S: Spirituality and purpose in life in alcoholism recovery, *Journal of Studies on Alcohol* 54(3):297–301, 1993.

This study examines the relationship between spirituality and recovery from alcoholism. Spirituality is defined as the extent of practice of Alcoholics Anonymous steps 11 and 12 and is measured by a step questionnaire developed by the researcher. Step 11 suggests prayer and meditation, and step 12 suggests assistance of other alcoholics. Expressed degree of purpose in life is also seen as a reflection of spirituality. It was postulated that the extent to which steps 11 and 12 were practiced would be positively correlated with the extent of purpose in life reported by 100 Alcoholics Anonymous members. The major findings affirm this. The findings suggest that a sense of purpose in life increases with continuing sobriety and practice of the spiritual principles of Alcoholics Anonymous. (Author abstract.)

Cinciripini PM, McClure JB: Smoking cessation: Recent developments in behavioral and pharmacologic interventions, *Oncology (New York)* 12(2):249–259, 1998. (59 refs.)

Smoking kills more than 430,000 people each year in the United States and is currently estimated to be responsible for 30.5% of all cancer-related deaths in our society. The majority of these deaths could be prevented, however, if people refrained from usage of tobacco products. It is, therefore, essential that smoking cessation treatment become an integral component of all types of health care. In order to help clinicians better serve their smoking patients, the authors present an overview of current trends in the behavioral and pharmacologic treatment of smoking cessation. Although popular with patients, standard self-help interventions provide little clinical utility. A review of the current literature supports the use of behavioral counseling and nicotine replacement therapy as the most efficacious forms of intervention, particularly when combined. Recent trends in cessation research have also included nonnicotine medications, such as antidepressants, anxiolytics, and nicotine antagonists. Although there is insufficient evidence to mandate inclusion of most of these medications in standard smoking cessation treatment at this time, preliminary studies have not ruled out their potential effectiveness. (Author abstract.)

Crnkovic AE, DelCampo RL: A systems approach to the treatment of chemical addiction, *Contemporary Family Therapy* 20(1):25–36, 1998. (11 refs.)

Therapists are increasingly considering chemical addiction from a family systems perspective. Effects of chemical dependency upon the family are discussed, and intervention approaches aimed toward assisting the family as families redefine themselves and change their structure are considered. The integration of chemical dependency treatment and family therapy is also discussed as it is practiced in an intensive outpatient program at a psychiatric hospital. (Author abstract.)

Epstein EE, McCrady BS: Behavioral couples treatment of alcohol and drug use disorders: Current status and innovations (review), *Clinical Psychology Review* 18(6):689–711, 1998. (108 refs.)

Research suggests that Behavioral Couples Therapy (BCT), tailored to treat alcohol problems, produces significant reduction in alcohol consumption and improvement in marital functioning. Having established basic clinical protocols for Alcohol Behavioral Couples Therapy (ABCT) and provided support for their efficacy, clinical researchers around the country continue to develop and study new applications of the basic ABCT treatment models, such as adding relapse prevention or Alcoholics Anonymous components. Recent research supporting the heterogeneity in the population of individuals with alcohol problems has prompted some researchers on ABCT to consider additional adaptations of the treatment models for specific subgroups of alcoholics, and for particular individual and couples characteristics. Adaptation of ABCT to treat new populations such as drug abusers, female alcoholics, and problem drinkers is under investigation. The current article provides an overview of theoretical and clinical aspects of ABCT, and research on efficacy of the basic model and on areas of innovation and adaptation to new populations. Directions for future research on ABCT are suggested. (Author abstract.)

Farren CK: The use of naltrexone, an opiate antagonist, in the treatment of opiate addiction (review), *Irish Journal of Psychological Medicine* 14(1):31–34, 1997. (25 refs.)

The objective of this article is to review the use of the opiate antagonist naltrexone as an alternative to opiate agonist maintenance in the treatment of opiate addiction. An extensive literature search via Medline, Biosis, Psycinfo, and other databases was carried out, which revealed that naltrexone has been used in the treatment of opiate addicts in a variety of settings. A number of methods of induction onto naltrexone of recently abstinent addicts have been used. Naltrexone has had a wide range of outcome success with different populations and associated treatment regimes. The benefits of naltrexone can be compared with alternatives such as methadone maintenance and therapeutic communities. Naltrexone can be made more effective in the general population of opiate addicts with the use of adjunctive therapies. (Author abstract.)

Finn P, Wilcock K: Levo-alpha acetyl methadol (LAAM): Its advantages and drawbacks, *Journal of Substance Abuse Treatment* 14(6):559–564, 1997. (10 refs.)

Levo-Alpha Acetyl Methadol, or LAAM, is a medication therapy for individuals addicted to opiates that provides an alternative to methadone. Because it is administered only three times a week and, therefore, requires fewer clinic trips, patient acceptance can be higher than with methadone. While blocking the effects of other opiates and preventing withdrawal, LAAM does not produce a subjective high. However, because most patients are not familiar with LAAM, they may be initially more anxious and need more counseling and support while receiving the medication than they would with the more familiar methadone medication. On balance, LAAM enables clinic administrators and counselors to offer an alternative medication to methadone that some clients prefer once they become adjusted to it because of LAAM's even, stable effect. Through hypothetical but true-to-life case studies of LAAM use, it is possible to gain a clearer understanding of the advantages and drawbacks of using LAAM. (Author abstract.)

Galanter M, Egelko S, and Edwards H: Rational recovery: Alternative to AA for addiction, *American Journal of Drug and Alcohol Abuse* 19(4): 499–510, 1993.

Rational Recovery (RR) is a new self-help movement for substance abusers, with a cognitive orientation, which has been suggested as an alternative to Alcoholics Anonymous. This study was designed to examine the nature of RR and its impact on those who join. A national sample of 433 substance-abusing people attending 63 established RR groups was evaluated, using codable self-report questionnaires completed at RR meetings. Members were mostly men with college experience who had previously attended AA. Among recruits who attended their first RR meeting in the last month, 38% were abstinent in the last month. Among members who had joined 3 or more months before, 73% were abstinent in the last month; they had attended an average of 4.1 RR meetings in that month and carried out exercises at home based on Rational Emotive Therapy. Among those who joined 6 or more months before, 58% reported at least 6 months of abstinence. Among members with a history of heavy cocaine use, the portion reporting abstinence in the last month was not significantly different from those who had never used cocaine. The minority of members who were engaged for 3 months were still drinking, though, and did so on an average of 9.9 days in the last month. RR succeeded in engaging substance abusers and promoting abstinence among many of them while presenting a cognitive orientation that is different from the spiritual one of AA. Its utility in substance abuse treatment warrants further assessment. (Author abstract.)

Howard MO, Elkins RL, Rimmele C, et al: Chemical aversion treatment of alcohol dependence, *Drug and Alcohol Dependence* 29(2):107–143, 1991.

Developments in the application of chemical aversion therapy to the treatment of alcohol dependence are discussed. Historical factors leading to the early use of chemical aversion therapies are delineated, and the theoretical underpinnings of chemical aversion interventions are evaluated. Ethical and procedural considerations are addressed, and an assessment of the efficacy of the therapy is attempted. Future research activities that would lead to refinement of chemical aversion therapy protocols are highlighted. The effectiveness of chemical aversion treatment of alcohol dependence is discussed vis-a-vis production of conditioned alcohol-aversion and treatment outcome. (Author abstract.)

Kosten TR, McCance E: A review of pharmacotherapies for substance abuse (review), *American Journal on Addictions* 5(4):S30–S37, 1996. (70 refs.)

New pharmacotherapies have been developed for acute withdrawal and maintenance treatments of alcohol and opioid dependence, but not for cocaine dependence. High-dose, long-acting benzodiazepines, beta-blockers, and two antiseizure agents—carbamazepine and valproate—are being used for alcohol withdrawal. For maintenance treatment, opioid antagonists and various serotonergic agents such as fluoxetine, and ondansetron, show promise. For opioid dependence, clonidine-naltrexone detoxification appears quite cost-effective, and buprenorphine and LAAM (levo-alpha-acetymethadol) show promise for both detoxification and maintenance. More work is needed however, to discover an effective agent for target populations of cocaine abusers. (Author abstract.)

Mendelson JH, Mello NK: Management of cocaine abuse and dependence (review), *New England Journal of Medicine* 334(15):965–972, 1996. (122 refs.)

This article addresses the management of cocaine abuse and dependence. The authors briefly note the historical trends and current epidemiology and patterns of cocaine use, including a significant pattern of polydrug use among some groups in the population. They then review diagnostic criteria, and provide tables summarizing the diagnostic criteria for cocaine abuse, dependence, and withdrawal. The discussion of pharmacotherapy is preceded by a discussion of the pharmacologic effects and mechanisms of abuse and dependence. The major classes of drugs discussed are the antidepressants, drugs affecting dopaminergic function, opioid antagonists and mixed agonist-antagonists, and carbazepine. In the conclusion the authors note that none of the drugs now available are considered highly effective for either detoxification or maintenance of abstinence. It is noted as well that data suggest many cocaine abusers have had major psychological and psychosocial impairments that may have been compounded by subsequent problems of drug dependence. These include cognitive and learning disorders, interpersonal and social problems, as well as legal and financial difficulties. The roles of behavior therapies and other psychotherapeutic/counseling interventions are highlighted.

Miller WR: Researching the spiritual dimensions of alcohol and other drug problems, *Addiction* 93(7):979–990, 1998.

Although religions have been far from silent on the use of psychoactive drugs, and spirituality has long been emphasized as an important factor in recovery from addiction, surprisingly little research has explored the relationships between these two phenomena. Current findings indicate that spiritual/religious involvement may be an important protective factor against alcohol/drug abuse. Individuals currently suffering from these problems are found to have a low level of religious involvement, and spiritual (re)engagement appears to be correlated with recovery. Reasons are explored for the lack of studies testing spiritual hypotheses, and promising avenues for future research are discussed. Comprehensive addictions research should include not only biomedical, psychological, and socio-cultural factors but spiritual aspects of the individual as well.

Olitzky KM, Copans SA: *Twelve Jewish steps to recovery,* Woodstock VT: Jewish Lights Publishing, 1991.

A personal guide to turning from alcohol and other addictions. The 12-step programs of Alcoholics Anonymous and Narcotics Anonymous are interpreted from the perspective of Judaism. Each of the steps is interpreted using biblical stories, history, prayers, and discussion. Resource organizations, a glossary of important words, and selected readings are included.

Pendery ML, Maltzman IM, West LJ: Controlled drinking by alcoholics? New findings and a reevaluation of a major affirmative study, *Science* 217(4555):169–175, 1982.[3]

Controlled drinking has recently become a controversial alternative to abstinence as an appropriate treatment goal for alcoholics. In this study we reexamine the evidence underlying a widely cited report by Sobell and Sobell of successful controlled drinking by a substantial proportion of gamma (physically dependent) alcoholic subjects in a behavior therapy experiment. A review of the evidence, including official records and new interviews, reveals that most subjects trained to do controlled drinking failed from the outset to drink safely. The majority were hospitalized for alcoholism treatment within a year after their discharge from the research project. A 10-year follow-up (extended through 1981) of the original 20 experimental subjects shows that only one, who apparently had not experienced physical withdrawal symptoms, maintained a pattern of controlled drinking; eight continued to drink excessively—regularly or intermittently—despite repeated damaging consequences; six abandoned their effort to engage in controlled drinking and became abstinent; four died from alcohol-related causes; and one, certified about a year after discharge from the research project as gravely disabled because of drinking, was missing. (Author abstract.)

Room R, Greenfield T: Alcoholics Anonymous, other 12-step movements and psychotherapy in the U.S. population, 1990. *Addiction* 88(4):555–562, 1993.

Based on the 1990 U.S. National Alcohol Survey, this note provides the first available comprehensive findings on self-reported use of a variety of sources of personal support and counseling for alcohol use and other problems. Respondents were queried about lifetime attendance and number of times they went to identified sources of help in the prior year. Twelve-step groups included Alcoholics Anonymous, Al-Anon, Adult Children of Alcoholics, and other nonalcohol-oriented groups like Gamblers Anonymous, Narcotics Anonymous, and Overeaters Anonymous; additional questions inquired about support or therapy groups and individual counseling for nonalcohol problems. Of the U.S. adult popula-

---

[3]This article and the one by the Sobells represent one of the most significant, strident, and continuing controversies in the alcohol-drug field, i.e., whether "controlled drinking" (or drug use) is a suitable alternative to abstinence as a treatment goal. See *Journal of Studies on Alcohol* 50(5):465–486, 1989, containing an article on the topic, an editorial note, and two invited responses.

tion, 9% have been to an AA meeting at some time, 3.6% in the prior year, only about one-third of these for problems of their own. About half these percentages, mostly women, have attended Al-Anon. Of the same population, 13.3% indicate ever attending a 12-step meeting (including nonalcohol-oriented groups), 5.3% in the last year. During the prior year a further 2.1% used other support/therapy groups and 5.5% sought individual counseling/therapy for personal problems other than alcohol. In contrast to this high reported use, only 4.9% (ever) and 2.3% (12 months) reported going to anyone, including AA, for a problem (of their own) related to drinking. (Authors' abstract.)

Rotunda RJ, O'Farrell TJ: Marital and family therapy of alcohol use disorders: Bridging the gap between research and practice. *Professional Psychology: Research and Practice* 28(3):246–252, 1997. (21 refs.)

Clients with alcohol and other substance use disorders are routinely encountered by practitioners in various treatment settings. This article traces the rationale for using marital and family therapy with alcoholics and describes an ongoing behavioral marital therapy program that exemplifies an integration of clinical practice and research in this area. Specific treatment suggestions are offered, and practical considerations for therapists working with families struggling with alcoholism are discussed, including the role of self-help groups in family treatment, the danger of having preconceived notions about "alcoholic families," and the necessity for clinics and clinicians to possess the capacity to assess and treat comorbid psychological disorders as well as addictive behavior. (Author abstract.)

Rousso J: Psychotherapy with the recovering alcoholic. *Alcoholism Treatment Quarterly* 9(3/4):201–206, 1992.

This article discusses in detail psychotherapeutic approaches in working with alcoholic patients in recovery. It stresses the principles of patience and acceptance on the part of the therapist. It also stresses ways to help alcoholics recognize and deal with feelings that have so long been buried under the influence of alcohol. (Author abstract.)

Snow MG, Prochaska JO, Rossi JS: Processes of change in Alcoholics Anonymous: Maintenance factors in long-term sobriety. *Journal of Studies on Alcohol* 55(3):362–371, 1994.

The change strategies associated with successful long-term sobriety remain an understudied area in addiction research. Researchers conducting this study recruited individuals in various stages of sobriety (range: 1 month to 27 years of continuous abstinence). Subjects (N = 191) were surveyed on demographic, problem history, degree of self-utilization, current process of change use, and self-efficacy measures. Subjects were differentiated based on varying experience with AA, including exposure, frequency of meeting attendance, and degree of affiliation. Analyses included comparisons on demographic, problem history, process of change, and self-efficacy markers (i.e., self-change vs. self-help; differing levels of self-help utilization). Few differences were found between groups on demographic or self-efficacy indices, although there was a trend for past or current AA attendees and medium affiliates to report slightly greater alcohol use before quitting compared to self-changers or low affiliates. There was a consistent, positive relationship between the use of behaviorally oriented change processes and increased involvement with AA, with current attendees and high affiliates using these particular strategies more frequently than either self-changers, past attendees, or the low-to-medium affiliate groups. The utility of process analyses in helping map the pattern of successful addictive behavior change is discussed. (Author abstract.)

Sobell MB, Sobell LC: *Behavioral treatment of alcohol problems.* New York: Plenum Press, 1978.
The Sobells have been among the most prolific researchers in the behavioral quarter of the research-treatment community. This work includes a summary of a project involving a training regimen using behavioral paradigms that was reported to successfully replace addicted uncontrolled use with a pattern of "controlled drinking."

Special Issue on Alcoholics Anonymous. *Journal of Substance Abuse Treatment* 11(2):1–166 (entire issue), 1994.
The lead article is entitled "How AA works and why it's important for clinicians to understand." It notes that alcoholism is associated with tremendous suffering, psychological denial, and physical and emotional debilitation. Much of the suffering that plagues alcoholics is rooted in core problems with self-regulation involving self-governance, feeling life (affects), and self-care. Alcoholics Anonymous is effective because it is a sophisticated group psychology that effectively accesses, corrects, or repairs these core psychological vulnerabilities. The traditions of storytelling, honesty, openness, and willingness to examine character defects ("take inventory") allow people to express themselves who otherwise would not feel or speak or are deceitful (to self and others) and would deny vulnerability and limitation to openly admit to it. This article is followed by 10 other articles specifically related to aspects of AA with attention to the use of self-help groups by professionals and what helping professionals need to know to use these resources effectively.

Tiebout HM: Surrender versus compliance in therapy, with special reference to alcoholism. *Quarterly Journal of Studies on Alcohol* 14:58–68, 1953. (This article is available as a monograph through the National Council on Alcohol and Other Drug Dependencies.) In distinguishing between surrender and compliance, Tiebout addressed a concept that had special meaning for the early members of AA. Some of the points in his work have influenced professional treatment approaches and continue to leave their mark within the Fellowship, particularly what is perceived as necessary to follow the therapeutic regimen of AA. Surrender is distinguished from compliance and seen as an essential precursor for "acceptance." It takes place at the conscious level but more importantly the unconscious level, with a recognition of a fundamental inability to solve problems (handle alcohol) alone. This in turn provides the alcoholic with the motivation and ability to reach out for help and allows one to achieve psychological growth and change. In contrast, "compliance" is viewed as a conscious or rational acceptance but unconscious resistance to the need for change, creating a state of tension, strain, and conflict and often blocking surrender.

Wilcox RE, McMillen BA: The rational use of drugs as therapeutic agents for the treatment of alcoholism. *Alcohol* 15(2):161–177, 1998. (244 refs.)
The most crucial question in alcohol research has been said to be, "Why do some people drink uncontrollably?" Thus one of the highest priorities is identifying and testing anticraving agents. The author sets forth several assumptions that would guide any such work on what constitutes craving. A theoretical framework is provided for understanding craving, and the role of psychiatric comorbidity as well as other substance use is examined. The role of mesocortical structures is considered, and current research is reviewed. The discussion focuses on the molecular mechanisms of action of possible therapeutic agents and the likely need to combine drugs with complementary actions on the limbic system. Data is summarized in 4 extended tables that outline different agents' effects on alcohol consumption, alcohol craving, voluntary cocaine consumption, and cocaine and craving. (Author abstract.)

Wynne RD, McCrady BS, Kahler CW, Liddle HA, Palmer RB, Horberg LK, et al: When addictions affect the family. In Harway M, ed: *Treating the changing family*. New York: John Wiley & Sons, Inc., 1996, pp. 293–317. (83 refs.)
While there has been a "war on drugs," the authors note that relatively little research has been conducted to determine the impact of drug and alcohol abuse on family functioning. Nonetheless, the clinical community is increasingly paying attention to the family, and a variety of treatment and prevention approaches have been advanced that focus on families and the impact of addiction on the family. This chapter discusses the impact of alcohol and drug abuse on family functioning, describes models for conceptualizing and treating the problems these families experience, and suggests directions family clinicians might take to improve research and practice in the field. It summarizes research to date, describes the impact on physical and psychological health, outlines theoretical models of addictions and family functioning and current clinical approaches, and concludes with a discussion of individual differences, the role of gender, and ethnic and cultural factors.

SPECIAL POPULATIONS

There may be remarkable similarities between the 15-year-old alcohol abuser, who also dabbles with cocaine, and the 72-year-old retired schoolteacher, who never drank anything stronger than a nice white wine, but that should not blind us to the equally significant differences! In this chapter, we focus upon the distinctive characteristics of special populations, particularly adolescents, college students, the elderly, women, and those in the workplace. Of course, there is no segment of the population untouched by alcohol or drug problems. The chapter concludes with some suggested ways to identify the needs and issues of groups not discussed here. The groups selected for special attention here are those that cut across all segments of society.

Space does not allow equal discussion of even the major racial and ethnic groups and their particular needs nor other populations that may be of particular interest to individual readers, be it gays and lesbians, members of the military, or rural laborers. Since we cannot adequately even begin to acquaint you with the characteristics and issues to bear in mind when working with clients from any particular ethnic, racial, or religious group, we must be content to urge you to speak with more experienced colleagues, as well as to turn to the ever-increasing body of literature on minority and high-risk groups, including Native Americans, African-Americans, Hispanics, migrant workers, and Asians. However, in thinking about the special considerations of the groups that are discussed, one of the hopes is to make you more sensitive to the characteristics of any client.

ADOLESCENTS

Adolescence is indeed a special period of life. It lies at the back door of childhood yet at the very doorstep of adulthood. At no comparable time in life do more physical and emotional changes take place in such a narrow span of time. *Adolescence* as a term is less than 150 years old. Before that time, one grew straight from childhood into adulthood. The needs of family and culture demanded earlier work and community responsibilities. Survival depended on it. With increasing industrialization, children left the factories and fields to spend more time in school, play, and idle time. Society became increasingly aware of the presence of teenagers as a group who had, and still have, fairly undefinable roles and rights. Most texts define adolescence as the period from 12 to 21 years of age. Physical and legal determinants would suggest otherwise. Physical changes indicative of the beginning of adolescence may begin as early as age 7 and not end until the mid-20s. Legal age differs between state and federal jurisdictions. Draft registration requirements and voting privileges at 18 have clouded the definition.

Physical changes

The most striking aspect of adolescence is the rapid physical growth. These changes are mediated by the sex hormones. The rough charts

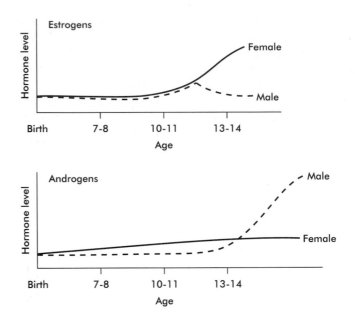

above indicate that the first recognizable change in the male is caused by fat increase dictated by a small but gradual increase in estrogen. Every boy gains weight at the expense of height during these years. Some boys due to become tall and muscular men are quite chubby during these early adolescent years. To add insult to injury, the next body part to grow is the feet, then the thighs, making him appear short waisted and gawky. This slows, allowing the rest of the body to catch up. Androgen influence appears later, with pigment changes in the scrotal sac, then enlargement of the testes and penis, the beginning of pubic hair, and early voice changes. The first nocturnal emission or "wet dream" may occur as early as age 10 or as late as age 15. Even so, the majority of boys remain "relatively sterile" until age 15. The major male growth spurt appears at age 14½ and is due primarily to growth in the backbone. This averages 4 to 4½ inches over an 18-month period. Some boys will shoot up 8 to 10 more inches during this time. Axillary and facial hair soon follow. Facial hair may develop entirely in 1 year. Other boys, equally normal but with different genes, may not complete the facial and body-hair growth until their mid to late 20s.

We are indeed taller than our ancestors, which can be shown from historical evidence. Clothing, doorways, and furniture were made for shorter men and women. Better nutrition is mainly responsible for the changes seen.

A girl's first hormonal response is around age 7 or 8 with a normal vaginal discharge called leukorrhea. The feet then grow, but this is rarely as noticeable a change as in the male. A breast "button" begins about age 11 under the skin of one breast first, to be followed in weeks or months under the remaining breast. The breasts develop into adult breasts over a span of 4 to 5 years. Pubic hair begins approximately 6 months after the breast button stage. The hips widen, and the backbone gains 3 to 4 inches before she is ready for her menses. Although a critical body weight is not the only initiator, the body is influenced by this. If other criteria are met, such as developing breasts, pubic hair, widened hips, and growth spurt, a sample of American girls will begin their menses weighing from 100 to 105 pounds. Nutrition has a great deal to do with the menarche (first menses); girls in countries with poor nutritional standards begin their menses 2 to 3 years later. The mean age for menarche in the United States is 12. (Pilgrim girls, who suffered from many nutritional deprivations, often had menarche delayed until age 17.) A regular menstrual cycle is not established immediately. Quite commonly a girl will have anovulatory (no egg) periods for 6 to 18 months before having ovulatory periods. This change may bring an increased weight gain, breast tenderness, occasional emotional lability, and cramps at the midcycle. These are consequences of progesterone, a hormone secreted by the ovary at the time of ovulation. An adult pattern in ovulation will not be completed until the early 20s.

Until puberty, boys and girls are equally strong in muscle strength (if corrected for height and weight). Total body fat increases in girls by 50% from ages 12 to 18, whereas a similar decrease occurs in boys. Muscle cell size and number increase in boys; muscle cell size alone increases in girls. Internal organs, such as the heart, double in size. Blood pressure increases with demands of growth. Pulse rate decreases, and the ability to break down fatigue metabolites in muscle prepares the male, especially, for the role of hunter and runner that was so important for survival centuries ago.

Marked fatigue coupled with overwhelming strength is often difficult to fully appreciate. An adolescent may wolf down several quarts of milk, a full meal or two, play many hours of active sports, and yet complain bitterly of severe fatigue at all times. This human metabolic furnace needs the food and rest as well as the drive to have the machine function and test itself out. These bodily inconsistencies often show in mood swings and unpredictable demands for self-satisfaction and physical expression.

The rapidity of these changes tends to produce almost a physiological confusion in many adolescents. Quite commonly, they become preoccupied with themselves. This can lead to an overconcern with their health. In some instances it is almost hypochondriacal. Adolescents may complain of things that to an adult appear very minor. The thing to remember is that their concern is very real and deep. Attention should be paid to their concerns. Remembering the rapid rate of physical changes that confront adolescents makes their preoccupation with their bodies understandable.

Characteristics

Adolescence characteristically is an extremely healthy time of life. In general, adolescents do not die off from the kinds of things that strike the rest of us, such as heart disease. The major causes of adolescent deaths are accidents, suicide, and homicide. Due to this healthiness, adults tend to assume that adolescents with problems are not really sick and thus do not give their complaints the attention they deserve. Furthermore, teens themselves may not perceive their health risk behaviors as dangerous or may be unable to articulate concerns that they may have. Another characteristic of adolescence is a truly tremendous need to conform to their peers. There is the need to dress alike, wear the same hairstyle, listen to the same music, and even think alike. A perpetual concern of the adolescent is that he or she is different. Although the sequence of physical development is the same, there is still variation in the age of onset and the rate of development. This can be a big concern for adolescents, whether the teenager is ahead, behind, or just on the norm. Worry about being different is a particular concern for the adolescent who may want or need professional help. The adolescent will not go unless it is "peer acceptable." Kids often stay away from care-givers out of fear. A big fear is that if they go, sure enough something really wrong will be found. This, to their minds, would officially certify them as different. They cannot tolerate that. They also fear that counselors will not respect confidentiality and will serve as parent surrogates rather than working with the teen in a true counselor-client relationship.

Also characteristic of adolescence is wildly fluctuating behavior. It frequently alternates between wild, agitated periods and times of quiescence. A flurry of even psychotic-type thinking is not uncommon. This does not mean that adolescents are psychotic for a time and then get over it. There are just some periods when their thinking really only makes sense to themselves and possibly to their friends. For example, if not selected for the play cast, he may be sure that he "proves" he will be a failure his entire life. If she is denied the use of the family car on Friday, she may overreact. With a perfectly straight face, she may accuse her parents of never letting her have the car, even as she stands there with the car keys ready to drive off.

Adolescence is very much a time of two steps forward and one step back, with an occasional jog to one side or the other. Despite the ups and downs, it is usually a continuing, if uneven, upward trip to maturity.

Another point of importance: in early adolescence, girls are developmentally ahead of boys. At the onset of puberty, girls are physically about 2 years ahead. This makes a difference in social functioning because social development takes place in tandem with physical development. This can cause problems in social interactions for boys and girls of the same age. Their ideas of what makes a good party or what is appropriate behavior may differ considerably. The girls may consider their male peers "total dweebs." The boys, aware of the girls' assessments, may be shaken up, while the girls feel dislocated, too. With the uneven development of boys and girls during early adolescence, girls may be a year ahead of boys. There is a catching-up period later, but in dealing with younger adolescents, keep this disparity in mind.

Developmental tasks   When does adolescence end? There are fairly clear-cut signs that mark the beginnings of the process. There is more to adolescence than just physical maturation. Defining the end can lead to philosophical discussions of "maturity." Doesn't everyone know a 45-year-old or 65-year-old "adolescent"? There is more to assigning an end point than just considering a numerical age.

One way of thinking about the adolescent period is to assign to it four tasks. From this point of view, once the tasks have been reasonably accomplished, the person is launched into adulthood. These tasks are not tackled in any neat order or sequence. It is not like the consistent pattern of physical development. They are more like four interwoven themes, the dominant issues of adolescence.

The first task of adolescence is acceptance of the *biological role*. This means acquiring some degree of comfort with one's identity as either male or female. It is an intellectual effort that has nothing to do with sexuality or experimentation with sexuality.

The second task is the struggle to become comfortable with one's *sexuality*. This does not mean struggling with the question of "how to make out at the drive in!" It is the much more important question: "Who am I as a sexual person and how do I get along with those to whom I am actually or potentially sexually attracted?" Before adolescence, children are far more casual with each other. With adolescence, those days are over. Simply to walk by someone that one could be sexually attracted to and say "Hi" without blushing, giggling, or throwing up can be a problem. To become a person capable of sexual and emotional intimacy—able to carry on all manner of social and eventually sexual activities with another person—does not come easily. It is fraught with insecurity and considerable self-consciousness. If you force yourself to remember your own adolescence, some memories of awkwardness and uncertainty come to the fore. Thus there is the adolescent who does not ask for a date because of the anticipated no. Being dateless is much more tolerable than hearing a no.

The third task is the choice of an *occupational identity*. It becomes important to find an answer to "What am I going to do (be)?" There are usually several false starts to this one. Think of the 5-year-old who wants to be a fireman. He probably never will be, but he gets a lot of mileage for awhile just thinking he is. It is not so different for adolescents. It is not helpful to pooh-pooh the first ideas they come up with. Nor is handing over an inheritance and saying "Go ahead" recommended. They need some time to work it out in their heads. A fair amount of indecision, plus some real "crazy" ideas, are to be expected.

The fourth task is the *struggle toward independence*. This is a real conflict. There is the internal push to break away from home and parents and, at the same time, the desire to remain comfortably cared for. The conflict shows up in rebellion, because there are not many ways to feel independent when living at home, being fed, checked on, prodded, and examined by parents. Rebellion of some type is common during this period, especially among male adolescents. It need not be over major issues, and may be relatively invisible and untraumatic for both adolescent and parent, if the parents can avoid being drawn into power struggles.

Rebellion Rebellion can be seen in such things as manner of dress and appearance. It is usually the opposite of what the parents' generation accepts. Little ways of testing out parents crop up in being late from a date, buying something without permission, or arguing with parents over just about anything. The kids are aware of their dependence, and they don't like it. There is even some shame over being in such a position. It is important that parents recognize the rebellion and respond to it. In the era of "Be friends with your kids," some well-meaning parents accepted any behavior from their kids. For example, if the kids, for the sake of rebellion, brought home some grass to smoke, their parents might just light up, too. Often the kids will do whatever they can just to get their parents angry. They are often reminded by others of how much they look or act like their father or mother, and they don't want that. Adolescents want to be themselves. They do not want to be carbon copies of their parents, whom they probably don't like much at the moment. Going out and drinking with the gang, doing something weird to their hair that Mom and Dad will hate, not cleaning their rooms, or helping the neighbors but not their parents are all fairly common ways of testing out and attempting to assert independence.

Destructive rebellion can occur when the parents either do not recognize the rebellion or do not respond to it. It can take many forms, such as running out of the house after an argument and driving off at 80 or 90 miles per hour, getting really drunk, running away, or, for girls, getting pregnant despite frequent warnings from their perhaps over-restrictive parents to avoid all sexual activities.

There are many roadblocks to completion of these four basic tasks. One results from a social paradox. Adolescents are physically ready for adult roles long before our society allows it. Studies of other societies and cultures point this out. In some societies adolescence doesn't cover a decade or more. Young people leave school at earlier ages to go to work or into apprenticeships, for example. Our society dictates instead that people stay in an adolescent position for a frightfully long time: junior high school, senior high school, college, graduate school. Another social paradox comes from the mixed messages. On the one hand, it's "Be heterosexual, get a date, "Get a job," "Be grown up." One the other, it's "Be back by 1 AM," "Save the money for college," "Don't argue with me." The confusion of "Grow up, but stay under my control" can introduce tensions. Another roadblock can be posed by alcohol and drug use. Of all groups, adolescents are those most likely to be involved with drugs other than alcohol. In considering adolescents, it is imperative to think broadly, in terms of substance use and abuse, or chemical dependency, not just in terms of alcohol and alcoholism.

This has been a very brief overview of adolescence. There are many excellent books on the subject should you want a more in-depth study. For our purposes here, it will suffice as a context in which to consider alcohol and other drug use.

Alcohol and other drug use

Alcohol and other drug use is common in adolescence. According to the annual survey of adolescent alcohol and other drug use, in 1998, by 8th grade, 52.5% of teenagers had tried alcohol, and 24.8% reported having been drunk. By the 12th grade, the percentage who had ever used alcohol increased to 81.4%, and 62.4% report having been drunk. Also 29% report having used an illicit drug by grade, with that number rising to 54% by 12th grade. See Table 10.1

In looking at trends, while illicit drug use had been increasing during the 1990s, the numbers showed a decline in 1998. The majority of this decrease is due to a reduction in marijuana use. Similarly, stimulant use has been declining since 1998. Also, in 1998, for the very first time, there was a drop in alcohol use for all three grades, both in terms of drinking in the past year or during the past 30 days. There was a similar though small reduction in reports of drunkenness during the preceding year. This survey, *Monitoring the Future,* also asks questions about kids' notion of the risks that accompany different drug use, as well as their sense of how easy it is to get either alcohol or other drugs, and their degree of disapproval of use. Consistently the level of use of a substance is related to the perceptions of riskiness and the individual's level of disapproval. As perceptions of risk go down, use goes up; similarly, as the level of disapproval goes down, use increases.

Despite widespread alcohol use, adolescents tend to be uninformed about the effects of alcohol as a drug. Short on facts, adolescents tend

TABLE 10.1 ALCOHOL AND OTHER DRUG USE BY EIGHTH, TENTH, AND TWELFTH GRADERS, 1998

Type of Substance	Lifetime use (%)			Use in past 30 days (%)		
	8th grade	10th grade	12th grade	8th grade	10th grade	12th grade
Alcohol	52.5	69.8	81.4	23.0	38.8	52.0
Cigarettes	45.7	57.7	65.3	19.1	27.6	35.1
Smokeless tobacco	15.0	22.7	26.2	4.8	7.5	8.8
Any illicit drugs	29.0	44.9	54.1	12.1	21.5	25.6
Any illicit drug other than marijuana	16.9	23.6	29.4	5.5	8.6	10.7
Any illicit drug including inhalants	37.8	49.3	56.1	14.9	22.5	26.6
Marijuana	22.2	39.6	49.1	9.7	18.7	22.8
Inhalants	20.5	28.3	15.2	4.8	2.9	2.3
Hallucinogens	4.9	9.8	14.1	1.4	3.2	3.8
Cocaine	4.6	7.2	9.3	1.4	2.1	2.4
Crack	3.2	3.9	4.4	0.9	1.1	1.0
Heroin	2.3	2.3	2.0	0.6	0.7	0.5
Stimulants	11.3	16.0	16.4	3.3	5.1	4.6
Tranquilizers	4.6	7.8	8.5	1.2	2.2	2.4
Steroids	2.3	2.0	2.7	0.5	0.6	1.1

From: *Monitoring the Future*, 1998 data. From press release data, December 18, 1998. Lloyd Johnston, principle investigator, The University of Michigan, Ann Arbor MI.

more than adults to rely on myths. For example, beer, the overwhelming favorite beverage, is thought to be less intoxicating than distilled spirits. One study showed that 42% thought 5 to 7 cans of beer could be drunk in 2 hours without risk of intoxication. Seventy percent believed cold showers could sober someone up, and 62% thought coffee would do it. Also, adolescents minimize the consequences of drinking. Only 8% thought their driving ability would be "much worse" under the influence. One part of adolescent thinking is the idea that they are invulnerable, that nothing can or will hurt them. As a result adolescents do not consider their being in an accident a real possibility, much less one that might result in serious injury or death.

Adolescents use alcohol in many different ways, some of which are a normal part of the whole process. The "try it on" thread runs throughout adolescence. Alcohol is just one of the things to be tried. With drinking being a massive part of adult society, it is natural that the adolescent struggling toward adulthood will try it. Drinking is also attractive for either rebellious or risk-taking behavior. In addition, it can also serve to anesthetize the pain of adolescents who are isolated or subject to abuse by family or peers.

Adolescent alcohol and drug problems

Not unexpectedly, there are also problems accompanying adolescent drinking and drug use. To cite just a few of the statistics from the ever-growing pile:

- 31% of high school seniors report having had 5 or more drinks in a row during a 2-week period.
- 13% of 12th graders report daily smoking of a half a pack of cigarettes or more.
- The three leading causes of death among adolescents—unintentional injuries, homicide, and suicide—as well as unsafe sexual behavior are closely yoked to alcohol use.
- A study of adolescents' emergency room visits found that 40% had a positive blood alcohol level.
- By the age of 17 approximately 12% of adolescents can be categorized as at risk for substance abuse.

One way to understand the high incidence of problems with substance abuse in adolescence is in terms of the adolescent developmental tasks cited earlier. The first task mentioned was the acceptance of one's biological role. For women the onset of their menstrual cycle provides clear biological evidence of their transition into adulthood. For males the transition may be more difficult. But for both in contemporary America the question of how to know you are an adult is often difficult. For many adolescents, drinking serves as a rite of passage. Not only is it an adult activity, it is also one way to be "one of the crowd." Drinking can provide entry to a group of peers. Even as an adult, one is often encouraged to drink and given messages that not to drink is to be antisocial. For adolescents with their intolerance of differences and their increased vulnerability to following along with peers' behavior, not drinking at a party where others are drinking may be even harder than for adults.

The second developmental task mentioned was the struggle to become comfortable with one's sexuality. This can be threatening to many adolescents. Alcohol can be used to avoid intimacy or to seek intimacy without responsibility. It can also help avoid dealing with concerns or confusion related to sexual orientation. "I wasn't myself last night, I was really plastered" can be said by either boys or girls to disavow what happened the night before. The same is true in the sexual realm, as a means of experimenting without taking responsibility. In our society, being drunk has long provided a "way out." Often people are not held accountable for actions that occur when they are drunk. Thus getting drunk can often help adolescents express these increasingly powerful impulses, without really taking direct responsibility for their behavior. This can include not taking proper precautions, as the rising number of AIDS cases among this group and the growing number of teenage pregnancies can testify. Very risky behavior, indeed.

Part of the task of attaining independence is learning to set limits for themselves, to develop self-control. For some adolescents, this is more difficult than for others. It is particularly difficult about issues like drinking where societal messages and alcohol advertising suggest that "having more than one" is appropriate adult behavior. In the process of learning self-control, adolescents react negatively to adults setting limits. If parents are too aggressive in forbidding alcohol use, it may backfire. Further confusing matters is the fact that adolescent development is characterized by changes in patterns of thinking. Before the age of 12 to 13 years, adolescents generally adhere to concrete rules for behavior. From ages 13 to 15 years, adolescents are likely to question the justification of set rules. They feel that conventions are arbitrary, so rules supporting them are invalid. By the age of 16, most of them begin to realize that some rules are necessary.

Another important task mentioned earlier is the development of a sense of identity. Part of the task of gaining an independent identity involves experimentation in all realms. Adolescents may use alcohol for help in experimenting with different roles and identities. Closely connected to this experimentation is risk taking. Some of this risk taking involves physical danger. Adolescents are said to have a "sense of invulnerability." Unfortunately, alcohol can further increase this sense of invulnerability and lead to risk taking with dangerous consequences. It is not surprising, as mentioned earlier, that accidents are the leading cause of death for adolescents and that alcohol use and abuse is heavily implicated in fatal accidents from all causes.

As these adolescent developmental tasks are accomplished, the number of problem drinkers decreases. But for a significant proportion of problem drinkers, these problems will persist and grow worse. For far too many, the problem drinking may end in death or disability.

Signs of alcohol/substance use problems　Often the temptation is to disregard adolescent alcohol or drug problems as "just a stage," or a normal feature of adolescence. The criteria for diagnosing alcohol abuse in adolescents are the same as those for adults. It involves a pattern of pathological use and impairments in major life areas. Common signs of a possible substance use problem are listed below. These signs are not exclusively linked to substance use. Thus, if an evaluation rules out substance use, further exploration is required to identify and address the behaviors of concern.

School activities
- unexplained drop in grades
- unexplained drop in school performance
- irregular school attendance

Health indicators
- accidents
- frequent "flu" episodes, chronic cough, chest pains, "allergy symptoms"
- feelings of loneliness or depression
- being unable to fight off common infections, fatigue, loss of energy
- short-term memory impairment
- more than "the normal" adolescent mood changes, irritability, anger

Family relationships
- decreased interest in school or family social activities, sports, and hobbies
- not bringing friends home
- not returning home after school
- unaccounted-for personal time
- failure to provide specific answers to questions about activities
- unexplained disappearance of possessions in the home
- verbal (or physical) mistreatment of younger siblings

Relationships with friends
- dropping old friends
- new group of friends
- attending parties where parents or adults are not present
- strange phone calls

Personal issues
- increased money or poor justification of how money was spent
- change in personal priorities
- wearing "druggie" clothing or jewelry
- possession of "drug" materials
- desire to be secretive or isolated

Indicators of a significant problem would include any "covering up" or lying about drug and alcohol use or about activities, losing time from school because of alcohol or drug use, being hospitalized or arrested because of drinking or drug-related behavior or truancy, plus alcohol or drug use themselves. Alcohol or drug use at school generally indicates heavy use. One should be particularly alert to these signs and symptoms in children of alcoholics, who have a genetic predisposition and a parent for whom alcohol is a loaded issue.

The progression of a substance use problem in adolescents is similar to the progression seen in adults and is described in Chapter 6. Table 10.2 summarizes the key features.

General considerations in working with adolescents In working with an adolescent, it is wise to avoid obvious authority symbols, such as white laboratory coats, framed diplomas dripping off the walls, and a remote clinical attitude. Adolescents are probably already having some degree of difficulty with authority figures anyway, and they don't need you added to that list. Being somewhat informal in dress and setting can remove one barrier. On the other hand, spiked hair, playing CDs, and sitting on a floor cushion sucking on a "roach" when they arrive won't go down very well either. They want you to know about those things, but not be into them; unless, of course, you really are (even then, leave the

TABLE 10.2 NATURAL HISTORY OF SUBSTANCE USE PROBLEMS: SIGNS AND SYMPTOMS OF ADOLESCENT SUBSTANCE USE

Stage	Pattern of use	School	Peers	Family	Self
Experimentation Regular use	Occasional	◄─────────────────── Few effects ───────────────────►			
(Seeking the mood swing)	Weekends Occasional weekdays	Grades may become erratic	Hanging around drug-using crowd	Some increase in family conflict	Changes in dress or choice of music, increased mood swings
Abuse					
(Preoccupation with use)	Occasional weekdays, e.g., before or after school	Decreased school performance	Avoids straight friends	Verbal and physical fights	Depression, stealing, fabrication, and misperception of events
Dependence					
(Use to feel normal or as a requisite for functioning)	Daily, instead of usual activities	May drop out or be expelled	Alienation from original friends; antisocial behavior, sexual acting out	Increased shame and conflict	Guilt, remorse, depression, anger, paranoia, physical deterioration

Modified from Kinney J: Alcohol use and its medical consequences. In Alcohol use, abuse, and dependence, Timonium, Md, 1989, Milner-Fenwick.

roach at home). An attempt to fake out the adolescent will fail. They are a hard group to fool, and they place a high premium on honesty. Respect this and honestly be yourself. This means asking for a translation of their vocabulary if you are not familiar with the lingo.

Empathy rather than sympathy is the goal. This is true of all therapeutic relationships. Sympathy is feeling like the other person. Empathy is knowing how the person feels but not feeling like he or she does at the moment. For instance, it is simply not helpful to be depressed along with the person.

In general, three types of therapy are done with adolescents. One involves *manipulation of the environment*. This can include arranging for the father to spend more time with his child, getting the kid who hates Shakespeare into a different school program, or organizing a temporary placement for the child whose parents are nonsupportive at the time. These can be very valuable interventions.

Standard insight therapy—psychologically or psychiatrically oriented therapy—is not often used. Not many adolescents are ready for, or even could benefit from, this kind of therapy. The ones who can benefit from it tend to be bright, advantaged young people, who seem more capable and older than their peers or their chronological age would suggest.

The most commonly productive therapy is what could be termed a *relational approach*. This requires time for you and the adolescent to become well acquainted and for the adolescent to feel comfortable with you. The counselor is a neutral person, available to the adolescent in a very different way than are parents or peers. For many adolescents AA, particularly a young persons group, can be a helpful way to be involved in a relational therapy, and also to have successful adult role models for sobriety.

The issue of confidentiality always comes up. It can be a mistake to guarantee that "nothing you say will ever leave this room." The therapist does have the responsibility for others as well as the adolescent client. Given blanket protection, what happens when the kid announces he plans to rob the local deli or another says she plans to drive the family car off the road at the first opportunity? A different approach was suggested by the late Dr. Hugh MacNamee. His practice was to tell whomever he saw that though most of what they said would be held in confidence, if they told him anything that scared him about what they might do, that would be harmful to themselves or others, he was going to blow the whistle. He made it clear he would not do so without telling them; nonetheless, he would do it. In his experience, adolescents accept this, maybe even with relief. It may help to know that someone else is going to exert some control, especially if adolescents are none too sure about their own inner controls at the moment.

In a similar vein, Dr. MacNamee suggested keeping the adolescent posted on any contacts you have with others about him or her. If a parent calls, start off the next session by informing the adolescent, "Hey, your Dad called me, and he wanted. . . ." If a letter needs to be written to a school, probation officer, or someone else, share what you are writing with the adolescent. The chances are fairly good his or her fantasy about what you might say is worse than anything you would actually say, no matter what the problem. Because trust is such an issue with adolescents, it is important that you be willing to say to them what you would say about them.

Although the aforementioned is a good general approach to the issue of confidentiality, you may need to be aware of other complicating factors. In particular, we refer to the legal issues of a child's right to care versus parental rights to be informed. There may be circumstances in which an adolescent has a legal right to be seen and treated without parental knowledge or consent. In any case, the ground rules you are following must be clear to the adolescent client.

Alcohol/drug assessment   Once the issue of confidentiality has been cleared up, it is important to take a family history. Ask about alcohol or drug problems, prescription or nonprescription. Include the grandparents, uncles, aunts, brothers and sisters, cousins, as well as the parents. Other important parts of the history include asking the adolescent how he spends his time. Ask him to describe a typical day. Ask what he and his friends do Saturday night. Ask about his peer group, about their ages, activities, and drug and alcohol use. Ask how they are seen and described by other groups in the high school, and then ask about his use of drugs and alcohol. Ask about parental relationships. Ask about sleep, appetite, depression, and the possibility of physical or sexual abuse. Also be able to discuss issues of sexuality and sexual orientation. It is also important to determine the adolescent's risk for HIV infection.

The fact that adolescent alcohol abuse can go on for as long as 6 years without being diagnosed is a tribute to the ability of these adolescents to hide their problems, to the ability of parents to avoid recognizing problems in their children, to the tendency of health providers not to address substance abuse and other sensitive issues, and to the ability of school systems to ignore or expel problem children. It is not unusual for parents to be actively protecting, rescuing, and taking care of a substance-abusing adolescent without realizing that this supports and prolongs the abuse. They make good on forged checks. They hire lawyers or pay to have legal charges dropped. They go to bat for them at school or blame school authorities for the problems. In our experience, parents must stop protecting these children and seek help for them instead.

When asking about drug and alcohol use, begin by asking about the first time they were drunk, how much they drink now, how often, if they have ever tried to stop or cut down. Ask about blackouts, legal problems, and school problems. Ask about pot, crack, cocaine, acid, stimulants. Increasingly, younger adolescents are beginning their experimentation with intoxication by using inhalants which are easily available in any supermarket or drug store. Finally, don't assume that an adolescent is providing a wholly accurate history about drug and alcohol use. Denial is a central characteristic of adolescent alcohol or drug abuse. It is important to get information from parents and teachers whenever you are concerned about adolescent alcohol or drug problems.

Getting adolescents into treatment   Although occasionally adolescents will spontaneously request treatment, more often they come to treatment under some duress. In working with them, it is important to make it clear that your task is to help them and that you are not an agent of their parents, the law, or the school system. At the same time, part of helping them may involve an intervention, which entails confrontation and, as was mentioned earlier, total confidentiality cannot be assured.

In dealing with adolescents, the importance of working with the family cannot be overemphasized. The parents need to deal with their child's alcohol/substance abuse. And they must consider their own behaviors, which may have protected, covered up, excused, or even in part created the problem. When it is clear that there is a significant problem and all efforts to involve the adolescent in treatment have failed, the parents may need to seek legal help. Most states allow for parents to request state assistance if they feel they cannot enforce safe limits for their child. Although this is a very drastic and difficult step to take, it can be important when alcohol-abusing adolescents are acting in ways that endanger their lives. Probation can also be a way of mandating treatment for adolescents, but again this only works if the parents can stop protecting the adolescent from the consequences of his behavior.

Adolescent alcohol/substance abuse treatment   Once it has been determined that an adolescent needs treatment and the adolescent has agreed to treatment, it is important to proceed in a careful way. Because medical and psychiatric complications frequently accompany adolescent substance abuse, a thorough medical and psychiatric evaluation should precede or be an early part of any treatment plan. Treatment options include outpatient, residential, or hospital-based care and can involve individual, group, and family counseling, plus self-help groups such as AA or NA (Narcotics Anonymous). Halfway houses may also be helpful for adolescents who are not ready to return home from a hospital-based program but who no longer need the structure of a hospital.

There are very good alcohol/drug treatment programs for adolescents. There are those, on the other hand, that might most kindly be described as "nontraditional" or those less concerned with therapeutics than with turning a profit. Don't forget the standard questions before referring an adolescent to any program. 'Does the program work?' 'Is the program drug free?' 'Is there a strong family component?' 'Is there a strong therapeutic component?' 'Is there a strong educational component?' 'Is the adolescent involved in treatment planning?' 'Is there a peer component?' 'Are there provisions for aftercare?' 'What are the costs and risks of treatment, including both financial cost and time cost?' 'What beliefs are instilled?' 'What are the staff's credentials, including training, experience, licensure, and certification?' 'Is there a full range of services, including pediatric, psychiatric, educational, psychological, and alcohol counselors?' 'Is there involvement with AA?' 'How does the program feel when you visit it?' 'Is the program accredited?' 'If so, by whom?'

When referring an adolescent for treatment, it is important to remember that alcoholism and drug addiction are chronic diseases. Treatment does not end with discharge. The conceptual model to use is not that of an acute illness like appendicitis, where the offending tissue can be surgically removed and the problem will never recur. It is rather a chronic illness like asthma or arthritis, where ongoing monitoring is always essential and whereas some cases are mild and require only outpatient treatment, others may require hospitalization.

Dual diagnosis   Other psychiatric disorders are not uncommon among adolescents with alcohol or drug use problems. Several studies of adolescents in treatment found that over 80% had another psychiatric disorder. This is not to suggest that this holds for all adolescents with substance use problems. Possibly the presence of other psychiatric disorders causes more disruptions and thus increases the likelihood of these teens entering treatment. Among female adolescents with alcohol problems, there is a greater incidence of other substance abuse disorders, as well as depression. There is also a higher incidence of post-traumatic stress disorder. For these girls there is often a history of childhood abuse. Attention deficit/hyperactivity disorder doubles the risk of alcohol or drug dependency in adolescents and also increases the likelihood of relapse following treatment.

Given the increasing reliance on medications in the treatment of psychiatric disorders in general, it is not surprising that they are being used with adolescents as well and for those with dual diagnoses. However, to date there are no specific studies of efficacy of these medications in teenage populations. The exception is the use of ritalin, a stimulant, for treatment of attention deficit/hyperactivity disorder (AD/HD). The down side with Ritalin is that stimulants can be abused. The other drugs sometimes used with AD/HD, the tricyclic antidepressants and certain blood pressure medications, also pose a risk if the adolescent drinks. Disulfiram has been used with adolescents, but with some reluctance. Given adolescents' greater impulsivity, clinicians are concerned about the greater risk of drinking and the associated disulfiram reaction.

Adolescents and AA   For the adolescent with an alcohol/substance abuse problem, how might AA be of use? The first thought might be that the adolescent would never identify with a group of predominantly 35- to 55-year-olds. In many areas, that stereotype of the AA group does not necessarily hold true; there are now in some locales what are called "young people's groups." There the average age is the low- to mid-20s. Even if there are no young people's groups in your vicinity, age need not be a barrier to an adolescent's affiliating with AA. On the contrary, several features of AA might attract and intrigue the adolescent. It is a group of adults who will definitely not preach at him. Furthermore, given the collective life experiences within AA, the members are not likely to be shocked, outraged, or, for that matter, impressed by any of the adolescent's behavior. The members will generally treat the adolescent as an adult, presumably capable of making responsible choices, although cognizant that to do so isn't easy for anyone. There is within AA a ready assortment of potential surrogate parents, aunts, uncles, and grandparents. The intergenerational contact, possibly not available elsewhere to the adolescent, can be a plus. Also, AA remains sufficiently "unacceptable" so as not to be automatically written off by the adolescent wary of traditional, staid, "establishment," and "out-of-it" adult groups. Because being alcoholic or a drug abuser is still a stigmatized condition, the parents may be more uncomfortable than their children about AA attendance for adolescents. The therapist may need to help parents with this. In making a referral, the same guidelines outlined in the section on AA would apply. The adolescent is full of surprises, and his willingness to attend AA may well be another.

Adolescents and AIDS   A growing concern is the rapid increase of AIDS among young adults. This inevitably means that HIV was contracted during adolescence. Any discussion of adolescents and AIDS requires thinking about the role of the other "A"—alcohol. Alcohol is definitely involved in this equation for two reasons. First, there's the well-known disinhibiting effect of alcohol and the impaired judgment that is a part of that. Sexual encounters are more likely when drinking. It is less likely that condoms will be used, increasing the risk of a variety of sexually transmitted diseases in addition to HIV. Sexual encounters are also more likely to be "casual," involving partners with little history and no ongoing relationship. With the advent of AIDS the important message to be conveyed is that there is no longer, if there ever was, such a thing as "casual" sex. The stakes are higher, and the costs are no longer simply psychological wounds.

The second important factor which has considerable significance in thinking about adolescents, alcohol, and AIDS goes beyond simply altered judgment. It appears that one of the effects of alcohol, in anyone, not just in those who are alcohol dependent or who drink heavily, is to interfere temporarily with the immune system. Possibly for a day or two alcohol has seemingly "turned down the volume." Thus, the body's usually available means of fighting off infections and viruses are not up to par. This allows infections to gain a foothold, which may otherwise not have happened.

Adolescent treatment and prevention programs need also to be involved in AIDS education. Some treatment programs, beyond including an educational component, also discuss the issue of HIV testing; there are several who have adopted this as a routine part of their procedures.

Beyond the fact that it really *does* matter if one is or is not HIV positive, these activities also serve to reinforce the point that HIV/AIDS is a real issue. It isn't something that can't or wouldn't touch an adolescent's life. These activities emphasize that it is the choices that adolescents make or don't make that have an impact on them.

Managed care   The advent of managed care has created problems in arranging care for adolescent patients. There has been an increase in the availability of day treatment options. For some adolescents, more structure and a protected environment is required to establish sobriety. Many managed care plans are very reluctant to approve residential care except for very limited periods. When adolescents fail in outpatient or day treatment settings, too often the adolescent is blamed for being un-motivated, rather than the treatment setting being recognized as unable to provide the level of care needed.

Prevention

One important task for anyone working with adolescents is to be aware of the potential problems that virtually every adolescent will encounter with respect to alcohol and drugs. Even if adolescents are not currently into drugs or alcohol, anticipatory discussion can be very helpful. This means speaking with them about how they can handle the situation when it inevitably does arise. Contacts with adolescents, for whatever reason, can be used. This might mean the school counselor who meets with the adolescent to discuss next year's course offerings. Or it may be the oc-casion of the mandatory physical examination required before participa-tion in high school athletics. For the adolescent who is having a problem of some kind, recording an alcohol/drug history is imperative.

In many communities, there are also efforts underway through parent groups and groups of adolescents to support the development of healthy peer values and norms about alcohol/drug use. It is almost impossible to speak of adolescent alcohol or other drug use without hearing the phrase "peer pressure." This for many conjures up the image of someone sidling up to a kid and saying, "want to try some beer?" or "How 'bout a joint?" The most potent form of peer pressure, however, is what adoles-cents *think* everyone else is doing. Teens are apt to overestimate the numbers of their peers who drink by up to 50%. Friends do have consid-erable influence; however, parents and adults do as well. The expecta-tions of adults in the community have a big impact.

In thinking about prevention, one is not only trying to prevent use and abuse. The other goal is to prepare adolescents to deal with possible al-cohol or other drug use emergencies. In fact, it may well fall to the kid who isn't drinking to be the one to do what needs to be done in such circumstances. This doesn't just mean figuring out alternative trans-portation. It is also important that they know how to respond to possible overdose, e.g., knowing the dangers of letting a really drunk kid "just sleep it off." Adolescents need to learn that when they are in the presence of drinking, they do need to be their "brother's—and sister's—keeper."

For some adults, there may be a tendency to "finally" take a stand regarding their children's drinking. Unfortunately, this often occurs after a lengthy period of vacillating behavior. Finally, something dramatic is done, which may not be well thought out. For example, several years ago there was a growing awareness and concern about alcohol use by our local high school students. There were the usual incidents for the age group—unchaperoned parties with drinking, parents allowing alcohol to be served in their homes, drinking and driving, bringing alcohol to school dances, or coming to dances after drinking. That year the soccer team had an outstanding season and made it to the play-offs for the state championship. A parent put a bottle of champagne on the bus. The team subsequently won. In the course of the celebrating, someone remembered the champagne on the bus. The players proceeded to pour it over one another. This led to a public uproar. In the aftermath, the team members refused to tell who got the champagne from the bus. Interestingly, the parent who provided the champagne never confessed either. As a result, the next year's team was not allowed to participate in any postseason games, regardless of their playing record. Beyond the questions of delaying punishment for such an extended period or penalizing players who may not have even been present, there was a further irony. Not only were the students following a well-established tradition witnessed at the conclusion of every professional championship series, but this incident may have represented the most appropriate, nondestructive use of alcohol ever displayed in the school. But, this was the time to "put the foot down." Although an extreme example, this points out the capacity to undermine one's efforts if action is taken precipitously. (See the box on page 377 for more information.)

Minority youth

Much of what has been said about the presentation and treatment of substance abuse does not capture the problems of many urban minority youth. Regardless of whether these youths are African American, Hispanic, or Native American, they are far more likely to live in substandard housing, be in families with fewer economic resources, have less access to medical care, attend substandard schools, or be dropouts. If they live in urban areas, they are more likely than their white peers to live in areas in which drug use is prevalent and accompanied by violence in the community.

COLLEGE STUDENTS

Patterns of use

Alcohol and drug use on the college campus has received considerable attention over the past decade. A national survey of college students and

SOME THOUGHTS FOR PARENTS — PARENTS DO MAKE A DIFFERENCE

SOME BASIC FACTS

- A major national study found that 4 out of 10 parents think they have little influence over their adolescent's decision to use or not use drugs. Not true.
- Approximately 45% of parents indicate that it is likely their teens will use illegal drugs.
- Teens and their parents suffer from "collective ignorance."
  High school students overestimate the proportion of students who are weekly drinkers by 100%. Unfortunately, drinking patterns change toward what adolescents mistakenly think is the norm. Parents underestimate use.
- Risk factors for adolescent drinking encompass sociocultural factors, such as alcohol availability; parental behavior and drinking patterns; the influence and drinking habits of siblings and peers; personality traits, particularly those related to impulsiveness and risk taking; and positive beliefs about alcohol's effects.
- Young people reared in home environments that have permissive or casual attitudes about alcohol and who are introduced to alcohol at an earlier age may be more vulnerable to alcohol-related problems in adolescence.
- Access via licensed premises is one of the strongest predictors of drinking and alcohol problems. Among 15- to 18-year-olds, the ability to get served is more significant than peer or parental influences.
- The earlier that children begin alcohol use, the greater the likelihood of later problems.
- Taking on adult roles too early—becoming a teenage parent, or living independently of parents or family, or dropping out of school—is more common among those who used alcohol or other drugs in early adolescence. These situations further increase the likelihood of substance use problems as young adults.
- Be concerned about teenage smoking, as a health risk and as a "gateway drug." Pack-a-day adolescent smokers are 3 times more likely to drink alcohol, 7 times more likely to use smokeless tobacco, and 10 to 30 times more likely to use illicit drugs than are nonsmokers.
  Appreciate how addictive nicotine is. Very quickly smoking moves beyond experimentation. For teens who do smoke, promote smoking cessation programs.

APPRECIATE YOUR INFLUENCE

- Parents are a *more* potent influence than are peers and siblings.
- Parents' influence operates as a natural harm-reduction mechanism that helps protect teenage drinkers from developing alcohol problems.
- Parents influence their children's drinking through family interactions, by modeling and reinforcing standards, and through the attitudes and skills they impart to guide behavior in new situations. Thus, parental influences endure.
- An important predictor of whether a teenage boy will have an alcohol-related driving offence or accident is whether his parents are neutral (rather than negative) about teenage drinking.
- The quality of family relationships and the amount of time adolescents spend with family is a more important influence on adolescents' substance use than is the kind of family in which teenagers are living—whether with both parents, with a parent and step-parent, in a single-parent home, or with nonfamily members.
- Adolescents' perceptions of the parenting style in their home are linked to adolescent substance use. Teens who view their parents as generally authoritative (know what they are talking about), as not permissive (who have standards and clear expectations), and as less authoritarian (not "Do it because I say so") do better in school and are less likely to abuse substances.
- Adolescent drinking behavior is found to be largely unrelated to the socioeconomic circumstances of the family. A supportive family environment is associated with lowered rates of alcohol use.
- Parents' who use illegal drugs have teens at much higher risk of drug use.
- Parents' health habits influence their children.
  This ranges from wearing bike helmets, to using seat belts, to having healthy drinking patterns, or to being a smoker. The younger the child, the more powerful is the parents' model. If you have any concern about your own substance use, act on this. Very few people worry about their alcohol or drug use needlessly.
  If you are a smoker, is now the time to quit?

BE REALISTIC

- Parents who recognize the potential for their adolescent's becoming involved with alcohol are more likely and able to intervene if this occurs. They are also more likely to supervise teen parties given at their home.
- Parents see substance use as motivated by factors with negative connotations, e.g., boredom, rebellion, loneliness, and social pressure. Their children are more likely to cite factors that are more positive, e.g., curiosity, fun, insight/experience.
- Appreciate the complexity of this issue.
  There is no one thing that leads to nor one single thing that prevents substance use.
- At some point every teen is in a situation in which alcohol or other drugs are present. Help your child anticipate how they can respond gracefully, to avoid embarrassing themselves or others.

WHAT YOU CAN DO?

- Use your influence . . . with your children,
  with the parents of your
  children's friends,
  within your community.
- Support policy initiatives to reduce access to alcohol.
- Provide anticipatory guidance.
- Expect others in your child's life—pediatrician, coach, clergyman/rabbi/ priest—to discuss substance use.

- Be sure your son or daughter knows how to respond to an alcohol/drug emergency.
- Help make the *real* norms in your community apparent.
- Become informed.
- Talk to other parents.
- Set an example. Let your children and others know where you stand on drug and alcohol use.
- Never forget that what you do or fail to do can be a matter of life or death.

*There are three major national surveys that gather information on alcohol and drug use patterns. One is conducted by the National Institute on Drug Abuse and is called *Monitoring the Future*. The survey is not restricted to college students but also includes young adults not attending college. There is also the *Core Survey* sparked by the funding of prevention and educational efforts on college campuses by the U.S. Department of Education's Fund for the Improvement of Secondary Education. The intent was to assure that each individual school would have information about the use and extent of alcohol/drug problems, as well as to provide a national snapshot of the situation among this age group. The third national survey is the College Alcohol Study, which uses a sample of 140 four-year institutions and is funded by the Robert Wood Johnson Foundation. It was first conducted in 1993 and was repeated in 1997. The results of these different surveys are generally comparable in terms of defining the nature of alcohol and drug use. However, each has some unique questions that allow one to look at different aspects of substance use and abuse.

young adults, conducted regularly by the National Institute on Drug Abuse, shows that, with a few significant exceptions, college students' substance use patterns are generally similar to those of their age peers who are not attending college. Interestingly, it is with licit drugs—nicotine and alcohol—where one finds the most significant differences. College students are only slightly more likely to be drinkers, but they are far more likely to be heavy drinkers. While there has been a recent upsurge in smoking by college students, they are, nonetheless, far less likely to be smokers than those who are not attending college.

The higher rates of both college student drinking and heavy drinking may, in part, be attributable to two demographic factors. One, alcohol use increases when young adults move away from their parents and begin living independently. And second, drinking declines after marriage for both men and women. Those who do not go to college are more likely to live at home or be married, both of which are associated with less drinking. In combination these two factors may explain some of these differences in drinking patterns.

According to the most recent Core Survey involving over 93,000 students, 84.5% of all students used alcohol in the preceding year; 50% tobacco; 9.5% hallucinogens; and 8.5% amphetamines. Less than one-half of one percent reported having used opiates, inhalants, designer drugs, steroids, or other illicit substances. How often do students drink? Of all students, 15% of college students are nondrinkers. Among those who drink, 17.5% drink infrequently; meaning 1–6 times in the past year. Forty-two percent are moderate drinkers, drinking between once per month and once a week. The remaining 24% are frequent drinkers, drinking 3 or more times per week. How about the amount of alcohol that is consumed? Not surprisingly, there is considerable variation. In the week prior to the Core Survey, 36% of students had not used alcohol;

SURVEYOR WHO doesn't understand The question

In our survey of over 47 college campuses, we found that almost 90% of college students abuse rugs. They spill beer on them. They vomit on them. They never vacuum or steam clean them.

12% had had only one drink; 30% reported from 2 to 10 drinks, and 23% reported 10 or more. Just as is true of the general population, there is no "average" college drinker.

Gender differences   Differences present during high school continue into college. Women drink less per occasion and drink less frequently. The proportion of women who drink approximates that for men, but they are less likely to be heavy drinkers or daily drinkers. Women are also less likely to use illicit substances. Their use of tranquilizers is on par with that of male students. Smoking, however, is different. In 1993 for the first time the NIDA survey found that the proportion of women who were daily smokers exceeded that of men. That trend has continued.

Racial and ethnic differences   The traditionally black schools have significantly lower levels of alcohol and other drug use and a lower rate of problems associated with use. In addition, African Americans drink less than white students, wherever they are attending school.

Trends   There has been a general overall decline in illicit drug use since 1980.

The most dramatic change in substance use is the increase in those who report episodes of heavy drinking. The particular concern is the level of binge drinking, defined as 5 or more drinks per drinking occasion for men and 4 or more for women. The 1997 Core Survey found 45% of students reporting at least one instance of binge drinking in the prior two weeks. Ten percent reported 2 occasions of binge drinking; and 21% reported 3 or more such occasions. This is a virtual 25% increase over the previous 2 years. However, there is one question that needs to be considered. What is the duration of 'the drinking occasion?' If students are attending a party that goes from 9 P.M. to 2 A.M., the five drinks that define a "binge" represent one drink per hour. That is the rate at which alcohol is metabolized; the student party-goer could go home with essentially a zero blood alcohol level. That is a different scenario than the group that heads to a local pub and has 5 beers in an hour and a half.

Interestingly, students' drinking practices did not change substantially following the changes in the legal drinking age that occurred in the 1980s. When the legal drinking age was raised, there was only a transient impact on college students' drinking. There was a decrease in consumption immediately after such legislation was passed, but with time the numbers of students drinking returned to the previous levels.

Problems associated with substance use

Data on the magnitude and nature of problems related to alcohol and substance use on college campuses were very scant for a long time. Colleges individually did not systematically gather data regarding different campus problems that would have allowed them to identify the contributing role of alcohol or drugs. When such data was gathered, it was generally treated as confidential information, and very rarely published in professional literature, in part because of the institution's concerns about its public image. There has always been the concern that if such data were available to the press, the institution might be viewed less favorably by the public, alumni, prospective students and their parents, potential donors, and, for public institutions, the state legislature, which controls funds. The Core Survey and Campus Alcohol Survey have significantly remedied this.

Effects on students   The proportion of students who report various types of problems is summarized in Table 10.3.

Table 10.3 indicates the frequency of various problems. However, an important question is to what extent do these problems reflect particular

TABLE 10.3   STUDENT REPORTS OF CONSEQUENCES OF ALCOHOL OR DRUG USE, 1997

Problem	Experienced the Problem During Past Year (%)			
	any time	1–2 times	3–5 times	6 or more time
Had a hangover	62.0	25.0	15.0	22.0
Nauseated or vomited	52.0	32.0	12.0	8.0
Had a memory loss	31.0	18.5	6.0	6.4
Been hurt or injured	14.0	10.5	2.0	1.0
Tried unsuccessfully to stop using	6.0	4.0	1.0	1.0
Thought I might have a problem	11.0	6.5	2.0	2.5
Thought about committing suicide	5.0	3.0	1.0	1.0
Tried to commit suicide	1.2	0.9	0.1	0.2
Performed poorly on a test or project	22.0	15.0	5.0	2.0
Missed class	32.5	16.5	8.5	7.5
Damaged property	7.5	5.0	1.5	1.0
Argument or fight	30.0	20.0	6.5	4.0
Been taken advantage of sexually	13.0	10.0	1.5	1.5
Have taken advantage of someone sexually	6.0	4.0	1.0	1.0
Done something I later regretted	38.0	24.5	7.5	5.8
Been criticized by someone I know	30.0	18.5	6.5	5.0
Trouble with police or campus authorities	14.0	12.0	2.0	1.0

From Presley CA, Leichliter JS, Meilman PW: *Alcohol and drugs on American college campuses*, Carbondale IL: Core Institute, Southern Illinois University, 1998.

TABLE 10.4   RATE OF ALCOHOL PROBLEMS FOR DIFFERENT
DRINKING PATTERNS

Problem	Binge Drinking Pattern (%)		
	None	Infrequently	Most Frequency
Have a hangover	30	75	90
Do something you regret	14	37	63
Miss a class	8	30	54
Argue with friends	6	21	46
Engage in unplanned sexual activity	8	22	42
Hurt or injured	2	8	22
Trouble with campus or local police	1	4	11
Five or more alcohol-related problems since the start of school year	3	14	47

From Wechsler H, Dowdall GW, Maenner G, Gledhill-Hoyt J, Lee H: Changes in binge
drinking and related problems among American college students between 1993 and 1997:
Results of the Harvard School of Public Health College Alcohol Study, *Journal of American
College Health* 47(2):57–68, 1998.

drinking patterns. The Campus Alcohol Survey summarized in
Table 10.4, clearly shows that the more frequently students report binge
drinking, the more likely they are to encounter these negative consequences.

Academic performance too is related to alcohol consumption. One
thing that distinguishes the D or F student from the A student is that the
poorer student drinks over twice as much per week.

Effects of problems on others   An individual's drinking has an impact on others. It is seen as affecting the quality and nature of the community life at the school or university. Again, the overall level of heavy
drinking within the campus community plays a role, as is evident in
Table 10.5.

Alcohol and drug use also is a factor in campus violence and harassment. The 1997 Core Survey shows that the consumption of alcohol or
drugs is tied to having been a victim of violence or harassment. This is
summarized in Table 10.6.

Did you know that students who get D's drink twice as much as those who get A's?

THe question is "which is the cause and which the effect."

Students at risk for acute problems

There are several groups of students who are at greater risk for acute
problems. Those with less drinking experience are among those with the
greatest risk. Many student health services find that freshmen are those
most likely to be seen for overdoses and acute alcohol poisoning. In the
vicinity of 15 to 20 percent of the typical freshman class describe themselves as being nondrinkers. Most of these nondrinkers become drinkers
during their first year of college. Many problems accompany this transition from nondrinker to drinker, as well as among those making the
transition from infrequent to regular drinker.

TABLE 10.5   SECONDARY EFFECTS OF OTHERS DRINKING

Problem reported by nonbinge drinkers	Percentage of students reporting problems by institutional levels of binge drinking (%)		
	Low Binge Rate	Mid-range Rate	High Rate
Being insulted or humiliated	21	30	34
Had serious argument or quarrel	13	18	20
Pushed, hit, or assaulted	7	10	13
Had property destroyed	6	13	15
Had to care for drunken student	31	47	54
Studying or sleep interrupted	42	64	68
Unwanted sexual advance	15	21	26
Victim of sexual assault or date rape	2	1	2
Experienced at least one of above	62	82	87

From Wechsler H, Davenport A, Dowdall G, Moeykens B, Castillo S: Health and behavioral consequences of binge drinking in college: A national survey of students at 140 campuses, *Journal of the American Medical Association* 272(21):1672–1677, 1994.

TABLE 10.6   HARASSMENT OR VIOLENCE AND ALCOHOL/DRUG CONSUMPTION

Type of incident	% reporting incident	% of reported who had consumed alcohol or drugs before incident
Ethnic or racial harassment	7.0	16.0
Threats of physical violence	11.0	58.0
Actual physical violence	5.0	70.0
Theft involving force or threat of force	2.0	50.0
Forced sexual touching or fondling	6.0	76.0
Unwanted sexual intercourse	4.0	82.0

From Presley CA, Leichliter JS, Meilman PW: *Alcohol and drugs on American college campuses*, Carbondale IL: Core Institute, Southern Illinois University, 1998.

Fraternity and sorority members are another group at special risk for acute problems. The social life of these organizations often revolves around drinking. Members of Greek organizations consistently are found more likely to be drinkers and heavy drinkers than those who do not belong to these organizations. As an associated problem, the folk wisdom has long been that involvement in athletics is associated with lower levels of alcohol use. The assumption was that the student athlete has less free time and that training rules would discourage alcohol use. This is not the case, however. The Core Survey found that those involved in intercollegiate athletics were more likely to be heavy drinkers than were nonathletes. Male athletes who were fraternity members had the highest levels of heavy alcohol use.

A number of years ago a study conducted at the University of Pennsylvania found that the best predictor of alcohol problems during college was the frequency of drinking to intoxication reported by incoming students. Incoming freshmen who were the heaviest drinkers in their class and who had had a prior alcohol-related incident were found to be at much higher risk for future problems. By the end of their sophomore year, these students had more overall visits to the health center, more alcohol-related visits to the health center, and a lower grade point average.

Campus initiatives

Impetus to institutional action   The earliest pressure to address alcohol and substance use problems—going back to the 1970—came from recovering alumni. Many campus alumni magazines have periodically printed first-person accounts by recovering alumni. Typically these individuals do not blame their alma mater for causing their alcohol dependence, but they claim that the campus environment provided fertile ground for its later emergence. Another factor in the 1970s that gave rise to campus initiatives was the availability of federal monies for pilot demonstration educational programs specially targeted to college students.

Much of the attention paid to alcohol problems on college campuses is a manifestation of society's increasing awareness of alcohol and substance use problems. However, some factors have been unique to the campus community. One of these factors has been concern about institutional liability. Although the number of cases that have been litigated has been small, they have received considerable attention. Under its "duty to care," a college is responsible for the well-being of its students. Although the institution's obligation to supervise student conduct may be limited, it cannot claim a total absence of responsibility. An important point is differentiating between student activities that are wholly personal versus those in which the institution is involved through sponsorship and/or its regulation of student organizations. Another domain in which there is potential liability is in the institution's role as proprietor, with the duty to maintain safe premises. This includes rowdiness at football games or parties or protecting others from a student who is known to be abusive. The rise in the legal drinking age served to highlight the issue of institutional liability.

Colleges must also contend with the issues of organized sports such as the National Collegiate Athletic Association (NCAA) mandatory drug testing to establish a student's or team's eligibility. The NCAA mandatory drug testing is, in theory, only one component of a larger substance use educational and prevention effort. However, testing has received the most attention and institutional resources. In addition, federal initiatives to establish drug-free campuses have provided further impetus for institutional action. The drug-free campus legislation has made distribution of federal funds contingent on colleges establishing programs to promote nonuse among students and employees. These mandated programs are to include clearly established disciplinary actions for those who are found to be in violation of the campus policy.

Impediments to campus programs   Although campus efforts to address student alcohol and substance use are no longer foreign to colleges and universities, they are still a recent phenomenon. For example, the American College Health Association (ACHA), which has a reputation for its progressive stance toward health-care issues, only created standards for member institutions in 1987. Although they are not disinterested, many campus administrators have little sophistication with respect to alcohol and substance use problems. Personal biases and impressions here as elsewhere often substitute for information and data.

There are also a number of myths that continue to hold sway. One is the view that heavy drinking is "just a stage"—a diploma, a little more maturity, some adult responsibilities and this developmental period marked by excessive alcohol consumption will pass. One problem with this stance is that given the dangerous situations that can occur, a student may not survive to outgrow this problem. There is sometimes the perspective that substance use problems represent an educational deficit, that students are merely uninformed about alcohol or other drugs. Thus education becomes the primary intervention. This overlooks the fact that students arrive on campuses having already been targets of educational programs in their high schools and communities. Educational efforts are often simplistic and insufficient. This position also overlooks the fact that changes in knowledge do not necessarily lead to changes in behavior.

There are those too who see substance use problems as a case of bad manners, which is often essentially a moral issue. Those with alcohol problems are regarded as having poor attitudes and questionable values. The goal therefore is to have students "shape up." Discussion of "responsible" drinking can reinforce this orientation. The obvious unspoken counterpoint to responsible drinking is irresponsible drinking. Many students may be at substantial risk but do not view themselves nor are they considered by peers as being irresponsible. Students too can mistakenly be viewed as nondrinkers who are thrust into a drinking culture. On the contrary, the majority of students enter college with an established drinking pattern. Not only do they arrive on campus as drinkers, but many qualify as heavy drinkers, having more than five drinks per occasion.

Both students and college faculty and administration can have a distorted view of the actual campus drinking patterns. This is especially true in a climate where there is widespread concern about student drinking. Without some sense of the distribution of drinking practices among students, we may unwittingly adopt a distorted perception of campus alcohol use. Students alcohol patterns tend to mirror those found among adults. Remember that 7% of the adult population consumes 50% of all alcohol; there is the same parallel on the campus. Campuses have fewer abstainers than are found in the general population, but similarly there is a heavy-drinking subgroup. A survey of alcohol use at a New England private college is instructive. The results of a campus survey of drinking patterns were examined by dividing students into four quartiles by levels

of drinking (each quartile represents 25% of the students). The lowest quartile consumed 1.5% of all alcohol, the second quartile consumed 11.5%, and the third quartile consumed 23.0%. The highest drinking quartile consumed 64%, close to two-thirds of all the alcohol. In translating that to a "typical week," 57% of students had had from 0 to 6 drinks. At the other end of the continuum there were the 2.3% of the students who reported having had between 40 to 50 drinks. What this means is that during your average week, less than 3% of students drink as much alcohol as *all* the alcohol consumed by a group representing 57% of their classmates.

One school found that providing accurate information about actual consumption on a large public university campus had a dramatic impact. Following a media campaign to correct student perceptions of the amount of binge drinking, there was a 19% drop in the number of students who perceived binge drinking as the norm (from 70% to 51%.) Also important there was a corresponding reduction in self-reported binge drinking of 9% (from 43% to 34%). This suggests that changing college students' perceptions of drinking norms may change drinking patterns and lower the proportion of students who engage in binge drinking.

Campus policy   An important component of an institution's effort is formulating an alcohol/drug policy. A policy should not read like a penal code. It should set forth a clear, direct statement of the institution's stance toward alcohol and other drug use and the steps and means it intends to use in addressing these. Consider as a parallel, the institutional statements on academic honesty. In such statements, the institution's stance is clear. The standards set for members' behavior are unambiguous. There is not, however, an effort to establish comprehensive policing efforts to assure compliance. However, if violations of the honor code come to the administration's attention, they will be treated without hesitation as serious breeches of the ethos underpinning the community's intellectual life.

A question that commonly comes to light when alcohol policies are discussed is, "Can we enforce the policy?" One response is opting to go no further than creating "all the policy we think we can enforce," which often is little. There has been the perception that more limited statements would reduce liability, which is not the case. No institution can protect itself from suit in our litigious society. The institution is often the deep pocket. The best protection for the institution if litigation occurs is a comprehensive student education and treatment referral program.

A comprehensive program needs to involve all sectors of the campus community. This does not mean that everyone need be a "true believer" in the same fashion. For some, public relations may be a major concern; for others it may be institutional liability; and for others it may be the record on the playing field or not jeopardizing the school's status with the NCAA by coming up with positive urine screens. For others, the quality of life will be a major motivation and for others the academic life. For some, it will be a health concern, and for others it may be personal identification with the issues of children of alcoholics or alcohol dependence. A model program can encompass all of these motives, not deeming some as more legitimate and noble than others. Ultimately, campuswide involvement occurs when alcohol issues are recognized as intruding on each of us.

In defining the need for change, one segment of the community often overlooked when formulating of policy initially is the students. Others formulate policy, make the basic decisions, and put it to the students for some review and comment, which is often unfavorable. Those charged with planning often become bogged down in attempting to determine how to engineer students' acceptance. Students' negative responses may speak as much to their exclusion from the process as to their resistance to the program efforts proposed. We suspect that if students are engaged in the process, they will become informed about the issues, recognize the need for action, perceive any proposed actions as reasonable and intrinsically inevitable in light of the data, and be able to support any actions that are eventually proposed.

Education is a common element of programs. Too often education may be nothing more than slogans, operationally defined by whatever information fits on a lapel button. Education is a continuous process; there isn't *the* event that will do it once and for all. Education efforts need to be tailored to specific groups and employ a variety of different modalities.

There are a limited but significant number of emergency responses that need to be part of everyone's fund of knowledge in a campus community. One of these is how to recognize and respond to an alcohol emergency. This might be considered the alcohol-use equivalent of CPR. On many campuses as prominent as emergency numbers for the campus police or fire department are instructions about what to do and not do in the case of an alcohol overdose. Haverford College includes the following in its student handbook and has the Emergency Guide prominently posted around campus.

ALCOHOL FIRST AID

Severe intoxication and/or alcohol poisoning can be quite dangerous. Here are some basic guidelines to help you size up the scene and decide how to help a drunken friend.

DO

1 Assist the person to a comfortable and safe place.
2 Use a calm, strong voice; be firm.
3 Assess if the person is in a life-threatening situation, and get help if you need it.
4 Lay the person down on their side with knees up so they won't choke if they vomit.

5 Check breathing every 10 minutes. Do not leave them alone!

6 Stay with them if they vomit, to be sure they don't swallow or breathe in the vomitus.

DON'T

1 Don't give cold showers.

2 Don't try to walk them around.

3 Don't provoke a fight by arguing or laughing at someone who is drunk.

4 Don't try to counsel the person—confront the behavior later when they are sober.

5 Don't give anything to eat or drink—coffee and food won't help and the person may choke.

6 Don't permit the person to drive.

7 Don't give any drugs; they will not help sober someone up, and in combination with alcohol they may be lethal.

8 Don't induce vomiting.

EMERGENCY GUIDE

Call Safety and Security if:

- the person cannot be aroused by shaking or shouting.
- the person's breathing is shallow, irregular, or slowed to less than 6–7 breaths per minute.
- the person drank alcohol in combination with any other drugs.
- the person sustained a blow to the head or any injury that caused bleeding.
- the person drank a large quantity within a short period and then collapsed.

> **If You Are Not Sure What to Do, But Think That the Person Needs Help, Call for Medical Advice**

Every campus alcohol program is required to determine the threshold of concern with respect to individuals. Or, phrased another way, what is the institution prepared to overlook? The threshold for concern should be low. Whether an alcohol incident represents an isolated event or a chronic problem will never be outwardly and immediately apparent. The consequences of acute problems can be as disastrous as those connected with alcohol dependence. The accepted stance is always to err on the conservative side.

The environment   Efforts to address alcohol and drug problems are increasingly looking at broader issues than might be included in formal alcohol/drug policies. Chief among these is the social fabric of the campus. This includes considering the nature of social life, and particularly the extent to which this is tied to Greek organizations and heavy

drinking. Are there any/many alternatives to Greek organizations, or is the campus dependent upon fraternities/sororities to provide social opportunities? Tied to this discussion is concern about the campus' ability to foster a community that consists of culturally and ethnically/racially diverse groups.

The campus community is certainly not immune from larger social pressures. More than that, the college community has also been the target of extensive marketing efforts by the brewing industry. The rationale for these efforts is obvious. This segment of the population is among the heaviest beer drinkers. Promotional efforts on the college campus involve a long-range investment by the beer producers. If new drinkers develop brand loyalty, which continues throughout a lifetime, and especially if these drinkers are heavy drinkers, the cost of promotion is easily recouped.

Promotional efforts directed to campuses have included providing kegs of beer as prizes for campus events such as blood drives. Some students are compensated for being campus promotional representatives, distributing advertising paraphernalia such as caps, posters, and napkins with the brewer's logo. Beer companies are major advertisers in campus newspapers and other campus publications. Many associations of college professionals have developed marketing guidelines for promotion of alcoholic beverages and requested that their members not allow alcohol beverage promotion on campus unless the marketers abide by the guidelines.

In terms of general advertising, women and minorities have become targets of special campaigns. Although spokesmen for the liquor and brewing industries describe the advertising as an effort to increase market share, there are those who are suspicious. Recognizing that women and minorities drink less than do white males, it is hard to imagine that special advertisements to these groups is not also intended to increase the total market by recruiting more and heavier drinkers.

Campuses are touched by the larger culture. The opposite is also true. This is particularly true in the sphere of athletics. In 1999, an invitational symposium on intercollegiate athletics was convened to consider steps to mitigate campus alcohol and other drug problems. Representatives were drawn from campuses ranging in size from Division I to Division III. This meeting was prompted by several factors. One was the recognition that college athletes are more prone to alcohol and other drug use and associated negative consequences. But also, college athletics can contribute to a range of problems on campus and surrounding communities. There is the impact of pro-drinking advertising that accompanies sports sponsorships. Other problems result from widespread drinking both before and during home game weekends. This is particularly true at larger institutions with their long-standing traditions such as pregame parties, tailgating, and postgame affairs.

Symposium participants agreed on the importance of reaffirming the educational mission as the top priority of colleges and universities. The school is, foremost, a place for students to learn and to develop ethical values, not an entertainment venue or business enterprise. The gathering adopted the following recommendations:

• The NCAA should reassess its policies for accepting alcohol advertising and sponsorship, because alcohol advertising of college sports sends a mixed message to underage students on campus and in the community. College and university presidents should consider following the lead of the University of North Carolina at Chapel Hill, the University of Minnesota, and the University of Kentucky and similarly divest their sports programs of alcohol advertising.

• Schools should enforce consistent alcohol control measures for public events, e.g., pregame tailgating and in-stadium alcohol availability, to avoid double standards. Schools should further ensure that such pregame events do not compete for student attention with scheduled classes. Control measures should focus on high-risk drinking and related behaviors, as well as on marketing practices that encourage high-risk consumption.

• Schools should work with their surrounding communities in collaborative prevention activities.

• Schools should examine their sports recruiting practices, and the attendant underage drinking by high school visitors during recruit weekends. They should encourage frank communication with recruits (and their parents) about the dangers of hazing, high-risk drinking, and campus policies prior to athletes' arrival on campus.

• Schools should reduce risks posed by postgame celebration and consolation occasions by encouraging coaches and team leaders to host such social gatherings in ways that do not involve alcohol and other drugs.

• Schools should examine the pros and cons of accepting support from the alcohol industry in whatever form, including so-called "responsible drinking" campaigns.

• Schools should be alert to the health status of their student athletes. For some students treatment may be indicated.

Closing thoughts

In conclusion, consider how campus efforts may be evaluated. There are a variety of parameters that can be used to measure program impact, such as levels of dorm damage, the numbers of emergency visits to the local hospital emergency department, the number of cases involving alcohol or other drug use that come before the campus judiciary system, and how each of these is handled. However, there is another dimension. It does not easily lend itself to measurement but is also important. This is captured by the following incident, related by a colleague, an encounter that he learned of only by chance:

At the prodding of concerned friends a fraternity member was seen by a substance use counselor and eventually entered treatment. This set off a wave of referrals from the student's fraternity, one of which turned out to be the current president. This student was treated as an outpatient on campus and became active in AA as part of continuing treatment. Following that year's fraternity rush, the first house meeting with the new pledge class was held. Of those present, each in turn introduced himself. In a parody of introductions at AA meetings, one of the first pledges to introduce himself, after giving his name, added, "and I'm an alcoholic." This was met with tittering and laughter. Each subsequent pledge introduced himself in a similar fashion, concluding with "and I'm an alcoholic." Finally it was the president's turn. He looked around at each person and introduced himself in a quiet but forthright way: "I'm Joe, and I really *am* an alcoholic." Dead silence.

Ultimately, the goal is for change to permeate the community, so that everyday encounters between persons, of the sort that go unnoticed by others, will embody increased awareness and an appreciation of the problems that can accompany alcohol and other drug use. Such moments as the one just described, in this case taking 10 seconds, represent the outcome of many years' work and are among the most eloquent testimonies to a campus's efforts.

THE ELDERLY

Dishonor not the old: we shall all be numbered among them.

APOCRYPHA: BENSIRA 8:6

On one of the earliest television talk shows—that only the elderly will remember—Art Linkletter, the host, was interviewing children. The topics as you will see were a bit different then! The children came up with the following answers to a question he posed: "You can't play with toys anymore . . . the government pays for everything . . . you don't go to work . . . you wrinkle and shrink." The question was, "What does it mean to grow old?" These responses contain many of the stereotypes our society attributes to the elderly. They also show that this negative picture develops from a very early age. There is a stigma about growing old. The notion is that for the elderly there is no play or fun, no money, no usefulness, and no attractiveness.

In considering the elderly, it is important to recognize that we all really are talking about ourselves. It is inevitable: we will all age; we will all become elderly. A participant at a geriatric conference reported being asked by a friend, "Give me the inside scoop, what can I do to keep from getting older?" The response the person received was simple: "Die now!" There is no other way to avoid aging. So, for those not yet elderly, in thinking about the older person, imagine yourself years in the future, because many of the circumstances will probably be the same.

It is now estimated that over 36 million persons are over age 65; this represents a larger percentage of the population than ever before. This is the group arbitrarily defined as the elderly or aged. Each day, 3000 people die and 4000 people reach their sixty-fifth birthdays, so there is a net gain of 1000 in the elderly population. The proportion of the population age 65 and over is the fastest-growing segment of the U.S. population. Between 1900 and 1975, the proportion of the elderly increased sevenfold, while the total population hadn't quite tripled. In 1970 the average age of the population was 28 years. The average age has now reached 35 years. Increased longevity has contributed to this change as has a declining birth rate among younger persons. The post-World War II baby boom generation is now in its forties and fifties, further contributing to the increase in the average age of the population. In the year 2000 it is estimated that the elderly will comprise 12.5% of the total population. Consequently, the problems of the elderly, including alcohol dependence, are become a growing concern for our society.

Stresses of aging

Despite the inevitability of aging and physical problems arising as the years pass, there is an important thing to keep in mind. It has been said many times and in many different ways that you are as young as you want to be. This is only possible, however, if a person has some strengths going for him or her. The best predictor of the future, specifically how someone will handle growing old, is how the individual has handled the previous years. Individuals who have demonstrated flexibility as they have gone through life will adapt best to the inevitable stresses that come with getting older. These are the people who will be able to feel young, regardless of the number of birthdays they have celebrated.

Interestingly, as people get older, they become less similar and more individual. One person commented that as people grow older they become 'more like themselves.' The only thing that remains alike for this group is the problems they face. There is a reason for this. In going through life, people rely most heavily on the coping styles that seem to have served them well previously. With years and years of living, gradually individuals narrow down their responses. What looks, at first glance, like an egocentricity or eccentricity of old age is more likely a lifelong behavior that has become one of the person's exclusive methods for dealing with stress. An example illustrating this point arose in the case of an elderly surgical patient for whom psychiatric consultation was requested. This man had a constant smile. In response to any question or statement by the nurse or doctors, he smiled, which was often felt to be wholly inappropriate. The treatment staff requested help in comprehending the patient's behavior. In the process of the psychiatric consultation, it became quite understandable. Friends, neighbors, and family of the man consistently described him as "good ole Joe, who always had a friendly word and a smile for everyone, the nicest man you'd ever want to meet." Now under the most fearful of situations, with many cognitive processes depleted, he was instinctively using his faithful, basic coping style. Very similarly, the person who goes through life with a pessimistic streak may become angry and sad in old age. People who have been fearful under stress may be timid and withdrawn in old age. On the other hand, people who have been very organized and always reliant on a definite schedule may try to handle everything by making lists in old age. What is true in each case is that the person settles into a style that was present and successful in earlier life.

Major stresses   In dealing with elderly people it is important to keep in mind that the particular stresses that are common to this group differ somewhat from those of younger people. Stresses may arise from social factors, psychological factors, or physical problems. Iatrogenic stresses (harm caused by efforts to heal) can also occur as the helping professions serve (or inadequately serve) elderly people.

Social stresses   Social stresses can be summarized under the phenomenon of the national addiction to youth. Television commercials highlight all types of products that can be used to disguise the process of aging. There is everything from hair colorings to dish detergents, which if used will make a mother's hands indistinguishable from her daughter's. Look around you. Who is being hired and who is being retired? Aging is equated with obsolescence and worthlessness. People who have been vital, contributing members of an organization suddenly find themselves with the title "honorary." It is often not an honor at all! It means these people have become figureheads; they have been replaced. The real work has been taken over by someone else—someone younger.

Social policy has also neglected the needs of older people. Despite the growth of the elderly population, for instance, the National Institute of Mental Health spent a mere 1.1% of its budget for research on problems of the elderly only one decade ago. Only 1% of its budget for services went to provide for care of elderly people. This figure is now changing, but it suggests an underlying attitude of disinterest in older people's needs.

The process of receiving medical care and paying medical bills can in itself be a stressor for older people. Elderly people have twice as many visits to a physician, their average hospital stay is three and one half times longer than for persons under age 65, and the hospital stay costs five times more than for the under-65 age group. Insurance coverage (including Medicare) is often inadequate, especially for preventive services. The chronic illnesses older people suffer often require much time and few "high tech" interventions; the American insurance system reimburses especially poorly for this type of care.

The real issue is one of attitude. If one examines the dynamics behind this attitude, then one can see why there has been disinterest and avoidance. Generally, the medical profession and other helping people, including family and friends, are overwhelmed by the multiplicity, chronicity, and confusing nature of the disorders of aging. Care-givers often feel helpless in dealing with the elderly and harbor self-doubts about whether they can contribute in a satisfactory manner that is also personally gratifying. To put it another way, most of us like to see results, to see things happen, to believe there is a "before" and "after" picture, in which the difference is clear. Also, it is important to feel that the part we have played, however big or small, has made a difference.

Helpers like it when someone puts out her hand and says "thank you." The elderly often say, "Don't bug me. I don't want help." If you consider who it is that voluntarily comes into most clinical agencies, it is not the elderly. Those elderly who do come have usually been coerced. Helpers do not like complainers. What do the elderly say? "This hurts; that hurts . . . you're not nice enough . . . you don't come soon enough . . . my old doctor was much better . . . do this, do that." Helpers like patients who receive maximum cures in the minimum of time. This certainly is not the elderly. There are more visits, for more problems, requiring more time. Helpers like patients who get well. How many of the elderly are cured? How can you take away their diabetes, their arthritis, the pain from the memory of a lost spouse? Helpers like patients who take their advice. With the elderly, you suggest A and they'll often do B.

These interactional dynamics are understandable but only aggravate the problem. They may rub the helper's instincts the wrong way. The result is that many potential care-givers decide they do not like working with the elderly, and it shows. Very few clinicians volunteer to take on elderly clients. If an elderly client comes into a helping agency, the chances are good that the person who sees the client may soon decide to transfer the case to someone more "appropriate" or refer the client to another agency.

Another factor that gets in the way of their receiving adequate care from helping people is that they may resent the helper's youth, just as the helper fears their elderliness. Also, the elderly generally dislike the dependent status that goes along with being a client or patient. It is the opposite of what they want, which is to be independent and secure and feel a sense of worth. Being in treatment implies that something is wrong with them. It also means that someone else is partially in charge and telling them how to run their lives.

Psychological stresses   The greatest psychological stress the elderly must face is loss. In the geriatric population losses are steady, predictable, and often come in bunches. And even if they do not, they are still numerous. What are the specific losses?

There is the loss that comes from the *illnesses and deaths* of family and friends. The older you get, statistically the more likely that those about you will begin to falter. So there are the obvious losses of support and companionship. Not necessarily as obvious is that the deaths of others also lead to questioning about loss of self, anticipation of one's own death. This may sometimes be the source of anxiety attacks among the elderly.

There is the loss that comes from the *geographical separations* of family. This begins earlier in life, as children go to school and later leave home for college or the service and then eventually marry. For the elderly, this may be especially difficult, because 50% of all grandparents do not have grandchildren living close by. As new generations are being born,

they are not accessible to the older generation whose lives are coming to a close.

There is the loss of *money* through earned income. Whether income is supplemented through pensions, social security, or savings, the elderly usually do not have as much money as they did earlier in their lives. Dollars do not only represent buying power; they also have symbolic values. Money represents power, stature, value, and independence. Lack of money has obvious implications in vital areas of self-esteem.

There are the losses that accompany *retirement:* loss of status, gratification, and often most important, identity. With retirement, you lose who you have been. This refers not only to retirement from a job; it includes retirement from anything—from being a mother, or a grandmother, or from just being a person who is capable of walking around the block. Often accompanying retirement is a loss of privacy. For married couples, retirement may mean more togetherness than they have had for years. Both spouses will have to change routines and habits and be forced to accommodate the presence of the other. The expectations may also be tremendous. Retirement, in most people's fantasies, is thought to usher in the "golden years" and provide the opportunity to do the things that have been put off. There may well be a letdown.

There is also the loss of *body functions and skills,* which may include a loss of attractiveness. Older people may develop body odors. They lose their teeth. They are more prone to infection. For women, the skin may become dry, including the skin of the vagina, which can lead to vaginal discharges and dyspareunia (painful intercourse). For men, there is general loss of muscle tone. Everything begins to stick out where it shouldn't. As physical problems arise, this may lead to loss of skills. The carpenter with arthritis or the tremors of Parkinson's disease will be unable to do the things that were formerly possible and rewarding.

The elderly may try to handle stress in a number of ways. One is the widely used defense of *denial.* In response to an observation that a client's hand is more swollen, he may well say, "Oh no, it's no different than it's always been." If a close friend is in the hospital and very seriously ill, she may dismiss the seriousness and claim it is just another of her spells—she'll be out, perky as ever, in a day or two.

Another common way of handling loss is by *somatization.* This means bringing the emotional content out in the open, but "saying" it in terms of it being the body that hurts. This is why so many of the elderly are labeled hypochrondriacal. When he says his knee hurts and he really cannot get up that day, what he also may be saying is that he hurts inside, emotionally. Because he may not get attention for emotional pains, having something wrong physically or "mechanically" is socially more acceptable.

Another way of handling loss is *restricting affect.* Instead of saying it does not exist, as with denial, there is a withdrawing. They become less involved, so they do not hear about the bad things happening. By being less a part of the world, they are less vulnerable.

Unfortunately, all these defenses boomerang and work against the elderly. How are love, affection, and concern expressed? Through words, behavior, and many nonverbal cues—a smile, a nod, a touch. After so many years of living, the elderly certainly know the signs of affection and caring as well as those of distancing and detachment. By withdrawing when they are fearful, they may well see others reciprocally withdrawing; the elderly may then be left without any source of affection, interest, or caring. This in turn they read as dislike, and they may feel their initial withdrawing was justified. Therefore one of the prime treatment techniques with the elderly is to reach out to them, literally. Smile, touch them, sit close to them. Attempt to reach through the barrier they may have erected with the "protective" psychological defenses mentioned.

The elderly frequently are hurt by what helping people instinctively say when reaching out to the aged. Statements like "you're lucky to be alive . . . quit worrying about things . . . grow old gracefully" are often misinterpreted by the elderly as someone telling them to ignore their losses, or that the person making such statements does not want to get close to them. The elderly's response is that they do not want to grow old gracefully, they do not want to be "easy to manage," they want to go out with a bang, leave a mark—they want to be individuals to the last day.

How about sex and the elderly? The most prevalent myth is that the elderly have no interest in sex. Physiologically, aging itself need not greatly affect sexual functioning. With advancing years, it takes a little longer to achieve an erection, a little more time to the point of ejaculation, orgasm is a little less intense, and a little more time is required before orgasms can be reexperienced. However, if the elderly are physically healthy, there is no reason why they should not be sexually active. The biggest factors influencing sexual activity in the elderly are the availability of a partner and social pressures. Among the elderly, when a partner dies, the survivor is often not encouraged to date or remarry. What is considered virility at age 25 is seen as lechery after age 65. Even when both partners are alive, if they are living in an institution or in the home of children, sexual activity may well be frowned upon or "not allowed."

Another loss is that of *sensation*. With aging, the senses become less acute. What this means is that the elderly are then deprived of accurate cues from their environment. This may be a big factor in the development of suspiciousness in older persons. Any paranoid elderly person should have hearing and vision evaluated. The most powerful loss, the loss no elderly person is prepared to understand or accept, is the loss of thinking ability. This loss may occur imperceptibly over time. It comes from the loss of cortical brain function. Suddenly a person who has been an accountant or a schoolteacher, for example, is adding $2+2$, and it doesn't equal 4 every time. This is embarrassing and scary. Although they may be able to stand losing other things, to "lose one's mind" is the ultimate indignity.

The result of all or any of these losses is that self-respect, integrity, dignity, and self-esteem are threatened. The implication can be that

usefulness is questioned and life is ebbing away. The feeling may well be that "my work is over."

Biological stresses Of the elderly, only 5% are institutionalized in nursing homes, convalescent centers, or similar facilities. However, about half of the elderly have some serious physical disability, such as heart disease, diabetes, lung disease, or arthritis. About 25% also have a significant functional psychological problem, with depression being the most prevalent. Understandably, as life expectancy increases and we live longer, there is more vulnerability to the natural course of disease.

Depressive illness is very prevalent among the elderly. There may well be a physiological basis for this. The levels of neurochemicals (serotonin, monoamine oxidase, and norepinephrine) thought to be associated with depression change in the brain as people get older. These depressions, then, are not necessarily tied solely to situational events. However, because so many things are likely to be going on in the surrounding environment for the elderly, it is too easy to forget the potential benefits of judiciously prescribed antidepressants. Malnourishment, for instance, is all too common in the elderly. Nutritional deficiency can cause several syndromes that may look like depressions. Many physical ailments, such as thyroid dysfunctions, and illnesses caused by the disease processes themselves, manifest themselves as depression.

Depression in the elderly may not be the same as depression in younger persons, with tearfulness, inability to sleep, or loss of appetite. Some of the tips for recognizing depression in the elderly are an increased sensitivity to pain, refusing to get out of bed when physical problems don't require bed rest, poor concentration, a marked narrowing of coping style, and an upsurge of physical complaints. Often, the poor concentration leads to absent-mindedness and inattentiveness, which are misdiagnosed as defective memory and ultimately as "senility," while the depression goes unrecognized and untreated. Senility is really a useless clinical term. The proper term should be dementia, which means irreversible cognitive impairment. However, all cognitive impairment should be considered reversible (delirium) until proven otherwise. It should also be remembered that alcohol abuse, as well as sometimes creating problems itself, can, in patients with dementia, make the confusion worse. The elderly deserve an aggressive search for potentially treatable, reversible causes of organic brain syndromes by qualified medical personnel.

Suicide among the elderly is a very big problem. Of those who commit suicide, 25% are over age 65. The rate of suicide for those over 65 is 5 times that of the general population. After age 75, the rate is 8 times higher. In working with the elderly, a suicide evaluation should not be neglected, because so many depressions are masked.

A variety of changes associated with aging make the elderly more vulnerable to the acute effects of alcohol. Body water content declines and the body fat content increases with age. Between the ages of 20 and 70, there is a 10% decrease in lean body mass. With a given amount of alcohol, these combined reductions lead to a higher blood alcohol level among the elderly. Furthermore, with aging there is diminished blood flow through the liver. This means that while the rate of metabolism is unaltered the alcohol is cleared more slowly. For any given amount, the peak blood alcohol level will be 20% higher for a 60-year-old than for a 20-year-old. At age 90, the peak blood alcohol level is 50% higher. Those elderly persons who may have some existing impairment in cognitive functioning have even greater sensitivity to alcohol. In addition to the increased acute effects of alcohol, a variety of other physical changes make the elderly more vulnerable to the medical consequences of use. By age 75, there is a 50% reduction in lung capacity, the kidneys work at only 45% of their earlier capacity, and heart function is reduced by 35%.

Iatrogenic stresses   *Iatrogenic* refers to harm caused by efforts to heal. Some of the stresses on the elderly are in fact the product of the health-care system and the insensitivities to the psychological and basic physiological changes in the elderly. All too often, medication is overprescribed in an attempt to keep behavior controlled rather than diagnosed. Too few clinicians take into account the dramatically altered way the elderly metabolize medications, which means that fewer medicines in combination and lowered doses of drugs are frequently required. There is also a tendency by everyone concerned to ignore the fact that alcohol, too, is a toxic drug. The combination of alcohol with other medications in light of the altered metabolism for both can create serious problems. Rarely is there any thought of whether the elderly patient can afford the medicine prescribed. Also the elderly person's ability to comply with directions for taking medications is overestimated.

A poignant example of the above was the case of an elderly woman who was discharged from the hospital with a number of medications. She had been admitted with severe congestive heart failure but had responded well to drug therapy for her hypertension and fluid retention. Within 2 weeks of her return home, her condition began to deteriorate, which was a source of dismay and consternation to her physicians. She was thought surely to be purposefully causing her ailments, and a psychiatrist, who was asked to consult on the case, decided to make a home visit. The woman knew which medications to take, when, and for what conditions. However, there was one problem. As she handed the bottle of capsules to the psychiatrist, with her crippled arthritic fingers, the "diagnosis" became obvious: the child-proof cap! She had been unable to open the bottles and therefore unable to take the medicine. This is a vivid reminder of the need to consider all the available information in assessing the problems of the elderly.

Patterns of alcohol and other drug use

Substance use patterns of the elderly differ considerably from those in other parts of the population. These are summarized below.

Alcohol   Elderly people generally have a somewhat lower rate of alcohol use than do middle aged and young adults. Nonetheless, several studies have shown that more than half of older people do use some alcohol. A large study by the National Institute on Aging questioned thousands of older adults about their drinking. The prevalence of alcohol use varied considerably by geographic location, but on average, 73% of men and 56% of women 65 and older used some alcohol. Depending on location, between 7% and 10% of women and 22% and 36% of men used 1 ounce or more of alcohol per day. As in other studies, men at all ages and in all locations were more likely than women to drink. The frequency of drinking decreased with increasing age. Nonetheless, even among women 75 and older in Iowa, the group with the lowest frequency of drinking, 30% still used some alcohol. Other surveys generally show similar results. Studies that have followed people over time have generally found a decrease in drinking with increasing age. Those who have used alcohol when younger are unlikely to become complete abstainers unless health problems intervene.

Drinking among older people is of importance even if it does not qualify as "alcohol abuse," for two reasons. First, safe levels of use have not been established. For instance, we know that, among middle-aged people, 2 drinks per day is enough to contribute to high blood pressure. In older people, who obtain higher blood alcohol levels per drink, the amount required to affect blood pressure is probably lower. The risk of hip fracture is also increased in heavy social drinkers. Nonabusive drinking can also become problematic when other medications are being used.

Little is known about the relationship of alcohol use to life stresses and changes, although there has been speculation. The advent of retirement communities has provided an interesting opportunity to examine some aspects of these questions. It appears that in these settings, which offer their residents a variety of leisure activities such as golf, swimming, crafts classes, and discussion groups, social isolation is not tied to higher levels of alcohol use. On the contrary, the heaviest drinkers, defined as drinking at least two or more drinks per day, who constituted 20% of those studied, were also those who were socially more active. Since entering the community, one-third of the individuals noted a change in drinking patterns, with three-fourths of those individuals reducing their alcohol use. But that leaves one-fourth who reported that their drinking had increased. One of the questions raised is whether social activity in retirement communities may be tied to alcohol use and may facilitate or even promote heavier drinking by some individuals.

Over-the-counter preparations   For many people, use of over-the-counter medications is the first response to an illness or a medical problem. Self-prescribed preparations are used more extensively than are prescription medications. The typical American household is estimated to have an average of 17 different over-the-counter products on hand. In response to the question of how they handle everyday health problems,

35% of elderly people report they do not treat the problem, 35% report using an over-the-counter medication, 15% use prescription medications available in the home, 11% use some other home remedy, and 13% contact their doctor or dentist. If elderly people take any action in response to a health-care problem, the odds are good that they will use an over-the-counter preparation.

When chronic illness accompanies aging, there is an understandable tendency to find preparations to ease discomfort. Elderly people are more likely than any other segment of the population to use these preparations. They take seven times more over-the-counter drugs than do members of any other age group. One study of healthy elderly people identified 54% as regularly using over-the-counter drugs. Fifty percent of that group reported that they typically used analgesics, laxatives, or antacids between 4 to 6 times per week. Of those who use over-the-counter drugs daily, 80% are believed to simultaneously be using prescribed drugs, alcohol, or both. Some may often use six or more preparations.

The number of over-the-counter preparations is growing. Potent medications that previously required a doctor's prescription, e.g., ibuprofen and naproxen, are now available without one. In addition, health-care professionals do not rank very high as a major source of information about over-the-counter preparations. Among elderly people, advertising has been identified as *the* primary source of information by a quarter of those surveyed. Friends, relatives, and neighbors constitute the next-largest group, acting as the source of information for 20% of those surveyed. The label on the product itself was noted by 13% as the source of information. Pharmacists were consulted as the source of information for 20%, and physicians were consulted by only 14%.

Prescription drugs   The elderly take a disproportionate percentage of all medication. Upward of 60% of elderly people have some medications that are prescribed; in many studies more than 80% do. Some of the drugs most commonly prescribed are also those with high potential for adverse drug reactions. Nonsteroidal anti-inflammatory drugs, for example, increase the risk of gastrointestinal bleeding, especially for older people. Central nervous system depressants, especially long-acting benzodiazepines, increase the risk of falls and hip fracture. These drugs also have notable abuse potential. When use of these drugs is sanctioned by physicians, defining "abuse" can be difficult. In such circumstances, it may be more useful to approach the problem by identifying functional or social impairments use causes rather than attempting to identify criteria for abuse.

Adverse drug reactions   Adverse drug reactions are more common among elderly people. One major reason for this is that they use more drugs than do younger people. Because of multiple chronic illnesses, they may be under the care of more than one physician, none of whom may be fully informed about the complete range of medications the patient is taking. As drug regimens become more complex, there is a greater probability of error by the patient as well as greater potential for interactions between drugs. Concurrent use of drugs, even 10 or more hours apart, can significantly affect absorption, distribution, metabolism, and toxicity. With more drugs being used, including alcohol, there is greater potential for adverse interactions. A study of hospitalized patients found that all patients taking more than 8 drugs had at least one interacting pair of drugs in that mix.

The unique physiological changes that accompany aging and affect drug distribution and metabolism also contribute to the increased risk of drug-alcohol interactions. The risk of an adverse drug reaction in those 50 to 59 years old may be as much as a third greater than for those in their forties. Above age 60 there appears to be a further twofold to threefold increase. Diagnosis of adverse drug reactions may be hampered because of their resemblance to illnesses common in old age, such as gait disturbances and cognitive impairment.

Many commonly prescribed drugs can interact with alcohol. Such interactions can occur by several mechanisms. Some of the effects are due to changes in liver metabolism that occur with age. Remember that normal changes in liver function are compounded by the presence of alcohol. For this reason medications as common as aspirin and acetaminophen, to oral anticoagulants, to oral medications used with diabetes, to antihistamines, and pain medications can present problems in the presence of alcohol. There are other interactions that occur for other reasons beside changed liver function. For example, anti-ulcer drugs, such as cimetidine, inhibit alcohol metabolism in the stomach, resulting in greater absorption of alcohol and higher blood alcohol levels per drink. Since elderly people already obtain higher blood alcohol levels per drink due to age-related changes in drug distribution, this effect is probably of even more importance to this group. Alcohol used at the same time as some nonsteroidal anti-inflammatory drugs may substantially increase the risk of the gastrointestinal inflammation and bleeding these drugs can cause. Then there is increased sedation, delirium, and psychomotor impairment that can occur when alcohol is used with benzodiazepines and other drugs that affect the CNS.

Illicit drug use   What in the vernacular is termed *illicit* drug use is quite uncommon among elderly people. The lifetime prevalence of drug abuse among those 65 years and older is in the vicinity of one-half of 1%. (0.5%) Little information is available about older persons involved in illicit drug use or older street addicts. A study of methadone maintenance patients in New York found 2% were over age 60. However, it is highly likely that the number of older persons with illicit drug use problems will increase dramatically over the next decade. Studies have found that within methadone maintenance programs, one-third of the patients are over age 40, and one-fourth are between the ages of 40 and 49. It has been estimated that given the drug use patterns of those now in middle age, within the next 10 years the number of those over age 60 with an illicit drug problem will quadruple.

Alcohol problems

Not only do the patterns of substance use, including alcohol, vary among elderly people, but the associated problems and presentations do as well. Between 2% and 4% of elderly people meet the criteria for alcohol abuse or alcoholism. Approximately 10% have problems related to drinking that are not severe enough to meet these criteria. In general, men have a much higher likelihood of being problem drinkers than do women, the prevalence decreases with increasing age, and there is considerable geographic variation in the prevalence of alcoholism. In medical settings, the prevalence is higher, and it appears to increase with increasing level of care. In primary care settings, 10%–15% of elderly patients are alcohol abusers or dependents, while up to 25% of hospitalized elderly people are. An analysis of Medicare billing data showed that elderly people nationally are hospitalized more often for alcohol-related problems than for heart attack. Recognizing alcohol problems among elderly people in medical settings can be very challenging, and in the past physicians have recognized and intervened with only a small proportion of these patients. Nonetheless, studies of treatment populations consistently find that about 10% of patients entering alcohol treatment programs are age 65 and older.

Types of alcohol dependence   Alcohol problems make their initial appearance at different points in life. A majority of elderly alcoholics have had a long history of alcohol use and abuse. Although these people have been relatively resistant to alcohol-related morbidity through middle age, they often begin to experience deterioration of physical and cognitive functioning as they reach their 60s and 70s. There is also a group of people who develop alcoholism in old age. For some of these people, the stresses of aging may have been too great or come too fast. They turned to alcohol as a coping mechanism. Reflecting these two different patterns, alcoholism among elderly people is commonly described as either *early onset* or *late onset*. Researchers have adopted different age cutoff points to distinguish these two varieties, cutoff points that fall anywhere between ages 40 to 60 years. Despite the differences in distinguishing between the two varieties, there is general agreement that of elderly people with alcohol dependence, approximately 50% began drinking heavily before age 40, and approximately two-thirds before age 60. Thus the ratio of early onset to late onset alcoholism is around 2:1.

Some differences identified between those with early and late onset alcohol dependence are summarized in Table 10.7.

Many factors may contribute to the development of late onset alcohol dependence. Problems from alcohol use sometimes emerge in later life

TABLE 10.7   CHARACTERISTICS OF EARLY AND LATE ONSET ALCOHOL DEPENDENCE

Characteristics	Early Onset (%)	Late Onset (%)
Separated or divorced	22	55
Widowed	33	9
Time spent in jail	78	55
Symptoms of organic brain disease	11	36
Serious health problem	44	91
Family history of alcoholism	86	40

From: Bienfeld D: Alcoholism in the elderly, *American Family Physician* 36(2):163–169. 1987.

with minimal changes in alcohol consumption. Because of the normal aging process, what had previously been a benign "heavy social" drinking pattern for some individuals becomes problematic. Some elderly people, however, seem to develop drinking problems as a maladaptive response to social stresses. These include retirement, loss of a spouse, grief responses, economic hardships, social isolation, and changes in living situations. The view that changing life circumstances and social isolation are specific factors that provoke alcohol problems in elderly people is largely speculative. At any age, alcohol may be used to cope with major life stresses. For elderly people, these stressors are predictable and more numerous.

An awareness of differences between early and late onset alcoholism is important both for screening and for treatment. For those with early onset alcoholism, the odds are greater that some of the usual social indicators of alcoholism can be elicited via eliciting the person's past medical and social history. For those with a past history of an identified alcohol problem, any current drinking should be of concern. Of those with significant alcohol problems, the number who return to nonproblematic social drinking is small. There is also a greater probability of prior alcohol treatment among early onset alcoholics. One treatment program found that slightly over one-third of early onset patients had had prior treatment. Even among those with late onset alcohol dependence, however, 17% had had some prior treatment. In treatment programs, emphasis on developing alternative coping strategies is of particular importance for late onset alcoholics.

Presentations   Alcohol problems among elderly people often have nonspecific presentations. Many of the negative consequences of alcohol and/or drug abuse among younger persons, such as job difficulties or family and legal problems, are less common. Elderly people who are alcohol dependent more commonly present with medical complications of their drinking. Among elderly people, some of the presentations are often mistaken for age-related illness such as malnutrition, falls, other accidents, incontinence, mood swings, depression, confusion, less attention

TABLE 10.8   CURRENT AND PAST MEDICAL DIAGNOSES IN ELDERLY PATIENTS WITH ALCOHOLISM

Diagnosis	Current Diagnosis number	Past Diagnosis number	Total Number	%
Alcoholic liver disease	37	2	39	18
Hypertension	71	2	73	33
Chronic obstructive pulmonary disease	65	1	66	31
Coronary artery disease	36	5	41	19
Arteriosclerosis	9	2	11	5
Neurological disorders				
Organic brain disease	52	2	54	25
Cerebral vascular disease	12	2	14	7
Cerebral degeneration	13	0	13	6
Diabetes	17	1	18	8
Peptic ulcer disease	4	29	33	15
Alcoholic gastritis	6	3	7	3
Prostate hypertrophy (men)	16	19	35	23
Psoriasis	8	3	11	5
Degenerative joint disease	38	6	44	20

Adapted from Hurt RD: Alcoholism in elderly persons: Medical aspects and prognosis of 216 inpatients, *Mayo Clinic Proceedings* 63:756. 1988.

to self-care, and unexpected reactions to prescribed medications. The results of one study of 216 patients, age 65 and above, admitted to the Mayo Clinic's substance abuse treatment service are summarized in Table 10.8.

Screening   The importance of taking an alcohol and drug use history does not decline with the patient's increasing age. One goal of history taking is to identify alcohol or drug dependence. An additional goal of history taking that assumes greater importance with increasing age is to identify medically hazardous alcohol use, including potential alcohol-drug interactions. Asking about quantity and frequency of use is therefore as important as asking about adverse consequences of drinking. Several techniques have been shown to help enhance the accuracy of self-reported quantity and frequency of drinking. Asking about each type of alcoholic beverage separately will increase the accuracy of reporting. The "timeline follow-back" procedure uses a calendar and visual aids to enhance reporting of alcohol consumption. This procedure asks about drinking on each specific day of the week for as far back as the interviewer deems important. Heavy drinking determined by this method has been shown to be a good indicator of problem drinking.

Obstacles to identification and intervention   Many of the screening instruments in common use are based on the behavior of young men and do not transfer well to older people. Since older people are often

retired, for instance, they will not have problems at work. Since they often live alone, they are less likely to have alcohol-induced marital problems. It is particularly challenging to identify problem drinking in people with cognitive impairment. Family, friends, and neighbors are important sources of information about those who are unable to give a good history themselves.

Other factors also contribute to poor recognition of alcohol problems in older people. Classic signs of alcohol dependence may be obscure. Tolerance, manifest by requiring more alcohol to achieve the same effect, is one classic component of alcohol dependence. Older people, who obtain higher blood alcohol levels per drink, may honestly report requiring less alcohol intake to get the same effect as before. Withdrawal, though its signs and symptoms are little different in older people, may not be recognized until late in the course. Many other possible causes of the tachycardia, hypertension, delirium, etc. will be thought of first in elderly people. Social decline is often marked by nonspecific features, described above, which differs from the presentation in younger people.

Elderly people, as well as other segments of the population, are likely to be protected by family, friends, or caretakers. They may fail to see the problem, ignore what they suspect, or justify not intervening in an alcohol problem, because no one wants to take away someone's "last pleasure." Thinking "What do they have to live for anyway? They have been drinking all these years, they'll never stop now, and I don't want to be the one who asks them to give up the bottle" is also common. Such enabling of an alcoholic is not unique to situations involving elderly people. It is probably more common, though, for those persons closest to an elderly problem drinker to actively facilitate the continuation of drinking. For example, a neighbor or housekeeper may ensure access to alcohol by purchasing it for the homebound person and thereby circumvent and sabotage others' efforts to intervene. In situations where family members or friends support problem drinking or are reluctant to intervene, it is important to point out that problem drinking is not pleasurable drinking. Such complications of heavy drinking as cognitive impairment, gait disturbances and other physical dependencies are greatly feared by most older people. These impairments often lead to nursing home placement, which most elderly people wish to avoid at almost any cost.

Detoxification and treatment   Detoxification protocols need to be adjusted for elderly people. Generally, because of autonomic and cardiovascular instability, detoxification is better managed in a hospital than on an outpatient basis. Although the general strategy is similar for managing withdrawal in younger patients, there are several caveats. Withdrawal is likely to take longer in elderly people, especially those with cognitive impairment. The use of benzodiazepines, as a preventive measure, in the absence of withdrawal symptoms is contraindicated, because it might provoke delirium. It is generally recommended that their use be delayed and only prescribed in response to specific signs and symptoms of withdrawal. Drugs with a short half-life are preferable to longer-acting agents. The usual dosage can be reduced by one-half to two-thirds. In a person also dependent on benzodiazepines, withdrawal may take considerably longer than alcohol withdrawal alone.

The use of Antabuse® (disulfiram) has been suggested by some as potentially useful. Careful consideration needs to be given to the risks and potential benefits. Among elderly people, the risks may be considerable. Physically they are more frail. Their metabolic ability to handle disulfiram is a factor. They may be less able to comply with the restrictions because of cognitive impairments. Their greater use of over-the-counter preparations increases the probability of inadvertent drug reactions. A disulfiram reaction that might be uncomfortable for someone younger may represent a medical crisis and have a lethal outcome for someone elderly.

Elderly people need the same type of rehabilitation services as younger persons—education, counseling, and involvement in self-help groups. Treatment programs typically incorporate elderly people in their general programs. The prognosis is at least as good for elderly people as it is for younger persons. In addition to the treatment program's standard regimen, elderly people also require a thorough medical evaluation and potentially more extensive social service involvement at discharge and as a part of aftercare.

Research in the early 1980s indicated that elderly alcoholics had comparable treatment outcomes to younger patients, which was interpreted as refuting the need for specially focused programs for older persons. However, more recent research has demonstrated that programs tailored to elderly people enhance outcomes by reducing treatment dropout, by increasing rates of aftercare, and significantly by dealing with relapses that occurred, and not losing these patients to treatment if they resume drinking.

For most clinicians, the issue of specialized versus standard programs is likely to be nothing more than an academic interest, because so few programs have been developed for elderly people. However, some of the benefits of programs designed for elderly people may be achieved within the standard programs, with some inventiveness. Referring agencies and health-care providers need to be sensitive to the accommodations that might be made to serve elderly people better. Matching patients with clinicians who are knowledgeable about and comfortable in treating elderly people within standard programs and who are able to work at a slower, gentler pace can be beneficial. Furthermore, abrasive confrontation, which is used in some programs, is not likely to be effective with elderly persons. Programs that emphasize that style of group work may be poor choices for a referral. However, groups are important to elderly people in reducing the sense of isolation, enhancing communication skills, providing a forum for problem solving, and dealing with denial. Small group sessions or individual therapy within a general treatment program can help develop the special skills the older person may need

for coping with losses, enjoying leisure time, and developing new relationships after the loss of old ones. A particular element found to be important for elderly people is referred to as *life review*. Groups need to allow for the elderly person's reminiscence and processing of the past. This is important for all elderly persons to see their lives as a whole. For those in treatment for alcohol problems, incorporating this process in a way that does not diminish self-esteem or devalue the elderly person's life is important. This is not only important in formal alcohol treatment but in contacts with health-care and social service professionals as well.

Treatment of the cognitively impaired alcoholic is especially difficult. Often a prolonged period of enforced abstinence from alcohol will be needed in order to determine if the person will recover sufficient cognitive function to pursue and participate in treatment. If not, a permanently supervised living situation, such as a nursing home or group home where alcohol is not available, will probably be needed.

Drug use problems

Illicit drug use, as mentioned earlier, is uncommon among elderly people. Prescription and over-the-counter drug use, however, is often problematic in this segment of the population. While now over a decade old, a major report mandated by 1988 federal legislation reviewed and made recommendations on drug use in the Medicare program. Among its findings was that those age 60 and above, though constituting only 17% of the population, account for 51% of all deaths from drug reactions. A significant portion of these were due to drug mismanagement.

Prevention

Your middle-age patient of today is some other clinician's elderly patient several years hence. Today's adolescent is establishing a framework for making independent decisions about self-care and health-care practices. These will have a bearing on lifelong health habits. What kind of questions should any individual consider before he or she decides to take medication? What specific questions are important for the particular patient? Patients rarely consult their doctor before making such decisions. In fact, no doctor would want to be contacted on that basis! A resource available to everyone is the pharmacist. Though almost always available, the pharmacist is an underutilized resource. One of his or her jobs is public education and information. Patients need instruction about the kind of questions to ask: Are there any contraindications when using this product? Is there a need for concern about interactions with this prescription medication? Are there any side effects?

General suggestions for working with elderly people

Remember that elderly people are survivors. Those who are old now have lived through hard times. Getting through the Great Depression and a world war or two has required strength. Those who survived have a wealth of experience to bring to coping with the stresses of aging. Make it clear that you respect their strengths and experience and that you have high expectations for their ability to overcome their problems.

Because many elderly persons are reluctant to seek or receive help, a family member is often the person to make the initial contact. The family's views of the situation, their ideas and fears, need to be discussed. Whatever the problem, the chances are good that something can be done to improve the picture and improve functional status. It often comes as a surprise to families that there is hope for recovery. Professionals can help the family too, as they cope with a difficult situation, e.g., arranging for Meals-on-Wheels or making simple suggestions about how to make routines easier.

In conversation with elderly people, do not stick with neutral topics like the weather all of the time. Discuss topics of common interest to you both such as gardening or baseball, as well as some controversial topic, something appealing. You can enhance self-esteem by letting the person know that you not only want their opinions, but you want them to listen to yours.

Multiple resources may be needed to assist elderly people. In many instances older adults with alcohol problems need to become reinvolved in the world. Meaningful contacts can come from a variety of people, not just from professional helpers. The janitor in the client's apartment building, a neighbor, or a crossing guard at the street corner may all be potential allies. If the person was once active in a church group, civic organization, or other community group, but has lost contact, recommend that he or she get in touch with the organization. There is often a member who will visit or be able to assist in other ways. Many communities have senior citizen centers that offer social programs, Meals-on-Wheels, counseling on Social Security and Medicare, and transportation.

When cognitive impairment is a factor, providing cues to orient the person may be helpful. Mention dates, day of the week, and current events. Do not, however, expect a cognitively impaired person to retain such information or to learn new skills. Since remote memory is usually preserved longer than recent memory, discussing past life events and interests may be socially rewarding.

If you give specific information to the client, write it down legibly. This makes it much easier for the client to comply. If family members are present, tell them the directions too. In thinking about compliance and what can be done to assist the elderly in participating in treatment, take some time to think about how your agency functions. What does it mean for an elderly person coming to see you? Are there long waits at several different offices on several different floors? Does it require navigating difficult stairs, elevators, and hallways in the process? Are there times of the day that make use of public transportation easier? Consider such factors, and make adjustments to make it much easier for your elderly clients. In specific terms, make every effort to do things in as uncomplicated, convenient, nonembarrassing, and economical a fashion as possible.

Separate sympathy and empathy. Sympathy is feeling sorry in company with someone. The elderly don't want that; it makes them feel like children. Empathy means you understand or want to understand. This is what they would like.

Be aware that you may be thought of and responded to as any number of important people in your client's long life. Also, you may alternately represent grandchild, child, parent, peer, and authority figure to them at various points in treatment, even within the same interview, and at the same time.

Have integrity with the elderly. Do not try to mislead or lie to them. They are too experienced with all the con games in life. If they ask you questions, give them straight answers. This, however, does not mean being brutal in the name of "honesty." For example, in speaking with a client you might well say, "Many other people I talk with have concerns about death, do you?" If the client responds, "No, I haven't thought much about it," you don't blurt out, "Well, you better think about it, since you only have 6 months to live." That is not integrity.

In working with the elderly, set specific goals. Make sure that the initial ones are easily attainable. This means they can have some surefire positive experiences. With that under their belts, they are more likely to take some risks and attempt other things.

Make home visits. Home visits are the key to working with this group. It may be the only thing that will break down their resistance and help them get treatment. Very few will seek help on their own initiative. So, if someone is not willing to come to your office, give him a call. Ask if you can make an appointment to see him at home. If the response you get is, "I don't want you to come," don't quit. Your next line is, "Well, if I'm ever in the area, I'd like to stop by." And try to do that. Bring some small token gift, such as a magazine or flowers. After your visit, you may well find his or her resistance has disappeared. The home visit can be vital in making an adequate assessment. Seeing the person in his or her own home, where security is at its peak, provides a much better picture of how the person is getting along, as well as the pluses and minuses of the environment. It also allows the client to be spontaneous in emotions and behavior. If you regularly make home visits, beware of making the person "stay in trouble" to see you. Don't just visit in a crisis. Instead, stop in to hear about successes. Your visits may be a real high point for the person, who may not like to think of losing this contact. Make a visit the day after the client's first day on a new volunteer job, for example.

Beware of those who arrange trivial activities for older people to occupy their time. Crafts classes, for instance, ought to teach real skills, not just keep people busy. Many elderly people also have something they can teach others. For example, the carpenter who is no longer steady enough to use tools will be able to provide consultation to people

who want to remodel their homes. Elderly people have a richness of life experiences and much to contribute.

It is always important that the substance abuse clinician work closely with the client's physician and health-care providers. There are few situations when it is more important that everyone is singing from the same page.

WOMEN

Alcoholism, heavy drinking, problem drinking, and other drug use were long assumed to be problems of men. Accordingly, research on substance abuse problems among women was very limited for a long time. With respect to alcohol, a literature review indicates that only 28 English-language studies of women with alcoholism were published between 1928 and 1970. Another assumption has been that when present, alcoholism is alcoholism and drug dependence, is drug dependence, regardless of gender.

Despite the growing attention to women's problems, the data available is not easily synthesized. One problem results from the fact that researchers frequently study women who enter treatment. This limits what can be said about the extent, nature, and magnitude of problems among women in general. Further complicating the situation is the fact that those being studied seemingly represent all of the possible combinations of alcohol and other substance use. Subjects of research studies range from alcohol dependent women to women with drug dependence to women with alcohol dependence who use/abuse/are dependent on other substances to female substance users who drink/drink heavily/are alcohol dependent. The extent to which these populations are distinctive or overlapping is unknown, so generalizations from any of these individual studies is difficult. In addition, some research to date has used relatively small samples and has focused on narrow topics, such as the use of day care by urban women in substance abuse treatment. While such details are very important, a multitude of detail doesn't necessarily make seeing the big picture easier. Although facts proliferate and there is more information, there is not always greater understanding.

Gender differences

Women represent a growing percentage of drinkers, including those with alcohol problems and also those with alcohol dependence. For younger women in the general population, the proportion of drinkers is beginning to equal that of men. Men, as a group, are statistically more likely than women to be drinkers primarily because of the greater number of abstainers among older women. These older women, born on the heels of prohibition, are of an era in which women's drinking was less socially acceptable and far less prevalent. The behavior of their granddaughters is quite different.

TABLE 10.9 SUBSTANCE USE IN THE PAST YEAR BY GENDER, 1995

Substance	% Men	% Women
Alcohol	70.1	61.1
Nicotine	34.6	29.5
Marijuana	10.5	6.6
Cocaine	2.3	1.2
Crack	0.6	0.4
Hallucinogens	1.9	1.3
Prescription*	3.1	2.7

*Nonmedical use

From Substance Abuse and Mental Health Services Administration: *National Household Survey on Drug Abuse: Main Findings 1995*, Rockville MD: Substance Abuse and Mental Health Services Administration, 1997.

TABLE 10.10 SUBSTANCE USE IN THE PAST YEAR FOR WOMEN OF DIFFERENT AGES, 1995

Substance	All women (%)	Age Groups (%)			
		12–17 yrs	18–25 yrs	26–34 yrs	>34 yrs
Alcohol	61.1	34.8	72.7	73.3	35.6
Nicotine	29.5	25.8	38.8	35.2	26.6
Marijuana	6.5	13.4	19.0	7.9	2.3
Cocaine	1.2	1.6	3.5	2.1	0.4
Crack	0.4	0.7	1.0	0.7	0.1
Hallucinogens	1.3	4.7	4.5	1.0	0.2
Prescription*	2.7	4.3	6.4	3.1	1.6
Heroin	0.6	0.6	0.8	1.0	0.4

*Nonmedical use

From Substance Abuse and Mental Health Services Administration, *National Household Survey on Drug Abuse: Main Findings 1996,* Rockville MD: Substance Abuse and Mental Health Services Administration, 1997.

Tables 10.9 and 10.10 summarize the substance use patterns of women with respect to those of men, and they also show differences among women by age group. Table 10.11 looks at differences among women in terms of race and ethnicity. This information is drawn from the most recently published Household Survey, conducted regularly on behalf of the National Institute on Drug Abuse.

Differences among women

Ethnic considerations   Ethnicity would be anticipated to be an important basis for differences among women. While data remain limited, there are differences with respect to patterns of use. White women are more likely than either Hispanic or African-American women to be drinkers and to be smokers. African-American women are more likely to have used illicit drugs in the past year, primarily attributable to higher

TABLE 10.11   WOMEN'S SUBSTANCE USE IN THE PAST YEAR BY RACE
AND ETHNICITY, 1996

Substance	% Women Reporting Use in Past Year			
	All women	White	African American	Hispanic
Alcohol	58.6	64.3	52.9	48.8
Nicotine	27.0	32.0	28.1	21.4
Any illicit drug	8.0	7.8	10.5	7.0
Marijuana	6.0	5.9	7.7	5.2
Cocaine	1.3	1.2	1.5	2.1
Crack	0.5	0.5	0.4	1.4
Inhalants	0.7	0.9	0.2	0.4
Prescription*	2.5	2.6	2.4	2.0
Stimulants	0.7	0.7	0.4	0.8
Sedatives	0.2	0.3	0.3	0.1
Tranquilizers	1.0	1.1	0.5	0.4

*Nonmedical use
From NIDA: *National Household Survey on Drug Abuse: Population Estimates 1996,*
Rockville MD: NIDA, 1997

levels of marijuana use. Where there are apparent racial ethnic differences, most noticeable in the category of illicit drug use, the differences disappear when age, education, and household income are taken into account. Table summarizes substance use for women from different ethnic/racial groups.

Sexual orientation   With the limited attention to substance use problems of women generally, it is not surprising that there has been very little discussion directed to lesbian and bisexual women. Beyond sexism, lesbian addiction goes unaddressed because of homophobia and the attendant societal stigma. Research is exceedingly limited, although work is being done. In larger cities there are treatment programs being conducted specifically for lesbian and bisexual women.

It has often been said that lesbians and bisexual women are at greater risk for substance use problems than are heterosexual women. Some have estimated that from 25% to 35% of lesbians have a serious substance use problem. This elevated level of substance use disorders was attributed in part to the "fact" that much of lesbian social life supposedly revolves around bars. However, in truth it appears that this reported higher risk was a consequence of the way in which the earliest research was conducted. A more recent study, the first to use *random* sampling methods, failed to support this perception. No significant differences were found between the lesbian/bisexual women and heterosexual women, either in terms of drinking patterns or rates of alcohol problems. Other studies have supported this. The one striking difference that has been found between lesbian/bisexual women and heterosexual women is in the proportion of lesbian women who are current smokers.

A subgroup of lesbians that may be particularly vulnerable to substance use problems are adolescents. A common theme in any study or report of lesbian, gay male, and bisexual youth is the chronic stress created by the verbal and physical abuse they receive from peers and adults. This can lead to a number of problematic outcomes, ranging from difficulties at school, to running away or being ejected from home, encounters with the law, prostitution, as well as substance abuse and suicide attempts.

Even though the rate of problems may not be elevated to the degree that had been presumed, there are unique treatment issues. Lesbian/bisexual women entering treatment will confront special issues, such as when and how to reveal their sexual orientation and deal with the associated prejudices. There is a small but rich literature with respect to treatment, the issues to be confronted, the perceptions of treatment, and the treatment process, both in formal treatment and in the use of self-help groups.

The toll of AIDS in the gay community is well known. Lesbian women are also at elevated risk for HIV/AIDS if sexually active with a partner who is an intravenous drug user. Data suggest that a very high percentage of all HIV/AIDS cases (possibly upward of 90%) reported among women who had only had a female partner involved intravenous use by the partner.

Age-related differences   Despite the fact that age has not received particular attention, it is repeatedly cited as *the* factor related to the differences that are identified among women. For example, among alcoholic women, younger women have been recognized as being at greater risk for other drug use. They have also been recognized as being at substantially higher risk for attempted or completed suicide attempts. One study of the effects of age demonstrated considerable differences between women under age 35 and those over age 35, as of 1989. Age 35 was chosen as the point for separating age groups to divide the sample into those who had reached adulthood before or after the early 1970s, a period in which there were dramatic cultural changes. The question being examined was: "Have shifts in cultural norms and behavior with respect to substance use, as well as women's roles, influenced the natural history of those who enter treatment?" This seemed to be the case. The age-related differences identified among women included are outlined below. Despite being a decade old, nonetheless these findings dramatically point out the impact of cultural eras and social change.

• *Substance-use patterns.* Younger women (then under age 35) were more likely than older women to be using marijuana, cocaine, stimulants, opiates, and hallucinogens on a weekly basis. One-third of younger women reported weekly use of marijuana, and one-third reported weekly use of cocaine. While 16% of younger women reported daily drinking, this was 2.5 times more common in older women, with 40% reportedly being daily drinkers.

- *Onset of use*. Over one-half of the younger women (56%) had started drinking before age 16, whereas only 14% of the older women had begun drinking by that age. If age 18 is the point of adulthood, 83% of the younger women, compared with less than one-half of the older women (46%), had spent their entire adult lives as drinkers. The differences based on age for drug use during adulthood are even more extreme. For the older women, 14% had been using drugs since age 18, but 74% of the younger women had been using drugs all their adult lives.

- *Settings for use*. Women's drinking has frequently been characterized as solitary, private, and hidden. This is less true of younger women, with slightly over one-half reporting their drinking or drug use to always or usually take place with others. Only 20% of older women reported that their use occurred primarily in the company of others. Thus the pattern of solitary, private use is true of older women.

- *Correlates of use*. Despite the lower percentage reporting daily drinking, younger women were not likely to have experienced binges and suffered signs of serious withdrawal, and they were more likely to have used alcohol or drugs during pregnancy. They were also more likely to have had incidents of consuming the equivalent of a fifth of liquor per day and more likely than older women to have hit someone or been violent toward others. Younger women had a 2.5 times higher incidence of eating disorders, with 25% having either anorexia or bulimia or alternating periods of starving and binging and purging. Rates of depression were similar across age groups. In comparison with older women, the younger group had considerably more work-related problems—e.g., in relationships with supervisors and coworkers, the quality of work performance, time off the job, and injuries on the job. Younger women were also more likely to have been the driver in a motor vehicle accident, to have been arrested, or to have been jailed overnight. In the year before treatment, younger women had more hospitalizations for psychiatric care, received more emergency room medical treatment, and had hospitalization and outpatient medical care similar to that of the older women.

- *Violence and abuse*. Younger women also had a history of greater physical abuse as children (36%). As adults, the prevalence of abuse escalated, with 48% of younger women reporting physical abuse and 32% reporting rape or coerced sexual intercourse. This is in contrast to older women, of whom 23% reported a history of physical abuse before age 18, rising to 35% after age 18. For younger women, relationships with boyfriends and spouses were marked by domestic violence and abuse. Among married women, younger women were 2.5 times more likely than were older women to have a spouse with an alcohol or substance abuse problem.

- *Past history*. Younger women demonstrated a wider range of problems and more incidents of social difficulties before age 15. These included truancy (30%), suspensions or expulsions from school (23%), being arrested (14%), running away from home more than once (28%), vandalism (19%), shoplifting and stealing (53%), and starting physical fights (27%). Younger women reported being more sexually active in early adolescence, with 20% having had sexual intercourse with more than one person before their fifteenth birthday.

• *The widowed.* Although elderly widows have not been identified as a subgroup at special risk, the question of the relationship of grief, bereavement, and the subsequent use of alcohol was examined among women admitted for substance abuse treatment. Tranquilizer use has been recognized as greater among widows, even in the absence of a therapeutic effect. Three-fourths of the widows had a history of heavy alcohol use before the deaths of their husbands. There was a significant subgroup who did appear to be at increased risk for the development of an alcohol problem after the death of their husbands. These were women who had no family history of alcohol problems but whose deceased husbands had been alcohol dependent and had been untreated. Alcohol problems emerged in these women as a response to pathological grief, which was the legacy of the alcoholic marriage.

Natural history

In what other ways do alcohol and drug problems of women differ from those of men? The major differences that have been described are noted below, admittedly in a very brief and cursory fashion.

• Apparently more alcoholic women than men can point to a specific trigger for the onset of heavy drinking.

This might be a divorce, an illness, the death of a spouse, children leaving home, or some other stressful event. If a woman seeks help at such a point, both a careful alcohol use history and education about the potential risks of alcohol use are warranted. The danger of relying upon alcohol or other drugs is that the crisis can take on a long-term life of its own. The challenge to those dealing with a woman in the face of any of the above difficulties is in providing empathy rather than sympathy. Either overtly or covertly, the danger is often to imply that if that had happened to us, we would probably have responded in the same fashion. The current dangerous misuse of alcohol and drugs can become lost in the forest of other problems.

• Women's alcohol dependence is often described as "telescoped."

This means the disease appears later and progresses more rapidly. The period of time between the onset of heavy drinking and entry into treatment is shorter among women, too.

• Women alcoholics are more susceptible to medical complications than are male alcoholics.

For men, the presence of medical complications is tied to long-term, regular heavy use. The several six-packs a day over time will take their toll. For women, the situation may be different. Medical complications among women may be less a product of the amount usually consumed but tied to the frequency of heavy drinking occasions. Thus, very heavy drinking once or twice a week may raise more havoc than if the same amount of booze were spread out over time. Women have particular susceptibility to liver disease. This may well be tied to the differences in the way men and women metabolize alcohol (see Chapter 2). Women with alcohol dependence have consumed significantly less alcohol during their drinking career than have men, perhaps 45% less, yet they still experience difficulties of a similar magnitude.

• Women alcoholics tend to come into treatment earlier than men.

The time between the onset of heavy drinking and a referral for treatment is likely to be shorter. This is believed to be due to higher rates of medical complications. Women too tend to exhaust the social supports and resources needed to continue alcohol use. Also, women have a greater number of alcohol-induced problems than do men, even when the length of drinking, the presence of psychiatric problems, and work status are taken into account. Men, however, outnumber women entering treatment by almost 4 to 1.

• In a marriage in which one spouse is alcoholic, when it is the woman, there is a significantly greater likelihood of divorce.

If the wife has alcoholism, there is a nine-times greater chance of divorce than is found for male alcoholics. An important consequence is that the family and emotional support systems that are an asset in recovery are less likely to be present. Interestingly, whatever the woman's marital situation, it has been found that women entering treatment do not receive the solid support for that decision that men generally receive from family and friends.

• Women with alcohol and/or other drug problems are more likely than are men to have a drug dependent partner.

• If the woman is unmarried or a divorced single parent, there are not only additional emotional demands but also economic burdens. In the aftermath of divorce, almost three-quarters of women and their children are economically less well off, if not downright poverty stricken. Entry into treatment may stretch an already difficult financial situation.

• Women have higher rates of use of other drugs and also other drugs in combination with alcohol than do men.

They are prescribed mood-altering drugs much more frequently than men. A sample of women alcoholics found that 70% had a past history of having been prescribed psychoactive drugs, a rate 1.5 times greater than for alcoholic men. Of the women prescribed psychoactive drugs, one-half could recall at least one occasion of having used alcohol in combination with the medication; also, one-half had been prescribed more than one category of drug. This suggests the need for obtaining a very careful drug use history, with a wary eye for multiple drug use and abuse.

• In the workplace and vocational spheres, differences between men and women are evident. With respect to employment and vocational status, women with substance use problems—just like women in the general population—have fewer vocational skills and training and are less likely to be employed, to hold high-status jobs, to be self-supporting, and, if drugs are involved, to be financing their own drug use. In

these circumstances, women may support their drug addiction with petty larceny, shoplifting, and prostitution. They also have fewer vocational skills and training. Women are more likely than men are to lose their jobs. Women with alcohol or other drug problems are more likely to be dependent on a family member or on public welfare for survival than are men.

• In terms of what prompts treatment and the perceptions of problems when entering care, women have been found to differ from men in several ways. Generally women report more depression, anxiety, sense of powerlessness, hopelessness, and guilt than men report. This is not the result of their having more psychiatric illness but is part of the female symptom pattern of alcohol dependence.

• Women entering treatment often have experienced recent episodes of violence.

• While reporting less support for entry into treatment, women, more than men, credit pressure from others as a major factor in their seeking treatment, whether from children, other relatives, coworkers, or their physician.

• More commonly women do not see either alcohol or drug use as their primary problem. Thus they are inclined to express concern about the ability of a substance abuse program to assist them. This also means that it is particularly important for treatment personnel to help them make the connection between their life problems and alcohol or drug use.

• A concern unique to women is fear of losing custody of children. This is especially an issue for women who are involved with illicit drug use.

• Among patients admitted to private hospitals for cocaine treatment, despite many similarities between the sexes, several significant differences were identified. Women had started to use cocaine at a younger age than the men, and the opposite is true for most other drugs and alcohol use. The appearance of crack is credited with many of these changes. Women's use of crack has rivaled, and in some cities, exceeded use by men.

• Women with dependence are reported to have lower expectations for their lives than men, and also to express more concern with survival and minimizing discomfort.

• Little is known about personality factors that may predate the emergence of alcohol dependence in women.

A follow-up in later life of a sample of women college students found that factors predictive of alcohol dependence in later life were considerably different from those among men. The best predictor for alcohol dependence in women might be termed *purposeful drinking*—that is, drinking to relieve shyness, to get high, to be happy, and to get along better. Research also indicates that women who are heavy social drinkers have the expectation that drinking will relieve worries, nervousness, and tension.

• A problem of growing concern is the rise of HIV infection and AIDS among women, primarily related to their own intravenous drug use or to their having a sexual partner with AIDS.

It appears that young women with alcohol and multiple substance-use problems are a population at particular risk. While a 3:1 ratio of male-to-female intravenous drug users has been frequently cited, among younger women this disparity is disappearing. Women appear to have a faster transition from drug use initiation to dependence, tend to be introduced to drug use by partners, have drug-using partners which promotes access to drugs, are more likely to engage in needle-sharing, and with the potential for prostitution, are likely to have greater ease in maintaining a steady supply of drugs. All of these factors contribute to an increased risk of HIV/AIDS infection. Beyond the risk to these women, the other issue of concern is perinatal transmission in pregnancy. A public health priority is intervention to reduce the spread of HIV/AIDS in this population.

• There are gender-based differences that are evident in women's relationships to family, and spouse or partner. Women who come from families where drugs were commonly used as a primary coping strategy are more likely to themselves become addicted. Women with substance use problems have often experienced greater familial disruption than have men with such problems. In contrast to men, both alcohol- and opiate-involved women come from drug-abusing and disorganized families. Female heroin addicts are more likely than are male heroin addicts to have first been introduced to heroin by family members or others close to them. The development of dependence is linked to the family's approval of use or the absence of clear disapproval of use, in combination with easy access to the drug.

• With respect to the drinking population, women are overly represented in emergency-room visits, as indicated by data drawn from the Drug Abuse Warning Network (DAWN).

It is speculated that this is due to women's greater vulnerability to overdoses at lower levels of consumption and their greater likelihood to use alcohol in combination with other drugs. With many overdoses reported as accidental, one important intervention is education about the effects of alcohol and other drugs, alone and in combination.

• Alcohol problems in women greatly increase the risk for suicide. A recent study determined that alcoholic women have a history of suicide attempts five times greater than that of nonalcoholic women, with 40% of the alcoholic women in this study reporting a suicide attempt. Furthermore, close to 50% who make one attempt will make a future suicide attempt. Youth and alcohol/drug use and abuse in women are a high-risk combination.

Treatment issues

Beyond the items already touched on that can influence the course of the disease process and when and how women are identified and diagnosed, there are also issues relevant to the treatment process itself.

Mothering and female sexuality are two aspects of self-esteem unique to women. If a woman has children, some of the questions she may well be asking herself include: "Am I a good mother? Can I be a good mother? Have I hurt my children? Can I ever cope with my children if I don't drink or use drugs?" These may not be explicit in the therapy sessions, but they do cross her mind. They begin to be answered, positively, one hopes, as she gains sober and straight time. Family meetings may also be one way she gains answers to these questions. However, in some cases where there has been child abuse or a child is having special difficulties, a referral to a children's agency, a family-service agency, or a mental health clinic may be important in dealing with these situations. One of the things any mother will need to learn if she is to regain her self-esteem as a mother is a sense of what the "normal" difficulties are in raising children.

In terms of sexuality, there may be a number of potential questions. If she has had a divorce or an affair, a woman may well be wondering about her worth and attractiveness as a woman. Even if the marriage is intact, there may be sexual problems. On one hand, the sexual relationship may have almost disappeared as the drinking progressed. On the other, it may have been years since she has had sexual intercourse without the benefit of a glass of wine or a couple of beers. Again, time in sobriety may well be the major therapeutic element. But couples therapy and/or sexual counseling may be needed if marital problems are not resolved. In cases where the sexual problems preceded the active drinking, professional help is certainly recommended. Sobering up is not likely to take away the existing problem in some miraculous fashion. To let it fester is to invite even more problems.

What about single women or women caught in an unsatisfactory marriage? It is not uncommon for them to find themselves "suddenly" involved in an affair or an extramarital relationship. With a little bit of sobriety, they are very ripe to fall in love. This may have several roots. The woman may be questioning her femininity, and the attentions of a man may well provide some affirmation of her status as a woman. Also possible is the fact that with sobriety comes a sense of being alive again. There is the reawakening of a host of feelings that have long been dormant, including sexual feelings. In this sense it may be like the bloom and intensity of adolescence. A romantic involvement may follow very naturally. Unfortunately, it can lead to disaster, if followed with abandon. This can be equally true for men.

A word of caution to male therapists working with women. If you are the first person in many years to accept her and if you have been making attempts to raise her self-esteem, she may mistake her gratitude for a personal emotional attachment to you. Your recognition of this "error" is imperative. If you provide contacts for her with other women in recovery, she may be better able to recognize this pitfall as well.

For women in treatment, children are another concern. If a woman has young children, long-term residential treatment may be very difficult to arrange. Many women have no husbands in the home, and extended family members do not always live down the street, as was once the case. However, for that very reason, it may be all the more important for the woman to begin her recovery in a residential center, where intense therapy may take place without the distractions of daily family life. Models of treatment to overcome this problem are being tried in many areas throughout the country. But in too many places the usual facilities are still the only ones available. You will need to stretch your creativity to the limit to deal with this problem. Potentially, friends, extended family—even if they are called in from a distance—or a live-in sitter can be used. When inpatient treatment is warranted, there may be no way to allow a client the optimum advantage of an extended residential treatment. If this is the case, intensive day treatment is a possible option. Even if inpatient care can be arranged, you may be faced with a woman's intense guilt over, and resistance to, leaving her children. There are no easy formulas, and the therapist is left to work out the best solution possible in each case.

The latest figures from the General Services Board of AA indicate that women represent a substantial number of AA members. It appears that whatever the differences between men and women, AA manages to achieve similar rates of success with both. It is as important to make a referral to AA or NA for your female clients as for male clients. A few trips to local meetings should assure her that it is no longer the male stronghold it once was. In many communities, one will also find groups that are predominantly women. A not uncommon criticism of Alcoholics Anonymous and the related 12-step programs is that they foster continuing female dependence. This, however, is not a universally accepted view. As one feminist author commented, "Those I see going into 12-step programs are basically trying to stay alive. They are not the people that one would see at political meetings. Without recovery they would probably be dead, and dead women don't have any politics."

There has been little systematic research on whether there are differences in treatment outcomes by gender. Both males and females with similar demographic characteristics, in comparable stages of their illness, are presumed to do equally well in similar treatment settings. A few recent studies do suggest that women may have more satisfactory outcomes one year posttreatment than do men. However, women's rates of entrance, retention, and completion of treatment are found to be significantly lower than rates for men.

Access to treatment may be a dimension on which men and women differ. For women there are the issues of child care and being able to afford treatment, because women have a greater chance of losing their jobs, having lower wages and benefits, and may be the family's sole source of support. Women may need more ancillary supports and services because of their status as single mothers or as victims of domestic violence or because of the absence of fewer supportive people in their environment. Training in and skillful application of the information on women's issues generally can minimize distrust of social-service system providers. Attitudes toward addicted women are often negative, and chemically dependent women are often subjected to sexual harassment. Pregnancy and childbirth are points where intervention is often effective with alcohol and drug-involved women.

Treatment issues for pregnant women

Pregnancy and childbirth are points when the potential for intervention is often greatest. Medical treatment for pregnant drug dependent women must include perinatal services, pharmacotherapy, health education, and referral. Perinatal services should encompass evaluation and treatment by a perinatologist and a perinatal nurse clinician. HIV counseling and testing and nutritional counseling are important. The mother should deliver in a hospital where emergency services are readily available in case of complications. Infants are frequently small and many need intensive care.

Methadone maintenance has proved very helpful in the treatment of pregnant opiate dependent women. Doses range from 10 to 90 milligrams with an average of 50 milligrams. It is clear that methadone is safe for pregnant women. The major problem encountered is withdrawal symptoms in the baby; other complications resulting from the medication do not occur. If methadone is used appropriately and coupled with comprehensive prenatal care, there is a decline in the complications of pregnancy, childbirth, and infant development.

Medical withdrawal of pregnant opiate dependent women from methadone generally is *not* indicated. Methadone doses should not be decreased, but continued at a level that provides comfort for the mother and decreases the chances of withdrawal of the mother as well as the fetus. In the third trimester, many women need an increase in methadone dose due to various physiological changes as well as weight gain at this time.

If a pregnant woman has any specific medical complications such as hyperthyroidism or diabetes, appropriate medical consultation is essential. Due to the impoverished conditions in which many of the women live, many problems are more common.

Policy and legal issues   Being a parent and a drug dependent woman presents many conflicts. One of the basic premises of child rearing and intervention models is that infant behavior is part of a communication system within the care-giving environment. This is a mutually responsive system in which feedback from one partner to the other is used to regulate this system. In early work with drug-exposed infants this complexity was not appreciated. As a consequence it was believed that drug exposure per se led to poor developmental outcome. If the mother was considered at all, it was thought that she could only lower the developmental outcome of the child. The *Maternal Lifestyles Study,* a multicenter, prospective longitudinal study, is now attempting to address these issues by studying the effects of prenatal drug exposure on the interplay between the neurobehavioral and regulatory capacities of the child and parenting and environment factors. There is the belief that here too there are often protective factors at work, that mitigate against some of the risks imposed by maternal drug use; and interventions that provide needed supports can make a difference.

With respect to social policy, a variety of approaches have been suggested to protect children born to drug dependent mothers. These include systematic and massive public education and support by community leaders to stress that no drugs be used during pregnancy; giving hospitals the legal power and financial resources to care for babies until they are medically ready for discharge and the home environment is ready to care for them; placing children into foster care if drug dependent parents cannot care for them; facilitating the adoption process when parents anticipate little chance for improvement. Special programs for children affected by prenatal drug exposure remain limited. Such programs are needed to address and prevent any developmental disabilities; to provide supportive services to parents or other caretakers such as foster parents or guardians who may be caring for the child because of the mother's continued drug use; and to help parents or caretakers cope with behavioral problems that could arise.

There are special considerations for children who remain in the home. Drug abuse treatment is necessary for drug dependent mothers. Among the most alarming statistics in terms of outcome for children born to mothers addicted to cocaine are those associated with child abuse and neglect. Child abandonment is common with infants who require extended care at birth or are later hospitalized. Intoxication from crack is associated with outbursts of violence, which increases the risk for battering. In many urban areas where crack use is prevalent, treatment programs have long waiting lists. Facilities that will accept pregnant women or women with infants are few. Unfortunately, even if treatment is provided, outcome studies suggest that compared with alcohol and opiate dependence, individuals dependent on cocaine, especially in the form of crack, have much more difficulty maintaining abstinence. Thus some oversight of children in the home is imperative. However, in urban areas in which child welfare systems are already overburdened, the probability of oversight to identify problems and intervene on the child's behalf is low.

A disturbing social development—the emergence of court actions filed against pregnant women who are dependent on cocaine—has received national attention. Women have been charged with child abuse on the basis of administering cocaine to the fetus through the umbilical cord. Unfortunately, judges, legislators, and prosecutors, like the public in general, have obtained most of their information about drug dependent pregnant and parenting women from the popular press. The coverage of the so-called "crack epidemic" and "crack babies" has been inaccurate and alarmist. Careful research and measured responses have not been widely covered, and thus there exists the prevailing assumption that children exposed prenatally to crack are inevitably and irremediably damaged.

The reactions to the problems of drug addicted pregnant women have thus been largely punitive. Hundreds of women have been prosecuted on unproven theories of fetal abuse and drug delivery through the umbilical cord. These prosecutions continue despite the fact that no appellate court in the country has upheld one. Thousands of women have also been reported under civil child neglect laws and investigated for being neglectful or abusive parents based solely on a positive urine toxicology specimen at the birth of the child. African-American women have been arrested and reported disproportionately to authorities despite evidence that white and African-American women in similar situations use illegal substances at approximately the same rate. Judges often assume, incorrectly, that drug dependent pregnant women have access to appropriate drug treatment, to contraceptive and abortion services, and to prenatal care. Moreover, they do not view addiction as a disease nor understand that relapse may be part of recovery. The public policy statements of leading medical and public health organizations opposing punitive responses has helped. Continued prosecution of pregnant women, cutbacks in services for pregnant and parenting drug users, and the continued belief among many leaders that children's physical and emotional health problems can be blamed exclusively on cocaine or other drugs suggests the need for extensive judicial and public education and organized opposition to punitive approaches to this health problem.

THE WORKPLACE

Some basic statistics

For the first time the Household Survey in 1994 included questions about alcohol and drug use in relation to work. Those surveyed were asked about work-related issues, e.g., missed work, being fired, workplace accidents, their occupation, size of the workplace, whether they had ever been provided with information about the alcohol and drug polices at work, the existence of an EAP, the use of drug testing, and their attitudes toward testing. What were the findings? In the total population ages 18–49, about 8% of full-time workers, 9% of part-time workers, and 16% of the unemployed reported current illicit drug use (i.e., any illicit drug use in the previous 30 days). For full-time workers, 9% reported heavy alcohol use, that is, 5 or more drinks per occasion in the past 30 days. Those who reported current illicit drug use were more likely to have had three or more employers in the past year, taken an unexcused absence, or either voluntarily left a job or been fired. The rate of current drug use is higher among 18- to 25-years olds, males, whites, and those with personal income of less than $9,000 or more than $75,000. The rate of current illicit drug use is higher among those working in smaller establishments, with 1–24 employees. The rate of heavy

THE GREAT MAJESTO JUMPS 100 Feet into A Wet SPONGE

I know his Secret. He wets the sponge with Cognac.

alcohol use is consistent for all size establishments. Thirty-five percent of full-time workers reported drug testing at hiring, 20% reported random drug testing, and 28% reported testing upon reasonable suspicion.

The majority of those who have alcohol or other drug problems are members of the work force. As business and industry began to recognize the costs to them of employees with alcohol problems, there was a rapid development of special programs to identify problems and initiate treatment. Studies have consistently found that substance use has a statistically significant effect on labor supply, absenteeism, and retention, and influences a variety of performance measures. The earliest work-based programs focused on alcohol and were sometimes called *occupational alcohol programs.* That term has been replaced by *employee assistance programs,* with a corresponding broadening in scope. Attention is no longer primarily or narrowly directed to alcohol or even substance use, but the array of issues that might influence job performance, be it family problems, financial problems, or mental health concerns. Programs too are increasingly interested not just with addressing problems but in preventing them. So now we see *employee wellness programs.* These can include stress reduction courses, programs on nutrition, or exercise programs, and in many places, fitness centers actually on site.

Historically, drinking has been interwoven with work. There has long been the office party, the company picnic, the wine and cheese reception, the martini lunches, the "drink date" to review business, the bar car on the commuter train, the old standby gift of a fifth for a business associate, the round of drinks to celebrate the closing of a business deal, or the construction crew stopping off for beers after work. Over the past several years the meshing of drinking and business has come under fire. First, the IRS decreed that the martini lunch was not a legitimate business expense. Then the growing interest in physical fitness took its toll. Concern about liability when alcohol is a part of company-sponsored parties has come into play. Though recently receiving more attention, court cases addressing this go back to the mid-1970s. Nonetheless, for too long drinking in many work situations was not only accepted but expected. Whenever alcohol use is tolerated, the potential for alcohol problems among susceptible individuals rises, more so if drinking is subtly encouraged.

With the passage of the *Drug-free Workplace Legislation* in the 1980s, drug use also became a workplace concern. Gradually more and more businesses inaugurated mandatory drug testing as a condition for initial hiring and continuing employment. Clearly the focus was on drugs as opposed to alcohol. At the same time, it also conveyed the message that alcohol no longer enjoys a status of being "okay," while all other drugs are "bad." Substance use of whatever variety can and does interfere with performance and productivity and is therefore a legitimate business concern. For a long period, smoking at work was an accepted practice. This is no longer the case, and many work sites have offered smoking cessation programs to help employees quit. No longer being able to smoke at work has certainly raised the quit rate. There is also the phenomenon of 'exiled' smoking, people taking smoking breaks, and questions are now being raised about the impact of this practice. Two different questions are being asked: what is the impact on performance of smoker's experiencing withdrawal, and what is the impact on non-smokers' morale as they witness coworkers taking authorized and unauthorized cigarette breaks?

Occupational high-risk factors

Although a job cannot be said to cause alcohol/drug dependence or abuse, it can contribute to its development. Some of the factors that Trice and Roman, authorities in the area of workplace alcohol issues, have identified as job-based risk factors include:

- absence of clear goals (and absence of supervision)
- freedom to set work hours (isolation and low visibility)
- low structural visibility (e.g., salespeople away from the business place)
- being a "work horse," overly invested in one's job
- occupational obsolescence (especially common in scientific and technical fields)
- new work status
- "required" on-the-job drinking (e.g., salespeople drinking with clients)
- reduction of social controls (occurs on college campuses and other less structured settings)
- severe role stress
- competitive pressure
- presence of illegal drug users

More recently researchers have recognized that working with alcohol itself can be a risk factor, e.g., in the hospitality industry. Another form of work-related drug problem comes not from the individual's use but others' use. The smoking ban in restaurants or bars may be appreciated by the patrons. The real beneficiaries are bartenders and the wait-staff, who never had the option of leaving and were trapped in a smoky haze for their 8-hour shifts.

The workplace cover-up

If bringing up the drinking practices and potential problems of a family member or close friend makes someone squirm, the idea of saying something to a coworker is virtually unthinkable. Almost everyone accepts a separation between work and home or professional and private life. So until the alcohol problem flows into the work world, the worker's use of alcohol is often considered no one else's business. That does not mean that no one sees a problem developing. Our suspicion is that someone

Portrait of a man who stops in a bar for 3 drinks on his way home from work every night.

There are two things that will be believed of a man whosoever, and one of them is that he has taken to drink.
BOOTH TARKINGTON

with even a little savvy can often spot potentially dangerous drinking practices. The office scuttlebutt or work crew's bull sessions plus simple observation make it common knowledge who "really put it away this weekend," or the "poor devil who just got picked up for a DWI," or "you can always count on Sue to join in whenever anyone wants to stop for a drink after work."

Even if an employee does show some problems on the job, whether directly or indirectly related to alcohol use, coworkers may try to "help out" by doing extra work or at least by not blowing the whistle. Because employee assistance programs, if they are available, are based on identifying work deterioration, any attempt by coworkers to help cover up job problems makes spotting the problem all the more difficult. If a company does not have a program to help those employees with alcohol/drug problems, odds for a cover-up by coworkers are even greater. Another important party in this concealment strategy is predictably the spouse, who usually doesn't want to do anything to threaten the paycheck.

In the past when the cover-ups no longer could hide a problem, the employee usually got fired; this may still happen in many companies. In such instances, the enterprise may lose a formerly valuable and well-trained worker, statistically a costly "solution." The current thinking is that it is cheaper for a company to identify problems earlier and to use the job as leverage to get the employee into treatment and back to work.

Workplace interventions

Facts and experience suggest that the occupational environment may be one of the most efficient and economical means of providing an opportunity for early identification and treatment of alcoholism and alcohol- and other drug-related problems. Early intervention increases the chances for recovery for the following reasons:

- physical health has not deteriorated significantly
- financial resources are not as depleted
- emotional supports still exist in the family and community
- threat of job loss can be used as leverage

Employee assistance programs (EAPs) are organized in a variety of ways, from an in-house counselor to contracts with outside groups for these services. Earlier programs were more narrowly restricted and focused upon alcohol and drugs alone. Now, these narrowly focused efforts have typically been replaced by what is known as the "broad brush" approach, that is, dealing with any of the many problems that may affect employees' performance.

The following are among the more common signs and symptoms that may point to a troubled employee and thereby help to identify the problem drinker or substance abuser:

- chronic absenteeism
- change in behavior

- physical signs
- spasmodic work pace
- lower quantity and quality of work
- partial absences
- avoidance of supervisors and coworkers
- on-the-job drinking or drug use
- on-the-job accidents and lost time from off-the-job accidents

Training supervisors and others to recognize these signs is important so that early detection can occur. Training is also critical in helping employers to document and not diagnose. Where there have been broad educational efforts through information sessions, posters, pamphlets, and so forth, there has been an increase in peer or self-referrals. Such referrals may often make up the bulk of referrals to a program. The culture of the workplace has a significant impact on the use and acceptance of EAP's. While supervisory personnel are a major factor, equally important are the attitudes of close coworkers.

An important technique in dealing with those in the workplace is called either *intervention, constructive coercion,* or *confrontation.* This approach, based on the Johnson intervention model, is used in the work setting to motivate the individual to seek help to improve job performance and retain the job. In the context of a formal program, the procedure is to identify, document, and then discuss the facts with the employee and extend an offer of referral for help.

Confrontation occurs within the company's normal evaluation and disciplinary procedures. A supervisor, manager, or union steward who notes certain behaviors and signs of deteriorating job performance documents them. If the confrontation is unsuccessful, the next phase would be a stepped-up disciplinary procedure, including a time limit and a formal referral with the "threat" of job loss if performance is not improved. However, it is believed that often despite such policies and procedures many supervisors are more apt to be informal (talking with workers, listening, and being supportive) than formal (referring workers to helping resources within the company or community). Supervisors are more likely to become involved if they have positive attitudes about help giving and seeking, are trained to identify and help workers, and are aware of what is going on in workers' lives.

The workplace medical clinic is also well positioned to promote screening and conduct brief office-based interventions. One recent Swedish study found that when employees were offered an alcohol screening as part of a routine occupational health visit, 98% took advantage of the opportunity. Of those screened, 21% were found to have excessive alcohol consumption and were contacted to arrange a follow-up visit. It was found that 80% of those contacted by telephone came in for a follow-up visit, compared to only 17% who were sent a letter. Of equal interest is that this program also prompted persons who had not been seen to call for an appointment.

Implications for treatment

It is important that substance abuse professionals be knowledgeable about workplace programs. They can thereby better coordinate treatment efforts for the employed client.

Does the individual's employer have an EAP? If so, who is the clinician? What services are offered? For any client, it is important that you be aware of any work-related problems. If so, what is the current job status? Has a disciplinary procedure been instituted, or has the employee been informally warned and referred for treatment? In addition, to avoid future conflict, learn about any union involvement. Such information can help in formulating realistic treatment plans.

It is important to be sensitive to the policies and politics of the employed client's work setting. Without this knowledge and awareness, there is the danger of violating confidentiality or, conversely, of not taking full advantage of the opportunity to cooperate with the employer on the client's behalf. If there is a company policy, learn about it so that you can plan realistically and avoid treatment-work conflicts. The nature of the client's work and the potential impact of any medication, if prescribed, must be considered. A follow-up plan must consider the working person's hours and geographical location. The flexibility and accessibility of the treatment facility can be a key factor in successful rehabilitation. Evening office hours and early-morning and weekend appointments may have to be arranged so that treatment will not interfere with the job. On the other hand, if there is an EAP with clinical personnel, this may be the most appropriate site for follow-up and continuing care, after the initial intensive treatment.

You may also find that some individuals will have to be treated as outpatients even when inpatient services are more appropriate. The employee may not be able to take the time off or may not have adequate insurance coverage. Insurance plans are far less likely to cover inpatient treatment, and if so the stay will be very limited. The rationale is that outpatient care is less expensive and that little or no evidence indicates that inpatient care provides better treatment outcomes. As noted earlier, these assumptions are based on data derived from group statistics. Both ends of the spectrum are lost to the statistical average. As we hope has become clear, all clients are not alike, and blanket assumptions regarding treatment can be hazardous to a client's health.

Many larger companies are also becoming involved in managed health-care plans. This means that there are designated providers, as in an HMO (Health Maintenance Organization), which provides either whatever medical care is needed or the required prior approval for a treatment referral, if the insurance is to cover the costs. The rationale for such arrangements is that unnecessary services will be eliminated and health-care dollars will be used more wisely. While laudable in concept, in practice this arrangement has caused concern. With respect to alcohol and substance abuse services, there are several problems that have been identified. Some managed health-care systems have developed contracts

Portrait of a man
who thinks he's clever
when he's drunk

with specific treatment agencies to provide all necessary services. Payment is often based on a per capita formula, with a set reimbursement paid for a diagnostic category, rather than reimbursements being made on the basis of actual costs incurred. Thus there is a clear incentive to limit services, for example to favor outpatient care over inpatient treatment, or to have outpatient treatment consist of a specified number of visits. This may work for the "average" client. However the average person in treatment is by analogy like the statistically average drinker we described in Chapter 1—virtually nonexistent. The provision of individualized treatment needed to ensure optimal care is sacrificed for indiscriminately delivering the statistically predetermined norm.

Workplace programs have made significant progress in demonstrating that the "human approach" is good business. Yet there is still a great deal to be done, and it can be better accomplished with cooperation among those involved in the occupational program field and substance abuse clinicians.

OTHER SPECIAL POPULATIONS

When caring for clients, the fact is that the "average client" is virtually nonexistent. All kinds of factors have an impact, particularly racial and ethnic background, in combination with age and gender. These have an important impact in several ways. These factors, for example, determine what kinds of behavior are viewed as evidence of a problem, to whom people turn for help and under what circumstances, and clients' comfort in using professional care.

In this chapter, neither racial nor ethnic groups are discussed specifically. In the United States the major racial and ethnic groups are African Americans, Hispanics, Asians, and Native Americans. In addition, there are other client groups, which though their characteristics may be less dramatic are just as real, e.g., the Portuguese New England fisherman, the Vermont farmer, the client from the hills of Appalachia, or the blue collar worker from the midwest. Furthermore, even within a particular group there can be considerable diversity, as is true of Hispanics. Differences include geographical location, whether the individual is from California, Texas, Florida, or New York, whether the client is a recent immigrant or native-born, and if native-born, what generation.

For the clinician working with the member of an ethnic or racial group, one of the most useful pieces of information will be the client's relationship to his or her traditional culture as well as to the larger, dominant culture. This is sometimes referred to as *cultural orientation,* meaning what sets of rules an individual instinctively follows. The basic question is to what extent the client identifies with a traditional ethnic group and to what extent he or she thinks and is comfortable in functioning not as a member of a particular ethnic group but as part of the American "mainstream." Some of the terms used to describe these different orientations is

TABLE 10.12   ASSESSING CULTURAL ORIENTATION

	Traditional culture or culture of origin	Majority culture
Social	• close friends from same ethnic background • leisure activities within ethnic community	• close friends not restricted to ethnic group • leisure not primarily within ethnic community
Language	• fluent in native language • uses primarily native language	• not fluent in native language
Spiritual/traditions	• familiar with and participates in ethnic ceremonies and celebrations	• unfamiliar with or does not participate in native festivities
Family	• defined by customs of the ethnic culture	• considers family the nuclear family unit, i.e. spouse, or parents and children

"assimilated" as opposed to "nonassimilated," or bicultural. In brief, those individuals who are not assimilated think of themselves in terms of the values and rules of behavior of their group of origin. Those who are assimilated may or may not be familiar with the traditional ways; they are most comfortable functioning in the usual style of the dominant American culture. Those described as bicultural are able to function by the rules either of their native culture or the majority American culture.

In working with clients who are members of ethnic groups, a sense of their cultural orientation is important. Table 10.12 indicates the different areas that might be considered.

Becoming acquainted with a different culture

In working with clients who are members of any cultural group other than your own, it is important to become familiar with the values, practices, and ways of seeing the world that are part of that group. Often a useful place to start is by considering the nature of your biases and the source of any preconceived notions.

Suggesting that a referral be made to a counselor or clinician who is also from the same ethnic or racial group as the client may be good advice. But it isn't always possible. At the very least it is important to know about the history and cultural traditions. In terms of alcohol problems, how are drinking problems defined? What are the behaviors that within the community would signal an alcohol problem? To whom do people tend to turn for help in time of trouble? Are there any particular biases against seeking professional care or getting help from an 'outsider?' Are there any particular customs that would make getting help more difficult? Be alert to any barriers caused by language. Therapists should be alert to and not be surprised to be watched closely for signs of prejudice or disinterest. As necessary, certainly acknowledge the limits and differences of your own experience and background. Wise advice that holds here as elsewhere is that "the patient is the best instructor," but it requires that you open yourself to learning.

RESOURCES AND FURTHER READING

Closser MH, Blow FC: Special populations: Women, ethnic minorities, and the elderly, *Psychiatric Clinics of North America* 16(1):199–209, 1993. (41 refs.)

Ubell V, Sumberg D: Heterosexual therapists treating homosexual addicted clients, *Journal of Chemical Dependency Treatment* 5(1):19–33, 1992. (8 refs.)

Adolescents

Alcohol Health and Research World: 22(2): entire issue, 1998.
   The entire issue is devoted to adolescent alcohol problems.

Alexander DE, Gwyther RE: Alcoholism in adolescents and their families: Family-focused assessment and management, *Pediatric Clinics of North America* 42(1):217–234, 1995. (102 refs.)

Bachman JG, Johnston LD, O'Malley PM: Explaining recent increases in students' marijuana use: Impacts of perceived risks and disapproval, 1976 through 1996, *American Journal of Public Health* 88(6):887–892, 1998. (17 refs.)

Bergmann PE, Smith MB, Hoffmann NG: Adolescent treatment: Implications for assessment, practice guidelines, and outcome management, *Pediatric Clinics of North America* 42(2):453–472, 1995. (11 refs.)

Denton RE, Kampfe CM: The relationship between family variables and adolescent substance abuse: A literature review, *Adolescence* 29(114): 475–495, 1994. (27 refs.)

Donovan C, McEwan R: A review of the literature examining the relationship between alcohol use and HIV-related sexual risk-taking in young people (review), *Addiction* 90(3):319–328, 1995. (35 refs.)

Epps RP, Manley MW, Glynn TJ: Tobacco use among adolescents: Strategies for prevention, *Pediatric Clinics of North America* 42(2):389–402, 1995. (67 refs.)

Farrell M, Strang J: Substance use and misuse in childhood and adolescence (review), *Journal of Clinical Psychiatry* 32(1):109–128, 1991. (139 refs.)

Hawkins JD, Catalano RF, Miller JY: Risk and protective factors for alcohol and other drug problems in adolescence and early adulthood: Implications for substance abuse prevention (review), *Psychological Bulletin* 112(1):6–105, 1992. (308 refs.)

Hennessy M: Adolescent syndromes of risk for HIV infection (review), *Evaluation Review* 18(3):312–341, 1994. (126 refs.)

Jones CL, Battjes RJ, eds: *Etiology of drug abuse: Implications for prevention, NIDA Research Monograph 56*, Rockville MD: National Institute on Drug Abuse, 1985.

Jurich AP, Polson CP: Family factors in the lives of drug users and abusers, *Adolescence* 20(77):143–159, 1985. (85 refs.)

Lamminpaa A: Alcohol intoxication in childhood and adolescence (review), *Alcohol and Alcoholism* 30(1):5–12, 1995. (78 refs.)

Leccese M, Waldron HB: Assessing adolescent substance use: A critique of current measurement instruments (review), *Journal of Substance Abuse Treatment* 11(6):553–563, 1994. (67 refs.)

McLellan AT, Dembo R: *Screening and assessment of alcohol- and other drug-abusing adolescents: Treatment Improvement Protocol (TIP) Series 3,* Rockville MD: Center for Substance Abuse Treatment, 1993.

Rogers PD, Speraw SR, Ozbek I: The assessment of the identified substance-abusing adolescent, *Pediatric Clinics of North America* 42(2): 351–370, 1995. (25 refs.)

Rotunda RJ, Scherer DG, Imm PS: Family systems and alcohol misuse: Research on the effects of alcoholism on family functioning and effective family interventions (review), *Professional Psychology: Research and Practice* 26(1):95–104, 1995. (106 refs.)

Schonberg SK: *Guidelines for the treatment of alcohol- and other drug-abusing adolescents: Treatment Improvement Protocol (TIP) Series 4,* Rockville MD: Center for Substance Abuse Treatment, 1993.

Shifrin F, Solis M: Chemical dependency in gay and lesbian youth, *Journal of Chemical Dependency Treatment* 5(1):67–76, 1992. (12 refs.)

College students

Bachman JG, Wadsworth KN, O'Malley PM, Johnston LD, Schulenberg JE: *Smoking, drinking and drug use in young adulthood: The impacts of new freedoms and new responsibilities,* Mahwah NJ: Lawrence Erlbaum, Inc., 1997.

Baer JS, Kivlahan DR, Marlatt GA: High-risk drinking across the transition from high school to college, *Alcoholism: Clinical and Experimental Research* 19(1):54–61, 1995. (27 refs.)

Engs RC, Hanson DJ: University students' drinking patterns and problems: Examining the effects of raising the purchase age, *Public Health Report* 133(6):647–673, 1988. (61 refs.)

Haines M, Spear SF: Changing the perception of the norm: A strategy to decrease binge drinking among college students, *Journal of American College Health* 45(3):134–140, 1996. (18 refs.)

Howard GS, Nathan PE, eds: *Alcohol use and misuse by young adults,* Notre Dame IN: University of Notre Dame Press, 1994.

Johnston LD, O'Malley PM, Bachman JG: *National survey results on drug use from the monitoring the future study, 1975–1997. Volume II: College students and young adults,* Rockville MD: National Institute on Drug Abuse, 1998.

Leichliter JS, Meilman PW, Presley CA, Cashin JR: Alcohol use and related consequences among students with varying levels of involvement in college athletics, *Journal of American College Health* 46(6):257–262, 1998. (27 refs.)

Presley CA, Meilman PW, Lyerla R: *Alcohol and drugs on American college campuses: Use, consequences, and perceptions of the campus environment, Volume III. 1989–1991.* Carbondale IL: Southern Illinois University, 1998

Wechsler H, Davenport AE, Dowdall GW, Grossman SJ, Zanakos SI: Binge drinking, tobacco, and illicit drug use and involvement in college athletics: A survey of students at 140 American colleges, *Journal of American College Health* 45(5):195–200, 1997. (19 refs.)

Wechsler H, Dowdall GW, Maenner G, Gledhill-Hoyt J, Lee H: Changes in binge drinking and related problems among American college students between 1993 and 1997: Results of the Harvard School of Public Health College Alcohol Study, *Journal of American College Health* 47(2): 57–68, 1998. (18 refs.)

The elderly

Adams WL, Yuan Z, Barboriak JJ, Rimm AA: Alcohol-related hospitalizations of elderly people: Prevalence and geographic variation in the United States, *Journal of the American Medical Association* 270(10): 1222–1225, 1993. (29 refs.)

Atkinson RM: Late onset problem drinking in older adults (review), *International Journal of Geriatric Psychiatry* 9(4):321–326, 1994. (28 refs.)

Barnea Z, Teichman M: Substance misuse and abuse among the elderly: Implications for social work intervention (review), *Journal of Gerontological Social Work* 21(3/4):133–148, 1994. (65 refs.)

Brower KJ, Mudd S, Blow FC, Young JP, Hill EM: Severity and treatment of alcohol withdrawal in elderly versus younger patients, *Alcoholism: Clinical and Experimental Research* 18(1):196–201, 1994. (12 refs.)

Egbert AM. The older alcoholic: Recognizing the subtle clinical clues, *Geriatrics* 48(7):63–69, 1993. (25 refs.)

Flaherty JH: Commonly prescribed and over-the-counter medications: Causes of confusion (review), *Clinics in Geriatric Medicine* 14(1): 101–121, 1998. (281 refs.)

Jennison KM: The impact of stressful life events and social support on drinking among older adults: A general population survey, *International Journal of Aging and Human Development* 35(2):99–123, 1992. (85 refs.)

Reid MC, Anderson PA: Geriatric substance use disorders (review), *Medical Clinics of North America* 81(4):999–1016, 1997. (104 refs.)

Scott RB, Mitchell MC: Aging, alcohol, and the liver, *Journal of the American Geriatrics Society* 36(3):225–265, 1988. (110 refs.)

Solomon K, Manepalli J, Ireland GA, et al: Alcoholism and prescription drug abuse in the elderly: St. Louis University grand rounds (review), *Journal of the American Geriatric Society* 41(1):57–69, 1993. (75 refs.)

Thibault JM, Maly RC: Recognition and treatment of substance abuse in the elderly, *Primary Care* 20(1):155–165, 1993. (35 refs.)

Women

Abbott AA: A feminist approach to substance abuse treatment and service delivery, *Social Work in Health Care* 19(3/4):67–83, 1994. (70 refs.)

Aldrich MR: Historical notes on women addicts, *Journal of Psychoactive Drugs* 26(1):61–64, 1994. (18 refs.)

Bepko C, ed: *Feminism and addiction,* New York: Haworth Press, 1991. (Chapter refs.)

Bradley KA, Boyd-Wickizer J, Powell SH, Burman ML: Alcohol screening questionnaires in women: A critical review, *Journal of the American Medical Association* 280(2):166–171, 1998. (54 refs.)

Center for Substance Abuse Treatment: *Practical approaches in the treatment of women who abuse alcohol and other drugs,* Rockville MD: Center for Substance Abuse Treatment, 1994. (Chapter refs.)

Finkelstein N, Duncan SA, Derman L, et al: *Getting sober, getting well: A treatment guide for caregivers who work with women,* Cambridge MA: CASPAR, 1990.

Gomberg ES: Women and alcohol: Use and abuse (review), *Journal of Nervous and Mental Disease* 181(4):211–219, 1993. (75 refs.)

Hall JM: Lesbians and alcohol: Patterns and paradoxes in medical notions and lesbians' beliefs (review), *Journal of Psychoactive Drugs* 25(2): 109–119, 1993. (109 refs.)

Henderson DJ: Drug abuse and incarcerated women: A research review, *Journal of Substance Abuse Treatment* 15(6):579–587, 1998. (89 refs.)

Roth P, ed: *Alcohol and drug issues are women's issues,* Metuchen NJ: Women's Action Alliance and The Scarecrow Press, Inc., 1991. (Chapter refs.)
Volume One: A review of the issues
Volume Two: The model program guide

Stein MD, Cyr MG: Women and substance abuse (review), *Medical Clinics of North America* 81(4):979–1007, 1997. (125 refs.)

Welsh DM, ed: *Alcohol health and research world* 18(3): entire issue, 1994.

The workplace

Delaney W, Grube JW, Ames GM: Predicting likelihood of seeking help through the employee assistance program among salaried and union hourly employees, *Addiction* 93(3):399–410, 1998. (54 refs.)

Eisner MD, Smith AK, Blanc PD: Bartenders' respiratory health after establishment of smoke-free bars and taverns, *Journal of the American Medical Association* 280(22):1909–1914, 1998. (64 refs.)

Forrest ARW: Ethical aspects of workplace urine screening for drug abuse, *Journal of Medical Ethics* 23(1):12–17, 1997. (25 refs.)

French MT: The effects of alcohol and illicit drug use in the workplace: A review, *Journal of Employee Assistance Research* 2(1):1–22, 1993. (63 refs.)

French MT: Zarkin GA, Bray JW, Hartwell TD: Costs of employee assistance programs: Findings from a national survey, *American Journal of Health Promotion* 11(3):219–222, 1997. (18 refs.)

Hartwell TD, Steele PD, Rodman NF: Workplace alcohol-testing programs: Prevalence and trends, *Monthly Labor Review* 121(6):27–34, 1998. (27 refs.)

Hermansson U, Knutsson A, Ronnberg S, Brndt L: Feasibility of brief intervention in the workplace for the detection and treatment of excessive alcohol consumption, *International Journal of Occupational and Environmental Health* 4(2):71–78, 1998. (30 refs.)

Hopkins KM: Influences on formal and informal supervisor intervention with troubled workers, *Employee Assistance Quarterly* 13(1):33–54, 1997. (20 refs.)

Karuntzos GT, Dunlap LJ, Zarkin GA, French MT: Designing an Employee Assistance Program (EAP) intervention for women and minorities: Lessons from the Rockford EAP Study, *Employee Assistance Quarterly* 14(1):49–67, 1998. (37 refs.)

Kramer RM: The role of the EAP in the identification and treatment of substance abuse, *Clinics in Laboratory Medicine* 18(4):747–759, 1998.

Shain M, Eakin J, Suurvali H, Currie A: Small business owners and the management of employees with problems: A descriptive study, *Employee Assistance Quarterly* 14(1):1–21, 1998. (19 refs.)

Special Issue. *Alcohol Health and Research World* 16(2):1–172, 1992.

Substance Abuse and Mental Health Services Administration, Office of Applied Studies, Hoffman JP, Larison C, Sanderson A: *An analysis of worker drug use and workplace policies and programs,* Rockville MD: Substance Abuse and Mental Health Services Administration, 1997. (20 refs.)

OTHER PSYCHIATRIC CONSIDERATIONS

Substance use disorders are in themselves psychiatric conditions. In this chapter, the focus is upon broader psychiatric issues of importance for the substance abuse clinician. These topics include suicide, the elements of the mental status examination, the major categories of psychiatric illness, and medications used in their treatment. The classifications for mental illness are important on several counts. One is that some clients will have a separate, coexisting psychiatric illness in addition to their alcohol or drug abuse or dependence. Another is that many colleagues are from the mental health field, and it is useful to be comfortable with the terminology and issues with which they deal. Finally, alcohol or other substance use problems will often mimic psychiatric conditions. Being informed about these conditions is vital when the task is determining if the behavior being observed or reported is a symptom of a substance use problem or another psychiatric illness.

SUICIDE EVALUATION AND PREVENTION

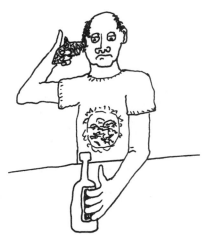

Substance use, alcohol use in particular, and suicide go together. Recall from Chapter 1 that in a substantial number of suicide attempts, the individual had been drinking and that approximately 40% of all completed suicides are alcohol related. The suicide rate for alcoholics is 55 times that of the general population. Before we all are overwhelmed by these statistics, we should consider why suicide and alcohol are connected and what we can do about them.

For practical purposes, there are several different groups to be considered when examining suicide. First are the completers, those who take their lives and intended to. Classically, these are lonely white men over 50 years of age or lonely teenagers. They use violent means such as a gun or hanging. Their methods are calculated and secretive. Second are those who succeed but did not intend to. These are the attempters. Classically they are white women, ages 20 to 40, often with interpersonal conflicts whose method is pills. The suicide attempt is often an impulsive response. Attempters die by mistake or as the result of miscalculation. For example, they lose track of dosage, or something goes wrong with their plans for rescue. The attempter's intent is not so much to die as to elicit a response from others. Emergency room psychology, which dismisses these clients with a firm kick in the pants, is inappropriate. Someone who is trying to gain attention by attempting suicide is in reality quite sick and deserves care. Third are the threateners. These are those individuals who use suicide as a lethal weapon: "If you leave me, I'll kill myself." They are often involved in a pathological relationship. These threateners usually do not follow through, but they are frightened and guilt-ridden. In responding to them the therapist will attempt to challenge the threat and thereby remove the deadlock it has created. Finally there is another group to be considered in suicide assessment. These people are termed parasuicidal. They are people who harm themselves either for release of tension or to relieve emotional pain. Not uncommonly, they have a history of physical or sexual abuse or severe neglect as children. Though they may intentionally seriously injure themselves, they usually do not have suicide in mind when they do so. They differ from attempters in that, unlike attempters, the impetus is not to get the attention of others, but to relieve internal emotional pain. However, here too, there are always errors and deaths occur.

Statistics and high-risk factors

The real statistic to keep in mind is that suicide is the second-leading recorded cause of death in people under 18 or over 65 years of age. Sixty percent give some prior indication of their intent, thereby making suicide preventable. Typical indications might be "I have a friend . . . ," or "What would you think if . . . ," or stockpiling drugs, or giving away possessions. New behaviors can be important cues. People doing things they have never done before may often indicate they have suddenly decided to commit suicide and are now at peace. Examples might be suddenly playing cards, dancing, or taking out the garbage when they have never made a practice of this before.

If present, certain high-risk factors should be identified. These include recent loss of a loved one or being single, widowed, and/or childless; living in an urban area; being unemployed, nonreligious, or "oppressed." High-risk emotional factors include anger plus hopelessness, broken or pathological family/friend communications, and isolation in a marriage or ongoing relationship. Verbal high-risk cues take the form of both direct statements: "I'm going to kill myself," or indirect indications: "I won't be around to give you any more trouble." People entering and leaving a depression are especially vulnerable, as are those with chronic illnesses like arthritis, high blood pressure, ulcers, and malignancies.

Recall that 65% of all suicide attempts are related to alcohol. Several reasons explain this correlation. First, the chemical nature of alcohol tends to release certain brain areas from control. The guarding mechanisms are let down. Hidden thoughts and impulses are released. (You may have witnessed incidents such as the intoxicated guy calling the boss a bastard.) Second, because of the chemical action of alcohol, a state is created wherein the integrative capacity of the brain is diminished. This is a condition in which aspects of memory and concentration are lost. Third, when alcohol is used as a medicine, it is unfortunately a good one to initially produce a mood of relaxation and pseudostability. In this state, people may think things are just the way they should be. They feel cool, calm, and collected so that suicide at this point may seem relevant and a good idea: "I'll just jump. It's the rational solution." More alcohol acts as a true depressant with obvious potential consequences. Finally, alcohol may also bring out psychological vulnerabilities. It may place people on the edge of reality, tip the scales, lead to loose associations, bring out psychosis, disinhibit normal fears, and produce voices saying: "The world is better off without you." In all these cases, alcohol acts as a catalyst, both physically and psychologically.

The most fertile ground for suicide is in cases of clinical depression. Most people who have the "blues" are not suicidal. They might think, "Gee, I wish I were dead, things are going so badly," or "I don't know how I'll make it. I might just drive off the road if things don't get better." Things usually do get better, however. On the other hand, clinical depression is characterized by a consistently low mood over a period of weeks, plus weight changes, sleep problems, and other physical symptoms. Pessimism is a symptom of the illness, just as fever is a symptom of the flu. Feelings of how bad things are are part of the depression. Depression, therefore, is bad enough alone, but combined with alcohol, it is a potent mix. "There is no way out." "I'm a bad person—the only way out is to kill myself."

How to ask

The therapist should always ask about suicide with any person who is depressed. The thing to remember is that we have never killed anybody by asking. We have certainly missed helping people we could have helped by not asking. There is no way to instigate a suicidal attempt by commonsense asking. It will come as a relief to your clients if you do ask them. Use your own emotional barometer to find out whether they are depressed or whether they are sad. Check yourself in an interview every so often. Block out the client for a moment and ask, "How am I feeling right now? Am I sad, angry, scared? What am I feeling?" It is probably a pretty good barometer of how the client is feeling. The client often says he feels great; check your own gut reactions and trust them.

Ask every client about suicide, but let rapport develop first. Do not just have the client come in and immediately ask him intimate questions like. "How's your sex life?" or "Been hallucinating lately?" or "Feel like killing yourself?" The client will probably want to kill you. Let rapport develop, and later say, "Now we've talked about a lot of things these last 20 minutes. Have any of them ever gotten you to the point of feeling you couldn't go on any longer?" Don't leave it there; explain that when you say that, you mean suicide. Always say the word "suicide." Do not just ask clients if they ever thought of "throwing in the towel" or some other euphemism. They can take you pretty literally and might say, "Well, no. I dried myself pretty well this morning." You have to get yourself to say "suicide." Practice. It is not so easy to come right out and say it. The first few times it bombs, something like this, "Gee, we've talked about a lot of things. Have any of them ever gotten you to the point of thinking about committing s—s-ah—s-th—." It's almost the kind of thing you need to practice in front of a mirror. "Su-i-cide. Suicide."

Clients may say, "Boy, you're kidding!" but it's not a hostile response. If anybody does say "Yes"—and the client probably will tell you if he or she has been thinking about it—obtain as much information as you can. Then go on to say, "Well, when was the last time you thought of it?" and "How about today?" Whenever the client was thinking of it last, find out what he was doing, how he thought about it, and when he thought of it, and ascertain his plans for it as specifically as possible. In cases of most serious intent, the client will probably say, "Well, not only have I been thinking of it today, but I've been cleaning my gun, it's in my car, my car's outside." In other words, get all the data.

What to do

Try to diffuse the situation psychologically and in a practical way. For instance, offer alternatives. Say something like, "On the other hand, what specific reasons do you have for living?" Try to get to a positive thing. Start initiating reasons to live. The more seriously depressed the client, the fewer reasons will come to mind. Remember, that is part of the illness. The client will say, "nothing," and cry. At that point, try to reiterate things he or she told you earlier about him- or herself that are reasons to live—a child, a spouse, a business. Provide the reason to live: "That child really needs you." If the client doesn't come up with anything, allow 60 seconds to think of something, even one reason, and then support that enthusiastically: "You're right. Tremendous!" Back the client up! Fill in the picture, and lead him or her into ways that can be acted upon practically. If it is a child, for example, ask where the child is now. How can the client as a parent be of help?

Another important thing is to make a referral, whenever possible, to a mental health clinic or mental health specialist. As a counselor, you have a key role in identifying potential suicides. You cannot expect yourself to single-handedly treat and manage the situation. Request a consultation for further evaluation. Possibly the person is in a real depression and needs medication or the supervision of an inpatient facility. So, call and make an appointment before the client leaves the office. In conjunction with the mental health clinic, a decision can be made about how quickly the person should be seen—immediately, later today, or tomorrow. If the client is already being seen by a therapist, contact the therapist. A therapist who is unaware of the situation will want to know and will also be able to provide guidance for you so that you are working together. Don't be afraid you are stepping on anyone's toes. Anybody contemplating suicide cannot have too many people in his or her corner.

Maybe here we can lay to rest any discomfort that arises from the philosophical debates on whether someone has a right to commit suicide. There is considerable discussion about the right to die. Looking at it from the practical side of the issue, anyone who thinks they do would just go ahead and do it. They wouldn't be in your office. Anyone who "happens" into a counselor's office, or phones, and acknowledges

suicidal thoughts, directly or indirectly, is not there by chance. They are seeking help in settling their internal debate over life versus death. The counselor, as do other helping people, must come down clearly on the side of living. When depressed, a client cannot rationally make this decision. Once the depression clears, most clients are very pleased that you prevented their action on suicide plans.

If a client has a weapon, ask that it be checked at the reception desk or elsewhere on the premises. If it is at home, ask that someone else take possession of it and notify you when that is done. Never let a client who is suicidal—and they usually improve during the interview—leave your office without your double-checking plans for the rest of the day. Be specific. Call home to make sure someone will be there if that is the expectation. Give the client chores and support. Get something for them to do. Have somebody there to watch the client around the clock and to give the attention he or she needs. Set up another appointment to see the person within 48 hours. Have them call you to check in later that day, or you call them. Be specific. Say, "I'd like to call you between 4 and 5," or at least "this afternoon." It is better not to give an exact time because that is often hard to meet. This kind of paternalism is needed at this time. The weaning of dependence and fostering of independence come later. Give reinforcements. "What do you like to do? What do you have to do? Do it and let me know how it goes."

In talking with a client, the only times that you may foresee something going wrong are in the following three situations. It's simple logic, but it's also a trap.

1 If the client's theme is rejection and loss, for example, be careful you do not reject or put him or her off.

2 If you agree with the client about how bad things are, for example, the client says, "I am a worthless person. I beat my child," you may easily get into your own negative feelings about this. You might communicate, "Well, you are right, that was a horrible thing to do." Do not crucify clients. Do not support their punitive guilt response.

3 Clients may say how bad they feel. You are tempted to say, "I understand how badly you feel. I often feel that way myself." You're trying to sympathize and share the misery, but clients interpret this as permission to feel the way they do. You are getting away from the reasons the client has to live and are underscoring their pessimism. It is better to reinforce the reasons to live.

Other thoughts about evaluation and prevention come to mind. Get histories of previous suicide attempts. Anyone who has tried it once has a poor track record. A family history of suicide or other losses in childhood from divorce or illnesses or a history of childhood sexual abuse also increase the risk. For someone who has either attempted suicide or is thinking about it, reduce the isolation from family and friends. Hospitalization under close supervision may be needed if supports are lacking. Remove guns, ropes, pills, and so on. Have the client give you the

weapon personally. Shake hands with the client as he or she leaves the office, and give "something of yourself" to take with them to put in their wallet or pocket, such as a piece of paper with your name and phone number. Try to make sure the client does not have what would constitute a lethal dosage of medication. Any supply of tricyclic antidepressants greater than 1000 mg or a 5-day supply of meprobamate (Miltown) (8000 mg) can be lethal.

Now consider a special situation. If you happen to get involved in an emergency where someone is about to shoot himself, jump from a window ledge, or do something else rash, try to be calm. Keep your voice down. Do not ask philosophical questions, but ask practical questions: "What's your name?" "Where are you from?" Try to have a nonthreatening conversation. This is a grueling situation and can last for hours. Wear the person down. Do not ever be a hero. Do not rush a person with a gun. Stay alive to help the people who can be helped.

Trust your gut reactions. Don't feel that if you are unsuccessful, it is your fault. Don't ever forget that your job with suicidal clients is not to be God. Being God's helper is enough.

MENTAL STATUS EXAMINATION

The *mental status examination* is one of the tools used by mental health professionals. Its purpose is to guide observation and assist the interviewer in gathering essential data about mental functioning. It consists of standard items, which are routinely covered, ensuring that nothing important is overlooked. The format also helps mental health workers record their findings in a fashion that is easily understood by their colleagues.

Three aspects of mental functioning are always included: mood and affect, thought processes, and cognitive functioning. Mood and affect refer to the dominant feeling state. They are deduced from the client's general appearance; what the client reports; and posture, body movements, and attitude toward the interviewer. Thought processes zero in on how the client presents his or her ideas. Are the thoughts ordered and organized, or does the client jump all over the place? Are his sentences logical? Is the content—what is discussed—sensible, or does it include delusions and bizarre ideas? Finally, cognitive functioning refers to intellectual functioning, memory, ability to concentrate, comprehension, and ability to abstract. This latter portion of the mental status examination involves asking specific questions, for example, about current events, definitions of words, or meanings of proverbs. The interviewer considers the individual's education, lifestyle, and occupation in making a judgment about the responses.

If the counselor can get some training in how to do a simple mental status examination, it can be helpful in spotting clients with particular problems. It can also greatly facilitate your communication with mental health workers. Just telling a psychiatrist or a psychiatric social worker that the person you are referring is "crazier than a bedbug" isn't very useful.

CO-OCCURRING PSYCHIATRIC ILLNESS

Understanding the relationship between alcohol or other drug use and mood or behavior is one of the most challenging and essential components of anyone's work in the substance abuse field. An effort to determine the relative contributions of addictive and nonaddictive psychiatric disorders to abnormal mental states is essential for several reasons. First, alcohol abuse is associated with other psychiatric conditions and can mask psychiatric disorders. Studies have shown the risk of having a problem with alcohol use increases 10 times if a person has schizophrenia or 15 times if a person has an antisocial personality disorder. Second, alcoholism and withdrawal from alcohol dependence can produce symptoms that resemble many other psychiatric disorders. For example, over one-third of persons treated for alcohol disorders report a psychotic episode in the preceding 6 months. For this reason, psychiatry, perhaps more than any other medical discipline, must respect alcoholism as "the great mimicker." Psychoactive substance-related disorders are the most common psychiatric disorders for people between the ages of 18 and 65. Because of this, it is imperative that all mental health workers include a thorough assessment of alcohol use for all people seeking mental health treatment. Furthermore, if alcohol or drug use co-occurs with another psychiatric disorder, both disorders should be treated concurrently and aggressively. Preferably this treatment should be based on an integrated approach.

In this text, we have placed considerable emphasis on the fact that psychological problems are not the cause of alcoholism per se. However, in trying to get that message across, it is important not to lose sight of the fact that an individual may have both alcohol dependence and another psychiatric condition. Whether alcoholism grows in the soil of some other psychiatric condition (sometimes termed secondary or reactive alcoholism) or whether it co-occurs with another psychiatric problem, when present, it develops a momentum of its own. On the other hand, the client's ability to establish and maintain sobriety may be dependent upon actively treating other psychiatric conditions as well. The clinician confronted by clients with dual diagnoses faces both diagnostic and treatment challenges, and all too frequently the client faces administrative and systemic barriers.

The next eight sections cover some of the major classes of psychiatric illness as they relate to alcohol use disorders.

Mood disorders

Mood and emotion are what you feel and how you show it. There are two extremes: people who are depressed and those who are manic, and people can fluctuate between these two extremes. This is called a *bipolar mood disorder*. People who are manic show characteristic behavior. Often they have grand schemes, which to others seem quite outlandish. Their conversation is very quick and pressured. Often they jump from topic to topic. If there were a conversation about the state of the union, a person when manic might say, "and, yes, Arkansas is a very pretty state. President Clinton was the governor of the state, and the governor of my car is out of kilter. The left tire is flat, out of air like a balloon Suzy got at the circus where she stained her best dress with cotton candy. . ." Although there is a logical connection between these thoughts, there is an inability to concentrate on any single thought. This pattern of thinking is termed "loose associations." One thought is immediately crowded out by the next. Someone who is manic may also be aggressive and irritable or feel themselves very attractive, sexually irresistible, or capable of superhuman performance. People when manic are perpetually in high gear, have difficulty sleeping, and may have trouble concentrating. Simply being in their company might well make you feel exhausted.

Depression, which is the other side of the mood coin and is far more common, has all the opposite characteristics. Rather than being hyped up, people when depressed grind to a halt. They find very little pleasure in most activities. Movements, speech, and thinking may be slowed down. Biological changes can accompany depression and are called vegetative symptoms. These include disturbances of normal sleep patterns, constipation, slowed motor activity, and weight loss or gain. In extremes, the person with depression stops eating, is unable to rest, experiences a complete depletion of energy, and expends available motor energy in repeated, purposeless motions such as hand-wringing and pacing. Such depression is associated with a sense of self-reproach, irrational guilt, worthlessness, hopelessness, and loss of interest in life. In full force, these phenomena may culminate in suicidal thoughts, plans, or actions. Severe depression is a life-threatening disorder.

Most depression and mania are believed to have a biological basis. They are also episodic disorders. Between episodes, the mood states typically return to a normal state. This is not to imply that one simply sits back and waits for the manic or depressive episode to pass. With individuals who are significantly depressed, suicide is an ever-present possibility. Individuals when manic can incur phenomenal life problems that can wreak havoc for themselves as well as for their families. These conditions are highly treatable with medications (see the following section). Talking therapies may be helpful in less severe conditions but are of little use when someone's perception of reality and thought processes are seriously altered.

Alcohol use and alcoholism are intertwined with mood disorders in several ways. The most important one is that alcohol consumption can cause depressive symptoms in anyone. Alcohol can produce a toxic depression that embraces the full range of depression's symptoms, including anorexia, insomnia, somatic complaints, suicidal thoughts, and despair. Experimental studies have demonstrated that heavy drinking can induce depressive symptoms in both alcoholics and nonalcoholics. A temporary depression is frequently described as a feature of alcoholism that can remit with abstinence. Depending on the diagnostic criteria used, depression may be seen in over one-half of those participating in alcohol rehabilitation. Women are more likely than are men to present with symptoms of depression. Beyond the acute effects of the drug alcohol, chronic alcohol abusers often confront deteriorating social relations, loss of employment, associated trauma, and loss of health, which are factors also associated with depressed states.

As mentioned in the section on suicide, any alcohol use by someone in a depression is contraindicated. This is an additional concern for alcoholics. It is estimated that 7% to 21% of alcoholics commit suicide. Although suicidal behavior in general increases with alcohol consumption, active alcoholics attempt suicide far more often than do nonalcoholics when drinking. Several factors contribute to this. Alcoholism may be an indicator of a suicide-prone individual; alcoholism itself can be considered a form of slow suicide. The loss of cognitive function resulting from alcohol abuse will create an increasing gap between personal expectations and actual performance, resulting in despair. The multiple losses mentioned before can compound a sense of hopelessness. In assessing an alcoholic's suicide potential, further risk factors to consider are the loss of a close interpersonal relationship within the previous 6 weeks, the presence of hopelessness, and negative attitudes toward the interviewer. The alcoholic with suicidal thoughts, above all, needs to be taken seriously whether he is inebriated or not. As an important aside, a reactive depression may also be seen in the family members of a substance abuser. Alcoholism is a family illness, and one out of three American families have direct contact with an alcoholic. These people may develop depression as their defenses are overwhelmed by the constant stress of dealing with emotional and physical abuse, economic instability, and their perceived impotence to change their loved one's behavior. Obviously, for most, referral to Al-Anon will be far more appropriate than the use of antidepressant medications.

Because depression is often a result of alcoholism, representing a reactive or secondary depression, usually the depressed symptoms seen in alcoholics do not require separate treatment, but research suggests that 10% to 15% of females and 5% of males seeking alcoholism treatment have a major affective disorder that preceded the alcohol abuse. In these instances, it is likely that the depression will not lift with abstinence and alcohol treatment. At the point of entry into treatment, it may be difficult to get the information needed to distinguish initially between an independent, primary depression and depression that results from alcoholism. The client may have difficulty providing an accurate chronology of events due to cognitive deficits that are a part of both alcoholism and depression. The most reliable information is often provided by family and friends.

The cause of depression for a person abusing alcohol may only become apparent over time. If the depressive symptoms lift with abstinence, then one can be confident that the affective disturbance was secondary to the alcohol abuse. If there are persistent depressed symptoms after several weeks of abstinence, then the clinician should consider the possibility of a co-occurring mood disorder and concurrent treatment for depression may be indicated. An extended period of sobriety before making the diagnosis of depression, though preferable, may not always be possible. On occasion, the clinician may be so impressed with the severity of depressive symptoms that waiting for several months cannot be justified. This is critically important, because without adequate concurrent treatment, these clients are likely to see themselves as treatment failures. For them, things have not gotten better with sobriety. Also, they may unwittingly be urged by AA friends or treatment personnel "to work the program harder." In fact, they have been giving it their all. All treatment for persons abusing alcohol must include education about depression, its biological basis, and why medications can be useful. Discomfort may surface around the use of medications, especially because many treatment programs caution clients about the dangers of psychoactive drug use. Clients need to be reassured that the medications prescribed for depression have no addiction potential and are not associated with abuse. It is also important to keep in mind that several medical conditions (e.g., thyroid disease) can cause mood disorders as well.

Another association between mood disorders and alcohol use is that drinking can escalate during the period of mood disturbance. Research indicates that 20% to 60% of clients with bipolar disorders report excessive use of alcohol during the manic phases of their illness. It is unclear whether this is an effort to "self-medicate" their disturbing manic symptoms or whether it is a result of the poor judgment that is part of this phase of the illness. Regardless of why alcohol use increases, the consequences of the disinhibiting effects of alcohol, laid on top of the impaired judgment generally present, are often disastrous. The focus of therapy for bipolar clients with alcohol abuse is two-pronged. The primary disorder may require medication (lithium and/or antipsychotic agents); counseling and education are necessary to address alcohol use issues. In individuals with primary depression, 20% to 30% report increased alcohol intake during their mood disturbance. Here, too, this can complicate their treatment.

Disorders involving psychosis

Psychosis refers to a disintegration of thought processes frequently associated with disturbances in function. While psychosis as a symptom may be associated with a variety of psychiatric disorders, including substance-related disorders, it is often prominent in schizophrenic disorders. *Schizophrenia* and other psychotic disorders are a group of chronic fluctuating disturbances that are among the most incapacitating of the mental disorders. They exact an enormous cost in human suffering and public and private resources. These disorders have a biochemical basis but are subject to environmental influences.

Schizophrenia occurs is about 1% of the general population. Schizophrenia is heterogeneous in its presentation. Those with schizophrenia

FORMAL THOUGHT
DISORDER

may have "positive" symptoms including hallucinations (a sensory perception with no corresponding stimulus), delusions (a fixed, false belief), or incoherence of thought with resultant disorganized speech. They may also have "negative" symptoms including shyness or withdrawal from social contacts, difficulty communicating, as well as a depressed mood. Attention and cognitive disturbances are frequently present. Attempts to communicate are very difficult because the person with schizophrenia may perceive reality very differently. The individual with schizophrenia often misinterprets environmental stimuli. This altered perception can be very subtle or very marked. Clients with schizophrenia may make connections between events that are not justified. For example, the client may hear a car backfire and see their landlord in the hallway and develop a concern that the landlord is "out to get me." If the client then hears imaginary voices saying, "He'll shoot first, ask questions later," their sense of paranoia becomes even greater. The treatment of schizophrenic disorders as well as other psychotic disorders includes medications (see following section) as well as ongoing supportive counseling and other rehabilitative efforts.

Some conditions associated with alcohol abuse closely resemble psychotic disorders. One study found a history of psychotic symptoms in over 40% of alcoholics who sought treatment. One such condition that may be misdiagnosed and lead to the inappropriate use of antipsychotic medication is that of *alcoholic hallucinosis*. Although seen in less than 3% of chronic alcoholics, it is so easily confused with schizophrenia that it should be considered in all cases of acute psychosis. It is often part of withdrawal states, but it can also occur in an actively drinking individual. Symptoms include auditory, tactile, or visual hallucinations. The person will typically develop delusions of a persecutory nature related to these hallucinations. Several features help to distinguish alcohol hallucinosis from schizophrenia. The client will have a history of heavy alcohol use. The majority of alcoholics with this condition will have their first episode after the age of 40, while schizophrenia typically appears earlier in life. The client usually has no family history of schizophrenia, but there may be a family history of alcoholism. Unlike schizophrenia, there is little evidence of a formal thought disorder, for example, loose associations and disorganization of thinking. The content of the hallucinations is fairly simple, unlike the less understandable or bizarre hallucinations of schizophrenia. In alcohol hallucinosis, the resolution of these symptoms is usually quick, occurring over the course of 1 to 6 days. Management should include hospitalization, close observation, some minor tranquilizers, and the limited use of antipsychotic medications. Wernicke-Korsakoff syndrome (see Chapter 3) also includes psychotic symptoms. This is an irreversible organic brain syndrome resulting from chronic alcohol abuse, which is characterized by prominent memory impairment and striking personality changes.

Aside from the psychotic symptoms that may result from alcohol use, estimates of the prevalence of alcohol use disorder co-occurring with schizophrenia range from 14% to 47%. This may occur with levels of alcohol consumption that would typically not be thought of as problematic in the general population. The combination of schizophrenia and alcohol abuse will often result in a rocky clinical course and a poor prognosis. Without specialized services, these individuals may have difficulty complying with any treatment plan. They will frequently not take medications as prescribed and may be unwilling or unable to follow recommendations for abstinence from alcohol. Efforts to end drinking in this population must be based on an assessment of what alcohol provides for the individual. If drinking is used to reduce anxiety around hallucinations, then increasing antipsychotic medication may be appropriate. If drinking is used to reduce uncomfortable side effects from antipsychotic medication, then a reduction or substitution of medications may be necessary. If drinking represents their effort to achieve peer acceptance, then nonalcohol social alternatives should be developed. For these clients, the need for compliance with prescribed medication cannot be overemphasized. Abstinence for some persons with schizophrenia may be indicated because even moderate drinking may, for them, be disruptive, suggesting a vulnerability to the affects of alcohol.

For these patients, the standard alcohol or drug regimen may be seen as threatening. Poor treatment outcomes in traditional alcohol treatment settings have been associated with the severity of psychiatric symptoms. Persons with schizophrenia tend to do poorly in group settings with lots of confrontation but can be treated quite effectively in less threatening groups. In recent demonstration projects, a phase model using treatment approaches matched to engagement, persuasion, active treatment, and relapse prevention phases has been effective in achieving treatment goals. Incorporating motivational interviewing techniques also appears promising. If AA is to be used as part of the treatment plan, then these persons must be thoroughly prepared for AA experiences after they have accepted the need for abstinence. The host group should be assessed in advance for receptiveness to the psychiatrically impaired. Specialized dual-diagnosis self-help groups for this are ideal and are increasingly available in many regions.

Anxiety disorders

Anxiety disorders are relatively common and involve incapacitating nervousness, tension, apprehension, and fear. These symptoms may appear episodically and "out of the blue," as in panic attacks. The anxiety may be a fear of particular places or situations, as in agoraphobia, or it may be a symptom of fearing a specific object (e.g., spiders), which is called a simple phobia. For others it may take the form of unrelenting recurrent ideas (obsessions) or the need to perform repetitive rituals (compulsions). The anxious person may experience physical symptoms including diaphoresis (sweating), tremor, diarrhea, pallor, rapid pulse, shortness of breath, headache, or fatigue. In contrast to other mental disorders, which may also be associated with a significant amount of anxiety, the anxiety disorders do not involve major disturbances in mood, thought, or judgment. Care must be taken to rule out other medical problems or medications as the cause of anxiety symptoms.

The relationship of anxiety disorders to alcoholism remains controversial. As with mood disorders, the anxiety experienced may be independent of or secondary to alcoholism. Most clinicians know of clients who drink to control symptoms of panic or phobic disorders. This self-medication may well take on a life of its own, leading to alcohol abuse or dependence. There is a high prevalence of anxiety disorders in alcoholics in treatment. Several studies have reported the rate of associated anxiety disorders to be in a range between 22% and 44%. Investigators concede that the sequence of anxiety and drinking is highly variable between individuals.

Understanding the relationship of anxiety symptoms to the drinking behavior is essential. Abstinence alone may "cure" the anxious symptoms if they are the consequences of drinking. On the other hand, severe anxiety may increase the vulnerability of the dually diagnosed client to relapse. Treatment decisions must be based on a careful history of symptoms and observation of the individual following detoxification. If a co-occurring anxiety disorder is felt to be present, an integrated treatment plan might include the use of psychotherapy, behavioral therapy, or medications. Participation in safe, supportive 12-step programs may also reduce symptoms from anxiety disorders. Antidepressants such as imipramine (Tofranil®) or sertraline (Zoloft®) may be effective with certain anxiety disorders and have very little abuse potential. Benzodiazepines are often effective for the symptoms of anxiety, but because of their high abuse potential, they should be lower on the list of medication alternatives. Buspirone (BuSpar), with a good safety profile, not euphorigenic, and with few drug interactions, can be useful in treating an anxiety disorder in individuals with alcoholism. Cautious prescribing practices and a regular monitoring of clinical progress will minimize the risk of drug abuse and maximize the chances of successful recovery.

Personality disorders

Everyone has a unique set of personality traits that they exhibit in a range of social situations. When these traits are so rigid and maladaptive that they repeatedly interfere with a person's social or occupational functioning, they constitute a personality disorder. People with these disorders have the capacity "to get under everyone's skin." There are 10 different types of personality disorders described in DSM-IV, but the two most commonly associated with alcoholism are the antisocial and borderline types.

A person with an antisocial personality disorder is frequently in trouble, getting into fights, conning others for personal profit, committing crimes, and having problems with authority. Antisocial personality disorders appear to be inherited independent of the predisposition to develop alcoholism. Although these two disorders are not genetically linked, those with antisocial personality disorder are at high risk for developing alcoholism. In addition, chronic alcohol consumption can lead to personality changes that closely resemble the antisocial personality. However, these behaviors may well disappear following abstinence. Studies have found that from 10% to 20% of men and about 5% to 10% of women in alcohol treatment facilities meet the criteria for antisocial personality, which appears to predate their alcoholism. For this group the prognosis is poor. Their social problems will not disappear with abstinence. They are generally resistant to any type of intervention, lack remorse for their behavior, and will frequently alienate care-givers and peer support groups.

A person with a borderline personality disorder may act impulsively with multiple suicide attempts, exhibit inappropriate emotions such as intense anger or ingenuine affection, have feelings of emptiness or boredom, and have frequent mood swings. They also frequently use alcohol in chaotic and unpredictable patterns, and 13% to 28% of alcoholics seeking treatment have been given this diagnosis. It is again important to attempt to separate out the sequence of behavioral problems and alcohol abuse in developing appropriate treatment plans. People with this disorder also evoke strong negative feelings from their care-givers. All suicidal behavior, from threats to attempts, must be taken seriously. Treatment objectives include the creation of a safe and secure relationship and environment.

Attention-deficit/hyperactivity disorders

It has been recognized that some children are unable to remain attentive in situations where it is socially necessary to do so. This is often most apparent in school, but it can also be apparent in the home. In the past, these conditions were termed hyperactivity or minimal brain dysfunction; they are now known as attention-deficit hyperactivity disorders (ADHD). Follow-up studies of children with ADHD have noted a tendency for the development of alcohol dependence in adulthood. The examination of alcoholics' childhoods also shows a higher incidence of ADHD. One hypothesis is that a subgroup of alcohol abusers begin to drink to stabilize areas of the brain that are "irritable" due to damage earlier in life. For them, alcohol can be considered self-medication. Alcohol may improve performance on cognitive tasks, allow better concentration, and offer a subjective sense of stability. Such a response to alcohol would be highly reinforcing and thereby increase the risk of addiction.

With adults, it is very difficult to sort out the cognitive impairment caused by alcohol from a preexisting, underlying deficit. Prolonged abstinence is once more desirable. On the other hand, these clients may be unable to achieve and maintain sobriety.

When confronted with an individual who has been through treatment several times and never been able to establish sobriety, take a careful childhood history. If there is evidence of difficulties in school

signs of hyperactivity

Signs of living with hyperactivity

or other problems suggesting ADHD, further evaluation and treatment with medication may be warranted. The medication prescribed in such cases may belong to the stimulant class; however, for such clients it has a paradoxical "calming" effect. In addition, the above data suggest it would be useful to discuss with parents of children currently diagnosed as having ADHD steps that might be taken to reduce a future risk of alcohol problems. Recent studies do not support any conclusions that the use of medication in childhood correlates with eventual substance abuse.

Organic mental disorders

A disorder is diagnosed as organic when it is caused by a known defect in brain function. The causes can vary. For example, organic mental disorders can result from trauma to the central nervous system, from a brain tumor, from a stroke, or from a variety of infections. These impairments in brain function limit the person's ability to think and respond meaningfully to the environment. Usually there are significant changes in cognitive function. Problems with memory, an inability to concentrate, or a loss of intellectual capacity are common.

These disorders can represent permanent impairment, or they can be completely reversible. Which of these outcomes occurs depends mostly on whether there has been only temporary interference with the brain's function (e.g., through ingestion of drugs or an active infection of the brain) or whether there has been permanent damage to brain tissue. Reversible organic mental disorders are referred to as *delirium*. Typically the onset of delirium is rapid, and if the cause is identified and treated, the person may return to his or her usual self within days. Another component of delirium can be visual hallucinations, especially at night, which can be particularly terrifying. *Dementia* generally refers to irreversible organic brain syndromes. Usually these have a more gradual onset, with there being a gradual deterioration of function over the course of years. In addition to the limitations these disorders create for an individual, an equally significant factor may be how the individual perceives them. If the symptoms appear slowly, the individual may be able to compensate, that is for the most part appear normal, especially if in a familiar environment with no new problems to solve. On the other hand, if the symptoms appear rapidly, the person may understandably be extremely upset. As the individual experiences a reduction in thinking capacity, anxiety often results and is very apparent.

The treatment of organic mental disorders attempts, when possible, to correct the underlying cause. If it is a tumor, surgery may be indicated; if it is drug-induced, withdrawal of the toxic agent is necessary. If permanent impairment is associated with organic mental disorders, rehabilitation measures will be initiated to assist the person in coping with limitations. In relation to alcohol use, there are a variety of organic mental disorders. Delirium may arise from acute intoxication, which clearly impairs mental functioning, or it may occur during withdrawal states, which can occur in the person physically dependent on alcohol.

Severe cognitive deficits in a chronic alcoholic may lead to the diagnosis of *alcoholic dementia*. This type of dementia develops insidiously and typically occurs during the drinker's fifth or sixth decade. The symptoms include a deteriorating memory and often dramatic personality changes. Mood swings are common; moods can swing from anger to euphoria. This condition is related to the widespread brain damage and actual shrinkage of brain tissue, which is apparent if the person has a CAT scan of the brain. With abstinence, there may be some recovery over the first 6 weeks. These improvements will be marked and be evident on a CAT scan. Abstinence, unfortunately, is difficult to achieve. The impairment in thinking doesn't allow the standard counseling and educational approaches to take hold. Generally some degree of dementia persists.

The elderly are particularly susceptible to mental disturbances caused by alcohol. Metabolism slows with age, leading to higher blood levels of alcohol with similar consumption in the geriatric population. Their increased use of prescribed medication also increases the likelihood of a medication/alcohol interaction, often leading to episodes of confusion. Among elderly patients seen in an emergency room, confusion was virtually three times more common for those with an alcohol problem. Older people have an apparent heightened sensitivity to all psychoactive compounds, leading to greater cognitive changes while drinking. Sometimes frank organic brain syndromes occur. As demographic changes result in a higher percentage of older people, practitioners will be increasingly challenged to identify alcohol-related cognitive deficits and not simply chalk them up to aging. The diagnosis is often missed in this population because the elderly tend to be protected by their friends and family. They may not meet strict DSM-IV criteria for alcohol abuse or alcohol dependence, but they still may be drinking pathologically.

Polysubstance dependence

Alcohol abuse among those who are primarily abusing other licit and illicit substances is frequently overlooked. In one study, 70% to 77% of clients entering treatment for benzodiazepine (antianxiety agents) abuse also met criteria for alcohol abuse. Of opioid addicts in treatment, 20% to 35% were found to have alcohol-related problems. The danger here is that an alcohol problem is treated lightly and without any real alcohol assessment done or alcohol treatment provided. The cocaine abuser who routinely uses alcohol to offset the stimulant's effects may not be aware of a developing alcohol dependence. It is also necessary to look for other drug dependencies in those with identified alcohol problems. The rate of other drug abuse or dependence in treatment samples of alcoholics ranges from 12% to 43%.

Other addictive behaviors

The concept of addiction is now being extended to behaviors that do not involve substance abuse. These behaviors include gambling, running, and eating disorders. Some people refuse food intake because they believe they are too fat, although the scales say differently (anorexia). Others stuff themselves and vomit, over and over (bulimia.) Case reports of associations between eating disorders and alcohol abuse are increasing as recognition of each illness improves. A striking phenomenon is the frequency of referral for alcohol treatment of individuals who had eating disorders in earlier years. There appears to be a higher incidence of a positive family history for alcoholism in persons with anorexia, which also increases their risk for developing this dependency. Although prospective studies are needed, the potential risk of alcoholism among those with eating disorders should be recognized.

Clinical considerations

When confronted with a possible dual diagnosis of alcoholism and another psychiatric condition, alcoholism treatment personnel should consider consultation from a psychiatrist or mental health worker. Treating both conditions simultaneously is necessary and may require a delicate balancing act. Under any circumstances, extra support and education is essential. The client needs to appreciate that he is being treated for two very different conditions. Efforts to help the client integrate information from both treatment perspectives require thoughtful treatment planning.

Homelessness, alcohol use, and chronic mental illness

Although homelessness is not an illness, it represents a point where chronic mental illness intersects with alcohol problems. Alcohol dependence is one pathway toward homelessness. On the other hand, homelessness can be a condition that precedes increased alcohol abuse. Either way, alcohol-related problems within the homeless population are enormous. On any given night, over 600,000 people in this country are without adequate shelter, and about two-fifths of them are affected by alcohol abuse. Certainly the "skid row bum," whose repeated detox and jail stints leave lasting impressions on providers, remains inextricably linked with homelessness in the popular consciousness. Historically, the "chronic public inebriate" frequently ended up on the streets. The odds for successful treatment then went down due to their social losses. Homeless persons with alcoholism have unique service and housing needs requiring creative responses.

The homeless alcohol abuser has been shown to be multiply disadvantaged with higher rates of physical, mental, and social problems than the nonalcohol-abusing homeless person. The homeless alcohol abuser tends to be male, white, and elderly. They often have troubled marital and family histories and poorer employment records, and they often are more transient and socially isolated. They are frequently incarcerated for petty crimes and often are victims of violent attacks. As many as one-half of alcohol-abusing homeless persons have an additional psychiatric diagnosis. Homeless alcohol abusers are at high risk for neurologic impairment, heart disease and hypertension, chronic lung disease, liver disease, and trauma. These clinical features complicate engagement, intervention, and recovery.

Successful treatment of alcoholism depends on social and physical environments where sobriety is positively supported. These are hardly the conditions encountered in a street existence. Therefore the service needs of the homeless go beyond the provision of substance abuse treatment. Providing only detoxification and short-term inpatient care will reinforce the revolving door scenario that too often typifies homeless persons with alcoholism. Assistance and support for finding appropriate, affordable, and alcohol-free housing is the backbone of treatment for this special population. To accomplish even this basic goal, bridging the person's disaffiliation, distrust, and disenchantment is necessary. Overcoming these adverse motivational forces requires a great deal of clinical skill. It also requires a great deal of patience, since the homeless alcoholic will be among the most severe and chronically ill clients that a counselor is likely to encounter. The needs of the homeless alcohol abuser go beyond the capacity of any one provider. Clinicians will need to continue to form coalitions with advocates, politicians, and community resources to develop adequate service systems for this disadvantaged population.

PSYCHOTROPIC MEDICATIONS

Neither alcohol nor drug problems exist in a vacuum. Those with substance abuse problems can have a variety of other problems, some physical, some psychiatric. These patients may be receiving treatment or treating themselves. The treatment may involve prescription or over-the-counter medications. The more one knows about medications in general, the more helpful one can be to a client. Those with substance-abuse dependence and particularly alcohol dependent people tend to seek instant relief from the slightest mental or physical discomfort. The active alcoholic may welcome any chemical relief and is at risk for using some psychotropic medications in an abusive manner. The recovering person, on the other hand, may be so leery of any medication that he or she may refuse to use those medications that are very much needed. Thus some familiarity with the types of psychotropic medications and their appropriate use is important. They are not alike, either in terms of their actions or in their potential for abuse.

Taking a good medication history is imperative in dealing with clients. Here are some of the questions you would want to have in mind: What medications do you currently take? Is it prescribed, when was it

prescribed, and by whom was it prescribed? Are you following the prescription? Do you take more or less or use a different schedule? Is the drug having the desired effects? What, if any, side effects exist? Do you have any medication allergies? What is your philosophy about medications? Have you ever abused medication in the past? These questions can help identify abuse of current medications and prevent future abuse in vulnerable recovering individuals.

Tremendous confusion may arise from a communication gap between the patient and the prescribing physician. The physician prescribes a medication intended to have a specific effect on a particular patient. The patient is sometimes unclear about (and usually doesn't question) the need for medication. There may be limited access to the physician for follow-up calls. Only feedback from the patient enables the doctor to make adjustments, if necessary. The regimen for taking a drug is important, also. Often, as the patient begins to feel better, he or she stops or cuts the dose of a prescribed drug. One danger in this is that enough has been taken to relieve the symptoms but not enough to remove the underlying cause. Clients should be encouraged to consult with the physician before altering the way medications are taken. Because treatment requires good communication, you should help the client to ask questions about the treatment and the drugs involved. Also be sensitive to the problems that the cost of medications can present for some clients. Those without insurance can find the cost prohibitive. This may mean that they skimp on taking medicines as prescribed to make their supply last longer. Or they may put off having a prescription refilled on schedule, because their budget simply can't be stretched that far, at that time.

Every drug has multiple simultaneous actions. Only a few of these effects are being sought when any drug is prescribed. These intended effects are the therapeutic effects. All other effects would be the side effects in that instance. In selecting a medication for a patient, the doctor seeks a drug with the maximum therapeutic impact and the fewest side effects. Ideally this should be a collaborative effort. Enough information must be exchanged to enable the client to give valid consent.

The group of medications of particular interest in relation to alcohol or other drug use are those with *psychotropic* effects. Any drug that influences behavior or mood falls into this category. Because of the abuse potential of some of them (particularly antianxiety medications) and their ability to mimic intoxicated states, these medications are of the greatest concern to the substance abuse clinician. At the same time, they may be the most widely misunderstood. There is no denying that psychotropic medications are widely prescribed and sometimes overprescribed. It ought to be noted though that the bulk of these mood-altering medications are not being prescribed by psychiatrists. Rather they are prescribed by family physicians and other medical specialties. Because of their mood-altering properties, such medications may be candidates for abuse. "Down with drugs" is not apt to be an effective banner for the substance abuse clinician, however. All psychotropic medications are not alike. Not all represent potential problems for clients.

A discussion of the four major categories of psychotropic medications follows. Each has different actions and is prescribed for different reasons. These are the antipsychotic agents, the antidepressant agents, the mood stabilizers, and the antianxiety agents.

Antipsychotic medications

The antipsychotic drugs are also called *neuroleptics* or *major tranquilizers*. These drugs relieve the symptoms of psychoses. In addition to the antipsychotic effect, they also have a tranquilizing and a sedative effect, calming behavior and inducing drowsiness. Antipsychotic medications have allowed many patients to live in the community rather than institutions. However, their potential for irreversible side effects mandates judicious use. Different medications in this group have differing side effects, making them either more or less sedating. The medication prescribed is selected on the basis of the patient's constellation of symptoms. Thus a drug with greater sedative effects might well be selected for a person exhibiting manic or agitated behavior. Some antipsychotic drugs are currently available in a long-acting injectable form called *decanoate*. These shots can be useful in ensuring medication compliance in clients with a history of poor compliance.

The antipsychotic medications most frequently encountered are listed in Table 11.1.

As with most medications, antipsychotic drugs interact with alcohol. A common effect of combining alcohol with sedating medications is *potentiation*. This implies that the two agents act in concert to exaggerate the sedative effects, which could cause problems. Alcohol can also increase brain chemicals that the neuroleptic agents are attempting to block, leading to reduced effectiveness. Another interaction worth noting is that alcohol has been reported to increase the likelihood of some side effects of neuroleptic agents.

Neuroleptic drugs are much less likely to be abused than the usual sedatives or antianxiety agents. They are not chemically similar to alcohol and are therefore not subject to cross-tolerance or addiction. The sensations they produce are generally not experienced as pleasurable and are therefore infrequently sought out. For these reasons, an antipsychotic agent may be prescribed not to relieve psychotic symptoms, but for its sedative or tranquilizing properties. Several of the side effects caused by neuroleptic medications are unpleasant and require additional medication to reduce. The medications that can be used to reduce these unpleasant side effects include benztropine (Cogentin) and trihexiphenidyl (Artane). They can induce pleasurable mental changes and may be abused by clients.

TABLE 11.1 ANTIPSYCHOTIC MEDICATIONS

Traditional Antipsychotic Medications

Action: Precise mechanism unknown. Thought to act primarily on dopamine receptors.

Drugs in category	Daily dose range	Potential overdose danger
Chlorpromazine (Thorazine®)	50–500 mg/day	Moderate
Thioridazine (Mellaril®)	50–400 mg/day	Moderate
Haloperidol (Haldol®)	1–15 mg/day	Moderate
Fluphenazine (Prolixin®)	25–100 mg IM q 1–4 weeks	Moderate
	5–60 mg/day p.o.	
Thiothixine (Navane®)	5–60 mg/day	Moderate
Perphenazine (Trilafon®)	4–24 mg/day	Moderate
Molindone (Moban®)	50–225 mg/day	Moderate

Potential side effects: sedation, dry mouth, parkinsonian side effects, dystonic reactions, tardive dysknesia, constipation, difficulty with urination, blurred vision, muscle rigidity and weakness, weight gain (except for *molindone*).

"Atypical" Antipsychotic Medications

Drugs in category	Daily dose range	Potential overdose danger

Action: (All atypicals except *clozapine*) Unknown. Believed to bind at some dopamine and serotonin receptors.

Olanzepine (Zyprexa®)	2.5–10 mg/day	Low

Potential side effects: sleepiness, postural hypotension, constipation, weight gain, dizziness, muscle rigidity and weakness, possible liver enzyme elevations.

Risperidone (Risperdal®)	0.5–6 mg/day	Low

Potential side effects: sleepiness, dizziness, palpitations, weight gain, sexual function complaints, increased fatigue, dose-related extrapyramidal effects.

Quetiapine (Seroquel®)	50–750 mg/day	Low

Potential side effects: Sleepiness, orthostatic hypotension, dizziness, constipation, dry mouth, weight gain.

Clozapine (Clozaril®)	100–900 mg/day	High

Action: Binds to dopamine receptors in limbic and striatal areas, may also act as antagonist at adrenergic, cholinergic, histaminergic, and serotonergic receptors.

Potential side effects: drowsiness, sedation, dizziness, headache, tremor, excessive salivation and sweating, dry mouth, rapid heart rate, hypotension, fainting, weight gain risk, seizures, possible agranulocytosis (requiring periodic white blood counts).

Antidepressant medications

The antidepressants, another major class of psychotropic medications, are used to treat the biological component of depression. They must be taken at a high enough dose to achieve a therapeutic level. A period of regular use (often 2 to 4 weeks) is also necessary before these medications have their full effect. Therefore an initial complaint of patients is that the medicine isn't helping. Side effects vary according to the category of antidepressant. These are most pronounced when the person first begins taking the drug. The physician may choose to have the patient take the medication at a particular time of the day to minimize side effects. There are several different types of antidepressants, grouped according to their chemical properties and how they act.

The *SSRIs*—the acronym for <u>s</u>elective <u>s</u>erotonin <u>r</u>euptake <u>i</u>nhibitors—are the most commonly prescribed and most widely used antidepressant medications. In general, they have fewer side effects than the other categories of antidepressant medications. The most commonly encountered side effects include gastrointestinal symptoms, headache, insomnia, and agitation.

Tricyclics are the oldest category of commonly used antidepressants. Common side effects include dry mouth and constipation. A third category known as <u>m</u>onoamine <u>o</u>xidase <u>i</u>nhibitors (MAOIs) require additional dietary restrictions to avoid bad side effects. Drugs in this category have numerous other side effects as well. *Buproprion* is another commonly prescribed antidepressant. It is presently the only medication in its category and is chemically unrelated to the other antidepressants. Common side effects include agitation, dry mouth, insomnia, headache, gastrointestinal symptoms, and tremor. Other medications not included in the above-mentioned categories include trazadone, amoxapine, and maprotiline. Of these, only trazadone is used with any frequency, and then more often for its side effect of sedation rather than its antidepressant effect.

The most common antidepressants are listed in Table 11.2.

There is no clear evidence that antidepressant medications invite abuse or create dependence. However, overdoses of some of these medications (e.g., the tricyclics) can be lethal. Again, in combination with alcohol, problems can arise because of their additive effects.

Mood stabilizers

Mood stabilizers are used to treat bipolar (manic-depressive) disorder (see Table 11.3). A few comments on lithium carbonate are worth mention. It can be helpful in either depression or mania and is a common medication used in controlling bipolar disorder. The dose is geared to body weight, and the level is monitored periodically through blood samples. Because lithium produces no pleasant effects it is unlikely to be abused. The opposite behavior is the more common problem. Feeling greatly improved, those on lithium may decide it's no longer necessary.

TABLE 11.2   ANTIDEPRESSANT MEDICATIONS

SSRIs (Selective Serotonin Reuptake Inhibitors)

Action: Believed to increase the neurotransmitter serotonin by preventing the usual reuptake of serotonin by the presynaptic (sending) nerve cell, making more available for transmission to the postsynaptic (receiving) nerve cell.

Drugs in category	Daily dose range	Potential overdose danger
Fluoxetine (Prozac)	10–80 mg	Low
Paroxetine (Paxil)	10–80 mg	Low
Sertraline (Zoloft)	25–200 mg	Low
Citralopram (Celexa)	20–40 mg/day	Low

Potential side effects: nausea, headache, nervousness, insomnia, drowsiness, diarrhea, decreased libido, sexual dysfunction.

Tricyclics

Action: Believed to involve potentiation of norepinephrine and possibly serotonin activity by blocking reuptake by the presynaptic (sending) nerve cell, making more available for transmission to the postsynaptic (receiving) nerve cell.

Drugs in category	Daily dose range	Potential overdose danger
Imipramine (Tofranil)	30–200 mg/day	High
Desipramine (Norpramin)	25–200 mg/day	High
Amitriptyline (Elavil)	10–200 mg/day	High
Nortriptyline (Pamelor)	30–150 mg/day	High
Doxepin (Sinequan)	25–300 mg/day	High
Protriptyline (Vivactil)	15–60 mg/day	High

Potential side effects: dry mouth, increased heart rate, EKG changes, urinary hesitation, constipation, blurred vision, sedation, weight gain.

Monamine-Oxidase Inhibitors (MAOIs)

Action: Believed to act by inhibiting the enzyme monamine oxidase, responsible for the breakdown of monoamines (norepinepherine, epinepherine, and serotonin). Inhibition results in increased levels of these neurotransmitters. Because of the possibility of major interactions with foods containing tyramine and multiple medications resulting in marked blood pressure elevation, use of the MAOIs requires that the patient be very diligent about his or her diet and the use of other medication. Thus, they are infrequently prescribed.

Drugs in category	Daily dose range	Potential overdose danger
Tranylcypromine (Parnate)	30–60 mg/day	High
Phenylzine (Nardil)	15–90 mg/day	High

Potential side effects: overstimulation, anxiety, agitation, mania, restlessness, insomnia, drowsiness, dizziness, insomnia, gastrointestinal symptoms, headaches, rapid heartbeat, hypertensive crisis when used with food containing tyramine or medications with sympathomimetic effects, such as cold preparations.

TABLE 11.2   (*continued*)

Other Antidepressant Medications

Drugs in category	Daily dose range	Potential overdose danger
Venlafaxine (Effexor)	75–225 mg/day	Low

Action: Believed to potentiate the action of serotonin, norepinephrine, and dopamine by inhibition of the reuptake mechanism.

Potential side effects: headache, sweating, elevated blood pressure, nausea, insomnia, dizziness, anorexia, anxiety, sleepiness, difficulty with orgasm (higher doses).

Bupropion (Wellbutrin,	100–450/day	Low
marketed as Zyban for smoking cessation)		

Action: Unknown, weak blocker of catecholamines.

Potential side effects: agitation, dry mouth, sweating, insomnia, seizures, dizziness.

Nefazadone (Serzone)	100–600 mg/day	Low
Trazadone (Desyrel)	50–600 mg/day	Low

Action: Unknown. Possible inhibition of reuptake of serotonin and norepinepherine.

Potential side effects: Both medications: dry mouth, nausea, constipation, sleepiness, dizziness, lightheadedness, vision problems, confusion. Trazadone: hypotension, sexual dysfunction in males.

Mirtazepine (Remeron)	15–45 mg/day	Low, but few reports

Action: Unknown. May enhance norepinepherine and serotonin by preventing reuptake.

Potential side effects: sleepiness, dizziness, increased appetite and weight gain, increased triglycerde and cholesterol levels.

However, maintaining stability often depends upon continuation of the medication.

In addition to lithium, tegretol (Carbamazepine) and valproic acid are used with patients who cannot take lithium because of side effects, or they are taken in addition to lithium. Use of alcohol with either of these is contraindicated because of possible additive effects and because there is the possibility that either of them, on their own, can cause liver damage. This would be made worse by alcohol use.

Antianxiety medications

The final group of psychotropic medications are the antianxiety agents. The major action of these drugs is to promote tranquilization and sedation. Quite properly, alcohol can be included in any list of drugs in this class. The antianxiety agents have sometimes been called the minor

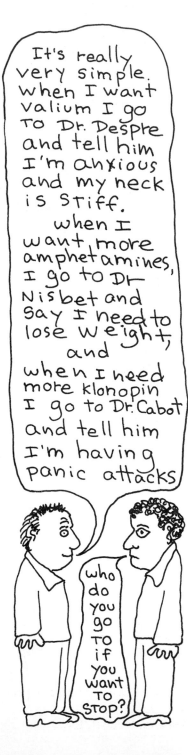

TABLE 11.3 MOOD STABILIZERS

Mood Stabilizers

Note: Used most commonly with patients with bipolar (manic-depressive) disorder to control and prevent mania

Drugs in category	Daily dose range	Potential overdose danger
Lithium	600–1800 mg/day	High

(Lithium Carbonate, Lithonate, Lithobid, Eskalith)

Action: Unknown. Alters sodium transport and causes a shift toward intraneuronal metabolism of catecholamines, but specific biochemical mechanism of action in mania is not known.

Potential side effects: hand tremor, nausea, weight gain, increased output of urine and increased fluid intake, fatigue, lethargy, hypothyroidism.

Divalproex (Depakote)	500–1500 mg/day	High

Valproic Acid (Depakene)

Action: Anticonvulsant. Mechanism of action/effectiveness in mania is unknown.

Potential side effects: gastrointestinal symptoms, asthenia, weight gain, sleepiness, dizziness, tremor, elevated liver function tests.

Carbamazepine (Tegretol)	400–1200 mg/day	High

Action: Anticonvulsant. Mechanism of action/effectiveness in mania is unknown.

Potential side effects: dizziness, drowsiness, unsteadiness, nausea, vomiting, skin rashes. Rare, but serious, effects on bone marrow and white blood count.

tranquilizers. They have no antipsychotic or significant antidepressant properties and are very effective in the treatment of anxiety disorders. Short-acting forms are frequently prescribed as sleeping aids. However, their high potential for abuse and dependence make them less likely to be the first medication prescribed for anxiety, especially in persons who have any history of abuse of alcohol or drugs. The most common antianxiety agents are listed in Table 11.4.

Medications in this class, along with barbiturates (now rarely prescribed), are those most likely to be troublesome for alcoholics. The potential for abuse of these antianxiety agents has become more broadly recognized. Valium, Xanax, and Ativan are the antianxiety agents that have been most widely associated with abuse and dependence. In the past, Quaalude and Placidyl—which interestingly are no longer available for prescription in this country—as well as Miltown and some barbiturates also caused major abuse/dependency problems. Newer antianxiety medications have demonstrated far less abuse potential, e.g., buspirone (BuSpar) and hydroxyzine (Atarax, Vistaril).

Beyond problems of possible abuse, there are other dangers with the antianxiety agents and alcohol. Taken in combination, they potentiate one another. There are those who will remember Karen Ann Quinlin, whose family was one of the first to have fought to have her removed from a respirator. She had been in a coma for almost a decade. Far fewer

TABLE 11.4 ANTIANXIETY AGENTS

Antianxiety Medications

Note: The table is restricted to the most commonly prescribed medications.

Action: Depression of activity at all excitable tissues. In general, acts at receptors on neurons that are linked with or potentiate the GABA (gamma-amino-butyric acid) system, which inhibits neuronal activity. Chloride ion flow into neurons is facilitated by the GABA system, resulting In sedation.

Benzodiazepines

Drugs in category	Daily dose range	Potential overdose danger
Alprazolam (Xanax)	0.25–6 mg	Low
Chlordiazepoxide (Librium)	5–100 mg	Low
Clonazepam (Klonopin)	0.5–4 mg	Low
Diazepam (Valium)	2–40 mg	Low
Lorazepam (Ativan)	1–6 mg	Low
Oxazepam (Serax)	10–90 mg	

Potential side effects: sedation, fatigue, ataxia, impaired motor function, thus possible difficulty operating machinery or automobiles.

I belong to idealists anonymous. We don't actually meet, but we think about meeting a lot.

people are aware that the cause of her irreversible coma was attributed to the combination of alcohol and Valium.

Because of their similar pharmacology, alcohol and the antianxiety agents are virtually interchangeable. This phenomenon is the basis of cross-addiction and is the rationale for their use for alcohol detoxification. It is their very interchangeability with alcohol that makes them very poor drugs for those with an alcohol problem, except for detoxification purposes.

On the whole, Americans are very casual about medications. Too often, prescriptions are not taken as directed, are saved up for the next illness, or are shared with family and friends. Over-the-counter preparations are treated as candy. The fact that a prescription is not required does not render these preparations harmless. Some possible ingredients in over-the-counter drugs are antihistamines, stimulants, and of course, alcohol. These can cause difficulty if taken in combination with alcohol or may themselves be abused.

RESOURCES AND FURTHER READING

Alexander MJ: Women with co-occurring addictive and mental disorders: An emerging profile of vulnerability (review), *American Journal of Orthopsychiatry* 66(1):61–70, 1996. (85 refs.)
    The heterogeneity of those with co-occurring addictive and mental disorders has only recently begun to be recognized, and treatment strategies for different segments of this population are still being developed. This article reviews the literature on alcohol and drug problems in women,

Every form of addiction is bad, no matter whether the narcotic be alcohol or morphine or idealism.

CARL JUNG

Eat not to fullness; drink not to elevation.

BENJAMIN FRANKLIN

and on women with severe mental illness who are at high risk for substance abuse—as well as other forms of abuse and deprivation—due to poverty and victimization. As public health and mental health agendas are threatened by budget cuts, it is critical that initial gains in acknowledging and addressing their needs not be lost or abandoned. (Author abstract.)

Allan CA: Alcohol problems and anxiety disorders: A critical review, *Alcohol and Alcoholism* 30(2):145–151, 1995. (44 refs.)

The assumption that, within clinical populations, anxiety reduction is a major factor in the etiology of drinking problems no longer appears to be a plausible explanation of the available data. There are many studies that document the occurrence of anxiety symptoms in problem drinkers, but the difficulty lies in deciding which comes first, the alcohol problem or the anxiety. Evidence is reviewed which indicates that anxiety is likely, in most instances, to be a consequence rather than a cause of heavy drinking. This has implications for the treatment of patients with both disorders. The assessment and management of patients with a dual diagnosis of alcohol dependence and anxiety is discussed in the light of these findings. (Author abstract.)

Berglund M, Ojehagen A: The influence of alcohol drinking and alcohol use disorders on psychiatric disorders and suicidal behavior, *Alcoholism: Clinical and Experimental Research* 22(7 Supplement):333S–345S, 1998. (112 refs.)

This review reports on the influence of alcohol drinking and alcohol use disorders on psychiatric disorders and suicidal behavior. The base of the study was previous reviews of the National Institute on Alcohol Abuse and Alcoholism publication *Alcohol and Health in 1993* and by Helgason in 1996. Using a defined search strategy in Medline, another 42 articles from 1994 to 1996 were included in the comorbidity part and 19 in the suicidal part. Epidemiological and clinical studies confirm high comorbidity of substance use disorders and other mental disorders. Alcohol abuse worsens the course of psychiatric disorders. Light to moderate alcohol consumption has no documented positive effect on the course. Levels of risk consumption of alcohol in psychiatric disorders have not been well defined. One-fifth to one-third of increased deaths rate among alcoholics is explained by suicide, in countries with high alcohol consumption, the suicide rate is also high and is increasing with total increased alcohol consumption. Comorbidity is common among suicide victims, and substance use disorders are most frequently combined with depressive disorders. Interpersonal loss within 6 weeks before suicide is more often present among alcoholics than among nonalcoholic suicide victims. (Author abstract.)

Buckley PF: Substance abuse in schizophrenia: A review, *Journal of Clinical Psychiatry* 59(Supplement):26–30, 1998. (60 refs.)

Approximately half of the patients who suffer from schizophrenia are also substance abusers at some time during their illness. The motivational drive toward abusive consumption is compounded in individuals with schizophrenia who turn toward substances with reinforcing properties to alleviate aspects of psychosis. This review examines the prevalence, etiology, and clinical effects of substance abuse (e.g., alcohol, nicotine, cocaine) among individuals with schizophrenia. Clearly, substance abuse persists in spite of treatment with typical antipsychotics. The efficacy of newer-generation antipsychotics in the reduction of substance abuse among the schizophrenic population has yet to be established, but clozapine has been shown to reduce alcohol, smoking, and cocaine use. Hence, clozapine is a therapeutic option for dually diagnosed patients because of its superior efficacy relative to conventional neuroleptics and its capacity to control substance abuse. (Author abstract.)

Covey LS, Glassman AH, Stetner F: Cigarette smoking and major depression (review), *Journal of Addictive Diseases* 17(1):35–46, 1998. (28 refs.)

The authors review recent literature that has demonstrated an association between cigarette smoking behavior and major depression. Persons with major depression are more likely to smoke and to have difficulty when they try to stop. When they manage to succeed in stopping, such persons are at increased risk of experiencing mild to severe states of depression, including full-blown major depression. The period of vulnerability to a new depressive episode appears to vary from a few weeks to several months after cessation. This knowledge suggests a relationship between smoking and depression that is complex, pernicious, and potentially lifelong. It is recommended that cessation treatments incorporate screening procedures that will identify those patients with a propensity to depression and monitor the emergence of postcessation depression, particularly in those with a history of depression. (Author abstract.)

Drake RE, Mercer-McFadden C, Mueser KT, McHugo GJ, Bond GR: Review of integrated mental health and substance abuse treatment for patients with dual disorders (review), *Schizophrenia Bulletin* 24(4): 589–608, 1998. (107 refs.)

Patients with severe mental disorders such as schizophrenia and co-occurring substance use disorders traditionally received treatments for their two disorders from two different sets of clinicians in parallel treatment systems. Dissatisfaction with this clinical tradition led to the development of integrated treatment models in which the same clinicians or teams of clinicians provide substance abuse treatment and mental health treatment in a coordinated fashion. We reviewed 36 research studies on the effectiveness of integrated treatment for dually diagnosed patients. Studies of adding dual-disorders groups to traditional services, studies of intensive integrated treatments in controlled settings, and studies of demonstration projects have thus far yielded disappointing results. On the other hand, 10 recent studies of comprehensive, integrated outpatient treatment programs provide encouraging evidence of the programs' potential to engage dually diagnosed patients in services and to help them reduce substance abuse and attain remission. Outcomes related to hospital use, psychiatric symptoms, and other domains are less consistent. Several program features appear to be associated with effectiveness: assertive outreach, case management, and a longitudinal, stagewise, motivational approach to substance abuse treatment. Given the magnitude and severity of the problem of dual disorders, more controlled research on integrated treatment is needed. (Author abstract.)

Drake RE, Muesser KT, Clark RE, Wallach MA: The course, treatment, and outcome of substance disorder in persons with severe mental illness, *American Journal of Orthopsychiatry* 66(1):42–51, 1996. (64 refs.)
Individuals with co-occurring substance abuse and severe mental illness are particularly vulnerable to negative outcomes. This paper reviews findings on the longitudinal course of dual disorders in traditional treatment systems, which provide separate mental health and substance abuse programs; describes the movement toward programs that integrate both types of treatment at the clinical level; reviews evidence related to outcomes in integrated treatment programs; and discusses health-care policy changes that would encourage effective treatments. (Author abstract.)

Faigel HC, Sznajderman S, Tishby O, Turel M, Pinus U: Attention deficit disorder during adolescence: A review, *Journal of Adolescent Health* 16(3): 174–184, 1995. (137 refs.)
Attention deficit disorder (ADD) in adolescents has received scant attention when compared with that given to children. With or without hyperactivity, ADD does not disappear at puberty and is an important factor in scholastic and social failure in adolescents. As a condition associated with decreased metabolism in the premotor and prefrontal superior cerebral cortex, ADD in adolescents responds well to treatment with stimulants, tricyclic antidepressants, and monoamine oxidase inhibitors. Nonpharmacologic modalities such as behavior modification, individual and family therapy, and cognitive therapy are useful adjuncts to psychopharmacologic management. Without effective treatment, ADD often results in increased risk of trauma, substance abuse, and conduct and affective disorders during adolescence, and marital disharmony, family dysfunction, divorce, and incarceration in adulthood. Properly treated with medication and counseling, adolescents with ADD succeed as well as their peers. (Author abstract.)

Fujita B, Nikkel R: *Dual diagnosis training: A workshop for assessing and treating the client with both substance abuse and mental illness diagnoses, Trainer's Manual,* Salem OR: Office of Alcohol and Substance Abuse, 1992.
This is one of three volumes that together comprise a training package on the subject of dual diagnosis. There are two participants' volumes. The first, Volume I, is directed toward providing mental health workers with substance abuse information. It was supplanted by Volume II, developed by the State of Oregon and directed toward providing information on psychopathology to substance abuse workers. This trainer's manual accompanies these two volumes. It is recommended as an introductory course. This manual reviews goals and general considerations for trainers and then outlines the 3 days of training.

Lehman AF, Dixon LB, eds: *Double jeopardy: Chronic mental illness and substance use disorders,* Chur Switzerland: Harwood Academic Publishers GmbH, 1995. (Chapter refs.)
This edited volume with 17 chapters and 30 contributing authors is part of a series on management of chronic mental illness. This volume dealing with dual diagnosis, i.e., those with coexisting chronic mental illness and substance use disorders, is organized into three major sections. The

first provides an overview, the epidemiology, ethnic and cultural factors, and assessment. The second section deals with treatment. It provides an overview of treatment principles and then focuses on treatment of substance use among those with different psychiatric illnesses, schizophrenia, mood disorders, and comorbidity among adolescents, the elderly, and chronic mental illness when secondary to substance abuse. HIV and chronic substance use and psychiatric illness is also discussed. The final section is directed to an examination of social systems, i.e., the family, housing, legal issues, models for integrating treatment, development of needed resources, and both policy and financing of care.

Marshall EJ, Alam F: Psychiatric problems associated with alcohol misuse and dependence (review), *British Journal of Hospital Medicine* 58(1):44–46, 1997. (37 refs.)
Psychiatric comorbidity is common in individuals with alcohol problems and has a significant effect on the outcome of alcohol problems. Problem drinkers should therefore be screened for psychiatric disorders and have access to appropriate treatment. Psychiatric comorbidity should be taken into account in the planning and development of treatment services for alcohol problems. (Author abstract.)

Mercer CC, Mueser KT, Drake RE: Organizational guidelines for dual disorders programs, *Psychiatric Quarterly* 69(3):145–168, 1998. (109 refs.)
Dual disorders—combined severe mental disorders and substance use disorders—were barely recognized two decades ago. As a result of the high prevalence and serious consequences of these disorders, they have received considerable attention over the last two decades. Knowledge has accumulated about dual disorders and their treatment, and treatment providers may now consider numerous options for clinical interventions and program designs. In this article, the authors offer guidelines concerning these options. They review the current knowledge about dual disorders and the results of recent research on the assessment and treatment of these disorders. They present treatment principles, recommendations on the components and organization of dual disorders programs, and suggestions for dealing with clinical issues that remain controversial. They conclude with comments on the demands of the managed care environment and the heightened importance of continued research in this area. (Author abstract.)

Mueser KT, Drake RE, Miles KM: Course and treatment of substance use disorder in persons with severe mental illness. In Onken LS, Blaine JD, Genser S, Horton AM Jr, eds: *Treatment of drug-dependent individuals with comorbid mental disorders: NIDA research monograph 172,* Rockville MD: National Institute on Drug Abuse, 1997, pp. 86–109. (76 refs.)
In this chapter the authors begin with a discussion of issues in the assessment of substance use disorders in persons with severe psychiatric disorders. Following this, an overview provides a natural history of substance use disorders in both the general population and among the chronically mentally ill. Next, the failure of the parallel treatment system for dually diagnosed clients is briefly reviewed, followed by a description of more recently developed integrated substance abuse and mental health methods. Preliminary data are then presented from a

3-year study by the New Hampshire-Dartmouth Psychiatric Research Center of integrated treatment for dual-diagnosis clients. The implications of research on integrated treatment approaches for policy decisions are discussed in a concluding section, as are future directions for research in this area.

Oei TPS, Loveday WAL: Management of comorbid anxiety and alcohol disorders: Parallel treatment of disorders, *Drug and Alcohol Review* 16(3):261–274, 1997. (71 refs.)

Comorbid alcohol-related disorders and anxiety disorders have been found to occur in alcohol treatment populations, anxiety treatment populations, and the general community. People suffering from co-occurring alcohol-related and anxiety disorders are more prone to relapse to alcohol abuse, and more likely to reenter the treatment system for either disorder than are sufferers of either disorder without a comorbid disorder. This review shows that it is no longer sustainable to conceptualize comorbidity of alcohol and anxiety disorders as a unitary concept, i.e., lumping alcohol-related and anxiety disorders as one global condition, but as separate distinct combinations of particular anxiety disor-ders, e.g., alcohol dependence and panic disorder, or alcohol dependence and generalized anxiety disorder. The recommended treatment approach, supported by the evidence, is to offer separate and parallel therapy for the alcohol-related and anxiety disorders, until empirical evidence from treatment outcome studies suggests otherwise. (Author abstract.)

Osher FC: A vision for the future: Toward a service system responsive to those with co-occurring addictive and mental disorders, *American Journal of Orthopsychiatry* 66(1):71–76, 1996. (16 refs.)

Identified by providers, family members, administrators, and consumers as an issue creating frustration, high costs, and a profoundly negative impact on quality of life, co-occurring addictive and mental disorders cry out for creative and alternative clinical responses. With empirical research and clinical experience supporting the effectiveness of integrated approaches, the time has come to reconsider the systematic division of addictive and mental health services. A change toward integrated systems of care is likely to benefit the mental health and addiction treatment needs of all people, not just those with co-occurring disorders. (Author abstract.)

Rosenberg SD, Drake RE, Wolford GL, Mueser KT, Oxman TE, Vidaver RM, et al: Dartmouth Assessment of Lifestyle Instrument (DALI): A substance use disorder screen for people with severe mental illness, *American Journal of Psychiatry* 155(2):232–238, 1998.

Seivewright N, Daly C: Personality disorder and drug use: A review, *Drug and Alcohol Review* 16(3):235–250, 1997. (110 refs.)

The concept of personality disorder (PD) is more relevant in the clinical management of drug users than are other approaches to personality assessment. A problem in diagnosis is separating behaviors inherent in the activity of drug misuse from true evidence of PD, especially the antisocial type (ASPD), and rating instruments vary in their ability to do this. Nevertheless, the available evidence suggests that approximately two-thirds of drug users in treatment have PD, with ASPD being the most common. Studies have mainly been in opiate users, while the prevalence of PD may be lower across the range of drugs, and in nontreatment settings. PD has been found to be associated with a range of complications and adverse outcomes in drug use, including psychiatric problems, poor social functioning, dropout from treatment, and increased HIV risk behaviors and infection rates. Outcomes for ASPD individuals in methadone maintenance treatment appear reasonable, however, and it may be that early recourse to such treatment is the most practical option for many PD opiate users, a potential criticism being that this does not directly address the PD problems. (Author abstract.)

Special Issue on Homelessness, *Alcohol Health and Research World* 11(3):1–91, Spring 1987.

Wilens TE, Biederman J, Spencer TJ: Attention-deficit hyperactivity disorder and the psychoactive substance use disorders (review), *Child and Adolescent Psychiatric Clinics of North America* 5(1):73–92, 1996. (107 refs.)

There has been increasing interest in the overlap between attention-deficit hyperactivity disorder (ADHD) and psychoactive substance use disorder (PSUD). In this article the relationship between PSUD and ADHD and associated concurrent disorders such as conduct disorder is addressed. A review of the literature suggests a robust association between ADHD and PSUD; however, the precise nature of this association remains unclear. Diagnostic and treatment strategies for adolescents and adults with ADHD plus PSUD are discussed. (Author abstract.)

Wittchen HU, Perkonigg A, Reed V: Comorbidity of mental disorders and substance use disorders, *European Addiction Research* 2(1):36–47, 1996. (45 refs.)

Recent major epidemiological surveys in general population samples throughout the world have demonstrated that substance use disorders are among the most frequent forms of mental disorders in the community, and are also frequently associated with other forms of mental disorders. This paper briefly reviews the concept of comorbidity of substance use disorders. The review is limited to studies in the general population using standardized diagnostic interviews. Specific emphasis is laid upon the most recent data from the National Comorbidity Survey, which specifically addressed comorbidity issues in detail. The clear majority of subjects with a definite substance use disorder according to the strict DSM-III-R definition has or has had at least one other comorbid mental disorder. Comorbidity rates between specific substance use disorders and other mental disorders are compared and discussed in light of several other international epidemiological studies. Furthermore, time sequences of substance use disorders and comorbid disorders are presented. Potential pathogenetic and clinical implications are addressed. (Author abstract.)

Zweben JE: Psychiatric problems among alcohol and other drug dependent women (review), *Journal of Psychoactive Drugs* 28(4):345–366, 1996. (69 refs.)

This article focuses on assessment and treatment of psychiatric disorders within the alcohol and drug treatment and recovery system. Inasmuch as women are represented in all categories of psychiatric disorders, the article begins with a discussion of basic principles of assessment and treatment, examines some of the barriers to good practice, and offers recommendations for reducing them. The article then reviews in greater detail the psychiatric disorders most frequently found in women seeking help in alcohol and drug treatment settings, adding considerations relevant to those particular disorders. A brief review of key elements to facilitate planning, ongoing monitoring, and evaluation by treatment and recovery service providers is provided. (Author abstract.)

ODDS 'N ENDS

BEYOND COUNSELING

There are other relevant issues for substance abuse clinicians. Space considerations prevent doing little more than mentioning them here. Clinicians frequently discover that although their formal job description is centered around serving clients, there are often other expectations. Such duties fall into the general area of *indirect services,* an awkward phrase used to cover all the other things the clinician is often required to do. Public education, case consultation, and planning for community programs are just a few examples. These aspects of a therapist's work are vital to the overall success of treatment efforts.

Educational activities

Counselors are often called upon to participate in public and professional education programs. The former might include presentations to high school students or church groups or might entail being a panelist on a radio or television talk show. The latter might take the form of in-service training for other professionals, supervision of trainees or students, or assisting with workshops.

Do's   In any educational endeavor, plan ahead—don't just "wing it." An effective presentation takes preparation. Find out from those organizing the program what they have in mind for a topic. You may wish to suggest an alternative. Who will be in the audience, and what will be its size? How long are you expected to speak? Are there others on the program? In choosing a topic, consider what would be of interest; ask yourself, "What kinds of questions are likely to be on the audience's mind?" Do not be overly ambitious and try to cover everything you think someone ought to know about alcohol. If your audience goes away understanding three or four major points, you can consider your presentation successful. Choose a subject about which you are more expert than your audience. A counselor might effectively talk about alcohol's effects on the body to a group of fifth or sixth graders. Any counselor who would attempt to lecture a group of doctors about medical complications is asking for trouble. Leave time for questions, and save some of your choice tidbits for a question-and-answer period.

Feel free to develop several basic spiels. Use films or videotapes. A film can be an excellent vehicle for stimulating conversation, but be sure it is appropriate. Three questions for sparking a discussion afterward are the following: "What kind of response did you (the audience) have?" "What new information did you learn?" and "What surprised you?"

If public speaking doesn't come easily, rather than trying hard to avoid such assignments or just struggling through with one eye on the clock, enroll in a public speaking course. A good place to look for such an offering is at a local community college or adult education program.

Feel free to borrow from colleagues. One of the things that marks effective speakers is having metaphors that somehow manage to capture the essence of a situation. By way of example, a colleague has a very effective response to the not uncommon question of "Can alcoholics drink again?" In responding to this, he uses the metaphor of someone's deciding to remove the spare tire from the trunk of the car. There may not be any problems the next day, the next week, or the next month. But sooner or later. . . . When the inevitable happens, it may be merely an inconvenience or the circumstances might make it an absolute nightmare.

Dont's   Avoid crusading, "drunkalogs," or horror stories. These approaches may shock your audience and titillate them, but (and it is an important "but") most audiences will not identify with what you are saying. The presentation will be unconnected to their experience. Such an approach is likely to leave those in the audience with a "That's not me!" response. There seems to be a widespread tendency to share personal past history of one's own alcohol or other drug use, especially when speaking with teenagers. Perhaps the motivation is to establish credibility. Perhaps it is intended to demonstrate to teenagers that, even though an adult, the speaker is in tune with the teenagers' experience. Whatever the motive, we have strong biases against this approach. It is an approach that is out of touch with adolescents' psychology.

Preaching is preaching, whatever the guise. It's also a bit presumptuous. Does the speaker really think that his or her past history is *so* compelling that the recital of past problems should motivate others to change? Another danger is that what the speaker wishes to describe as problems are heard by those in the audience as escapades. There is the danger too that a degree of romanticism and bravado creeps into the telling. The speaker lived dangerously, at the edge, and beat the odds. Most importantly, it doesn't really go down with kids and accomplish what is intended. A middle school student, in response to a parental query as to what the mandatory drug education program was like, rolled his eyes and groaned. He recounted the "episode of the day," attributed to the educator's "friend." The educator, having grown up in the sixties, managed to produce a succession of "close friends," each of whom had had some experience with whatever the drug they happened to be discussing. In summing up what they were learning, the student wryly noted," I guess what we're really learning is that Mr. J. has some problems picking his friends." Whatever factual information was intended to be conveyed got lost. The general impression was that the sessions were contrived. The unfortunate effect too was to trivialize the subject.

Finally, clinical vignettes as well are usually inappropriate with lay audiences. With professional audiences, if case material is used, great care must be taken to obscure identifying information. For either audience, avoid using jargon. Instead, look for everyday words to convey what you mean or use examples or metaphors that capture what you are trying to say.

Training others

Substance abuse professionals have a special contribution to make in the training of other professionals. A common complaint of many substance abuse counselors is how ill-equipped other professional helpers may be to work with alcoholics. However, this situation is not likely to change unless and until the experts, such as counselors, begin to participate in education. Consider this a priority activity.

It is especially important to stick to your area of expertise. Your single unique skill is your ability to interact therapeutically with those with substance abuse problems. Your specialized knowledge and experience is the most important thing you can share. Often this is most effectively communicated by examples of the kinds of questions you ask clients and the type of responses you make in return, rather than by lecturing. However, one trap you should avoid is giving the impression that what you do and know is a mystery that others could never hope to learn. This can come across to your students in subtle ways, through statements such as, "Well, I've been there, so I know what it's like," or the offhanded comment that, "If you really want to know what alcoholism's all about, what you have to do is (1) spend 2 weeks working on an alcohol unit, (2) go to at least 20 AA meetings, (3) talk firsthand to recovering alcoholics," (4) (and so on). Any or all of these might be advisable and valuable educational experiences. However, you ought to be able also to explain in very concrete terms what information such experiences can provide and why they are valuable.

A few words on supervision of trainees or students may be helpful. Do not be fooled by the notion that the arrival of a student or a trainee is going to ease your workload. It shouldn't. Doing a good job of supervision requires a big investment of your time and energy. Whether the student is with you for a single day, several weeks, or a semester, serious thought must be given to structuring the time to ensure a valuable experience for the student. There are some basic questions to consider in planning a reasonable program. Do you want the trainee to acquire specific skills or just become "sensitized" to treatment techniques? What are the student's goals? What will prove most useful to the student later on? What is the student's background in terms of academic training and experience with alcoholism? The social worker trainee, the clergy member, the recovering alcoholic with 10 years of AA experience—each is starting from a different point. Each has different strengths and weaknesses, different things to learn and unlearn. In planning the educational experience, map out how you will incorporate the trainee. In what activities will the trainee participate? Generally, you will want to have the student at least "sample" a broad range of agency activity but also have a more in-depth continuing involvement in selected areas.

Probably the single most important thing is to allow a trainee ample time to discuss what goes on, either with you or with other staff. The idea is not to run a student ragged with a jam-packed schedule and no chance to sit down with anyone to talk about what has been observed.

If a student is going to be joining you for an interview, be sure you set aside at least 10 to 15 minutes ahead of time as a pre-interview briefing. Also, at the conclusion, spend some time reviewing the session and responding to questions. Do not expect that what the student is to learn is obvious.

Be sure to introduce or discuss with clients the presence of trainees. Clients do not need to be provided a student's résumé nor be given a brochure describing in complete detail the nature of the training program. However, they do need to be told who the trainees are and to be reassured that they are working with the staff in a trainee capacity. Clients have every right to be uncomfortable and apprehensive at the thought either that the merely curious are passing through to observe them or that they are being used as guinea pigs. In our experience, most clients do not object to being involved with students if the situation is properly presented and if they recognize they have the right to say no.

Prevention efforts

Prevention is receiving much attention at the national, state, and local levels. The first concerted attention to prevention appeared more than a decade ago when the NIAAA and NIDA first earmarked funds for prevention programs. On the heels of that a special federal agency was then created, first known as the Office for Substance Abuse Prevention. It combined the previously separate alcohol and drug prevention initiatives and soon thereafter was renamed the Center for Substance Abuse Prevention (CSAP). However, what prevention means is not necessarily as clear-cut as might be presumed.

Before commenting on current efforts, some background on prevention and its terminology is useful. Activities directed at preventing the occurrence of disease have been the mainstay of all public health efforts. This is true whether it is the notion of vaccination to prevent smallpox, polio, or measles or efforts to ensure that the town water supply is uncontaminated so as to prevent cholera outbreaks. The emphasis on and approaches to prevention within the addictions field are probably more closely linked to prevention efforts as they developed in the community mental health movement in the 1950s and early 1960s. Attempts at primary, secondary, and tertiary prevention were first widely introduced in that context. What these three different kinds of prevention activity all have in common is that each is intended to reduce the total number of people who suffer from a disease. If you think about it for a moment, you will realize that reducing the total number of cases can be accomplished in only three ways. One way is to prevent the illness in the first place; thus no new cases develop. This is what is meant by *primary prevention*. A second way to reduce those who have an illness is to identify and treat those who contract the disease, as quickly as possible. By restoring health to those having the disease, you reduce the total number of existing cases. This is *secondary prevention*. A third way to keep the total

number of cases down is to initiate specific efforts to avoid relapse and maintain the health of those who have been treated. This is *tertiary prevention*. While possibly a bit confusing, secondary and tertiary prevention within this public health framework involve treatment personnel.

This public health framework has generally been applied to diseases or illnesses. Accordingly, when prevention was first introduced into the alcohol field, the emphasis was the same. The focus was on preventing alcohol*ism*. In applying the public health framework to alcohol dependence, primary prevention efforts are activities directed at reducing the number of people who develop alcoholism. Secondary prevention is essentially early detection and intervention. Tertiary prevention efforts include follow-up care and continued monitoring after active intensive treatment to avoid relapse and reactivating of the disease.

However, within the addiction field, prevention has now moved beyond just efforts to prevent the disease of addiction. It is now recognized that there are a number of serious problems that can accompany alcohol or other drug use that occur in the absence of addiction. So prevention efforts have emerged to reduce the frequency and severity of negative consequences of use. In these instances, in terms of alcohol, the goal is to prevent not a disease, but the negative consequences of drinking. In this context primary prevention is directed toward achieving low-risk alcohol use. Similarly, secondary prevention would be the steps taken to prevent problems if/when intoxication occurs. Efforts to avoid repetition of such situations in the future would constitute tertiary prevention. The difference in attempting to prevent the disease alcoholism versus the problems associated with use may be obvious to us now, but this was not always the case. Nor was it always fully recognized that efforts that may be effective for preventing acute problems cannot be expected automatically to be effective in dealing with the problems of chronic use. Programs successful at one level of prevention may not work well at another level. Consider SADD (Students Against Drunk Driving). This program may help reduce the toll associated with teenage driving and alcohol use; however, it would not be a promising means by which to prevent alcoholism in teenagers now or as they grow to adulthood. As another example, in the drug field, needle exchange programs are effective in reducing the spread of disease, including HIV/AIDS that accompanies intravenous drug use. This approach is not seen as an effort to prevent drug use. In any discussion of prevention, it is very important that we be clear as to what it is we are trying to prevent. In the absence of such specification, people tended to lump different kinds of problems together. In such situations, there is the ever-too-likely outcome that the programs implemented will be ill suited to accomplish what the planners had hoped to achieve.

The very earliest prevention effort was conducted by treatment agencies as part of their outreach efforts. These programs by today's standards were rather primitive. There was little research to guide efforts; these programs were clearly "add-ons" to the agencies' basic mission.

For the most part they were educational efforts. Also, they were generally directed at the single element that we have since come to recognize carries the least weight; that is, the individual. Realistically this is probably the only point at which most agencies or individual clinicians were even able to consider intervening. A counseling center is not set up to do biomedical research to uncover the genetic basis of addiction nor about to embark on gene therapy; neither is the agency likely to be able to undertake a massive campaign to change U.S. drinking practices, or even a campaign to change its own community norms.

In comparison, current prevention efforts have changed dramatically. Special programs and agencies have been established with this as the major mission. There is an ever-growing body of research to guide activities. At the same time, prevention is emerging as a new and separate professional discipline within the substance abuse field. In terms of its evolution and development, the role of prevention specialist may be comparable to the position of substance abuse clinicians a decade or two ago. The expertise required and the knowledge base for this new profession are not yet clearly defined nor agreed upon. However, when one looks at the nature of the work, one can guess what some of the essential elements may prove to be. There is much to be gotten from the substance abuse fields, such as knowledge of the etiology of substance use, abuse, and dependence. At the same time there are vital elements to be learned from other disciplines, such as the nature of child and adult development, family dynamics, information from health education and promotion as to the underlying principles that influence health habits and behavior, interpersonal skills, educational skills, and principles of community organization. The list could surely be extended.

There has also been a growing refinement in our thinking about prevention models. As a complement to the public health model, other frameworks have emerged. They are not in conflict but represent other useful distinctions. One important addition is a model that clarifies how we define the *target of prevention* activities. The following schema is one used widely by the Center for Substance Abuse to focus attention on the particular group to whom the prevention effort is directed:

• General population. These are also commonly termed "universal approaches." A universal approach is something that is directed to *everyone*. There is no effort to target it to a special subset of people. Good examples of universal approaches are media campaigns.

• At-risk groups. There are also called "selective approaches." Here the target is not the entire population but specific *subgroups*. Mention prevention and we almost automatically think of adolescents. However, there are other groups that might well be the target of a selected intervention, for example, pregnant women or the elderly who use over-the-counter medications. Selected approaches might also be targeted to specific subgroups among teenagers, such as teenage drivers, teen athletes; or to parents.

- At-risk individuals. Another term used for these kinds of interventions is "indicated approaches." Such initiatives are directed to *specific individuals* who are known to be at risk. Oftentimes it includes those who have been identified as having had some kind of problem, or those who are in a high-risk situation, such as school dropouts.

Prevention efforts are also being conceptualized as focusing not only on risk factors but on protective factors as well. Accordingly a program may not simply try to counter and moderate risk factors, but it may also try to enhance protective factors.

At the policy level there is other terminology used with respect to prevention. One hears of *demand reduction* or *supply reduction* prevention strategies. These terms are borrowed from the field of economics. They draw upon the notion of the marketplace, and the fact that the availability of any commodity is dependent upon two factors. One is the amount produced by manufacturers and the other is the level of interest consumers have in purchasing it. If no one wants to buy a widget, fewer are made. If fewer are manufactured, there are fewer available for people to purchase. To apply this to alcohol and other drugs, demand reduction initiatives include any activities that make these substances less attractive to potential users and thus reduces the size of the market. One obvious way is through treatment; abstinence removes a customer. Another demand strategy would be to raise taxes on licit drugs, thus increasing their cost and reducing the numbers who purchase them. Supply reduction efforts, on the other hand, are those efforts directed to making drugs or alcohol less available. Examples include border patrols to reduce traffic in illicit drugs, or reducing the number of package stores or bars within a neighborhood.

A number of demonstration prevention programs have been implemented, and their effectiveness has been evaluated. Handbooks and programs guides are available from the Center for Substance Abuse Prevention that outline these approaches. While these are available as guides, anyone who is involved in prevention efforts needs also to think critically about how to apply any program to one's own situation. Also, what is seemingly apparent is that there is no single wonderful program that will do the whole thing. A question to be considered is what different components might be combined, without spreading oneself so thin that the likelihood of achieving anything is diminished. Attention needs to be directed to setting priorities. If one can't do everything, what are the most pressing concerns, and what is achievable? In terms of program evaluations, attention also needs to be paid to negative findings. Being dearly loved doesn't make a program effective. Some programs at best have a limited impact in changing behavior. Also, changes that take place may soon fade away. Some programs have even been found to have a negative impact—upon completion of the program the participants are more likely to use alcohol or other drugs than those who did not participate. This has raised the question, not entirely with tongue in cheek, as to whether informed consent is as appropriate in the prevention arena as it is in the treatment realm.

The first prevention programs were primarily educational endeavors. The second generation included other elements, such as providing social alternatives, or efforts to build self-esteem or to teach drink refusal skills. Many prevention initiatives are now multipronged and draw upon other components as well, combining legal approaches, public education, media campaigns, or outreach efforts targeted to specific high-risk groups and individuals. Within these, greater attention is paid to the role of community organizations and their potential role in changing community norms. Community groups too may become involved in lobbying for changes in laws, or to get more police patrols. Much is being done to mobilize parents to respond collectively to teenagers' substance use. This may involve helping parents define their collective expectations, for example, around issues such as teenagers having parties without a parent or adults present, or parents allowing alcohol to be consumed in their homes. Other activities involving parents may focus upon organizing substance-free high school graduation parties, or providing mini-courses on parenting skills. What these approaches are doing is making changes in the environment and changing attitudes toward substance use, as well as imparting concrete skills.

A dilemma   Within the context of current program policies at the federal level, the Center of Substance Abuse Prevention places almost exclusive attention upon adolescents and the promotion of abstinence. Thus, the goal of most prevention efforts is nonuse of alcohol or other drugs. Accordingly, there is discomfort incorporating harm reduction efforts into these programs, the predominant approach elsewhere in the world. A goal of nonuse may be laudable. It may not be achievable, but to debate that is to be sidetracked. The fact remains that many adolescents *are* using alcohol and/or other drugs. Research indicates that there are significant differences between kids' responses to such programs depending if they are or are not already involved with alcohol. A harm reduction message and no use messages need not be incompatible. For example, one can make a case that everyone should know how to deal with an alcohol emergency. To provide this information to teens should not be equated with condoning or encouraging use. For one thing, they know that alcohol is used by some peers, so we are not telling them anything that they don't already know. As a practical matter, it may well fall to those who do not drink to respond if/when a problem arises.

There is ever-growing literature on prevention, including research findings. In general, this research suggests that prevention is less successful than we might have initially hoped. For one reason, behavior changes that may occur immediately after participation in a program tend not to be very long lasting. Or, students learn the material and have more information, yet this doesn't get translated into changes in their behavior. What this suggests is that any prevention effort cannot be a one-shot deal but needs to be ongoing. In fact, the larger issue really is prevention of substance use problems throughout the life span. The hope of preventing all alcohol or other drug use by teens is probably unrealistic. But what is clear is that anything that can be done to delay the onset of use is worth it. The later one starts to use alcohol or drugs, the lower the chances of the individual's having serious or long-term problems. In the drug field, there is debate about "gateway" drugs, that is, whether there are particular drugs that lead to the use of others. If there is a single major gateway drug, it appears to be nicotine. As is usually the case, alcohol and drug prevention efforts can't be separated, and what is clear is that these efforts cannot afford to leave smoking out of the picture.

Even if particular prevention programs have only a modest impact on adolescent alcohol and drug use, they may make a significant difference in other ways. Their presence may well promote secondary prevention, by changing the views, increasing the awareness of the potential dangers, and thereby increasing the likelihood of earlier intervention if a problem does occur.

THE REAL WORLD

Being a professional colleague

Historically the substance abuse field developed outside of mainstream medicine and the other helping professions. Alcohol treatment programs, for example, initially developed for the very reason that those with alcoholism were excluded or poorly served by the traditional helping professions. The first alcohol treatment programs were often staffed by recovering people. The basic therapeutic program consisted of helping the client establish sobriety and attempting to orient him or her to the Fellowship of AA.

With the establishment of the NIAAA, alcohol treatment as we now know it began. Although no longer functioning in isolation, separate and outside the mainstream, some tensions need to be dealt with because of that history. Different professions in the field are just now learning to collaborate. Being the "new kid on the block," it may fall to the substance abuse professionals to work a bit harder at this. One of the difficulties that may go unrecognized is problems in communication. Each profession has its own distinctive language (terminology and jargon) that often is not understood by the outsider. For example, a counselor reports to the client's physician that the client has "finally taken the 'first step.' " The counselor shouldn't be surprised if the physician has no idea what he means. In such situations, it may be tempting to get a little testy, "Well, doctors should know about AA," etc, etc. Of course they should, but they'll not learn if you don't use language they can understand. Remember, you expect them to use language you can understand when discussing your client's medical condition. Return the favor.

Be sensitive also to the fact that many other professionals have a distorted view of alcohol treatment's effectiveness. In large part, this is

because they never see the successes. However, those patients who come in again and again in crisis (though this may only be a very small minority of clients) are all too memorable. In fact, Vaillant found that as few as one-half of 1% of all the clients at a detoxification center accounted for as many program admissions as did 50% of the clients who only entered once. Of the 5,000 clients seen in a 78-month span, it seems that the 2,500 who never returned were easily forgotten while the 25 who were admitted 60 times or more were always remembered. So encourage recovering clients to recontact the physician, social worker, or nurse who may have been instrumental in their entering treatment but who have no idea of the successful outcome.

Also make yourself available to other professionals for consultation. One of the surest ways to establish an ongoing working relationship with someone is to have been helpful in managing a difficult case. Consider offering to join a physician during an appointment with a person he thinks may be alcoholic. Or similarly, sit in with a member of the clergy. Your availability may make their task of referral far easier. They may be reluctant to make a referral to an alcohol treatment program because that would imply they had already made a definitive diagnosis. Alcohol clinicians should be sensitive to the fact that in "just making a referral," the counselor, physician, or clergy is being forced to deal with the alcoholic's denial, resistance, and ignorance of the disease. That's the hard part, especially for someone who doesn't do it day in and day out. So anything you can do at that stage will be very helpful.

Being a professional also, means being open to new ideas. One of the observations made of the alcohol field is that practitioners tend to keep using the "tried-and-true" rather than paying attention to new information. One article has suggested that there are "taboo topics" that govern how care is provided but that have not been validated by research, and furthermore are seemingly not even open to question. While we may not like to hear such suggestions, there is some truth to this observation. Some of the examples the author cited included questions about the necessity of Alcoholics Anonymous for maintaining abstinence; the existence of spontaneous remission; the lack of empirical support for the addictive personality concept; the value of smoking cessation in early recovery; overuse of the addiction concept; and the lack of empirical support for the disease concept of codependency. Some of these we might recognize as now behind us, such as the disease concept of codependency, or belief in "an addictive personality." It is always easier to identify the taboos from a former era. In the future, undoubtedly there will be current approaches, similarly seen as topics "off-limits." Possible nominees include the use of drug therapies for treatment of the addiction as opposed to their use in treating comorbid psychiatric conditions; the insistence on abstinence as the central focus of prevention; and discomfort with harm reduction approaches, be it needle exchange or decriminalization of marijuana use.

Whether the substance abuse field is more guilty of such behavior than other fields is probably not an argument worth waging. And, to the extent these charges are true, there may be some historic explanation. When the alcohol field was founded, care was provided in a manner that contradicted what was then the accepted mainstream way of doing things. In fact, those who remember the early days of the field can recall when alcohol counselors often thought their job, in part, was to protect clients from the established professionals, who, however well intentioned, didn't then have a very good track record. But that is now a very old battle, one that no longer needs to be fought. What is true is that it is always easier for any of us to continue doing what we have been doing. Don't our clients effectively remind us of this every day! Part of being a professional is evaluating new information and modifying our approaches based on the evidence.

Selecting a professional position

In seeking and selecting professional employment, there are a number of points to consider. By analogy, accepting any employment is almost like entering into a marriage. When it works, it's marvelous, and when there's a mismatch, it's quite the opposite. Many positions may have the title of "addictions counselor" or "therapist," but there will be considerable variation among them, depending on the agency setting and its clientele. Beyond looking closely at the facility, it is equally important to look closely at yourself. Take a professional inventory. What are your clinical strengths, and what are areas of lesser competence? What are you most comfortable doing, and which things are more stressful? Is "routine" a comfort or is it likely to invite boredom? Because of the differences between people, one person's perfect job is another person's nightmare.

In considering agencies, you are your own best counsel. But at the same time, consult with colleagues and use the grapevine. What should you give thought to? Among the long list of things worth considering is: What is the work atmosphere like? Does the agency have frequent staff turnover or is it fairly stable? Why do people leave? Is there a sense of camaraderie? How do the various professionals on staff interact with one another? How does the counselor/therapist fit into the hierarchy? What are the opportunities for professional development, both formal and informal? How is clinical supervision handled? Does the agency support and encourage continuing education? Will the agency help cover costs of attending conferences and workshops? What are the routes for promotion? To what are promotions tied—formal credentials, experience, certification? Is the position part of a well-established program or a new venture just getting off the ground? What kind of security does the position provide? How much security do you want and need? Where do you want to be professionally 5 years from now; how will the position you are considering facilitate attaining that goal? What are the skills you would like to develop, and can they be learned in the position being considered?

Then there are always the nuts and bolts of personnel practices. Is the salary appropriate for the position, and can you live on it? Are the benefits comparable with those for other professional staff? What are the hours? Is there "on call" or evening or weekend work? How many hours a week do comparable staff typically work? In both alcohol and human service agencies there is too often chronic understaffing. So conscientious workers pitch in, work extra hours, and somehow never have the opportunity to take that time off later!

Before managed care many clinicians found themselves considering private practice. Now, with the changes that are taking place in healthcare delivery, this is a less inviting option. On the surface, private practice may seem very attractive. On the other hand, it can be very lonely. Those who are in private practice need to take specific steps to develop and maintain professional contacts. (This is in addition to developing referral sources to assure clients get the services they need, beyond those that you can offer.) More than any of us can appreciate is the extent to which our colleagues are responsible for helping us maintain our balance and are invaluable and needed resources for us. While it is difficult to set any minimum length of experience before setting up a private practice, this certainly is not the place for a newcomer to the field.

Being a professional

What it is   Addictions counseling is a growing profession. The professional counselor has mastered a body of knowledge, has special skills, and has a code of ethics to guide the work. Being a professional does not mean you have to know it all. Do yourself a favor right now. Give yourself permission to give up any pretense that it is otherwise. Feel free to ask questions, seek advice, request a consultation, say you don't know. Alcohol treatment requires diverse skills and talents. Treatment programs are staffed by people with different kinds and levels of training, for the very reason that no one person or specialty can do the job alone. Being a professional also means constantly looking at what you are doing, evaluating your efforts. There is always more than one approach. You cannot make sober people by grinding drunks through an alcohol treatment machine. Being open to trying new things is easier if you aren't stuck with the notion that you are supposed to be the big expert. And of course you will make mistakes—everyone does.

What it isn't   Overwhelming numbers of people need and ask for help. The tendency is to overburden yourself because of the obvious need. Spreading yourself too thin is a real problem and danger. One also needs to develop assertiveness to resist agency pressures to take on increasing responsibilities. In either instance it creates resentment, anger, frustration, and a distorted view of the world. "No one else seems to care! Somebody's got to do it." It's a trap. Unless you're an Atlas, you'll get mashed.

Your personal life must be preserved—try to keep that in mind. The people who live with you deserve some of your attention, too. It is hard to maintain a relationship with anyone if all you can manage is "What a day!" before you lapse into silence and soon fall asleep. Save your own space. Collapsing might give you a nice sense of martyrdom, but it won't help anybody. Better to be more realistic in assessing just what you can do productively, devoting your energy to a realistic number of clients, and giving your best. Keep a clear eye on your own needs for time off, trips, and visits to people who have nothing to do with your work. Some compromise may be necessary between being your version of the "ideal therapist" and your own needs.

Give some thought about handling the calls that come after working hours. Some workers ruefully decide on unlisted home phone numbers. Intoxicated clients and their upset families are notoriously inconsiderate. "Telephone-itis" sets in with a few drinks or a few hits. You may think you do want to be available at all hours; if so, think that one over carefully. Many agencies have emergency services to handle after-hours calls. If there are situations when you decide it is important to be available to a client outside of the working day, have them contact the emergency service who can in turn contact you.

You cannot take total responsibility for clients. Rarely does someone make it or not because of one incident. This does not mean that you should adopt a laissez-faire policy; however, just as you cannot take all the credit for a sober, happy alcoholic, neither can you shoulder all the blame when the client fails to remain sober.

Professional development

Part of the work life of any professional is properly directed not to serving clients, developing programs, or promoting the broad interests of the substance abuse field, but to nurturing the clinician's own professional growth. This can take many forms, for example, attending workshops, going to conferences, seeking consultation from colleagues, visiting other programs, or reading. It is important that you provide for your own continuing professional development.

It has been said that the half-life of medical and scientific knowledge is 8 years. This means that half of what will be known 8 years from now has not yet been discovered. On the other hand, half of what is now taken as fact will be out of date! Consequently, education must be a continuing process. What can so easily happen is that in the press of day-to-day work, you find you do not have enough time to keep up. Sadly, what can occur is that a clinician may have a résumé with 10 years' job experience, but it is the first year's experience repeated nine more times. As with any specialty, the daily pressures make keeping current a real problem. Get on NIAAA's and NIDA's mailing list, subscribe to a journal or two, and then make the time to read them. Area or regional meetings of addiction workers of all disciplines are also a way to keep up to date.

There is one final factor worth mentioning with respect to remaining current. One of the things that confronts the alcohol counselor is that much of the information that he or she needs to know comes from many different fields—from medicine, from psychology, from anthropology, from law, and so forth. Because of this, keeping current isn't simply a matter of time. In many instances it means having access to an "interpreter," someone who can explain things in everyday language, in a way that you can understand. In turn, part of your work becomes translating relevant information for clients. Beyond taking part in formal education programs, every alcohol clinician needs to have someone to whom they can turn, with whom they are comfortable saying, "Explain this to me."

Certification and licensure

If you plan to work as an alcohol and/or drug counselor, the issue of certification and licensure is important. In the past, certification by a counselor's association or licensure by a state board may have been primarily important for your own sense of professionalism. Now it is becoming virtually a necessity. More and more frequently, a clinician's being certified or licensed as an alcohol counselor is a hiring requirement. Groups that accredit treatment programs are concerned about staff qualifications, as a way of assessing the ability of a program to provide good care. Also, insurance companies are paying attention to the credentials of those who provide care and making this a basis for reimbursement. Clinical agencies may no longer be able to bill for alcohol treatment provided by noncertified or nonlicensed counselors. The same is true for counselors in private practice.

Certification and licensure are two different approaches to accomplishing the same goal. They differ chiefly in terms of the type of group that is certifying that an individual has demonstrated a minimal level of competency, or training, and is therefore qualified to do a particular line of work. *Certification* is the term used when a special association or professional group confers the "seal of approval." *Licensure* is the term used when an officially designated state governmental body awards the credential. Certification or licensure is something that takes place at a state level. Each state has its own individual requirements. The same is true of teachers, lawyers, nurses, social workers, as well as barbers, beauticians, or some tradespeople, like plumbers or electricians. For professions that have been around longer, such as law, nursing, medicine, there is generally reciprocity between states. In part, this is based on the fact that there are clear professional standards that have emerged over the years. Also, there is a national examination that all states use and recognize. In addictions counseling there is much more variation between states, even though the areas assessed are similar. These areas are summarized in Table 12.1. But the differences between states are narrowing. Clearly on the horizon is the requirement that clinicians have master's-level training, rather than having only a certificate

TABLE 12.1 OVERVIEW OF CERTIFICATION/LICENSURE REQUIREMENT

Certifying group	Varies by state, most commonly an alcohol counselors' association. Some states have more than one group offering certification.
Types of certification	States typically have different types of certification available.
	Distinctions may be made between alcohol and drug counselors.
	Some states offer an administrative or supervisory certificate as well as a clinician certificate.
	Levels of certification may distinguish more senior clinicians from those entering the field or those in training.
Requirements	Counseling experience
	Education/training
	Clinical supervision
	The biggest differences between states is in the time requirements for each; whether there is a formula for substituting formal educational programs for work experience; or to what extent the subject area of education and training is stipulated. Several states specify clinical competencies that must be covered, several require specific educational programs in the area of ethics.
	States may have additional special requirements, such as length of sobriety for those in recovery.
Testing	There is generally a written examination, a personal interview, as well as some "sample" of clinical work, whether preparation of a portfolio, making a case presentation, or providing a videotape of a clinical encounter.
Recertification	Length of certification ranges from 2 to 4 years.
	Recertification requires evidence of continuing education.

program or a bachelor's degree. The best way to find out the requirements for a particular state are to contact the State Office of Alcohol/Drug Programs, which will be able to provide the name and address of the certifying group.

ETHICS

Basic principles

Being a helping professional means being allied to a set of ethical standards. National groups and state counselor associations have adopted specific codes of ethics for their members. The principles that underlie these codes are the same as those for other helping professions. What these codes really are is a series of statements of the most basic rules you are striving to follow in working with clients. For counselors, ultimately the most basic tool you have to help others is yourself. Therefore, *how* you think about the responsibilities of working with others is vitally

I thought you said a "coat of Ethics" so I went to a second-hand clothing store in Harvard Square and bought a tweed topcoat that once belonged to a philosophy professor.

important. Ethical codes are intended to serve as guidelines. They have a history and have developed from experience.

Quite a few years ago, the graduation speaker for a group of counselor trainees at Dartmouth Medical School spoke on what constituted being a professional. The question raised was, "How is a professional counselor different from the kindly neighbor, who one speaks to over the backyard fence?" The answer provided was that the professional counselor is able "to profess." That raised a few eyebrows, the meaning not being immediately obvious. What was being referred to as distinguishing the trained helping person from ordinary well-intentioned people is that the professional is able to state i.e., profess, what it is he or she does. A professional functions deliberately and thoughtfully. The professional doesn't rely on "seat of the pants" intuition or instinctive responses. The other important distinction is that the counselor or therapist has made a commitment to a set of beliefs as to how one interacts with clients. The counselor has an explicit set of ethical standards to guide helping behavior.

While a commonly used word, *ethics* nonetheless warrants a definition. One definition is that ethics encompasses the rules that define the "ought-ness" of our behavior. Ethics is a statement of how we believe that we ought to behave. Those who study ethics have identified three basic principles that are germane to determining standards and values with respect to clinical work. If the clinician's behavior does not incorporate these values, there is considerable risk of doing harm. One such ethical principle for those in a helping relationship is a belief in a client's right to autonomy. Simply put, that refers to the belief that clients have the ultimate right to make the decisions that affect their lives. Another is the principle of beneficence. This represents a commitment to respect those in our care, compassion, a commitment to "doing good" and not behaving in a way that places our interests above those of the client. The third principle is that of justice. This too means being respectful. But it refers as well to behavior that promotes social justice, a self-imposed obligation both to be fair and to not discriminate in one's clinical work.

Even if a specific code of ethics for counselors did not exist and were not written down, these are basic ethical principles that are presumed by your other professional coworkers. What is required by those in helping professionals is above and beyond that which may be expected of others or expected of us in other situations. It also needs to be pointed out that how these principles are put into practice is all too often neither clear-cut nor obvious. For example, consider the issue of autonomy. With respect to those who are alcohol dependent and drinking, one struggles with the question of whether a client is capable of acting in his or her own self-interest. If the principle of beneficence is also factored in, it may be felt that some degree of pressure or coercion to prompt treatment is warranted. Yet, there are limits to the degree of coercion and how it is exercised.

There are two ethical concerns that deserve special comment. One is confidentiality. The other is establishing and maintaining boundaries between what is professional and personal, between work and the rest of your life, and between your professional efforts and your personal participation in AA or other self-help groups.

Confidentiality

For the alcohol professional, as for anyone in the helping professions, confidentiality is a crucial issue. Most of us simply do not consider how much of our conversation includes discussion about other people. When we think about it, it can be quite a shock. It is especially difficult when we are really concerned about someone and are looking for aid and advice. There is only one place for this in a professional relationship with a client. That is with your supervisor or therapist coworkers. It is never okay to discuss a client with your spouse, friends, even other alcohol workers from different facilities. Even without using names, enough usually slips out to make the client easily identified some time in the future. Unfortunately, the confidentiality standard is not kept all the time; there are occasional slips by even the most conscientious workers. You will do it accidentally, and you will hear it from time to time. All you can do is try harder in the first instance and deliberately forget what you heard in the second. What your client shares with you is privileged information. That includes where he is and how he is doing. Even good news is his or hers alone to share.

If you are heading up an outreach office, rather than functioning within the main agency, it is up to you to inform your secretary and other staff about confidentiality. The same is true for any volunteers working in the office. Of necessity they have some knowledge about the people being seen, at least who they are. It must be stressed that any information they acquire there is strictly private. You do not need to get huffy and deliver a lecture, but you should make the point very clearly and set some standards in the workplace.

There are federal regulations with respect to confidentiality of client information and records in alcohol and drug services. Information cannot be released to any outside party without the client's permission. This means friends, physician, employer, or another treatment facility. A treatment facility is not even allowed to say if anyone has ever been or is currently in treatment. Generally, one always has a client sign a statement agreeing to release information before anything written is sent out. This then becomes part of the client or medical record. Similarly, if you want to get information from another facility or party, you need to seek the client's permission and get a written release to forward to those from whom the information is being requested. The only exceptions to this are if the life of the client or someone else is at risk.

Setting boundaries

An ever-important and ongoing dilemma is establishing appropriate boundaries in relationships with clients. This can turn up in many forms, but ultimately the question is doing what is required to maintain a professional relationship. One situation that may occasionally arise is when clients will show up with presents. While they are actively working with you, the general guideline is no gifts. This is especially true if something of real monetary value is offered. In such cases, it is important to discuss what is being said by the gift. Use your common sense, though; there are times when clearly the thing to do is accept graciously. (If you have a fantasy of a Range Rover being delivered anonymously to your door, and it comes true . . . unfortunately, our experience doesn't cover that.)

Similarly, social engagements with a client alone or with the family are not recommended. It could be a "plot" to keep you friendly and avoid problems that have to be worked out. During office time, deal with the invitation and gently refuse.

Helping professionals are expected to avoid romantic entanglements with clients. If a romantic inclination on the part of either client or counselor begins to show up, it should be worked out—and not in bed. This is the time to run, not walk, to an experienced coworker. It may be hard on our egos, but the fact is that people with problems are as confused about their emotions as everything else. They may be feeling so needy that they "love" anyone who seems to be hearing their cry. It really isn't you personally. If they had drawn Joe or Amy as their counselor, then one of them would be the object of the misplaced emotion right now. So talk it over with a supervisor, guide, or mentor, not just a buddy. Then, follow his or her advice. It may have to be worked through with the client, or referral to another counselor may be necessary if it cannot. It is never acceptable to have a sexual relationship with a client.

The need to keep counseling and personal relationships separate does not only apply when the client is in actual treatment. It is also applicable afterward. This can be particularly difficult when the paths of a clinician and a former client intersect in other areas of life, such as if both are members of AA or NA. However, as cruel as it may sound, former clients are forever off-limits.

These ethical standards are not arbitrary nonsense set up by a bunch of Puritans. They are protections designed to protect both you and the client before you from needless hurt. The hurts can be emotional or range all the way to messy court actions. Those who have walked the road before you have discovered what keeps upsets to a minimum, your sense of self-worth realistic, and your helpfulness at its optimum level.

Another ethical concern is how to keep your professional life and private life separate. Don't do a counseling number on your friends; you are likely to end up with fewer of them if you do. It is just as inappropriate to turn friends or family into clients as it is to turn clients into friends. When you see a friend exhibiting behavior that you think indicates he or she is heading for trouble, it is hard not to fall into your professional role. Don't. Bite your tongue. A friend knows what business you're in. If that person wants help, he or she will ask. Should that day come, refer him to see someone else. And stay out of the picture. Counseling friends and relatives is another no-no. Vital objectivity is impossible. No matter how good you are with your clients, almost anyone else will be better equipped to work with your family or friends. If you are concerned about a close friend, then you see a therapist, as a client, to assess whether you want to or can become part of an intervention process.

Considerably greater attention is now being paid to the ethical issues that arise in alcohol and other drug use counseling. This is the result of two factors. One is that the field of medical ethics in general is becoming better established. Ethics committees in fact have been created in many institutions to help staff consider ethical dilemmas. The other factor is that alcohol and other drug addictions are no longer on the outside, looking in, but have become a part of health and medical care. Thus the issues that are raised in other areas of medicine are now also being considered in respect to substance abuse clients. There are a number of ethical issues that have gotten particular attention. One of these arises around illicit drug use during pregnancy. The question becomes how one considers and balances the welfare of the unborn child and that of the mother. Another area in which there has been increasing discussion is around the question of organ transplants. Should alcohol dependent people be considered candidates for a liver transplant, given that the number of those who need liver transplants far exceeds the number of organs available?

Ethics also enters into the area of research. Anyone who works in a setting that conducts research needs to be familiar with the guidelines for ethical research practices. Federal regulations that involve human subjects are very strict. Any research project that involves human subjects is required to take very careful steps to protect the subjects. First it must be demonstrated that the answers to the questions being raised require human research, that mice, rats, or baboons wouldn't do. With that established, virtually all institutions have a committee to review how the research is to be conducted. These committees are required to review the risks to those involved, to consider how it is proposed that subjects will be recruited, and to review the steps to be taken so that potential subjects understand what is entailed, what the risks are, and that no coercion is involved. This is not as straightforward as it sounds. Consider the situation in which the researcher is also the individual's counselor or doctor. There is an established relationship. Given the trust that is present, the client or patient may agree to virtually anything. It is not that they are being pressured, they are simply apt to comply with any request because you make it. They may not even really listen to your explanation but tend to do whatever you ask. On the other hand, they may not be wild about the idea. However, they are afraid of what the consequences might be if they say no. Will you be angry? Might you stop seeing them? These worries may seem unfounded to you, but they are very common. Another source of confusion is that clients and patients in general assume that any research will actually benefit them if they are involved. In some abstract way, all knowledge probably benefits all of us. But that isn't really the case with medical research conducted in health-care settings. Such research is only justified when we truly don't know the answer. Is drug A more effective than drug B? Is the use of this counseling approach more effective than another? If the answer is clear—that means scientifically established, opposed to the answer being based on our hunches and impressions—then it is unethical to do research on that question. Occasionally one will see articles in the newspaper referring to a research project that has been discontinued early, when it became evident that those receiving an experimental treatment were doing better than those receiving an alternative therapy, or no treatment at all.

Anyone who works in an organization that conducts research needs to think about this. Here is just a smattering of some of the ethical questions being raised in the alcohol/drug field related to research issues. Should it be permissible for researchers to design a study that involves giving alcohol to alcoholics? What safeguards are needed to do this? What obligations are there to provide or at least offer treatment after the research is completed? What kinds of criteria might one feel are necessary to decide who could or could not be included in such a study? Another research-related ethical issue is the role of the liquor and brewing industries as well as the tobacco industry in the sponsorship of research. What biases might this introduce, and what potential conflicts of interest? Another ethical issue in the field centers on the role of drug testing in the workplace, and the balance between public safety concerns and an individual's right to privacy.

Cases that raise ethical concerns do not have clear-cut solutions. One can examine the case from different perspectives and possibly arrive at very different conclusions. To further complicate the situation, it is important to recognize that the course of action that different professions may deem ethical can differ. This is sometimes the source of unfortunate misunderstandings. It is most likely to come to the fore around cases that involve resistant clients. Counselors may well determine that terminating with a client who is in denial and for whom every reasonable effort has been made to intervene is the best and ethical course of action. To do otherwise may seem to the clinician to facilitate the continuation of drinking. One of the hard things that substance abuse clinicians have had to learn to say to clients is that "the way things are going, I don't see how I can help you." Counselors may fail to appreciate that this option may not be open to other professionals. The physician who is caring for a patient doesn't have the right to simply say, "I will not see you anymore." The person has a right to medical care, and the physician is ethically required to make a referral before terminating care. The issue is further compounded by the fact that the patient probably did not come to the physician for help with alcohol or drug problems but for some other condition. Counselors not understanding this have at times erroneously viewed physicians as enabling continued drinking or drug use because the doctor continued to provide medical care even if the patient refuses to deal with these issues.

Hopefully, in your first years of counseling, you will have a supervisor to help you through such sticky wickets. Use him or her. The real pros are the ones who used all the help they could get when they needed it. That is how they got to be pros.

COUNSELORS WITH "TWO HATS"

Many workers in the addictions field are themselves recovering people. Long before national attention was focused on alcoholism, for example, private rehabilitation centers were operated and often staffed by sober alcoholics. In the course of recovery, many alcoholics find themselves working in many capacities, in many different types of facilities. Being a recovering person no longer qualifies one as a professional. There is more to it than that. That view ignores the skill and special knowledge that recovering people working in the field have gained. They may have had a harder row to hoe and deserve a lot of respect for sticking to it.

Being a recovering person has some potential advantages for a counselor, but it also has some clear disadvantages. Being a counselor may, at times, be most confusing for the recovering clinician who is also in AA or NA. Doing 12-step work and calling it counseling won't do, from the individual's or the 12-step program's point of view. Twelfth-step work is voluntary and has no business being used for bread earning; AA's and NA's traditions are clearly against this. They are not opposed to their members working in the field, if they are qualified to do so. If you are a member of a 12-step program and also a counselor, it is important to keep the dividing line in plain sight. The trade calls it "wearing two hats." There are some good AA/NA pamphlets on the subject, and the AA monthly magazine, *The Grapevine,* publishes articles for two-hatters from time to time.

A particular bind for two-hat counselors comes if attending meetings of 12-step programs becomes tied to their jobs more than their own sobriety. They might easily find themselves sustaining clients at meetings and not being there for themselves. A way to avoid this is to find a meeting you can attend where you are less likely to see clients. On the occasions when clients do see you at meetings and bring up problems or questions about their treatment, gently tell them you will discuss it with them in the office. On the other hand if they are questioning some aspect of the meeting, introduce them to another member present.

It is too easy for both you and the clients to confuse AA or NA with the other therapy. The client benefits from a clear distinction as much, if not more, than you do. There is always the difficulty of keeping your priorities in order. You cannot counsel if you are drinking yourself. So, whatever you do to keep sober, whether it includes self-help or not, keep doing it. Again, when so many people out there seem to need you, it is very difficult to keep from overextending. A recovering person simply cannot afford this. (If this description fits you, stop reading right now and choose one thing to scratch off your schedule.) It is always easy to

justify skimping on your own sober regimen because "I'm working with alcoholics all the time." Retire that excuse. Experience has shown it to be a counselor killer.

Another real problem is the temptation to discuss your job at a 12-step or self-help meeting or to discuss clients with other members. The members don't need to be bored by you any more than by a physician member describing the surgical removal of a gallbladder. Discussing your clients, even with another AA or NA member, is a serious breach of confidentiality. This will be particularly hard, especially when a really concerned member asks you point-blank about someone. The other side of the coin is keeping the confidences gained at self-help meetings and not reporting to coworkers about what transpired with clients. Hopefully, your nonalcoholic coworkers will not put you in a bind by asking. It is probably okay to talk with your AA or NA sponsor about your job if it is giving you fits. However, it is important to stick with the subject of you and leave out work details and/or details about clients.

Watch out if feelings of superiority creep in toward other "plain" members or colleagues without a personal history of alcohol/drug problems. Recovery from alcohol or drug dependence does not accord you magical insights. On the other hand, the absence of a personal alcohol or drug history is not a guaranteed route to knowing what is going on either. Keep your perspective as much as you're able. After all, you are all in the same boat, with different oars. To quote an unknown source: "It's amazing how much can be accomplished if no one cares who gets the credit."

Clinician impairment and relapse

Before proceeding further, it should be noted that the issue of impairment caused by alcohol and drug use is not solely a concern for the alcohol and substance abuse fields. While some professions have come further than others, virtually every professional group—physicians, nurses, social workers, psychologists—has recognized the problem and developed policies and programs to address it. These efforts are conducted under the auspices of an impaired professionals committee, which may be affiliated with the professional association or a state licensing board. The general thrust is to encourage reporting by concerned individuals, be it family members, colleagues, or patients; to initiate a nonprejudicial review; and, where impairment is suspected to, then endeavor to have the individual evaluated and, as indicated, provided with treatment. In many of these instances, considerable leverage is provided by the obligation to report findings to licensing boards and the threat of disciplinary action if treatment is refused.

While every profession has members who are recovering alcoholics or drug dependent individuals—as well as those who go untreated—the alcohol and substance abuse field is a special case, given its history. There would appear to be greater numbers of recovering people in this field, and their recovery status is relevant to the work they perform. For those professionals who are recovering, we have alluded to a variety of situations that may spell potential trouble: burnout, inappropriate relationships with clients, slackening self-help attendance, overinvolvement with the job, and unrealistic expectations. For the clinician who is a recovering alcoholic, all of these can lead to a relapse. Becoming a professional in no way confers immunity to relapse. Unfortunately, this fact of life has not been very openly discussed by the alcohol counseling profession. It has been the profession's big taboo topic. On the occasions where it has occurred, the situation has too often been handled poorly. There is either a conspiracy of silence or a move to drive the counselor out of the field. The coworkers can very readily assume all the roles of "the family," and the counselor's coworkers can get caught up in functioning as enablers.

What suggestions do we have? Ideally, the time to address the issue of possible relapse is at the time of hiring. To our minds, both the counselor and the agency have a mutual responsibility to be alert to possible danger signs, and they should agree to address them openly. This does not mean the recovering professional is always under surveillance. It simply is a means of publicly acknowledging that relapses can and do occur and that they are too serious to ignore. We would suggest that if a counselor relapses, it is his or her responsibility both to seek help and to inform the agency. The job status will be dependent on evaluating the counselor's ability to continue serving clients and to participate in treatment for himself or herself. The time to agree upon an arbitrator/consultant or referral is before relapse, not in the midst of it.

Some people favor an arbitrary ironclad rule: any drinking and you're out of your job. However, that seems to miss the point. There is the recovering professional, who buys a six-pack, has 1 or 2 beers, sees what is going on, picks up the phone, and calls for help. Another case is the person who "nips" off and on for weeks, who subsequently exhibits loss of control, and shows up at the office intoxicated. Though it is important not to treat the former case lightly, nonetheless the disease process has not been wholly reactivated as it has in the latter case. Interestingly, those we have known who have had a single drinking incident, as in the example given, have tended to take a brief sick leave and reengage themselves in a brief period of intensive care. They have interpreted the drinking as a very serious sign that something in their life is out of balance, warranting serious attention. What is essential in any case is securing adequate treatment for the clinician and not jeopardizing the care of the clients.

If you are a clinician known to your clients as a recovering alcoholic, your relapse can have a profound effect on some of them. If you are off the job and enter treatment, you can count on the news rapidly becoming public knowledge. It is our belief that the agency and the coworkers dealing with your case load have a responsibility to inform your clients. Certainly, any details are a private matter, but that a relapse has occurred cannot be seen as none of their business.

A word to coworkers covering for a relapsed counselor: if you are the coworker, be prepared to deal with clients' feelings of betrayal, hopelessness, anger, and fear. You will need to provide extra support. Be very clear about who is available to them in their counselor's absence. Also recognize that this can be a difficult, painful experience for you and other coworkers, who may well share many of the client's feelings. Be prepared to call upon extra reinforcements in the form of consultation and supervision.

If you are a counselor who has relapsed and you return to work after a leave, there is no way you can avoid dealing with the fact of the relapse. How this is handled should be dealt with in supervision and with lots of input from more seasoned colleagues. You will be trying to walk along a difficult middle ground. On one hand, your clients do not need apologies, nor will they benefit from hearing all the details or in any way being put in the role of your therapist. Yet neither can it be glossed over, treated as no big deal and of no greater significance than your summer vacation. In short, you have to, in your own counseling, come to grips with the drinking or relapse so that you do not find yourself working it out on the job with your clients.

A different but similar situation is posed by the clinician who enters the alcohol field as a nonalcoholic but who comes to recognize a budding alcohol problem. In the cases of which we are aware, the individuals were in very early stages of the disease. This raises interesting questions. Since there has been ample evidence of the wisdom of not having recovering alcoholics enter the field until sober a minimum of 2 years, how does the "2 years of sobriety principle" apply in such situations? Does that automatically mean that those who have been good clinicians must exit from the field for the same length of time? To jump to that conclusion is premature. As a profession, we need to determine what the dynamics in this situation are, when an extended leave is needed and when it is not. In the meantime, common sense dictates that this situation needs to be carefully evaluated and monitored. Possibly a brief leave of absence might be indicated, although not necessarily because the counselor has to enter a residential program. A leave provides the opportunity to work intensely on personal issues, which then reduces the risk that they will be dealt with inappropriately in sessions with clients. At the very least, it will be imperative that lots of clinical supervision occurs and that both a sponsor and a therapist for the counselor be an integral part of the recovery.

The foregoing may seem a very grim note on which to conclude this text. It is sobering, but it is reality, too. Maybe one of the hardest things to learn in becoming a clinician is how to take care of yourself. Like everything else, that takes a lot of practice too. One aspect of caring for yourself professionally as well as personally is to place yourself in the company of nurturing people.

A mention of nurturing cannot help but bring to mind faces of those who have been important to each of us. On behalf of all of us, thank you.

RESOURCES AND FURTHER READING

Issues of the profession

Anderson SC, Wiemer LE: Administrators' beliefs about the relative competence of recovering and non-recovering chemical dependency counselors, *Families in Society* 73(10):596–603, 1992.

The authors review the literature on the relative competence of recovering and non-recovering counselors and report the findings of a study on the beliefs, preferences, and practices of administrators regarding these two groups. Most administrators believe that the two groups have no differences in effectiveness. Administrators are equally divided between preferring a balance of recovering and nonrecovering counselors and having no preference. The implications for policy, practice, and research are discussed. (Author abstract.)

Blume SB: *Confidentiality of patient records in alcoholism and drug treatment programs,* New York: American Medical Society on Alcoholism and Other Drug Dependencies and National Council on Alcoholism, 1987.

The pamphlet reviews the 1987 revisions of federal regulations governing confidentiality of alcohol and drug abuse patient records. It addresses the records covered by the regulations; types of communications covered; written informed consent; the application of consent to situations involving minors, incompetent, or deceased persons; types of information to be released with consent; and the security of records.

Chiauzzi EJ, Liljegren S: Taboo topics in addiction treatment: An empirical review of clinical folklore (review), *Journal of Substance Abuse Treatment* 10(3):303–316, 1993.

This article reviews 11 taboo topics, that is, research findings that question traditional assumptions and teachings of addiction treatment. These topics include (1) the lack of empirical support for the Minnesota Model, (2) questions about the necessity of Alcoholics Anonymous for maintaining abstinence, (3) the existence of spontaneous remission, (4) the detrimental aspects of labeling, (5) the value of addicted individuals' self-reports, (6) the lack of empirical support for the addictive personality concept, (7) cue exposure as an underutilized intervention, (8) the interactional nature of motivation, (9) the value of smoking cessation in early recovery, (10) the overuse of the addiction concept, and (11) the lack of empirical support for the disease concept of codependency. Misconceptions arise due to the lack of communication between disciplines and the experiential bias of current addiction treatment modalities. Emphasis is placed upon the importance of empiricism to advance the addiction field beyond faith and supposition. (Author abstract.)

NAADAC Education and Research Foundation: *Salary and compensation study of alcoholism and drug abuse professionals, 1993,* Arlington VA: NAADAC, 1993.

The study of alcoholism and drug abuse counselor salaries and incomes was commissioned by NAADAC's Education and Research Foundation to provide a national profile of the profession's compensation. The results also provide insight into several career pathways common to the profession and help to confirm or dispel many notions regarding compensation in a variety of occupations held by those trained as counselors. Information was gathered from 746 NAADAC members who completed a 4-page mailed questionnaire. This information is presented in 40 tables and covers some of the following areas: normal weekly hours and length of service in primary employment, earnings from primary employment for government employees compared with other professionals, respondents' years of experience and formal education, completed formal education and subject of highest degree earned by salaried respondents, and characteristics of employing organization.

Shipko JS, Stout CE: A comparison of the personality characteristics between the recovering alcoholic and non-alcoholic counselor, *Alcoholism Treatment Quarterly* 9(3/4):207–214, 1992.

Graduate students in social work have been described as often being pessimistic about the treatment outcomes of alcoholics; such an attitude hinders treatment, diagnosis, and recovery for the patient. Within the field of alcoholism treatment, personality characteristics may exist that differentiate recovering alcoholic counselors from counselors who are nonalcoholic. In addition, the nonalcoholic counselors may use a treatment approach based on academic training and theory versus recovering alcoholic counselors who, in addition to theory and training, may tend to use their subjective experiences and participation in Alcoholics Anonymous as a primary mode of alcoholism counseling. The combination of personality factors and of theoretical approaches may influence treatment outcome. (Author abstract.)

Ethics

Editor: Enhancing the quality of our endeavors: The Farmington consensus, *Journal of Psychoactive Drugs* 29(3):299–300, 1997. (0 refs.)

In July of 1997, editors from 25 psychoactive substance use journals convened to discuss issues related to the quality of their publications. The meeting was international in scope. This is a publication of the consensus statement, "The Farmington Statement," that was drafted at the meeting. It represents a commitment to the peer review process, sets forth expectations of authors, identifies formal responses to breeches of those expectations, and sets forth means of maintaining editorial independence from sources of support. The group also addressed the limitations imposed by the "English language hegemony." (Author abstract.)

Hannum H: The Dublin Principles of Cooperation among the beverage alcohol industry, governments, scientific researchers, and the public health community (editorial), *Alcohol and Alcoholism* 32(6):639–640, 1997. (0 refs.)

This is a reprinting of the principles known as the 'Dublin Principles,' which were adopted as a consensus statement and suggested for adoption by the alcohol industry, governmental groups, and researchers. It addresses the mutual responsibility of the beverage industry and researchers to comport themselves in an ethical fashion, to avoid conflicts of interest or the appearance of same; the obligation in situations of providing educational information to do so in an unbiased fashion; that alcohol policies should reflect a combination of government regulation, industry self-regulation, and individual responsibility. Only legal responsible consumption of alcohol should be promoted by the beverage alcohol industry. (Author abstract.)

Plant M, Plant M, Vernon B: Ethics, funding and alcohol research, *Alcohol and Alcoholism* 31(1):17–25, 1996. (31 refs.)

The field of alcohol research is a multidisciplinary area of inquiry. Moreover the debate about alcohol issues is highly politicized, involving not only researchers but also 'advocates' and those with strong ideological orientations or who represent powerful vested interests. Researchers may easily be caught in the crossfire in polemics involving such people. From time to time ethical malpractice is evident, yet there are often neither clear guidelines to delineate which behaviors are unacceptable nor how ethical violations are to be handled. This paper considers a number of key issues currently topical in the field. These are specifically concerned with the relationships between funders or sponsors and policy makers and researchers. Such issues include the ownership of data, sponsor control, and the divergent cultures and outlooks of researchers and sponsors/funders. It is concluded that the field of alcohol research requires a code of ethics to regulate the relationship between researchers and funders. This should provide protection for subjects, patients, clients, researchers, and those who pay for research. Some tentative suggestions are put forward for discussion. (Author abstract.)

Clinical care

Anderson M, Elk R, Andres RL: Social, ethical and practical aspects of perinatal substance use, *Journal of Substance Abuse Treatment* 14(5): 481–486, 1997. (69 refs.)

Substance use in pregnancy has garnered increasing attention over the last decade as a particularly concerning facet of the larger national drug problem. This concern stems from the unique circumstance presented by pregnancy, in which the fetus may suffer harm as a result of maternal behavior. Furthermore, organizing a response to this problem is complicated by the ethically and legally challenging nature of the maternal-fetal relationship. The medical implications of perinatal substance use are profound. A discussion of these associated medical and obstetrical complications lies outside the focus of this paper, and the reader is referred to other reviews. This article is intended to aid clinicians in their approach to the substance-using pregnant patient. It first reviews the scope of this problem in social and financial terms and then reviews the important ethical and legal issues involved in current policymaking. Lastly, the authors suggest a clinical intervention focusing on education and improvement in identification and management of this subset of patients. (Author abstract.)

Cranford M: Drug testing and the right to privacy: Arguing the ethics of workplace drug testing, *Journal of Business Ethics* 17(16):1805–1815, 1998.

As drug testing has become increasingly used to maximize corporate profits by minimizing the economic impact of employee substance abuse, numerous arguments have been advanced that draw the ethical justification for such testing into question, including the position that testing amounts to a violation of employee privacy by attempting to regulate an employee's behavior in her own home, outside the employer's legitimate sphere of control. This article first proposes that an employee's right to privacy is violated when personal information is collected or used by the employer in a way which is irrelevant to the terms of employment. This article then argues that drug testing is relevant and therefore ethically justified within the terms of the employment agreement, and therefore does not amount to a violation of an employee's right to privacy. Arguments to the contrary, including the aforementioned appeal to the employer's limited sphere of control, do not account for reasonable constraints on employee privacy which are intrinsic to the demands of the workplace and implicit in the terms of the employment contract. (Author abstract.)

Doyle K: Substance abuse counselors in recovery: Implications for the ethical issue of dual relationships, *Journal of Counseling and Development* 75(6):428–432, 1997. (16 refs.)

The issue of dual relationships is a significant ethical challenge for all counselors. For the counselor recovering from an addiction to substances, this issue can be even more problematic. Existing codes of ethics offer insufficient guidance to the recovering counselor. Following an overview of dual relationships, the author reviews the ethical codes of the American Counseling Association and the National Association of Alcoholism and Drug Abuse Counselors, with particular attention paid to their applicability to the recovering counselor. Potentially difficult situations are considered, and recommendations are offered both for the recovering counselor and for the counseling field in general to minimize the incidence of unethical behavior due to dual relationship issues. (Author abstract.)

Forrest ARW: Ethical aspects of workplace urine screening for drug abuse, *Journal of Medical Ethics* 23(1):12–17, 1997. (25 refs.)

The author's objective was to review the ethical and legal implications of the involvement of medical practitioners in workplace screening for drug misuse, which raises many ethical issues. If screening is considered as being part of medical practice with the involvement of occupational health physicians, as suggested by the Faculty of Occupational Medicine, then the ethical requirements of a normal medical consultation are fully applicable. The employee's full and informed consent to the process must be obtained, and the employee should have an unfettered right of access to all the relevant records and to the urine sample he/she has provided in the event that he/she wishes to challenge the opinion expressed by the physician. If the process is not part of medical practice, then employees should have the same rights as they would have if required to provide intimate body samples in the course of a criminal investigation, given the potentially serious consequences of an erroneous positive finding for their livelihood. (Author abstract.)

Hall W: The role of legal coercion in the treatment of offenders with alcohol and heroin problems, *Australian and New Zealand Journal of Criminology* 30(2):103–120, 1997. (71 refs.)

This article discusses the ethical justification for and reviews the American evidence on the effectiveness of treatment for alcohol and heroin dependence that is provided under legal coercion to offenders whose alcohol and drug dependence has contributed to the commission of the offense with which they have been charged or convicted. The article focuses on legally coerced treatment for drunk-driving offenders and heroin dependent property offenders. It outlines the various arguments that have been made for providing such treatment under legal coercion. The ethical objections to legally coerced drug treatment are briefly discussed before the evidence on the effectiveness of legally coerced treatment for alcohol and other drug dependence is reviewed. The evidence, which is primarily from the United States, gives qualified support for some forms of legally coerced drug treatment, provided that these programs are well resourced, carefully implemented, and their performance is monitored to ensure that they provide a humane and effective alternative to imprisonment. (Author abstract.)

Marshall MJ, Marshall S: Treatment paternalism in chemical dependency counselors, *International Journal of the Addictions* 28(2):91–106, 1993. This study investigated the degree of paternalism in the treatment philosophies of chemical dependency counselors in three categories of treatment center: adolescent-only, adult, and religious/minority. Counselors were shown picture arrays of either adolescent patients or adult patients and asked to choose a preferred treatment policy, either paternalistic or compensatory in nature. Results showed religious/minority counselors preferred a significantly greater paternalistic approach to all patients than did the adolescent-only and adult center counselors. The adolescent-only counselors responded more paternalistically to the adolescent patients than to the adult patients, while the adult and religious/minority counselors did not respond significantly differently to either group. (Author abstract.)

Modell JG, Glaser FB, Mountz JM: The ethics and safety of alcohol administration in the experimental setting to individuals who have chronic, severe alcohol problems, *Alcohol and Alcoholism* 28(2):189–197, 1993. There is a popular belief that the experimental administration of alcohol to individuals who have chronic, severe alcohol problems (alcoholics) is inherently dangerous or unethical. This creates an environment in which researchers who desire to conduct a study involving the administration of alcohol to persons with severe alcohol problems must defend the relative safety and reasonableness of this practice when, in fact, scientific justification for not using this important methodological technique in alcohol research is lacking. The primary purpose of this article is to present and discuss the safety, ethical, and practical considerations of research involving administration of alcohol to subjects who have had difficulty refraining from harmful alcohol use in the natural setting. It is concluded that there is no overriding reason why alcohol cannot, with due precaution, be safely and ethically administered in the experimental setting to human subjects who suffer from alcohol problems. (Author abstract.)

Richmond R: Ethical dilemmas in providing tobacco to developing countries: The case of China, *Addiction* 92(9):1137–1141, 1997. (26 refs.) We should recognize that we have a responsibility to people who live outside our own borders, and view ourselves as part of the global community. Looking at China, we are faced with ethical dilemmas that require consideration. First, there is the ethical dilemma of business versus health. The opening and development of the tobacco business in China, which includes vigorous marketing, is considered against the health consequences of tobacco use, which is estimated to cost 600,000 lives annually in China, rising to 2 million by 2025 without effective tobacco control programs. A second ethical dilemma is employment versus impoverishment, in which the opportunities for work in the tobacco industry are considered against a background of malnutrition caused in part by a proportion of household budgets used to buy tobacco, and the erosion of the land, as trees are used to produce tobacco. Gains have already been made in tobacco control in China, with the way open for much development in the future. (Author abstract.)

Schonberg SE, Lee SS: Identifying the real EAP client: Ensuing ethical dilemmas, *Ethics and Behavior* 6(3):203–212, 1996. (26 refs.)
As employee assistance programs (EAPs) have evolved and expanded their scope in the past decade, many factors have contributed to meeting the demands of conflicting client constituencies in a multifaceted client environment. This article enumerates several of these factors, notes consequences of ensuing conflicts, and ultimately proposes some methods to counter some of these ethical dilemmas in the future. It is the hope that greater recognition and understanding of ethical conflicts in client loyalty within a host organization will foster increased sensitivity on the part of the EAP practitioner toward resolving these conflicts. (Author abstract.)

St. Germaine J: Ethical practices of certified addiction counselors: A national survey of state certification boards, *Alcoholism Treatment Quarterly* 15(2):63–72, 1997. (11 refs.)
Fifty-five addiction counselor certification boards were surveyed to determine the frequency and categories of ethical complaints filed against certified addiction counselors and the board actions taken during the years 1991 and 1992. Certification boards also were asked to respond to questions about their policies and procedures relating to ethical complaints and training requirements. The most common complaints against addiction counselors were for having a sexual relationship with a current client, being unable to practice with skill and safety due to alcohol, drugs, or other mental or physical condition, and practicing without a certificate. (Author abstract.)

Weinstein BA, Raber MJ: Ethical assessment of structured intervention with chemically dependent clients, *Employee Assistance Quarterly* 13(3):19–31, 1998. (22 refs.)
Structured intervention is a widely accepted approach to helping the chemically dependent client get treatment. Because this method departs from the tradition of the client directly seeking help, it raises unique ethical dilemmas, for both client and practitioner, including issues of self-determination, secrecy, coercion, environmental manipulation, and "fair exchange." Analysis of these issues using a model for ethical decision-making is followed by discussion of four ethical options for the practitioner. The authors identify a preferred ethical position based on theoretical and practice knowledge plus professional and personal values. (Author abstract.)

Wright N, McGovern T: Ethics for the alcoholism and drug abuse counselor, *The Counselor* 6(3):17–19, 1988. This article discusses the revised and, as of 1994, most recent Code of Ethics adopted by the NAADAC Board of Directors, July, 1987.

Prevention

Abt Associates, eds: *Drug abuse prevention research, dissemination and application materials* (6 volumes), Rockville MD: NIDA, 1997. (volume refs.)

This set of materials is organized into six volumes, intended to promote more effective drug abuse prevention programs. The different volumes are as follows:

1. "Drug Abuse Prevention: What Works" provides an overview of the theory and research on which the materials are based. It includes definitions of prevention, description of risk and protective factors, and a discussion of the key features of three different approaches to prevention—universal, selective, and indicated.

2. "Community Readiness for Drug Abuse Prevention: Issues, Tips, and Tools" is a resource manual that introduces the concept of community readiness for prevention efforts. It defines the concept of "readiness," provides a rationale for and seven factors central to assessment of the community, and sets forth strategies for increasing areas of weakness.

3. "Drug Abuse Prevention and Community Readiness" is an accompanying training manual. It is a 9-hour, modular training curriculum, designed for use by training facilitators to induce prevention practitioners and community members to the basic theory and strategies. It includes lecture outlines, exercises, handout materials, and overheads.

4. "General Population (universal intervention)" describes prevention efforts for the general population.

5. "At-Risk Groups (selective interventions)" describes prevention efforts for selected groups considered to be at high risk for substance abuse.

6. "At-Risk Individuals (indicated intervention)" provides illustrative examples of intervention for different individuals, using different representative prevention program efforts.

Bukoski W, ed: *Meta-analysis of drug abuse prevention research, NIDA Monograph 170,* Rockville MD: National Institute on Drug Abuse, 1997. (Chapter refs.)

The development of prevention policy and the design of prevention initiatives will be significantly enhanced by an understanding of which prevention programs have proven efficacious, under which circumstances, and with which populations. To provide such knowledge, the National Institute on Drug Abuse consulted with evaluation research experts to assess the published studies of drug abuse prevention and to integrate those results into a meaningful and objective meta-analysis to identify promising approaches. This report is based on papers from a technical review meeting. The papers address both programmatic issues and methodological concerns. The first section addresses the meta-analysis of adolescent drug abuse prevention efforts; the meta-analysis of integrity test for predicting drug and alcohol abuse; and an approach for meta-analysis of risk and protective factors. The second section considers special methodological issues pertinent in drug abuse prevention research, including methods to calculate effect size, issues in coding intervention studies, differences in outcomes produced by experimental and quasi-experimental studies; and issues related to causal inferences related to program effects. Collectively this report provides a current overview of the efficacy of prevention programs and related measurement systems, and helps to define research approaches.

Center for Substance Abuse Prevention: *Selected findings in prevention*, Rockville MD: Center for Substance Abuse Prevention, 1997. (36 refs.) This report summarizes the results of prevention research sponsored by the Center for Substance Abuse Prevention. That agency has made considerable investment in funding of demonstration programs for state and local communities, which have been submitted to rigorous evaluation. This document assembles the results of those efforts. The introduction to the report serves as an executive summary and then presents the major findings with respect to the following topics: correlations of the initiation of substance abuse; findings related to the efficacy of prevention activities; findings related to program implementation; findings related to cost and financing of programs. It also sets forth a number of working hypotheses in areas in which outcome data remains limited. (Author abstract.)

Donaldson SI, Sussman S, MacKinnon DP, Severson HH, Glynn T, Murray DM, et al: Drug abuse prevention programming: Do we know what content works? (review), *American Behavioral Scientist* 39(7):868–883, 1996. (78 refs.) This article summarizes the theoretical underpinnings, substantive contents, and limitations of comprehensive social-influences-based drug abuse prevention programming. This type of programming has produced the most consistently successful preventive effects. There is some evidence that one major part of these programs, changing social norms, is an essential ingredient for successful drug abuse prevention programming. Because programs, when disseminated to the public, often contain only a subset of lessons from the social influences curriculum, there remains the potential error of implementing a combination of lessons that may not be effective. Some types of prevention programming may be successful in some situations. Finally, social-influences-based programming may not be as effective with some subpopulations, such as high-risk youths. (Author abstract.)

Harrison-Burns B, Kunisawa B: *A guide to multicultural drug abuse prevention,* Rockville MD: Department of Health and Human Services, 1981. (36 refs.) This booklet, the second in a series of six, presents information on the conducting of community needs assessments. It points out some things to be aware of when planning a prevention program, and what resources are available. When developing an evaluation design (which must begin at the earliest planning stages) it is important that the needs assessment and evaluation complement each other. The six-booklet series includes: Introduction, Needs Assessment, Strategies, Resources, Funding, and Evaluation.

Hawkins JD, Catalano RF: *Communities that care: Action for drug abuse prevention,* San Francisco: Jossey-Bass Publishers, 1992. (195 refs.) This volume is intended as a comprehensive guide for alcohol and other prevention efforts. It is organized into three sections, with each section consisting of multiple chapters. The first section is entitled "Preventing Drug Abuse Among Youth at Risk." Its three chapters provide an overview of the problem, outline the theoretical and empirical underpinnings for the strategy presented, termed "Communities that Care," and considers risk factors and protective factors within the framework of social developmental theory. It also describes the community mobilization process, including who needs to be involved, at what stage, how to involve community members, developing a strategy, and assessing resources available. The second section, "Community Action Strategies," consists of 11 chapters. It begins with an overview of community action strategies. The subsequent chapters address strategies for different development stages, ranging from early infancy through preschool, and school years. Parent education as well as approaches to working through the schools are considered. It concludes with an examination of the importance of public policy and the role of the media in promoting long-term campaigns. The final section, "Supporting Community Prevention Programs," addresses one of the most common problems, i.e., the absence of resources.

Foxcroft DR, Listershen D, Lowe G: Alcohol misuse prevention for young people: A systematic review reveals methodological concerns and lack of reliable evidence of effectiveness (review), *Addiction* 92(5):531–537, 1997. (45 refs.)

In a systematic review this study considered over 500 papers that reported prevention programs. Only 33 studies merited inclusion in the review, and most of these had some methodological shortcomings. Twenty-one studies reported some significant short- and medium-term reductions in drinking behavior. Of two studies that carried out longer-term evaluations, only one reported a significant longer-term effect, with small effect sizes. No factors clearly distinguished partially effective from ineffective or harmful prevention programs. In conclusion, the lack of reliable evidence means that no one type of prevention program can be recommended. In particular, there is a need to carry out well-designed scientific evaluations of the effectiveness of current or new prevention efforts that target young people's alcohol misuse. (Author abstract.)

Hall NW, Zigler E: Drug-abuse prevention efforts for young children: A review and critique of existing programs (review), *American Journal of Orthopsychiatry* 67(1):134–143, 1997. (62 refs.)

Children under age 5 are increasingly the target of formal interventions aimed at deterring subsequent drug abuse. These prevention efforts are characterized, however, by a lack of empirical research on the variables involved in inoculating very young children against later drug use, and the lack of assessment research demonstrating their effectiveness. Curriculum-based antidrug programs for preschool children are reviewed, and developmental and early intervention research is used as the basis of recommendations for strengthening such efforts. (Author abstract.)

Herrmann DS, McWhirter JJ: Refusal and resistance skills for children and adolescents: A selected review, *Journal of Counseling and Development* 75(3):177–187, 1997. (71 refs.)

The authors review the literature on refusal and resistance skill (RRS) training implemented with children and adolescents. RRS training is critically evaluated across different target behaviors and outcomes. RRS efficacy is considered for tobacco use, including smoking and smokeless tobacco, alcohol and substance abuse, and sexual activity. Factors that influence RRS training are identified and process variables are discussed. These include age and gender, media formats (video or live), and teacher-led versus peer-led approaches. Conclusions are drawn based on the reviewed literature. (Author abstract.)

Hittner JB, Levasseur PW, Galante V: Primary prevention of alcohol misuse: Overview and annotated bibliography, *Substance Use & Misuse* 33(10):2131–2178, 1998. (24 refs.)

Following an overview of conceptual and methodological issues related to alcohol misuse primary prevention and a brief discussion of the most frequently employed primary prevention strategies, a comprehensive annotated bibliography of the alcohol misuse primary prevention literature is presented. Several benefits of presenting detailed annotations, such as allowing readers to (a) examine the various prevention program components, (b) identify the presence or absence of methodological shortcomings, (c) identify whether or not high-risk groups were included as program participants, and (d) evaluate the feasibility of program implementation, are also highlighted. (Author abstract.)

McNeil A: Preventing the onset of tobacco use. In Bolliger CT, Fagerstrom KO, eds: *Progress in respiratory research: The tobacco epidemic,* Basel: Karger, 1997, pp. 213–219. (97 refs.)

This chapter updates earlier reviews on smoking prevention. It addresses the onset of use, prevalence trends, characteristics of those who experiment with tobacco, prevention interventions through the schools, media campaigns, cessation efforts, smoking policies, and communitywide efforts, restrictions on sales, advertising bans, and fiscal policy, i.e., taxation. Tables are provided on real price vs. adolescent daily smoking, and the percentage of 15-year-olds who smoke at least once weekly for 25 European countries. (Author abstract.)

Pentz MA, Bonnie RJ, Shopland DR: Integrating supply and demand reduction strategies for drug abuse prevention (review), *American Behavioral Scientist* 39(7):897–910, 1996. (30 refs.)

Historically, demand and supply reduction approaches to the prevention and control of tobacco, alcohol, and other drug abuse have been treated as independent efforts in the United States, vying for public attention and funding. Separate reviews of research suggest that the more effective components of each approach can reduce potential drug use by 20% to 40% for 3 years and sometimes longer. This article briefly reviews demand and supply reduction approaches to drug abuse prevention and presents hypothetical models of change in drug use behavior based on program and policy interventions that are introduced sequentially into communities. (Author abstract.)

Sorensen G, Emmons K, Hunt MK, Johnston D: Implications of the results of community intervention trials (review), *Annual Review of Public Health* 19:379–416, 1998. (229 refs.)

This paper examines the results of population-level interventions conducted in three settings: entire communities, worksites, and schools. Four major conclusions are discussed: (a) Directions for the next generation of community-based interventions include targeting multiple levels of influence; addressing social inequalities in disease risk; involving communities in program planning and implementation; incorporating approaches for "tailoring" interventions; and utilizing rigorous process evaluation. (b) In addition to randomized controlled trials, it is time to use the full range of research phases available, from hypothesis generation and methods development to dissemination research. (c) The public health research agenda may have contributed to observed secular trends by placing behavioral risk factors on the social and media agendas. (d) The magnitude of the results of community intervention trials must be judged according to their potential public health or population-level effects. Small changes at the individual level may result in large benefits at the population level. (Author abstract.)

Wallace SK, Staiger PK: Informing consent: Should 'providers' inform 'purchasers' about the risks of drug education? *Health Promotion International* 13(2):167–171, 1998. (47 refs.)

This paper argues that most drug education is problematic as an "evidence-based" intervention, as it either lacks sufficient empirical support for its implementation, or it continues in the face of negative results. It is argued that drug education is a good example of an entrenched but risky public health intervention which is unimpeded by any burden of evidence, but this fact is not well known in the purchasing communities, which often mandate such preventive programs universally. A morally informed public health policy would suggest that such quality assurance data is mandatory for the continuation or maintenance of any preventative drug education. (Author abstract.)

WORLD WIDE WEB (WWW) SITES

The following are a selection of many World Wide Web (WWW) sites that address substance abuse. Those included are noteworthy for their substantive information, authoritative materials, unique and distinctive content, as well as their links to other Internet resources.

Addiction Research Foundation (Canada)
www.arf.org

The Addiction Research Foundation is supported by the Ontario provincial government. Among the materials on its site are the publication of professional staff, organized by topical areas; excellent public information fact sheets; and the table of contents of *The Journal,* a long-standing quarterly newspaper directed to the substance abuse field and the general public.

Cable News Network (CNN, health section)
www.cnn.com/HEALTH/

Produced by CNN, this site features current news stories that generally include substance abuse-related topics. Beyond summarizing the issue, frequently there are associated background materials, statistical summaries, graphs, charts, links to related www sites, and further reference sources.

Canadian Centre on Substance Abuse (CSSA)
www.ccsa.ca

Established as a national agency in 1988 by an Act of Parliament, CCSA provides public information on the nature, extent, and consequences of substance use, and provides support to Canadian treatment, prevention, and educational programs. CCSA coordinates the Canadian Substance Abuse Information Network (CAIN), a group of electronically linked regional and provincial resource centres. The website provides a listing of courses on the Internet, a calendar of events, Centre publications, resource lists, bibliographies, and access for on-line searching of its specialized databases.

Center for Substance Abuse Prevention (CSAP)
www.samhsa.gov/csap

CSAP provides access to information on prevention of alcohol and other drug problems. Copies of a variety of materials such as curricula can be downloaded. It sponsors the National Clearinghouse of Alcohol and Drug Information [see p. 507] and also maintains a workplace helpline. Both are accessible through this site.

Columbia University Health Service, Go Ask Alice
www.columbia.edu/cu/healthwise

Mounted by the Student Health Service at Columbia University, this site deals with sexuality, sexual health, relationships, general health, fitness and nutrition, and emotional well-being. The subsection on substance abuse issues uses a question-and-answer format. It provides factual, authoritative information using a harm reduction perspective.

Indiana Prevention Resource Center (IPRC)
www.drugs.indiana.edu

The IPRC provides technical assistance through the provision of information, materials, and consultations to public and private prevention programs. The site is well organized, and it contains a wealth of information, in many instances, unique, such as a dictionary of drug-related slang terms. It maintains several searchable databases and links to other groups, e.g., the National PTA's website, Resources for School Educators.

Join Together
www.jointogether.org

Join Together provides technical assistance to community prevention initiatives. The major sections of this site include community action; news; public policy; funding sources; and other Internet resources, including e-mail discussion lists. There is a database of over 74,000 persons searchable by name, organization, city, state, or zip code. There is also a listing of publications, with the capacity to order on-line. Single copies are free.

Lindesmith Center
www.lindesmith.org

Lindesmith Center is a drug policy research institute. Its site features full-text articles from both the academic and popular press that address drug policy from economic, criminal justice, and public health perspectives. It also carries information about its public policy seminar series.

Marin Institute
www.marininstitute.org

The Marin Institute promotes a public health approach to prevention, focusing not on individual-based risk factors but on environmental conditions that support and glamorize alcohol use. It provides information on the beverage industry and marketing practices. There is information on its publications, prevention initiatives, particularly at the local level, the beverage industry, training, and a searchable database on The Alcohol Industry and Policy. There are links to other prevention and advocacy sites.

National Inhalant Prevention Coalition
www.inhalants.org

This site is a source of information and resource materials on inhalants, including videos for adults and youth, posters, curriculum, and brochures/comic books. Includes related information for emergency medical personnel, public policy initiatives with retailers, and educational initiatives cosponsored with the U.S. Consumer Product Safety Commission.

National Clearinghouse for Alcohol and Drug Information (NCADI)
www.niaaa.nih.gov/

This site contains information on the activities of the NIAAA, grants and contracts, an organizational chart, a directory of telephone and e-mail addresses for staff; publications; news and current events; and links to other groups. Access to the ETOH and Quick Facts searchable databases is provided.

National Institute on Drug Abuse (NIDA)
www.nida.nih.gov

In addition to outlining activities and programs of NIDA, there is a list of its publications and communiqués about upcoming events at the regional, national, and international level. Information about its grant programs is posted. The site also includes a description of NIDA's organizational structure and a searchable database to contact Institute personnel. There are links to other related websites.

Online AA Resources
www.cast.co/aa

This site includes information about AA, including literature (English and non-English), history, intergroup telephone numbers, regional resources, on-line meeting information, AA-related computer programs, and gatherings and conventions.

Project Cork, State of Vermont (ADAP)
www.state.vt.us/adap/

This site contains a variety of materials of interest to health-care and human service professionals, a well as those in the substance abuse field. Subject bibliographies are posted on over 100 substance abuse-related areas, with new bibliographies added quarterly. Issues of the quarterly current awareness newsletter, *Library Watch,* are posted; these are directed to the areas of adolescents, clinical issues, medical aspects, prevention, primary care, and policy. There are also annotated resource lists, e.g., periodicals on substance abuse; and a directory of over 50 substance abuse-related organizations. This page provides access to CORK, a searchable on-line database with over 36,000 records that represent materials in the CORK collection and encompasses the literature back to the late 1970s. Database documentation is also available—a thesaurus, scope notes, and a list of the subject terms used for indexing records.

Rutgers University Center of Alcohol Studies, Library
www.rci.rutgers/~cas2.edu

The Rutgers Center is internationally recognized for its research, education, clinical services, and information. The Center's library houses the world's largest collection of alcohol information and can provide individualized information services, specialized bibliographies, and document delivery services.

U.S. Information Agency (USIA), Narcotics and Substance Abuse
www.usia.org/topical/global/drugs/subab.htm

Produced by the federal agency charged with organizing and distributing information to citizens of other countries, this website has over 80 topical areas, including a section on narcotics and substance abuse. Information is organized by publications, government policy, statistics, education and research, drugs and crime, self-help groups, and List-servs.

Web of Addictions
www.well.com/user/woa

This privately produced site consists primarily of links to web resources. It is one of the best and easiest means to explore substance abuse resources on the Internet.

This list was developed by the Project Cork Resource Center, Vermont Department of Health, Office of Alcohol & Drug Abuse Programs, 108 Cherry Street, PO Box 70, Burlington, VT 05402-0070. E-mail: cork@vdh.state.vt.us

ORGANIZATIONS IN THE SUBSTANCE ABUSE FIELD

The following organizations are of interest to librarians and information specialists for two major reasons. These groups provide information services; also many prepare and distribute quality publications. Organizations are listed alphabetically, drawn from the following categories:

- Clearinghouses
- Hotlines
- Library-related Organizations
- Special Focus of Group by Population
- Self-help Groups
- Professional Organizations
- Canadian-Based
- U.S.-Based

Addiction Research Foundation, Division Library (ARF)
Address: 33 Russell St., Toronto, ON, Canada M5S 2S1
Phone: (416) 595-6144; (800) 661-1111 U.S. and Canada
Fax: (416) 595-6601
E-mail: isd@arf.org
Web: www.arf.org or sano.arf.org

Description: Organized in 1949 as an agency of the government of Ontario, the ARF provides treatment, conducts research, and disseminates information about alcoholism and drug addiction. The ARF is a collaborating center for research and training on drug dependence of the World Health Organization. The Foundation is significant to those beyond the province for its research, educational materials, and information services. In 1998, the Foundation merged with the Clarke Institue of Psychiatry of the Donwood and Queen Street Mental Health Center to form the Centre for Addiction and Mental Health.

Publications:
- Product catalogue. Free.
- *Projection.* Bimonthly. $18 (Canadian) $23. An objective audiovisual review service.

Addictions Foundation of Manitoba, William Potoroka Memorial Library

Address: 1031 Portage Ave., Winnipeg, MB, Canada R3G OR8
Phone: (204) 944-6233
Fax: (204) 772-0225

Description: The library has almost 4,000 books, about 400 videotapes and films, and an in-house database. It collects and disseminates alcohol and drug information on behalf of the Foundation and serves professionals, students, and the general public throughout the province. It responds to short queries from others.

Publications:
• *Directions.* Quarterly newsletter. For addictions professionals, educators, general public. Free.
• *Audiovisual Resource Catalog.* 42 pp. Free.
• *Directory of Manitoba Addictions Services and Programs.* Irregular. Free.
• *Directory of Services: Addictions Foundation of Manitoba.* Irregular. Free.
• Pamphlets, booklets, and reports. Free to Manitoba residents.

Adult Children of Alcoholics (ACoA) World Service Organization, Inc.

Address: PO Box 3216, Torrance, CA 90510-3216
Phone: (310) 534-1815
E-mail: info@adultchildren.org
Web: www.adultchildren.org

Description: A 12-step, 12-tradition program of recovery for those who grew up in an alcoholic or otherwise dysfunctional household. The World Service Organization provides information about and referral to meetings throughout the country and offers assistance to those organizing new groups. For information send a self-addressed, stamped, business-size envelope, or leave a phone message, or send an e-mail request (the fastest response).

African-American Family Service (A-AFC)

Contact: Kathy Boese, Information Specialist
Address: 2616 Nicollet Ave. South, Minneapolis, MN 55408
Phone: (612) 871-7878
Fax: (612) 871-2567
E-mail: being updated

Description: Formerly the Institute on Black Chemical Dependency, A-AFC responds to phone or mail requests with photocopies of articles and bibliographies. It provides a range of substance abuse treatment, education, prevention, and professional training services.

Publications:
• *Info Agency.* Newsletter. Free.
• Publications catalog. Free.

Al-Anon Family Group Headquarters, Inc.

Address: 1600 Corporate Landing Parkway, Virginia Beach, VA 23454
Phone: (757) 563-1600

Fax: (757) 563-1655
E-mail: wso@al-anon.org
Web: www.al-anon.alateen.org

Description: Al-Anon is a self-help program for family members and friends of those with an alcohol problem. The headquarters serve both Al-Anon and Alateen. Alateen is directed to teenagers with an alcoholic parent. In 1997 Al-Anon had over 30,000 groups in more than 100 countries, including 3,500 Alateen groups. Al-Anon was founded by Lois Wilson, wife of one of the founders of AA, and was originally known as the AA Auxiliary.

Publications:
- Publications catalog. Free.
- Directory. Lists worldwide offices. Free.
- *Al-Anon Speaks Out.* Quarterly newsletter for professionals. Free.

Alcohol Research Information Service (ARIS)
Contact: Robert L. Hammond, Director
Address: 1106 East Oakland Ave., Lansing, MI 48906
Phone: (517) 485-9900
Fax: (517) 485-1928

Description: The Alcohol Research Information Service is a nonprofit organization whose purpose is to collect, correlate, and disseminate information regarding alcohol and alcoholic products, their manufacture, sale, and use for beverage, industrial, or other purposes, and their impact on health and well-being in the United States. The organization admits to a bias, namely that the use of beverage alcohol, individually and collectively, has a net harmful effect. ARIS invites walk-in visitors and phone queries from 9 A.M. to 5 P.M.

Publications:
- *The Bottom Line on Alcohol and Society.* Quarterly journal. Subscription.
- *Monday Morning Report.* Bimonthly subscription newsletter.
- *The Globe.* Journal. Subscription.

Alcoholic Beverage Medical Research Foundation (ABMRF)
Contact: Robin A. Kroft, Deputy Executive Director
Address: 1122 Lennilworth Dr., Suite 407, Baltimore, MD 21204
Phone: (410) 821-7066
E-mail: info@abmrf.org
Web: www.abmrf.org/

Description: Established in 1982 with support from the malt beverage industries of the United States and Canada, supports medical, behavioral, and social research and information dissemination on the use of alcoholic beverages and the prevention of alcohol-related problems. Grant recipients are from U.S. and Canadian academic institutions. The Foundation's Library and Resource Center on Moderate Drinking provides literature searches on request.

Publications:
- *Journal of the ABMRF.* Quarterly. Free. Abstracts of current literature on the psychosocial and medical effects of moderate drinking, news about the Foundation, and selected statistical tables.

Alcoholics Anonymous General Service Office (AA)

Contact: Adrienne Brown (liaison to professional community)
Address: Box 459, Grand Central Station, New York, NY 10163
Phone: (212) 870-3400
Fax: (212) 870-3003
Web: www.alcoholics-anonymous.org

Description: The General Service Office responds to inquiries about the Fellowship, prepares and distributes literature, including lists of the thousands of AA groups around the world, and maintains links with each AA group. AA literature and audiovisual materials are directed to alcoholics, AA members, and human service and health-care professionals.

Publications:
• Catalog. Free.

American Academy of Addiction Psychiatry (AAAP)

Contact: Jeanne G. Trumble, MSW
Address: 7301 Mission Road, Suite 252, Prairie Village, KS 66208
Phone: (913) 262-6161
Fax: (913) 262-4311
E-mail: addicpsych@aol.com
Web: member.aol.com/addicpsych/private/homepage.htm

Description: Founded in 1985 to improve education, prevention, treatment and research in the field of alcoholism and addictions and to strengthen the training of psychiatrists in the addiction field, the Academy holds annual meetings and edits a peer-reviewed journal.

Publications:
• *The American Journal on Addictions.* Quarterly. Subscription.

American Academy of Health Care Providers in the Addictive Disorders

Contact: Richard E. Rogers, Executive Director
Address: 767 Concord Ave., Cambridge MA 02138
Phone: (617) 661-6248
Fax: (617) 492-3183

Description: Founded to determine standards of training and clinical experience in the field of addiction treatment, the Academy requires these standards for health-care providers who receive certification, regardless of discipline. The Academy recognizes those who have satisfied the training and experience requirements necessary to be considered as a qualified health-care provider in the addictive disorders. The Academy's information and referral service for professionals and managed care companies provides information about specialty providers.

Publications:
• *International Register of Health Care Providers in the Addictive Disorders.* Semiannual. $15 (members); $25 (nonmembers).

American Council for Drug Education (ACDE)

Address: 164 West 74th St., New York, NY 10023
Phone: (800) 488-3784

Fax: (212) 595-2553
E-mail: mgagne@phoenixhouse.org
Web: www.acde.org

Description: Founded in 1977, the ACDE provides information on health hazards associated with the use of tobacco, alcohol, marijuana, cocaine, crack, and other psychoactive drugs. It prepares and publishes educational materials for employees and employers, parents, children, educators, students, policy makers, and constituents.

Publications:
- Publications catalog. Free.
- *The Drug Educator.* Quarterly membership newsletter.

American Library Association (ALA)

Address: 50 East Huron St., Chicago, IL 60611
Phone: (800) 545-2433
Fax: (800) 448-9374
Web: www.ala.org

Description: The largest library association in the world, the ALA has 57,000 members working in all types of libraries—public, school, academic, state and federal agencies. The Association publishes and distributes journals, monographs, and reference works and organizes two conferences each year.

Publications:
- Publications catalog. Free.

American Medical Association (AMA)

Contact: John J. Ambre, MD, Ph.D. Director, Department of Toxicology
            and Drug Abuse
Address: 515 North State St., Chicago, IL 60610
Phone: (312) 464-4559 (Department of Toxicology and Drug Abuse)
Fax: (312) 464-4184 (Department of Toxicology and Drug Abuse)
Web: www.ama.org/library/

Description: The AMA's Department of Toxicology and Drug Abuse has successfully pressed for recognition of alcoholism as a major public health problem. It continues its work defining the physician's responsibilities in caring for addicted persons, promoting physician education, tackling the problem of the impaired physician, and advocating enlightened public policy toward addictions.

Publications:
- *The Busy Physician's Guide to the Management of Alcohol Problems.* Pamphlet. Free.
- *AMA's Guidelines for Physician Involvement in the Care of Substance Abuse Patients.* Free.
- Special reports.
- AMA policy statements.

American Public Health Association (APHA)

Address: 1015 Fifteenth Street NW, Washington, DC 20005

Phone: (202) 789-5600. (Ask for chair of Section on Alcohol and Drugs)
Fax: (202) 789-5661
Web: www.apha.org/

Description: The Alcohol and Drugs Section of the APHA aims to enhance the visibility and effectiveness of public health policy relating to alcohol and other drug prevention and treatment. The Section initiates policy resolutions for APHA adoption, sponsors sessions at the Annual Meeting, and contributes to the review of the scientific basis for public health policies and programs involving alcohol, tobacco, and other drugs. Founded in 1872, APHA is the largest organization of public health professionals in the world, representing more than 32,000 members from 77 occupations of public health.

Publications:
- *American Journal of Public Health.* Monthly.
- *The Nation's Health.* Newspaper. Monthly.
- Publications catalog. Free.

American Society of Addiction Medicine (ASAM)
Contact: James F. Callahan, DPA, Executive Vice President
Address: 4601 North Park Ave., Arcade Suite 10, 1 Chevy Chase, MD 20815
Phone: (301) 655-3920
E-mail: www.asam.org
Web: http://207.201.181.5

Description: ASAM is a national medical specialty society of physicians in the field of alcohol and other drug dependencies. It was admitted to the American Medical Association's House of Delegates as a voting member in June 1988, and in June 1990 the AMA added addiction medicine (ADM) to its list of self-designated specialties. Members encompass all medical specialties and subspecialties. Physician certification is offered.

Publications:
- *ASAM News.* Bimonthly membership newsletter.
- *Journal of Addictive Diseases.* Subscription. Quarterly.
- ASAM Membership Directory
- Position statements and guidelines.
- Syllabi for Certification Program Review Course

Association for Medical Education and Research in Substance Abuse (AMERSA)
Contact: Doreen Maclane-Baeder
Address: Center for Alcohol and Addiction Studies, Box G-BH, Brown University, Providence, RI 02912
Phone: (401) 785-8263
Fax: (401) 444-1850
E-mail: amersa@Caas.Caas.Biomed.brown.edu
Web: center.butler.brown.edu/AMERSA

Description: Started in 1976 by the federally funded Career Teachers in Alcohol and Drug Abuse, AMERSA is a national organization directed to education of health professionals in the field of alcohol and drug abuse. Full membership is available to those holding faculty appointments as well as others, as determined by the membership committee. AMERSA arranges field placements for students and trainees who desire experience in alcohol and drug abuse treatment, research, and education.

Publications:
• *Substance Abuse.* Quarterly.

Association of Canadian Distillers

Contact: Sandi Bokij, Information Specialist
Address: Suite 1100-90, Sparks St., Ottawa, ON, Canada K1P 5T8
Phone: (613) 238-8444, ext. 214 (library)
Fax: (613) 238-3411

Description: The Association of Canadian Distillers is a national trade association established to protect and advance the interests of its ten members, all of whom are licensed manufacturers and marketers of distilled spirits products. The Association's mandate involves promoting and protecting the viability of the Canadian distilled spirits industry and proactively encouraging more socially responsible attitudes towards consumption.

Publications:
• Annual report.
• Brochure. Provides history of distilleries and describes the Association.

Association of Research Libraries (ARL)

Address: 21 Dupont Circle, Suite 800, Washington, DC 20036
Phone: (202) 296-2296
Fax: (202) 872-0884
E-mail: arlhq@arl.org
Web: www.arl.org/

Description: The ARL includes 121 research libraries in the United States and Canada. It serves as a forum for the exchange of ideas and an agent for collective action.

Publications:
• Publications catalog

Brewers Association of Canada

Address: 155 Queen St., Suite 1200, Ottawa, ON, Canada K1P 6L1
Phone: (613) 232-9601
Fax: (613) 232-228
E-mail: officeff@brewers.ca
Web: www.brewers.ca/

Description: National trade association for Canadian brewing companies, both conventional and microbreweries. Information primarily serves organizational members. It compiles international statistical information on consumption, taxation, and control policies.

Publications:
• Publications catalog. Free.
• Legislation digest. Irregular publication. $100/volume (Canadian, for first year of subscription, $40, subsequent years)

• *1997 International Survey—Alcoholic Beverage Taxation and Control Policies* (9th edition). $508 Canadian; $350 U.S.

Brown University Center for Alcohol and Addiction Studies

Contact: David Lewis, M.D., Director
Address: Brown University, Butler Hospital, Box G, Providence, RI 02912
Phone: (401) 444-1800
Fax: (401) 863-1850
Web: center.butler.brown.edu

Description: Established in 1982 with assistance from NIAAA and NIDA, the Center is directed to research, education, and training, and the development of public health policy. In addition to curriculum materials, it offers a postdoctoral training program for physicians and doctoral-level professionals in human services and education.

Publications:
• Project ADEPT. Curriculum and associated materials for primary care physicians and other health-care professionals.

Canadian Centre on Substance Abuse (CCSA)

Address: 75 Albert St., Suite 300, Ottawa, ON, Canada K1P 5E7
Phone: (613) 235-4048
Fax: (613) 235-8101
E-mail: webmaster@ccsa.ca
Web: www.ccsa.ca

Description: CCSA is a national agency, established in 1988 by an Act of Parliament. Funded by Canada's Drug Strategy and through its own revenue-generating efforts, the Centre: (1) promotes informed debate on substance abuse issues and encourages public participation in reducing the harm associated with drug abuse; (2) disseminates information on the nature, extent, and consequences of substance abuse; and (3) supports and assists organizations involved in substance abuse treatment, prevention, and educational programming.

Publications:
• *Directory of Substance Abuse Organizations in Canada*
• *Canadian Profile: Alcohol, Tobacco and Other Drugs*
• *Treatment. Canadian Directory of Substance Abuse Services.*
• Publications list.
• *Action News/Action Nouvelles*. Newsletter.

Canadian HIV/AIDS Clearinghouse

Address: Canadian Public Health Association, 1565 Carling Ave., 4th Floor, Ottawa, ON, Canada K1Z 8R1
Phone: (613) 725-3434
Fax: (613) 725-1205
E-mail: AIDS/SIDA@cpha.ca

Description: The Clearinghouse serves AIDS educators across Canada and throughout the world. It is the central Canadian documentation centre on AIDS/HIV in Canada. The Clearinghouse offers distribution of free materials, a lending library, and information and referral services in English and French.

Publications:
- Canadian HIV/AIDS newsletter. Free.
- Catalogue of materials distributed by the Clearinghouse. Free.
- Catalogue of videos. Videos available for loan within Canada. Free.

Center for Medical Fellowships in Alcoholism and Drug Abuse

Contact: Marc Galanter, M.D., Director
Address: Division of Alcoholism and Drug Abuse, NB20N31, Department of Psychiatry, NYU School of Medicine, 550 First Ave., New York, NY 10016
Phone: (212) 263-6960
Fax: (212) 263-8285
E-mail: marcgalanter@nyu.edu

Description: The Center is jointly sponsored by the American Academy of Addiction Psychiatry (AAAP), the Association for Medical Education in Substance Abuse (AMERSA), and the American Society of Addiction Medicine (ASAM). It promotes postgraduate medical training in the addictions, establishes training standards for medical training in the addictions, disseminates information on existing postgraduate programs, and promotes the establishment of new programs in qualified medical training centers.

Publications:
- *Postgraduate Medical Fellowships in Alcoholism and Drug Abuse.* Annual. Describes training programs in the United States. (60 pages.)

Center for Substance Abuse Prevention (CSAP)

Contact: Karol L. Kumpfer, Ph.D., Director
Address: 5600 Fishers Lane, Rockwall II Building, 9th floor, Rockville, MD 20857
Phone: (301) 443-0365
Fax: (301) 443-5447
Web: www.samhsa.gov/csap

Description: CSAP, a part of the Substance Abuse and Mental Health Services Administration (SAMHSA) of the Public Health Service, U.S. Department of Health and Human Services, was created by the Anti-Drug Abuse Act of 1986. It oversees and coordinates national drug prevention efforts, funds demonstration grant programs, coordinates a national training system for prevention, and manages an information clearinghouse. It also runs a regionally based network of programs to promote prevention at the state level, the RADAR (Regional Alcohol and Drug Awareness Resources) Network

Publications:
- Catalog. Available from NCADI. Phone: (800) 729-6686

Center for Substance Abuse Treatment (CSAT)

Contact: Camille T. Barry, RN, Ph.D., Acting Director
Address: Rockwall II Bldg., Suite 618, 5600 Fishers Lane, Rockville, MD 20857
Phone: (301) 443-5052
Hotline: (800) 662-HELP Drug information and treatment referral hotline.
Fax: (301) 434-7801
Web: www.samhsa.gov/csat

Description: The Center for Substance Abuse Treatment (CSAT), within the Substance Abuse and Mental Health Services Administration of the U.S. Department of Health and Human Services, was established to direct and coordinate federal efforts to promote treatment of alcohol and other drug problems.

Publications:
- *CSAT Treatment Improvement Protocols* (TIPS). Free. Available from NCADI.
- *CSAT Treatment Assistance Publications* (TAPS). Free. Available from NCADI.

Children of Alcoholics Foundation, Inc.
Contact: Director of Public Information
Address: W. 60th St., 5th Floor, New York, NY 10023
Phone: (800) 359-COAF (359-2623)
Fax: (212) 754-2208
Web: www.lafn.org/community/aca

Description: A voluntary nonprofit organization established in 1982. Primary purposes are to reach, help, and offer hope to young and adult children of alcoholics; to inform and educate the public and professionals about this group; to disseminate research and new data on the effects of family alcoholism on children; and to encourage federal, state, and local decision-makers to respond to the needs of this high-risk group.

Publications:
- Catalog. Free.

Cocaine Anonymous World Services, Inc. (CA)
Address: 3740 Overland Ave., Suite G, Culver City, CA 90034
Phone: (310) 559-5833. Administrative office.
             (800) 347-8998. 24-hour referral line.
Fax: (310) 559-2554
E-mail: CAWSO@co.org
Web: www.ca.org/

Description: Founded in 1982, CA is a fellowship of people who help each other recover from their addiction to cocaine and other mind-altering substances. Its structure is similar to that of AA, with meetings held throughout the United States. The World Service Office maintains a 24-hour referral line. The Co-Anon program is available for affected family members.

Publications:
- Fact file. Free.
- *Hope, Faith and Courage: Stories from the Fellowship of Cocaine Anonymous*

CSAP Workplace Helpline
Phone: (800) 843-4971

Description: Operated by the Center for Substance Abuse Prevention, the helpline is staffed Monday through Friday, 9 A.M. to 8 P.M. It offers telephone consultation, resource referrals, and publications to business, industry, and unions to assist in planning, development, and implementation of comprehensive drug-free workplace programs.

Distilled Spirits Council of the United States (DISCUS)
Contact: Matthew Vellucci, Librarian
Address: 1250 Eye Street NW, Washington, DC 20005
Phone: (202) 628-3544
Fax: (202) 682-8888
Web: www.discus.health.org/

Description: This trade association for liquor producers and marketers in the United States, monitors national, state, and local alcohol legislation; maintains statistics on production and sales; maintains a library; and welcomes inquiries from the general public.

Publications:
• Legislative summary. Organized by state. Free.

Drug and Alcohol Nursing Association, Inc. (DANA)
Contact: Susan Piscator, Executive Director
Address: 660 Lonely Cottage Dr., Upper Black Eddy, PA 18972-9313
Phone: (610) 847-5396
Fax: (610) 847-5063

Description: Established in 1979 as a professional organization for nurses involved in alcohol and other drug use fields, DANA is concerned with standards of practice, quality of care, and specialty practice. Its annual conference includes continuing education programs.

Publications:
• *DANA.* Membership newsletter.

Drug Dependency Services Library, Newfoundland Department of Health
Address: PO Box 8700, St. John's, NF, Canada A1B 4J6
Phone: (709) 729-0623
Fax: (709) 729-5824
Web: www.gov.nf.ca/health/commhlth/factlist/factlist.htm

Description: A service within the Provincial Department of Health, Community Services Division. The agency coordinates alcohol/drug education, prevention, and treatment services within Newfoundland and Labrador. Its library offers information services to residents of the province and responds to brief questions of those from elsewhere.

Publications:
• Catalogs of audiovisuals for youth, books, journals, reports, and Drug Dependency Services information.
• Family series. Brochures.
• *Fast Facts.* Information on different drugs.

Drug Information & Strategy Clearinghouse (DISC)
Address: PO Box 8577, Silver Spring, MD 20907
Phone: (800) 578-3472. [Note: There are several voice mail menus before callers reach the Clearinghouse.]
Fax: (301) 519-6655
Web: www.ocsc.org

Description: DISC provides housing officials, residents, and community leaders with information and assistance on drug abuse prevention and drug trafficking control techniques. It operates and maintains databases with information about national and community-based antidrug programs. The Clearinghouse acquires and reviews more than 1,500 reports, articles, news items, videos, grant applications, and other materials annually. Information specialists conduct searches of specialized databases for materials about antidrug programs and strategies.

Publications:
- Information packages. Information on drug-free workplaces, eviction legislation, grantsmanship, and technical assistance for Public Housing Drug Elimination Program grant applications.
- Resource lists. Other public and private information sources
- How-to brochures. Descriptions of strategies and resources for drug prevention, drug treatment, law enforcement, security, and housing management.
- Flyers. New HUD regulations and funding opportunities.

Drug Policy Foundation (DPF)

Address:	4455 Connecticut Ave. NW, Suite B-500, Washington, DC 20008-2302
Contact:	Whitney Taylor
Phone:	(202) 537-5005
Fax:	(202) 537-3007
E-mail:	dpf@dpf.org
Web:	www.dpf.org

Description: The Foundation is an independent, nonprofit organization with more than 18,000 supporters. Its goal is to educate about alternatives to current drug control strategies. The DPF believes that current drug policies are expensive, create a new class of criminals, and do not address the health aspects of the drug control issue. The DPF aims to educate political leaders and the public about alternative policies and programs that exist both abroad and in the United States. It has a large uncatalogued collection of drug policy print and audiovisual materials that is open to the public for on-site use. Library services are not available. The DPF hosts an annual conference for policy makers and medical and legal professionals.

Publications:
- *Drug Policy Letter.* Quarterly. $35 U.S.; $50 international
- *Conference Manual.* Annually. $20.

Drugs and Policy Clearinghouse, Office of National Drug Control Policy

Address:	1600 Research Boulevard, Rockville, MD 20850
Phone:	(800) 666-3332

Description: Funded by the Office of National Drug Control Policy (ONDCP) and managed by the Bureau of Justice Statistics, Department of Justice, the clearinghouse distributes data on drugs and crime. In 1994 it became a part of the National Criminal Justice Reference Service. The Clearinghouse focuses on serving the data needs of federal, state, and local government agencies and policy makers. The Clearinghouse can arrange access to Bureau of Justice Statistics data sets and other criminal justice data that are available on public computer tapes, CD-ROMs, and disks.

Publications:
- Catalog, selected federal publications. Free.
- *Drugs, Crime, and the Justice System.* National annual report compiling drug data from various sources. Free.

Employee Assistance Professionals Association (EAPA)
Contact: Sylvia A. Straub, Ph.D., CAC, Chief Operating Officer
Address: 2101 Wilson Boulevard, Suite 500, Arlington, VA 22201
Phone: (703) 522-6272
Fax: (703) 522-4585
E-mail: eapamain@aol.com; or eapprescen@aol.com
Web: www.eap-association.com/

Description: Founded in 1971 as the Association of Labor-Management Administrators and Consultants on Alcoholism (ALMACA), the organization changed its name in 1989. It currently has 7,000 members engaged directly in providing employee assistance services. In 1987 it established a Certification Commission for certification of employee assistance professionals under an examination system. The Association publishes an extensive selection of brochures, books, and research publications on prevention, treatment, and education. The Resource Center responds to professional information requests without charge.

Publications:
- Publications catalog. Free.

Hazelden Foundation, Library and Information Resources
Contact: Barbara Weiner, MLS, Librarian
Address: Box 11, Center City, MN 55012
Phone: (651) 213-4411, Library.
    (800) 328-9000, Publishing.
Fax: (651) 213-4411
E-mail: bweiner@hazelden.org
Web: www.hazelden.org

Description: Founded in 1949 as a residential treatment program, the Foundation also provides education and training, at its Minnesota Center as well as at other sites. Of special note is a weeklong "Professionals in Residence Program" which offers experiential learning in addition to lectures and discussions with program staff. Hazelden also offers comprehensive prevention training to teachers, counselors, and community leaders working with at-risk youth. Hazelden is a major publisher in the alcohol-drug field. Its library will respond to questions from professionals.

Publications:
- Educational materials catalog. Free.
- Calendar of continuing education opportunities. Workshop descriptions. Free.
- *Hazelden Voice.* Newsletter for professionals and alumni. Free.

Health Canada
Address: Departmental Library, Jeanne Mance Building, Floor 2, Ottawa, ON, Canada K1A 0K9
Phone: (613) 954-8593

Fax: (613) 957-0292
Web: www.hc-sc.gc.ca/ or, for catalog: www.ils.ca/hc

Description: Health Canada (Federal Department of Health) assists Canadians to maintain and advance their physical and mental well-being. The departmental library was established in 1991. Its collections focus on health policy, health promotion, health financing and service delivery, mental health, as well as health and well-being of specific populations (e.g., aged, children, natives, etc.). All library services are available to the public. Online services are only available to Health Canada employees.

International Lawyers in Alcoholics Anonymous (ILAA)

Contact: Eliseo D.W. Gauna
Address: 14643 Sylvan St., Van Nuys, CA 91411-2327
Phone: (818) 785-6541
Fax: (818) 785-3887

Description: ILAA serves as a clearinghouse to assist attorneys seeking help for alcohol and other drug problems and holds an annual convention.

Join Together

Address: 441 Stuart St., Floor -7 Boston, MA 02116
Phone: (617) 437-1500
Fax: (617) 437-9394
E-mail: info@jointogether.org
Web: www.jointogether.org/

Description: Started in 1991, Join Together is a national program to help communities fight substance abuse. It is funded by a grant from the Robert Wood Johnson Foundation to the Boston University School of Public Health. Program components include: public policy panels, a national leadership fellows program, a national computer network, a communications program, and technical assistance to community programs. Although Join Together does not have a formal information service, professionals respond to phone queries. Its National Computer Network, a part of Handsnet, is available to the public by subscription.

Publications:
• Reports and recommendations of policy panels and related community action guides.
• Annual survey of community substance abuse prevention activity.
• *FASA Update*. Newsletter. Quarterly. Free.

Lesbian, Gay, Bisexual and Transgender Specialty Center at the Lesbian and Gay Community Services Center

Address: 208 West 13th Street, New York, NY 10011
Phone: (212) 620-7310

Description: Founded in 1994, the center addresses related to issues of the gay, bisexual, transgender, and lesbian community with respect to substance abuse.

Library Development Centre, National Library of Canada (LDC)

Address: 395 Wellington St., Ottawa, ON, Canada K1A 0N4

Phone: (613) 995-9481
Fax: (613) 943-1112

Description: LDC supports the development of library and information resources in Canada by providing reference and information services on all aspects of library and information science to the Canadian library community.

Marin Institute

Address: 24 Belvedere St., San Rafael, CA 94901
Phone: (415) 456-5692
Fax: (415) 456-0491
E-Mail: erisw@marininstitute.org
Web: www.marininstitute.org

Description: Established in 1987 and designated to receive long-term core funding from the Beryl Buck Trust, the Institute's goal is to reduce the toll of alcohol and other drug problems on Marin County and on society in general. The Institute develops, implements, evaluates, and disseminates innovative approaches to prevention locally, nationally, and internationally. The Resource Center is a state-of-the-art information system designed to support the work of the Institute staff and their constituencies. It has two major collections. The Industry Database, which is a unique collection of nearly 8,000 abstracts by and about the alcoholic beverage industry, and the Online Catalog, which contains about 3000 items on prevention of alcohol, tobacco, and other drug problems. The Thesaurus developed by the Institute includes more than 1,000 alcohol and other drug prevention terms in the social sciences, business, and health fields.

Publications:
• *Marin Institute Thesaurus.* Print version, $50. ASCII (must be ordered with print version), $10.
• *Alcohol Industry Database Report.* Quarterly. $32 year.

Medical Library Association (MLA)

Address: 65 East Wacker Place, Suite 1900, Chicago, IL 60601-7298
Phone: (312) 419-9094
Fax: (312) 419-8950

Description: The Association includes more than 5,000 individuals and institutions in the health information field. It has developed professional standards and credentialing and offers continuing education at annual and regional chapter meetings and locally.

Publications:
• Publications catalog. Free.

Narcotics Anonymous World Services, Inc. (NA)

Contact: Jeff Gershoff, Public Information
Address: PO Box 9999, Van Nuys, CA 91409
Phone: (818) 773-9999, ext 131
Fax: (818) 700-0700
E-mail: jeffg@na.org
Web: www.na.org/

Description: Narcotics Anonymous is a 12-step program, modeled after AA, for persons for whom drugs have become a problem and who wish to stop using.

Publications:
• Products listing. Free.

National AIDS Information Clearinghouse (CDC NAC)
Address: CDC National Prevention Information Network, PO Box 6003, Rockville MD 20849-6003
Phone: (800) 458-5231. TTY (800) 243-7012.
E-mail: info@cdcnpin.org
Web: www.cdcnpin.org

Description: The Clearinghouse has been incorporated as a part of the CDC National Prevention Information Network. A reference, referral, and publication distribution service for HIV and AIDS information, the Clearinghouse offers information on all aspects of HIV/AIDS prevention, care, and social support. Its collection includes descriptions of over 19,000 AIDS-related programs and over 11,000 materials on topics ranging from general information to education and training programs in over 50 languages. The bilingual, multidisciplinary staff of the Clearinghouse offer reference and referral services and document delivery. Services are accessible by phone, by Internet services, by FAX, and by mail. The Internet services include E-mail and a listserv that is a read-only mailing list for those who wish to receive AIDS-related documents from CDC.

Publications:
• Brochure. Describes services. Free.

National Association for Children of Alcoholics (NACoA)
Address: 1426 Rockville Pike, Suite #100, Rockville, MD 20852
Phone: (301) 468-0985
Fax: (301) 468-0987
E-mail: nacoa@erols.com
Web: www.health.org/nacoa

Description: Founded in 1983 the National Association for Children of Alcoholics (NACoA) provides public and professional information, education, advocacy, and community networking on behalf of children and families affected by alcoholism and other drug dependencies. NACoA programs and members work to increase public awareness and services for children of alcoholics.

Publications:
• *NACoA NETWORK Newsletter.* Bimonthly membership newsletter.
• *Poor Jennifer . . . She's Always Losing Her Hat.* Educational video, with trainer's guide, posters, and audio cassette.

National Association for Native American Children of Alcoholics (NANACOA)
Address: 130 Andover Park E #230, Seattle WA 98188
Phone: (206) 248-3539

Fax: (206) 248-3678
E-mail: nanacoa@nanacoa.org
Web: www.nanacoa.org

Description: NANACOA was organized at the 1988 Annual Convention of the National Association for Children of Alcoholics by more than 70 Native Americans from 30 different tribes. It serves as a source of information, training, and support for Native American communities around the needs of children of alcoholics. Activities include planning a National Conference for Native American Children of Alcoholics and regional training programs, and increasing community awareness and recognition of the needs of Native American children of alcoholics.

National Association of Alcoholism and Drug Abuse Counselors (NAADAC)

Address: 1911 North Fort Myer Dr., Suite 900, Arlington, VA 22209
Phone: (800) 548-0497
Fax: (800) 377-1136
E-mail: naadac@naadac.org
Web: www.naadac.org

Description: NAADAC is a national professional organization for alcoholism and drug abuse professionals with over 17,000 members. It runs a credentialing program with two levels of certification for counselors who are certified in their states. Certification requirements include education, clinical experience, and successful completion of an exam that is offered two times a year.

Publications:
- *The Counselor.* Bimonthly journal.
- *NAADAC Newsletter.*
- Study guide (for certification exam) $45 (members, $25).

National Association of Lesbian and Gay Addiction Professionals (NALGAP)

c/o: Progressive Research & Training for Action (PRTA)
Address: 440 Grand Ave., Suite 401, Oakland, CA 94610-5012
Phone: (510) 465-0547
Web: www.prta.com/nalgap.html

Description: NALGAP is a national membership organization comprised of professionals and other concerned individuals whose mission is to address and counteract the effect of heterosexual bias and homophobia on those affected by substance abuse and addictions through advocacy, training, networking, and resource development. NALGAP is in the process of reorganizing as a section within Progressive Research & Training for Action. It is establishing a National Clearinghouse on Lesbian/Gay/Bisexual/Transgender Substance Abuse Information.

Publications:
- Berg S, Finnegan D, McNally E, NALGAP: *Annotated bibliography: Alcoholism, substance abuse and lesbians/gay men,* 1987, 900 entries, 259 pages. $10.
- Quarterly membership newsletter

National Association of State Alcohol and Drug Abuse Directors (NASADAD)

Contact: Kathleen Sheehan, Director of Public Policy
Address: 808 17th St. NW, Suite 410, Washington, DC 20006
Phone: (202) 293-0090. Ext. 106.
Fax: (202) 293-1250
Web: www.nasadad.org

Description: NASADAD is a private association that endeavors to facilitate cooperative efforts between the federal government and state agencies and among states on alcohol and drug abuse treatment, prevention, and public policy.

Publications:
• Publications catalog. Free. [Selected publications distributed by NCADI.]

National Center on Addiction and Substance Abuse at Columbia University (CASA)

Contacts: David Mann, MLS, Librarian
Address: 152 West 57th St., New York, NY 10019
Phone: (212) 841-5200
Fax: (212) 956-8020
Web: www.casacolumbia.org/

Description: Founded in 1992, CASA is an independent, nonprofit corporation affiliated with Columbia University. It works with experts in medicine, law enforcement, business, law, economics, communications, teaching, social work, and the clergy. Its goals are to explain the social and economic cost of substance abuse, identify what prevention and treatment programs work for whom and under what circumstances, and encourage individuals and institutions to take responsibility to prevent and combat substance abuse. The library will respond to questions from professionals.

Publications:
• Catalog of publications. Free.
• *Cigarettes, Alcohol, Marijuana: Gateways to Illicit Drug Use.* $8. 64 pages.

National Clearinghouse for Alcohol and Drug Information (NCADI)

Address: PO Box 2345, Rockville, MD 20847-2345
Phone: (800) 729-6686 or (301) 468-2600
Fax: (301) 468-6433
E-mail: info@health.org
Web: www.health.org

Description: NCADI is the information service of the Substance Abuse and Mental Health Services Administration of the U.S. Department of Health and Human Services. It acts as the central point within the federal government for current print and audiovisual materials about alcohol, tobacco, and other drug problems. Information specialists respond to more than 20,000 alcohol and other drug-related inquiries each month. It distributes bibliographies and publications, posters, videotapes, and prevention curricula. NCADI maintains an extensive full-service library. It coordinates the Regional Alcohol and Drug Awareness (RADAR) Network which facilitates access to state and local sources of information about alcohol and other drugs.

Publications:
- Publications catalog. Free.
- *Prevention Pipeline.* Current awareness. Bimonthly.

National Clearinghouse on Family Violence (Canada)
Contact: Stephanie Wilson
Address: 1918C2, Floor-18 Jeanne Mance Bld. Tunney's Pasture, Ottawa, ON, Canada K1A 1B4
Phone: (800) 267-1291; (613) 957-2938 [local]; (800) 561-5643 [TTY]
Fax: (888) 267-1233; (613) 941-8930 [local]
Web: www.hc-sc.gc.ca./nc-cn

Description: The Clearinghouse is a national resource center for information and solutions to violence in the family. It provides information to front-line workers, researchers, and community groups as well as answering queries from individuals. The Clearinghouse maintains a reference collection with on-line bibliographic searching of approximately 10,000 titles.

Publications:
- Brochures and pamphlets. Free. Available in English and French.
- *The Family Violence Film and Video Catalogue.* Films and videos available for rental through the offices of the National Film Board of Canada.

National Clearinghouse on Substance Abuse (Canada) (NCSA)
Address: 75 Albert St., Suite 300, Ottawa, ON, Canada K1P 5E7
Phone: (613) 235-4048
Fax: (613) 235-8101
E-mail: webmaster@ccsa.ca
Web: www.ccsa.ca

Description: The National Clearinghouse has a collection of over 7,000 items unique to Canadian substance abuse and addictions issues. It provides information services and maintains specialized databases on Canadian substance abuse resources, treatment services, and organizations. It coordinates the Canadian Substance Abuse Information Network (CSAIN), a nationwide consortium whose members exchange information, share resources, and develop new information products. The NCSA fulfills information requests or directs them to an appropriate source. It develops and produces electronic and printed information products including databases, directories, inventories, and bibliographies. It distributes the publications of the Canadian Centre on Substance Abuse (CCSA)

National Clearinghouse on Tobacco and Health, Canadian Council for Tobacco Control
Address: 170 Laurier Ave. West, Suite 1000, Ottawa, ON, Canada K1P 5V5
Phone: (613) 567-3050
Fax: (613) 567-2730
E-mail: info-services@cctc.ca
Web: www.cctc.ca

Description: Founded in 1989, the Clearinghouse is a program of the Canadian Council for Tobacco Control. Provides information on tobacco use, prevention, and reduction issues, programs, resources, and initiatives to eligible professionals. It is an integral component of the National Strategy to Reduce Tobacco Use in Canada.

Publications:
- Publications catalog
- *Update on Smoking and Health.* Three issues annually.
- *Youth and Tobacco Fact Sheet Series.* Single copies free.
- *Tobacco and Health Network Directory.* $20 (Canadian)
- *Smoke and Mirrors: The Canadian Tobacco War.* $25 (Canadian)

National Consortium of Chemical Dependency Nurses, Inc. (NCCDN)
Contact: Randy Bryson, Executive Director
Address: 1720 Willow Creek Circle, Suite 519, Eugene, OR 97402
Phone: (800) 87-NCCDN or (503) 485-4421
Fax: (541) 485-7372

Description: A nonprofit corporation, the Consortium is an association of RNs and LPNs engaged in the practice of, or interested in, chemical dependency nursing. The Consortium also supports and advocates for the recovery and reinstatement of the impaired professional. NCCDN offers certification for nurses practicing in the field of chemical dependency.

Publications:
- *CD Nurse Briefing.* Newsletter.

National Council on Alcoholism and Drug Dependence, Inc. (NCADD)
Contact: Jeffrey Hon, Director for Public Information
Address: 12 W. 21st Street, New York, NY 10010
Phone: (212) 206-6770 or (800) NCA-CALL Hotline, for referrals.
Fax: (212) 645-1690
E-mail: national@ncadd.org
Web: www.ncadd.org

Description: Founded in 1944, NCADD currently works in partnership with nearly 200 affiliates throughout the nation. It actively advocates government policies to reduce alcohol and other drug addictions and to provide for the treatment needs and rights of affected people. Its annual meetings and publications are excellent continuing education opportunities and information resources.

Publications:
- Catalog of publications. Free.
- *NCADD Amethyst.* Quarterly newsletter. $50.
- *NCADD Washington Report.* Monthly newsletter. $50.

National Institute on Alcohol Abuse and Alcoholism (NIAAA)
Contact: Enoch Gordis, M.D., Director
Address: 6000 Executive Boulevard, MSC 7003, Rockville, MD 20892-7003
Phone: (301) 443-3885
Fax: (301) 443-7043
Web: www.niaaa.nih.gov

Description: NIAAA is one of 16 research institutes that comprise the National Institutes of Health. NIAAA conducts and supports biomedical and behavioral research, health services research, research training, and health information dissemination regarding the prevention of alcohol abuse and the treatment of alcoholism. The National Clearinghouse for Alcohol and Drug Abuse responds to questions about the NIAAA and distributes its publications. Its database, "ETOH" is available from OVID, a commercial database vendor, and also searchable through the NIAAA website.

Publications:
- *Alcohol Health and Research World.* Quarterly journal. $18 (domestic) $22.50 (foreign).
- Research monograph series.

National Institute on Drug Abuse (NIDA)

Contact: Alan I. Leshner, Director
Address: Parklawn Building, 5600 Fishers Lane, Rockville, MD 20857
Phone: (301) 443-6480
Fax: (301) 433-9127
Web: www.nida.nih.gov

Description: One of 16 research institutes overseen by the National Institutes of Health. NIDA conducts and supports biomedical and behavioral research, health services research, research training, and health information dissemination regarding the prevention and treatment of drug abuse. The Institute is organized into five divisions: Intramural Research, Extramural Research, Education and Research Training, Research Dissemination, and Epidemiological Studies.

Publications:
- *NIDA Notes.* Quarterly newsletter for professionals.
- *NIDA Capsules.* Irregular newsletter.
- Publications catalog. Available from NCADI.

National Nurses Society on Addictions (NNSA)

Contact: Kim Bains, Executive Director
Address: 4101 Lake Boone Trail, Suite 201, Raleigh, NC 27607
Phone: (919) 550-8868
Web: www.nnsa.org

Description: NNSA is a professional organization for nurses whose field of practice is substance abuse/addictions nursing, including clinicians, educators, managers, and researchers. Full membership is available to registered professional nurses; others may become associate members. The organization is dedicated to providing quality comprehensive care to addicted persons and their families. Certification for nurses in the specialty was developed in collaboration with the National Consortium of Chemical Dependency Nurses.

Publications:
- Quarterly newsletter.
- *The Role of Nurses in Alcoholism, The Impaired Nurse, Educating Nurses on Addiction.*
- *Standards of Addictions Nursing Practice with Selected Diagnoses and Criteria*, 58 pp., 1988, published with the American Nurses' Association.

- *The Care of Clients with Addictions: The Dimensions of Nursing Practice*, 32 pp., 1987, published with the American Nurses' Association.
- *Nursing Care Planning with the Addicted Client.*
- Other position papers.

National Self-Help Clearinghouse

Contact: Audrey Gartner, Executive Director
Address: 25 West 43rd St., Room 620, New York, NY 10036
Phone: (212) 354-8525
Fax: (212) 642-1956
E-mail: info@selfhelpweb.org
Web: www.selfhelpweb.org

Description: The Clearinghouse conducts training for professional and lay people about self-help methods, carries out research activities, maintains an information and referral databank, publishes materials, and addresses professional audiences about policies affecting self-help groups.

Publications:
- *How to Organize a Self-Help Group.*
- *Organizing a Self-Help Clearinghouse.*
- *New Dimensions in Self-Help.*
- *Directory of Regional Self-Help Clearinghouses.*

New Jersey Alcohol/Drug Resource Center

Contact: Penny Page, MLS, Director
Address: Center of Alcohol Studies, Smithers Hall-Busch Campus, Rutgers University, 607 Allison Rd., Piscataway, NJ 08854-8001
Phone: (732) 445-5528
Fax: (732) 445-5944

Description: The Clearinghouse is housed at the Library of the Rutgers Center of Alcohol Studies. It serves institutions of higher education, state agencies, communities, and school districts throughout the state by providing resources in alcohol and other drug abuse education and prevention. It responds to information requests from the general public in New Jersey and beyond with subject bibliographies, fact sheets, resource guides, videos on loan, copies of articles, prepared handouts, and more.

Publications:
- Publications list. Free.
- Fact sheet series. Free to NJ residents

Nicotine Anonymous World Services (NA)

Address: NAWSO, P.O. Box 591777, San Francisco, CA 94159-1777
Phone: (415) 750-0328
Web: www.nicotine-anonymous.org

Description: NA helps members and others to live without smoking using the 12-step self-help program model adapted from Alcoholics Anonymous.

Publications:
- *Seven Minutes: A Forum for Smokers Who Don't Smoke.* Newsletter. Quarterly.
- National list of meeting places and contacts.

- Information pamphlets.
- Starter kits for new meetings.

Office of Minority Health Resource Center (OMHRC)

Contact: Odette Wynter-Tuckson
Address: PO Box 202, Washington, DC 20013-7337
Phone: (800) 444-6472; (301) 565-4020
Fax: (732) 565-5112
Web: www.omhrc.gov/

Description: The Office of Minority Health (OMH) established the OMH Resource Center as a national resource for minority health information. The Resource Center facilitates access to minority health information, health promotion activities, preventive health services, and public health education. It offers assistance in the analysis of issues and problems that relate to minority health and provides assistance to organizations and individuals working in minority health professions. The Center maintains information, resources, and publications on health-specific topics that target African-American, Asian-American, Alaska Native, Hispanic/Latino, Native American, and Pacific Islander people. It provides information services and maintains five minority health databases.

Publications:
- Publications list.

Parents' Resource Institute for Drug Free Education (PRIDE)

Contact: Thomas Gleaton, Ed.D., President
Address: 3610 DeKalb Technology Parkway, Suite 105, Atlanta, GA 30340
Phone: (404) 577-4500
Fax: (404) 688-6937
E-mail: Prideprc@mindspring.com
Web: www.prideusa.org

Description: A nonprofit organization devoted to alcohol, tobacco, and other drug prevention. It offers information to the public and programs for parents, youth, educators, businesses, and governments.

Publications:
- Catalog. Free.

Prevention Source BC (British Columbia)

Contact: Jo-Anne Lauzer, MEd
Address: Suite 210, 2730 Commercial Dr., Vancouver, BC, Canada V5N 5P4
Phone: (604) 874-8452; (800) 663-1880, British Columbia residents.
Fax: (604) 874-9348
E-mail   info@preventionsource.bc.ca
Web: www.preventionsource.bc.ca

Description: Prevention Source BC is funded by the Province of British Columbia. The Centre provides toll-free information services to residents of the province seeking information about prevention, organizations, programs, materials, and research in the area of substance misuse. In addition, Prevention Source BC has a collection of materials available for on-site use.

Publications:
- Resource catalogue.
- *The Source.* Newsletter, three times per year.

Project Cork

Contact: Jean Kinney, MSW, Director
Address: Vermont Department of Health, Office of Alcohol and Drug Abuse Programs, 108 Cherry St., PO Box 70, Burlington, VT 05402
Phone: (802) 651-1616
Fax: (802) 652-4151
E-mail: cork@vdh.state.vt.us
Web: www.state.vt.us/adap/

Description: The Institute was founded in 1978, at Dartmouth College Medical School, as part of a medical education curriculum development effort. In 1997 it relocated to the State of Vermont Department of Health. Project Cork produces CORK, an online bibliographic database of substance abuse materials of interest to clinicians, educators, and those involved in public policy. It produces curriculum and other resource materials, and provides current awareness services. It disseminates these materials via its website.

Rutgers University Center of Alcohol Studies, Library

Contact: Penny Page, MLS, Library Director
Address: 607 Allison Rd., Smithers Hall, Busch Campus, Piscataway, NJ 08854-8001
Phone: (732) 445-4442
Fax: (732) 445-5944
E-mail: ppage@rci.rutgers.edu
Web: www.rci.rutgers/~cas2.edu

Description: The Center is internationally recognized for its research, education, clinical services, and information. The Center's library houses the world's largest collection of alcohol information and can provide individualized information services, specialized bibliographies, and document delivery services.

Publications:
- Publications catalog. Free.
- Alcohol bibliography series.

Saskatchewan Health Resource Centre

Contact: Kathy Donovan, Addictions Co-ordinator
Address: 3475 Albert St., Regina, S4S 6X6 Canada
Phone: (306) 787-3090
Fax: (306) 787-3823
E-mail: library@health.gov.sk.ca

Description: The Resource Centre collection of approximately 8,000 books, 500 journals, 600 audiovisuals, and a pamphlet resource file reflects current health policies, and prevention, treatment, and program support. It includes extensive holdings in the addictions field. The Resource Centre provides interlibrary loans and information services. The audiovisual collection is available for loan within the province.

Publications:
- *Alcohol and Other Drug Services Directory*. Annual. Overview of alcohol and other drug-related community resources in Saskatchewan.
- *Film and Video Directory on Alcohol and Other Drugs*. Video titles in the Resource Centre.

Society of Teachers of Family Medicine (STFM)

Contact: Roger A. Sherwood, Executive Director
Address: PO Box 8729, Kansas City, MO 64114
Phone: (800) 274-2237
Fax: (816) 333-3884
E-mail: sherwood@stfm.org
Web: www.stfm.org

Description: Founded in 1967 to support family medicine as an academic discipline, STFM's 4,800 members hold annual meetings and workshops. Its Group on Substance Abuse presents at meetings and works with the U.S. Center for Substance Abuse Prevention.

Publications:
- *Family Medicine*. Monthly subscription journal.
- *STFM Messenger*. Bimonthly newsletter.
- STFM bookstore. Free.

Special Libraries Association (SLA)

Address: 1700 Eighteenth Street, NW, Washington, DC 20009-2508
Phone: (202) 234-4700
Fax: (202) 265-9317
Web: www.sla.org

Description: The second-largest library and information-related association in North America, SLA was founded in 1900. It offers support, services, and opportunities for special librarians (librarians working in specialized libraries) and information managers. Its annual meeting offers opportunities for members to update their professional skills and improve their communications and marketing techniques. SLA provides scholarship aid, employment assistance, continuing education, and consultation to members and is a major publisher of books on library techniques.

Publications:
- Publications catalog. Free.

Substance Abuse Librarians and Information Specialists (SALIS)

Address: Box 9513, Berkeley, CA 94709-0513
Phone: (510) 642-5208 (Andrea Mitchell)
Fax: (510) 642-5208
E-mail: salis@arg.org
Web: www.salis.org

Description: An international association of individuals and organizations with special interests in the exchange and dissemination of alcohol, tobacco, and other drug information, created in 1978, SALIS's annual meetings offer members opportunities for professional development, information exchange, and networking. SALIS is an affiliate member of the International Council on Alcohol and Addictions (ICAA). It actively collaborates with the

Center for Substance Abuse Prevention (CSAP) RADAR Network and the NIAAA-CSAP Alcohol and Other Drug Thesaurus project.

Publications:
- *SALIS News*. Quarterly newsletter. Includes reviews of reference books and videos. Free to members; $20 for nonmembers.
- SALIS directory.

Trauma Foundation

Contact:	Robin Tremblay-McGaw, MLS, Information Services Director
Address:	1001 Potrero Ave., Building One, Room 300, San Francisco General Hospital, San Francisco, CA 94110
Phone:	(415) 821-8209, ext. 26
Fax:	(415) 282-2363
E-mail:	robintm@traumafdn.org
web:	www.traumafdn.org

Description: The Trauma Foundation is the home office for the San Francisco Injury Center and the Pacific Center for Violence Prevention. It houses a special library on injury and violence prevention that includes a wealth of alcohol and drug information. The library offers full reference services.

Publications:
- *Resources for Injury and Alcohol Problem Prevention.*

This list was developed by the Project Cork Resource Center, Vermont Department of Health, Office of Alcohol & Drug Abuse Programs, 108 Cherry Street, PO Box 70, Burlington, VT 05402-0070. E-mail: cork@adap.adp.state.vt.us

THE INTERACTION EFFECTS OF ALCOHOL WITH OTHER DRUGS

Type of drug	Generic name	Trade name	Interaction effect with alcohol
Analgesics Nonnarcotic	Salicylates	(Products containing aspirin) Bayer Aspirin Bufferin Alka-Seltzer	Heavy concurrent use of alcohol with analgesics can increase the potential for GI bleeding. Special caution should be exercised by individuals with ulcers. Buffering of salicylates reduces possibility of this interaction.
Narcotic	Codeine Morphine Opium Oxycodone Propoxyphene Pentazocine Meperidine	 Pantopon Parepectolin (paregoric) Percodan Darvon Darvon-N Talwin Demerol Tylox	The combination of narcotic analgesics and alcohol interact to reduce functioning of the CNS and can lead to loss of effective breathing function and respiratory arrest: death may result.
Antianginal	Nitroglycerin Isosorbide dinitrate	Nitrosat Isordil, Sorbitrate	Alcohol in combination with antianginal drugs may cause the blood pressure to lower—creating a potentially dangerous situation.
Antibiotics Antiinfective agents	Furazolidone Metronidazole Nitrofurantoin	Furoxone Flagyl Cyantin Macrodantin	Certain antibiotics, especially those taken for urinary tract infections and *Trichomonas* infections, have been known to produce disulfiram-like reactions (nausea, vomiting, headaches, hypotension) when combined with alcohol.

Anticoagulants	Warfarin sodium
	
	Acenocoumarol
	Coumarin
	  derivatives
		Coumadin,
		  Panwarfin
		Sintrom
		Dicumarol
			With chronic alcohol use, the anticoagulant effect of these drugs is inhibited. With acute alcohol use the anticoagulant effect is enhanced: hemorrhaging could result.

Anticonvulsants	Phenytoin Carbamazepine Primidone Phenobarbital	Dilantin Tegretol Mysoline Luminal	Chronic heavy drinking can reduce the effectiveness of anticonvulsant drugs to the extent that seizures previously controlled by these drugs can occur if the dosage is not adjusted appropriately. Enhanced CNS depression may occur with concurrent use of alcohol.

(continued)

THE INTERACTION EFFECTS OF ALCOHOL WITH OTHER DRUGS (*continued*)

Antidiabetic agents Hypoglycemics	Chlorpropamide Acetohexamide Tolbutamide Tolazamide Insulin	Diabinese Dymelor Orinase Tolinase Iletin	The interaction of alcohol and either insulin or oral antidiabetic agents may be severe and unpredictable. The interaction may induce hypoglycemia or hyperglycemia; also disulfiram-like reactions may occur.
Antidepressants Tricyclics	Nortriptyline Amitriptyline Desipramine Doxepin Imipramine	Aventyl Elavil, Endep Pertofrane Sinequan Tofranil	Enhanced CNS depression may occur with concurrent use of alcohol and antidepressant drugs. Alcohol itself can cause or exacerbate clinical states of depression.
Monoamine oxidase inhibitors (MAOI)	Pargyline Isocarboxazid Phenelzine Tranylcypromine	Eutonyl Marplan Nardil Parnate	Alcoholic beverages (such as beer and wines) contain tyramine, which will interact with an MAOI to produce a hypertensive hyperpyrexic crisis. Concomitant use of alcohol with MAOIs may result in enhanced CNS depression.
Antihistamines	(For example) Chlorpheniramine Diphenhydramine	(Many cold & allergy remedies) Coricidin Allerest Benadryl	The interaction of alcohol and these drugs enhances CNS depression.
Antihypertensive agents	Rauwolfia preparations Reserpine Guanethidine Hydralazine Pargyline Methyldopa	Rauwiloid Serpasil Ismelin Apresoline Eutonyl Aldomet	Alcohol, in moderate dosage, will increase the blood pressure-lowering effects of these drugs, and can produce postural hypotension. Additionally, an increased CNS-depressant effect may be seen with the rauwolfia alkaloids and methyldopa. Alcohol itself causes hypertension and may counteract the therapeutic effect of antihypertensive agents.
Antimalarials	Quinacrine	Atabrine	A disulfiram-like reaction and severe CNS toxicity may result if antimalarial drugs are combined with alcohol.
CNS depressants Barbiturate sedative hypnotics	Phenobarbital Pentobarbital Secobarbital Butabarbital Amobarbital	Luminal Nembutal Seconal Butisol Amytal	Since alcohol is a depressant, the combination of alcohol and other depressants interact to further reduce CNS functioning. It is extremely dangerous to mix barbiturates and alcohol. What would be a nondangerous dosage of either drug by itself can interact in the body to the point of coma or fatal respiratory arrest. Many accidental deaths of this nature have been reported. A similar danger exists in mixing the nonbarbiturate hypnotics with alcohol.
Nonbarbiturate sedative hypnotics	Methaqualone Glutethimide Bromides Flurazepam Chloral hydrate	Quaalude Doriden Neurosine Dalmane Noctec	Disulfiram-like reactions have been reported with alcohol use in the presence of chloral hydrates.

THE INTERACTION EFFECTS OF ALCOHOL WITH OTHER DRUGS (*continued*)

Tranquilizers (major)	Thioridazine Chlorpromazine Trifluoperazine Haloperidol	Mellaril Thorazine Stelazine Haldol	The major tranquilizers interact with alcohol to enhance CNS depression, resulting in impairment of voluntary movement such as walking or hand coordination; larger doses can be fatal. Increases incidence and severity of extrapyramidal side effects of these drugs.
Tranquilizers (minor)	Diazepam Meprobamate Chlordiazepoxide Oxazepam Lorazepam Alprazolam	Valium Equanil Miltown Librium Serax Ativan Xanax	The minor tranquilizers depress CNS functioning. Serious interactions can occur when using these drugs and alcohol.
CNS stimulants	Caffeine Amphetamines Methlyphenidate Dextroamphetamine Methamphetamine	(in coffee and cola) Vanquish Benzedrine Ritalin Dexedrine Desoxyn Ritalin	The stimulant effect of these drugs can reverse the depressant effect of alcohol drugs on the CNS, resulting in a false sense of security. They do not help the intoxicated person gain control over coordination or psychomotor activity.
Disulfiram (anti-alcohol preparation)	Disulifiram	Antabuse	Severe CNS toxicity follows ingestion of even small amounts of alcohol. Effects can include headache, nausea, vomiting, convulsions, rapid fall in blood pressure, unconsciousness, and—with sufficiently high doses—death.
Diuretics (also antihypertensive)	Hydrochlorothiazide Chlorothiazide Furosemide Quinethazone	Hydrodiuril, Esidrix Diuril Lasix Hydromax	Interaction of diuretics and alcohol enhances the blood pressure—lowering the effects of the diuretic; could possibly precipitate hypotension.

INDEX